500 COOKIE RECIPES

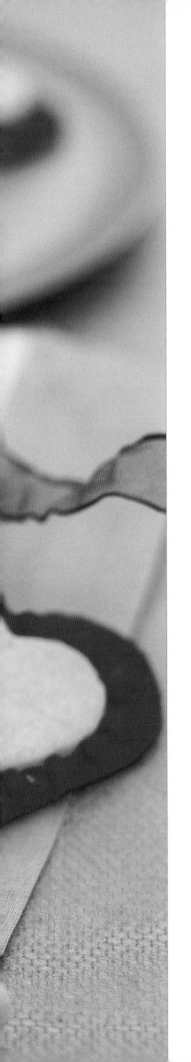

500 COOKIE RECIPES

AN IRRESISTIBLE COLLECTION OF COOKIES, BISCUITS, BARS, BROWNIES, SLICES, SCONES, MUFFINS, CUPCAKES, SHORTBREADS, FLAPJACKS, CRACKERS, CANDIES AND MORE   CATHERINE ATKINSON

greene&golden

This edition is published by greene&golden,
an imprint of Anness Publishing Ltd, Blaby Road, Wigston,
Leicestershire LE18 4SE; info@anness.com

www.annesspublishing.com

If you like the images in this book and would like to investigate
using them for publishing, promotions or advertising, please visit
our website www.practicalpictures.com for more information.

Publisher: Joanna Lorenz
Editorial Director: Helen Sudell
Editor: Simona Hill
Recipes: Pepita Aris, Catherine Atkinson, Alex Barker,
Ghillie Basan, Angela Boggiano, Carol Bowen, Georgina
Campbell, Carla Capalbo, Maxine Clark, Carole Clements,
Elizabeth Wolf-Cohen, Matthew Drennan, Tessa Evelegh, Joanna
Farrow, Christine France, Brian Glover, Nicola Graimes, Carole
Handslip, Biddy White Lennon, Sara Lewis, Gilly Love, Lesley
Mackley, Norma MacMillan, Sue Maggs, Sally Mansfield, Jane
Milton, Sally Morris, Anna Mosseson, Janice Murfitt, Rena Salman,
Anne Sheasby, Young Jin Song, Marlena Spieler,
Christopher Trotter, Laura Washburn, Kate Whiteman,
Judy Williams, Jeni Wright, Carol Wilson and Annette Yates
Photographers: Karl Adamson, Edward Allwright, Martin
Brigdale, James Duncan, John Freeman, Michelle Garrett,
Amanda Heywood, David Jordan, William Lingwood,
Debbie Patterson and Sam Stowell
Reader: Molly Perham
Production Controller: Mai-Ling Collyer

© Anness Publishing Ltd 2012

A CIP catalogue record for this book is available from
the British Library.

NOTES

Bracketed terms are intended for American readers.
For all recipes, quantities are given in both metric and imperial
measures and, where appropriate, in standard cups and spoons.
Follow one set of measures, but not a mixture, because they
are not interchangeable.
Standard spoon and cup measures are level.
1 tsp = 5ml, 1 tbsp = 15ml, 1 cup = 250ml/8fl oz.
Australian standard tablespoons are 20ml.
Australian readers should use 3 tsp in place of 1 tbsp for
measuring small quantities.
American pints are 16fl oz/2 cups. American readers should use
20fl oz/2.5 cups in place of 1 pint when measuring liquids.
Electric oven temperatures in this book are for conventional
ovens. When using a fan oven, the temperature will probably
need to be reduced by about 10–20°C/20–40°F. Since ovens
vary, you should check with your manufacturer's instruction
book for guidance.
The nutritional analysis given for each recipe is calculated per
portion (i.e. serving or item), unless otherwise stated. If the
recipe gives a range, such as Serves 4–6, then the nutritional
analysis will be for the smaller portion size, i.e. 6 servings.
The analysis does not include optional ingredients,
such as salt added to taste.
Medium (US large) eggs are used unless otherwise stated.
Granulated (white) sugar is used unless otherwise stated.

Front cover shows Mini Chocolate Marylands – for recipe,
see page 64.

PUBLISHER'S NOTE

Contents

Introduction

Nothing equals the satisfaction of home baking, and no other culinary skill can produce fabulous results in such a short time and with so few ingredients. No commercial cake mix, or shop-bought cookie, can match one that is home-made for taste, texture and flavour and neither can it create the delicious aroma and sweet wafts of baking that permeate the kitchen, stimulating the appetite and offering the enticing promise of a sweet treat to follow.

Baking at home gives the cook complete control of the choice of ingredients, and choosing the best that you can afford to buy is a good way to start. Baking can be enjoyed by all the family, and it offers a great opportunity to get children interested in preparing and making the food that they will eat. It's a therapeutic activity too, and sharing the results is a sociable and pleasing way to spend time with family and friends. Above all, nothing beats the taste of fresh-from-the-oven baked produce. And there is pride in being the provider of such filling fare. So whether you're looking for a mid-morning or mid-afternoon snack to share with friends,

Below: *Bars and squares can be filled with healthy ingredients for a delicious snack.*

Above: *Crunchy chocolate chip cookies are everybody's favourites.*

feeding ravenous schoolchildren returning home, or are in need of a sweet taste to signal the finale of a meal, this fabulous book is guaranteed to contain the ideal recipe. It's packed full of recipes and lavish colour photographs to inspire your culinary choices,

Whatever your taste and food requirements, this appealing book contains every cookie recipe imaginable. Every well known favourite is included, from soft and chewy flapjacks to crisp and crunchy all-butter cookies, to rich and sinful double chocolate brownies, from plain and wholesome oat biscuits to spicy and fruity confections, as well as moreish and comforting sweet treats.

There are recipes for cookies, bars, slices, scones, muffins, crackers and pastries, including plenty of innovative ideas using ingredients that were once only available from specialist outlets but are now more standard fare. There are recipes suitable for baking in batches to satisfy the needs of the cake stall, lavishly decorated confections for birthday parties, and indulgent recipes for special events. Recipes from many countries

Above: *Savoury crackers can be eaten plain or served with cheese.*

are here and a special chapter is devoted to baking cookies for annual festivals and events, such as wedding celebrations, Christmas, Easter and New Year.

Baking is an exact science and needs to be approached in an ordered way. Having said that, making cookies is a relatively simple introduction to baking. First read the recipe through from beginning to end to ensure that you understand the cooking method. Set out all the required ingredients and equipment before you begin, just to make sure that you have everything in stock. Eggs and butter should be at room temperature for best results, unless otherwise stated. Sift the flour after you have measured it. If you sift the flour from a fair height, it will have more chance to aerate and lighten.

No two ovens are alike. Buy a reliable oven thermometer and test the temperature of your oven. When possible bake the cookies in the centre of the oven where the heat is more likely to be constant. If you are using a fan-assisted oven, follow the manufacturer's guidelines for baking. Choose good quality baking tins. They can improve your results, as they conduct heat more efficiently. Finally, if you are baking cookies on baking sheets,

swap the positions of the sheets midway through baking to ensure an even distribution of heat.

There are many ways of making cookie dough, but most cookies are made according to just three or four methods, which are all simple to master. Once the batter is thoroughly mixed, the cookies are either rolled out, shaped using a piping (pastry) bag, dropped from a teaspoon on to a baking sheet, piped and/or pressed into a mould, depending on the consistency of the batter. The quantity of each ingredient in the recipe and the combination of ingredients determines whether the cookie is soft-centred and chewy, hard and crunchy, or flaky with a melt-in-the-mouth consistency.

Everyday cookies may be left plain or lightly dusted with icing (confectioners' sugar) or unsweetened cocoa powder, while those for special occasions may be decorated with an assortment of toppings, or sandwiched together with a sweet and creamy filling, and then drizzled with topping.

Whatever your baking requirements, with 500 tried-and-tested delicious recipes to choose from, this book contains the only cookie selection you'll ever need.

Below: *Macaroons contain no fat, so are a healthy choice for those watching their diet.*

Measuring Ingredients

Cooks with years of experience may not need to measure ingredients, but if you are a beginner or are trying a new recipe for the first time, it is best to follow instructions carefully. Also, measuring ingredients precisely will ensure consistent results. Always use the best quality ingredients that are within their "use-by" date.

I For liquids measured in pints or litres, use a glass or clear plastic measuring jug (cup). Put it on a flat surface and pour in the liquid. Check that the liquid is level with the marking specified in the recipe.

2 For liquids measured in spoons, pour the liquid into the measuring spoon, to the brim, and then pour it into the mixing bowl. Do not measure it over the mixing bowl in case of spillages.

3 For measuring dry ingredients in a spoon, fill the spoon, scooping up the ingredients. Level the surface with the straight edge of a knife.

4 For measuring dry ingredients by weight, scoop or pour on to the scales, watching the dial and reading carefully. Balance scales give more accurate readings than spring scales.

5 For measuring syrups, set the mixing bowl on the scales and turn the gauge to zero, or make a note of the weight. Pour in the required weight of syrup.

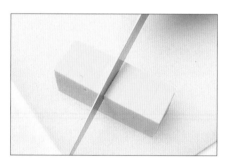

6 For measuring butter, cut with a sharp knife and weigh, or cut off the specified amount following the markings on the wrapping paper.

Rubbing-in Method

Plain cookies are usually made by rubbing the fat into the flour. For this, the fat, whether butter, margarine or lard, should not be rock hard or too warm. It is first chopped into small pieces, then added to the dry ingredients. The mixture is lifted high and the lumps of fat rubbed between the fingertips as the mixture is allowed to fall back into the bowl.

I Sift the flour into a bowl from a height, adding the raising agents, salt and any sugar or spices. Mix the dry ingredients evenly together. Sift in any other dry ingredients.

2 Add the diced butter, and use your fingertips to rub the fat into the flour. Cold fingertips produce the best results, rubbing in the fat without melting it. Sprinkle on any liquid ingredients.

3 Mix with a fork and then gather the ingredients together with your fingertips until the dough forms a ball. If it is too dry add more liquid. Turn on to a lightly floured surface and knead lightly.

Beating Method

To make cookies by the beating method, the fat and sugar are beaten together before the eggs and dry ingredients are added. The fat (usually butter) should be soft enough to be beaten so, if necessary, remove it from the refrigerator and leave for at least 30 minutes. For best results, the egg should be at room temperature too.

1 Sift the flour with the salt, raising agent and any other dry ingredients, such as spices or unsweetened cocoa powder into a bowl. Set aside.

2 Put the fat in a bowl and beat with an electric mixer or a wooden spoon until soft and pliable. Add the sugar and beat until the mixture is pale and fluffy.

3 Add the eggs or egg yolks, one at a time, beating well after each addition. Scrape the bowl often so all the ingredients are evenly combined.

4 Add the sifted dry ingredients to the mixture. Beat at low speed just until smoothly combined, or fold in with a large metal spoon.

5 If the recipe calls for any liquid, add it in small portions, alternately with portions of the dry ingredients.

6 Drop spoonfuls of the ingredients on to the prepared baking sheet and bake as directed for the recipe.

Melting Method

Cookies such as flapjacks and gingernuts are made by first melting the fat and sugar or syrup together. The dry ingredients are then stirred in to make a soft dough that firms as it cools. The baked cookies become crisp as they cool, so should be quickly shaped or left on the baking sheets for a few minutes before transferring to a wire rack.

1 Put the butter, any syrup, milk and sugar in a heavy pan and heat gently over a low heat until the butter has just melted. The heat should be low so that the sugar does not burn, but melts instead into the butter. If the mixture boils it will alter the proportions.

2 Remove the pan from the heat and leave the mixture to cool for a few minutes. This is particularly important if you are going to add eggs to the mixture. Sift over the flour and any flavourings, salt and raising agents and stir well until the mixture is smooth.

3 Add the sifted dry ingredients to the mixture. Beat at low speed just until smoothly combined, or fold in with a large spoon. Shape the cookie dough as soon as possible before the raising agents start to work. Bake as directed for the recipe.

Butter Cookies

These crunchy, buttery cookies make a delicious afternoon treat served with a cup of tea or a glass of milk. The dough can be made in advance, wrapped in foil, and chilled in the refrigerator until you are ready to bake the cookies.

Makes 25–30
175g/6oz/3/4 cup unsalted (sweet) butter, at room temperature, diced
90g/3 1/2 oz/1/2 cup golden caster (superfine) sugar
250g/9oz/2 1/4 cups plain (all-purpose) flour
demerara (raw) sugar, for coating

1 Put the butter and sugar in a bowl and beat until light and fluffy.

2 Add the flour, mix in, then, using your hands, gradually work in the crumbs until the mixture forms a smooth dough. Roll into a sausage shape about 30cm/12in long, then pat the sides flat to form a square log.

3 Sprinkle a thick layer of demerara sugar on a piece of baking parchment. Press each side of the dough into the sugar to coat. Wrap and chill for 30 minutes until firm.

4 Preheat the oven to 160°C/325°F/Gas 3.

5 Remove the dough from the refrigerator and unwrap. Cut it into thick slices and place slightly apart on lightly greased baking sheets. Bake for 20 minutes until just beginning to turn brown. Transfer to a wire rack to cool.

Variations
• To flavour the cookies, add ground cinnamon, grated lemon or orange rind, or vanilla or almond extract to the butter mixture, or add whole glacé (candied) cherries, chocolate chips, chopped nuts or dried fruit such as chopped apricots to the dough.
• As an alternative, coat the outside in sugar or chopped toasted nuts.

Orange Buttery Cookies

These rich, buttery cookies with a smooth and crisp texture can be scented with rose water or vanilla instead of orange flower water and are delicious served with tea.

Makes 20–25
200g/7oz/scant 1 cup butter
130g/4 1/2 oz/generous 1 cup icing (confectioners') sugar, sifted
5–10ml/1–2 tsp orange flower water
250g/9oz/2 1/4 cups plain (all-purpose) flour, sifted
handful of blanched almonds

1 Melt the butter in a pan and leave to cool until lukewarm.

2 Stir the icing sugar and orange flower water into the melted butter, then gradually beat in the flour to form a smooth, stiff dough. Wrap in clear film (plastic wrap) and chill for 15 minutes.

3 Preheat the oven to 180°C/350°F/Gas 4. Lightly grease a baking sheet.

4 Break off walnut-size pieces of dough and roll into balls. Place on the baking sheet and flatten slightly. Press a nut into the centre of each.

5 Bake for 20 minutes, or until golden. Allow to cool slightly on the baking sheet; when firm, transfer to a wire rack.

Chocolate-tipped Cookies

Wrap cold winter hands around a mug of steaming hot chocolate and dunk these cookies in for a special treat. The sweet taste and crunchy texture make these a moreish addition to the cookie jar.

Makes 14–16
115g/4oz/1/2 cup butter, softened
45ml/3 tbsp icing (confectioners') sugar, sifted
150g/9oz/2 1/4 cups plain (all-purpose) flour
few drops vanilla extract
75g/3oz plain (semisweet) chocolate

1 Preheat the oven to 180°C/350°F/Gas 4. Lightly grease two baking sheets.

2 In a large bowl, beat together the butter and icing sugar until very soft. Mix in the flour and vanilla extract. The mixture should be quite stiff.

3 Put the mixture in a large piping (pastry) bag fitted with a large star nozzle and pipe 10–13cm/4–5in straight lines on the prepared baking sheets.

4 Bake for 15–20 minutes until pale golden brown. Allow to cool slightly before lifting on to a wire rack. Leave to cool completely.

5 Put the chocolate in a small heatproof bowl and set over a pan of gently simmering water. Heat gently, stirring frequently until melted. Dip both ends of each cookie in the chocolate. Place the dipped cookies on a wire rack and leave to set.

Butter Cookies Energy 84kcal/350kJ; Protein 0.8g; Carbohydrate 9.6g, of which sugars 3.3g; Fat 4.9g, of which saturates 3.1g; Cholesterol 12mg; Calcium 14mg; Fibre 0.3g; Sodium 36mg.
Orange Buttery Cookies Energy 131kcal/546kJ; Protein 2.3g; Carbohydrate 9.5g, of which sugars 3.5g; Fat 9.6g, of which saturates 2.9g; Cholesterol 16mg; Calcium 28mg; Fibre 0.7g; Sodium 5mg.
Chocalate-tipped Cookies Energy 120kcal/503kJ; Protein 1.2g; Carbohydrate 13.2g, of which sugars 6.1g; Fat 7.3g, of which saturates 4.6g; Cholesterol 16mg; Calcium 17mg; Fibre 0.4g; Sodium 44mg.

Brittany Butter Cookies

These lightly glazed little cookies are similar to shortbread, but are richer. Traditionally, they are made with lightly salted butter.

Makes 18–20
6 egg yolks, lightly beaten
15ml/1 tbsp milk
250g/9oz/2¼ cups plain (all-purpose) flour
175g/6oz/¾ cup caster (superfine) sugar
200g/7oz/scant 1 cup butter at room temperature, diced

1 Preheat the oven to 180°C/350°F/Gas 4. Lightly grease two heavy baking sheets.

2 Mix 15ml/1 tbsp of the egg yolks with the milk to make a glaze. Set aside.

3 In a bowl, beat together the sugar and butter until light and creamy. Add the egg yolks and mix to combine. Add the flour in batches and stir well. Use your fingertips until it is all incorporated and the mixture forms a slightly sticky dough. Gather it together.

4 Using floured hands, pat out the dough to about 5mm/¼in thick and stamp out rounds using a 7.5cm/3in cutter. Transfer the rounds to the prepared baking sheet, brush each with a little of the reserved egg and milk glaze, then, using the back of a knife, score gently with lines to create a lattice pattern.

5 Bake for about 12 minutes or until golden. Cool on the baking sheet to firm up, then transfer to a wire rack and leave to cool completely.

Variation
To make a large Brittany butter cake, pat the dough with well-floured hands into a 23cm/9in loose-based cake tin (pan). Brush with the glaze and score the lattice pattern on top. Bake for 45–60 minutes until firm to the touch and golden brown.

Buttery Vanilla Cookies

These crisp, buttery cookies are perfect with strawberries and cream. They are known as refrigerator cookies as the mixture is chilled until it is firm enough to cut neatly into thin slices. The dough can be frozen and when thawed enough to slice, can be freshly baked, but do allow a little extra baking time.

Makes 28–30
275g/10oz/2½ cups plain (all-purpose) flour
200g/7oz/scant 1 cup unsalted (sweet) butter
90g/3½oz/scant 1 cup icing (confectioners') sugar, plus extra for dusting
10ml/2 tsp vanilla extract

1 Put the flour in a food processor. Add the butter and process until the mixture resembles coarse breadcrumbs.

2 Add the icing sugar and vanilla, and process until the mixture comes together to form a dough. Knead lightly and shape into a thick sausage, 30cm/12in long and 5cm/2in in diameter.

3 Wrap and chill for at least 1 hour, until firm.

4 Preheat the oven to 200°C/400°F/Gas 6. Lightly grease two baking sheets.

5 Using a sharp knife, cut 5mm/¼in thick slices from the dough and space them slightly apart on the baking sheet.

6 Bake for 8–10 minutes. Leave for 5 minutes, then transfer to a wire rack to cool. Serve dusted with icing sugar.

Cook's Tip
Alternate the position of the baking sheets in the oven halfway through cooking, if necessary, until the cookies are cooked evenly and have just turned pale golden around the edges.

Buttery Vanilla Cookies Energy 84kcal/350kJ; Protein 0.8g; Carbohydrate 9.6g, of which sugars 3.3g; Fat 4.9g, of which saturates 3.1g; Cholesterol 12mg; Calcium 14mg; Fibre 0.3g; Sodium 36mg.
Brittany Butter Cookies Energy 170kcal/711kJ; Protein 2.2g; Carbohydrate 19g, of which sugars 9.4g; Fat 10g, of which saturates 5.7g; Cholesterol 82mg; Calcium 32mg; Fibre 0.4g; Sodium 65mg.

Vanilla Crescents

These attractively shaped cookies are sweet and delicate, ideal to serve with creamy ice cream or a light and fluffy fruit fool for dessert. Kids love them with chocolate ice cream.

Makes 36
175g/6oz/1¼ cups unblanched almonds
115g/4oz/1 cup plain (all-purpose) flour
pinch of salt
225g/8oz/1 cup unsalted (sweet) butter at room temperature, diced
115g/4oz/½ cup sugar
5ml/1 tsp vanilla extract
icing (confectioners') sugar, for dusting

1 Grind the almonds with a few tablespoons of the flour in a food processor, blender or nut grinder and process in short pulses until finely ground.

2 Sift the remaining flour with the salt into a bowl. Set aside.

3 In a large bowl, beat together the butter and sugar until light and fluffy.

4 Add the almonds, vanilla extract and the sifted flour and salt. Stir to mix well. Gather the dough into a ball, wrap in baking parchment, and chill for at least 30 minutes.

5 Preheat the oven to 160°C/325°F/Gas 3. Lightly grease two baking sheets.

6 Break off walnut-size pieces of dough and roll them into small cylinders about 1cm/½in in diameter. Bend them into crescent shapes and place on the baking sheets, spaced well apart.

7 Bake for about 20 minutes until dry but not brown. Transfer to a wire rack to cool only slightly. Set the rack over a baking sheet and dust with an even layer of icing sugar. Leave to cool completely.

Sugar-topped Stars

These cookies are great for little ones to help make.

Makes 10
115g/4oz/½ cup butter
175g/6oz/1½ cups plain (all-purpose) flour, plus extra for dusting

50g/2oz/¼ cup caster (superfine) sugar

For the topping
30ml/2 tbsp golden (light corn) syrup
30ml/2 tbsp preserving sugar

1 Put the butter and flour in a bowl and rub together until the mixture looks like breadcrumbs. Stir in the caster sugar and knead together to make a ball. Chill for 30 minutes.

2 Preheat the oven to 180°C/350°F/Gas 4 and lightly grease two baking sheets.

3 Roll out the dough on a lightly floured surface to a 5mm/¼in thickness and use a 7.5cm/3in cookie cutter to stamp out the stars.

4 Arrange the cookies on the baking sheet. Press the trimmings together and keep rolling out and cutting more biscuits until all the mixture has been used.

5 Bake for 10–15 minutes, until they are golden brown. Transfer to a wire rack to cool completely.

6 Heat the golden syrup in a pan over a low heat. Brush over the cookies and sprinkle the sugar on top. Leave to cool.

Quick Vanilla Cookies

Just a few drops of vanilla extract give these cookies their defining flavour. Beware, they're very moreish.

Makes 32
150g/5oz/10 tbsp butter, softened
150g/5oz/¾ cup caster (superfine) sugar
1 egg, lightly beaten
2.5ml/½ tsp vanilla extract
225g/8oz/2 cups plain (all-purpose) flour, sifted

1 Put all the ingredients in a bowl and beat together until a smooth, firm dough is formed.

2 Lightly knead on a floured surface then roll the dough into a log shape about 5cm/2in diameter and 20cm/8in long. Wrap the log in clear film (plastic wrap) and chill for at least 1 hour or until firm enough to slice.

3 Preheat the oven to 190°C/375°F/Gas 5. Lightly grease two large baking sheets.

4 Cut the dough into 5mm/¼in slices. Place the cookies about 2.5cm/1in apart on the baking sheets. Bake for 12 minutes, or until just golden around the edges. Leave on the baking sheets for 2–3 minutes, then transfer to a wire rack to cool.

Vanilla Crescents Energy 62kcal/258kJ; Protein 2.5g; Carbohydrate 6.3g, of which sugars 3.6g; Fat 3.1g, of which saturates 0.3g; Cholesterol 3mg; Calcium 19mg; Fibre 0.5g; Sodium 4mg.
Sugar-topped Stars Energy 186kcal/778kJ; Protein 1.8g; Carbohydrate 24.4g, of which sugars 11.1g; Fat 9.7g, of which saturates 6g; Cholesterol 25mg; Calcium 31mg; Fibre 0.5g; Sodium 79mg.
Quick Vanilla Cookies Energy 80kcal/334kJ; Protein 0.9g; Carbohydrate 10.4g, of which sugars 5g; Fat 4.1g, of which saturates 2.5g; Cholesterol 16mg; Calcium 14mg; Fibre 0.2g; Sodium 31mg.

Sablés with Caramel Glaze

These are very buttery cookies with a dark caramel glaze. Eat on the day of baking for the best taste.

Makes about 18
200g/7oz/1¾ cups plain
   (all-purpose) flour
pinch of salt
75g/3oz/⅔ cup icing
   (confectioners') sugar
130g/4½oz/generous ½ cup
   unsalted (sweet) butter, diced

3 egg yolks
2.5ml/½ tsp vanilla extract
1 egg yolk, for glazing

For the caramel syrup
50g/2oz/¼ cup sugar
20ml/4 tsp water
2.5ml/½ tsp lemon juice
50ml/2fl oz/¼ cup water

1 To make the caramel syrup, put the sugar, 20ml/4 tsp water and lemon juice into a pan. Place over a gentle heat and stir until clear. Boil to a rich golden brown. Remove from the heat and immediately plunge the base of the pan into cold water to stop the cooking. Stir in the 50ml/2fl oz/¼ cup water. Cool.

2 Put the cookie ingredients, except the egg yolks and vanilla, into a food processor then process until the mixture resembles breadcrumbs. Add the egg yolks and vanilla and blend until a firm dough forms. Form into a ball, wrap in clear film (plastic wrap) then chill for 15 minutes.

3 Preheat the oven to 180°C/350°F/Gas 4. Lightly grease two baking sheets.

4 Roll the dough out on baking parchment 5mm/¼in thick. Using a 7.5cm/3in cookie cutter, stamp out rounds and place them on the baking sheets.

5 In a bowl, beat the egg yolk with 15ml/1 tbsp of the glaze. Brush sparingly over the cookies. Leave to dry, then apply a second layer. Make a pattern using the fork tines.

6 Bake for about 10–15 minutes, or until crisp and golden brown. Transfer to a wire rack to cool.

Sugar-topped Vanilla Cookies

Buttery, crumbly vanilla cookies with an irresistible crunchy sugar topping, these are great with a cup of tea but also delicious served with luxury vanilla ice cream for a quick dessert.

Makes about 24
115g/4oz/½ cup unsalted
   (sweet) butter, at room
   temperature, diced
50g/2oz/¼ cup vanilla caster
   (superfine) sugar

1 egg, beaten
1.5ml/¼ tsp vanilla extract
200g/7oz/1¾ cups self-raising
   (self-rising) flour, plus extra
   for dusting
45ml/3 tbsp cornflour
   (cornstarch)

For the topping
1 egg white
15ml/1 tbsp vanilla caster
   (superfine) sugar
75g/3oz sugar cubes, crushed

1 Preheat the oven to 180°C/350°F/Gas 4.

2 In a bowl, beat the butter and sugar together until light and fluffy. Beat in the egg and vanilla extract. Sift together the flour and cornflour over the mixture and mix to a soft dough.

3 Roll the mixture out on a lightly floured surface. Using a cookie cutter, stamp out the cookies and place on a lightly greased baking sheet.

4 For the topping, put the egg white in a small bowl and whisk until foamy. Whisk in the vanilla sugar. Using a pastry brush, spread generously on each cookie. Sprinkle with the crushed sugar cubes.

5 Bake for about 15 minutes, or until the topping is just beginning to turn golden brown. Remove from the oven and transfer to a wire rack to cool.

> **Cook's Tip**
> To make vanilla sugar, split a vanilla pod (bean) open down one side. Place in a jar of sugar and leave to infuse for a few days.

Sablés with Caramel Glaze Energy 129kcal/541kJ; Protein 1.6g; Carbohydrate 15.9g, of which sugars 7.5g; Fat 7g, of which saturates 4g; Cholesterol 49mg; Calcium 24mg; Fibre 0.3g; Sodium 46mg.
Sugar-topped Vanilla Cookies Energy 96kcal/405kJ; Protein 1.2g; Carbohydrate 14.2g, of which sugars 6.2g; Fat 4.3g, of which saturates 2.6g; Cholesterol 18mg; Calcium 35mg; Fibre 0.3g; Sodium 66mg.

Sugar-crusted Shortbread Rounds

Shortbread should melt in the mouth, taste buttery but never greasy. It tastes best when eaten freshly made with a cup of tea.

Makes about 24
450g/1lb/2 cups butter
225g/8oz/1 heaped cup caster (superfine) sugar

450g/1lb/4 cups plain (all-purpose) flour
225g/8oz/scant 1½ cups ground rice or rice flour
5ml/1 tsp salt
demerara (raw) sugar, to decorate
golden caster (superfine) sugar, for dusting

1 Preheat the oven to 190°C/375°F/Gas 5.

2 Make sure all the ingredients are at room temperature. Put the butter and sugar in a bowl and beat together until light, pale and fluffy.

3 Sift together the flour, ground rice or rice flour and salt and stir into the butter and sugar with a wooden spoon, until the mixture resembles fine breadcrumbs.

4 Gather the dough together with your hands, then put it on a clean work surface. Knead lightly until it forms a ball but do not over-knead or the shortbread will be tough and greasy. Roll into a sausage, about 7.5cm/3in thick. Wrap in cling film (plastic wrap) and chill until firm.

5 Pour the demerara sugar on to a sheet of baking parchment. Unwrap the dough and roll in the sugar until evenly coated. Slice the roll into discs about 1cm/½in thick.

6 Place the discs on to two lightly greased baking sheets lined with baking parchment, spacing them well apart to allow for spreading. Bake for 20–25 minutes until very pale gold.

7 Remove the cookies from the oven and sprinkle immediately with the golden caster sugar. Allow to cool on the baking sheet for 10 minutes before transferring to a wire rack to cool completely.

Shortbread Shells

These interesting shaped cookies are made by pressing the dough into a queen scallop shell prior to baking. If you don't have shells you could stamp out rounds with a cookie cutter instead.

Makes 12
100g/3½oz/½ cup butter, softened
50g/2oz/¼ cup caster (superfine) sugar, plus extra for sprinkling
150g/5½oz/1¼ cups plain (all-purpose) flour

1 Preheat the oven to 200°C/400°F/Gas 6. Lightly grease one large baking sheet and line with baking parchment.

2 Put the butter and sugar into a bowl and beat until light and fluffy. Sift the flour over and stir it in until the mixture can be gathered into a ball of soft dough.

3 Divide the dough into 12 and with your hands form into equal-sized balls.

4 Sprinkle the inside of a scallop shell with sugar, gently press a ball of dough into it, spreading it evenly so the shell is filled. Invert on to the prepared baking sheets, pressing it down to flatten the base and to mark it with the impression of the shell. Lift the shell off, carefully prising out the dough. Alternatively, press or roll the dough balls into plain round cookies measuring about 5cm/2in in diameter.

5 Bake for about 10 minutes until set. Traditionally, they should not be allowed to brown, but should have crisp golden edges.

6 Sprinkle with a little extra sugar, transfer to a wire rack and leave to cool completely.

Cook's Tip
Although shaping the first shell-shape biscuit may seen tricky, the shell will coat with sugar and the rest will slip out easily. You could flavour the mixture with vanilla or spices in step 2.

Sugar-crusted Shortbread Rounds Energy 275kcal/1147kJ; Protein 2.5g; Carbohydrate 32g, of which sugars 10.2g; Fat 15.7g, of which saturates 9.8g; Cholesterol 40mg; Calcium 37mg; Fibre 0.8g; Sodium 197mg.
Shortbread Shells Energy 121kcal/506kJ; Protein 1.2g; Carbohydrate 14.1g, of which sugars 4.6g; Fat 7g, of which saturates 4.4g; Cholesterol 18mg; Calcium 21mg; Fibre 0.4g; Sodium 51mg.

Almond Shortbread Fingers

This easy all-in-one recipe makes a very light, crisp shortbread with an excellent flavour, and it keeps well. Serve with tea or coffee, or to accompany light desserts.

Makes about 48
225g/8oz/1 cup butter, softened
75g/3oz/6 tbsp caster
  (superfine) sugar
275g/10oz/2½ cups plain
  (all-purpose) flour
25g/1oz/¼ cup ground almonds
grated rind of ½ lemon

1 Preheat the oven to 180°C/350°F/Gas 4. Lightly grease a large Swiss roll tin (jelly roll pan).

2 Beat the butter and sugar together in a mixing bowl until light and fluffy. Set aside.

3 Sift the flour and almonds into a clean mixing bowl. Turn the creamed mixture on to the flour and almonds, then work it together first using a wooden spoon and then using your fingers to make a smooth dough.

4 Turn the mixture out on the prepared tray and flatten it out to the edges with the back of a wooden spoon until it is an even thickness all over.

5 Bake for 20 minutes, or until pale golden brown. Remove from the oven and immediately mark the shortbread into fingers or squares with a sharp knife, while the mixture is soft.

6 Leave the shortbread in the tin to cool for a few minutes, and then transfer to a wire rack and leave to cool completely.

7 If stored in an airtight container, the shortbread can be kept for up to two weeks.

> **Variation**
> *Replace the lemon rind with the grated rind of two oranges, if you like.*

Shrewsbury Cakes

These are crisp, lemony shortbread cookies with fluted edges, which have been made and sold in the town of Shrewsbury, in England, since the 17th century.

Makes about 20
115g/4oz/½ cup butter, softened
140g/5oz/¾ cup caster
  (superfine) sugar
2 egg yolks
225g/8oz/2 cups plain
  (all-purpose) flour, plus extra
  for dusting
finely grated rind of 1 lemon

1 Preheat the oven to 180°C/350°F/Gas 4. Lightly grease two baking sheets.

2 In a mixing bowl, beat together the butter and sugar until pale, light and fluffy. Beat in each egg yolk one at a time, beating thoroughly after each addition.

3 Sift the flour over the top and add the lemon rind. Stir in with a wooden spoon at first and then gather up the mixture with your fingertips to make a stiff dough. Knead the dough lightly on a floured surface then roll it out evenly to about 5mm/¼in thick.

4 Using a 7.5cm/3in fluted cookie cutter, stamp out rounds and arrange on the baking sheets. Gather up the trimmings and roll out again to make more cookies until all the dough has been used up.

5 Bake for about 15 minutes, until firm to the touch and lightly browned.

6 Transfer to a wire rack and leave to cool completely.

> **Variations**
> • *Omit the lemon rind and sift 5ml/1 tsp mixed (apple pie) spice with the flour in step 3.*
> • *Add 25g/1oz/2 tbsp currants or raisins to the mixture in step 3.*

Almond Shortbread Fingers Energy 64kcal/266kJ; Protein 0.7g; Carbohydrate 6.1g, of which sugars 1.8g; Fat 4.2g, of which saturates 2.5g; Cholesterol 10mg; Calcium 11mg; Fibre 0.2g; Sodium 29mg.
Shrewsbury Cakes Energy 115kcal/482kJ; Protein 1.4g; Carbohydrate 16.1g, of which sugars 7.5g; Fat 5.4g, of which saturates 3.2g; Cholesterol 32mg; Calcium 023mg; Fibre 0.4g; Sodium 37mg.

Butter and Almond Shortbreads

Moist shortbread cookies, flavoured with almonds, are cut into shapes of your choice and given a generous dusting of sugar so that they are pure white.

Makes 20–22
225g/8oz/1 cup unsalted (sweet) butter
150g/5oz/2/3 cup caster (superfine) sugar
2 egg yolks
5ml/1 tsp vanilla extract
2.5ml/1/2 tsp bicarbonate of soda (baking soda)
45ml/3 tbsp brandy
500g/1 1/4lb/5 cups plain (all-purpose) flour, plus extra for dusting
pinch of salt
150g/5oz/1 1/4 cups blanched almonds, toasted and coarsely chopped
350g/12oz/3 cups icing (confectioners') sugar

1 Preheat the oven to 180°C/350°F/Gas 4. Lightly grease two large baking sheets.

2 In a large bowl, beat together the butter and caster sugar until light and fluffy. Beat in the egg yolks one at a time, then add the vanilla extract.

3 In a small bowl, mix the baking soda with the brandy and stir into the butter and sugar mixture.

4 Sift together the flour and salt over the mixture and mix to a firm dough. Knead lightly with your fingertips, add the almonds and knead again.

5 Roll out the dough to 2.5cm/1in thick on a lightly floured surface. Press out shapes, using cookie cutters. Place on the baking sheets and bake for 20–25 minutes, or until pale golden. Do not let the cookies become brown.

6 Sift a quarter of the icing sugar on to a plate. Set aside. As soon as the cookies come out of the oven, dust them generously with sifted icing sugar. Leave to cool for a few minutes, then place them on the sugar-coated plate. Sift the remaining icing sugar over them. The aim is to give them a generous coating, so they are pure white.

Sweet Almond Cookies

Serve these crisp cookies with ice cream or fruit fool, or more simply with fresh fruit salad, yogurt or a spoonful of thick cream. Make a batch in advance and keep them in an airtight tin.

Makes about 25
25g/1oz/2 tbsp butter
30ml/2 tbsp milk
1 egg yolk
225g/8oz/2 cups ground almonds, plus extra for rolling out
25g/1oz/2 tbsp caster (superfine) sugar
5ml/1 tsp baking powder
2.5ml/1/2 tsp vanilla extract

1 Preheat the oven to 190°C/375°F/Gas 5.

2 Melt the butter in a pan and leave to cool until lukewarm.

3 Blend together the milk and egg yolk.

4 Mix the ground almonds, sugar and baking powder in a bowl then stir in the melted butter, vanilla extract and milk and egg mixture.

5 Knead the mixture with your hands to form a moist dough and then roll out to about 5mm/1/4in thick on a cool surface lightly dusted with extra ground almonds.

6 Cut the dough into rounds using a 6cm/2 1/2in cookie cutter. Gather the trimmings together and keep rolling out and cutting more cookies until all the mixture has been used up.

7 Transfer the dough rounds to a non-stick baking sheet and bake for about 10 minutes until lightly browned. Transfer to a wire rack and leave to cool completely.

Variation
The egg yolk is not essential but helps to bind the mixture together. If preferred, use an extra 15ml/1 tbsp milk.

Butter and Almond Shortbreads Energy 325kcal/1363kJ; Protein 4.4g; Carbohydrate 46.1g, of which sugars 26.9g; Fat 14.3g, of which saturates 6.4g; Cholesterol 44mg; Calcium 71mg; Fibre 1.3g; Sodium 72mg. **Sweet Almond Cookies** Energy 69kcal/288kJ; Protein 2.1g; Carbohydrate 1.7g, of which sugars 1.5g; Fat 6.1g, of which saturates 1g; Cholesterol 10mg; Calcium 25mg; Fibre 0.7g; Sodium 8mg.

Almond Cookies

Fine sugar and butter combine to give these cookies a light, delicate texture. They can be made days ahead, and are delicious with desserts or coffee.

Makes about 25

115g/4oz/1 cup plain
   (all-purpose) flour, plus extra
   for dusting
175g/6oz/1½ cups icing
   (confectioners') sugar
pinch of salt
50g/2oz/½ cup chopped almonds
2.5ml/½ tsp almond extract
115g/4oz/½ cup unsalted
   (sweet) butter, softened
icing (confectioners') sugar,
   for dusting
halved almonds, to decorate

1 Preheat the oven to 180°C/350°F/Gas 4. Lightly grease two large baking sheets.

2 Combine the flour, icing sugar, salt and chopped almonds in a bowl. Add the almond extract.

3 Put the softened butter in the centre of the flour mixture and use your fingertips to draw the dry ingredients into the butter until a dough is formed. Knead until smooth. Shape the dough into a ball.

4 Place the dough on a lightly floured surface and roll it out to a thickness of about 3mm/⅛in. Using a 7.5cm/3in cookie cutter, stamp out 25 rounds, re-rolling the dough as necessary to use up any trimmings. Place the rounds on the baking sheets, leaving a little space between them. Decorate the cookies halved almonds.

5 Bake for 25–30 minutes until pale golden. Leave for 10 minutes, then transfer to wire racks to cool. Dust thickly with icing sugar before serving,

> **Cook's Tip**
> Use fancy cookie cutters such as hearts and crescents to make these cookies look even more interesting.

Almond Tiles

These cookies are named after the French roof tiles they resemble. Making them is a little fiddly, so bake a few at a time until you get the knack.

Makes about 24

70g/2½oz/½ cup whole
   blanched almonds, lightly
   toasted
70g/2½oz/⅓ cup caster
   (superfine) sugar
40g/1½oz/3 tbsp unsalted
   (sweet) butter, softened
2 egg whites
2.5ml/½ tsp almond extract
35g/1¼oz scant ¼ cup plain
   (all-purpose) flour, sifted
55g/2oz/⅔ cup flaked
   (sliced) almonds

1 Preheat the oven to 200°C/400°F/Gas 6. Generously grease two baking sheets.

2 Put the almonds and 30ml/2 tbsp of the sugar in a food processor fitted with the metal blade, and pulse until ground.

3 In a large bowl, beat the butter until creamy, then add the remaining sugar and beat until light and fluffy. Gradually beat in the egg whites until well blended, then add the almond extract. Sift in the flour and fold in, then fold in the ground almond mixture.

4 Drop tablespoons of mixture on to the baking sheets about 15cm/6in apart. With the back of a wet spoon, spread each mound into a paper-thin 7.5cm/3in round. Sprinkle each round with a few flaked almonds.

5 Bake one sheet at a time, for 5–6 minutes until the edges are golden and the centres still pale. Working quickly, use a thin metal spatula to loosen the edges of each cookie. Lift on the spatula and place over a rolling pin, then press down the sides of the cookie to curve it.

6 Continue shaping the cookies, transferring them to a wire rack as they cool and crisp. If the cookies become too crisp to shape, return the baking sheet to the oven for 15–30 seconds to soften them, then continue as above.

Almond Cookies Energy 188kcal/788kJ; Protein 3.5g; Carbohydrate 22.5g, of which sugars 10.9g; Fat 10g, of which saturates 4.4g; Cholesterol 45mg; Calcium 44mg; Fibre 0.8g; Sodium 58mg.
Almond Tiles Energy 59kcal/246kJ; Protein 1.4g; Carbohydrate 4.5g, of which sugars 3.1g; Fat 4.1g, of which saturates 1.1g; Cholesterol 4mg; Calcium 16mg; Fibre 0.4g; Sodium 16mg.

Iced Almond Cookies

Crisp and crunchy, these small cookies are flavoured with ground almonds. They are delicious served with a bowl of vanilla ice cream.

Makes about 25
115g/4oz/½ cup butter
115g/4oz/generous ½ cup caster (superfine) sugar
1 egg, separated
5ml/1 tsp vanilla extract
115g/4oz/1 cup ground almonds

115g/4oz/1 cup plain (all-purpose) flour

To decorate
50g/2oz/½ cup icing (confectioners') sugar
75–100 crystallized alpine pink petals (rose petals, primroses or violets could also be used)

1 Preheat the oven to 180°C/350°F/Gas 4. Lightly grease two large baking sheets.

2 In a large bowl, beat together the butter and sugar until light and fluffy. Add the egg yolk and vanilla extract and mix together. Stir in the ground almonds. Sift the flour over the mixture, stir in with a wooden spoon at first, and then knead together with your fingertips until the dough forms a ball.

3 With your hands, roll the dough into small balls about 2.5cm/1in diameter, then place on the prepared baking sheet. Flatten slightly with the back of a spoon.

4 Lightly beat the egg white and brush over the cookies. Bake for about 15 minutes. Using a metal spatula, transfer the cookies to a wire rack and leave to cool.

5 To decorate the cookies, sift the icing sugar into a bowl. Add about 1 tsp of hot water and stir until the mixture is smooth and thick enough to coat the back of a wooden spoon.

6 Spoon the icing on top of each cookie and while still wet secure the crystallized alpine pink petals to the top. Leave to set for about 30 minutes before serving. Store in an airtight container for 2–3 days.

Big Macs

These giant macaroons are crisp on the outside, chewy in the middle and naturally free from gluten and cow's milk. Ground almonds are a great alternative to the flour used in most cookies, and macaroons don't need butter for their deliciously moist, rich taste.

Makes 9
2 egg whites
5ml/1 tsp almond extract
115g/4oz/1 cup ground almonds
130g/4½oz/generous 1 cup light muscovado (brown) sugar

1 Preheat the oven to 180°C/350°F/Gas 4. Line a large baking sheet with baking parchment.

2 Put the egg whites in a large, clean bowl and whisk until they form stiff peaks.

3 Add the almond extract to the egg whites and whisk to combine. Sprinkle over the ground almonds and sugar and gently fold in using a large metal spoon.

4 Place nine tablespoonfuls of the mixture, spacing them well apart to allow room for spreading, on to the prepared baking sheet and flatten slightly with the back of a spoon. Bake for 15 minutes until risen, deep golden and beginning to turn crisp.

5 Leave the macaroons on the baking sheet for 5 minutes, then transfer to a wire rack and leave to crisp up and cool completely.

Cook's Tips
• These macaroons will store well in an airtight container; do not store in the refrigerator because they'll turn soft and lose their lovely crisp and chewy texture.
• To make a macaroon with a milder flavour, use caster (superfine) sugar in place of the light muscovado sugar.

Iced Almond Cookies Energy 115kcal/481kJ; Protein 1.5g; Carbohydrate 15g, of which sugars 10.1g; Fat 5.8g, of which saturates 2.4g; Cholesterol 9mg; Calcium 24mg; Fibre 0.5g; Sodium 27mg.
Big Macs Energy 138kcal/577kJ; Protein 3.4g; Carbohydrate 16g, of which sugars 15.6g; Fat 7.1g, of which saturates 0.6g; Cholesterol 0mg; Calcium 39mg; Fibre 0.9g; Sodium 16mg.

Microwave Almond Cookies

These cookies are great to make if you want a sweet treat and are short of time. They look paler than conventionally baked cookies, but are just as delicious. Store in an airtight container once cool and eat within 24 hours.

Makes 12
50g/2oz/¼ cup butter
50g/2oz/¼ cup soft light brown sugar
1 egg yolk
75g/3oz/⅔ cup plain (all-purpose) flour
25g/1oz/¼ cup ground almonds

1 In a large bowl, beat the butter and sugar together until light and fluffy. Beat in the egg yolk.

2 Sift over the flour and gently fold into the butter mixture together with the ground almonds.

3 Place six tablespoonsfuls of the mixture in a circle on a microwave-proof dish or a piece of baking parchment. Cook for 1¾–2½ minutes on full (100 per cent) power or until the surface of the cookies is dry.

4 Remove the cookies carefully from the microwave as the edges will be soft. Leave to stand for 1 minute before lifting them on to a wire rack. They will finish cooking and become firmer as they cool.

Double Peanut Cookies

Packing up a party picnic? Got another birthday party coming up? Make sure that some of these fabulous nutty cookies are on the menu.

Makes 25
225g/8oz/1 cup butter
30ml/2 tbsp smooth peanut butter
115g/4oz/1 cup icing (confectioners') sugar
50g/2oz/¼ cup cornflour (cornstarch)
225g/8oz/2 cups plain (all-purpose) flour
115g/4oz/1 cup unsalted peanuts

1 Preheat the oven to 180°C/350°F/Gas 4. Lightly grease two baking sheets.

2 Put the butter and peanut butter in a bowl and beat together. Add the icing sugar, cornflour and plain flour and mix together to make a soft dough.

3 Roll the mixture into 25 small balls, using the palms of your hands, and place on the baking sheets. Leave plenty of room for the cookies to spread.

4 Press the tops of the balls of dough flat, using the back of a fork. Press a few of the peanuts into each of the cookies.

5 Bake for about 15–20 minutes, until lightly browned. Leave to cool for a few minutes before lifting the cookies carefully on to a wire rack with a metal spatula to cool completely.

Almond Ice Cream Sandwiches

These crisp, nutty wafer cookies make perfect ice cream sandwiches for a summer-time treat.

Makes 6 sandwiches
50g/2oz/¼ cup unsalted (sweet) butter
2 egg whites
75g/3oz/scant ½ cup caster (superfine) sugar
50g/2oz/½ cup plain (all-purpose) flour
40g/1½oz/scant ½ cup ground almonds
30ml/2 tbsp flaked (sliced) almonds (optional)
raspberry ripple or vanilla ice cream, to serve
icing (confectioners') sugar, for dusting

1 Preheat the oven to 200°C/400°F/Gas 6. Line two large baking sheets with baking parchment.

2 Put the butter in a small pan and melt over a very low heat.

3 Put the egg whites and sugar in a bowl and whisk lightly with a fork until the egg whites are broken up. Add the flour, melted butter and ground almonds and mix until evenly combined.

4 Drop 6 level tablespoonfuls of mixture on to each baking sheet, spacing them well apart. Spread each tablespoonful of mixture into circles about 7cm/2¾in in diameter. Sprinkle with almonds, if using, and bake for 10–12 minutes until golden around the edges.

5 Remove from the oven, peel away the paper and transfer to a wire rack to cool.

6 Place a scoop of slightly softened ice cream on to one cookie and top with another, gently pressing them together. Dust with sugar and serve.

Cook's Tip
Don't be tempted to use greaseproof (waxed) paper instead of baking parchment as the cookies may stick to it.

Microwave Almond Cookies Energy 87kcal/362kJ; Protein 1.3g; Carbohydrate 9.4g, of which sugars 4.6g; Fat 5.1g, of which saturates 2.4g; Cholesterol 26mg; Calcium 19mg; Fibre 0.4g; Sodium 27mg.
Double Peanut Cookies Energy 130kcal/543kJ; Protein 1.2g; Carbohydrate 13.9g, of which sugars 5.1g; Fat 8.2g, of which saturates 4.9g; Cholesterol 19mg; Calcium 17mg; Fibre 0.3g; Sodium 60mg.
Almond Ice Cream Sandwiches Energy 184kcal/771kJ; Protein 3.3g; Carbohydrate 20.1g, of which sugars 13.5g; Fat 10.7g, of which saturates 4.7g; Cholesterol 18mg; Calcium 36mg; Fibre 0.8g; Sodium 73mg.

Ladies' Kisses

These old-fashioned cookies are sweet, light and a moreish treat. With their delicious soft chocolate centre they are ideal for an elegant afternoon tea.

Makes 20
150g/5oz/10 tbsp butter, softened
115g/4oz/generous ½ cup caster (superfine) sugar
1 egg yolk
2.5ml/½ tsp almond extract
115g/4oz/1 cup ground almonds
175g/6oz/1½ cups plain (all-purpose) flour
50g/2oz plain (semisweet) chocolate

1 In a large bowl, beat the butter and sugar together until light and fluffy. Beat in the egg yolk, almond extract, ground almonds and flour until evenly mixed. Chill in the refrigerator for about 2 hours until firm.

2 Preheat the oven to 160°C/325°F/Gas 3. Line several baking sheets with baking parchment.

3 Break off small pieces of dough and roll into balls with your hands, making 40 altogether. Place the balls on the baking sheets and flatten slightly with the back of a spoon. Space them well apart as they will spread in the oven.

4 Bake for 20 minutes or until golden. Remove the baking sheets from the oven, lift off the parchment with the cookies still on it, then place on wire racks. Leave to cool. Repeat with the remaining mixture.

5 Lift the cooled cookies off the paper. Melt the chocolate in a bowl over a pan of hot water. Use to sandwich the cookies in pairs, then leave to cool and set before serving.

> **Cook's Tip**
> *These cookies look dainty served in frilly petit fours cases.*

Salted Peanut Cookies

The combination of salty and sweet flavours in these little cookies is delicious. The texture is delightfully crunchy and will appeal particularly to adult tastes.

Makes 70
250g/9oz/generous 1 cup soft light brown sugar, plus extra for dipping
350g/12oz/3 cups plain (all-purpose) flour
2.5ml/½ tsp bicarbonate of soda (baking soda)
115g/4oz/½ cup butter at room temperature, diced
115g/4oz/½ cup margarine
2 eggs
10ml/2 tsp vanilla extract
225g/8oz/2 cups salted peanuts

1 Preheat the oven to 190°C/375°F/Gas 5. Lightly grease two baking sheets. Grease the base of a small glass and dip in sugar. Set aside.

2 In a small bowl, sift together the flour and bicarbonate of soda and set aside.

3 In a large bowl, beat together the butter, margarine and sugar until the mixture is light and fluffy. Beat in the eggs, one at a time, and then the vanilla extract. Gently fold in the sifted flour mixture using a metal spoon.

4 Add the peanuts and gently stir them into the butter mixture until evenly combined.

5 On to the prepared baking sheets drop teaspoonfuls of the mixture, spaced 5cm/2in apart to allow room for spreading. Flatten each slightly with the prepared glass, dipping the base of the glass in the sugar after each use.

6 Bake the cookies in the oven for about 10 minutes, until lightly coloured. Remove from the oven and leave to set for a minute or two. With a metal spatula, carefully transfer the cookies to a wire rack and leave to cool completely before serving.

Ladies Kisses Energy 159kcal/665kJ; Protein 2.4g; Carbohydrate 14.8g, of which sugars 8g; Fat 10.5g, of which saturates 4.7g; Cholesterol 26mg; Calcium 32mg; Fibre 0.8g; Sodium 47mg.
Salted Peanut Cookies Energy 77kcal/322kJ; Protein 1.5g; Carbohydrate 7.9g, of which sugars 4g; Fat 4.6g, of which saturates 1.2g; Cholesterol 9mg; Calcium 11mg; Fibre 0.3g; Sodium 38mg.

Peanut Butter Cookies

These cookies must be close to the top of the list of America's favourite cookies, ever since peanut butter was introduced at the 1904 St Louis, Missouri, World Fair.

Makes 24
115g/4oz/½ cup butter at room temperature, diced
125g/4½oz/¾ cup firmly packed soft light brown sugar
1 egg
5ml/1 tsp vanilla extract
225g/8oz/1 cup crunchy peanut butter
115g/4oz/1 cup plain (all-purpose) flour
2.5ml/½ tsp bicarbonate of soda (baking soda)
pinch of salt

1 In a large bowl, beat together the butter and sugar until light and fluffy.

2 In another bowl, mix the egg and vanilla extract, then gradually beat the liquid into the butter mixture.

3 Stir in the peanut butter and blend thoroughly.

4 Sift over the bowl the flour, bicarbonate of soda and salt and stir into the mixture to form a soft dough. Chill the dough for at least 30 minutes, until firm.

5 Preheat the oven to 180°C/350°F/Gas 4. Lightly grease two baking sheets.

6 Roll rounded teaspoonfuls of the dough into balls. Place on the baking sheets and press flat with a fork into rounds about 6cm/2½in in diameter, making a criss-cross pattern.

7 Bake for about 12 minutes or until lightly coloured. Transfer to a wire rack and leave to cool.

Variation
For extra crunch, add 50g/2oz/½ cup chopped peanuts with the peanut butter.

Lemony Peanut Pairs

These simple-to-make cookies are filled with peanut butter, but you could use buttercream or chocolate-and-nut spread instead. Make a selection with different fillings and let the kids choose.

Makes 8–10
40g/1½oz/3 tbsp soft light brown sugar
50g/2oz/¼ cup butter, softened
5ml/1 tsp grated lemon rind
75g/3oz/¾ cup wholemeal (whole-wheat) flour, plus extra for dusting
50g/2oz/¼ cup chopped crystallized (candied) pineapple
25g/1oz/2 tbsp smooth peanut butter
sifted icing (confectioners') sugar, for dusting

1 Preheat the oven to 190°C/375°F/Gas 3. Lightly grease a baking sheet.

2 In a large bowl, beat together the sugar, butter and lemon rind until light and fluffy. Beat in the flour, then knead until a smooth dough forms. On a lightly floured surface roll out the dough thinly.

3 Stamp out eight to 10 rounds using a cookie cutter. Space well apart on the baking sheet to allow room for spreading.

4 Press a piece of chopped pineapple on to each cookie. Bake for 20 minutes until golden brown. Transfer to a wire rack and leave to cool completely.

5 Sandwich two cookies together with the peanut butter. Serve lightly dusted with sifted sugar.

Variation
To make an alternative buttercream filling, beat 15g/½oz/1 tbsp butter until soft. Sift in 25g/1oz/2 tbsp icing (confectioners') sugar and beat together until smooth.

Peanut Butter Cookies Energy 154kcal/641kJ; Protein 3.4g; Carbohydrate 13.7g, of which sugars 8.3g; Fat 9.9g, of which saturates 4g; Cholesterol 18mg; Calcium 19mg; Fibre 0.8g; Sodium 71mg.
Lemony Peanut Pairs Energy 103kcal/431kJ; Protein 1.6g; Carbohydrate 12.3g, of which sugars 7.5g; Fat 5.6g, of which saturates 3g; Cholesterol 11mg; Calcium 13mg; Fibre 1.1g; Sodium 54mg.

Rich Peanut Crunch Cookies

These delicious sweet and nutty cookies are so easy to make. They puff up into lovely domed rounds during baking, giving them a really professional look. If you prefer cookies with a slightly less "nutty" texture, use smooth peanut butter rather than the crunchy variety.

Makes 25
150g/5oz/1¼ cups self-raising
    (self-rising) flour
2.5ml/ ½ tsp baking powder
115g/4oz/½ cup unsalted
    (sweet) butter, at room
    temperature, diced
115g/4oz/generous ½ cup light
    muscovado (brown) sugar
1 egg
150g/5oz/generous ½ cup
    crunchy peanut butter
icing (confectioners') sugar,
    for dusting

1 Preheat the oven to 190°C/375°F/Gas 5. Lightly grease two baking sheets.

2 Sift the flour and baking powder together into a bowl.

3 Put the butter and sugar in a mixing bowl and beat until pale and creamy.

4 Beat in the egg, then add the sifted flour mixture and the peanut butter. Beat together until the ingredients are thoroughly mixed.

5 Place heaped teaspoonfuls of the mixture on to the baking sheets; space well apart to allow the cookies to spread while baking. (If necessary, spoon the dough on to the baking sheets in batches.)

6 Bake the cookies for about 20 minutes until risen; they will still be quite soft to the touch.

7 Leave the cookies on the baking sheets to set for about 5 minutes, then using a metal spatula carefully transfer them to a wire rack and leave to cool completely. To serve, lightly dust with icing sugar. Store in an airtight container for 2–3 days.

Hazelnut Cookies

Serve these sweet little nut cookies as petits fours with after-dinner coffee. As a healthy bonus, they are rich in vitamin E.

Makes about 25
115g/4oz/8 tbsp butter
75g/3oz/¾ cup icing
    (confectioners') sugar
115g/4oz/1 cup plain
    (all-purpose) flour
75g/3oz/¾ cup ground hazelnuts
1 egg yolk
blanched hazelnuts, to decorate
icing (confectioners') sugar,
    for dusting

1 Preheat the oven to 180°C/350°F/Gas 4. Lightly grease and then line three or four baking sheets with baking parchment.

2 In a large bowl, beat together the butter and sugar until light and fluffy.

3 Beat in the flour, ground hazelnuts and egg yolk until evenly mixed.

4 Take a teaspoonful of mixture at a time and shape it into a smooth ball with your fingers. Place the rounds well apart on the baking parchment, to allow room for spreading. Flatten slightly with your thumb and then press a whole hazelnut into the centre of each one to decorate.

5 Bake the cookies, one tray at a time, for about 10 minutes or until golden brown. Allow to set slightly for 1 or 2 minutes then transfer them to a wire rack using a metal spatula.

6 While still warm, sift icing sugar over each cookie to cover and then leave to cool completely before serving. Store in an airtight container interleaved with baking parchment.

> **Variation**
> *Instead of the ground hazelnuts other ground nuts can be used, such as pecans, walnuts, macadamia and Brazil nuts.*

Peanut Crunch Cookies Energy 112kcal/466kJ; Protein 2.1g; Carbohydrate 10.3g, of which sugars 5.3g; Fat 7.2g, of which saturates 3.2g; Cholesterol 18mg; Calcium 15mg; Fibre 0.5g; Sodium 50mg.
Hazelnut Cookies Energy 86kcal/359kJ; Protein 1.1g; Carbohydrate 6.9g, of which sugars 3.4g; Fat 6.2g, of which saturates 2.7g; Cholesterol 26mg; Calcium 15mg; Fibre 0.3g; Sodium 29mg.

Chocolate-dipped Hazelnut Crescents

Dipped in melted chocolate, these cookies look professionally made, yet they are surprisingly easy to make.

Makes about 35
285g/10oz/2 cups plain (all-purpose) flour
pinch of salt
225g/8oz/1 cup unsalted (sweet) butter
55g/2oz/¹/₃ cup caster (superfine) sugar
15ml/1 tbsp hazelnut liqueur or water
5ml/1 tsp vanilla extract
175g/6oz milk chocolate, grated
85g/3oz/¹/₂ cup hazelnuts, toasted and finely chopped
icing (confectioners') sugar, for dusting
175g/6oz milk chocolate, for decorating

1 Preheat the oven to 160°C/325°F/Gas 3. Lightly grease two large baking sheets.

2 Sift the flour and salt into a bowl.

3 In another large bowl, beat the butter until creamy. Add the sugar and beat until fluffy, beat in the hazelnut liqueur and vanilla. Gently stir in the flour, until just blended, then fold in the grated chocolate and hazelnuts.

4 With floured hands, shape the dough into 5 ×1cm/2 × ½in crescents and place on the prepared baking sheets spaced widely apart to allow room for spreading.

5 Bake in the oven for 20–25 minutes until the edges are set and the biscuits slightly golden. Remove the crescents from the baking sheets and transfer to a wire rack to cool for 10 minutes.

6 Break the milk chocolate into a small heatproof bowl and set over a pan of gently simmering water. Heat gently, stirring frequently, until melted. Remove from the heat.

7 Dust the crescents with icing sugar. Dip half of each crescent into melted chocolate. Place on a baking sheet lined with baking parchment and leave to cool. Chill until the chocolate has set.

Cashew Nut Button Cookies

These light little cookies, flavoured with ground cashew nuts, are coated in toasted hazelnuts. You will need a food processor to grind the cashew nuts.

Makes about 20
150g/5oz/1¼ cups unroasted cashew nuts
1 egg white
25g/1oz/2 tbsp caster (superfine) sugar
50g/2oz/¹/₃ cup dates, finely chopped
5ml/1 tsp finely grated orange rind
30ml/2 tbsp pure maple or maple-flavoured syrup
90g/3¹/₂oz/scant 1 cup toasted hazelnuts, chopped

1 Preheat the oven to 190°C/375°F/Gas 5. Lightly grease two baking sheets.

2 Put the cashew nuts in a food processor, fitted with a metal blade, and process until finely ground.

3 In a large bowl, whisk the egg white until stiff. Whisk in the sugar. Stir in the ground cashews, dates, orange rind and syrup. Mix together well.

4 Put the chopped hazelnuts in a small bowl. Drop small spoonfuls of the cookie mixture into the hazelnuts and toss until well coated.

5 Place the coated cookies on the prepared baking sheets and bake in the oven for about 10 minutes until lightly browned. Leave the cookies on the baking sheets to firm up slightly, then using a metal spatula carefully transfer them to a wire rack and leave to cool completely.

> **Variation**
> *You could buy ground almonds, rather than grinding your own, and use them to replace the ground cashew nuts. For coating the cookies substitute toasted almonds in place of the toasted hazelnuts.*

Chocolate-dipped Hazelnut Crescents Energy 102kcal/427kJ; Protein 1.9g; Carbohydrate 13.8g, of which sugars 7.6g; Fat 4.7g, of which saturates 2g; Cholesterol 2mg; Calcium 38mg; Fibre 0.5g; Sodium 9mg. **Cashew Nut Button Cookies** Energy 92kcal/382kJ; Protein 2.4g; Carbohydrate 5.9g, of which sugars 4.8g; Fat 6.7g, of which saturates 1g; Cholesterol 0mg; Calcium 11mg; Fibre 0.6g; Sodium 29mg.

Pecan Nut Puffs

As they don't keep very well, you have the perfect excuse to enjoy these melt-in-the-mouth, light-as-air cookies as freely as you like.

Makes 24

115g/4oz/1 cup plain (all-purpose) flour
pinch of salt
115g/4oz/½ cup unsalted (sweet) butter at room temperature, diced
30ml/2 tbsp sugar
5ml/1 tsp vanilla extract
115g/4oz/1 cup pecan nuts
icing (confectioners') sugar, for dusting

1 Preheat the oven to 150°C/300°F/Gas 2. Lightly grease two baking sheets.

2 Sift the flour and salt together into a bowl.

3 In a large bowl, beat together the butter and sugar until light and fluffy. Stir in the vanilla extract.

4 Grind the pecan nuts in a food processor, blender or nut grinder. Stir several times to prevent the nuts from becoming oily.

5 Push the ground nuts through a sieve (strainer) set over a bowl to aerate them. Any pieces that are too large to go through the sieve can be ground again.

6 Stir the nuts and sifted flour into the butter mixture to make a dough. Roll the dough into marble-size balls between the palms of your hands.

7 Place the balls on the prepared baking sheets, spaced well apart to allow room for spreading. Bake in the oven for 45 minutes.

8 Leave the puffs to cool slightly, then, while they are still hot, roll them in icing sugar. Leave to cool completely on a wire rack, then roll once more in icing sugar.

Mini Pecan Fudge Bites

These cute little cookies have the flavour of butterscotch and fudge and are topped with chopped pecan nuts for a delicious crunch – just the right size for an afternoon treat with tea or coffee.

Makes 30

200g/7oz/1¾ cups self-raising (self-rising) flour
115g/4oz/½ cup butter, at room temperature, diced
115g/4oz/generous ½ cup dark muscovado (molasses) sugar
75g/3oz vanilla cream fudge, diced
1 egg, beaten
25g/1oz/½ cup pecan nut halves, sliced widthways

1 Preheat the oven to190°C/375°F/Gas 5. Lightly grease two or three baking sheets.

2 Put the flour in a bowl, and using your fingertips, rub in the butter until the mixture resembles fine breadcrumbs. Alternatively, put the flour and butter in a food processor and process until the mixture resembles breadcrumbs.

3 Add the muscovado sugar and diced vanilla cream fudge to the flour mixture and stir well until combined. Add the beaten egg and mix in well.

4 Bring the dough together with your hands, then knead gently on a lightly floured surface. It will be soft yet firm.

5 Roll the dough into two cylinders, 23cm/9in long. Cut into 1cm/½in slices and place on the baking sheets. Sprinkle over the pecan nuts and press in lightly.

6 Bake for about 12 minutes until browned at the edges. Transfer to a wire rack to cool.

Variation
Use walnut halves, sliced, instead of the pecan nuts.

Pecan Nut Puffs Energy 90kcal/373kJ; Protein 0.9g; Carbohydrate 5.3g, of which sugars 1.6g; Fat 7.4g, of which saturates 2.8g; Cholesterol 10mg; Calcium 11mg; Fibre 0.4g; Sodium 29mg.
Min Pecan Fudge Bites Energy 86kcal/359kJ; Protein 1g; Carbohydrate 11.3g, of which sugars 6.2g; Fat 4.4g, of which saturates 2.3g; Cholesterol 15mg; Calcium 17mg; Fibre 0.2g; Sodium 29mg.

Walnut Cookies

These cookies are for lovers of walnuts, but the same recipe can be used for pecan nut lovers too.

Makes 60
115g/4oz/½ cup butter
175g/6oz/scant 1 cup caster
    (superfine) sugar
115g/4oz/1 cup plain
    (all-purpose) flour
10ml/2 tsp vanilla extract
115g/4oz/⅔ cup walnuts,
    finely chopped

1 Preheat the oven to 150°C/300°F/ Gas 2. Lightly grease two baking sheets.

2 In a mixing bowl, beat the butter until soft. Add 100g/4oz/ ½ cup of the sugar and continue beating until light and fluffy. Stir in the flour, vanilla extract and walnuts.

3 Drop teaspoonfuls of the batter 5cm/2in apart on the prepared baking sheets and flatten slightly. Bake for about 25 minutes.

4 Transfer to a wire rack set over a baking sheet and sprinkle with the remaining sugar.

Walnut Crescents

Although delicious just as they are, these cookies are also good when one end is dipped and coated in melted chocolate.

Makes 9
115g/4oz/⅔ cup walnuts
225g/8oz/1 cup unsalted
    (sweet) butter
115g/4oz/generous ½ cup sugar
2.5ml/½ tsp vanilla extract
225g/8oz/2 cups plain
    (all-purpose) flour
pinch of salt
icing (confectioners') sugar,
    for dusting

1 Preheat the oven to 180°C/350F/Gas 4.

2 Grind the walnuts in a food processor, blender or nut grinder until they are almost a paste. Transfer to a bowl.

3 Add the butter to the walnuts and mix with a wooden spoon until blended. Add the sugar and vanilla, and stir to blend.

4 Sift the flour and salt into the walnut mixture. Work into a dough.

5 Shape the dough into small cylinders about 4cm/1½in long. Bend into crescents and place evenly spaced on an ungreased baking sheet.

6 Bake for about 15 minutes until lightly browned. Transfer to a rack to cool slightly. Set the rack over a baking sheet and dust lightly with icing sugar. Leave to cool completely. Store in an airtight container.

Pecan Tassies

These cookies are made in two parts, a rich cream cheese base is filled with a sweet and nutty filling.

Makes 24
115g/4oz/½ cup cream cheese
115g/4oz/½ cup butter, diced
115g/4oz/1 cup plain
    (all-purpose) flour, plus extra
    for dusting

For the filling
2 eggs
115g/4oz/½ cup soft dark
    brown sugar
5ml/1 tsp vanilla extract
pinch of salt
25g/1oz/2 tbsp butter, melted
115g/4oz/⅔ cup pecan nuts

1 Place a baking sheet in the oven and preheat to 180°C/ 350°F/Gas 4. Lightly grease 24 mini-muffin tins.

2 Put the cream cheese and butter in a mixing bowl. Sift over the flour in two batches and mix well to a smooth paste after each addition.

3 Roll out the dough thinly on a lightly floured surface. Try not to add too much flour to the rolling pin. With a floured cookie cutter, stamp out 24 6cm/2½in rounds. Gather the trimmings together and continue to roll and stamp out rounds. Line the mini-muffin tins with the rounds and chill for 30 minutes.

4 To make the filling, lightly whisk the eggs in a bowl. Gradually whisk in the brown sugar, and add the vanilla extract, salt and melted butter. Set aside.

5 Reserve 24 pecan halves and chop the rest coarsely with a sharp knife.

6 Place a spoonful of chopped nuts in each muffin tin and cover with the filling. Set a pecan half on the top of each.

7 Place the muffin tins on top of the hot baking sheet and bake in the oven for about 20 minutes until puffed and set. Using a metal spatula, carefully transfer the tassies to a wire rack to cool. Serve at room temperature.

Walnut Cookies Energy 107kcal/449kJ; Protein 1.7g; Carbohydrate 16.2g, of which sugars 16.1g; Fat 4.4g, of which saturates 0.4g; Cholesterol 0mg; Calcium 14mg; Fibre 0.2g; Sodium 15mg.
Walnut Crescents Energy 51kcal/212kJ; Protein 0.5g; Carbohydrate 3.7g, of which sugars 1.6g; Fat 3.9g, of which saturates 1.9g; Cholesterol 7.5mg; Calcium 6.7mg; Fibre 0.1g; Sodium 28mg.
Pecan Tassies Energy 139kcal/576kJ; Protein 1.6g; Carbohydrate 9g, of which sugars 5.3g; Fat 10.9g, of which saturates 4.9g; Cholesterol 33mg; Calcium 20mg; Fibre 0.4g; Sodium 56mg.

Walnut Biscotti

These light crunchy cookies with toasted walnuts are flavoured with orange and coriander seeds.

Makes about 40
115g/4oz/1/2 cup unsalted (sweet) butter, diced
200g/7oz/1 cup sugar
2 eggs
15ml/1 tbsp walnut or olive oil

finely grated rind of 1 large orange
350g/12oz/3 cups plain (all-purpose) flour
7.5ml/1 1/2 tsp baking powder
75g/3oz/3/4 cup cornmeal
115g/4oz/1 cup walnuts, toasted and chopped
10ml/2 tsp coriander seeds, crushed

1 Preheat the oven to 160°C/325°F/Gas 3.

2 Put the butter and sugar in a large bowl and beat together until light and fluffy. Add the eggs, walnut or olive oil and orange rind and mix well.

3 Sift the flour and baking powder over the mixture and add the cornmeal, walnuts and coriander seeds. Mix thoroughly and with your hands bring together to form a soft but not sticky dough.

4 Shape the dough into four logs, each measuring about 18cm/7in long and 5cm/2in in diameter. Place slightly apart on non-stick baking sheets. Bake in the oven for 35 minutes until lightly golden.

5 Transfer to wire racks and leave the logs for 10 minutes to cool slightly, then slice diagonally into 1cm/1/2in slices. Return the slices to the baking sheets and bake for 10 minutes. Transfer to wire racks to cool completely.

Cook's Tip
To toast the nuts, spread them on a baking sheet and place in the oven at 160°C/325°F/Gas 3 for 5–7 minutes until just beginning to brown.

Almond Biscotti

This Italian speciality is a traditional recipe. It does not contain butter or oil but uses the eggs to bind the mixture together.

Makes 48
200g/7oz/generous 1 cup whole unblanched almonds
215g/7 1/2oz/scant 2 cups plain (all-purpose) flour

90g/3 1/2oz/1/2 cup caster (superfine) sugar
pinch of salt
pinch of saffron threads
2.5ml/1/2 tsp bicarbonate of soda (baking soda)
2 eggs
1 egg white, lightly beaten

1 Preheat the oven to 190°C/375°F/Gas 5. Lightly grease and sift flour over two baking sheets.

2 Spread the almonds in a baking tray and bake for about 15 minutes until lightly browned. When cool, put 50g/2oz/1/3 cup of the almonds in a food processor, blender, or nut grinder and process until finely ground. Coarsely chop the remaining almonds into two or three pieces each. Set aside.

3 Combine the flour, sugar, salt, saffron, bicarbonate of soda and ground almonds in a bowl and mix to blend. Make a well in the centre and add the eggs. Stir to form a rough dough. Transfer to a floured surface and knead until well blended. Knead in the chopped almonds.

4 Divide the dough into three equal parts. Roll into logs about 2.5cm/1in in diameter. Place on one of the prepared sheets, brush with the egg white and bake for 20 minutes.

5 Slice each log at an angle, making 1cm/1/2in slices. Return the slices to the baking sheets and bake at 140°C/275°F/Gas 1 for 25 minutes more. Transfer to a rack to cool.

Cook's Tip
Dunk biscotti in sweet white wine, such as an Italian Vin Santo.

Walnut Biscotti Energy 104kcal/434kJ; Protein 1.8g; Carbohydrate 13.5g, of which sugars 5.4g; Fat 5g, of which saturates 1.8g; Cholesterol 16mg; Calcium 20mg; Fibre 0.4g; Sodium 22mg.
Almond Biscotti Energy 51kcal/216kJ; Protein 1.6g; Carbohydrate 5.7g, of which sugars 2.2g; Fat 2.6g, of which saturates 0.3g; Cholesterol 8mg; Calcium 18mg; Fibre 0.4g; Sodium 5mg.

Coffee Biscotti

These crisp cookies are made twice as delicious with both freshly roasted ground coffee beans and strong aromatic brewed coffee in the mixture.

Makes about 30
25g/1oz/⅓ cup espresso-roasted coffee beans
115g/4oz/⅔ cup blanched almonds
200g/7oz/scant 2 cups plain (all-purpose) flour
7.5ml/1½ tsp baking powder
pinch of salt
75g/3oz/6 tbsp unsalted (sweet) butter, cubed
150g/5oz/¾ cup caster (superfine) sugar
2 eggs, beaten
25–30ml/1½–2 tbsp strong brewed coffee
5ml/1 tsp ground cinnamon, for dusting

1 Preheat the oven to 180°C/350°F/Gas 4. Lightly grease two baking sheets.

2 Put the espresso coffee beans in a single layer on one side of a large baking sheet and the almonds on the other. Roast in the oven for 10 minutes. Leave to cool.

3 Put the coffee beans in a blender or food processor and process until fairly fine. Tip out and set aside. Process the almonds until finely ground.

4 Sift the flour, baking powder and salt into a bowl. Rub in the butter until the mixture resembles fine breadcrumbs. Stir in the caster sugar, ground coffee and almonds. Add the beaten eggs and enough brewed coffee to make a fairly firm dough.

5 Lightly knead for a few seconds until smooth and shape into two rolls about 7.5cm/3in in diameter. Place on the baking sheet and dust with cinnamon. Bake for 20 minutes.

6 Using a sharp knife, cut the rolls into 4cm/1½in slices on the diagonal. Arrange the slices on the baking tray and bake for another 10 minutes, or until lightly browned. Transfer to a wire rack and leave to cool.

Orange Biscotti

These crisp, crunchy cookies are based on a traditional Italian recipe in which the cookies are packed with nuts and twice baked. This version is flavoured with orange instead of nuts and shaped into long, thin sticks. They are a little softer than the classic biscotti, which are very hard.

Makes about 20
50g/2oz/¼ cup unsalted (sweet) butter, at room temperature, diced
90g/3½oz/½ cup light muscovado (brown) sugar
1 egg
finely grated rind of 1 small orange, plus 10ml/2 tsp juice
175g/6oz/1½ cups self-raising (self-rising) flour
7.5ml/1½ tsp baking powder
good pinch of ground cinnamon
50g/2oz/½ cup polenta
icing (confectioners') sugar, for dusting

1 Preheat the oven to 160°C/325°F/Gas 3. Lightly grease a large baking sheet.

2 In a large bowl, beat together the butter and sugar until smooth and creamy. Beat in the egg, then the orange rind and juice, flour, baking powder, cinnamon and polenta.

3 Tip the mixture on to a lightly floured surface and knead until well blended. Place the dough on the baking sheet and flatten out with the palm of your hand to make a rectangle about 25 x 18cm/10 x 7in.

4 Bake the dough for 25 minutes, then remove from the oven and leave to stand for about 5 minutes until slightly cooled.

5 Using a sharp knife, cut the mixture widthways into thin sticks, about 1cm/½in wide.

6 Space the cookies out slightly on the baking sheet so there's a gap between each one, then return to the oven and bake for another 20 minutes until crisp. Transfer the biscotti to a wire rack and leave to cool. Serve dusted with a little icing sugar.

Coffee Biscotti Energy 97kcal/409kJ; Protein 2g; Carbohydrate 12.9g, of which sugars 5.7g; Fat 4.4g, of which saturates 1.4g; Cholesterol 12mg; Calcium 37mg; Fibre 0.6g; Sodium 54mg.
Orange Biscotti Energy 80kcal/337kJ; Protein 1.4g; Carbohydrate 13.6g, of which sugars 5.1g; Fat 2.5g, of which saturates 1.4g; Cholesterol 15mg; Calcium 17mg; Fibre 0.3g; Sodium 19mg.

Mandelbrot

These crisp, twice-baked cookies, studded with almonds, are similar to biscotti. Serve them with coffee, tea or a glass of schnapps.

Makes 24–36
375g/13oz/3¼ cups plain (all-purpose) flour
115g/4oz/1 cup ground almonds
5ml/1 tsp bicarbonate of soda (baking soda)
pinch of salt
3 eggs
250g/9oz/1¼ cups caster (superfine) sugar
grated rind of 1 lemon
5ml/1 tsp almond extract
5ml/1 tsp vanilla extract
130g/4½oz/1 cup blanched almonds, roughly chopped

1 Preheat the oven to 180°C/350°F/Gas 4. Lightly grease two baking sheets.

2 Sift together the plain flour, ground almonds, bicarbonate of soda and salt.

3 Using a whisk, beat together the eggs and sugar until light and fluffy, then beat in the lemon rind and almond and vanilla extracts. Slowly add the flour and ground almonds, a little at a time, mixing until well blended. Add the chopped almonds and mix well.

4 Turn the mixture on to a floured surface and knead gently for about 5 minutes. Divide the dough into two pieces and form each into a long, flat loaf. Place on the baking sheets and bake for 35 minutes, or until golden brown.

5 Remove the loaves from the oven and leave for 15 minutes to cool slightly. Cut them into 1cm/½in diagonal slices, taking care not to break or crush the soft insides of the loaves.

6 Arrange the slices on clean baking sheets (working in batches). Bake for 6–7 minutes until the undersides are golden and flecked with brown. Turn the slices over and bake for another 6–7 minutes. Transfer to wire racks to cool.

Amaretti

These moreish cookies are great with afternoon tea, although they are equally delicious served with a sweet white dessert wine later in the day.

Makes 36
200g/7oz/1¾ cups almonds plain (all-purpose) flour, for dusting
225g/8oz/generous 1 cup caster (superfine) sugar
2 egg whites
2.5ml/½ tsp almond extract or 5ml/1 tsp vanilla extract
icing (confectioners') sugar, for dusting

1 Preheat the oven to 160°C/325°F/Gas 3.

2 Skin the almonds by dropping them into a pan of boiling water for 1–2 minutes. Drain well, then rub the almonds in a clean dish towel to remove the skins.

3 Spread out the almonds on a baking sheet and let them dry out in the oven for 10–15 minutes but do not allow them to turn brown. Remove them from the oven and leave to cool. Dust the almonds with a little flour. Increase the oven temperature to 180°C/350°F/Gas 4.

4 Put the almonds and half of the sugar in a food processor and process until finely ground.

5 Whisk the egg whites in a grease-free bowl until they form soft peaks. Gradually add half the remaining sugar and whisk until stiff peaks form. With a metal spoon, gently fold in the remaining sugar, the almond or vanilla extract and the almonds.

6 Spoon the almond mixture into a piping (pastry) bag and, using a plain nozzle, pipe the mixture in walnut-size rounds on to a baking sheet. Sprinkle lightly with the icing sugar and leave to stand for 2 hours.

7 Bake for 15 minutes, until pale golden brown. Transfer to a wire rack and leave to cool.

Mandelbrot Energy 111kcal/466kJ; Protein 3g; Carbohydrate 15.8g, of which sugars 7.7g; Fat 4.4g, of which saturates 0.5g; Cholesterol 16mg; Calcium 37mg; Fibre 0.8g; Sodium 8mg.
Amaretti Energy 37kcal/155kJ; Protein 1.1g; Carbohydrate 3.2g, of which sugars 3.1g; Fat 2.3g, of which saturates 0.2g; Cholesterol 0mg; Calcium 12mg; Fibre 0.3g; Sodium 4mg.

Oatmeal Lace Rounds

Any-time-of-day cookies, these are delicious with morning coffee or as a great after-school treat for hungry children. These cookies can also be served with ice cream as an unusual alternative to wafers, and makes for a more substantial dessert.

Makes 14
150g/5¹/₂oz/²/₃ cup butter at room temperature, diced
125g/4¹/₂oz/³/₄ cup rolled oats
165g/5³/₄oz/³/₄ cup dark brown sugar
150g/5¹/₄oz/³/₄ cup caster (superfine) sugar
45g/1¹/₂oz/¹/₃ cup plain (all-purpose) flour
pinch of salt
1 egg, lightly beaten
5ml/1tsp vanilla extract
70g/2¹/₂oz/¹/₂ cup pecans or walnuts, finely chopped

1 Preheat the oven to 180°C/359°F/Gas 4. Lightly grease two baking sheets.

2 Melt the butter in a pan over a low heat, stirring occasionally. Remove from the heat and set aside.

3 Put the oats in a large bowl. Sift over the brown sugar, caster sugar, flour and salt. Mix well to combine.

4 Make a well in the centre and add the melted butter, egg and vanilla extract. Mix until blended, using a wooden spoon, then stir in the chopped nuts.

5 Drop rounded teaspoonfuls of the mixture about 2in/5cm apart on the prepared baking sheets, to allow room for spreading during baking.

6 Bake in the oven for 5–8 minutes until lightly browned around the edges and bubbling. Allow to cool on the baking sheet for 2 minutes.

7 With a metal spatula, transfer the cookies to a wire rack and leave to cool completely.

Nut Lace Wafers

These cookies look so pretty, it almost seems a shame to eat them, but if you didn't, you would certainly be missing out on a treat. Serve them with smooth and creamy desserts.

Makes 18
50g/2oz/¹/₂ cup blanched almonds
50g/2oz/¹/₄ cup butter
45ml/3 tbsp plain (all-purpose) flour
115g/4oz/¹/₂ cup sugar
30ml/2 tbsp double (heavy) cream
2.5ml/¹/₂ tsp vanilla extract

1 Preheat the oven to 190°C/375°F/Gas 5. Thoroughly grease two baking sheets.

2 With a sharp knife, chop the almonds as finely as possible, or put them in a food processor or blender fitted with a metal blade and process until finely ground.

3 Melt the butter in a small pan over a low heat. Remove from the heat and stir in the ground almonds, plain flour, sugar, double cream and vanilla extract until well combined.

4 Drop teaspoonfuls of the mixture 6cm/2¹/₂in apart on the prepared baking sheets, to allow room for spreading during baking.

5 Bake in the oven for about 5 minutes, or until golden brown. Allow to cool on the sheets briefly, until the cookies are just firm.

6 With a metal spatula, transfer the cookies to a wire rack and leave to cool completely. These cookies have a soft and chewy texture, but will harden.

> **Variation**
> Add 40g/1¹/₂oz/¹/₄ cup finely chopped candied orange peel to the mixture with the almonds in step 3.

Nut Lace Cookies Energy 78kcal/327kJ; Protein 1g; Carbohydrate 7.2g, of which sugars 5.5g; Fat 5.2g, of which saturates 2.2g; Cholesterol 8mg; Calcium 16mg; Fibre 0.3g; Sodium 18mg.
Oatmeal Lace Rounds Energy 103kcal/431kJ; Protein 1g; Carbohydrate 13.2g, of which sugars 9.7g; Fat 5.5g, of which saturates 2.5g; Cholesterol 15mg; Calcium 11mg; Fibre 0.4g; Sodium 32mg.

Spiced Lace Cookies

Very pretty, delicate and crisp, these lacy cookies are ideal for serving with elegant creamy or iced desserts, or to be eaten with a cup of coffee mid morning. Don't be tempted to bake more than four on a sheet.

Makes about 14
75g/3oz/6 tbsp butter, diced
75g/3oz/¾ cup rolled oats
115g/4oz/generous ½ cup golden
   caster (superfine) sugar
1 egg, beaten
10ml/2 tsp plain
   (all-purpose) flour
5ml/1 tsp baking powder
2.5ml/½ tsp mixed spice (apple
   pie spice)

1 Preheat the oven to 180°C/350°F/Gas 4. Lightly grease and then line three or four baking sheets with baking parchment.

2 Put the butter in a medium pan and set over a low heat until just melted. Remove from the heat.

3 Stir the rolled oats into the melted butter. Add the sugar, egg, flour, baking powder and mixed spice and mix well to combine.

4 Place only 3 or 4 heaped teaspoonfuls of the mixture, spaced well apart, on each of the lined baking sheets.

5 Bake in the oven for about 5–7 minutes, or until a deepish golden brown all over. Leave the cookies on the baking sheets for about 1–2 minutes to firm up slightly.

6 Carefully cut the parchment so you can lift each cookie singly using a metal spatula. Invert on to a wire rack and remove the parchment. Leave to cool completely, while you cook the remaining batches.

Variation
Replace the mixed spice (apple pie spice) with ground cinnamon.

Oaty Biscuits

In England oats have been one of the principal crops since the days of the Anglo-Saxons and King Alfred the Great. By the 14th century, the grain had become a major export. Nutritious and delicious, oats are a major ingredient in these biscuits.

Makes about 18
115g/4oz/½ cup butter
115g/4oz/½ cup soft brown
   sugar
115g/4oz/½ cup golden (light
   corn) syrup
150g/5oz/1¼ cups self-raising
   (self-rising) flour
150g/5oz rolled oats

1 Preheat the oven to 180°C/350°F/Gas 4. Lightly grease two or three baking sheets with butter.

2 Gently heat the butter, sugar and golden syrup in a pan, stirring occasionally until the butter has melted and the sugar has dissolved. Remove from the heat and leave to cool slightly.

3 Sift the flour over the mixture in the pan and stir well to combine. Add the oats, to make a soft dough.

4 With your hands, roll small pieces of the dough into small balls and arrange them on the prepared baking sheets, leaving plenty of room for them to spread. Flatten each ball slightly with a metal spatula.

5 Put one tray into the oven and cook for 12–15 minutes until golden brown and cooked through.

6 Leave to cool on the baking sheet for 1–2 minutes, then carefully transfer to a wire rack to crisp up and cool completely, while you cook the remaining batches.

Variation
Add 25g/1oz/¼ cup finely chopped toasted almonds or walnuts, or a small handful of dried fruit such as raisins or sultanas (golden raisins) in step 3.

Spiced Lace Cookies Energy 101kcal/425kJ; Protein 1.3g; Carbohydrate 13.1g, of which sugars 8.6g; Fat 5.3g, of which saturates 2.9g; Cholesterol 25mg; Calcium 11mg; Fibre 0.4g; Sodium 40mg.
Oaty Biscuits Energy 151kcal/637kJ; Protein 1.8g; Carbohydrate 23.9g, of which sugars 11.9g; Fat 6g, of which saturates 3.3g; Cholesterol 14mg; Calcium 22mg; Fibre 0.8g; Sodium 59mg.

Oaty Coconut Cookies

Toasting the oats and coconut before mixing them with the other ingredients is the secret of both the delicious flavour and the lovely crunchy texture of these cookies. You'll need to keep an eye on the oats and coconut and give them the occasional stir, as they will burn if cooked too long.

Makes 18

115g/4oz/½ cup sugar
175g/6oz/2 cups rolled oats
75g/3oz/1 cup dessicated (dry unsweetened shredded) coconut
225g/8oz/1 cup butter, at room temperature, diced
40g/1½oz/¼ cup firmly packed soft dark brown sugar
2 eggs
60ml/4 tbsp milk
7.5ml/1½ tsp vanilla extract
115g/4oz/1 cup plain (all-purpose) flour
2.5ml/½ tsp bicarbonate of soda (baking soda)
pinch of salt
5ml/1 tsp ground cinnamon

1 Preheat the oven to 200°C/400°F/Gas 6. Lightly grease two baking sheets. Grease the base of a small glass and dip it in some sugar.

2 Spread the oats and coconut on an ungreased baking sheet. Bake in the oven for 8–10 minutes until golden brown, stirring occasionally.

3 In a large bowl, beat the butter and sugars together until light and fluffy. Beat in the eggs, then add the milk and vanilla extract. Sift the flour, bicarbonate of soda, salt and cinnamon together and fold into the creamed mixture. Stir in the oat and coconut mixture.

4 Drop spoonfuls of the mixture on to the baking sheets, spaced well apart to allow for spreading while baking. Flatten each with the sugared glass. Bake for 8–10 minutes until golden brown.

5 Transfer the cookies to a wire rack and leave to firm up and cool completely. The cookies will keep stored in an airtight container for 3–4 days.

Melting Moments

As the name suggests, these crisp cookies really do melt in the mouth. They have a texture like shortbread but are covered in rolled oats to give a crunchy surface and extra flavour, and are traditionally topped with a nugget of glacé cherry.

Makes 16–20

40g/1½oz/3 tbsp butter, softened
65g/2½oz/5 tbsp lard
85g/3oz/6 tbsp caster (superfine) sugar
1 egg yolk, beaten
few drops of vanilla or almond extract
150g/5oz/1¼ cups self-raising (self-rising) flour
rolled oats, for coating
4–5 glacé (candied) cherries

1 Preheat the oven to 180°C/350°F/Gas 4.

2 In a large bowl, beat together the butter, lard and sugar until light and fluffy, then gradually beat in the egg yolk and vanilla or almond extract.

3 Sift the flour over the creamed mixture and stir together to make a soft dough. With your hands, gently roll into 16–20 small balls.

4 Spread the rolled oats on to a sheet of baking parchment and roll the dough balls in them until evenly coated.

5 Place the balls, spaced slightly apart, on two baking sheets. Flatten each ball a little with your thumb.

6 Cut the cherries into quarters and place a piece of cherry on top of each cookie.

7 Bake in the oven for 15–20 minutes, until the cookies are lightly browned.

8 Allow the cookies to set slightly for 1–2 minutes on the baking sheets. With a metal spatula, transfer the cookies to a wire rack and leave to cool completely. Store in an airtight container for 2–3 days.

Oaty Coconut Cookies Energy 84kcal/352kJ; Protein 1.1g; Carbohydrate 8.3g, of which sugars 3.8g; Fat 5.4g, of which saturates 3.4g; Cholesterol 18mg; Calcium 11mg; Fibre 0.5g; Sodium 34mg.
Melting Moments Energy 88kcal/370kJ; Protein 0.7g; Carbohydrate 10.9g, of which sugars 5.4g; Fat 5g, of which saturates 2.4g; Cholesterol 7mg; Calcium 30mg; Fibre 0.3g; Sodium 40mg.

Tea Swirls

These cookies are very quick and easy to make. If you don't want to pipe the mixture, simply spoon it on to the baking parchment and press it down with a fork.

Makes 20
150g/5oz/⅔ cup butter, softened
75g/3oz/¾ cup caster (superfine) sugar, sifted
1 egg, beaten
a few drops almond extract
225g/8oz/2 cups plain (all-purpose) flour
2–3 large pieces candied peel, cut into small diamond shapes

1 Preheat the oven to 230°C/450°F/Gas 8. Line two baking sheets with baking parchment.

2 Beat together the butter and sugar in a large bowl until light and fluffy, then beat in the egg yolk and almond extract.

3 Sift the flour over the mixture in batches and beat well until smooth.

4 Spoon the mixture into a piping (pastry) bag fitted with a large star nozzle and pipe 10 rosette shapes on each of the baking sheets, spacing them slightly apart. It is best to work with cold hands so that the consistency of the mixture is not affected by heat.

5 Press a piece of candied peel diamond gently into the centre of each cookie. Bake in the oven for 5 minutes until golden brown.

6 Leave to cool for a few minutes, then using a metal spatula, transfer the cookies to a wire rack to cool completely. These cookies can be stored in an airtight container for several days.

> **Variation**
> Use 10 halved glacé (candied) cherries instead of the candied peel and cut each in half.

Crunchy Jumbles

Making up your mind about whether you prefer milk or plain chocolate chips is the perfect excuse for baking another batch of these tasty cookies.

Makes 36
115g/4oz/½ cup butter at room temperature, diced
225g/8oz/1 cup sugar
1 egg
5ml/1 tsp vanilla extract
175g/6oz/1¼ cups plain (all-purpose) flour
2.5ml/½ tsp bicarbonate of soda (baking soda)
pinch of salt
115g/4oz/2 cups crisped rice cereal
175g/6oz/1 cup chocolate chips

1 Preheat the oven to 180°C/350°F/Gas 4. Lightly grease two or three large baking sheets.

2 In a large bowl, beat together the butter and sugar until light and fluffy. Beat in the egg and vanilla extract.

3 Sift the flour, bicarbonate of soda and salt over the mixture and fold in until just mixed.

4 Add the cereal and chocolate chips to the mixture and stir thoroughly to mix. Drop spoonfuls of the dough on to the baking sheets, spacing them well apart to allow room for spreading during baking.

5 Bake the cookies in the oven for 10–12 minutes until golden brown. Leave to firm up slightly on the baking sheet for 1–2 minutes. Use a metal spatula to transfer the cookies to a wire rack to cool completely.

> **Variation**
> To make Crunchy Walnut Jumbles, add 50g/2oz/½ cup walnuts, coarsely chopped, with the cereal and chocolate. Alternatively you could try adding different breakfast cereals for different textures and tastes.

Tea Swirls Energy 113kcal/471kJ; Protein 1.4g; Carbohydrate 12.7g, of which sugars 4.1g; Fat 6.6g, of which saturates 4g; Cholesterol 26mg; Calcium 21mg; Fibre 0.4g; Sodium 50mg.
Crunchy Jumbles Energy 95kcal/398kJ; Protein 0.9g; Carbohydrate 14.2g, of which sugars 9.8g; Fat 4.2g, of which saturates 2.5g; Cholesterol 12mg; Calcium 18mg; Fibre 0.3g; Sodium 31mg.

Farmhouse Cookies

Packed with cereal, these are true farmhouse cookies that your grandmother would have made but with the addition of peanut butter. With the muesli, and peanut butter, these cookies are high in fibre and children will love them as much as the adults.

Makes 18

115g/4oz/¹/₂ cup butter, at room temperature
90g/3¹/₂oz/generous 1 cup light brown sugar
65g/2¹/₂oz/¹/₄ cup crunchy peanut butter
1 egg
50g/2oz/¹/₂ cup plain (all-purpose) flour
2.5ml/¹/₂ tsp baking powder
2.5ml/¹/₂ tsp ground cinnamon
pinch of salt
175g/6oz/1¹/₂ cups muesli (granola)
50g/2oz/¹/₃ cup raisins
50g/2oz/¹/₂ cup chopped walnuts

1 Preheat the oven to 180°C/350°F/Gas 4. Lightly grease one or two baking sheets.

2 In a large bowl, beat together the butter and sugar until light and fluffy. Beat in the peanut butter, until mixed, then beat in the egg.

3 Sift the flour, baking powder, cinnamon and salt over the peanut butter mixture in batches and stir well after each addition. Stir in the muesli, raisins and walnuts. (Taste the mixture to see if it needs more sugar, as muesli varies.)

4 Drop rounded tablespoonfuls of the mixture on to the prepared baking sheet about 2.5cm/1in apart to allow room for spreading during baking. Press each gently with the back of a spoon to spread each mound into a circle.

5 Bake in the oven for about 15 minutes until lightly coloured. Leave to firm up slightly on the baking sheets, then with a metal spatula, transfer the cookies to a wire rack and leave to cool completely. Store the cookies in an airtight container.

Crunchy Oatmeal Cookies

This combination of crunchy cereal and oats is highly nutritious, providing protein, carbohydrate, vitamins and minerals – and the cookies taste wonderful.

Makes 14

175g/6oz/³/₄ cup butter, at room temperature, diced
125g/4¹/₂oz/³/₄ cup caster (superfine) sugar
1 egg yolk
175g/6oz/1¹/₂ cups plain (all-purpose) flour, plus extra for dusting
5ml/1 tsp bicarbonate of soda (baking soda)
pinch of salt
40g/1¹/₂oz/¹/₂ cup rolled oats
40g/1¹/₂oz/¹/₂ cup crunchy nugget cereal

1 In a large bowl, beat together the butter and sugar until light and fluffy. Mix in the egg yolk.

2 Sift over the flour, bicarbonate of soda and salt, then stir into the butter mixture. Add the oats and cereal and stir to blend. Chill for at least 20 minutes.

3 Preheat the oven to 190°C/375°F/Gas 5. Lightly grease a baking sheet. Flour the base of a wide, heavy glass.

4 Using two spoons, drop teaspoons of the dough on to the prepared baking sheet, spaced well apart. Gently flatten them with the floured base of the glass, dusting it with more flour if necessary.

5 Bake for 10–12 minutes until golden. With a metal spatula, transfer the cookies to a wire rack. Allow to cool completely before serving or storing.

Variation
To make nutty oatmeal cookies, substitute an equal quantity of chopped walnuts or pecan nuts for the cereal, and prepare as described in the recipe.

Crunchy Oatmeal Cookies Energy 220kcal/923kJ; Protein 2.3g; Carbohydrate 27.6g, of which sugars 14.3g; Fat 11.9g, of which saturates 6.8g; Cholesterol 41mg; Calcium 33mg; Fibre 0.8g; Sodium 81mg.
Farmhouse Cookies Energy 165kcal/688kJ; Protein 2.9g; Carbohydrate 16.9g, of which sugars 10.1g; Fat 10g, of which saturates 4.1g; Cholesterol 24mg; Calcium 25mg; Fibre 1.1g; Sodium 94mg.

Luxury Muesli Cookies

It is best to use a "luxury" muesli for this recipe, preferably one with 50 per cent mixed cereal and 50 per cent fruit, nuts and seeds. These buttery, crunchy cookies are ideal for a snack at any time.

Makes about 20
115g/4oz/½ cup unsalted (sweet) butter
45ml/3 tbsp golden (light corn) syrup
115g/4oz/generous ½ cup demerara (raw) sugar
175g/6oz/1½ cups "luxury" muesli (granola)
90g/3½oz/¾ cup self-raising (self-rising) flour
5ml/1 tsp ground cinnamon

1 Preheat the oven to 160°C/325°F/Gas 3. Line two or three baking sheets with baking parchment.

2 Put the butter, syrup and sugar in a large pan and heat gently. Stir constantly until the butter has completely melted.

3 Remove the pan from the heat, then stir in the muesli, flour and cinnamon and mix together until well combined. Set aside to cool slightly.

4 Place spoonfuls of the mixture, slightly apart, on the baking sheets to allow room for spreading during baking.

5 Bake for 15 minutes until the cookies are just beginning to brown around the edges. Leave to cool for a few minutes on the baking sheets.

6 With a metal spatula, carefully transfer the cookies to a wire rack and leave to cool completely before serving or storing.

> **Variation**
> *Tropical muesli containing coconut and dried tropical fruits makes an interesting alternative to regular luxury muesli. Try different versions using your favourite muesli flavours.*

Fruit and Nut Cookies

The mixture for these cookies can be made ahead of time and stored in the refrigerator. The muscovado sugar lends a rich addition to these flavoursome chocolate chip, fruit and nut cookies.

Makes about 20
115g/4oz/½ cup unsalted (sweet) butter, at room temperature, diced
115g/4oz/generous ½ cup sugar
115g/4oz/generous ½ cup light muscovado (brown) sugar
1 large (US extra large) egg
5ml/1 tsp vanilla extract
200g/7oz/1¾ cups self-raising (self-rising) flour
150g/5oz/scant 1 cup chocolate chips
50g/2oz/½ cup hazelnuts or walnuts, chopped and toasted
50g/2oz/scant ½ cup raisins

1 Preheat the oven to 180°C/350°F/Gas 4. Line two baking sheets with baking parchment.

2 Put the butter and sugars in a mixing bowl and beat together until light and fluffy. Add the egg and vanilla extract and beat to combine.

3 Add the flour, chocolate chips, chopped toasted hazelnuts or walnuts, and raisins and mix together. The dough will now have a crumbly texture.

4 Place teaspoonfuls of the mixture, spaced well apart, on the baking sheets. Bake for 15 minutes until golden. Leave for 5 minutes, then use a metal spatula to transfer to a wire rack to cool.

> **Cook's Tip**
> *If you don't want to bake the mixture all at once, spoon it into a plastic container, cover the surface tightly with clear film (plastic wrap) and replace the lid. Keep in the refrigerator for up to 1 week. When required, remove the dough from the refrigerator 15 minutes before you want to bake the cookies, and stir well.*

Fruit and Nut Cookies Energy 187kcal/786kJ; Protein 2.1g; Carbohydrate 26.5g, of which sugars 18.7g; Fat 8.8g, of which saturates 4.5g; Cholesterol 22mg; Calcium 30mg; Fibre 0.7g; Sodium 41mg.
Luxury Muesli Cookies Energy 120kcal/502kJ; Protein 1.4g; Carbohydrate 17.2g, of which sugars 9.3g; Fat 5.5g, of which saturates 3.1g; Cholesterol 12mg; Calcium 15mg; Fibre 0.8g; Sodium 46mg.

Malted Oat Cookies

This recipe is packed with oats, which produces a crisp, chewy cookie. Flavoured with malt, they are hard to resist.

Makes 18
175g/6oz/1½ cups rolled oats
75g/3oz/½ cup light muscovado (brown) sugar
1 egg
60ml/4 tbsp sunflower or vegetable oil
30ml/2 tbsp malt extract

1 Preheat the oven to 190°C/375°F/Gas 5. Lightly grease two baking sheets.

2 Mix the rolled oats and brown sugar in a bowl, breaking up any lumps in the sugar.

3 Beat the egg in a small bowl and add it together with the sunflower oil and malt extract to the oats and sugar mixture. Set the mixture aside to soak for 15 minutes, then beat together to combine thoroughly.

4 Using a teaspoon, place small heaps of the mixture well apart to allow room for spreading on the prepared baking sheets. Press the heaps into 7.5cm/3in rounds with the back of a dampened fork.

5 Bake the cookies in the oven for 10–15 minutes, until golden brown. Leave on the baking sheets for 1 minute to cool slightly.

6 With a metal spatula, transfer the cookies to a wire rack and leave to cool completely.

> **Variation**
> *Try replacing 25g/1oz/¼ cup of the rolled oats with ground Brazil nuts. This will provide a healthy dose of selenium and make a cookie with a slightly different texture as well as a strong nutty taste.*

Ker-runch Cookies

An unusual coating of bran flakes covers these small cookies – a painless way of making sure that you have plenty of fibre in your diet. Children will find them fun to make, too.

Makes about 18
175g/6oz/¾ cup butter
175g/6oz/¾ cup light muscovado (brown) sugar
1 egg
175g/6oz/1½ cups self-raising (self-rising) wholemeal (whole-wheat) flour
115g/4oz/generous 1 cup rolled oats
115g/4oz/⅔ cup mixed dried fruit
50g/2oz/2 cups bran flakes breakfast cereal

1 Preheat the oven to 160°C/325°F/Gas 3. Line two baking sheets with baking parchment.

2 Put the butter and sugar in a large bowl and beat together until pale and creamy.

3 Add the egg to the butter mixture and beat in until thoroughly combined. Stir in the flour, oats and fruit.

4 Roll the mixture into walnut-size balls between the palms of your hands.

5 Spread out the bran flakes on a shallow plate and roll the balls in them to coat. Place on the prepared baking sheets and flatten each one gently with your hand.

6 Bake the cookies in the oven for about 20 minutes until firm and golden brown. Remove from the baking sheets while still hot as these cookies firm up very quickly.

7 Transfer to a wire rack and leave to cool completely.

> **Variation**
> *Coat the cookies in oats instead of bran flakes.*

Malted Oat Cookies Energy 86kcal/364kJ; Protein 1.6g; Carbohydrate 12.8g, of which sugars 5.7g; Fat 3.6g, of which saturates 0.4g; Cholesterol 11mg; Calcium 9mg; Fibre 0.7g; Sodium 12mg.
Ker-runch Cookies Energy 196kcal/825kJ; Protein 2.9g; Carbohydrate 27.5g, of which sugars 15.4g; Fat 9.1g, of which saturates 3.6g; Cholesterol 12mg; Calcium 20mg; Fibre 1.8g; Sodium 110mg.

Florentine Cookies

These are not traditional Florentines but an utterly yummy version with a soft crumbly base and a wonderfully chewy topping.

Makes 24
115g/4oz/¹/₂ cup unsalted
  (sweet) butter, at room
  temperature, diced
115g/4oz/generous ¹/₂ cup caster
  (superfine) sugar
1 egg
a few drops of almond extract
  (optional)
225g/8oz/2 cups self-raising
  (self-rising) flour, plus extra
  for dusting

For the topping
175g/6oz/1¹/₂ cups ready-to-eat
  dried apricots, chopped
50g/2oz/¹/₂ cup dried mango
  pieces, chopped
100g/3¹/₂oz/scant 1 cup flaked
  (sliced) almonds
60ml/4 tbsp plain (all-purpose)
  flour
50g/2oz/¹/₄ cup unsalted
  (sweet) butter
50g/2oz/¹/₄ cup golden caster
  (superfine) sugar
60ml/4 tbsp golden (light
  corn) syrup

1 Preheat the oven to 190°C/375°F/Gas 5. Lightly grease two baking sheets.

2 In a large bowl, beat together the butter and sugar until the mixture is light and fluffy, then beat in the egg. Stir in the almond extract, if using, and the flour, using a wooden spoon and then your hands to make a firm soft dough.

3 Roll the dough out on a floured surface and, using a 7.5cm/3in round cookie cutter, stamp out 24 rounds. Place them on the baking sheets, spaced slightly apart.

4 To make the topping, combine the apricots, mango, almonds and flour in a bowl. Put the butter, sugar and syrup in a small pan and heat gently until the butter has melted and the mixture is combined. Pour over the fruit and nuts and mix together.

5 Spoon the mixture on top of the cookies. Bake for 12–14 minutes until golden and crisp. Leave the cookies on the baking sheets for 5 minutes, then transfer to a wire rack to cool.

Microwave Fruit and Nut Cookies

These irresistible cookies make the best of familiar flapjacks and old-fashioned, chocolate-coated Florentines.

Makes 16
75g/3oz/6 tbsp butter
45ml/3 tbsp/¹/₄ cup golden (light
  corn) syrup
115g/4oz/1¹/₄ cups rolled oats
25g/1oz/2 tbsp soft brown sugar
25g/1oz/2 tbsp chopped mixed
  candied peel
25g/1oz/2 tbsp glacé (candied)
  cherries, coarsely chopped
25g/1oz/¹/₄ cup hazelnuts,
  coarsely chopped
115g/4oz/²/₃ cup plain
  (semisweet) chocolate

1 Lightly grease a 20cm/8in square microwave-proof shallow dish and line the base with a sheet of rice paper.

2 Place the butter and golden syrup in a microwave-proof bowl and microwave on full (100 per cent) power for 1¹/₂ minutes until melted. Stir well together.

3 Add the oats, sugar, peel, cherries and hazelnuts and mix well.

4 Spoon the mixture into the dish and level the surface with the back of a spoon. Microwave on full (100 per cent) power for 6 minutes, giving the dish a half turn every 2 minutes. Allow to cool slightly, then cut into 16 fingers and place on a wire rack to cool.

5 Break the chocolate into pieces and put in a microwave-proof bowl. Microwave on full (100 per cent) power for 2–3 minutes, stirring twice, until melted and smooth.

6 Spread the chocolate over the tops of the cookies and mark in a zig-zag pattern with the prongs of a fork. Leave to set.

Cook's Tip
Rice paper is used for cooking in traditional recipes as well as in microwave methods. It prevents mixtures, such as this sweet oat base, from sticking by cooking on to them. When cooked, the rice paper can be eaten with the biscuits or other items.

Florentine Cookies Energy 167kcal/699kJ; Protein 2.5g; Carbohydrate 22.1g, of which sugars 13g; Fat 8.2g, of which saturates 3.8g; Cholesterol 15mg; Calcium 39mg; Fibre 1.3g; Sodium 51mg.
Microwave Cookies Energy 133kcal/555kJ; Protein 1.5g; Carbohydrate 15.7g, of which sugars 10.4g; Fat 7.5g, of which saturates 3.7g; Cholesterol 10mg; Calcium 14mg; Fibre 0.9g; Sodium 44mg.

Fruits and Millet Treacle Cookies

These little cookies are quick to make, and will no doubt disappear just as quickly when they come out of the oven. However, if you are not fond of treacle then golden syrup can be used equally successfully as an alternative.

Makes about 25–30
90g/3¹/₂oz/7 tbsp butter
150g/5oz/²/₃ cup light muscovado (brown) sugar
30ml/2 tbsp black treacle (molasses)
I egg
150g/5oz/1¹/₄ cups plain (all-purpose) flour
50g/2oz/¹/₂ cup millet flakes
50g/2oz/¹/₂ cup almonds, chopped
200g/7oz/generous I cup luxury mixed dried fruit

I Preheat the oven to 190°C/375°F/Gas 5. Lightly grease two large baking sheets.

2 Put the butter, muscovado sugar, treacle and egg in a large bowl and beat together until well combined and the mixture is light and fluffy.

3 Stir in the flour and millet flakes, the almonds and dried fruit. Put tablespoonfuls of the mixture on to the prepared baking sheets, spaced well apart to allow room for spreading during baking.

4 Bake in the oven for about 15 minutes until golden brown.

5 Leave the cookies on the baking sheets to firm up for a few minutes, then use a metal spatula to transfer them to a wire rack and leave to cool completely.

Cook's Tip
Make sure that you use millet flakes for these cookies rather than millet grains. The grains will swell too much during cooking and spoil the cookies.

Candied Peel Crumble Cookies

Crumbly, melt-in-the-mouth cookies, these incorporate candied peel, walnuts and white chocolate chips and are coated with a zingy lemon glaze.

Makes about 24
175g/6oz/³/₄ cup unsalted (sweet) butter, at room temperature, diced
90g/3¹/₂oz/¹/₂ cup caster (superfine) sugar
I egg, beaten
finely grated rind of I lemon

200g/7oz/1³/₄ cups self-raising (self-rising) flour
90g/3¹/₂oz/generous ¹/₂ cup candied peel, chopped
75g/3oz/³/₄ cup chopped walnuts
50g/2oz/¹/₃ cup white chocolate chips

For the glaze
50g/2oz/¹/₂ cup icing (confectioners') sugar, sifted
15ml/I tbsp lemon juice
thin strips of candied peel, to decorate (optional)

I Preheat the oven to 180°C/350°F/Gas 4. Lightly grease two baking sheets.

2 Put the butter and sugar in a large bowl and beat together until light and fluffy. Add the egg and beat well together.

3 Add the lemon rind and flour and stir together gently. Fold the candied peel, walnuts and chocolate chips into the mixture.

4 Place tablespoonfuls of the mixture, spaced slightly apart, on the baking sheets and bake in the oven for 12–15 minutes, until cooked but still pale in colour. Transfer the cookies to a wire rack using a metal spatula and to leave to cool completely.

5 For the glaze, put the icing sugar in a bowl and stir in the lemon juice. Spoon some glaze over each cookie. Decorate with candied peel, if using.

Variation
Replace the candied peel in the cookies with glacé (candied) cherries and decorate with a small piece of cherry on top.

Fruit and Millet Treacle Cookies Energy 99kcal/416kJ; Protein 1.2g; Carbohydrate 15.8g, of which sugars 10.5g; Fat 3.7g, of which saturates 1.2g; Cholesterol 7mg; Calcium 20mg; Fibre 0.4g; Sodium 32mg. Candied Peel Crumble Cookies Energy 150kcal/626kJ; Protein 1.8g; Carbohydrate 16.2g, of which sugars 9.8g; Fat 9.2g, of which saturates 4.4g; Cholesterol 23mg; Calcium 31mg; Fibre 0.5g; Sodium 61mg.

Toffee Apple and Oat Crunchies

An unashamedly addictive
mixture of chewy oats, soft
apple and wonderfully
crunchy toffee, this cookie
won't win large prizes in the
looks department but is top
of the class for flavour.

Makes about 16
150g/5oz/10 tbsp unsalted
  (sweet) butter
175g/6oz/scant 1 cup light
  muscovado (brown) sugar
90g/3¹/₂oz/¹/₂ cup sugar

1 large (US extra large)
  egg, beaten
75g/3oz/²/₃ cup plain
  (all-purpose) flour
2.5ml/¹/₂ tsp bicarbonate of soda
  (baking soda)
pinch of salt
250g/9oz/2¹/₂ cups rolled oats
50g/2oz/scant ¹/₂ cup sultanas
  (golden raisins)
50g/2oz dried apple rings,
  coarsely chopped
50g/2oz chewy toffees, coarsely
  chopped

1 Preheat the oven to 180°C/350°F/Gas 4. Line two or three
baking sheets with baking parchment.

2 In a large bowl, beat together the butter and both sugars
until light and creamy. Add the beaten egg and beat well until
thoroughly combined.

3 Sift together the flour, bicarbonate of soda and salt. Add
to the butter, sugar and egg mixture and mix in well. Finally add
the oats, sultanas, chopped apple rings and toffee pieces and
stir gently until just combined.

4 Using a large tablespoon, place heaps of the mixture well
apart on the prepared baking sheets to allow room for
spreading during baking. Bake for about 10–12 minutes, or
until lightly set in the centre and just beginning to brown at
the edges.

5 Remove the cookies from the oven and leave to firm up on
the baking sheets for a few minutes.

6 Using a metal spatula, transfer the cookies to a wire rack
and leave to cool completely. Store in an airtight container
for 3–4 days.

Apple and Elderflower Stars

These delicious, crumbly
apple cookies are topped
with a sweet yet very
sharp icing. Packaged in
a pretty box, they would
make a delightful gift for
someone special.

Makes about 18
115g/4oz/¹/₂ cup unsalted
  (sweet) butter, at room
  temperature, diced
75g/3oz/scant ¹/₂ cup caster
  (superfine) sugar
2.5ml/¹/₂ tsp mixed spice (apple
  pie spice)

1 large (US extra large) egg yolk
25g/1oz dried apple rings,
  finely chopped
200g/7oz/1³/₄ cups self-raising
  (self-rising) flour
5–10ml/1–2 tsp milk, if necessary

For the topping
200g/7oz/1³/₄ cups icing
  (confectioners') sugar, sifted
60–90ml/4–6 tbsp elderflower
  cordial
sugar, for sprinkling

1 Preheat the oven to 190°C/375°F/Gas 5. Lightly grease two
baking sheets.

2 Beat together the butter and sugar until light and fluffy. Beat
in the mixed spice and egg yolk. Add the chopped apple and
flour and stir together well. The mixture should form a stiff
dough but if it is too dry, add some milk.

3 Roll the dough out on a floured surface to 5mm/¹/₄in thick.
Using a star cookie cutter, stamp out the cookies.

4 Place on the baking sheets and bake for about 10–15
minutes, or until beginning to brown around the edges. Using a
metal spatula, transfer the cookies to a wire rack to cool.

5 To make the topping, sift the icing sugar into a bowl and add
just enough elderflower cordial to mix to a fairly thick but still
pourable consistency.

6 When the cookies are completely cool, trickle the icing
randomly over the stars. Immediately sprinkle with sugar and
leave to set.

Toffee Apple and Oat Crunchies Energy 249kcal/1047kJ; Protein 3.1g; Carbohydrate 38.8g, of which sugars 23.2g; Fat 10.1g, of which saturates 5.3g; Cholesterol 32mg; Calcium 34mg; Fibre 1.3g; Sodium 79mg.
Apple and Elderflower Stars Energy 157kcal/659kJ; Protein 1.4g; Carbohydrate 26.6g, of which sugars 18.1g; Fat 5.7g, of which saturates 3.4g; Cholesterol 25mg; Calcium 27mg; Fibre 0.4g; Sodium 42mg.

Date and Orange Oat Cookies

The fragrant aroma of orange permeates the kitchen when these cookies are baking. Orange is a classic partner with dates and both add a richness to these healthy crumbly oat cookies.

Makes 25
150g/5oz/¾ cup soft dark
  brown sugar
150g/5oz/10 tbsp butter
finely grated rind of 1 unwaxed
  orange
150g/5oz/1¼ cups self-raising
  (self-rising) wholemeal
  (whole-wheat) flour
5ml/1 tsp baking powder
75g/3oz/⅔ cup medium oatmeal
75g/3oz/½ cup dried dates,
  roughly chopped

1 Preheat the oven to 180°C/350°F/Gas 4. Lightly grease two baking sheets.

2 Put the sugar and butter in a large bowl and beat together until light and fluffy. Stir in the orange rind.

3 In a separate bowl, sift the flour with the baking powder. Fold the flour mixture and then the oatmeal in to the butter and sugar mixture until well combined. Add the dates and mix well.

4 Place heaped tablespoonfuls of the mixture on to the prepared baking sheets, spacing them well apart to allow the mixture room for spreading. Bake in the oven for 15–20 minutes, until golden.

5 Leave the cookies to firm up slightly on the baking sheet for 1–2 minutes. Use a metal spatula to carefully transfer the cookies to wire racks and leave to cool completely. Store in an airtight container for 3–4 days.

> **Variation**
> *Replace the dates with dried chopped apricots, raisins, sultanas (golden raisins) or figs.*

Apricot and Hazelnut Oat Cookies

These cookie-cum-flapjacks have a chewy, crumbly texture. They are sprinkled with apricots and toasted hazelnuts, but any combination of dried fruit and nuts can be used.

Makes 9
115g/4oz/1 cup self-raising
  (self-rising) flour, sifted
115g/4oz/1 cup rolled oats
75g/3oz/scant ½ cup chopped
  ready-to-eat dried apricots
115g/4oz/½ cup unsalted
  (sweet) butter

75g/3oz/scant ½ cup golden
  caster (superfine) sugar
15ml/1 tbsp clear honey

For the topping
25g/1oz/2 tbsp chopped
  ready-to-eat dried apricots
25g/1oz/¼ cup toasted and
  chopped hazelnuts

1 Preheat the oven to 160°C/325°F/Gas 3. Lightly grease a large baking sheet.

2 Put the flour, oats and chopped apricots in a large mixing bowl.

3 Put the butter, sugar and honey in a pan and cook over a gentle heat until the butter melts and the sugar dissolves, stirring the mixture occasionally. Remove the pan from the heat.

4 Pour the honey and sugar mixture into the bowl containing the flour, oats and apricots. Mix with a wooden spoon to form a sticky dough.

5 Divide the dough into nine pieces and place on the prepared baking sheet. Press into 1cm/½in thick rounds.

6 Scatter over the topping of apricots and hazelnuts and press into the dough. Bake the cookies for about 15 minutes, until they are golden and slightly crisp. Leave to cool on the baking sheet for 5 minutes, then transfer to a wire rack to cool completely.

Date and Orange Oat Cookies Energy 121kcal/508kJ; Protein 1.5g; Carbohydrate 17.4g, of which sugars 8.4g; Fat 5.5g, of which saturates 3.1g; Cholesterol 13mg; Calcium 17mg; Fibre 0.7g; Sodium 39mg. **Apricot and Hazelnut Oat Cookies** Energy 262kcal/1098kJ; Protein 3.7g; Carbohydrate 33.2g, of which sugars 14.4g; Fat 13.6g, of which saturates 6.8g; Cholesterol 27mg; Calcium 71mg; Fibre 2.1g; Sodium 130mg.

Sultana Cornmeal Cookies

These little yellow biscuits come from Italy, where cornmeal is produced in the north of the country and Marsala is produced in Sicily.

Makes 48
75g/3oz/¹/₂ cup sultanas (golden raisins)
115g/4oz/1 cup finely ground yellow cornmeal
175g/6oz/1¹/₂ cups plain (all-purpose) flour
7.5ml/1¹/₂ tsp baking powder
pinch of salt
225g/8oz/1 cup butter
225g/8oz/1 cup sugar
2 eggs
15ml/1 tbsp Marsala or 5ml/1 tsp vanilla extract

1 Soak the sultanas in a small bowl of warm water for 15 minutes. Drain.

2 Preheat the oven to 180°C/350°F/Gas 4. Lightly grease two or three baking sheets.

3 Sift the cornmeal, flour, baking powder and salt together into a mixing bowl. Set aside.

4 Put the butter and sugar in a large bowl and beat together until light and fluffy. Beat in the eggs, one at a time. Beat in the Marsala or vanilla extract. Add the dry ingredients to the butter mixture, beating until well blended. Stir in the sultanas.

5 Drop heaped teaspoons of the mixture on to the prepared baking sheet in rows about 5cm/2in apart to allow room for spreading while baking.

6 Bake in the oven for 7–8 minutes, until the cookies are golden brown at the edges.

7 Leave to firm up slightly on the baking sheets for 1–2 minutes before carefully transferring the cookies to a wire rack using a metal spatula.

8 Leave to cool completely before serving. Store the cookies in an airtight container for up to 5 days.

Prune and Peel Rock Buns

These buns are quick and easy to make and taste absolutely wonderful.

Makes 12
225g/8oz/2 cups plain (all-purpose) flour
10ml/2 tsp baking powder
75g/3oz/²/₃ cup demerara (raw) sugar
50g/2oz/¹/₂ cup chopped ready-to-eat dried prunes
50g/2oz/¹/₃ cup chopped mixed (candied) peel
finely grated rind of 1 lemon
60ml/4 tbsp sunflower oil
75ml/5 tbsp milk

1 Preheat the oven to 200°C/400°F/Gas 6. Lightly grease a large baking sheet.

2 Sift the flour and baking powder, then stir in the sugar, prunes, peel and lemon rind.

3 Mix the oil and milk, then stir into the mixture, to make a dough which just binds together.

4 Spoon into rocky heaps on the baking sheet and bake for about 20 minutes, until golden. Transfer to a wire rack and leave to cool completely.

Lemon and Raisin Rock Cakes

These lightly spiced, fruity rock buns are easy to make, and delicious to eat.

Makes 16
225g/8oz/2 cups self-raising (self rising) wholemeal (whole-wheat) flour
pinch of salt
115g/4oz/¹/₂ cup butter
115g/4oz/ generous ¹/₂ cup golden caster (superfine) sugar
5ml/1 tsp ground mixed spice (apple pie spice)
finely grated rind of 1 lemon
115g/4oz/²/₃ cup raisins
1 egg, beaten
milk, to mix
pared lemon rind, to decorate

1 Preheat the oven to 200°C/400°F/Gas 6. Lightly grease two baking sheets.

2 Put the flour and salt in a bowl and lightly rub in the butter until the mixture resembles breadcrumbs.

3 Add the sugar, spice, lemon rind and raisins to the flour mixture and mix together.

4 Stir in the egg and enough milk to make a stiff, but crumbly mixture.

5 Using two spoons, put rough heaps of the mixture on to the prepared baking sheets. Bake for 15–20 minutes, until lightly browned and firm to the touch. Leave to firm up on the baking sheet for 1–2 minutes.

6 Using a metal spatula, transfer the rock cakes to a wire rack and leave to cool completely. Serve the cookies decorated with lemon rind.

Sultana Cornmeal Cookies Energy 60kcal/254kJ; Protein 1.1g; Carbohydrate 9.6g, of which sugars 3.3g; Fat 2.1g, of which saturates 1.2g; Cholesterol 12mg; Calcium 10mg; Fibre 0.3g; Sodium 17mg.
Prune and Peel Rock Buns Energy 132kcal/559kJ; Protein 2.1g; Carbohydrate 25.3g, of which sugars 11g; Fat 3.2g, of which saturates 0.4g; Cholesterol 0mg; Calcium 44mg; Fibre 1g; Sodium 16mg.
Lemon and Raisin Rock Cakes Energy 147kcal/617kJ; Protein 1.9g; Carbohydrate 21.6g, of which sugars 10.9g; Fat 6.5g, of which saturates 3.9g; Cholesterol 27mg; Calcium 27mg; Fibre 0.6g; Sodium 72mg.

Cinnamon Treats

These simple cookies really are a treat and there's no better accompaniment than a large pot of tea.

Makes 50
250g/9oz/2¼ cups plain (all-purpose) flour
pinch of salt
10ml/2 tsp ground cinnamon
225g/8oz/1 cup unsalted (sweet) butter, at room temperature
225g/8oz/generous 1 cup caster (superfine) sugar
2 eggs
5ml/1 tsp vanilla extract

1 In a large bowl, sift together the flour, salt and cinnamon. Set aside.

2 In a large bowl, beat the butter until soft. Add the sugar and continue beating together until the mixture is light and fluffy.

3 Beat the eggs and vanilla, then gradually stir into the butter mixture. Stir in the dry ingredients.

4 Divide the mixture into four equal parts, then roll each into 5cm/2in diameter logs. Wrap tightly in foil and chill in the refrigerator until firm.

5 Preheat the oven to 190°C/375°F/Gas 5. Lightly grease two baking sheets.

6 With a sharp knife, cut the logs into 5mm/¼in slices. Place the rounds on the prepared sheets, spaced slightly apart, and bake for about 10 minutes, until lightly coloured. Leave on the baking sheet for 1–2 minutes until the cookies firm up slightly.

7 With a metal spatula, transfer the cookies to a wire rack and leave to cool completely.

Variation
Replace the ground cinnamon with mixed spice (apple pie spice), if you like.

Cinnamon-coated Cookies

The aroma that fills the kitchen while these cookies are baking is mouthwatering. They are too good to resist.

Makes 30
115g/4oz/½ cup butter, at room temperature
350g/12oz/1¾ cups caster (superfine) sugar
5ml/1 tsp vanilla extract
2 eggs
50ml/2fl oz/¼ cup milk
400g/14oz/3½ cups plain (all-purpose) flour
5ml/1 tsp bicarbonate of soda (baking soda)
50g/2oz/½ cup finely chopped walnuts

For the coating
65g/2½oz/5 tbsp sugar
30ml/2 tbsp ground cinnamon

1 Preheat the oven to 190°C/375°F/Gas 5. Lightly grease two baking sheets.

2 In a large bowl, beat the butter until light. Add the sugar and vanilla extract and continue mixing until pale and fluffy. Add one egg at a time, beating well after each addition, then add the milk and mix well together.

3 Sift the flour and bicarbonate of soda over the butter mixture and stir in until combined. Stir in the chopped walnuts. Put in the refrigerator to chill for 15 minutes.

4 For the coating, mix the sugar and cinnamon. Roll tablespoonfuls of the dough mixture into walnut-size balls. Roll the balls in the sugar mixture.

5 Place the cookies 5cm/2in apart on the prepared sheets to allow for spreading during baking and flatten slightly with the back of a spoon. Bake in the oven until golden brown, about 10 minutes.

6 Leave to firm up slightly on the baking sheets for a few minutes, then using a metal spatula carefully transfer the cookies to a wire rack. Leave to cool completely before serving.

Cinnamon Treats Energy 71kcal/298kJ; Protein 0.8g; Carbohydrate 8.6g, of which sugars 4.8g; Fat 4g, of which saturates 2.4g; Cholesterol 17mg; Calcium 11mg; Fibre 0.2g; Sodium 31mg.
Cinnamon-coated Cookies Energy 65kcal/273kJ; Protein 0.9g; Carbohydrate 7.8g, of which sugars 3.1g; Fat 3.6g, of which saturates 2.2g; Cholesterol 14mg; Calcium 15mg; Fibre 0.2g; Sodium 28mg.

Clementine Shortbread Fingers

Light and mouthwatering, these citrus shortbreads are a real tea-time treat. Made with clementines, they are subtly sweet.

Makes 18
115g/4oz/¹/₂ cup unsalted (sweet) butter
50g/2oz/¹/₄ cup caster (superfine) sugar, plus extra for sprinkling
finely grated rind of 4 clementines
175g/6oz/1¹/₂ cups plain (all-purpose) flour, plus extra for dusting

1 Preheat the oven to 190°C/375°F/Gas 5. Lightly grease a large baking sheet.

2 Beat together the butter and sugar until soft and creamy, then add the grated clementine rind and beat well until it is fully incorporated.

3 Gradually add the flour, using a wooden spoon at first, and then with your hands gently pull the dough together to form a soft ball. Roll out the dough on a lightly floured surface to about 1cm/¹/₂in thick.

4 Cut into fingers, sprinkle over a little extra sugar and put on to the baking sheet spaced well apart. Prick lightly with a fork.

5 Bake for 20 minutes, or until light golden brown. Carefully lift the cookies on to a wire rack with a metal spatula and leave to cool completely.

Cook's Tip
The shortbread fingers will keep in an airtight container.

Variation
Substitute the grated rind of one Ugli fruit for the clementine rind and sprinkle the shortbread fingers well with sugar before baking.

Five-spice Fingers

These light, crumbly cookies have an unusual Chinese five-spice flavouring. Pipe them into finger shapes.

Makes 28
115g/4oz/¹/₂ cup butter, at room temperature, diced, plus extra for greasing
50g/2oz/¹/₂ cup icing (confectioners') sugar
115g/4oz/1 cup plain (all-purpose) flour
10ml/2 tsp Chinese five-spice powder
grated rind and juice of ¹/₂ orange

1 Preheat the oven to 180°C/350°F/Gas 4. Lightly grease two baking sheets.

2 Put the butter and half the icing sugar in a bowl and beat well with a wooden spoon, until the mixture is smooth and creamy.

3 Add the flour and five-spice powder and beat again until thoroughly mixed. Spoon the mixture into a large piping (pastry) bag fitted with a large star nozzle.

4 Pipe short lines of mixture, about 7.5cm/3in long, on the prepared baking sheets. Leave enough room for them to spread.

5 Bake for 15 minutes, until lightly browned. Leave to cool slightly before transferring to a wire rack using a metal spatula.

6 Sift the remaining icing sugar into a small bowl and stir in the orange rind. Add enough juice to make a thin icing. Brush over the cookies while they are still warm.

Variation
Substitute syrup from a jar of preserved stem ginger for the orange juice in the icing.

Clementine Shortbread Fingers Energy 87kcal/362kJ; Protein 0.7g; Carbohydrate 9.5g, of which sugars 4.7g; Fat 5.4g, of which saturates 3.3g; Cholesterol 14mg; Calcium 15mg; Fibre 0.3g; Sodium 47mg.
Five-spice Fingers Energy 53kcal/221kJ; Protein 0.5g; Carbohydrate 5.3g, of which sugars 2g; Fat 3.5g, of which saturates 2.2g; Cholesterol 9mg; Calcium 8mg; Fibre 0.1g; Sodium 25mg.

Almond Orange Cookies

The combination of lard and almonds gives these traditional cookies a lovely short texture, so that they melt in the mouth, but you could use white cooking fat, if you like. Serve them whenever you have guests – they are perfect with coffee or hot chocolate.

Makes 36
250g/9oz/1½ cups lard, softened
125g/4½oz/generous ½ cup
  caster (superfine) sugar
2 eggs, beaten
grated rind and juice of
  1 small orange
300g/11oz/2¾ cups plain
  (all-purpose) flour, plus extra
  for dusting
5ml/1 tsp baking powder
200g/7oz/1¾ cups ground
  almonds

For dusting
50g/2oz/½ cup icing
  (confectioners') sugar
5ml/1 tsp ground cinnamon

1 Preheat the oven to 200°C/400°F/Gas 6. Lightly grease two or three large baking sheets.

2 Place the lard in a large bowl and beat until light and fluffy. Gradually beat in the caster sugar.

3 Beat in the eggs, orange rind and juice until well combined, then sift over the flour and baking powder in batches and stir in after each addition. Add the almonds and bring together to form a dough.

4 Roll out on a lightly floured surface to 1cm/½in thick. Stamp out 36 rounds with a cookie cutter.

5 Lift the rounds on to the prepared baking sheets and bake for about 10 minutes, until golden. Leave on the baking sheets for 10 minutes to cool and firm slightly before transferring with a metal spatula to a wire rack to cool.

6 Place the wire rack over the baking sheet. Combine the icing sugar with the cinnamon and sift evenly over the cookies. Leave to cool completely.

Orange Cookies

Easy to make and even easier to eat, these cookies are just perfect with a cup of steaming hot chocolate on a winter's afternoon or with ice cream on a warm summer's evening.

Makes 30
115g/4oz/½ cup butter, at room
  temperature
200g/7oz/1 cup sugar
2 egg yolks
15ml/1 tbsp fresh orange juice
grated rind of 1 large orange
200g/7oz/1¾ cups plain
  (all-purpose) flour
15ml/1 tbsp cornflour
  (cornstarch)
pinch of salt
5ml/1 tsp baking powder

1 In a large bowl, beat together the butter and sugar until light and fluffy. Add the egg yolks, orange juice and rind, and continue beating to blend. Set aside.

2 In another bowl, sift together the flour, cornflour, salt and baking powder. Add to the butter mixture and stir until it forms a dough.

3 Wrap the dough in baking parchment and chill in the refrigerator for 2 hours.

4 Preheat the oven to 375°F/190°C/Gas 5. Lightly grease two baking sheets.

5 Roll spoonfuls of the dough into balls and place 1–2in/2.5–5cm apart on the prepared sheets.

6 Press down with a fork to flatten. Bake for about 8–10 minutes, until golden brown. Leave to firm up slightly for 1–2 minutes. With a metal spatula, transfer the cookies to a wire rack and leave to cool completely.

Cook's Tip
When rolling the dough into balls, try not to handle it too much or it may become greasy.

Almond Orange Cookies Energy 148kcal/617kJ; Protein 2.3g; Carbohydrate 12.1g, of which sugars 5.6g; Fat 10.4g, of which saturates 3.1g; Cholesterol 17mg; Calcium 29mg; Fibre 0.7g; Sodium 5mg.
Orange Cookies Energy 83kcal/350kJ; Protein 0.9g; Carbohydrate 12.6g, of which sugars 7.1g; Fat 3.6g, of which saturates 2.1g; Cholesterol 22mg; Calcium 15mg; Fibre 0.2g; Sodium 25mg.

Citrus Drops

These soft, cake-like treats are deliciously tangy, with a zesty, crumbly base filled with sweet, sticky lemon or orange curd. The crunchy topping of almonds makes the perfect finish.

Makes about 20
175g/6oz/¾ cup unsalted (sweet) butter, at room temperature, diced
150g/5oz/¾ cup caster (superfine) sugar
finely grated rind of 1 large lemon
finely grated rind of 1 orange
2 egg yolks
50g/2oz/½ cup ground almonds
225g/8oz/2 cups self-raising (self-rising) flour
lemon and/or orange curd
milk, for brushing
flaked (sliced) almonds, for sprinkling

1 Preheat the oven to 160°C/325°F/Gas 3. Lightly grease two baking sheets.

2 In a large bowl, beat the butter and sugar together until light and fluffy, then stir in the citrus rinds.

3 Stir the egg yolks into the mixture, then add the ground almonds and flour and mix well.

4 Divide the mixture into 20 pieces and shape each into a smooth ball with your hands. Place on the baking sheets. Using the handle of a wooden spoon, make a hole in the centre of each cookie.

5 Put about 2.5ml/½ tsp lemon or orange curd into each hole and gently pinch the opening together with your fingers to semi-enclose the curd.

6 Brush the top of each cookie with milk and sprinkle with flaked almonds.

7 Bake for about 20 minutes, until pale golden brown. Leave to cool slightly on the baking sheets to firm up, then transfer to a wire rack using a metal spatula and leave to cool completely.

Raspberry Sandwich Cookies

Children will love these sweet, sticky treats. If you need to store them, layer with baking parchment in an airtight container.

Makes 32
115g/4oz/1 cup blanched almonds
175g/6oz/1½ cups plain (all-purpose) flour, plus extra for dusting
175g/6oz/¾ cup butter
115g/4oz/generous ½ cup caster (superfine) sugar
grated rind of 1 lemon
5ml/1 tsp vanilla extract
1 egg white
pinch of salt
40g/1½oz/⅓ cup flaked (sliced) almonds, chopped
350g/12oz/1¼ cups raspberry jam (jelly)
15ml/1 tbsp lemon juice

1 Preheat the oven to 160°C/325°F/Gas 3. Lightly grease two baking sheets.

2 In a processor or nut grinder, finely grind the almonds with 45ml/3 tbsp of the flour.

3 Beat together the butter and sugar until light and fluffy. Stir in the lemon rind and vanilla.

4 Add the ground almonds and remaining flour and mix to form a dough. Gather it into a ball, wrap in baking parchment and chill for 1 hour.

5 Roll out on a lightly floured surface to 3mm/⅛in thick. With a floured 6cm/2½in cookie cutter, stamp out rounds, then stamp out the centres from half of them. Place them 1cm/½in apart on the baking sheets.

6 Whisk the egg white with the salt until just frothy. Brush only the rings with the egg white, then sprinkle over the chopped almonds. Bake for 12–15 minutes, until lightly browned. Cool for 2–3 minutes on the sheets before transferring to a wire rack.

7 In a small, heavy pan, heat the jam with the lemon juice until it melts and comes to a simmer. Brush the jam over the cookie rounds and sandwich together with the rings.

Citrus Drops Energy 157kcal/658kJ; Protein 2.1g; Carbohydrate 16.8g, of which sugars 8.2g; Fat 9.6g, of which saturates 4.9g; Cholesterol 39mg; Calcium 31mg; Fibre 0.6g; Sodium 55mg.
Raspberry Sandwich Cookies Energy 133kcal/554kJ; Protein 2g; Carbohydrate 13.9g, of which sugars 9.5g; Fat 8.1g, of which saturates 3.1g; Cholesterol 12mg; Calcium 27mg; Fibre 0.6g; Sodium 39mg.

Apple Sauce Cookies

Apple sauce, nuts and cinnamon are the perfect combination for cookies for winter.

Makes 36

455g/1lb cooking apples, peeled, cored and chopped
45ml/3 tbsp water
115g/4oz/¼ cup sugar

115g/4oz/½ butter
175g/6oz/1 cup plain (all-purpose) flour
2.5ml/½ tsp baking powder
1.5ml/¼ tsp bicarbonate of soda (baking soda)
pinch of salt
2.5ml/½ tsp ground cinnamon
50g/2oz/½ cup chopped walnuts

1 Cook the apples with the water in a covered pan over a low heat until the apple is tender. Leave to cool slightly then purée it in a blender or mash the apple with a fork. Measure out 175ml/6fl oz/¾ cup. Set aside and leave to cool.

2 Preheat the oven to 190°C/375°F/Gas 5. Lightly grease two or three baking sheets.

3 In a bowl, beat together the sugar and butter until pale and fluffy. Beat in the apple sauce.

4 Sift the flour, baking powder, bicarbonate of soda, salt and cinnamon into the mixture, and stir to blend. Fold in the chopped walnuts.

5 Drop teaspoonfuls of the dough on to the prepared baking sheets, spacing them well apart to allow room for spreading while baking.

6 Bake the cookies for 8–10 minutes, until they are golden brown. Using a metal spatula, transfer them to a wire rack and leave to cool before serving.

Cook's Tip
If the apple sauce is too runny, put it in a sieve (strainer) over a bowl and let it drain for 10 minutes before measuring it out.

Banana Cream Cookies

These delicious cookies are inspired by the classic childhood dessert bananas and cream. The warm banana cookies are coated in crisp sugar-frosted cornflakes and, for the ultimate indulgence, are delicious served warm drizzled with clear honey.

Makes about 24

2 eggs
250g/9oz/1¼ cups soft light brown sugar
5ml/1 tsp vanilla extract

100ml/3½fl oz/scant ½ cup sunflower oil
90g/3½oz/scant ½ cup crème fraîche
200g/7oz/1¾ cups plain (all-purpose) flour
200g/7oz/1¾ cups self-raising (self-rising) flour
50g/2oz/2½ cups frosted cornflakes
125g/4¼oz dried small bananas, chopped, or 2 bananas, peeled and chopped
icing (confectioners') sugar, sifted, for dredging

1 Put the eggs and sugar in a large bowl and whisk together until well blended. Stir in the vanilla extract.

2 Add the oil and crème fraîche and stir well to combine. Add the flours and mix well. (The mixture will be quite runny at this stage.) Cover with clear film (plastic wrap) and chill for about 30 minutes.

3 Preheat the oven to 180°C/350°F/Gas 4. Lightly grease two or three baking sheets.

4 Put the frosted cornflakes in a large bowl. Remove the cookie dough from the refrigerator and stir in the bananas.

5 Using a tablespoon, drop heaps of the cookie mixture into the cornflakes. Lightly toss so that each cookie is well coated, then remove and place on the prepared baking sheets. Flatten slightly with your fingertips.

6 Bake for 15–20 minutes, or until risen and golden brown and crispy. Transfer the cookies to a wire rack and dredge with sifted icing sugar. Serve while still warm.

Apple Sauce Cookies Energy 54kcal/227kJ; Protein 0.7g; Carbohydrate 5g, of which sugars 1.3g; Fat 3.7g, of which saturates 1.8g; Cholesterol 7mg; Calcium 9mg; Fibre 0.4g; Sodium 20mg.
Banana Cream Cookies Energy 159kcal/669kJ; Protein 2.5g; Carbohydrate 27.7g, of which sugars 13.1g; Fat 5g, of which saturates 1.5g; Cholesterol 20mg; Calcium 34mg; Fibre 0.6g; Sodium 29mg.

Rose Water Biscuits

These light, crunchy cookies are easy to make. They are perfect served with mint tea – the two flavours are made for each other. The mixture makes about 60 cookies, so bake them in batches, two trays at a time.

Makes 60

225g/8oz/1 cup butter, softened
    at room temperature
225g/8oz/generous 1 cup caster
    (superfine) sugar
1 egg
15ml/1 tbsp single (light) cream
15ml/1 tbsp rose water
300g/11oz/2¾ cups plain
    (all-purpose) flour
pinch of salt
5ml/1 tsp baking powder
caster (superfine) sugar,
    for sprinkling

1 In a large bowl, beat together the butter and sugar until light and fluffy.

2 Break in the egg, pour in the cream and rose water and beat until well combined.

3 Sift over the flour, salt and baking powder a little at a time, combining well after each addition. Use your fingertips to combine to a firm dough.

4 Mould the mixture into an even roll and wrap in clear film (plastic wrap). Chill for 1–1½ hours.

5 Preheat the oven to 190°C/375°F/Gas 5. Lightly grease two large baking sheets.

6 Using a sharp knife, thinly slice the cookie dough into rounds. Arrange the cookies on the prepared baking sheets, allowing enough space for them to spread during cooking. Sprinkle with a little caster sugar and bake for about 10 minutes, until they are just turning brown at the edges.

7 Using a metal spatula, transfer the cookies to a wire rack and leave to cool completely.

Lavender Heart Cookies

These delicate and fragrant cookies make an unusual treat and their pretty heart shape is sure to charm both family and friends.

Makes about 18

115g/4oz/½ cup unsalted
    (sweet) butter at room
    temperature, diced
50g/2oz/¼ cup caster
    (superfine) sugar
175g/6oz/1½ cups plain
    (all-purpose) flour
30ml/2 tbsp fresh lavender florets
    or 15ml/1 tbsp dried culinary
    lavender, coarsely chopped
30ml/2 tbsp caster (superfine)
    sugar, for sprinkling

1 Preheat the oven to 200°C/400°F/Gas 6. Lightly grease a large baking sheet.

2 In a large bowl, beat together the butter and sugar until light and fluffy.

3 Stir in the flour and lavender and bring the mixture together in a soft ball. Cover with clear film (plastic wrap) and chill for about 15 minutes.

4 Roll out the dough on a lightly floured surface and stamp out about 18 cookies, using a 5cm/2in cookie cutter. Place on the baking sheet and bake for about 10 minutes, until golden.

5 Leave the cookies for 5 minutes to set. Using a metal spatula, transfer carefully from the baking sheet on to a wire rack to cool completely.

6 The cookies can be stored in an airtight container for up to 1 week.

> **Cook's Tip**
> *If you are using fresh lavender, make sure that it has not been sprayed with any chemicals or subjected to traffic pollution.*

Rose Water Biscuits Energy 61kcal/257kJ; Protein 0.6g; Carbohydrate 7.8g, of which sugars 4g; Fat 3.3g, of which saturates 2g; Cholesterol 11mg; Calcium 10mg; Fibre 0.2g; Sodium 24mg.
Lavender Heart Cookies Energy 97kcal/406kJ; Protein 1g; Carbohydrate 11.9g, of which sugars 4.5g; Fat 5.4g, of which saturates 3.4g; Cholesterol 14mg; Calcium 17mg; Fibre 0.3g; Sodium 39mg.

Orange Oaties

These are so delicious that it is difficult to believe that they are healthy too. As they are packed with flavour and are wonderfully crunchy, the whole family will love them.

Makes about 16

175g/6oz/³⁄₄ cup clear honey
120ml/4fl oz/¹⁄₂ cup orange juice
90g/3¹⁄₂oz/1 cup rolled oats,
  lightly toasted
115g/4oz/1 cup plain
  (all-purpose) flour
115g/4oz/generous ¹⁄₂ cup golden
  caster (superfine) sugar
finely grated rind of 1 orange
5ml/1 tsp bicarbonate of soda
  (baking soda)

1 Preheat the oven to 180°C/350°F/Gas 4. Line two baking sheets with baking parchment.

2 Put the honey and orange juice in a small pan and simmer over a low heat for 8–10 minutes, stirring occasionally, until the mixture is thick and syrupy. Remove the pan from the heat and set aside to cool slightly.

3 Put the oats, flour, sugar and orange rind into a bowl. Mix the bicarbonate of soda with 15ml/1 tbsp boiling water and add to the flour mixture, together with the honey and orange syrup. Mix well with a wooden spoon.

4 Place spoonfuls of the mixture on to the prepared baking sheets, spaced slightly apart, and bake for 10–12 minutes, or until golden brown.

5 Leave to firm up slightly on the baking sheets for 5 minutes, then using a metal spatula, carefully transfer the cookies to a wire rack and leave to cool completely.

Variation
For additional flavour and aroma, use orange blossom honey for making the orange syrup in step 2.

Oat and Apricot Clusters

Here is a variation on an old favourite, which children can easily make themselves, so have plenty of dried fruits ready for them to add. No baking is involved with these cookies.

Makes 12

50g/2oz/¹⁄₄ cup butter
50g/2oz/¹⁄₄ cup clear honey
50g/2oz/¹⁄₂ cup medium
  rolled oats
50g/2oz/¹⁄₂ cup chopped
  ready-to-eat dried apricots
15ml/1 tbsp dried banana chips
15ml/1 tbsp shredded coconut or
  desiccated (dry unsweetened
  shredded) coconut
50–75g/2–3oz/2–3 cups
  cornflakes or crisped rice cereal

1 Place the butter and honey in a small pan and warm over a low heat, stirring until the butter melts. Remove the pan from the heat.

2 Add the oats, apricots, banana chips, coconut and cornflakes or crisped rice cereal and stir well with a wooden spoon until combined.

3 Spoon the mixture into 12 paper muffin cases, piling it up roughly. Transfer to a baking sheet and chill in the refrigerator until set and firm.

Variations
• To make Oat and Cherry Clusters, use rinsed and chopped glacé (candied) cherries in place of the apricots.
• To make Chocolate Chip Clusters, substitute 75g/3oz/¹⁄₂ cup chocolate chips.

Cook's Tip
The ingredients can be changed according to what you have in your store cupboard (pantry) – try peanuts, pecan nuts, raisins or dried dates.

Orange Oaties Energy 110kcal/466kJ; Protein 1.5g; Carbohydrate 26.2g, of which sugars 16.6g; Fat 0.6g, of which saturates 0g; Cholesterol 0mg; Calcium 18mg; Fibre 0.6g; Sodium 4mg.
Oat and Apricot Clusters Energy 97kcal/407kJ; Protein 1.2g; Carbohydrate 11.7g, of which sugars 5.2g; Fat 5.4g, of which saturates 3.5g; Cholesterol 9mg; Calcium 7mg; Fibre 0.9g; Sodium 70mg.

Rosemary-scented Citrus Tuiles

These delicious crisp cookies are flavoured with tangy orange and lemon rind, and made beautifully fragrant with fresh rosemary – an unusual but winning combination.

Makes 18–20
50g/2oz/¼ cup unsalted (sweet) butter, diced
2 egg whites
115g/4oz/generous ½ cup caster (superfine) sugar
finely grated rind of ½ lemon
finely grated rind of ½ orange
10ml/2 tsp finely chopped fresh rosemary
50g/2oz/½ cup plain (all-purpose) flour

1 Preheat the oven to 190°C/375°F/Gas 5. Lightly grease two baking sheets.

2 Melt the butter in a pan over a low heat. Remove the pan from the heat and leave to cool.

3 Whisk the egg whites until stiff, then gradually whisk in the sugar.

4 Fold the lemon and orange rinds, rosemary, flour and then the melted butter into the egg white mixture.

5 Place two large tablespoonfuls of mixture on a baking sheet. Spread each to a thin disc about 9cm/3½in in diameter. Bake for 5–6 minutes until golden.

6 Remove from the oven and carefully lift the tuiles using a metal spatula and drape over a rolling pin. Transfer to a wire rack when set in a curved shape. Bake the rest of the mixture in the same way.

Cook's Tip
Don't be tempted to bake more than two tuiles at a time or they will set firm before you have time to shape them.

Honey Crunch Creams

Different types of honey lend a different character to the flavour of these cookies. Try using orange blossom or lavender honey.

Makes 20
250g/9oz/2¼ cups self-raising (self-rising) flour
10ml/2 tsp bicarbonate of soda (baking soda)
50g/2oz/¼ cup caster (superfine) sugar
115g/4oz/½ cup unsalted (sweet) butter, diced

finely grated rind of 1 large orange
115g/4oz/½ cup clear honey
25g/1oz/¼ cup pine nuts or chopped walnuts

For the filling
50g/2oz/¼ cup unsalted (sweet) butter, at room temperature, diced
115g/4oz/1 cup icing (confectioners') sugar, sifted
15ml/1 tbsp clear honey

1 Preheat the oven to 200°C/400°F/Gas 6. Lightly grease three or four baking sheets.

2 Sift the flour, bicarbonate of soda and caster sugar into a bowl. Add the butter and rub in until the mixture resembles breadcrumbs. Stir in the orange rind.

3 Put the honey in a small pan and heat until just runny but not hot. Pour over the dry mixture and mix to a firm dough.

4 Shape half of the dough into 20 small balls. Place on the baking sheets, spaced well apart, and gently flatten. Bake for 6–8 minutes, until golden. Leave for a few minutes. Use a metal spatula to transfer the cookies to a wire rack to cool.

5 Shape the remaining dough into 20 balls and dip one side of each into the pine nuts or walnuts. Place the cookies, nut sides up, on the baking sheets, and bake as before.

6 To make the filling, put the butter, icing sugar and honey in a bowl and beat together. Use the mixture to sandwich the cookies together in pairs using a plain cookie for the base and a nut-coated one for the top.

Rosemary-scented Citrus Tuiles Energy 51kcal/214kJ; Protein 0.6g; Carbohydrate 8g, of which sugars 6.1g; Fat 2.1g, of which saturates 1.3g; Cholesterol 5mg; Calcium 7mg; Fibre 0.1g; Sodium 22mg.
Honey Crunch Creams Energy 164kcal/688kJ; Protein 1.5g; Carbohydrate 23.4g, of which sugars 13.9g; Fat 7.8g, of which saturates 4.4g; Cholesterol 18mg; Calcium 24mg; Fibre 0.4g; Sodium 52mg.

Apricot and Coconut Kisses

These tangy, fruity treats make a colourful addition to the tea table. Although they are easy to make and can be mixed and shaped in a matter of a few minutes, allow plenty of time for the apricots to soak and also for the cookies to chill before serving.

Makes 12

130g/4½oz/generous ½ cup ready-to-eat dried apricots

100ml/3½fl oz/scant ½ cup orange juice

40g/1½oz/3 tbsp unsalted (sweet) butter, at room temperature, diced

75g/3oz/¾ cup icing (confectioners') sugar, plus extra for dusting

90g/3½oz/generous 1 cup desiccated (dry unsweetened shredded) coconut, lightly toasted

2 glacé (candied) cherries, cut into wedges

1 Finely chop the dried apricots, then tip them into a bowl. Pour in the orange juice and leave to soak for about 1 hour, until all the juice has been absorbed.

2 In a large bowl, beat together the butter and sugar with a wooden spoon until pale and creamy. Gradually add the soaked apricots to the creamed butter and sugar mixture, beating well after each addition. Stir in the toasted coconut.

3 Lightly grease a small baking tray. Place teaspoonfuls of the coconut mixture on to the baking sheet, piling them up into little pyramids. Gently press the mixture together with your fingers to form neat shapes.

4 Top each cookie with a wedge of cherry. Chill in the refrigerator for about 1 hour until firm, then serve lightly dusted with icing sugar.

> **Cook's Tip**
> It is essential that all the orange juice has been absorbed by the apricots before adding them to the butter mixture, otherwise the cookies will be too moist to set properly.

Tea Finger Cookies

The unusual ingredient in these cookies is Lady Grey tea – similar to Earl Grey but with the addition of Seville orange and lemon peel – which imparts a subtle flavour.

Makes about 36

150g/5oz/⅔ cup unsalted (sweet) butter, at room temperature, diced

115g/4oz/generous ½ cup light muscovado (brown) sugar

15–30ml/1–2 tbsp Lady Grey tea leaves

1 egg, beaten

200g/7oz/1¾ cups plain (all-purpose) flour, plus extra for dusting

demerara (raw) sugar, for sprinkling

1 Preheat the oven to 190°C/375°F/Gas 5. Lightly grease two or three baking sheets.

2 Beat the butter and sugar until light and creamy. Stir in the tea leaves until combined. Beat in the egg, then fold in the flour.

3 Using your hands, roll the dough on a lightly floured surface into a long cylinder, about 23cm/9in long. Gently press down on the cylinder to flatten slightly. Wrap the dough in clear film (plastic wrap) and chill for about 1 hour until the dough is firm enough to slice.

4 Cut the dough cylinder into 5mm/¼in slices and place slightly apart on the prepared baking sheets.

5 Sprinkle the cookies with a little demerara sugar, then bake for 10–15 minutes, until lightly browned. Transfer the cookies to a wire rack with a metal spatula and leave to cool.

> **Variation**
> You could use other exotic types of tea for making these cookies. Try Earl Grey, flavoured with bergamot, or aromatic flower or fruit teas, such as jasmine, rose congou or pouchong, chrysanthemum, passion fruit or strawberry.

Tea Finger Cookies Energy 65kcal/270kJ; Protein 0.7g; Carbohydrate 7.7g, of which sugars 3.4g; Fat 3.7g, of which saturates 2.2g; Cholesterol 14mg; Calcium 11mg; Fibre 0.2g; Sodium 28mg.
Apricot and Coconut Kisses Energy 115kcal/480kJ; Protein 1g; Carbohydrate 11.7g, of which sugars 11.7g; Fat 7.5g, of which saturates 5.7g; Cholesterol 7mg; Calcium 14mg; Fibre 1.7g; Sodium 25mg.

Coconut Pyramids

Deliciously moist and melt-in-the-mouth, these golden-topped cookies are great favourites with children. A special but strictly adult treat would be to serve them with a glass of rum.

Makes 15
225g/8oz/1 cup desiccated (dry unsweetened shredded) coconut
115g/4oz/1/2 cup caster (superfine) sugar
2 egg whites

1 Preheat the oven to 190°C/375°F/Gas 5. Lightly grease a large baking sheet.

2 Put the desiccated coconut and caster sugar into a bowl and mix well. Set aside.

3 In a grease-free bowl lightly whisk the egg whites. Fold enough egg white into the coconut and sugar to make a fairly firm mixture. You may not need all the egg whites.

4 Form the mixture into pyramids by taking a teaspoonful and rolling it first into a ball. Flatten the base and press the top into a point. Arrange the pyramids on the prepared baking sheet, spaced well apart.

5 Bake for 12–15 minutes on a low shelf. The tips should begin to turn golden and the pyramids should be just firm, but still soft inside.

6 Slide a metal spatula under the pyramids to loosen them and leave to cool before transferring to a wire rack.

Cook's Tips
• The heat in conventional ovens tends to be uneven, so, if necessary, turn the sheets around during baking for the pyramids to brown evenly. However, this is not necessary in a fan-assisted oven.
• Keep an eye on the use-by date as desiccated coconut, like all nuts and nut products, can quickly become rancid.

Almond Macaroons

Freshly ground almonds that have been lightly toasted to intensify the flavour give these cookies their rich taste and texture. So, for best results, avoid using ready-ground almonds as a shortcut.

Makes 12
120g/4oz/1 cup blanched almonds, toasted
160g/5 1/2oz/generous 3/4 cup caster (superfine) sugar
2 egg whites
2.5ml/1/2 tsp almond or vanilla extract
icing (confectioners') sugar, for dusting

1 Preheat the oven to 180°C/350°F/Gas 5. Lightly grease a large baking sheet.

2 Reserve 12 almonds for decorating. In a food processor fitted with a metal blade, process the rest of the almonds and the sugar until finely ground.

3 With the machine running, slowly pour in enough of the egg whites to form a soft dough. Add the almond or vanilla extract and pulse to mix.

4 With moistened hands, shape the mixture into walnut-size balls and arrange on the baking sheet. Press a reserved almond on to each, flattening slightly, and dust lightly with icing sugar.

5 Bake the macaroons for about 10–12 minutes, until the tops are lightly golden and feel slightly firm. Transfer the baking sheet to a wire rack, leave to cool slightly, then transfer the cookies to a wire rack using a metal spatula and leave to cool completely.

Coconut Macaroons

These macaroons should be soft and chewy on the inside with a crisp texture on the outside.

Makes 24
40g/1 1/2oz/1/3 cup plain (all-purpose) flour
pinch of salt

215g/7 1/4oz/2 1/2 cups desiccated (dry unsweetened shredded) coconut
150ml/1/2 pint/2/3 cup sweetened condensed milk
5ml/1 tsp vanilla extract

1 Preheat the oven to 180°C/350°F/Gas 4. Line two baking sheets with baking parchment and lightly grease the paper.

2 Sift the flour and salt into a large bowl. Add the dessicated coconut and stir to combine.

3 Pour in the sweetened condensed milk. Add the vanilla extract and stir together from the centre. Continue stirring until a very thick batter is formed.

4 Drop heaped tablespoonfuls of batter 2.5cm/1in apart on the prepared baking sheets. Bake for about 20 minutes, until golden brown. Transfer the macaroons to a wire rack using a metal spatula and leave to cool completely.

Coconut Pyramids Energy 122kcal/509kJ; Protein 1.3g; Carbohydrate 9g, of which sugars 9g; Fat 9.3g, of which saturates 8g; Cholesterol 0mg; Calcium 8mg; Fibre 2.1g; Sodium 13mg.
Almond Macaroons Energy 102kcal/426kJ; Protein 2.8g; Carbohydrate 7.8g, of which sugars 7.5g; Fat 6.9g, of which saturates 0.6g; Cholesterol 13mg; Calcium 33mg; Fibre 0.9g; Sodium 5mg.
Coconut Macaroons Energy 86kcal/358kJ; Protein 1.3g; Carbohydrate 5.8g, of which sugars 4.6g; Fat 6.6g, of which saturates 5.5g; Cholesterol 3mg; Calcium 25mg; Fibre 1.3g; Sodium 37mg.

Creamed Coconut Macaroons

Finely grated creamed coconut gives these soft-centred cookies a rich creaminess. Use coconut cream if creamed coconut is not available. For a tangy flavour, or to ring the changes, add the grated rind of one lime to the mixture in step 2. The cooked macaroons can be stored in an airtight container for up to 1 week.

Makes 16–18
50g/2oz creamed coconut, chilled, or 120ml/8 tbsp coconut cream
2 large (US extra large) egg whites
90g/3½oz/½ cup caster (superfine) sugar
75g/3oz/1 cup desiccated (dry unsweetened shredded) coconut

1 Preheat the oven to 180°C/350°F/Gas 4. Line a large baking sheet with baking parchment.

2 Finely grate the creamed coconut, if using.

3 Use an electric beater to whisk the egg whites in a large, grease-free bowl until stiff.

4 Whisk in the sugar, a little at a time, to make a stiff and glossy meringue. Fold in the grated creamed coconut, or coconut cream, and desiccated coconut, using a metal spoon.

5 Place dessertspoonfuls of the mixture, spaced slightly apart, on the baking sheet. Bake for 15–20 minutes, until slightly risen and golden brown. Leave to cool on the parchment, then transfer to an airtight container.

> **Variation**
> *For very rich, sweet and tempting petits fours, make the macaroons smaller, and when cooked coat them in melted plain (semisweet) chocolate. Place on greaseproof (waxed) paper and leave until the chocolate is hard. Serve with small cups of strong, black coffee after a dinner party.*

Coconut and Lime Macaroons

These pretty pistachio nut-topped cookies are crunchy on the outside and soft and gooey in the centre. The zesty lime topping contrasts wonderfully with the sweetness of the coconut.

Makes 12–14
4 large (US extra large) egg whites
250g/9oz/3 cups desiccated (dry unsweetened shredded) coconut
150g/5oz/¾ cup sugar
10ml/2 tsp vanilla extract
25g/1oz/¼ cup plain (all-purpose) flour
115g/4oz/1 cup icing (confectioners') sugar, sifted
grated rind of 1 lime
15–20ml/3–4 tsp lime juice
about 15g/½oz/1 tbsp pistachio nuts, chopped

1 Preheat the oven to 180°C/350°F/Gas 4. Line two baking sheets with baking parchment.

2 Put the egg whites, desiccated coconut, sugar, vanilla extract and flour in a large, heavy pan. Mix well. Place over a low heat and cook for 6–8 minutes, stirring constantly to ensure it does not stick. When the mixture becomes the consistency of thick porridge (oatmeal), remove from the heat.

3 Place spoonfuls of the mixture in rocky piles on the lined baking sheets. Bake for 12–13 minutes, until golden. Leave to cool completely on the baking sheets.

4 To make the topping, put the icing sugar and lime rind into a bowl and add enough lime juice to give a thick pouring consistency. Place a spoonful of icing on each macaroon and allow it to drip down the sides. Sprinkle over the pistachio nuts and serve.

> **Variation**
> *If you prefer, make Coconut and Lemon Macaroons by substituting grated lemon rind and juice.*

Coffee and Hazelnut Macaroons

Macaroons are traditionally made with ground almonds. This recipe uses hazelnuts, which are lightly roasted before grinding, but you can use walnuts instead.

Makes 20
edible rice paper
115g/4oz/1 cup skinned hazelnuts
225g/8oz/generous 1 cup caster (superfine) sugar
15ml/1 tbsp ground rice
10ml/2 tsp ground coffee
2 egg whites
caster (superfine) sugar, for sprinkling

1 Preheat the oven to 180°C/350°F/Gas 4. Line two baking sheets with rice paper.

2 Place the skinned hazelnuts on another baking sheet and cook in the oven for 5 minutes. Cool, then place in a food processor fitted with a metal blade and grind the nuts until fine.

3 Mix the ground nuts with the sugar, ground rice and coffee. Stir in the egg whites to make a fairly stiff paste.

4 Spoon into a piping (pastry) bag fitted with a 1cm/½in plain nozzle. Pipe rounds on the rice paper, leaving room for the cookies to spread.

5 Sprinkle each macaroon with a little caster sugar, then bake for 20 minutes, or until pale golden.

6 Using a metal spatula, transfer the macaroons to a wire rack and leave to cool completely. Remove the excess rice paper when completely cold.

Cook's Tip
Rice paper, traditionally used as a base for macaroons, is an edible, smooth, flavourless, glossy paper made from the pith of a tropical tree.

Cherry Coconut Munchies

You'll find it hard to stop at just one of these munchies, which make a wonderful morning or afternoon treat. If you like, drizzle 25–50g/ 1–2oz melted chocolate over the cold munchies and leave to set before serving.

Makes 20
2 egg whites
115g/4oz/1 cup icing (confectioners') sugar, sifted
115g/4oz/1 cup ground almonds
115g/4oz/generous 1 cup desiccated (dry unsweetened shredded) coconut
few drops of almond extract
75g/3oz/⅓ cup glacé (candied) cherries, finely chopped

1 Preheat the oven to 150°C/300°F/Gas 2. Line two baking sheets with baking parchment.

2 Place the egg whites in a grease-free bowl and whisk until stiff peaks form.

3 Gently fold in the icing sugar using a metal spoon and a figure-of-eight stirring motion. Fold in the ground almonds, coconut and almond extract to form a sticky dough. Finally, fold in the chopped glacé cherries.

4 Place mounds on the baking sheets. Bake for 25 minutes. Allow to cool and set briefly on the baking sheets, then transfer to a wire rack.

Cook's Tips
• These cookies are at their best when just baked, but may be stored in an airtight container for up to 3 days.
• When whisking egg whites, avoid using a plastic bowl, as plastic scratches easily.

Variation
Use ground hazelnuts in place of the almonds and omit the almond extract.

Coffee and Hazelnut Macaroons Energy 64kcal/267kJ; Protein 1.2g; Carbohydrate 7g, of which sugars 6.2g; Fat 3.7g, of which saturates 0.3g; Cholesterol 0mg; Calcium 11mg; Fibre 0.4g; Sodium 7mg.
Cherry Coconut Munchies Energy 103kcal/431kJ; Protein 1.9g; Carbohydrate 9.3g, of which sugars 9.1g; Fat 6.8g, of which saturates 3.3g; Cholesterol 0mg; Calcium 20mg; Fibre 1.2g; Sodium 10mg.

Golden Ginger Macaroons

With their warm, spicy, ginger flavour, these slightly chewy little cookies are good served with ice cream and will go beautifully with mid-morning or after-dinner coffee.

Makes 18–20
1 egg white
75g/3oz/scant ½ cup soft light brown sugar
115g/4oz/1 cup ground almonds
5ml/1 tsp ground ginger

1 Preheat the oven to 180°C/350°F/Gas 4.

2 In a large, grease-free bowl, whisk the egg white until stiff and standing in peaks, but not crumbly, then whisk in the brown sugar.

3 Sprinkle the ground almonds and ginger over the whisked egg white and gently fold them together.

4 Using two teaspoons, place spoonfuls of the mixture on baking trays, leaving plenty of space between each.

5 Bake for about 20 minutes, until pale golden brown and just turning crisp.

6 Leave to cool slightly on the baking trays before using a metal spatula to transfer the cookies to a wire rack. Leave to cool completely.

Cook's Tip
Use non-stick baking trays or line trays with baking parchment to make sure the cookies don't stick.

Variation
You can substitute other ground nuts, such as hazelnuts or walnuts, for the almonds. Ground cinnamon or mixed spice (apple pie spice) could be added to the mixture instead of ginger for another variation.

Ginger Snaps

When these cookies are baked their tops craze and crack into an attractive pattern that is characteristic of this traditional family favourite cookie.

Makes about 24
115g/4oz/½ cup butter, diced
115g/4oz/generous ½ cup caster (superfine) sugar
115g/4oz/½ cup golden (light corn) syrup
225g/8oz/2 cups plain (all-purpose) flour
10ml/2 tsp ground ginger
5ml/1 tsp bicarbonate of soda (baking soda)

1 Preheat the oven to 180°C/350°F/Gas 4. Line two or three baking sheets with baking parchment.

2 Put the butter, sugar and syrup into a pan and heat gently, stirring occasionally, until the butter has melted and the sugar has dissolved. Remove the pan from the heat and leave to cool slightly.

3 Sift the flour, ginger and bicarbonate of soda and stir into the mixture in the pan to make a soft dough.

4 Shape the dough into about 24 balls and arrange them on the prepared baking sheets, well spaced out. Flatten each ball slightly with a metal spatula.

5 Put one tray into the hot oven and cook for about 12 minutes until golden brown (they burn easily). Leave to cool on the baking sheet for 1–2 minutes, then using a metal spatula, carefully transfer to a wire rack to crisp up and cool completely.

6 Cook the remaining cookies in the same way.

Cook's Tip
Measuring syrup is easier if you dip a metal spoon in very hot water first, then quickly dry it.

Golden Ginger Macaroons Energy 5kcal/21kJ; Protein 0.1g; Carbohydrate 0.4g, of which sugars 0.4g; Fat 0.3g, of which saturates 0g; Cholesterol 1mg; Calcium 2mg; Fibre 0g; Sodium 0mg.
Ginger Snaps Energy 101kcal/424kJ; Protein 1g; Carbohydrate 16.1g, of which sugars 9g; Fat 4.1g, of which saturates 2.5g; Cholesterol 10mg; Calcium 17mg; Fibre 0.3g; Sodium 43mg.

Double Ginger Cookies

These are a supreme treat for ginger lovers – richly spiced cookies packed with chunks of succulent preserved stem ginger. They are sure to give a boost when your energy flags.

Makes 20 large cookies

350g/12oz/3 cups self-raising (self-rising) flour
pinch of salt
200g/7oz/1 cup golden caster (superfine) sugar
15ml/1 tbsp ground ginger
5ml/1 tsp bicarbonate of soda (baking soda)
115g/4oz/½ cup unsalted (sweet) butter, diced
90g/3½oz/generous ¼ cup golden (light corn) syrup
1 large (US extra large) egg, beaten
150g/5oz preserved stem ginger in syrup, drained and coarsely chopped

1 Preheat the oven to 160°C/325°F/Gas 3. Lightly grease three baking sheets.

2 Sift the flour into a large bowl, add the salt, caster sugar, ground ginger and bicarbonate of soda and stir to combine.

3 Put the butter in a small pan with the syrup. Heat gently, stirring, until the butter has melted. Remove from the heat and set aside to cool until just warm.

4 Pour the butter mixture over the dry ingredients, then add the egg and two-thirds of the chopped ginger. Mix thoroughly, then use your hands to bring the dough together.

5 Shape the dough into 20 balls. Place them, spaced well apart, on the baking sheets and gently flatten them with your fingers or a metal spatula.

6 Press a few pieces of the remaining preserved stem ginger into the top of each of the cookies.

7 Bake for about 12–15 minutes, until golden. Leave to cool for 1 minute on the baking sheets to firm up. Using a metal spatula, transfer the cookies to a wire rack to cool completely.

Treacly Ginger Cookies

Packed with flavour and an extra hint of spice, these fabulous cookies will be a sure-fire hit with children and adults alike.

Makes 36

225g/8oz/generous 1 cup caster (superfine) sugar
90g/3½oz/generous 1 cup soft light brown sugar
115g/4oz/½ cup butter, at room temperature
115g/4oz/½ cup margarine, at room temperature
1 egg
90ml/6 tbsp black treacle (molasses)
250g/9oz/2¼ cups plain (all-purpose) flour
10ml/2 tsp ground ginger
2.5ml/½ tsp freshly grated nutmeg
5ml/1 tsp ground cinnamon
10ml/2 tsp bicarbonate of soda (baking soda)
pinch of salt

1 Preheat the oven to 170°C/325°F/Gas 3. Lightly grease two or three baking sheets.

2 In a large bowl, beat together half the caster sugar, the brown sugar, butter and margarine until light and fluffy. Add the egg and continue beating to blend well. Add the treacle and stir until fully incorporated.

3 Sift the flour, ginger, nutmeg, cinnamon, bicarbonate of soda and salt into the mixture and gently stir in. Cover with cling film (plastic wrap) and chill in the refrigerator for about 30 minutes.

4 Place the remaining sugar in a shallow dish. Roll tablespoonfuls of the cookie mixture into balls, then roll the balls in the sugar to coat.

5 Place the balls on the prepared baking sheets, spaced about 5cm/2in apart to allow for spreading during baking, and flatten slightly with your fingers or a metal spatula. Bake for 12–15 minutes, until golden brown around the edges but still soft in the middle. Leave to stand on the baking sheets for 5 minutes, then using a metal spatula, transfer to a wire rack to cool completely.

Double Ginger Cookies Energy 114kcal/479kJ; Protein 1.4g; Carbohydrate 20.4g, of which sugars 11.5g; Fat 3.5g, of which saturates 2.1g; Cholesterol 15mg; Calcium 23mg; Fibre 0.4g; Sodium 42mg.
Treacly Ginger Cookies Energy 57kcal/239kJ; Protein 0.6g; Carbohydrate 10.3g, of which sugars 6.8g; Fat 1.7g, of which saturates 1g; Cholesterol 7mg; Calcium 16mg; Fibre 0.1g; Sodium 15mg.

Gingerbread Men

These perennially popular little figures are easy to make and a guaranteed success. Made without sugar, these cookies are good for anyone diabetic.

Makes 8

115g/4oz/1 cup plain (all-purpose) flour, sifted, plus extra for dusting
7.5ml/1 1/2 tsp ground ginger
grated rind of 1 orange and 1 lemon
75ml/5 tbsp pear and apple jam
25g/1oz/2 tbsp butter
16 currants and 8 raisins, to decorate (optional)

1 Preheat the oven to 180°C/350°F/Gas 4.

2 Mix the sifted flour, ginger and grated orange and lemon rind in a bowl.

3 Melt the pear and apple jam and the butter in a small pan over a low heat. Stir it into the dry ingredients. Mix to a firm dough, wrap in clear film (plastic wrap) and chill for 2–3 hours.

4 Roll out the dough on a lightly floured surface to a thickness of 5mm/1/4in. Cut out gingerbread men, using a cutter.

5 Give the gingerbread men currant eyes and raisin noses. Using the point of a knife, draw a mouth on each. Place the cookies on a lightly floured baking sheet and bake for 8–10 minutes. Using a metal spatula, transfer to a wire rack and leave to cool completely.

Ginger Bites

Delightfully crisp, these tasty cookies make a delicious accompaniment to rich desserts and ice cream. They are equally good with a cup of strong tea or coffee, and perfect for feeding large groups of people.

Makes about 50

150g/5 1/2oz/1/2 cup plus 3 tbsp butter
400g/14oz/2 cups sugar
50ml/2fl oz/1/4 cup golden (light corn) syrup
15ml/1 tbsp black treacle (molasses)
15ml/1 tbsp ground ginger
30ml/2 tbsp ground cinnamon
15ml/1 tbsp ground cloves
5ml/1 tsp ground cardamom
5ml/1 tsp bicarbonate of soda (baking soda)
250ml/8fl oz/1 cup water
150g/5oz/1 1/4 cups plain (all-purpose) flour, plus extra for dusting

1 Put the butter, sugar, syrup, treacle, ginger, cinnamon, cloves and cardamom in a heavy pan and heat gently, stirring frequently, until the butter has melted and the sugar has dissolved. Remove the pan from the heat.

2 Mix together the bicarbonate of soda and measured water in a large heatproof bowl. Pour in the warm spice mixture and stir well with a wooden spoon until thoroughly blended, then add the flour and stir in well. Cover the bowl with clear film (plastic wrap) and put it into the refrigerator overnight to rest.

3 Preheat the oven to 220°C/425°F/Gas 7. Line several baking sheets with baking parchment.

4 Briefly knead the dough, then roll out on a lightly floured surface as thinly as possible. Stamp out flower shapes with a cookie cutter or cut the dough into shapes of your choice. Place them on the baking sheets spaced well apart.

5 Bake the cookies in the oven for about 5 minutes until golden brown, cooking in batches until all the cookies are cooked. Leave to cool on the baking sheet. Store in an airtight container for 1–2 days.

> **Cook's Tip**
> If you have time, you could add extra decoration to the cookies. For example, make a row of currant buttons down the front of each gingerbread man's body before baking, or pipe a colourful waistcoat (vest) with glacé icing afterwards. You could also add small sweets (candies) stuck on to the baked cookies with a dab of icing.

Ginger Bites Energy 31kcal/130kJ; Protein 0.2g; Carbohydrate 5.8g, of which sugars 4.2g; Fat 0.8g, of which saturates 0.5g; Cholesterol 2mg; Calcium 5mg; Fibre 0.1g; Sodium 13mg.
Gingerbread Men Energy 143kcal/600kJ; Protein 1.5g; Carbohydrate 17.7g, of which sugars 6.7g; Fat 7.9g, of which saturates 4.9g; Cholesterol 20mg; Calcium 23mg; Fibre 0.5g; Sodium 60mg.

Ginger Glass Cookies

As thin, delicate and elegant as fine glass, these ginger cookies are ideal served with creamy desserts, syllabubs, sorbets and luxury ice creams.

Makes about 18
50g/2oz/¼ cup unsalted (sweet) butter, diced
40g/1½oz/3 tbsp liquid glucose (clear corn syrup)
90g/3½oz/½ cup caster (superfine) sugar
40g/1½oz/⅓ cup plain (all-purpose) flour
5ml/1 tsp ground ginger

1 Put the butter and liquid glucose in a heatproof bowl set over a pan of gently simmering water. Stir together until melted. Set aside.

2 Put the sugar in a bowl and sift over the flour and ginger. Stir into the butter mixture, then beat well until combined. Cover with clear film (plastic wrap) and chill for about 25 minutes, until firm.

3 Preheat the oven to 180°C/350°F/Gas 4 and lightly grease two or three baking sheets.

4 Roll teaspoonfuls of the cookie mixture into balls between your hands and place them, spaced well apart to allow room for spreading, on the prepared baking sheets.

5 Place a second piece of baking parchment on top and roll the cookies as thinly as possible. Peel off the top sheet, then stamp each cookie with a 7.5 or 9cm/3 or 3½in cookie cutter.

6 Bake for 5–6 minutes, or until golden. Leave for a few seconds on the baking sheets to firm up slightly, then either leave flat or curl over in half. Leave to cool completely.

Cook's Tip
Use unlipped baking sheets so you can roll the cookies thinly.

Iced Ginger Cookies

If your children enjoy cooking with you, mixing and rolling the dough, or cutting out different shapes, this is the ideal recipe to let them practise on.

Makes about 16
115g/4oz/½ cup soft brown sugar
115g/4oz/½ cup butter
pinch of salt
few drops vanilla extract
175g/6oz/1⅓ cups wholemeal (whole-wheat) flour, plus extra for dusting
15g/½oz/1 tbsp unsweetened cocoa powder, sifted
10ml/2 tsp ground ginger
a little milk
glacé icing and glacé (candied) cherries, to decorate

1 Preheat the oven to 190°C/375°F/Gas 5. Lightly grease two baking sheets.

2 In a large bowl, beat together the sugar, butter, salt and vanilla extract until soft and fluffy. Work in the flour, cocoa powder and ginger, adding a little milk, if necessary, to bind the mixture. Knead lightly on a floured surface until smooth.

3 Roll out the dough on a lightly floured surface to about 5mm/¼in thick. Stamp out shapes using cookie cutters and place on the prepared baking sheets.

4 Bake the cookies for 10–15 minutes, leave to cool on the baking sheets until firm, then transfer to a wire rack to cool completely. Decorate with glacé icing and glacé cherries.

Chocolate Gingerbread

Chocolate and ginger form a classic partnership in these fabulous cookies.

Makes 12
175g/6oz/1½ cup plain (all-purpose) flour, plus extra for dusting
10ml/2 tsp mixed spice (apple pie spice)
pinch of salt
2.5ml/½ tsp bicarbonate of soda (baking soda)
25g/1oz/¼ cup unsweetened cocoa powder
75g/3oz/6 tbsp unsalted (sweet) butter, diced
75g/3oz/1/3 cup light muscovado (brown) sugar
1 egg

1 Sift together the flour, spice, salt, bicarbonate of soda and cocoa powder. Blend in a food processor, with the butter, until the mixture resembles fine breadcrumbs.

2 Add the sugar and egg and mix to a firm dough. Knead lightly. Wrap in clear film (plastic wrap) and chill for 30 minutes.

3 Preheat the oven to 180°C/350°F/Gas 4. Lightly grease two large baking sheets.

4 Roll out the dough to 10mm/½in thickness. Stamp out shapes and transfer to the prepared baking sheets.

5 Bake for 12 minutes until the cookies are just beginning to colour around the edges. Transfer to a wire rack to cool.

Ginger Glass Cookies Energy 55kcal/231kJ; Protein 0.3g; Carbohydrate 8.9g, of which sugars 6.2g; Fat 2.3g, of which saturates 1.5g; Cholesterol 6mg; Calcium 6mg; Fibre 0.1g; Sodium 21mg.
Iced Ginger Cookies Energy 119kcal/497kJ; Protein 1.6g; Carbohydrate 14.7g, of which sugars 7.8g; Fat 6.4g, of which saturates 3.9g; Cholesterol 15mg; Calcium 11mg; Fibre 1.1g; Sodium 53mg.
Chocolate Gingerbread Energy 133kcal/560kJ; Protein 2.3g; Carbohydrate 18.1g, of which sugars 6.8g; Fat 6.5g, of which saturates 3.7g; Cholesterol 29mg; Calcium 29mg; Fibre 0.7g; Sodium 64mg.

Shaker-style Spiced Cookies

These delicious spicy cookies can be packed up in pretty boxes to make elegant gifts for all ages. They are great to give to children or to make with children, as a gift for older relatives.

Makes about 25
50g/2oz/4tbsp butter
100g/4oz/scant ½ cup soft light brown sugar
45ml/3 tbsp clear honey

30ml/2 tbsp orange juice or milk
225g/8oz/2 cups plain (all-purpose) flour, plus extra for dusting
2.5ml/½ tsp bicarbonate of soda (baking soda)
5ml/1 tsp ground ginger
1.25ml/¼ tsp ground allspice
1.25ml/¼ tsp ground cinnamon

To decorate
45ml/3 tbsp orange juice or water
100g/4oz/1 cup icing (confectioners') sugar

1 Brush two baking sheets with a little oil.

2 Put the butter, sugar and honey into a pan and heat gently, stirring occasionally, until the butter has melted.

3 Add the orange juice or milk to the pan. Sift the flour, bicarbonate of soda and spices into the pan and mix with a wooden spoon, until you have a smooth dough. Leave the mixture to cool for 15 minutes.

4 Preheat the oven to 160°C/325°F/Gas 3. Turn out the ginger dough on to a floured surface, knead lightly and then roll out. Use cookie cutters to stamp out heart and hand shapes.

5 Transfer to the baking sheets. Cook for 8–10 minutes, until browned. Leave to cool on the baking sheet, then transfer to a wire rack to cool completely.

6 To make the icing, gradually mix the orange juice or water with the icing sugar to make a thick paste. Pipe borders of lines and dots, to decorate.

7 Leave to dry overnight before packing into boxes or tins. Keep for up to 10 days at room temperature.

Golden Gingerbread

Maple syrup is the secret ingredient that gives this spicy gingerbread its extra special flavour and lovely rich colour.

Makes 20
175g/6oz/1½ cups plain (all-purpose) flour, plus extra for dusting
1.5ml/¼ tsp bicarbonate of soda (baking soda)

pinch of salt
5ml/1 tsp ground ginger
5ml/1 tsp ground cinnamon
65g/2½oz/5 tbsp unsalted (sweet) butter, diced
75g/3oz/scant ½ cup caster (superfine) sugar
30ml/2 tbsp maple or golden (light corn) syrup
1 egg yolk, beaten

1 In a large bowl, sift together the flour, bicarbonate of soda, salt and spices.

2 Rub the butter into the flour until the mixture resembles fine breadcrumbs. Alternatively, blend in a food processor.

3 Add the sugar, syrup and egg yolk and mix or process to a firm dough. Knead lightly. Wrap in clear film (plastic wrap) and chill in the refrigerator for 30 minutes.

4 Preheat the oven to 180°C/350°F/Gas 4. Lightly grease two large baking sheets.

5 Roll out the dough on a lightly floured surface to 10mm/½in thick. Stamp out shapes using your choice of cookie cutter and transfer to the prepared baking sheets.

6 Bake for 12 minutes, until the cookies are just beginning to colour around the edges. Transfer to a wire rack and leave to cool completely.

> **Cook's Tip**
> If you want to make the darker cocoa gingerbread, substitute 15g/½oz flour for unsweetened cocoa powder.

Shaker-style Spiced Cookies Energy 67kcal/285kJ; Protein 0.9g; Carbohydrate 12.7g, of which sugars 5.8g; Fat 1.8g, of which saturates 1.1g; Cholesterol 4mg; Calcium 16mg; Fibre 0.3g; Sodium 13mg.
Golden Gingerbread Energy 1555kcal/6541kJ; Protein 21.7g; Carbohydrate 241.9g, of which sugars 105.1g; Fat 62.5g, of which saturates 36g; Cholesterol 340mg; Calcium 343mg; Fibre 5.4g; Sodium 497mg.

Ginger-topped Shortbread Fingers

Topping a ginger shortbread base with a sticky ginger mixture may be gilding the lily, but it tastes delicious!

Makes about 40
225g/8oz/2 cups plain
(all-purpose) flour
5ml/1 tsp ground ginger
75g/3oz/6 tbsp caster
(superfine) sugar

3 pieces preserved stem ginger, finely chopped
175g/6oz/¾ cup butter

For the topping
15ml/1 tbsp golden (light corn) syrup
50g/2oz/¼ cup butter
60ml/4 tbsp icing (confectioners') sugar, sifted
5ml/1 tsp ground ginger

1 Preheat the oven to 180°C/350°F/Gas 4. Lightly grease a shallow rectangular 28 x 18cm/11 x 7in baking tin (pan).

2 Sift the flour and ground ginger into a bowl and stir in the sugar and preserved stem ginger.

3 Rub in the butter until the mixture begins to bind together. Press the mixture into the prepared tin and smooth over the top with a metal spatula.

4 Bake for 40 minutes, until the ginger shortbread base is very lightly browned.

5 To make the topping, put the syrup and butter in a small pan. Heat gently until both have melted. Stir in the sifted icing sugar and ginger.

6 Remove the shortbread from the oven and pour the topping over the base while both are still hot. Leave to cool slightly, then cut into fingers. Remove to wire racks to cool completely.

> **Cook's Tip**
> Use the syrup from the jar of preserved stem ginger instead of golden syrup in the topping, if you prefer.

Lebkuchen

These luxurious and elegant cookies would make a delightful and special gift.

5ml/1 tsp ground ginger
2.5ml/½ tsp ground cloves
1.5ml/¼ tsp chilli powder

Makes 40
115g/4oz/½ cup unsalted
(sweet) butter
115g/4oz/½ cup light muscovado
(brown) sugar
1 egg, eaten
155g/4oz/⅓ cup black treacle
(molasses)
400g/14oz/3½ cups self-raising
(self-rising) flour, plus extra
for dusting

For the decoration
115g/4oz plain (semisweet)
chocolate
115g/4oz milk chocolate
115g/4oz white chocolate
chocolate sprinkles
unsweetened cocoa powder or
icing (confectioners') sugar,
for dusting

1 Beat together the butter and sugar until pale and fluffy. Beat in the egg and black treacle. Sift the flour, ginger, cloves and chilli powder into the bowl. Using a wooden spoon, gradually mix the ingredients together to make a stiff paste.

2 Turn out on to a lightly floured work surface and knead lightly until smooth. Wrap and chill for 30 minutes.

3 Preheat the oven to 180°C/350°F/Gas 4. Lightly grease two large baking sheets.

4 Roll out the dough to 8mm/¾in thickness and stamp out your choice of shapes using cookie cutters. Roll dough balls with the trimmings and flatten them. Place on the prepared baking sheets and bake for 8–10 minutes, until just beginning to colour around the edges. Transfer to a wire rack to cool.

5 For the decoration, melt the chocolate in separate bowls over a pan of gently simmering water. Spoon a little of each into three piping (pastry) bags. Cover a third of the cookies with plain chocolate, a third with milk chocolate, and a third with white chocolate. Pipe decorations on some cookies. Sprinkle icing sugar, cocoa or chocolate sprinkles over the rest.

Ginger-topped Shortbread Fingers Energy 62kcal/257kJ; Protein 0.5g; Carbohydrate 6.7g, of which sugars 3.2g; Fat 3.8g, of which saturates 2.4g; Cholesterol 10mg; Calcium 9mg; Fibre 0.1g; Sodium 29mg.
Lebkuchen Energy 105kcal/444kJ; Protein 2.4g; Carbohydrate 16.3g, of which sugars 11.7g; Fat 3.9g, of which saturates 0.4g; Cholesterol 19mg; Calcium 33mg; Fibre 0.7g; Sodium 16mg.

Sake and Ginger Cookies

Light and crisp, these cookies have a unique taste created by a combination of maple syrup and sake, complemented by a hint of ginger. They are delicious served with green tea.

Makes 20–30

250g/12oz/3 cups plain
  (all-purpose) flour, plus extra
  for dusting
45ml/3 tbsp sesame oil
25g/1oz fresh root ginger, peeled
  and grated

90ml/6 tbsp sake or rice wine
90ml/6 tbsp maple syrup or
  golden (light corn) syrup
2.5ml/½ tsp white pepper
30ml/2 tbsp pine nuts
vegetable oil, for deep-frying
salt

For the syrup

250ml/8fl oz/1 cup water
200g/7oz/1 cup sugar
30ml/2 tbsp clear honey
5ml/1 tsp ground cinnamon
pinch of salt

1 Sift the flour into a large bowl. Add the sesame oil. Mix in the grated ginger, sake, syrup, pepper and a splash of water. Knead into an elastic dough.

2 Roll out on a floured surface to about 1cm/½in thick. Use a cookie cutter to stamp out the dough into rounds.

3 To make the syrup, place the water, sugar and honey in a pan, and add a pinch of salt. Bring to the boil without stirring, then add the cinnamon and stir until the syrup thickens and becomes sticky. Pour into a bowl and set aside.

4 Grind the pine nuts to a fine powder in a mortar and pestle or using a food processor fitted with a metal blade.

5 Pour a generous amount of vegetable oil into a pan, and heat over medium heat until a small piece of day-old bread browns in about 20 seconds. Add the cookies, in batches if necessary, and deep-fry until golden brown.

6 Drain well to remove any excess oil and dip the cookies into the syrup to coat. Arrange on a serving plate and dust with ground pine nuts.

Three-colour Ribbon Cookies

These crisp twists of wafer-thin dough have a hint of gingery spiciness.

Makes 12–15

vegetable oil, for deep-frying
30ml/2 tbsp pine nuts,
  finely ground

For the green cookies

115g/4oz/1 cup plain
  (all-purpose) flour
2.5ml/½ tsp salt
10g/¼oz grated fresh root ginger
30ml/2 tbsp seaweed,
  finely ground

For the yellow cookies

115g/4oz/1 cup plain
  (all-purpose) flour

2.5ml/½ tsp salt
10g/¼oz grated fresh root ginger
50g/2oz sweet pumpkin, finely
  minced (ground)

For the pink cookies

115g/4oz/1 cup plain
  (all-purpose) flour
2.5ml/½ tsp salt
10g/¼oz grated fresh root ginger
50g/2oz apricot flesh, finely
  minced (ground)

For the syrup

250ml/8fl oz/1 cup water
200g/7oz/1 cup sugar
30ml/2 tbsp clear honey
2.5ml/½ tsp ground cinnamon
pinch of salt

1 To make the green cookies, sift the flour and salt into a large bowl and mix in the grated ginger, ground seaweed and a splash of water. Knead gently into a smooth, elastic dough. Place on a lightly floured surface and roll out the dough to about 3mm/⅛in thick. Cut into strips approximately 2 × 5cm/¾ × 2in. Make the yellow and pink cookies in the same way.

2 Score three cuts lengthways into each cookie, and bring one end of the strip back through the centre slit to form a knot.

3 Put the water, sugar and honey in a pan, and add a pinch of salt. Bring to the boil. Add the cinnamon and continue to boil, stirring until the syrup becomes sticky. Pour into a bowl.

4 Pour a generous amount of vegetable oil into a heavy pan, and heat over medium heat. Add the cookies and deep-fry until golden brown. Drain on kitchen paper, then dip into the cinnamon syrup. Dust with the ground pine nuts.

Sake and Ginger Cookies Energy 95kcal/403kJ; Protein 0.9g; Carbohydrate 16g, of which sugars 10.2g; Fat 3.3g, of which saturates 0.4g; Cholesterol 0mg; Calcium 14mg; Fibre 0.25g; Sodium 8.8mg.
Three-colour Ribbon Cookies Energy 178kcal/753kJ; Protein 2.6g; Carbohydrate 16.8g, of which sugars 16.1g; Fat 69.2g, of which saturates 0.5g; Cholesterol 0mg; Calcium 41mg; Fibre 0.8g; Sodium 132mg.

Viennese Whirls

These crisp, melt-in-the-mouth piped cookies are filled with a creamy coffee buttercream.

Makes 20
175g/6oz/12 tbsp butter
50g/2oz/½ cup icing
  (confectioners') sugar
2.5ml/½ tsp vanilla extract
115g/4oz/1 cup plain
  (all-purpose) flour
50g/2oz/½ cup cornflour
  (cornstarch)

icing (confectioners') sugar and
  unsweetened cocoa powder,
  for dusting

For the filling
15ml/1 tbsp ground coffee
60ml/4 tbsp single (light) cream
75g/3oz/6 tbsp butter, softened
115g/4oz/1 cup icing
  (confectioners') sugar, sifted

1 Preheat the oven to 180°C/350°F/Gas 4. Lightly grease a baking sheet.

2 Beat together the butter, icing sugar and vanilla extract until light and fluffy.

3 Sift in the flour and cornflour and beat until smooth. Spoon into a piping (pastry) bag fitted with a 1cm/½in fluted nozzle. Pipe small rosettes well apart on greased baking sheets. Bake for 12–15 minutes, until golden. Transfer to a wire rack to cool.

4 To make the filling, put the coffee in a bowl. Heat the cream to near-boiling and pour it over. Infuse for 4 minutes, then strain through a fine sieve (strainer).

5 Beat the butter, icing sugar and coffee-flavoured cream until light. Use to sandwich the cookies in pairs. Dust with icing sugar and unsweetened cocoa powder.

Variation
For mocha Viennese whirls, substitute 25g/1oz/¼ cup unsweetened cocoa powder for 25g/1oz/¼ cup of the flour.

Spicy Pepper Cookies

Hot and spicy, these little nuggets are perfect for a cold winter's day.

Makes 48
200g/7oz/ cups plain
  (all-purpose) flour
55g/2oz cornflour (cornstarch)
2.5ml/½ tsp ground cardamom
2.5ml/½ tsp ground cinnamon
2.5ml/½ tsp grated nutmeg
2.5ml/½ tsp ground ginger
2.5ml/½ tsp ground allspice

pinch of salt
2.5ml/½ tsp freshly ground
  black pepper
225g/8oz/1 cup butter, softened
100g/3½oz light brown sugar
2.5ml/½ tsp vanilla extract
5ml/1tsp finely grated lemon rind
65g/2fl oz whipping cream
85g/3oz finely ground almonds
30ml/2 tbsp icing (confectioners')
  sugar, for dusting

1 Preheat the oven to 180°C/350°F/Gas 4.

2 Sift the flour, cornflour, spices, salt and pepper into a bowl. Set aside.

3 Beat the butter and sugar together until light and fluffy. Beat in the vanilla extract and lemon rind.

4 Add the flour and spice mixture in batches, alternating it with the cream, and beating well after each addition. Begin and end with the flour.

5 Stir in the ground almonds until all the ingredients are thoroughly combined.

6 Shape the dough into 2cm/¾in balls in the palms of your hands. Place them on ungreased baking trays set about 2.5cm/1in apart to allow room for spreading during baking. Bake in the oven for 15–20 minutes until the cookies are golden brown.

7 Leave the cookies to firm up on the baking sheets for 1–2 minutes then, using a metal spatula, carefully transfer them to a wire rack to cool completely. Sift icing sugar over the surface before serving.

Viennese Whirls Energy 210kcal/877kJ; Protein 2.2g; Carbohydrate 21.3g, of which sugars 11.2g; Fat 13.5g, of which saturates 7.6g; Cholesterol 22mg; Calcium 28mg; Fibre 0.8g; Sodium 64mg.
Spicy Pepper Cookies Energy 75kcal/314kJ; Protein 0.8g; Carbohydrate 6.8g, of which sugars 2.6g; Fat 5.2g, of which saturates 2.8g; Cholesterol 11mg; Calcium 12mg; Fibre 0.2g; Sodium 30mg.

Coffee Ice Cream Sandwiches

The perfect treat for a summer's afternoon or an unusual way to end an *al fresco* dinner party, these cookies are guaranteed to hit the spot.

Makes 8
115g/4oz/½ cup butter, at room temperature
50g/2oz/¼ cup caster (superfine) sugar
115g/4oz/1 cup plain (all-purpose) flour
2 tbsp instant coffee powder
icing (confectioners') sugar, for dusting
450ml/16fl oz/2 cups coffee ice cream
2 tbsp unsweetened cocoa powder, for dusting

1 In a large bowl, cream the butter until soft. Beat in the sugar. Add the flour and coffee and mix by hand to form an evenly blended dough. Wrap in a plastic bag and chill for 1 hour.

2 Lightly sprinkle the work surface with icing sugar. Knead the dough on the sugared surface for a few minutes to soften it. Lightly grease two or three baking trays.

3 Using a rolling pin dusted with icing sugar, roll out the dough to ⅛in/3mm thick. With a 2½in/6cm cookie cutter, stamp out 16 rounds. Transfer the rounds to the baking trays. Chill for at least 30 minutes.

4 Preheat the oven to 300°F/150°C/Gas 2. Bake the cookies for about 30 minutes, until they are lightly golden. Let them firm up for a couple of minutes before removing them to a wire rack to cool completely.

5 Remove the ice cream from the freezer and let soften for 10 minutes at room temperature. With a metal spatula, spread the ice cream evenly on the flat side of eight of the cookies. Top with the remaining cookies, flat side down.

6 Arrange the ice cream sandwiches on a baking tray. Cover and freeze for at least 1 hour, longer if a firmer sandwich is desired. Sift the cocoa powder over the tops before serving.

Cappuccino Swirls

A melt-in-the-mouth, mocha-flavoured cookie drizzled with white and dark chocolate is just the thing to have with that mid-morning caffé latte.

Makes 18
10ml/2 tsp instant coffee powder
10ml/2 tsp boiling water
225g/8oz/1 cup unsalted (sweet) butter, at room temperature, diced
50g/2oz/¼ cup golden caster (superfine) sugar
150g/5oz/1¼ cups plain (all-purpose) flour
115g/4oz/½ cup cornflour (cornstarch)
15ml/1 tbsp unsweetened cocoa powder

For the decoration
50g/2oz white chocolate
25g/1oz dark (bittersweet) chocolate

1 Preheat the oven to 190°C/375°F/Gas 5. Line two baking sheets with baking parchment.

2 Put the coffee powder in a cup, add the boiling water and stir until dissolved. Set aside to cool.

3 In a bowl, beat the butter and sugar until pale and creamy. Stir in the coffee. Sift in the flour, cornflour and cocoa powder. Mix well.

4 Spoon into a piping (pastry) bag fitted with a plain nozzle. Pipe 18 spirals, slightly apart, on to the prepared baking sheets.

5 Bake for 10–15 minutes, until firm but not browned. Leave on the baking sheets for 1 minute, then transfer to a wire rack to cool. Place the cooled cookies on kitchen paper.

6 Melt the white and dark chocolate separately in heatproof bowls set over a pan of hot water.

7 Using a teaspoon, take some white chocolate and moving your hand speedily from left to right create small lines of chocolate drizzle over the cookies. Repeat the process with the dark chocolate, flicking it over the cookies. Leave until the chocolate has set and then remove the cookies from the paper.

Cappuccino Swirls Energy 179kcal/746kJ; Protein 1.3g; Carbohydrate 18.1g, of which sugars 5.7g; Fat 11.8g, of which saturates 7.3g; Cholesterol 27mg; Calcium 19mg; Fibre 0.5g; Sodium 88mg.
Coffee Ice Cream Sandwiches Energy 281kcal/1176kJ; Protein 3.4g; Carbohydrate 31.7g, of which sugars 20.2g; Fat 16.5g, of which saturates 10.4g; Cholesterol 45mg; Calcium 88mg; Fibre 0.5g; Sodium 122mg.

Dark Chocolate Fingers

With their understated elegance and distinctly grown-up flavour, these deliciously decadent chocolate fingers are ideal for serving with after-dinner coffee and liqueurs.

Makes about 26

115g/4oz/1 cup plain (all-purpose) flour
2.5ml/½ tsp baking powder
30ml/2 tbsp unsweetened cocoa powder
50g/2oz/¼ cup unsalted (sweet) butter, softened
50g/2oz/¼ cup caster (superfine) sugar
20ml/4 tsp golden (light corn) syrup
150g/5oz dark (bittersweet) chocolate
chocolate-flavour mini flakes, for sprinkling

1 Preheat the oven to 160°C/325°F/Gas 3. Line two baking sheets with baking parchment.

2 Put the flour, baking powder, cocoa powder, butter, caster sugar and golden syrup in a large mixing bowl. Work the ingredients together with your fingertips to combine and form into a dough.

3 Roll the dough out between sheets of baking parchment to an 18 × 24cm/7 × 9½in rectangle. Remove the top sheet. Cut in half lengthways, then into bars 2cm/¾in wide. Place on the baking sheets.

4 Bake for about 15 minutes, taking care not to allow the bars to brown or they will taste bitter. Transfer to a wire rack to cool.

5 Melt the chocolate in a heatproof bowl set over a pan of gently simmering water. Half-dip the cookies, place on baking parchment, sprinkle with chocolate flakes, then leave to set.

> **Variation**
> If you're making these cookies for children, dip them in melted plain (semisweet) or milk chocolate.

Chunky Chocolate Drops

Do not allow these cookies to cool completely on the baking sheet or they will become crisp and may break when you try to lift them on to a wire rack.

Makes 18

175g/6oz plain (semisweet) chocolate, chopped
115g/4oz/½ cup unsalted (sweet) butter, diced
2 eggs
90g/3½oz/½ cup sugar
50g/2oz/¼ cup soft light brown sugar
40g/1½oz/⅓ cup plain (all-purpose) flour
25g/1oz/¼ cup unsweetened cocoa powder
5ml/1 tsp baking powder
10ml/2 tsp vanilla extract
pinch of salt
115g/4oz/1 cup pecan nuts, toasted and coarsely chopped
175g/6oz/1 cup plain (semisweet) chocolate chips
115g/4oz good-quality white chocolate, chopped into 5mm/¼in pieces
115g/4oz good-quality milk chocolate, chopped into 5mm/¼in pieces

1 Preheat the oven to 160°C/325°F/Gas 3. Lightly grease two large baking sheets.

2 Melt the plain chocolate and butter in a pan over a low heat, stirring constantly. Remove from the heat and set aside to cool.

3 In a large mixing bowl, whisk the eggs and sugars until pale and creamy. Gradually pour in the melted chocolate mixture, beating until blended.

4 Beat in the flour, cocoa powder, baking powder, vanilla extract and salt until just blended. Stir in the nuts, chocolate chips and white and milk chocolate pieces.

5 Drop mounded tablespoonfuls of the mixture on to the baking sheets, 10cm/4in apart. Flatten each to 7.5cm/3in rounds. Bake for 8–10 minutes, until the edges look crisp.

6 Leave to cool for 2 minutes, then transfer to a wire rack to cool completely.

Dark Chocolate Fingers Energy 72kcal/303kJ; Protein 0.9g; Carbohydrate 9.9g, of which sugars 6.3g; Fat 3.5g, of which saturates 2.1g; Cholesterol 4mg; Calcium 11mg; Fibre 0.4g; Sodium 25mg.
Chunky Chocolate Drops Energy 264kcal/1101kJ; Protein 3.4g; Carbohydrate 21.1g, of which sugars 20.7g; Fat 19.1g, of which saturates 9.1g; Cholesterol 37mg; Calcium 48mg; Fibre 0.9g; Sodium 73mg.

Chocolate Crackle-tops

Older children will enjoy making these distinctive-looking cookies. The dough needs to be chilled for an hour, but then is easy to handle and roll.

Makes 38
200g/7oz plain (semisweet) chocolate, chopped
90g/3¹/₂oz/scant ¹/₂ cup unsalted (sweet) butter
115g/4oz/generous ¹/₂ cup caster (superfine) sugar
3 eggs
5ml/1 tsp vanilla extract
215g/7¹/₂oz/scant 2 cups plain (all-purpose) flour
25g/1oz/¹/₄ cup unsweetened cocoa powder
2.5ml/¹/₂ tsp baking powder
pinch of salt
175g/6oz/1¹/₂ cups icing (confectioners') sugar, for dusting

1 In a pan set over a low heat, melt the chocolate and butter until smooth, stirring frequently. Remove from the heat.

2 Stir in the sugar and continue stirring for 2–3 minutes, until it dissolves. Add the eggs, one at a time, beating well after each addition. Stir in the vanilla extract.

3 Sift the flour, cocoa powder, baking powder and salt into the chocolate mixture, in batches, until blended. Cover and chill for 1 hour, until the dough is cold and is able to hold its shape.

4 Preheat the oven to 160°C/325°F/Gas 3. Lightly grease two or three large baking sheets.

5 Sift the icing sugar into a bowl. Using a teaspoon, scoop out the cold dough and roll into 4cm/1¹/₂in balls. Drop each ball into the icing sugar and roll until heavily coated. Shake to remove any excess icing sugar.

6 Place on the baking sheets about 4cm/1¹/₂in apart. Bake for 10–15 minutes, until the tops feel slightly firm when touched.

7 Remove to a wire rack for 2–3 minutes, then transfer the cookies to the wire rack to cool completely.

Chewy Chocolate Cookies

The texture of these dark and delicious cookies is sublime – soft on the inside with a crisper, crunchier outside – matched only by their subtle mocha flavour.

Makes 18
4 egg whites
300g/11oz/2¹/₂ cups icing (confectioners') sugar
115g/4oz/1 cup unsweetened cocoa powder
30ml/2 tbsp plain (all-purpose) flour
5ml/1 tsp instant coffee powder
15ml/1 tbsp water
115g/4oz/1 cup walnuts, finely chopped

1 Preheat the oven to 180°C/350°F/Gas 4. Line two or three baking sheets with baking parchment and grease the paper well.

2 Whisk the egg whites in a grease-free bowl until frothy, using an electric whisk. Sift the sugar, cocoa powder, flour and coffee into the egg whites.

3 Add the water and continue beating on low speed to blend, then on high speed for a few minutes until the mixture thickens. Gently fold in the walnuts with a flexible spatula or metal spoon.

4 Place spoonfuls of the mixture 2.5cm/1in apart on the baking sheets. Bake in batches for 12–15 minutes until firm and cracked on top but soft inside. Using a metal spatula, transfer the cookies to a wire rack to cool.

Cook's Tip
• These cookies are best eaten the day they are cooked, but can be stored for 24 hours in an airtight container.
• Always buy fresh nuts in small quantities, as they quickly become rancid, and chop them only when you need to use them to prevent them from tasting stale.
• You could substitute pecans for the walnuts, if you like.

Chewy Chocolate Cookies Energy 138kcal/580kJ; Protein 3g; Carbohydrate 19.7g, of which sugars 17.6g; Fat 5.8g, of which saturates 1.2g; Cholesterol 0mg; Calcium 26mg; Fibre 1.1g; Sodium 76mg.
Chocolate Crackle-tops Energy 102kcal/428kJ; Protein 1.5g; Carbohydrate 15.8g, of which sugars 11.4g; Fat 4.1g, of which saturates 2.3g; Cholesterol 20mg; Calcium 17mg; Fibre 0.4g; Sodium 27mg.

Mini Chocolate Marylands

These delicious little cookies are perfect for any age group and for any time of day. They're quick and easy to make, too, and because they're small they bake super-fast.

Makes 40–45
125g/4¹/₄oz/generous ¹/₂ cup unsalted (sweet) butter, at room temperature, diced
90g/3¹/₂oz/ ¹/₂ cup caster (superfine) sugar
1 egg
1 egg yolk
5ml/1 tsp vanilla extract
175g/6oz/1¹/₂ cups self-raising (self-rising) flour
90g/3¹/₂oz/scant ¹/₂ cup milk
90g/3¹/₂oz/generous ¹/₂ cup chocolate chips

1 Preheat the oven to 180°C/350°F/Gas 4. Lightly grease two or three baking sheets.

2 In a large bowl, beat together the butter and sugar until pale and creamy. Add the egg, egg yolk, vanilla extract, flour, milk and half the chocolate chips and stir well with a wooden spoon until thoroughly combined.

3 Using two teaspoons, place small mounds of the mixture on the baking sheets, spacing them slightly apart to allow room for spreading.

4 Press the remaining chocolate chips on to the mounds of cookie dough and press down gently.

5 Bake for 10–15 minutes, until pale golden brown. Leave the cookies on the baking sheets for 2 minutes to firm up slightly, then, using a metal spatula, carefully transfer them to wire racks to cool completely.

> **Cook's Tip**
> *This recipe makes quite a large quantity. If you like, you can freeze half of the cookies for another time. Simply thaw, then return to the oven for a few minutes to re-crisp before serving.*

Chocolate and Walnut Chip Cookies

Rich-tasting and crunchy, these wonderful cookies are just perfect at any time of day.

Makes 24
115g/4oz/¹/₂ cup butter, at room temperature
50g/2oz/¹/₄ cup caster (superfine) sugar
90g/3¹/₂oz/scant ¹/₂ cup soft dark brown sugar
1 egg
2.5ml/¹/₂ tsp vanilla extract
175g/6oz/1¹/₂ cups plain (all-purpose) flour
2.5ml/¹/₂ tsp bicarbonate of soda (baking soda)
pinch of salt
175g/6oz/1 cup chocolate chips
50g/2oz/¹/₂ cup walnuts, chopped

1 Preheat the oven to 180°C/350°F/Gas 4. Lightly grease two large baking sheets.

2 In a large bowl, beat the butter and two sugars together until light and fluffy.

3 In a small bowl, mix the egg and vanilla, then gradually beat the liquid into the butter mixture. Sift over the flour, bicarbonate of soda and salt and beat to combine. Add the chocolate chips and walnuts and mix well.

4 Place heaped teaspoonfuls of the dough 5cm/2in apart on the prepared sheets. Bake for 10–15 minutes until lightly coloured. Transfer to a wire rack to cool.

Chocolate Chip Cookies

The lovely light texture of these cookies gives an old favourite a new twist.

Makes 16
75g/3oz/6 tbsp butter
50g/2oz/¹/₄ cup light soft brown sugar
50g/2oz/¹/₄ cup caster (superfine) sugar
1 egg
5ml/1 tsp vanilla extract
75g/3oz/³/₄ cup cornmeal
75g/3oz/³/₄ cup rice flour
5ml/1 tsp baking powder
pinch of salt
115g/4oz/²/₃ cup plain (semisweet) chocolate chips, or a mixture of milk and white chocolate chips

1 Preheat the oven to 190°C/375°F/Gas 5. Lightly grease two baking sheets.

2 Place the butter and sugars in a bowl and beat together until light and fluffy.

3 Beat in the egg and vanilla extract. Fold in the cornmeal, rice flour, baking powder and salt, then fold in the chocolate chips with a flexible spatula.

4 Place spoonfuls of the mixture on the prepared baking sheets, leaving space for spreading between each one. Bake for 10–15 minutes, until the cookies are lightly browned.

5 Remove the cookies from the oven and leave to cool for a few minutes, then transfer to a wire rack and leave to cool.

Mini Chocolate Marylands Energy 54kcal/227kJ; Protein 0.7g; Carbohydrate 6.4g, of which sugars 3.5g; Fat 3g, of which saturates 1.8g; Cholesterol 10mg; Calcium 19mg; Fibre 0.2g; Sodium 33mg.
Chocolate and Walnut Chip Cookies Energy 138kcal/578kJ; Protein 1.7g; Carbohydrate 16.5g, of which sugars 10.9g; Fat 7.7g, of which saturates 3.9g; Cholesterol 19mg; Calcium 20mg; Fibre 0.5g; Sodium 33mg. **Chocolate Chip Cookies** Energy 139kcal/581kJ; Protein 1.7g; Carbohydrate 16.7g, of which sugars 11.1g; Fat 7.7g, of which saturates 3.9g; Cholesterol 19mg; Calcium 20mg; Fibre 0.5g; Sodium 33mg.

Giant Triple Chocolate Cookies

Here is the ultimate cookie, packed full of chocolate and macadamia nuts. You will have to be patient when they come out of the oven, as they are too soft to move until completely cold.

Makes 12 large cookies
90g/3½oz milk chocolate
90g/3½oz white chocolate
300g/11oz dark (bittersweet) chocolate (minimum 70 per cent cocoa solids)
90g/3½oz/7 tbsp unsalted (sweet) butter, at room temperature, diced
5ml/1 tsp vanilla extract
150g/5oz/¾ cup light muscovado (brown) sugar
150g/5oz/1¼ cups self-raising (self-rising) flour
100g/3½oz/scant 1 cup macadamia nut halves

1 Preheat the oven to 180°C/350°F/Gas 4. Line two baking sheets with baking parchment.

2 Coarsely chop the milk and white chocolate and put them in a bowl. Chop 200g/7oz of the dark chocolate into very large chunks, at least 2cm/¾in in size. Put them into another bowl and set aside.

3 Break the remaining dark chocolate into pieces and place them in a heatproof bowl set over a pan of barely simmering water. Heat, stirring frequently, until the chocolate has melted and is smooth. Remove the bowl from the heat and stir in the butter. Add the vanilla extract and muscovado sugar and stir well until fully incorporated.

4 Add the flour and mix gently. Add half the dark chocolate chunks, all the milk and white chocolate and the nuts and fold together.

5 Spoon 12 mounds on to the prepared baking sheets, spacing them well apart. Press the remaining dark chocolate chunks into the top of each cookie. Bake for abut 12 minutes, until just beginning to colour. Remove from the oven and leave the cookies on the baking sheets to cool completely.

Chunky Double Chocolate Cookies

Twice the flavour and twice the fun, these crunchy cookies are packed with chunks of plain and white chocolate for the maximum taste impact.

Makes 18–20
115g/4oz/½ cup unsalted (sweet) butter, softened
115g/4oz/½ cup light muscovado (brown) sugar
1 egg
5ml/1 tsp vanilla extract
150g/5oz/1¼ cups self-raising (self-rising) flour
75g/3oz/¾ cup rolled oats
115g/4oz plain (semisweet) chocolate, coarsely chopped
115g/4oz white chocolate, coarsely chopped

1 Preheat the oven to 190°C/375°F/Gas 5. Lightly grease two baking sheets.

2 Beat the butter with the sugar in a bowl until pale and fluffy. Add the egg and vanilla extract and beat well.

3 Sift the flour over the mixture and fold in lightly with a metal spoon, then add the oats and chopped plain and white chocolate and stir until evenly mixed.

4 Place small spoonfuls of the mixture in 18–20 rocky heaps on the baking sheets, leaving space for spreading.

5 Bake for 12–15 minutes, or until the cookies are beginning to turn pale golden. Cool for 2–3 minutes on the baking sheets, then, using a metal spatula, lift on to wire racks to cool completely. The cookies will be soft when freshly baked but will harden on cooling.

> **Variation**
> Instead of the rolled oats, use 75g/3oz/¾ cup ground almonds. Omit the chopped chocolate and use 175g/6oz/1 cup chocolate chips instead. Top each heap of cookie mixture with half a glacé (candied) cherry before baking.

Giant Triple Chocolate Cookies Energy 416kcal/1738kJ; Protein 4.3g; Carbohydrate 47.6g, of which sugars 37.8g; Fat 24.4g, of which saturates 11.8g; Cholesterol 21mg; Calcium 71mg; Fibre 1.6g; Sodium 84mg. **Chunky Double Chocolate Cookies** Energy 169kcal/710kJ; Protein 2.3g; Carbohydrate 21.6g, of which sugars 13.1g; Fat 8.8g, of which saturates 5.1g; Cholesterol 22mg; Calcium 36mg; Fibre 0.6g; Sodium 47mg.

Chocolate Chip Nut Cookies

You can bake a batch of these nutty delights in no time at all – and they'll be eaten just as fast.

Makes 36
115g/4oz/1 cup plain (all-purpose) flour
5ml/1 tsp baking powder
5ml/1 tsp salt
75g/3oz/6 tbsp butter
115g/4oz/generous ½ cup caster (superfine) sugar
50g/2oz/¼ cup soft light brown sugar
1 egg
5ml/1 tsp vanilla extract
115g/4oz/⅔ cup plain (semisweet) chocolate chips
50g/2oz/½ cup hazelnuts, chopped

1 Preheat the oven to 180°C/350°F/Gas 4. Lightly grease two or three baking sheets.

2 Sift the flour, baking powder and salt into a small bowl. Set the bowl aside.

3 In a large bowl, beat the butter and sugars together until light and fluffy. Beat in the egg and vanilla extract. Sift the dry ingredients into the mixture and beat well.

4 Stir in the chocolate chips and half of the hazelnuts. Drop teaspoonfuls of the mixture on to the prepared baking sheets, to form 2cm/¾in mounds. Space the cookies about 5cm/2in apart to allow room for spreading.

5 Flatten each cookie lightly with a wet fork. Sprinkle the remaining hazelnuts on top of the cookies and press lightly into the surface.

6 Bake for 10–12 minutes, until golden brown. Transfer the cookies to a wire rack and leave to cool.

> **Variation**
> *If you like, you could substitute almonds or macadamia nuts for the hazelnuts – both go well with chocolate.*

Chocolate Delights

These crispy cookies are simply packed with flavour and are irresistible for a mid-morning coffee break.

Makes 50
25g/1oz plain (semisweet) chocolate
25g/1oz dark (bittersweet) cooking chocolate
225g/8oz/1 cup unsalted (sweet) butter, at room temperature
225g/8oz/generous 1 cup caster (superfine) sugar
2 eggs
5ml/1 tsp vanilla extract
225g/8oz/2 cups plain (all-purpose) flour
pinch of salt
115g/4oz/1 cup finely chopped walnuts

1 Melt the chocolates in a heatproof bowl set over a pan of gently simmering water. Set aside.

2 In a large bowl, beat the butter and sugar together until the mixture is light and fluffy.

3 Mix the eggs with the vanilla, then gradually stir into the butter mixture. Stir in the melted chocolate. Sift the flour and salt into the mixture and stir to combine. Stir in the nuts.

4 Divide the mixture into four and roll each into 5cm/2in diameter logs. Wrap tightly in foil and chill until firm.

5 Preheat the oven to 190°C/375°F/Gas 5. Lightly grease two baking sheets. Cut the logs into 5mm/¼in slices. Place the rounds on the baking sheets and bake for about 10 minutes until lightly coloured. Transfer to a rack to cool.

> **Variation**
> *For two-tone cookies, melt half the chocolate. Combine all the ingredients as above except the chocolate. Divide the mixture in half. Add the chocolate to one half. Roll out the plain mixture on to a flat sheet. Roll out the chocolate mixture, place on top of the plain one and roll up. Slice and bake as above.*

Chocolate Chip Nut Cookies Energy 64kcal/271kJ; Protein 0.8g; Carbohydrate 9.9g, of which sugars 5g; Fat 2.7g, of which saturates 1.2g; Cholesterol 4mg; Calcium 14mg; Fibre 0.3g; Sodium 68mg.
Chocolate Delights Energy 90kcal/377kJ; Protein 1.1g; Carbohydrate 8.9g, of which sugars 5.5g; Fat 5.8g, of which saturates 2.7g; Cholesterol 17mg; Calcium 13mg; Fibre 0.2g; Sodium 31mg.

Chocolate Chip Oat Cookies

The lovely texture of these cookies is matched by the delicious chocolate and vanilla flavour – a perfect thank you gift.

Makes 60

115g/4oz/1 cup plain (all-purpose) flour
2.5ml/½ tsp bicarbonate of soda (baking soda)
1.5ml/¼ tsp baking powder
pinch of salt
115g/4oz/½ cup butter
115g/4oz/generous ½ cup caster (superfine) sugar
90g/3½oz/scant ½ cup light brown sugar
1 egg
2.5ml/½ tsp vanilla extract
75g/3oz/¾ cup rolled oats
175g/6oz/1 cup chocolate chips

1 Preheat the oven to 180°C/350°F/Gas 4. Grease three or four baking sheets.

2 Sift the flour, bicarbonate of soda, baking powder and salt into a mixing bowl.

3 Beat together the butter and the two sugars. Add the egg and vanilla extract and beat until light and fluffy. Beat in the flour mixture until blended.

4 Stir in the oats and chocolate chips. The dough should be crumbly. Drop teaspoonfuls of the dough on to the baking sheets, spacing the cookies well apart so that they can spread during baking.

5 Bake for 15 minutes, until firm around the edge but soft to the touch in the centre. Transfer the cookies to a wire rack and leave to cool completely.

Variations
• Use either milk chocolate or plain (semisweet) chocolate chips, as both go well with the nutty texture.
• If you like, decorate the cookies by drizzling them with zig-zag lines of melted chocolate once they have cooled.

Chocolate Amaretti

As an alternative decoration lightly press a few coffee sugar crystals on top of each cookie before baking.

Makes 24

140g/5oz/1¼ cup blanched whole almonds
100g/3½oz/½ cup caster (superfine) sugar
15ml/1 tbsp unsweetened cocoa powder
30ml/2 tbsp icing (confectioners') sugar
2 egg whites
pinch of cream of tartar
5ml/1 tsp almond extract
flaked (sliced) almonds, to decorate

1 Preheat the oven to 180°C/350°F/Gas 4. Line a large non-stick baking sheet with baking parchment. Place the almonds on the baking sheet and bake until golden, 12 minutes. Leave to cool. Reduce the oven temperature to 160°C/325°F/Gas 3.

2 In a processor or blender fitted with a metal blade, process the almonds with half of the sugar until finely ground. Transfer to a medium bowl and sift the cocoa and icing sugar on top. Stir to blend. Set aside.

3 In a medium mixing bowl, using an electric mixer, beat the egg whites and cream of tartar until stiff peaks form. Sprinkle in the remaining sugar, a tablespoon at a time, beating well after each addition, and continue beating until the mixture is glossy and stiff. Beat in the almond extract.

4 Sprinkle the almond-sugar mixture over the beaten egg whites and fold in gently until just blended. Spoon the mixture into a large piping (pastry) bag fitted with a plain 1cm/½ in nozzle. Pipe 4cm/1½ in rounds about 2.5cm/1in apart on the prepared baking sheets. Press a flaked almond into the centre of each.

5 Bake the cookies for 12–15 minutes, or until they appear crisp. Remove to a wire rack to cool completely. When cool, store in an airtight container.

Chocolate Chip Oat Cookies Energy 207kcal/864kJ; Protein 3.2g; Carbohydrate 22.1g, of which sugars 12g; Fat 12.4g, of which saturates 5g; Cholesterol 32mg; Calcium 30mg; Fibre 1.1g; Sodium 46mg.
Chocolate Amaretti Energy 65kcal/270kJ; Protein 1.8g; Carbohydrate 5.8g, of which sugars 5.5g; Fat 4g, of which saturates 0.4g; Cholesterol 0mg; Calcium 20mg; Fibre 0.6g; Sodium 12mg.

Chunky Pecan Chocolate Drops

Toasted pecan nuts, chocolate chips and a mixture of white and milk chocolate chunks make these larger cookies extra special.

Makes 18
175g/6oz plain (semisweet) chocolate, chopped
115g/4oz/½ cup unsalted (sweet) butter, chopped
2 eggs
90g/3½oz/½ cup caster (superfine) sugar
50g/2oz/¼ cup light brown sugar
40g/1½oz/⅓ cup plain (all-purpose) flour
25g/1oz/¼ cup unsweetened cocoa powder
5ml/1 tsp baking powder
10ml/2 tsp vanilla extract
pinch of salt
115g/4oz/1 cup pecan nuts, toasted and coarsely chopped
175g/6oz/1 cup chocolate chips
115g/4oz fine quality white chocolate, chopped into 5mm/¼in pieces
115g/4 oz fine quality milk chocolate, chopped into 5mm/¼in pieces

1 Preheat the oven to 160°C/325°F/Gas 3. Lightly grease two baking sheets.

2 In a heatproof bowl set over a pan of gently simmering water, melt together the plain chocolate and butter. Remove from the heat and set aside to cool.

3 In a large bowl and using an electric mixer, beat the eggs and sugars for about 2 minutes, until creamy.

4 Pour in the melted chocolate mixture, beating until well blended. Sift in the flour, cocoa powder, baking powder, vanilla extract and salt in batches into the egg mixture and beat well after each addition. Stir in the nuts and remaining chocolate.

5 Drop tablespoonfuls of mixture on to the baking sheets. Bake for 8–10 minutes, until crisp.

6 Remove the baking sheets to a wire rack to cool for 2 minutes, then transfer the cookies to the wire rack.

Chocolate Caramel Nuggets

Inside each of these buttery cookies lies a soft-centred chocolate-coated caramel. They're at their most delicious served an hour or so after baking, so you might want to shape them in advance, then put the baking sheet of uncooked nuggets in the refrigerator until you are ready to bake them.

Makes 14
150g/5oz/1¼ cups self-raising (self-rising) flour, plus extra for dusting
90g/3½oz/7 tbsp unsalted (sweet) butter, chilled and diced
50g/2oz/¼ cup golden caster (superfine) sugar
1 egg yolk
5ml/1 tsp vanilla extract
14 soft-centred chocolate caramels
icing (confectioners') sugar and unsweetened cocoa powder, for dusting

1 Put the flour and butter in a food processor and process until the mixture resembles fairly fine breadcrumbs.

2 Add the sugar, egg yolk and vanilla extract to the food processor and process to a smooth dough. Wrap the dough in clear film (plastic wrap) and chill for 30 minutes.

3 Preheat the oven to 200°C/400°F/Gas 6. Lightly grease two large baking sheets.

4 Roll out the dough thinly on a lightly floured surface and cut out 28 rounds using a 5cm/2in cutter.

5 Place one chocolate caramel on a cookie round, then place a second round on top. Pinch the edges of the dough together so that the chocolate caramel is completely enclosed, then place on the prepared baking sheet. Make the remaining cookies in the same way. Bake for about 10 minutes, until pale golden.

6 Using a metal spatula transfer the cookies to a wire rack and leave to cool. Serve lightly dusted with sifted icing sugar and unsweetened cocoa powder.

Chocolate Cinnamon Tuiles

These crisp French cookies are classically plain – this special version is flavoured with cocoa and cinnamon.

Makes 12
1 egg white
50g/2oz/¼ cup caster
   (superfine) sugar

30ml/2 tbsp plain
   (all-purpose) flour
40g/1½oz/3 tbsp butter, melted
15ml/1 tbsp unsweetened
   cocoa powder
2.5ml/½ tsp ground cinnamon

1 Preheat the oven to 200°C/400°F/Gas 6. Lightly grease two baking sheets.

2 Whisk the egg white in a grease-free bowl until it forms soft peaks. Gradually whisk in the sugar.

3 Sift the flour over the mixture and fold in evenly. Stir in the melted butter. Transfer about 45ml/3 tbsp of the mixture to a small bowl and set aside.

4 Sift together the cocoa and ground cinnamon over the flour and butter mixture, in batches, stirring well after each addition.

5 Leaving room for spreading, drop spoonfuls of the chocolate-flavoured mixture on to the prepared baking sheets, then spread each gently with a metal spatula to make a neat round.

6 Using a small spoon, carefully drizzle the reserved unflavoured mixture over the rounds to create a softly marbled effect.

7 Bake for 4–6 minutes, until just set. Using a metal spatula, lift each cookie carefully and quickly drape it over a rolling pin to give a curved shape as it hardens.

8 Leave the tuiles to cool until set, then remove them gently and place on a wire rack to cool completely. Serve on the same day.

Fruity Chocolate Cookie Cakes

The combination of spongy cookie, fruity preserve and dark chocolate makes irresistible eating. As cookies go, these are a little fiddly to make.

Makes 18
90g/3½oz/½ cup caster
   (superfine) sugar
2 eggs
50g/2oz/½ cup plain
   (all-purpose) flour
75g/3oz/6 tbsp orange
   marmalade or apricot jam
125g/4¼oz plain (semisweet)
   chocolate

1 Preheat the oven to 190°C/375°F/Gas 5. Lightly grease 18 patty tins (muffin pans), preferably non-stick.

2 Stand a mixing bowl in very hot water for a couple of minutes to heat through, keeping the inside of the bowl dry. Put the sugar and eggs in the bowl and whisk with a hand-held electric mixer until light and frothy and the beaters leave a ribbon trail when lifted. Sift the flour over the mixture and stir in gently using a large metal spoon.

3 Divide the sponge mixture among the patty tins. Bake for 10 minutes, until just firm and pale golden around the edges. Using a metal spatula, carefully lift from the sponges from the tins and transfer to a wire rack to cool.

4 Press the marmalade or jam through a sieve (strainer) to remove any rind or fruit pieces. Spoon a little of the smooth jam on to the centre of each sponge.

5 Break the chocolate into pieces and place in a heatproof bowl set over a pan of gently simmering water. Heat, stirring frequently, until melted and smooth.

6 Spoon a little chocolate on to the top of each cookie and spread to the edges, covering the jam completely. Once the chocolate has just started to set, very gently press it with the back of a fork to give a textured surface. Leave to set for at least 1 hour.

Chocolate Cinnamon Tuiles Energy 55kcal/229kJ; Protein 0.8g; Carbohydrate 6.5g, of which sugars 4.4g; Fat 3g, of which saturates 1.9g; Cholesterol 7mg; Calcium 8mg; Fibre 0.2g; Sodium 38mg.
Fruity Chocolate Cookie Cakes Energy 84kcal/353kJ; Protein 1.3g; Carbohydrate 14.7g, of which sugars 12.5g; Fat 2.6g, of which saturates 1.3g; Cholesterol 22mg; Calcium 12mg; Fibre 0.3g; Sodium 11mg.

Chocolate Pretzels

These scrumptious snacks look so charming twisted into little knots. Sweet pretzels are a speciality of Germany and Austria.

Makes 28

115g/4oz/1 cup plain
  (all-purpose) flour
pinch of salt
45ml/3 tbsp unsweetened
  cocoa powder
115g/4oz/1/2 cup butter
150g/5oz/3/4 cup caster
  (superfine) sugar
1 egg
1 egg white, lightly beaten,
  for glazing
sugar crystals, for sprinkling

1 Sift together the flour, salt and cocoa powder. Set aside. Lightly grease two baking sheets.

2 In a large bowl, beat the butter until pale and soft. Add the sugar and continue beating until light and fluffy. Beat in the egg.

3 Add the dry ingredients and stir to blend. Gather the dough into a ball, wrap in greaseproof (waxed) paper and chill for 1 hour or freeze for 30 minutes.

4 Preheat the oven to 190°C/375°F/Gas 5.

5 Roll the dough into 28 small balls. Roll each ball into a rope about 25cm/10in long. With each rope, form a loop with the two ends facing you. Twist the ends and fold back on to the circle, pressing in, to make a pretzel shape.

6 Place on the prepared baking sheets. Brush with the egg white and sprinkle sugar crystals over the tops to decorate.

7 Bake for 10–12 minutes, until firm. Transfer to a wire rack to cool.

Cook's Tip

To make mocha-flavoured pretzels, replace 10ml/2 tsp of the unsweetened cocoa powder with instant coffee powder.

Chocolate-filled Cookies

Concealed chunks of plain chocolate are baked inside these delectable cookies to make a wonderful, melt-in-the-mouth surprise when you bite into them.

Makes about 16

150g/5oz/2/3 cup butter, softened
150g/5oz/3/4 cup caster
  (superfine) sugar
1 egg yolk
15ml/1 tbsp ground almonds
225g/8oz/2 cups self-raising
  (self-rising) flour, plus extra
  for dusting
25g/1oz/1/4 cup unsweetened
  cocoa powder
150g/5oz plain (semisweet)
  chocolate
icing (confectioners') sugar,
  for dusting

1 Preheat the oven to 190°C/375°F/Gas 5. Lightly grease two baking sheets.

2 Beat together the butter and sugar until pale and fluffy. Beat in the egg yolk and ground almonds.

3 Sift the flour and unsweetened cocoa powder over the mixture and gently fold in with a flexible spatula to make a firm dough. Knead lightly for a few seconds, then wrap in clear film (plastic wrap) and chill in the refrigerator for about 30 minutes.

4 Cut off slightly more than one-third of the dough. Cover the remaining dough with clear film until required. Roll out the smaller piece of dough on a lightly floured surface to a thickness of about 3mm/1/8in. Stamp out 16 rounds using a 4cm/1½in cookie cutter. Break the chocolate into 16 squares and put one square into the centre of each dough round.

5 Roll out the remaining dough and cut into 16 larger rounds using a 5cm/2in cutter. Place these over the chocolate-covered cookie rounds and press the edges together. Bake for 10 minutes, until firm.

6 Dust the cookies with icing sugar and, using a metal spatula carefully transfer to a wire rack. Serve warm while the filling is still soft and melted.

Variations

• For a fruity flavour and a different texture, substitute 30ml/2 tbsp dried sour cherries or dried cranberries for the ground almonds.
• For a moister mix, use desiccated (dry unsweetened shredded) coconut instead of the ground almonds.
• For an unusual and more sophisticated filling, use dark (bittersweet) chocolate and add candied chillies. Put 25g/1oz/2 tbsp caster (superfine) sugar into a small pan and add 30ml/2 tbsp water. Heat gently, stirring until the sugar has dissolved, then add 2 seeded and very finely chopped red chillies. Bring to the boil and boil for 2 minutes, without stirring. Remove from the heat, strain the chillies and leave to cool. Discard the syrup. Divide the chillies among the cookie rounds with the squares of chocolate.

Chocolate Pretzels Energy 72kcal/303kJ; Protein 1g; Carbohydrate 9.1g, of which sugars 5g; Fat 3.8g, of which saturates 2.3g; Cholesterol 16mg; Calcium 13mg; Fibre 0.3g; Sodium 37mg.
Chocolate-filled Cookies Energy 215kcal/902kJ; Protein 2.5g; Carbohydrate 26.7g, of which sugars 15.9g; Fat 11.7g, of which saturates 6.8g; Cholesterol 33mg; Calcium 65mg; Fibre 0.9g; Sodium 124mg.

Triple Chocolate Sandwiches

Chocolate shortbread is a great base for sandwiching or coating in lashings of melted chocolate.

Makes 15
125g/4¹/₄oz/generous ¹/₂ cup unsalted (sweet) butter, chilled and diced
150g/5oz/1¹/₄ cups plain (all-purpose) flour

30ml/2 tbsp unsweetened cocoa powder
50g/2oz/¹/₄ cup caster (superfine) sugar

For the filling
75g/3oz white chocolate
25g/1oz/2 tbsp unsalted (sweet) butter
115g/4oz milk chocolate

1 Put the butter, flour and cocoa in a food processor. Process until the mixture resembles breadcrumbs. Add the sugar and process again until the mixture forms a dough.

2 Transfer the dough to a clean surface and knead lightly. Wrap in clear film (plastic wrap) and chill for 30 minutes.

3 Preheat the oven to 200°C/400°F/Gas 6. Lightly grease a large baking sheet.

4 Roll out the chilled dough on a floured surface to a 33 × 16cm/13 × 6¼in rectangle. Place on the baking sheet. Cut the dough in half lengthways, then cut across at 2cm/¾in intervals to make 30 small bars. Prick each bar with a fork.

5 Bake for 12–15 minutes, until just beginning to darken. Leave for 2 minutes, then transfer to a wire rack to cool.

6 To make the filling, break the white chocolate into a heatproof bowl. Add half the butter and set the bowl over a pan of gently simmering water. Stir frequently until melted.

7 Spread a little of the filling on to half of the bars. Place another bar on top and push together to sandwich the cookies.

8 Melt the milk chocolate with the remaining butter. Using a teaspoon, drizzle over the cookies, then leave to set.

Chocolate Thumbprint Cookies

Chunky, chocolatey and gooey all at the same time, these gorgeous cookies are filled with a spoonful of chocolate spread after baking to really add to their indulgent quality.

Makes 16
115g/4oz/¹/₂ cup unsalted (sweet) butter, at room temperature, diced
115g/4oz/¹/₂ cup light muscovado (brown) sugar

1 egg
75g/3oz/²/₃ cup plain (all-purpose) flour
25g/1oz/¹/₄ cup unsweetened cocoa powder
2.5ml/¹/₂ tsp bicarbonate of soda (baking soda)
115g/4oz/generous 1 cup rolled oats
75–90ml/5–6 tbsp chocolate spread

1 Preheat the oven to 180°C/350°F/Gas 4. Lightly grease two large baking sheets.

2 In a bowl, beat together the butter and sugar until creamy.

3 Add the egg and beat well. Sift over the flour, cocoa powder and bicarbonate of soda and stir to combine. Add the rolled oats to the bowl and mix well.

4 Using your hands, roll spoonfuls of the mixture into balls. Place the balls on the baking sheet, spacing them well apart to allow room for spreading. Flatten slightly.

5 Dip a thumb in flour and press into the centre of each cookie to make an indent. Bake the cookies for 10 minutes. Leave for 2 minutes, then transfer to a wire rack to cool.

6 Spoon a little chocolate spread into the centre of each indented cookie.

Cook's Tip
Use chocolate and hazelnut spread instead of the plain one.

Chocolate Thumbprint Cookies Energy 163kcal/682kJ; Protein 2.3g; Carbohydrate 19.3g, of which sugars 10.3g; Fat 9g, of which saturates 4.1g; Cholesterol 27mg; Calcium 19mg; Fibre 0.8g; Sodium 66mg. Triple Chocolate Sandwiches Energy 189kcal/790kJ; Protein 2.4g; Carbohydrate 18.8g, of which sugars 11g; Fat 12.1g, of which saturates 7.5g; Cholesterol 22mg; Calcium 50mg; Fibre 0.6g; Sodium 88mg.

Chocolate and Prune Cookies

When freshly baked, these cookies have a deliciously gooey centre. As they cool down the mixture hardens slightly to form a firmer, fudge-like consistency.

Makes 18

150g/5oz/²/₃ cup butter, at room temperature, diced
150g/5oz/³/₄ cup caster (superfine) sugar
I egg yolk

250g/9oz/2¹/₄ cups self-raising (self-rising) flour
25g/1oz/¹/₄ cup unsweetened cocoa powder
about 90g/3¹/₂oz plain (semisweet) chocolate, coarsely chopped

For the topping

50g/2oz plain (semisweet) chocolate
9 ready-to-eat prunes, halved

1 Preheat the oven to 190°C/375°F/Gas 5. Line two baking sheets with baking parchment.

2 Beat the butter and sugar together until light and creamy. Beat in the egg yolk. Sift over the flour and cocoa powder and stir in to make a firm yet soft dough.

3 Roll out a third of the dough on baking parchment. Using a 5cm/2in cookie cutter, stamp out 18 rounds and place them on the baking sheets. Sprinkle the chopped chocolate in the centre of each cookie.

4 Roll out the remaining dough in the same way and, using a 7.5cm/3in round cookie cutter, stamp out 18 "lids". Place the lids over the cookie bases and press the edges together to seal.

5 Bake for about 10 minutes, until the cookies have spread a little and are just firm to the touch. Leave them on the baking sheets for a few minutes to firm up, then, using a metal spatula, transfer to a wire rack to cool completely.

6 For the topping, melt the chocolate in a heatproof bowl set over a pan of gently simmering water. Dip the cut side of the prunes in the chocolate, then place one on top of each cookie. Spoon any remaining chocolate over the prunes.

Chocolate Marzipan Cookies

These crisp little cookies are deliciously sweet and have a delightful almond surprise inside. Piped with zig-zag lines of white chocolate, they make a perfect party treat.

Makes 36

200g/7oz/scant 1 cup unsalted (sweet) butter at room temperature, diced

200g/7oz/scant 1 cup light muscovado (brown) sugar
I egg
300g/11oz/2³/₄ cups plain (all-purpose) flour, plus extra for dusting
60ml/4 tbsp unsweetened cocoa powder
200g/7oz white almond paste
115g/4oz white chocolate, chopped

1 Preheat the oven to 190°C/375°F/Gas 5. Lightly grease two large baking sheets.

2 In a bowl, beat the butter with the sugar until pale and fluffy. Add the egg and beat well.

3 Sift the flour and cocoa powder over the mixture. Stir in, first with a wooden spoon, then with clean hands, pressing the mixture together to make a fairly soft dough. If the dough seems sticky, wrap it in clear film (plastic wrap) and chill for about 30 minutes.

4 Roll out half the dough on a lightly floured surface to a thickness of about 5mm/¹/₄in. Using a 5cm/2in cutter, stamp out rounds until you have about 36 rounds.

5 Cut the almond paste into 36 equal pieces. Roll into balls, flatten slightly and place one on each dough round. Roll out the remaining dough, stamp out more rounds, then place on top of the almond paste. Press the dough edges to seal. Bake the cookies for 10–12 minutes, until well risen.

6 Transfer the cookies to a wire rack, using a spatula, and leave to cool completely. Melt the white chocolate, spoon into a paper piping (pastry) bag and pipe zig-zag lines on to the cookies. Leave to set before serving.

Chocolate and Prune Cookies Energy 197kcal/825kJ; Protein 2.3g; Carbohydrate 26.4g, of which sugars 15.5g; Fat 9.8g, of which saturates 5.9g; Cholesterol 29mg; Calcium 33mg; Fibre 1.1g; Sodium 66mg. **Chocolate Marzipan Cookies** Energy 137kcal/576kJ; Protein 1.9g; Carbohydrate 18.1g, of which sugars 11.6g; Fat 6.9g, of which saturates 3.8g; Cholesterol 17mg; Calcium 31mg; Fibre 0.6g; Sodium 57mg.

Chocolate Treacle Snaps

These elegantly thin, treacle-flavoured snap cookies have a delicate hint of spice and a decorative lick of chocolate on top. They are particularly good with a steaming cup of hot coffee.

Makes about 35
90g/3¹/₂oz/7 tbsp unsalted (sweet) butter, diced
175ml/6fl oz/³/₄ cup golden (light corn) syrup
50ml/2fl oz/¹/₄ cup black treacle (molasses)
250g/9oz/2¹/₄ cups plain (all-purpose) flour
150g/5oz/³/₄ cup golden caster (superfine) sugar
5ml/1 tsp bicarbonate of soda (baking soda)
1.5ml/¹/₄ tsp mixed spice (apple pie spice)
100g/3¹/₂oz milk chocolate
100g/3¹/₂oz white chocolate

1 Preheat the oven to 180°C/350°F/Gas 4. Line two or three baking sheets with baking parchment.

2 Put the butter, syrup and treacle in a small pan. Heat gently, stirring constantly, until the butter has melted. Remove from the heat and set aside until required.

3 Sift the flour into a large mixing bowl. Add the sugar, bicarbonate of soda and mixed spice and mix well using a wooden spoon. Slowly pour in the butter and treacle mixture and stir to combine well.

4 Place large teaspoonfuls of the mixture well apart on the prepared baking sheets. Bake the cookies for 10–12 minutes, until just beginning to brown around the edges. Leave them to cool for a few minutes on the baking sheets. When firm enough to handle, using a metal spatula, transfer the cookies to a wire rack to cool completely.

5 Melt the milk chocolate and white chocolate separately in heatproof bowls set over pans of gently simmering water. Stir frequently. Swirl a little of each into the centre of each cookie and leave to set.

Mocha Viennese Swirls

Sophisticated cookies that look elegant and taste superb, these swirls can be served with morning coffee to impress your guests or just please your friends.

Makes 20
250g/9oz plain (semisweet) chocolate, chopped
200g/7oz/scant 1 cup unsalted (sweet) butter at room temperature, diced
50g/2oz/¹/₂ cup icing (confectioners') sugar
30ml/2 tbsp strong black coffee
200g/7oz/1³/₄ cups plain (all-purpose) flour
50g/2oz/¹/₂ cup cornflour (cornstarch)
about 20 blanched almonds

1 Preheat the oven to 190°C/375°F/Gas 5. Lightly grease two large baking sheets.

2 Melt 115g/4oz of the chocolate in a heatproof bowl set over a pan of gently simmering water, then remove from the heat and leave to cool slightly.

3 Beat the butter with the icing sugar in a bowl until smooth and pale. Beat in the melted chocolate, then the black coffee.

4 Sift the flour and cornflour over the mixture. Fold in lightly and evenly to make a soft mixture. Spoon the mixture into a piping (pastry) bag fitted with a large star nozzle and pipe 20 swirls on the baking sheets, allowing room for spreading.

5 Press an almond into the centre of each swirl. Bake for about 15 minutes, until the cookies are firm and just beginning to brown. Leave to cool for about 10 minutes on the baking sheets, then, using a metal spatula, transfer to a wire rack to cool completely.

6 Melt the remaining chocolate in a heatproof bowl over a pan of gently simmering water. Dip the base of each swirl into the chocolate to coat. Place on a sheet of baking parchment and leave to set.

Chocolate Treacle Snaps Energy 109kcal/459kJ; Protein 1.2g; Carbohydrate 18.2g, of which sugars 12.8g; Fat 4g, of which saturates 2.4g; Cholesterol 6mg; Calcium 35mg; Fibre 0.2g; Sodium 38mg.
Mocha Viennese Swirls Energy 231kcal/965kJ; Protein 2.4g; Carbohydrate 23.5g, of which sugars 12.4g; Fat 14.8g, of which saturates 8.3g; Cholesterol 24mg; Calcium 31mg; Fibre 0.9g; Sodium 70mg.

Chocolate Truffle Cookies

Deeply decadent, chocolatey truffle cookies are given a wicked twist by the addition of cherry brandy – the perfect way to end dinner.

Makes 18

50g/2oz/½ cup plain (all-purpose) flour
25g/1oz/¼ cup unsweetened cocoa powder
2.5ml/½ tsp baking powder
90g/3½oz/½ cup caster (superfine) sugar
25g/1oz/2 tbsp butter, diced
1 egg, beaten
5ml/1 tsp cherry brandy
50g/2oz/½ cup icing (confectioners') sugar

1 Preheat the oven to 200°C/400°F/Gas 6. Line two baking sheets with baking parchment.

2 Sift together the flour, unsweetened cocoa powder and baking powder into a large bowl and stir in the caster sugar. Add the butter and rub in lightly with your fingertips until the mixture resembles breadcrumbs.

3 Mix together the beaten egg and cherry brandy and stir into the flour mixture. Cover with clear film (plastic wrap) and chill for 30 minutes.

4 Put the icing sugar into a bowl. Shape walnut-size pieces of dough roughly into a ball between the palms of your hands and drop into the icing sugar. Toss until thickly coated, then place on the baking sheets.

5 Bake for about 10 minutes, or until just set. Transfer to a wire rack, and leave to cool completely.

Variations
• Other liqueurs with an affinity with chocolate, such as amaretto and Cointreau, could also be used.
• If you're making these cookies for children, use orange juice instead of the cherry brandy.

Carob Chip Shorties

Perfect for anyone on a gluten-free or dairy-free diet, these lovely cookies are best eaten freshly made, preferably while still slightly warm.

Makes 12

175g/6oz/1½ cups gluten-free flour
25g/1oz/2 tbsp soft light brown sugar
75g/3oz/6 tbsp vegetable margarine
50g/2oz/⅓ cup carob chips
15–25ml/1–1½ tbsp clear honey, warmed
demerara (raw) or caster (superfine) sugar, for sprinkling

1 Preheat the oven to 160°C/325°F/Gas 3. Line one large baking sheet with baking parchment.

2 Put the flour and brown sugar in a mixing bowl and rub in the margarine.

3 Add the carob chips, then stir in just enough honey to bring the mixture together but not make it sticky.

4 Roll out the dough between two sheets of baking parchment to about 8mm/⅓in thick. Stamp out 12 rounds using a plain 5cm/2in round cookie cutter. Place the rounds on the prepared baking sheet, spaced apart to allow room for spreading. Prick each cookie once with a fork and sprinkle lightly with demerara or caster sugar.

5 Bake for about 15–20 minutes, until firm and golden brown. Using a metal spatula, carefully transfer the cookies to a wire rack to cool completely.

Cook's Tips
• Gluten-free flour can be bought at most health-food stores.
• Some margarines contain animal products, such as whey. The health-conscious and vegetarians should check the label.

Iced Carob Cookies

If you are unable to eat chocolate but still crave it, these heavenly cookies, with their creamy topping, may provide the answer.

Makes 12–16
115g/4oz/½ cup butter
10ml/2 tsp carob powder
115g/4oz/1 cup wholemeal (whole-wheat) flour
5ml/1 tsp baking powder

75g/3oz/⅓ cup dark muscovado (molasses) sugar
50g/2oz/generous ½ cup rolled oats

For the topping
50g/2oz carob bar, coarsely chopped
45ml/3 tbsp double (heavy) cream
15ml/1 tbsp chopped ready-to-eat dried apricots

1 Preheat the oven to 190°C/375°F/Gas 5. Line the base and sides of an 18cm/7in square shallow cake tin (pan) with baking parchment.

2 Put the butter in a large pan and add the carob powder. Stir over a low heat until the butter has melted and the mixture is smooth and thoroughly combined. Remove the pan from the heat, stir in the flour, baking powder, sugar and rolled oats and mix well.

3 Press the mixture into the prepared tin and bake for about 20–25 minutes, until just set. Mark into squares or bars while still hot. Leave to cool in the tin.

4 To make the topping, stir the carob bar and cream in a small pan over a low heat until combined. Remove the pan from the heat and spread the mixture over the cookies. Sprinkle the apricots on top and leave to cool completely and set.

> **Cook's Tip**
> Carob is derived from the carob bean, which has a nutritious, flavoursome pulp. Its taste is similar to chocolate and it has a high sugar content, but unlike chocolate, it does not contain any caffeine.

Carob and Cherry Cookies

Simplicity itself to make, these little cookies are given a chocolate-like flavour by the addition of carob powder and are deliciously crisp and crunchy.

Makes about 20
90g/3½oz/7 tbsp unsalted (sweet) butter, at room temperature, diced
75g/3oz/scant ½ cup caster (superfine) sugar

75g/3oz/⅓ cup light muscovado (brown) sugar
1 egg
150g/5oz/1¼ cups self-raising (self-rising) flour
25g/1oz/2 tbsp carob powder
50g/2oz/¼ cup glacé (candied) cherries, quartered
50g/2oz carob bar, chopped

1 Preheat the oven to 180°C/350°F/Gas 4. Line two large baking sheets with baking parchment.

2 Put the butter, both sugars and the egg in a large mixing bowl and beat well until the mixture is smooth and creamy.

3 Add the flour, carob powder, cherries and chopped carob bar to the mixture and mix well.

4 Shape the mixture into walnut-size balls and place, spaced slightly apart to allow room for spreading, on the prepared baking sheets.

5 Bake for about 15 minutes, until golden brown and just firm. Leave on the baking sheets for 5 minutes to cool slightly, then, using a metal spatula, carefully transfer the cookies to a wire rack to cool completely.

> **Variations**
> • If you aren't on a diet, use unsweetened cocoa powder and a bar of chocolate instead of the carob.
> • Use raisins, dried cranberries or dried sour cherries instead of cherries, if you like.

Iced Carob Cookies Energy 140kcal/585kJ; Protein 1.7g; Carbohydrate 14.3g, of which sugars 7.4g; Fat 8.9g, of which saturates 5.3g; Cholesterol 19mg; Calcium 12mg; Fibre 1.1g; Sodium 52mg.
Carob and Cherry Cookies Energy 114kcal/481kJ; Protein 1.4g; Carbohydrate 16.9g, of which sugars 11.2g; Fat 5g, of which saturates 3g; Cholesterol 19mg; Calcium 36mg; Fibre 0.5g; Sodium 71mg.

Chocolate Florentines

These big, flat, crunchy cookies are just like traditional Florentines but use tiny seeds instead of nuts. Rolling the edges of the cookies in milk or white chocolate turns them into a real treat.

Makes 12
50g/2oz/ ¼ cup unsalted (sweet) butter
50g/2oz/¼ cup caster (superfine) sugar
15ml/1 tbsp milk
25g/1oz/scant ¼ cup pumpkin seeds
40g/1½oz/generous ¼ cup sunflower seeds
50g/2oz/scant ½ cup raisins
25g/1oz/2 tbsp multi-coloured glacé (candied) cherries, chopped
30ml/2 tbsp plain (all-purpose) flour
125g/4¼oz milk or white chocolate

1 Preheat the oven to 180°C/350°F/Gas 4. Lightly grease two baking sheets.

2 Put the butter and sugar into a pan and set over a low heat, stirring constantly, until the butter has melted and the sugar has dissolved, then cook until bubbling. Remove the pan from the heat and stir in the milk, pumpkin and sunflower seeds, raisins, glacé cherries and flour. Mix well with a wooden spoon until thoroughly incorporated.

3 Spoon 6 teaspoonfuls of the mixture on to each baking sheet, spacing them well apart.

4 Bake for 8–10 minutes, until the cookies are turning dark golden. Using a metal spatula, push back the edges of the cookies to neaten them. Leave on the baking sheets for about 5 minutes to firm up, then carefully transfer to a wire rack to cool completely.

5 Break up the chocolate and put in a heatproof bowl set over a pan of gently simmering water. Heat, stirring frequently, until melted. Roll the edges of the cookies in the chocolate and leave to set on a clean sheet of baking parchment for about 1 hour.

Mini Florentines with Grand Marnier

Orange liqueur adds a note of glorious luxury to these ever-popular nut and dried fruit cookies. These mini versions would be delicious with dessert or after-dinner coffee and liqueurs.

Makes about 24
50g/2oz/¼ cup soft light brown sugar
15ml/1 tbsp clear honey
15ml/1 tbsp Grand Marnier
50g/2oz/¼ cup butter
40g/1½oz/⅓ cup plain (all-purpose) flour
25g/1oz/¼ cup hazelnuts, coarsely chopped
50g/2oz/½ cup flaked (sliced) almonds, chopped
50g/2oz/¼ cup glacé (candied) cherries, chopped
115g/4oz dark (bittersweet) chocolate, melted, for coating

1 Preheat the oven to 180°C/350°F/Gas 4. Line two or three baking sheets with baking parchment.

2 Combine the sugar, honey, Grand Marnier and butter in a small pan and melt over a low heat.

3 Remove the pan from the heat and tip in the flour, hazelnuts, almonds and cherries. Stir well.

4 Spoon small heaps of the mixture on to the baking sheets. Bake for about 10 minutes, until golden brown. Leave the cookies on the baking sheets until the edges begin to harden a little, then remove and cool on a wire rack.

5 Spread the melted chocolate over the underside of each Florentine with a round-bladed knife. When the chocolate is just beginning to set, drag a fork through to make wavy lines. Leave to set completely.

> **Variation**
> *For an extra decoration, pour melted milk, plain (semisweet) or white chocolate into a paper piping (pastry) bag, snip off the end and pipe zig-zag lines over the plain side of each Florentine.*

Chocolate Florentines Energy 157kcal/656kJ; Protein 2.2g; Carbohydrate 17.5g, of which sugars 14.8g; Fat 9.1g, of which saturates 4.3g; Cholesterol 11mg; Calcium 40mg; Fibre 0.6g; Sodium 38mg.
Mini Florentines with Grand Marnier Energy 82kcal/342kJ; Protein 1g; Carbohydrate 8.6g, of which sugars 7.2g; Fat 4.9g, of which saturates 2g; Cholesterol 5mg; Calcium 13mg; Fibre 0.4g; Sodium 14mg.

Florentine Bites

Very sweet and rich, these little mouthfuls are great with after-dinner coffee and liqueurs, and would also make an ideal and special gift to offer to a dinner party host.

Makes 36
200g/7oz good-quality dark
    (bittersweet) chocolate
    (minimum 70 per cent
    cocoa solids)

50g/2oz/2½ cups cornflakes
50g/2oz/scant ½ cup sultanas
    (golden raisins)
115g/4oz/1 cup toasted flaked
    (sliced) almonds
115g/4oz/½ cup glacé (candied)
    cherries, halved
50g/2oz/⅓ cup cut mixed
    (candied) peel
200ml/7fl oz/scant 1 cup
    sweetened condensed milk

1 Line the base of a shallow 20cm/8in cake tin (pan) with baking parchment. Lightly grease the sides.

2 Break the chocolate into pieces and put them into a small heatproof bowl set over a pan of gently simmering water. When the chocolate has melted, remove from the heat and spread it evenly over the base of the prepared tin. Chill in the refrigerator until set.

3 Preheat the oven to 180°C/350°F/Gas 4.

4 Put the cornflakes, sultanas, almonds, cherries and mixed peel in a large bowl. Pour over the condensed milk and toss the mixture gently, using a fork.

5 Spread the mixture evenly over the chocolate base and bake for 12–15 minutes, until golden brown. Cool in the tin, then chill for 20 minutes. Cut into squares.

> **Cook's Tip**
> *Condensed milk is creamy and rich and may be sweetened or unsweetened. Do not confuse it with evaporated milk, which is not sweetened and has a slightly "boiled" flavour.*

Black-and-White Ginger Florentines

These Florentines can be kept in the refrigerator in an airtight container for one week.

Makes 30
120ml/4fl oz/½ cup double
    (heavy) cream
50g/2oz/¼ cup unsalted
    (sweet) butter
90g/3½oz/½ cup sugar
30ml/2 tbsp clear honey
150g/5oz/1¼ cups flaked
    (sliced) almonds

40g/1½oz/⅓ cup plain
    (all-purpose) flour
2.5ml/½ tsp ground ginger
50g/2oz/⅓ cup diced candied
    orange peel
65g/2½oz/½ cup diced
    preserved stem ginger
200g/7oz plain (semisweet)
    chocolate, chopped
150g/5oz fine quality white
    chocolate, chopped

1 Preheat the oven to 180°C/350°F/Gas 4. Lightly grease two large baking sheets.

2 In a medium pan over a medium heat, stir the cream, butter, sugar and honey until the sugar dissolves. Bring the mixture to the boil, stirring constantly.

3 Remove from the heat and stir in the almonds, flour and ground ginger. Stir in the orange peel, preserved stem ginger and 50g/2oz/⅓ cup chopped plain chocolate.

4 Drop teaspoons of the mixture on to the baking sheets, spaced 7.5cm/3in apart. Spread thinly.

5 Bake for 8–10 minutes until the edges are golden brown. Leave to firm up for 10 minutes. Transfer to a wire rack to cool.

6 In separate heatproof bowls set over pans of gently simmering water, melt the remaining plain chocolate and the white chocolate. Cool slightly.

7 Spread plain chocolate on the flat side of half the Florentines. Spread the remaining Florentines with the white chocolate. Chill for 10–15 minutes to set.

Florentine Bites Energy 87kcal/364kJ; Protein 1.6g; Carbohydrate 12g, of which sugars 10.7g; Fat 3.9g, of which saturates 1.4g; Cholesterol 2mg; Calcium 30mg; Fibre 0.5g; Sodium 27mg.
Black-and-White Ginger Florentines Energy 71kcal/298kJ; Protein 0.9g; Carbohydrate 8.6g, of which sugars 7.8g; Fat 3.9g, of which saturates 1.3g; Cholesterol 2mg; Calcium 16mg; Fibre 0.3g; Sodium 11mg.

Late Night Cookies

Crisp yet crumbly and packed with chocolate chips, these are a must with tall glasses of ice-cold milk or stacked with a large amount of ice cream.

Makes about 12 large or 20 small cookies

75g/3oz/6 tbsp butter, softened
75g/3oz/scant ½ cup golden caster (superfine) sugar
75g/3oz/⅓ cup soft light brown sugar, sifted
1 large (US extra large) egg, beaten
2.5ml/½ tsp vanilla extract
150g/5oz/1¼ cups self-raising (self-rising) flour
25g/1oz/¼ cup unsweetened cocoa powder
pinch of salt
100g/4oz chopped chocolate or plain (semisweet) chocolate chips
ice cream, to serve

1 Preheat the oven to 180°C/350°F/Gas 4. Lightly grease two non-stick baking sheets.

2 Beat the butter and sugars together until pale and fluffy. Beat in the egg and vanilla extract.

3 Sift the flour with the cocoa and salt. Gently fold into the egg mixture with the chopped chocolate or chocolate chips, using a flexible spatula.

4 Place four heaped tablespoonfuls of the mixture, spaced well apart, on each baking sheet. Press down and spread out with the back of a wet spoon.

5 Bake the cookies for about 12 minutes, until a rich golden brown. Leave on the baking sheets for 1 minute to firm up slightly, then using a metal spatula, carefully transfer to a wire rack to cool completely.

6 When the baking sheets have cooled, lightly grease them again. Place teaspoons of the remaining mixture on them as before and bake. Continue in this way until all the cookies have been baked. When cold, serve sandwiched together with ice cream or on their own.

Chocolate and Pistachio Wedges

These cookies are rich and grainy textured, with a bitter chocolate flavour. They go extremely well with vanilla ice cream and are especially delicious with bananas and custard.

Makes 16

200g/7oz/scant 1 cup unsalted (sweet) butter, at room temperature, diced
90g/3½oz/½ cup golden caster (superfine) sugar
250g/9oz/2¼ cups plain (all-purpose) flour
50g/2oz/½ cup unsweetened cocoa powder
25g/1oz/¼ cup shelled pistachio nuts, finely chopped
unsweetened cocoa powder, for dusting

1 Preheat the oven to 180°C/350°F/Gas 4. Line a shallow 23cm/9in round sandwich tin (layer cake pan) with baking parchment.

2 In a large bowl, beat the butter and sugar together until light and creamy.

3 Sift the flour and cocoa powder over the butter mixture and mix in first with a wooden spoon, then work in with your hands until the mixture is smooth. Knead until soft and pliable.

4 Spread the mixture evenly in the tin. Sprinkle the pistachio nuts over the top and press in gently. Prick with a fork, then mark into 16 segments using a knife.

5 Bake for about 15–20 minutes. Do not allow to brown or the cookies will taste bitter.

6 Remove from the oven and dust the cookies with cocoa powder. Cut through the marked sections with a round-bladed knife and leave to cool before removing from the tin.

> **Cook's Tip**
> *Always sift cocoa powder before dusting cookies.*

Late Night Cookies Energy 170kcal/711kJ; Protein 2.8g; Carbohydrate 21g, of which sugars 11.5g; Fat 8.9g, of which saturates 5.2g; Cholesterol 34mg; Calcium 72mg; Fibre 0.7g; Sodium 117mg.
Chocolate and Pistachio Wedges Energy 188kcal/783kJ; Protein 2.4g; Carbohydrate 18.6g, of which sugars 6.3g; Fat 12g, of which saturates 7.1g; Cholesterol 27mg; Calcium 33mg; Fibre 1g; Sodium 115mg.

Chocolate and Coconut Slices

Rich, sweet and delicious, these slices will keep hunger at bay.

Makes 24

175g/6oz/ cups digestive biscuits
115g/4oz/½ cup butter
115g/4oz walnuts
55g/2oz/½ cup caster
  (superfine) sugar
pinch of salt

85g/3oz/ cup desiccated (dry
  unsweetened shredded)
  coconut
260g/9oz/ cups plain (semisweet)
  chocolate chips
250ml/8fl oz/ cups sweetened
  condensed milk

1 Preheat the oven to 180°C/350°F/Gas 4.

2 Put half the digestive biscuits in a clear plastic bag and use a rolling pin to crush them into small pieces, slightly larger than crumbs. Decant the contents of the bag into a bowl and repeat with the remaining cookies.

3 In a small pan set over a low heat, gently melt the butter, stirring occasionally.

4 In a blender or processor fitted with a metal blade, grind the walnuts, or chop them finely using a sharp knife.

5 Add the sugar and salt to the bowl with the crushed biscuits and pour on the melted butter. Mix well to combine.

6 Press the mixture evenly over the bottom of an ungreased 33 x 23cm/13 x 9in baking dish using the back of a spoon.

7 Sprinkle the coconut over the biscuit base, then sprinkle over the chocolate chips. Pour the condensed milk over the chocolate. Top the condensed milk with the chopped walnuts.

8 Bake in the oven for 30 minutes until just beginning to turn golden brown. Leave to firm up slightly, then unmould on to a wire rack and leave to cool, preferably overnight. Use a sharp knife to cut into slices.

Ice Cream Sandwich Cookies

These are great when you get those midnight munchies – keep them in an airtight container and sandwich together each time with ice cream of your choice or make the sandwiches complete with ice cream and coating and freeze until required.

Makes 12

115g/4oz/½ cup unsalted
  (sweet) butter, at room
  temperature, diced
115g/4oz/generous ½ cup caster
  (superfine) sugar
1 egg, beaten
200g/7oz/1¾ cups plain
  (all-purpose) flour
25g/1oz/¼ cup unsweetened
  cocoa powder, sifted
ice cream, to fill
toasted nuts, cookie crumbs,
  chocolate flakes or demerara
  (raw) sugar, to coat

1 Preheat the oven to 180°C/350°F/Gas 4. Lightly grease two baking sheets.

2 In a bowl, beat the butter and sugar together until light and fluffy, then beat in the egg. Stir in the flour and cocoa powder to make a firm dough.

3 Roll the dough out to a thickness of 5mm/¼in on baking parchment. Using a 7.5cm/3in plain round cookie cutter, stamp out 24 rounds and place on the baking sheets. Bake the cookies for about 15 minutes. Set aside on the baking sheets to cool.

4 To serve, spread 2 spoonfuls of softened ice cream on a cookie and press a second cookie on top.

5 Put your chosen coating on a plate and roll the cookies in it.

> **Cook's Tip**
> For super deluxe cookies, half-dip the ice cream cookies in melted chocolate. When the chocolate has set, either eat or wrap in foil and freeze for up to 2 weeks.

Nutty Marshmallow and Chocolate Squares

Unashamedly sweet, with chocolate, marshmallows, cherries, nuts and coconut, this recipe is a favourite with sweet-tooths.

Makes 9

200g/7oz digestive biscuits (graham crackers)
90g/3½oz plain (semisweet) chocolate

200g/7oz coloured mini marshmallows
150g/5oz/1¼ cups chopped walnuts
90g/3½oz/scant ½ cup glacé (candied) cherries, halved
50g/2oz/⅔ cup desiccated (dry unsweetened shredded) coconut
350g/12oz milk chocolate

1 Put the digestive biscuits in a plastic bag and, using a rolling pin, crush them until they are fairly small. Transfer the crumbs to a bowl.

2 Melt the plain chocolate in a heatproof bowl set over a pan of gently simmering water. Pour the melted plain chocolate over the broken biscuits and stir well.

3 Spread the mixture in the base of a 20cm/8in square shallow cake tin (pan).

4 Put the marshmallows, walnuts, cherries and coconut in a large bowl.

5 Melt the milk chocolate in a heatproof bowl set over a pan of gently simmering water. Pour the melted milk chocolate over the marshmallow and nut mixture and toss gently together until almost everything is coated. Spread the mixture over the chocolate base. Chill until set, then cut into squares.

> **Variation**
> Other nuts can be used instead of the walnuts – the choice is yours.

Almond-scented Chocolate Cherry Wedges

These cookies are a chocoholic's dream, and use the very best quality chocolate. Erratically shaped, they are packed with crunchy cookies, juicy raisins and munchy nuts.

Makes about 15

50g/2oz ratafia biscuits (almond macaroons) or small amaretti
90g/3½oz shortcake biscuits (cookies)
150g/5oz/1 cup jumbo raisins

50g/2oz/¼ cup natural glacé (candied) cherries, quartered
450g/1lb dark (bittersweet) chocolate (minimum 70 per cent cocoa solids)
90g/3½oz/scant ½ cup unsalted (sweet) butter, diced
30ml/2 tbsp amaretto liqueur (optional)
25g/1oz/¼ cup toasted flaked (sliced) almonds

1 Line a baking sheet with baking parchment.

2 Put the ratafia biscuits in a large bowl. Break half of them into coarse pieces. Break the shortcakes into three or four pieces and add to the bowl. Add the raisins and glacé cherries and mix well.

3 Melt the chocolate and butter with the liqueur, if using, in a heatproof bowl set over a pan of gently simmering water, stirring until smooth and combined. Remove from the heat and set aside to cool slightly.

4 Pour the chocolate over the cookie mixture and toss lightly together until everything is coated in chocolate. Spread out over the prepared baking sheet.

5 Sprinkle over the almonds and push them in at angles so they stick well to the chocolate-coated cookies. Leave in a cool place until set.

6 When the mixture is completely cold and set, cut into long thin triangles.

Nutty Marshmallow and Chocolate Squares Energy 603kcal/2523kJ; Protein 8.6g; Carbohydrate 69.7g, of which sugars 53.2g; Fat 34.1g, of which saturates 14.7g; Cholesterol 19mg; Calcium 133mg; Fibre 2.5g; Sodium 179mg. **Almond-scented Chocolate Cherry Wedges** Energy 288kcal/1206kJ; Protein 2.7g; Carbohydrate 34.6g, of which sugars 29.7g; Fat 16.4g, of which saturates 9.5g; Cholesterol 20mg; Calcium 31mg; Fibre 1.3g; Sodium 75mg.

Rich Chocolate Cookie Slice

These rich, dark chocolate refrigerator cookies are perfect served with strong coffee, either as a mid-morning treat or even in place of dessert. They are always very popular.

Makes about 10
275g/10oz fruit and nut plain (semisweet) chocolate
130g/4½oz/½ cup unsalted (sweet) butter, diced
90g/3½oz digestive biscuits (graham crackers)
90g/3½oz white chocolate

1 Lightly grease and line the base and sides of a 450g/1lb loaf tin (pan) with baking parchment.

2 Break the fruit and nut chocolate into even-size pieces and place in a heatproof bowl together with the butter.

3 Set the bowl over a pan of barely simmering water and stir gently until melted and smooth. Remove the bowl from the heat and set aside to cool for 20 minutes.

4 Break the digestive biscuits into small pieces. Finely chop the white chocolate.

5 Stir the broken biscuits and white chocolate into the cooled, melted fruit and nut chocolate until combined. Turn the mixture into the prepared tin and pack down gently. Chill for 2 hours, or until set.

6 To serve, turn out the mixture and remove the lining paper. Cut into slices with a sharp knife.

> **Variations**
> *You can use this simple basic recipe for all kinds of variations.*
> *• Try different kinds of chocolate, such as ginger, hazelnut, honey and almond, peanut or mocha.*
> *• Substitute different cookies for the digestive biscuits (graham crackers) – shortbread, Petit-Beurre, Marie, ginger nuts (gingersnaps) or peanut butter cookies.*

Rocky Road Wedges

Free from gluten and wheat, these crumbly chocolate wedges contain home-made popcorn in place of broken cookies, which are the classic ingredient in many no-bake cookies. This recipe uses an orange-flavoured chocolate bar, but any flavour can be used.

Makes 8
15ml/1 tbsp vegetable oil
25g/1oz/2½ tbsp popping corn
150g/5oz orange-flavoured plain (semisweet) chocolate
25g/1oz/2 tbsp unsalted (sweet) butter, diced
75g/3oz soft vanilla fudge, diced
icing (confectioners') sugar, for dusting

1 Heat the oil in a heavy pan. Add the popping corn, cover with a lid and heat, shaking the pan once or twice, until the popping noises die down. (It is important not to lift the lid until the popping stops.)

2 Remove the pan from the heat and leave for about 30 seconds before removing the lid. Be careful, as there may be quite a lot of steam trapped inside. Transfer the popcorn to a bowl and leave to cool for about 5 minutes.

3 Meanwhile, line the base of an 18cm/7in sandwich tin (layer cake pan) with baking parchment.

4 Once cooled, tip the corn into a plastic bag and tap with a rolling pin to break up into small pieces.

5 Break the chocolate into a heatproof bowl. Add the butter and set the bowl over a pan of gently simmering water. Stir frequently until melted. Remove the bowl from the heat and leave to cool for 2 minutes.

6 Stir the popcorn and fudge into the cooled melted chocolate mixture until well coated, then turn the mixture into the prepared tin and press down firmly in an even layer. Leave to set for about 30 minutes.

7 Turn the cookie out on to a board and cut into eight wedges. Serve lightly dusted with icing sugar.

Rich Chocolate Cookie Slice Energy 326kcal/1361kJ; Protein 2.7g; Carbohydrate 29g, of which sugars 23.8g; Fat 23g, of which saturates 13.9g; Cholesterol 33mg; Calcium 44mg; Fibre 0.9g; Sodium 144mg. **Rocky Road Wedges** Energy 191kcal/798kJ; Protein 1.5g; Carbohydrate 21g, of which sugars 19.3g; Fat 11.8g, of which saturates 5.9g; Cholesterol 11mg; Calcium 19mg; Fibre 0.5g; Sodium 33mg.

Ice Mountain

To create an alternative shape to rounds and squares, this refrigerator cookie is set in the corner of a cake tin, giving it a "pyramid" shape for slicing into triangles.

Makes 12
75g/3oz malted milk cookies
90g/3½oz milk chocolate
75g/3oz white chocolate
  mint sticks
250g/9oz white chocolate
60ml/4 tbsp double (heavy)
  cream
several clear mints (hard mint
  candies), to decorate

1 Cut one 23cm/9in square of baking parchment. Grease one side, and 5cm/2in of the base of an 18cm/7in square cake tin (pan). Line one side and the base of the tin.

2 Break the cookies into small pieces, chop the milk chocolate into small dice and break the chocolate mint sticks into short lengths. Keep these ingredients separate.

3 Reserve 50g/2oz of the white chocolate. Put the remainder in a small heatproof bowl with the cream and set the bowl over a pan of gently simmering water. Melt, stirring frequently. Remove from the heat.

4 Stir the cookies into the white chocolate mixture followed by the chocolate mint sticks. Add the milk chocolate, stir quickly to combine, then turn the mixture into the lined section of the tin. Hold the tin at an angle, then smooth the surface of the chocolate. Chill the mixture in the refrigerator, propping the tin up to maintain the angle to form the pyramid shape. Leave to set. Remove from the tin, place on a flat plate and peel off the paper.

5 In their wrappers, crush the mints with a rolling pin. Melt the reserved white chocolate in a heatproof bowl set over a pan of hot water.

6 Spread the white chocolate over the top sloping side of the pyramid, sprinkle with the crushed mints and press in lightly.

Chocolate Salami

This after-dinner sweetmeat resembles a salami, hence its name. It is very rich and will serve a lot of people. Slice it very thinly and serve with espresso coffee and amaretto liqueur.

Serves 8–12
24 Petit Beurre cookies, broken
  into pieces
350g/12oz plain (semisweet)
  chocolate, broken into squares
225g/8oz/1 cup unsalted (sweet)
  butter, softened
60ml/4 tbsp amaretto liqueur
2 egg yolks
50g/2oz/½ cup flaked (sliced)
  almonds, lightly toasted and
  thinly shredded lengthways
25g/1oz/¼ cup ground almonds

1 Place the cookies in a food processor and process until crushed into coarse crumbs.

2 Put the chocolate, a small knob (pat) of the butter and the liqueur in a heatproof bowl, set over a pan of barely simmering water. Heat until the chocolate melts, stirring occasionally.

3 Remove the bowl from the heat, leave to cool for a minute or two, stir in the egg yolks, then the remaining butter, a little at a time. Tip in most of the crushed cookies, leaving behind a good handful, and stir well. Stir in the flaked almonds. Leave the mixture in a cold place for 1 hour.

4 Process the remaining crushed cookies in the food processor until they are very finely ground. Mix with the ground almonds. Cover and set aside.

5 Turn the chocolate and cookie mixture on to a sheet of lightly oiled baking parchment, then shape into a 35cm/14in long sausage using a metal spatula. Wrap securely in the paper and freeze the roll for at least 4 hours, until solid.

6 To serve, spread the finely ground cookies and almonds out on a clean sheet of baking parchment and roll the salami in them until evenly coated. Transfer to a board and leave to stand for about 1 hour before cutting into slices with a sharp knife to serve.

Ice Mountain Energy 234kcal/977kJ; Protein 3.2g; Carbohydrate 24.8g, of which sugars 21.5g; Fat 14.2g, of which saturates 8.4g; Cholesterol 11mg; Calcium 100mg; Fibre 0.2g; Sodium 63mg.
Chocolate Salami Energy 453kcal/1885kJ; Protein 4.5g; Carbohydrate 36.6g, of which sugars 26.9g; Fat 32.3g, of which saturates 16.8g; Cholesterol 96mg; Calcium 47mg; Fibre 1.4g; Sodium 173mg.

Midnight Cookies

These cookies are so-called because you can make them up before you go to bed and leave them to bake slowly in the switched-off oven. Hey presto – there they are in the morning, lightly crunchy on the outside and deliciously soft in the middle.

Makes 9
1 egg white
90g/3¹/₂oz/¹/₂ cup caster
   (superfine) sugar
50g/2oz/¹/₂ cup ground almonds
90g/3¹/₂oz/generous ¹/₂ cup milk
   chocolate chips
90g/3¹/₂oz/scant ¹/₂ cup glacé
   (candied) cherries, chopped
50g/2oz/²/₃ cup dessicated
   (dry unsweetened
   shredded) coconut

1 Preheat the oven to 220°C/425°F/Gas 7. Line a baking sheet with baking parchment.

2 Put the egg white in a large, clean, grease-free bowl and whisk until stiff peaks form.

3 Add the sugar to the egg white, a spoonful at a time, whisking well between each addition until the sugar is fully incorporated. The mixture should be completely smooth and glossy in appearance.

4 Fold in the ground almonds, chocolate chips, glacé cherries and shredded coconut with a flexible spatula. Place 9 spoonfuls of the mixture on the baking sheet, spaced apart. Place the baking sheet in the oven, close the door and turn the oven off. Leave overnight (or for at least 6 hours) and don't open the oven door. Serve for breakfast or store in airtight container.

Cook's Tip
Given that time is always short in the morning, these cookies make a great breakfast treat – even children will find time to eat them. For a nourishing start to the day, serve them with fresh fruit. Alternatively, quickly whiz up a fresh fruit smoothie in the blender.

Chocolate Macaroons

The Italians claim to have invented these little cookies during the Renaissance and this classic combination of almonds and chocolate certainly suggests that this is true.

Makes 20
50g/2oz plain (semisweet)
   chocolate, chopped into
   small pieces
2 egg whites
200g/7oz/1 cup caster
   (superfine) sugar
2.5ml/¹/₂ tsp vanilla extract
1.5ml/¹/₄ tsp almond extract
115g/4oz/1 cup ground almonds
icing (confectioners') sugar,
   for dusting

1 Preheat the oven to 150°C/300°F/Gas 2. Line two baking sheets with baking parchment.

2 Melt the chocolate in a heatproof bowl placed over a pan of barely simmering water, stirring occasionally. Leave to cool.

3 In a grease-free bowl, whisk the egg whites until they form soft peaks. Gently fold in the sugar, vanilla and almond extracts, ground almonds and melted chocolate. The mixture should just hold its shape. If it is too soft, chill it for 15 minutes.

4 Place mounded teaspoonfuls of the mixture, spaced well apart, on the prepared baking sheets and flatten slightly. Brush each with a little water and sift over a thin layer of icing sugar.

5 Bake the macaroons for 20–25 minutes until just firm. Transfer to a wire rack to cool.

Cook's Tip
To make Chocolate Pine Nut Macaroons, spread 75g/3oz/ ³/₄ cup pine nuts in a shallow dish. Press the balls of chocolate macaroon dough into the nuts to cover one side of each ball and place them, nut side up, on lined baking sheets, then bake as above.

Midnight Cookies Energy 185kcal/777kJ; Protein 2.7g; Carbohydrate 23.5g, of which sugars 23.4g; Fat 9.6g, of which saturates 5g; Cholesterol 2mg; Calcium 48mg; Fibre 1.3g; Sodium 21mg.
Chocolate Macaroons Energy 94kcal/393kJ; Protein 2.1g; Carbohydrate 11.6g, of which sugars 11.4g; Fat 4.7g, of which saturates 0.7g; Cholesterol 0mg; Calcium 23mg; Fibre 0.6g; Sodium 9mg.

Sweet Hearts

These cookies are for Valentine's Day or an anniversary, but you could use different-shaped cutters in the same way to make cookies for other occasions.

Makes 12–14

50g/2oz/¼ cup unsalted (sweet) butter, softened

75g/3oz/scant ½ cup caster (superfine) sugar
1 egg yolk
150g/5oz/1¼ cups plain (all-purpose) flour
25g/1oz dark (bittersweet) chocolate, melted and cooled
25–50g/1–2oz dark (bittersweet) chocolate, to decorate

1 Preheat the oven to 180°C/350°F/Gas 4. Line two baking sheets with baking parchment.

2 Put the butter, sugar and egg yolk in a mixing bowl and beat well. Stir in the flour and then knead until smooth.

3 Divide the dough in half, then knead the melted chocolate into one half until it is evenly coloured.

4 Roll out each piece of dough between sheets of baking parchment, to 3mm/⅛in thick.

5 Stamp out shapes from both doughs using a 7.5cm/3in cookie cutter. Place the cookies on the prepared baking sheets.

6 Using a smaller cookie cutter, stamp out the centres from all the cookies. Place a light-coloured cookie in the centre of a larger chocolate cookie and vice versa.

7 Bake the cookies for 10 minutes, or until just beginning to turn brown. Remove from the oven and leave to cool.

8 To decorate, melt the chocolate in a heatproof bowl set over a pan of hot water. Leave to cool slightly. Put into a piping (pastry) bag. Pipe dots on to the outer part of the large chocolate hearts. Pipe zig-zags on the pale part of the large plain hearts. Leave in a cool place until they are set.

Chinese Fortune Cookies

Whether you're a rabbit or a dragon, a snake or a tiger, these charming cookies are sure to delight and are a wonderful way to celebrate the Chinese New Year with family and friends.

Makes about 35

2 egg whites
50g/2oz/½ cup icing (confectioners') sugar, sifted, plus extra for dusting
5ml/1 tsp almond or vanilla extract

25g/1oz/2 tbsp unsalted (sweet) butter, melted
50g/2oz/½ cup plain (all-purpose) flour
25g/1oz/⅓ cup desiccated (dry unsweetened shredded) coconut, lightly toasted
tiny strips of paper with "good luck", "health, wealth and happiness" and other appropriate messages typed or written on them, to decorate

1 Preheat the oven to 190°C/375°F/Gas 5. Line two or three baking sheets with baking parchment.

2 Put the egg whites into a grease-free bowl and whisk until foamy and white. Whisk in the icing sugar, a little at a time, beating well after each addition. Beat in the almond or vanilla extract and the melted butter. Fold in the flour with a flexible spatula and mix gently until smooth.

3 Place three seperate teaspoonfuls of mixture on to each prepared baking sheet and spread out evenly with the back of a spoon. Sprinkle with a little coconut. Bake one sheet at a time (as you will only have enough time to shape one sheetful of cookies before they set) for about 5 minutes, or until very lightly brown on the edges.

4 Remove the cookies from the oven, immediately loosely fold in half and place on the rim of a glass. Leave until firm, then transfer to a wire rack. Continue baking one sheet of cookies at a time.

5 Tuck the messages into the side of each cookie. Dust very lightly with icing sugar before serving.

Sweet Hearts Energy 107kcal/449kJ; Protein 1.4g; Carbohydrate 16.2g, of which sugars 8g; Fat 4.5g, of which saturates 2.6g; Cholesterol 22mg; Calcium 21mg; Fibre 0.4g; Sodium 23mg.
Chinese Fortune Cookies Energy 21kcal/87kJ; Protein 0.4g; Carbohydrate 2.7g, of which sugars 1.6g; Fat 1g, of which saturates 0.8g; Cholesterol 2mg; Calcium 3mg; Fibre 0.1g; Sodium 8mg.

Oznei Haman

These little cookies, shaped like three-cornered hats, are eaten at the Jewish summer feast of Purim.

Makes about 20
115g/4oz/½ cup unsalted
    (sweet) butter, at room
    temperature, diced
115g/4oz/generous ½ cup caster
    (superfine) sugar
2.5ml/½ tsp vanilla extract
3 egg yolks
250g/9oz/2¼ cups plain
    (all-purpose) flour, plus extra
    for dusting

beaten egg, to seal and glaze

For the filling
40g/1½oz/3 tbsp poppy seeds
15ml/1 tbsp clear honey
25g/1oz/2 tbsp caster
    (superfine) sugar
finely grated rind of 1 lemon
15ml/1 tbsp lemon juice
40g/1½oz/⅓ cup ground
    almonds
1 small (US medium) egg, beaten
25g/1oz/scant ¼ cup raisins

1 Beat the butter with the sugar until light and creamy. Beat in the vanilla and egg yolks. Sift over the flour, stir in, then work into a dough with your hands. Knead until smooth. Wrap in clear film (plastic wrap) and chill.

2 For the filling, put the poppy seeds, honey, sugar, lemon rind and juice into a pan with 60ml/4 tbsp water and bring to the boil, stirring. Remove from the heat and beat in the almonds, egg and raisins. Leave to cool.

3 Preheat the oven to 180°C/350°F/Gas 4. Line two large baking sheets with baking parchment.

4 Roll out the dough on a lightly floured surface to 3mm/⅛in thick. Using a 7.5cm/3in cookie cutter, stamp out rounds. Place a heaped teaspoon of filling on each round. Brush the edges with beaten egg, then bring the sides to the centre to form a tricorne shape. Seal and place on the prepared baking sheets, spaced slightly apart.

5 Brush with beaten egg and bake for 20–30 minutes, or until golden brown. Transfer to a wire rack and leave to cool.

Ma'amoul

Jews eat these date and nut cookies at Purim, Christians enjoy them at Easter and Muslims serve them at Iftar, the after-sunset meal that breaks the Ramadan fast. They are made in special wooden moulds, which seal the rose-scented pastry around the filling.

Makes 35–40
450g/1lb/4 cups plain
    (all-purpose) flour
225g/8oz/1 cup unsalted (sweet)
    butter, diced
45ml/3 tbsp rose water

60–75ml/4–5 tbsp milk
icing (confectioners') sugar,
    for dusting

For the filling
225g/8oz/1⅓ cups dried dates,
    stoned (pitted) and chopped
175g/6oz/1½ cup walnuts,
    finely chopped
115g/4oz/1 cup blanched
    almonds, chopped
50g/2oz/½ cup pistachio nuts,
    chopped
120ml/4fl oz/½ cup water
115g/4oz/½ cup sugar
10ml/2 tsp ground cinnamon

1 Preheat the oven to 160°C/325°F/Gas 3. Lightly grease one or two large baking sheets.

2 To make the filling, place the dates, walnuts, almonds, pistachio nuts, water, sugar and cinnamon in a small pan and cook over a low heat, until the dates are soft and the water has been absorbed. Set aside.

3 Place the flour in a bowl and add the butter, working it into the flour with your fingertips. Add the rose water and milk and knead until soft. Take walnut-size pieces of dough. Roll each into a ball and hollow with your thumb. Pinch the sides.

4 Place a spoonful of date mixture in the hollow, then press the dough back over the filling to enclose it, pressing the edges together to seal.

5 Arrange the cookies on the prepared baking sheets, spaced well apart. Press gently to flatten them slightly. Bake for 20 minutes. Do not allow them to brown or they will become hard. Leave to cool slightly and sprinkle with icing sugar.

Oznei Haman Energy 156kcal/653kJ; Protein 2.8g; Carbohydrate 18.7g, of which sugars 9.1g; Fat 8.3g, of which saturates 3.6g; Cholesterol 52mg; Calcium 46mg; Fibre 0.7g; Sodium 42mg.
Ma'amoul Energy 163kcal/680kJ; Protein 2.8g; Carbohydrate 16.1g, of which sugars 7.4g; Fat 10.1g, of which saturates 3.4g; Cholesterol 12mg; Calcium 35mg; Fibre 1g; Sodium 43mg.

Easter Cookies

These traditional English cookies are sweet, lightly spiced and flecked with currants. They have a soft and crunchy texture and are a filling treat.

Makes 16–18
115g/4oz/½ cup soft butter
75g/3oz/scant ½ cup caster (superfine) sugar, plus extra for sprinkling

1 egg
200g/7oz/1¾ cups plain (all-purpose) flour, plus extra for dusting
2.5ml/½ tsp mixed spice (apple pie spice)
2.5ml/½ tsp ground cinnamon
50g/2oz/¼ cup currants
15ml/1 tbsp chopped mixed (candied) peel
15–30ml/1–2 tbsp milk

1 Preheat the oven to 200°C/400°F/Gas 6. Lightly grease two baking sheets.

2 Beat together the butter and sugar until light and fluffy.

3 Separate the egg, reserving the white, and beat the yolk into the butter mixture.

4 Sift the flour and spices over the mixture, then fold in the currants and peel, adding sufficient milk to make a fairly soft dough.

5 Knead the dough lightly on a floured surface, then roll out to 5mm/¼in thick. Stamp out rounds using a 5cm/2in fluted cookie cutter. Arrange on the baking sheets, spaced well apart, and bake for 10 minutes.

6 Beat the egg white and brush gently over the cookies. Sprinkle with caster sugar and return to the oven for 10 minutes, until golden. Using a metal spatula, transfer to a wire rack to cool.

Variation
Substitute freshly grated nutmeg for the cinnamon.

Simnel Cookies

Enjoy these mini variations on the sweet, marzipan-covered simnel cake that is traditionally eaten at Easter and, originally, Mothering Sunday in Britain.

Makes about 18
175g/6oz/¾ cup unsalted (sweet) butter, at room temperature, diced
115g/4oz/generous ½ cup caster (superfine) sugar

finely grated rind of 1 lemon
2 egg yolks
225g/8oz/2 cups plain (all-purpose) flour
50g/2oz/¼ cup currants

For the topping
400g/14oz marzipan
200g/7oz/1¾ cups icing (confectioners') sugar, sifted
2–3 shades of food colouring
mini sugar-coated chocolate Easter eggs

1 Preheat the oven to 180°C/350°F/Gas 4.

2 Put the butter, sugar and lemon rind in a bowl and beat until light and fluffy. Beat in the egg yolks, then stir in the flour and currants and mix to a firm dough. If it is a little soft, chill in the refrigerator until firm.

3 Roll out the dough on baking parchment to 5mm/¼in thick. Using a 9cm/3½in cookie cutter, stamp out rounds and place, spaced slightly apart, on non-stick baking sheets.

4 To make the topping, roll out the marzipan to 5mm/¼in thick and use a 6cm/2½in cookie cutter to stamp out the same number of rounds as there are cookies. Place a marzipan round on top of each cookie and press down gently.

5 Bake the cookies for about 12 minutes, or until just golden. Remove from the oven and leave to cool on the baking sheets.

6 Put the icing sugar in a bowl and add water to mix to a smooth consistency. Colour the icing as desired. Three different colours have been used here.

7 Ice the cooled cookies. While the icing is still wet, press a few sugar-coated eggs on top of each cookie and leave to set.

Simnel Cookies Energy 285kcal/1197kJ; Protein 2.9g; Carbohydrate 45g, of which sugars 35.4g; Fat 11.6g, of which saturates 5.5g; Cholesterol 43mg; Calcium 48mg; Fibre 0.9g; Sodium 66mg.
Easter Cookies Energy 116kcal/485kJ; Protein 1.5g; Carbohydrate 15.4g, of which sugars 7g; Fat 5.7g, of which saturates 3.4g; Cholesterol 24mg; Calcium 25mg; Fibre 0.4g; Sodium 46mg.

Fourth of July Blueberry Softbakes

These are simply wonderful when eaten still warm from the oven. However, they are also good if allowed to cool and then packed for a traditional Independence Day picnic.

Makes 10
150g/5oz/1¼ cups plain (all-purpose) flour
7.5ml/1½ tsp baking powder
5ml/1 tsp ground cinnamon
50g/2oz/¼ cup unsalted (sweet) butter, at room temperature, diced
50g/2oz/¼ cup demerara (raw) sugar, plus extra for sprinkling
120ml/4fl oz/½ cup sour cream
90g/3½oz/scant 1 cup fresh blueberries
50g/2oz/½ cup semi-dried cranberries

1 Preheat the oven to 190°C/375°F/Gas 5. Line two baking sheets with baking parchment.

2 Sift together the flour, baking powder and cinnamon into a large mixing bowl. Add the diced butter and rub in with your fingers until the mixture resembles fine breadcrumbs. Stir in the demerara sugar.

3 Add the sour cream, blueberries and cranberries and stir until just combined.

4 Spoon ten mounds of the mixture, spaced well apart, on to the prepared baking sheets. Sprinkle with the extra demerara sugar and bake for about 20 minutes, or until golden and firm in the centre. Serve warm.

> **Variations**
> • For Thanksgiving, substitute fresh cranberries for the blueberries and chopped preserved stem ginger for the semi-dried cranberries.
> • For Halloween, substitute chocolate chips and chopped almonds for the fruit.
> • For Christmas, substitute raisins soaked in rum for 20 minutes for the blueberries.

Neuris

These melt-in-the-mouth sweet and spicy samosas are traditionally eaten during the Hindu festival of Diwali and are also given as little gifts to friends and family.

Makes 12
75g/3oz/1 cup desiccated (dry unsweetened shredded) coconut
50g/2oz/¼ cup light muscovado (brown) sugar
25g/1oz/¼ cup cashew nuts, chopped
50g/2oz/⅓ cup seedless raisins
250ml/8fl oz/1 cup evaporated milk
large pinch grated nutmeg
2.5ml/½ tsp ground cinnamon
12 sheets filo pastry, about 28 x 18cm/11 x 7in each
sunflower oil, for brushing

For the topping
15ml/1 tbsp evaporated milk
15ml/1 tbsp caster (superfine) sugar
desiccated (dry unsweetened shredded) coconut

1 For the filling, put the coconut, sugar, cashews, raisins and evaporated milk into a pan. Bring to the boil, stirring occasionally. Reduce the heat and cook for 10 minutes, stirring, until the milk is absorbed. Add the nutmeg and cinnamon. Cool.

2 Preheat the oven to 180°C/350°F/Gas 4. Line two baking sheets with baking parchment.

3 Brush one sheet of filo pastry with sunflower oil. Fold the sheet in half lengthways, then brush with more oil and fold widthways. Brush the edges of the folded pastry with water.

4 Put a spoonful of filling on one half of the pastry sheet. Fold the other half over the filling, and press the edges together. Place on the baking sheet. Repeat with the remaining mixture.

5 To make the topping, put the evaporated milk and sugar into a pan and heat gently, stirring until the sugar has dissolved. Brush over the cookies and sprinkle them with the coconut.

6 Bake for about 20 minutes, until golden brown. Transfer to a wire rack and leave to cool.

Fourth of July Blueberry Softbakes Energy 185kcal/775kJ; Protein 3.3g; Carbohydrate 25.2g, of which sugars 9.8g; Fat 8.4g, of which saturates 4.6g; Cholesterol 78mg; Calcium 48mg; Fibre 0.8g; Sodium 42mg. **Neuris** Energy 164kcal/689kJ; Protein 4.2g; Carbohydrate 24.6g, of which sugars 11.6g; Fat 6.1g, of which saturates 4.1g; Cholesterol 4mg; Calcium 88mg; Fibre 1.5g; Sodium 37mg.

Panellets

The Catalan name for these nutty festival cakes means "little bread", but they are, in fact, much closer to marzipan, with a slightly soft centre that is produced by their secret ingredient – sweet potato. Patisseries make hundreds of these little cakes for All Saints' Day, on 1st November, when families take flowers to the graveyards of their relatives.

Makes about 24
115g/4oz sweet potato
butter, for greasing
1 large (US extra large) egg, separated
225g/8oz/2 cups ground almonds
200g/7oz/1 cup caster (superfine) sugar, plus extra for sprinkling
finely grated rind of 1 small lemon
7.5ml/1½ tsp vanilla extract
60ml/4 tbsp pine nuts
60ml/4 tbsp pistachio nuts, chopped

1 Peel and dice the sweet potato and cook it in a pan of boiling water for about 15 minutes, until soft but not falling apart. Drain well and leave to cool.

2 Preheat the oven to 200°C/400°F/Gas 6. Line one or two baking sheets with foil and grease well with butter.

3 Put the cooled sweet potato into a food processor and process to a smooth purée. Gradually work in the egg yolk, ground almonds, caster sugar, lemon rind and vanilla extract, processing to make a soft dough. Transfer the dough to a bowl, cover with clear film (plastic wrap) and chill in the refrigerator for 30 minutes.

4 Spoon walnut-size balls of dough on to the prepared baking sheets, spacing them about 2.5cm/1in apart, then flatten them out slightly.

5 Lightly beat the egg white and brush over the cookies. Sprinkle half with pine nuts, slightly less than 5ml/1 tsp each, and half with pistachio nuts. Sprinkle lightly with sugar. Bake for 10 minutes, or until lightly browned.

6 Leave to cool on the foil, then lift off with a metal spatula.

Speculaas

These Dutch cookies are made from a spicy dough wrapped around a wonderfully rich marzipan filling. They are eaten in Holland around the Feast of St Nicholas on 6 December.

Makes about 35
175g/6oz/1½ cups ground hazelnuts
175g/6oz/1½ cups ground almonds
175g/6oz/scant 1 cup caster (superfine) sugar
175g/6oz/1½ cups icing (confectioners') sugar

1 egg, beaten
10–15ml/2–3 tsp lemon juice

For the pastry
250g/9oz/2¼ cups self-raising (self-rising) flour, plus extra for dusting
5ml/1 tsp mixed spice (apple pie spice)
75g/3oz/⅓ cup brown sugar
115g/4oz/½ cup unsalted (sweet) butter, diced
2 eggs
15ml/1 tbsp milk
15ml/1 tbsp caster (superfine) sugar
about 35 blanched almond halves

1 For the filling, mix the hazelnuts, almonds, sugars, egg and 10ml/2 tsp lemon juice to a firm paste, adding more lemon juice if needed. Halve the paste and roll into sausages 25cm/10in long. Wrap and chill.

2 For the pastry, sift the flour and spice into a bowl, then stir in the brown sugar. Add the butter and rub in well. Add one egg and mix to form dough. Knead, wrap and chill for 15 minutes.

3 Preheat the oven to 180°C/350°F/Gas 4. Line a large baking sheet with baking parchment.

4 Roll out the pastry on a lightly floured surface to a 30cm/12in square and cut in half to make two equal rectangles. Beat the remaining egg and brush some over the pastry.

5 Place a roll of filling on each piece of pastry and roll the pastry around it. Place, join side down, on the baking sheet. Beat the remains of the egg with the milk and sugar and brush over the rolls. Press almond halves along the top. Bake for 35 minutes, until golden brown.

Panellets Energy 130kcal/541kJ; Protein 3.1g; Carbohydrate 10.7g, of which sugars 9.6g; Fat 8.6g, of which saturates 0.8g; Cholesterol 8mg; Calcium 32mg; Fibre 1g; Sodium 20mg.
Speculaas Energy 168kcal/703kJ; Protein 3.1g; Carbohydrate 19.4g, of which sugars 13.7g; Fat 9.2g, of which saturates 2.3g; Cholesterol 23mg; Calcium 39mg; Fibre 0.9g; Sodium 28mg.

Christmas Honey Cookies

Gloriously sticky, these spicy cookies are an irresistible festive treat.

Makes 20
2.5ml/½ tsp bicarbonate of soda
    (baking soda)
grated rind and juice of
    1 large orange
150ml/¼ pint/⅔ cup extra virgin
    olive oil
75g/3oz/scant ½ cup caster
    (superfine) sugar

60ml/4 tbsp brandy
7.5ml/1½ tsp ground cinnamon
400g/14oz/3½ cups self-raising
    (self-rising) flour sifted with a
    pinch of salt
115g/4oz/1 cup shelled walnuts,
    chopped

For the syrup
225g/8oz/1 cup clear honey
115g/4oz/generous ½ cup caster
    (superfine) sugar

1 Mix together the bicarbonate of soda and orange juice.

2 Beat the oil and sugar with an electric mixer until blended. Beat in the brandy and 2.5ml/½ tsp of the cinnamon, then the orange juice and soda. Using your hands, gradually work the flour and salt into the mixture. Add the orange rind and knead for 10 minutes, or until the dough is soft and pliable.

3 Preheat the oven to 180°C/350°F/Gas 4.

4 Flour your hands and pinch off small pieces of the dough. Shape them into 6cm/2½in long ovals and place on ungreased baking sheets. Using a fork dipped in water, flatten each cookie. Bake for 25 minutes, until golden. Cool slightly, then transfer to a wire rack to harden.

5 To make the syrup, put the honey, sugar and 150ml/¼ pint/ ⅔ cup water in a small pan. Bring gently to the boil, skim, then lower the heat and simmer for 5 minutes.

6 Immerse the cold cookies, about six at a time, into the hot syrup and leave them for 1–2 minutes.

7 Lift them with a slotted spoon and place on a platter in a single layer. Sprinkle with the walnuts and remaining cinnamon.

Christmas Tree Cookies

These cookies make an appealing gift. They look wonderful hung on a Christmas tree.

Makes 12
175g/6oz/1½ cups plain
    (all-purpose) flour, plus extra
    for dusting

75g/3oz/⅓ cup butter, chopped
40g/1½oz/3 tbsp caster
    (superfine) sugar
1 egg white
30ml/2 tbsp orange juice
225g/8oz coloured fruit
    sweets (candies)
coloured ribbons, to decorate

1 Preheat the oven to 180°C/350°F/Gas 4. Line two baking sheets with baking parchment.

2 Sift the flour into a mixing bowl. Add the butter and rub into the flour with your fingertips until the mixture resembles fine breadcrumbs. Stir in the sugar, egg white and enough orange juice to form a soft dough. Turn out on to a lightly floured surface and knead lightly until smooth.

3 Roll out thinly and stamp out as many shapes as possible using a floured Christmas tree cookie cutter. Transfer the shapes to the prepared baking sheets, spacing them well apart. Knead the trimmings together.

4 Using a 1cm/½in round cutter or the end of a large plain piping nozzle, stamp out and remove six rounds from each tree shape. Cut each sweet into three and place a piece in each hole. Make a small hole at the top of each tree to thread through the ribbon. Repeat until you have used up the remaining cookie dough and sweets.

5 Bake for 15–20 minutes, until the cookies are slightly gold in colour and the sweets have melted and filled the holes. If the holes for threading the ribbons have closed up during baking, pierce them again while the cookies are still hot. Leave to cool on the baking sheets.

6 Thread short lengths of ribbon through the holes so that the trees can be hung up.

Christmas Honey Cookies Energy 173kcal/724kJ; Protein 2.7g; Carbohydrate 19.5g, of which sugars 4.6g; Fat 9.2g, of which saturates 1.1g; Cholesterol 0mg; Calcium 78mg; Fibre 0.8g; Sodium 73mg.
Christmas Tree Cookies Energy 147kcal/622kJ; Protein 1.9g; Carbohydrate 28.7g, of which sugars 16g; Fat 3.6g, of which saturates 2.1g; Cholesterol 15mg; Calcium 31mg; Fibre 0.5g; Sodium 45mg.

Christmas Tree Angels

Why not make these charming edible decorations to brighten your Yuletide?

Makes 20–30
90g/3½oz/scant ½ cup
  demerara (raw) sugar
200g/7oz/scant1 cup golden
  (light corn) syrup
5ml/1 tsp ground ginger
5ml/1 tsp ground cinnamon
1.5ml/¼ tsp ground cloves
115g/4oz/½ cup unsalted
  (sweet) butter, diced

10ml/2 tsp bicarbonate of soda
  (baking soda)
1 egg, beaten
500g/1¼lb/5 cups plain
  (all-purpose) flour, sifted

For the decoration
1 egg white
175–225g/6–8oz/1½–2 cups
  icing (confectioners')
  sugar, sifted
silver and gold balls
fine ribbon

1 Preheat the oven to 160°C/325°F/Gas 3. Line two or three large baking sheets with baking parchment.

2 Put the sugar, syrup, ginger, cinnamon and cloves into a heavy pan and bring to the boil over a low heat, stirring constantly. Once the mixture has boiled, remove the pan from the heat.

3 Put the butter in a heatproof bowl and pour over the hot sugar and syrup mixture. Add the bicarbonate of soda and stir until the butter has melted. Beat in the egg, then stir in the flour. Mix thoroughly and then knead to form a smooth dough.

4 Divide the dough into four. Roll each out between sheets of baking parchment, to a 3mm/⅛in thickness. Stamp out angels using a cookie cutter.

5 Using a skewer, make a hole in the cookies through which ribbon can be threaded. Place on the baking sheets. Bake for 10–15 minutes, until golden. Transfer to a wire rack to cool.

6 For the decoration, beat the egg white. Whisk in icing sugar until a soft-peak consistency forms. Put the icing in a piping (icing) bag fitted with a plain nozzle and decorate the cookies. Add silver and gold balls. Thread ribbon through the holes.

Stained Glass Windows

Baking coloured sweets inside a cookie frame creates a stained glass effect, particularly if you hang the cookies in the light.

Makes 12–14
175g/6oz/1½ cups plain
  (all-purpose) flour, plus extra
  for dusting
2.5ml/ ½ tsp bicarbonate of soda
  (baking soda)

2.5ml/½ tsp ground cinnamon
75g/3oz/6 tbsp unsalted (sweet)
  butter, chilled and diced
75g/3oz/scant ½ cup caster
  (superfine) sugar
30ml/2 tbsp golden (light
  corn) syrup
1 egg yolk
150g/5oz brightly coloured, clear
  boiled sweets (hard candies)
fine ribbon

1 Put the flour, bicarbonate of soda, cinnamon and butter into a bowl and rub the fat into the flour until the mixture resembles breadcrumbs. Add the sugar, syrup and egg yolk and mix until the mixture starts to cling together in a dough. Turn the dough out on to a lightly floured surface and knead until smooth. Wrap in clear film (plastic wrap) and chill for at least 30 minutes.

2 Preheat the oven to 180°C/350°F/Gas 4. Line two large baking sheets with baking parchment.

3 Roll out the dough thinly on a lightly floured surface. Stamp out 12 diamonds using a cookie cutter. Cut a smaller diamond from the centre of each and remove to leave a 1cm/½in frame. Make a hole at one end for hanging. Bake for 5 minutes.

4 Lightly crush the sweets with a rolling pin. Remove the cookies from the oven and fill the centre of each with two crushed sweets of the same colour.

5 Return the cookies to the oven for another 5 minutes until the sweets have melted. Spread the melted sweets to fill the space with the tip of a skewer. Leave to cool.

6 Thread ribbon through the holes in the cookies, then hang up the cookies as decorations.

Stained Glass Windows Energy 145kcal/612kJ; Protein 1.2g; Carbohydrate 26.4g, of which sugars 16.8g; Fat 4.6g, of which saturates 2.8g; Cholesterol 11mg; Calcium 22mg; Fibre 0.4g; Sodium 42mg.
Christmas Tree Angels Energy 147kcal/622kJ; Protein 1.9g; Carbohydrate 28.7g, of which sugars 16g; Fat 3.6g, of which saturates 2.1g; Cholesterol 15mg; Calcium 31mg; Fibre 0.5g; Sodium 45mg.

Christmas Cookies with Walnuts

At Christmas time, these are individually wrapped in small squares of brightly coloured tissue paper and arranged in large bowls. Transform them into gifts by wrapping five or six into packages and tying them with pretty coloured ribbons.

Makes 24
115g/4oz/½ cup lard, softened
  and diced

75g/3oz/¾ cup icing
  (confectioners') sugar
5ml/1 tsp vanilla extract
150g/5oz/1¼ cups unbleached
  plain (all-purpose) flour
75g/3oz/¾ cup broken walnuts,
  finely chopped

For the topping
50g/2oz/½ cup icing
  (confectioners') sugar
10ml/2 tsp ground cinnamon

1 Preheat the oven to 190°C/375°F/Gas 5. Lightly grease two baking sheets.

2 Place the lard in a large bowl and beat with an electric whisk until light and aerated. Gradually beat in 75g/3oz/¾ cup icing sugar, then add the vanilla extract and beat well.

3 Add the flour by hand, working it gently into the mixture. Do not be tempted to use a spoon or the mixture will be too sticky. Add the walnuts and mix in.

4 Divide the dough evenly into 24 small pieces, roll each into a ball and space well apart on baking sheets. Bake for 10–15 minutes, until golden. Leave to cool on wire racks.

5 Put the remaining icing sugar in a bowl and stir in the cinnamon. Add a few cookies at a time, shaking them in the icing sugar until they are heavily coated. Shake off the excess sugar. Serve wrapped in coloured paper.

Cook's Tip
These cookies should be crumbly and light to eat. Pecan nuts can be used instead of the walnuts, if you like.

Festive Cookies

These cookies are great fun to make as gifts. For a change, omit the lemon rind and add 25g/1oz/¼ cup ground almonds and a few drops of almond extract.

grated rind of 1 lemon
1 egg yolk
175g/6oz/1½ cups plain
  (all-purpose) flour, plus extra
  for dusting
pinch of salt

Makes about 12
75g/3oz/6 tbsp butter
50g/2oz/½ cup icing
  (confectioners') sugar

To decorate
2 egg yolks
red and green food colourings

1 In a large bowl, beat together the butter, sugar and lemon rind until fluffy. Beat in the egg yolk and then sift in the flour and the salt. Knead to form a dough. Wrap in clear film (plastic wrap) and chill for 30 minutes.

2 Preheat the oven to 190°C/375°F/Gas 5. Lightly grease two large baking sheets.

3 On a lightly floured surface, roll out the dough thinly. Using a cookie cutter, stamp out the cookies. Transfer the cookies to the baking sheets.

4 Mark the tops with a holly leaf cutter and use a plain piping nozzle for the berries. Chill for about 10 minutes, until firm. Put each egg yolk into a cup. Mix red food colour into one and green into the other. Paint the leaves and berries.

5 Bake for 10–12 minutes, or until they begin to colour around the edges. Leave to cool slightly on the baking sheets, and then transfer them to a wire rack to cool completely.

Cook's Tip
You can freeze the cookies, raw or baked. Baked cookies that have been frozen will benefit from being refreshed in the oven after they have thawed.

Christmas Cookies with Walnuts Energy 141kcal/591kJ; Protein 1.7g; Carbohydrate 15.4g, of which sugars 9g; Fat 8.5g, of which saturates 2g; Cholesterol 4mg; Calcium 22mg; Fibre 0.5g; Sodium 1mg.
Festive Cookies Energy 118kcal/494kJ; Protein 1.7g; Carbohydrate 15.7g, of which sugars 4.6g; Fat 5.8g, of which saturates 3.4g; Cholesterol 30mg; Calcium 26mg; Fibre 0.5g; Sodium 39mg.

Festive Gingerbreads

These brightly decorated gingerbread cookies are fun to make and may be used as tasty edible Christmas tree decorations.

Makes 20
30ml/2 tbsp golden (light corn) syrup
15ml/1 tbsp black treacle (molasses)
50g/2oz/¼ cup light soft brown sugar
25g/1oz/2 tbsp butter

175g/6oz/1½ cups plain (all-purpose) flour, plus extra for dusting
¾ tsp bicarbonate of soda (baking soda)
½ tsp ground mixed spice (apple pie spice)
1½ tsp ground ginger
1 egg yolk

To decorate
small quantity royal icing
red, yellow and green food colourings
brightly coloured ribbons

1 Preheat the oven to 190°C/375°F/Gas 5. Line several baking sheets with baking parchment.

2 Put the syrup, treacle, sugar and butter into a pan. Heat gently, stirring occasionally, until the butter has melted.

3 Sift the flour, bicarbonate of soda and mixed spice and ginger into a bowl. Stir in the treacle mixture and the egg yolk. Mix to a soft dough. Knead on a lightly floured surface until smooth.

4 Roll out the dough thinly. Using cookie cutters, stamp out as many shapes as possible. Arrange well spaced on the baking sheets. Make a hole in the top of each.

5 Bake in the oven for 15–20 minutes, or until risen and golden. Leave to cool slightly before transferring to a wire rack.

6 Divide the royal icing into four and colour one part red, one part yellow and one part green using food colouring. Fill a piping (icing) bag fitted with a writing nozzle with each.

7 Pipe lines, dots, and zig-zags on the cookies. Leave to dry. Thread ribbons through the holes in the cookies.

Christmas Cookies

These cookies taste rich and buttery. If you want Christmas cookies for adults you could add your choice of Christmas spices to the recipe.

Makes 30
175g/6oz/¾ cup unsalted (sweet) butter, at room temperature
275g/10oz/scant 1½ cups caster (superfine) sugar

1 egg
1 egg yolk
5ml/1 tsp vanilla extract
grated rind of 1 lemon
pinch of salt
275g/10oz/2½ cups plain (all-purpose) flour, plus extra for dusting

For the decoration
coloured icing
small decorations

1 Preheat the oven to 350°F/180°C/Gas 4.

2 In a large bowl, beat the butter until soft. Add the sugar and continue beating until light and fluffy.

3 Using a wooden spoon, gradually mix in the whole egg and the egg yolk. Add the vanilla extract, lemon rind and salt. Stir until thoroughly combined.

4 Add the flour and stir until blended. Gather the mixture into a ball with your fingertips, wrap in cling film (plastic wrap), and chill in the refrigerator for at least 30 minutes.

5 On a lightly floured surface, roll out the mixture to 3mm/⅛in thick.

6 Stamp out Christmas shapes or rounds with cookie cutters and place on a non-stick baking sheet. Gather up the trimmings and continue rolling and stamping out cookies until the mixture has been used up.

7 Bake the cookies in the oven for about 8 minutes until lightly coloured. Leave to stand for a few minutes before transferring to a wire rack with a metal spatula to cool completely. Ice and decorate, as you like.

Festive Gingerbreads Energy 2kcal/217kJ; Protein 0.6g; Carbohydrate 6.3g, of which sugars 2.4g; Fat 2.9g, of which saturates 1.8g; Cholesterol 9.4mg; Calcium 9.6mg; Fibre 0.1g; Sodium 20mg.
Christmas Cookies Energy 118kcal/495kJ; Protein 1.3g; Carbohydrate 17.3g, of which sugars 10.1g; Fat 5.3g, of which saturates 3.2g; Cholesterol 26mg; Calcium 21mg; Fibre 0.3g; Sodium 39mg.

New Mexico Christmas Biscochitos

The aniseed flavour in these cookies is very unusual, and the addition of brandy makes them a distinctly adult cookie.

Makes 24
175g/6oz/1½ cups plain (all-purpose) flour, plus extra for dusting
5ml/1 tsp baking powder
pinch of salt
50g/2oz/¼ cup unsalted (sweet) butter, softened
90g/3½oz/scant ½ cup sugar
1 egg
5ml/1 tsp whole aniseed
15ml/1 tbsp brandy
50g/2oz/¼ cup sugar mixed with 2.5ml/½ tsp ground cinnamon, for sprinkling

1 Sift together the flour, baking powder and salt into a large bowl. Set aside.

2 In another bowl, beat the butter with the sugar until soft and fluffy. Add the egg, aniseed and brandy and beat until incorporated. Fold in the dry ingredients until just blended to a dough. Shape into a ball, wrap in clear film (plastic wrap) and chill in the refrigerator for at least 30 minutes.

3 Preheat the oven to 180°C/350°F/Gas 4. Lightly grease two baking sheets.

4 On a lightly floured surface, roll out the chilled cookie dough to about 3mm/⅛in thick.

5 Using cookie cutters, stamp out shapes from the dough.

6 Place the cookies on the prepared baking sheets and sprinkle lightly with the cinnamon sugar.

7 Bake for about 10 minutes, until just barely golden. Leave to cool on the baking sheets for 5 minutes, then, using a metal spatula, carefully transfer the cookies to a wire rack to cool completely.

8 The cookies can be stored in an airtight container for up to 1 week.

Cinnamon and Orange Tuiles

The tempting aroma of cinnamon and orange evokes a feeling of Christmas and, served with coffee, these chocolate-dipped tuiles are perfect for festive occasions.

Serves 15
2 egg whites
90g/3½oz/½ cup caster (superfine) sugar
7.5ml/1½ tsp ground cinnamon
finely grated rind of 1 orange
50g/2oz/½ cup plain (all-purpose) flour
75g/3oz/6 tbsp butter, melted

For the dipping chocolate
75g/3oz plain (semisweet) chocolate
45ml/3 tbsp milk
75–90ml5–6 tbsp double (heavy) or whipping cream

1 Preheat the oven to 200°C/400°F/Gas 6. Lightly grease two or three large baking sheets.

2 In a grease-free glass bowl, whisk the egg whites until softly peaking, then whisk in the sugar until smooth and glossy.

3 Add the cinnamon and orange rind, sift over the flour and fold in with the melted butter. When well blended, add 15ml/1 tbsp of recently boiled water to thin the mixture.

4 Place 4–5 teaspoons of the mixture on each tray, well apart. Flatten out and bake, one sheet at a time, for 7 minutes, until just golden. Cool for a few seconds, then remove from the sheet with a metal spatula and immediately roll around the handle of a wooden spoon. Place on a rack to cool.

5 Melt the chocolate in the milk, then stir in the cream. Dip one or both ends of the cookies in the chocolate and leave to cool and set.

> **Variation**
> *You could substitute 5ml/1 tsp ground ginger or a few drops of peppermint extract for the cinnamon, if you like.*

New Mexico Christmas Biscochitos Energy 68kcal/286kJ; Protein 1g; Carbohydrate 11.8g, of which sugars 6.2g; Fat 2g, of which saturates 1.2g; Cholesterol 12mg; Calcium 15mg; Fibre 0.2g; Sodium 16mg. **Cinnamon and Orange Tuiles** Energy 125kcal/523kJ; Protein 1.2g; Carbohydrate 12.3g, of which sugars 9.7g; Fat 8.3g, of which saturates 5.2g; Cholesterol 18mg; Calcium 17mg; Fibre 0.2g; Sodium 42mg.

Festive Orange and Almond Cookies

Lightly spiced and delicately flavoured with orange flower water and almonds, these crisp little crescents are perfect for parties and festive occasions such as christenings and weddings.

Makes about 20
115g/4oz/1/2 cup unsalted (sweet) butter, softened
pinch of ground nutmeg
10ml/2 tsp orange flower water
50g/2oz/1/2 cup icing (confectioners') sugar, plus extra for dusting
90g/31/2oz/3/4 cup plain (all-purpose) flour
115g/4oz/1 cup ground almonds
25g/1oz/1/4 cup whole almonds, toasted and chopped

1 Preheat the oven to 160°C/325°F/Gas 3. Line two large baking sheets with baking parchment.

2 In a large bowl, beat the butter until soft and creamy. Add the nutmeg and orange flower water and beat to combine. Add the icing sugar and beat the mixture until fluffy.

3 Add the flour, ground and chopped almonds and mix well, then use your hands to bring the mixture together to form a dough, being careful not to overwork it.

4 Shape pieces of dough into sausages about 7.5cm/3in long. Curve each one into a crescent and place, spaced well apart, on the prepared baking sheets.

5 Bake for about 15 minutes, or until firm but still pale in colour. Leave to stand for about 5 minutes, then dust with a little icing sugar and, using a metal spatula, transfer the cookies to a wire rack to cool completely.

Cook's Tip
Made from the blossoms of the bitter orange, orange flower water has a wonderful fragrance that lends an exotic touch to these cookies. It is widely available from supermarkets.

New Year Honey Cakes

This classic honey cake is richly spiced with sweet, aromatic scents. For this reason it is a favourite at Rosh Hashanah, Jewish New Year, when sweet foods, particularly honey, are eaten in the hope of a sweet New Year.

Serves about 8
175g/6oz/11/2 cups plain (all-purpose) flour
75g/3oz/scant 1/2 cup caster (superfine) sugar
2.5ml/1/2 tsp ground ginger
2.5–5ml/1/2–1 tsp ground cinnamon
5ml/1 tsp mixed spice (apple pie spice)
5ml/1 tsp bicarbonate of soda (baking soda)
225g/8oz/1 cup clear honey
60ml/4 tbsp vegetable or olive oil
grated rind of 1 orange
2 eggs
75ml/5 tbsp orange juice
10ml/2 tsp chopped fresh root ginger, or to taste

1 Preheat the oven to 180°C/350°F/Gas 4. Line a 25 x 20cm/ 10 x 8in baking tin (pan) with baking parchment.

2 In a bowl, mix together the flour, sugar, ginger, cinnamon, mixed spice and bicarbonate of soda. Make a well in the centre.

3 Pour in the honey, oil, orange rind and eggs. Using a wooden spoon, beat until smooth, then add the orange juice. Stir in the chopped ginger.

4 Pour the cake mixture into the prepared tin, then bake for about 50 minutes, or until firm to the touch.

5 Leave to cool in the tin, then turn out and wrap in foil. Store at room temperature for 2–3 days before serving to allow the flavours of the cake to mature.

Cook's Tip
This honey cake keeps very well. It can be made in two loaf tins (pans), so that one cake can be eaten, while the other is wrapped in clear film (plastic wrap) and frozen for a later date.

Festive Orange and Almond Cookies Energy 131kcal/546kJ; Protein 2.3g; Carbohydrate 9.5g, of which sugars 3.5g; Fat 9.6g, of which saturates 2.9g; Cholesterol 16mg; Calcium 28mg; Fibre 0.7g; Sodium 5mg. **New Year Honey Cakes** Energy 152kcal/640kJ; Protein 1.9g; Carbohydrate 23.6g, of which sugars 13g; Fat 6.3g, of which saturates 3.8g; Cholesterol 26mg; Calcium 30mg; Fibre 0.4g; Sodium 49mg.

Mexican Wedding Cookies

Almost hidden beneath their veil of icing sugar, these little shortbread cookies are traditionally served at weddings, and are absolutely delicious. Serve them after dinner with coffee.

Makes 30
225g/8oz/1 cup butter, softened
175g/6oz/1½ cups icing
    (confectioners') sugar
5ml/1 tsp vanilla extract
300g/11oz/2¾ cups plain
    (all-purpose) flour
pinch of salt
150g/5oz/1¼ cups pecan nuts,
    finely chopped

1 Preheat the oven to 190°C/375°F/Gas 5. Lightly grease two baking sheets.

2 In a large mixing bowl, beat the butter until it is light and fluffy, then beat in 115g/4oz/1 cup of the icing sugar, with the vanilla extract.

3 Gradually add the flour and salt to the creamed mixture, using a wooden spoon at first until it starts to form a dough. Add the finely chopped pecans with the remaining flour. Pull the dough together with your hands and then knead the dough lightly.

4 Divide the dough into 30 equal pieces and roll them into balls. Space about 5mm/¼in apart on baking sheets. Press each ball lightly with your thumb, to flatten it slightly.

5 Bake the cookies for 10–15 minutes, until they start to brown. Leave to stand on the baking sheets for 10 minutes, then, using a metal spatula, carefully transfer the cookies to wire racks to cool completely.

6 Put the remaining icing sugar in a bowl. Add a few cookies at a time, shaking them in the icing sugar until they are heavily coated.

7 Store them, interleaved with baking parchment in an airtight container for up to 3 days.

Cinnamon-spiced Wedding Cookies

These melt-in-the-mouth cinnamon and vanilla cookies are also served at Mexican weddings. They are perfect for serving with coffee.

Makes about 40
225g/8oz/1 cup butter, softened
50g/2oz/¼ cup caster
    (superfine) sugar
5ml/1 tsp vanilla extract
225g/8oz/2 cups plain
    (all-purpose) flour
115g/4oz/1 cup cornflour
    (cornstarch)

For the topping
50g/2oz/½ cup icing
    (confectioners') sugar
5ml/1 tsp ground cinnamon

1 Preheat the oven to 160°C/325°F/Gas 3. Lightly grease two or three baking sheets.

2 In a bowl, beat the butter with the caster sugar until light and fluffy. Add the vanilla extract. Sift the flour and cornflour together over the mixture and gradually work into the creamed butter and sugar mixture in batches.

3 Roll heaped teaspoons of the mixture into balls and place on the baking sheets. Bake for 30 minutes, or until pale golden. Loosen on the baking tray and leave to cool slightly.

4 Sift the icing sugar and ground cinnamon into a bowl. While the cookies are still warm, toss them in the icing sugar mixture. Leave on a wire rack to cool.

5 Store in an airtight container for up to 2 weeks.

Variation
For a special surprise, shape the dough balls around squares of chocolate or pieces of crystallized (candied) fruit.

Cook's Tip
The cookie mixture can be prepared in a food processor.

Mexican Wedding Cookies Energy 147kcal/615kJ; Protein 1.5g; Carbohydrate 14.2g, of which sugars 6.5g; Fat 9.8g, of which saturates 4.2g; Cholesterol 16mg; Calcium 22mg; Fibre 0.5g; Sodium 46mg.
Cinnamon-spiced Wedding Cookies Energy 81kcal/339kJ; Protein 0.6g; Carbohydrate 9.7g, of which sugars 2.7g; Fat 4.7g, of which saturates 2.9g; Cholesterol 12mg; Calcium 11mg; Fibre 0.2g; Sodium 36mg.

Persian Celebration Cookies

These prettily decorated cookies are traditionally served on special occasions with black tea. However, they taste as good with coffee or even a glass of chilled dry white wine.

Makes about 22
75g/3oz/³⁄₄ cup icing
   (confectioners') sugar, sifted
225g/8oz/1 cup unsalted (sweet)
   butter, softened
300g/10oz/2¹⁄₂ cups rice flour

75g/3oz/³⁄₄ cup self-raising
   (self-rising) flour
1 egg yolk
15ml/1 tbsp rose water

For the topping
150g/5oz/1¹⁄₄ cups icing
   (confectioners') sugar, sifted
rose water
pink food colouring
crystallized rose petals or violets
   or pink sugar balls or
   sugar sprinkles

1 In a large bowl, beat together the sugar and butter until light and fluffy. Add the flours, egg yolk and rose water and mix first with a wooden spoon and then with your hands until a dough forms. Gather into a ball. Wrap with cling film (plastic wrap) and chill for 30 minutes.

2 Preheat the oven to 160°C/325°F/Gas 3. Line two baking sheets with baking parchment.

3 Shape small pieces of the dough into balls. Place well apart on the prepared baking sheets and flatten each one slightly.

4 Bake for 15–20 minutes, until firm but still quite pale in colour. Leave to cool completely on the baking sheets.

5 To make the topping, put the icing sugar into a bowl and add just enough rose water to mix to a thick, flowing consistency. Add just a light touch of pink food colouring to make a very pale shade.

6 Drizzle the icing in random squiggles and circles over all the cookies. Place a few crystallized rose petals or violets or pink sugar balls on top, or sprinkle with a little sugar sprinkles. Leave to set completely.

Striped Party Cookies

These cookies can be made in different flavours and colours and look wonderful tied in bundles or packed into decorative jars or boxes. Eat them with ice cream or light desserts.

Makes 25
2 egg whites
90g/3¹⁄₂oz/¹⁄₂ cup caster
   (superfine) sugar
50g/2oz/¹⁄₂ cup plain
   (all-purpose) flour
50g/2oz/¹⁄₄ cup unsalted (sweet)
   butter, melted
25g/1oz white chocolate, melted
red and green food colouring

1 Preheat the oven to 190°C/375°F/Gas 5. Line two baking sheets with baking parchment. Lightly grease several wooden spoon handles.

2 Place the egg whites in a bowl and whisk until stiff. Add the sugar gradually, whisking well after each addition.

3 Add the flour and melted butter and whisk until smooth. Drop four separate teaspoonfuls of the mixture on to the prepared baking sheets and spread into thin rounds.

4 Divide the melted chocolate in half and add a little food colouring to each half. Fill piping (icing) bags with coloured chocolate. Pipe lines or zig-zags of green and red chocolate over each round of cookie mixture.

5 Bake one sheet at a time for about 3 minutes, until pale golden. Loosen the rounds with a metal spatula and return to the oven for a few seconds to soften.

6 Taking one cookie at a time, turn it over and roll it around a spoon handle. Leave for a few seconds to set. Repeat to shape the remaining cookies.

7 When the cookies are set, slip them off the spoon handles on to a wire rack. If the cookies are too hard to shape, simply return them to the oven for a few seconds to soften. Store in an airtight container for 2–3 days.

Persian Celebration Cookies Energy 180kcal/753kJ; Protein 1.4g; Carbohydrate 24.3g, of which sugars 10.8g; Fat 8.8g, of which saturates 5.4g; Cholesterol 31mg; Calcium 24mg; Fibre 0.4g; Sodium 76mg. **Striped Cookies** Energy 42kcal/177kJ; Protein 0.5g; Carbohydrate 5.9g, of which sugars 4.4g; Fat 2g, of which saturates 1.2g; Cholesterol 4mg; Calcium 8mg; Fibre 0.1g; Sodium 18mg.

Celebration Hearts and Stars

These soft, sweet cookies have a wonderfully chewy texture and a deliciously warm, fragrant flavour. Serve with coffee at the end of a festive meal, or make them as a gift on a special occasion.

50g/2oz/1½ tbsp golden (light corn) syrup
50g/2oz/1½ tbsp black treacle (molasses)
400g/14oz/3½ cups self-raising (self-rising) flour, plus extra for dusting
10ml/2 tsp ground ginger

Makes about 25
115g/4oz/½ cup unsalted (sweet) butter, softened
115g/4oz/½ cup light muscovado (brown) sugar
1 egg

For the toppings
200g/7oz plain (semisweet) or milk chocolate
150g/5oz/1¼ cups icing (confectioners') sugar, sifted

1 In a large bowl, beat together the butter and sugar until light and creamy.

2 Beat in the egg, syrup and treacle, stirring carefully after each addition. Sift in the flour and ginger and mix to form a firm dough. Chill for 20 minutes.

3 Preheat the oven to 180°C/350°F/Gas 4. Lightly grease two large baking sheets.

4 Roll out the dough on a lightly floured surface to just under 1cm/½in thick and use cookie cutters to stamp out heart and star shapes. Place, spaced slightly apart to allow for spreading during baking, on the prepared baking sheets and bake in the oven for about 10 minutes, or until risen. Leave to cool on a wire rack.

5 To make the toppings, melt the chocolate in a heatproof bowl set over a pan of barely simmering water. Use the melted chocolate to coat the heart-shaped cookies.

6 Put the icing sugar into a bowl and mix with warm water to make a coating consistency, then use this to glaze the stars.

Black Russian Party Cookies

The ingredients of the famous cocktail – coffee and vodka – flavour these fabulous and unusual adult party cookies.

1 egg
225g/8oz/2 cups plain (all-purpose) flour
5ml/1 tsp baking powder
pinch of salt

Makes 16
30ml/2 tbsp ground espresso or other strong-flavoured coffee
60ml/4 tbsp near-boiling milk
115g/4oz/½ cup butter
115g/4oz/½ cup soft light brown sugar

For the icing
115g/4oz/1 cup icing (confectioners') sugar
about 25ml/1½ tbsp vodka

1 Preheat the oven to 180°C/350°F/Gas 4. Lightly grease two baking sheets.

2 Put the coffee in a small bowl and pour the hot milk over. Leave to infuse (steep) for 4 minutes, then strain through a fine sieve (strainer) and leave to cool.

3 Beat the butter and sugar together until light and fluffy. Gradually beat in the egg. Sift the flour, baking powder and salt together and fold in with the coffee-flavoured milk to make a fairly stiff mixture.

4 Place dessertspoonfuls of the mixture on the baking sheets, spacing them slightly apart to allow room for a little spreading. Bake the cookies for about 15 minutes, until lightly browned. Using a metal spatula, carefully transfer the cookies to a wire rack to cool.

5 To make the icing, mix the icing sugar and enough vodka together to make a thick icing. Spoon into a small baking parchment piping (icing) bag.

6 Snip off the end of the piping bag and lightly drizzle the icing over the top of each cookie. Leave the icing to set before serving.

Black Russian Party Cookies Energy 168kcal/706kJ; Protein 2g; Carbohydrate 26.2g, of which sugars 15.5g; Fat 6.5g, of which saturates 3.9g; Cholesterol 27mg; Calcium 35mg; Fibre 0.4g; Sodium 51mg.
Celebration Hearts and Stars Energy 185kcal/781kJ; Protein 2.3g; Carbohydrate 31.5g, of which sugars 19.3g; Fat 6.5g, of which saturates 3.8g; Cholesterol 18mg; Calcium 44mg; Fibre 0.7g; Sodium 41mg.

Italian Glazed Lemon Party Rings

These delicately flavoured, pretty cookies look almost too good to eat. The icing is flavoured with Italian liqueur, so they are strictly for adults.

Makes about 16
200g/7oz/1¾ cups self-raising (self-rising) flour
50g/2oz/¼ cup unsalted (sweet) butter, at room temperature, diced

25ml/1½ tbsp milk
50g/2oz/¼ cup caster (superfine) sugar
finely grated rind of ½ lemon
1 egg, beaten

For the topping
150g/5oz/1¼ cups icing (confectioners') sugar, sifted
30ml/2 tbsp Limoncello liqueur
15ml/1 tbsp chopped candied angelica

1 Preheat the oven to 180°C/350°F/Gas 4. Lightly grease two large baking sheets.

2 Put the flour into a bowl and rub in the butter with your fingertips until the mixture resembles breadcrumbs.

3 Put the milk, sugar and lemon rind in a small pan and stir over a low heat until the sugar has dissolved. Add to the flour mixture, together with the egg, and mix well. Knead lightly until smooth.

4 Roll walnut-size pieces of dough into strands 15cm/6in long. Twist two strands together and join the ends to make a circle. Place on the prepared baking sheets and bake for 15–20 minutes, or until golden.

5 To make the topping, stir the icing sugar and liqueur together. Dip the top of each cookie into the topping and sprinkle with angelica.

> **Variation**
> *If you are baking these cookies for children, use lemon syrup instead of the liqueur.*

Festival Shortbreads

This Greek version of shortbread is one of the world's most popular sweet treats.

Makes 24–28
250g/9oz/generous 1 cup unsalted (sweet) butter
65g/2½oz/⅓ cup caster (superfine) sugar
1 large (US extra large) egg yolk
30ml/2 tbsp Greek ouzo, Pernod or brandy

115g/4oz unblanched almonds
65g/2½oz/⅔ cup cornflour (cornstarch)
300g/11oz/2¾ cups plain (all-purpose) flour

For the decoration
about 60ml/4tbsp triple-distilled rose-water
500g/1¼lb/5 cups icing (confectioners') sugar

1 Preheat the oven to 180°C/350°F/Gas 4. Lightly grease two or three baking sheets.

2 In a bowl, beat together the butter and add the sugar until light and fluffy. Add the egg yolk and alcohol and mix well.

3 Grind the almonds in a processor or nut grinder to a coarse texture and mix into the butter mixture. Beat in the cornflour and enough flour to give a firm dough-like mixture.

4 Divide the dough into 24–28 equal portions. Form each into a crescent around a finger. Place on the prepared baking sheets, spaced well apart, and bake in the oven for 20–25 minutes. Check the cookies during baking and lower the oven temperature if they seem to be colouring too much. Loosen with a metal spatula and leave on the baking sheets to cool completely.

5 Pour the rose water into a small bowl and tip the sifted icing sugar into a larger one. Dip a cookie briefly first into the rose water and then into the icing sugar. Repeat until all the cookies are thoroughly coated. Set aside on waxed paper until dry.

6 Place in an airtight container, packing the cookies loosely or they will stick together.

Italian Glazed Lemon Party Rings Energy 125kcal/530kJ; Protein 1.7g; Carbohydrate 23.5g, of which sugars 14g; Fat 3.1g, of which saturates 1.8g; Cholesterol 19mg; Calcium 28mg; Fibre 0.4g; Sodium 25mg. **Festival Shortbreads** Energy 220kcal/926kJ; Protein 2.1g; Carbohydrate 31.9g, of which sugars 21.5g; Fat 10g, of which saturates 4.9g; Cholesterol 26mg; Calcium 38mg; Fibre 0.6g; Sodium 58mg.

Tiramisu Special Occasion Cookies

These delicate cookies taste like the wonderful Italian dessert with its flavours of coffee, chocolate, rum and rich creamy custard.

Makes 14
50g/2oz/¼ cup butter, at room
   temperature, diced
90g/3½oz/½ cup caster
   (superfine) sugar
1 egg, beaten
50g/2oz/½ cup plain
   (all-purpose) flour

For the filling
15ml/1 tbsp dark rum
2.5ml/½ tsp instant
   coffee powder
150g/5oz/⅔ cup mascarpone
15ml/1 tbsp light muscovado
   (brown) sugar

For the topping
75g/3oz white chocolate
15ml/1 tbsp milk
30ml/2 tbsp crushed
   chocolate flakes

1 To make the filling, in a large bowl, mix together the rum and coffee powder, stirring well until the coffee has dissolved. Add the mascarpone and muscovado sugar and beat well. Cover with clear film (plastic wrap) and chill until required.

2 Preheat the oven to 200°C/400°F/Gas 6. Line two or three baking sheets with baking parchment.

3 To make the cookies, in a bowl, beat together the butter and sugar until light and fluffy. Add the beaten egg and mix well. Stir in the flour and mix thoroughly.

4 Put the mixture into a piping (pastry) bag fitted with a 1.5cm/½in plain nozzle and pipe 28 small heaps on to the baking sheets, spaced slightly apart. Cook for about 6–8 minutes until firm in the centre and just beginning to brown on the edges. Set aside to cool.

5 Spread a little of the filling on to half the cookies and place the other halves on top.

6 Put the chocolate and milk in a heatproof bowl and melt over a pan of hot water. Spread evenly over the cookies, then sprinkle with crushed chocolate flakes to finish.

Party Cookies with Praline

These almond cookies, filled with vanilla cream and coated in praline, are just the thing for an afternoon gathering of friends.

Makes 17–18
150g/5oz/1¼ cups plain
   (all-purpose) flour
75g/3oz/¾ cup ground almonds
75g/3oz/6 tbsp unsalted
   (sweet) butter, at room
   temperature, diced
1 egg yolk
5ml/1 tsp vanilla extract
icing (confectioners') sugar, sifted,
   for dusting

For the praline
25g/1oz/¼ cup whole blanched
   almonds
50g/2oz/¼ cup caster
   (superfine) sugar

For the filling
150g/5oz/1¼ cups icing
   (confectioners') sugar, sifted
75g/3oz/6 tbsp unsalted
   (sweet) butter, at room
   temperature, diced
5ml/1 tsp vanilla extract

1 To make the praline, lightly oil a baking sheet and place the almonds on it. Melt the sugar in a non-stick pan over a very low heat until it turns dark golden brown. Pour immediately over the almonds. Set aside to cool. Crush the praline finely.

2 Preheat the oven to 160°C/325°F/Gas 3. Line three baking sheets with baking parchment.

3 Put the flour, ground almonds and butter in a bowl. Rub together. Add the egg and vanilla and work together using your hands to make a soft dough. Roll out to 5mm/¼in thick on baking parchment. Using a 5cm/2in round cookie cutter, stamp out rounds and place them on the prepared baking sheets.

4 Bake for about 15–20 minutes, until golden brown. Leave to stand for 5 minutes to firm up. Transfer to a wire rack to cool.

5 To make the filling, beat together the icing sugar, butter and vanilla until creamy. Use to sandwich the cookies in pairs. Roll the edges of each cookie in the praline until thickly coated. Dust the tops of the cookies with icing sugar.

Tiramisu Special Occasion Cookies Energy 124kcal/519kJ; Protein 2.3g; Carbohydrate 14.1g, of which sugars 11.4g; Fat 6.6g, of which saturates 4g; Cholesterol 26mg; Calcium 27mg; Fibre 0.1g; Sodium 34mg. **Party Cookies with Praline** Energy 172kcal/717kJ; Protein 2.2g; Carbohydrate 18.5g, of which sugars 12g; Fat 10.4g, of which saturates 4.7g; Cholesterol 29mg; Calcium 34mg; Fibre 0.7g; Sodium 53mg.

Summer Shortcakes

Irresistibly pretty, these delicious cookies are the perfect treat for a special summer occasion.

Makes 6
75g/3oz/¾ cup plain (all-purpose) flour
50g/2oz/4 tbsp butter, diced
25g/1oz/2 tbsp caster (superfine) sugar

grated rind of ½ orange
extra sugar, for sprinkling

For the filling
175g/6oz Greek (US strained plain) yogurt
15ml/1 tbsp icing (confectioners') sugar
250g/9oz/2¼ cups strawberries
5ml/1 tsp Cointreau (optional)
2 sprigs of fresh mint, to decorate

1 Preheat the oven to 180°C/350°F/Gas 4.

2 Place the flour and butter in a bowl, and rub the fat into the flour until the mixture resembles fine breadcrumbs. Stir in the sugar and orange rind and mix to a dough.

3 Knead the dough lightly, then roll out on a floured surface to 5mm/¼in thick. Stamp out 9cm/3½in fluted rounds with a cookie cutter.

4 Place the shapes on a baking sheet, prick with a fork and sprinkle with a little extra sugar. Bake for 10–12 minutes, until pale golden, then leave to cool on the baking sheet.

5 For the filing, blend the yogurt with the sugar. Reserve eight strawberries and process the rest in a blender, then press through a sieve (strainer).

6 Put 45ml/3 tbsp of the yogurt in a bowl and stir in the Cointreau, if using. Slice four strawberries and halve two, place on a plate and cover.

7 Spoon purée over the plates to cover completely. Put one cookie on each plate, spoon the reserved yogurt on top, then add the sliced strawberries. Top with the remaining cookies. Decorate with the yogurt mixed with Cointreau, strawberry halves and mint sprigs.

Raspberry and Rose Petal Shortcakes

Rose water-scented cream and fresh raspberries form the filling for this delectable cookie dessert.

Makes 6
115g/4oz/½ cup unsalted (sweet) butter, softened
50g/2oz/¼ cup caster (superfine) sugar
½ vanilla pod (bean), split and seeds reserved
115g/4oz/1 cup plain (all-purpose) flour, plus extra for dusting
50g/2oz/⅓ cup semolina
icing (confectioners') sugar, for dusting

For the filling
300ml/½ pint/1¼ cups double (heavy) cream
15ml/1 tbsp icing (confectioners') sugar
2.5ml/½ tsp rose water
450g/1lb/2⅔ cups raspberries

For the decoration
12 miniature roses, unsprayed
6 fresh mint sprigs
1 egg white, beaten
caster (superfine) sugar, for dusting

1 In a bowl, beat the butter, caster sugar and vanilla seeds until pale and fluffy. Sift in the flour and semolina and mix to a dough. Knead gently on a lightly dusted surface, then roll out thinly and prick with a fork. Stamp out 12 rounds with a 7.5cm/3in cookie cutter. Place on a lightly greased baking sheet and chill for 30 minutes.

2 To make the filling, whisk the cream with the sugar until soft peaks form. Fold in the rose water and chill until required.

3 Preheat the oven to 180°C/350°F/Gas 4. To make the decoration, paint the roses and leaves with the egg white. Dust with sugar, then dry on a wire rack.

4 Bake the cookies until lightly golden, about 15 minutes. Transfer to a wire rack and allow to cool.

5 Cover half the cookies with the filling, add the raspberries and top with a second cookie. Dust with icing sugar and decorate with the roses and mint.

Summer Shortcakes Energy 175kcal/734kJ; Protein 34.6g; Carbohydrate 198.1g, of which sugars 61.7g; Fat 10g, of which saturates 5.9g; Cholesterol 17.8mg; Calcium 73mg; Fibre 0.9g; Sodium 74.5mg.
Raspberry and Rose Petal Shortcakes Energy 547kcal/2273kJ; Protein 4.7g; Carbohydrate 37.1g, of which sugars 16g; Fat 43.2g, of which saturates 26.8g; Cholesterol 109mg; Calcium 81mg; Fibre 2.7g; Sodium 132mg.

Brandy Snaps with Cream

Brandy snaps were once considered a special treat for high days and holidays.

Makes about 12
50g/2oz/4 tbsp butter
50g/2oz/¼ cup caster (superfine) sugar
30ml/2 tbsp golden (light corn) syrup
50g/2oz/½ cup plain (all-purpose) flour
2.5ml/½ tsp ground ginger
5ml/1 tsp brandy
150ml/¼ pint/⅔ cup double (heavy) or whipping cream

1 Preheat the oven to 180°C/350°F/Gas 4. Line two or three baking sheets with baking parchment.

2 Gently heat the butter, sugar and golden syrup in a pan until the butter has melted and the sugar has dissolved. Remove the pan from the heat.

3 Sift the flour and ginger and stir into the butter mixture with the brandy.

4 Put small spoonfuls of the mixture on the lined baking sheets, spacing them about 10cm/4in apart to allow for spreading. Bake for 7–8 minutes, or until bubbling. Meanwhile, grease the handles of several wooden spoons.

5 Allow the cookies to cool on the baking sheet for 1 minute, then loosen with a metal spatula and quickly roll around the spoon handles. Leave to set for 1 minute, before sliding them off the handles and cooling completely on a wire rack.

6 Whip the cream until soft peaks form, spoon into a piping (pastry) bag and pipe into both ends of each brandy snap.

Cook's Tip
Store unfilled brandy snaps in an airtight container for up to 1 week. Fill with cream just before serving.

Giant Birthday Cookie

This enormous cookie is one for cookie-lovers of any age. Complete with candles and a personalized icing message, if you like, it makes the perfect centrepiece.

Makes one 28cm/11in cookie
175g/6oz/¾ cup unsalted (sweet) butter, at room temperature, diced
125g/4¼oz/⅔ cup light muscovado (brown) sugar
1 egg yolk
175g/6oz/1½ cups plain (all-purpose) flour
5ml/1 tsp bicarbonate of soda (baking soda)
finely grated rind of 1 orange or lemon
75g/3oz/scant 1 cup rolled oats

For the decoration
125g/4¼oz/generous ½ cup cream cheese
225g/8oz/2 cups icing (confectioners') sugar
5–10ml/1–2 tsp lemon juice
birthday candles
white and milk chocolate-coated raisins or peanuts
unsweetened cocoa powder, for dusting
gold or silver balls, for sprinkling

1 Preheat the oven to 190°C/375°F/Gas 5. Lightly grease a 28cm/11in metal flan tin (tart pan) and place on a large baking sheet.

2 In a bowl, beat the butter and sugar together until pale and creamy. Stir in the egg yolk. Add the flour, bicarbonate of soda, grated rind and oats and beat well.

3 Turn the mixture into the tin and flatten. Bake for 15–20 minutes, until golden. Leave to cool in the tin. Slide the cookie from the tin on to a large serving plate.

4 To decorate, beat the cream cheese in a bowl, then add the icing sugar and 5ml/1 tsp of the lemon juice. Beat until smooth and peaking, adding more juice if required.

5 Spoon the mixture into a piping (pastry) bag and pipe swirls around the edge of the cookie. Press the candles into the frosting. Sprinkle with chocolate raisins or peanuts and dust with cocoa powder. Finish by sprinkling with gold or silver balls.

Brandy Snaps with Cream Energy 121kcal/505kJ; Protein 0.6g; Carbohydrate 11.7g, of which sugars 10g; Fat 7.9g, of which saturates 5g; Cholesterol 21mg; Calcium 16mg; Fibre 0.1g; Sodium 24mg.
Giant Birthday Cookie Energy 4188kcal/17559kJ; Protein 35.3g; Carbohydrate 557.4g, of which sugars 369.4g; Fat 217.5g, of which saturates 130.2g; Cholesterol 694mg; Calcium 649mg; Fibre 10.5g; Sodium 1496mg.

Mini Party Pizzas

These cute confections look amazingly realistic and older children will love them. They're fun to make and are simply a basic cookie topped with icing, marzipan and dark cherries.

Makes 16
90g/3½oz/7 tbsp unsalted
  (sweet) butter, at room
  temperature, diced
90g/3½oz/½ cup golden caster
  (superfine) sugar
15ml/1 tbsp golden (light
  corn) syrup
175g/6oz/1½ cups self-raising
  (self-rising) flour, plus extra
  for dusting

For the topping
150g/5oz/1¼ cups icing
  (confectioners') sugar
20–25ml/4–5 tsp lemon juice
red food colouring
90g/3½oz yellow marzipan,
  grated (shredded)
8 dark glacé (candied)
  cherries, halved
a small piece of angelica,
  finely chopped

1 Preheat the oven to 180°C/350°F/Gas 4. Lightly grease two baking sheets.

2 In a bowl, beat together the butter and sugar until light and creamy. Beat in the syrup and then the flour.

3 Turn the mixture on to a lightly floured surface and cut into 16 even-size pieces. Roll each piece into a ball, then space well apart on the baking sheets, slightly flattening each one.

4 Bake for about 12 minutes, or until pale golden. Leave on the baking sheets for 3 minutes, then transfer to a wire rack to cool.

5 To make the topping, put the icing sugar in a bowl and stir in enough lemon juice to make a fairly thick, spreadable paste. Mix in enough food colouring to make the paste a deep red colour.

6 Spread the icing to within 5mm/¼ in of the edges of the cookies. Sprinkle with the shredded marzipan and place a halved cherry in the centre. Arrange a few pieces of chopped angelica on top so that the cookies resemble little cheese and tomato pizzas.

Chocolate Crispy Cookies

These little chocolate-coated cornflake cookies are always a hit with kids. They couldn't be easier to make – and are great for young aspiring cooks who want to get involved in the kitchen. The challenge is giving the cookies time to set before they're gobbled up by hungry helpers.

Makes 10
90g/3½oz milk chocolate
15ml/1 tbsp golden (light
  corn) syrup
90g/3½oz/3½ cups cornflakes
icing (confectioners') sugar,
  for dusting

1 Break the chocolate into a heatproof bowl and add the syrup. Set the bowl over a pan of gently simmering water and leave until melted, stirring frequently.

2 Put the cornflakes in a plastic bag and, using a rolling pin, lightly crush them, breaking the cornflakes into fairly small pieces.

3 Remove the bowl from the heat and tip in the cornflakes. Mix well until the cornflakes are thoroughly coated in the chocolate mixture.

4 Using paper muffin cases, put a spoonful of the chocolate mixture in the centre. Pack down firmly with the back of the spoon to make a thick cookie.

5 Continue making cookies in this way until all the mixture has been used up. Chill for 1 hour.

6 Put a little icing sugar in a small bowl. Lift each cookie from the paper and roll the edges in the icing sugar to finish.

Variation
You can also use other breakfast cereals, such as rice crispies or puffed rice. These may not need breaking up.

Mini Party Pizzas Energy 163kcal/687kJ; Protein 1.4g; Carbohydrate 28.8g, of which sugars 20.4g; Fat 5.5g, of which saturates 3g; Cholesterol 12mg; Calcium 28mg; Fibre 0.4g; Sodium 39mg.
Chocolate Crispy Cookies Energy 84kcal/355kJ; Protein 1.4g; Carbohydrate 14.2g, of which sugars 7.2g; Fat 2.8g, of which saturates 1.7g; Cholesterol 2mg; Calcium 21mg; Fibre 0.2g; Sodium 112mg.

Silly Faces

Silly faces are great fun for kids to decorate as they can experiment with different hairstyles and features.

Makes 14
115g/4oz/½ cup unsalted (sweet) butter, at room temperature, diced
115g/4oz/generous ½ cup golden caster (superfine) sugar
1 egg
115g/4oz/scant ⅓ cup golden (light corn) syrup
400g/14oz/3½ cups self-raising (self-rising) flour, plus extra for dusting

For the decoration
75g/3oz/6 tbsp unsalted (sweet) butter, at room temperature, diced
150g/5oz/1¼ cups icing (confectioners') sugar
strawberry, apple or liquorice strands
glacé (candied) cherries, halved
tubes red and black writing icing
small multi-coloured sweets (candies)

1 In a large bowl, beat together the butter and sugar until pale and creamy. Beat in the egg and golden syrup, then the flour.

2 Turn the mixture on to a lightly floured surface and knead until smooth. Wrap in clear film (plastic wrap) and chill.

3 Preheat the oven to 180°C/350°F/Gas 4. Lightly grease two baking sheets.

4 Roll out the dough on a floured surface and stamp out rounds using a 9cm/3½in cookie cutter. Transfer to the baking sheets. Bake for 10–12 minutes until turning golden around the edges. Transfer to a wire rack to cool.

5 To decorate, beat together the butter and icing sugar in a bowl until smooth and creamy. Spread a little buttercream along the top edge of each cookie, then secure the strawberry, apple or liquorice strands for hair. Use a dot of buttercream to secure a cherry for a nose. Pipe eyes and mouths using the icing, then add halved sweets, attached with buttercream, for the centres of the eyes.

Gingerbread House Cookies

For a party of young children, these gingerbread house cookies provide plenty of entertainment. You could incorporate a house decorating session as one of the party games, allowing the children to design their own house and take it home after the party.

Makes 10
115g/4oz/½ cup unsalted (sweet) butter, at room temperature, diced
115g/4oz/½ cup light muscovado (brown) sugar
1 egg
115g/4oz/scant ⅓ cup black treacle (molasses) or golden (light corn) syrup
400g/14oz/3½ cups self-raising (self-rising) flour, plus extra for dusting
5ml/1tsp ground ginger (optional)

For the decoration
1 tube white decorating icing
1 tube pastel-coloured decorating icing
selection of small multi-coloured sweets (candies), sugar flowers and silver balls

1 In a large bowl, beat together the butter and sugar until pale and creamy. Beat in the egg and treacle or syrup, then add the flour and ginger, if using. Mix together to make a thick paste.

2 Turn the mixture on to a floured surface and knead until smooth. Wrap in clear film (plastic wrap) and chill.

3 Preheat the oven to 180°C/350°F/Gas 4. Lightly grease three baking sheets. On a piece of cardboard, draw an 11 × 8cm/4½ × 3¼in rectangle. Add a triangle to the top for the roof. Cut out the shape to use as a template.

4 Roll out the dough on a lightly floured surface. Using the template, cut out the houses. Transfer to the baking sheets. Bake for 12–15 minutes, until risen and golden. Transfer the cookies to a wire rack to cool.

5 Use the icing in the tubes to pipe roof tiles, window and door frames and other decorative touches. Secure sweets and decorations to finish, cutting them into smaller pieces if necessary.

Silly Faces Energy 300kcal/1261kJ; Protein 3.2g; Carbohydrate 48g, of which sugars 26.7g; Fat 11.9g, of which saturates 7.2g; Cholesterol 43mg; Calcium 116mg; Fibre 0.9g; Sodium 213mg.
Gingerbread House Cookies Energy 275kcal/1156kJ; Protein 4.5g; Carbohydrate 43.2g, of which sugars 12.7g; Fat 10.5g, of which saturates 6.2g; Cholesterol 44mg; Calcium 67mg; Fibre 1.2g; Sodium 79mg.

Jelly Bean Cones

Chocolate-dipped cookie cones filled with jelly beans make great treats for kids of all ages. The filled cones look very pretty arranged in glasses to keep them upright. This way they can double as a tasty treat and a delightful table decoration.

Makes 10

3 egg whites
90g/3½oz/½ cup caster (superfine) sugar
25g/1oz/2 tbsp unsalted (sweet) butter, melted
40g/1½oz/⅓ cup plain (all-purpose) flour
30ml/2 tbsp single (light) cream
90g/3½oz plain (semisweet) chocolate
jelly beans or other small sweets (candies)

1 Preheat the oven to 190°C/375°F/Gas 5. Line two baking sheets with baking parchment and lightly grease them.

2 Put the egg whites and sugar in a bowl and whisk lightly until the egg whites are broken up. Add the melted butter, flour and cream and stir well to make a smooth batter.

3 Using a 15ml/1 tbsp measure, place a rounded tablespoon of the mixture on one side of a baking sheet. Spread to a 9cm/3½in round with the back of the spoon. Spoon more mixture on to the other side of the baking sheet and spread out to make another round.

4 Repeat with the cookie mixture on the second baking sheet.

5 Bake both sheets of cookies for about 8–10 minutes, until the edges are golden.

6 Peel away the paper from the baked cookies and roll them into cones. Leave to set. Continue until you have 10 cones.

7 Break the chocolate into a heatproof bowl set over a pan of simmering water and stir until melted. Dip the wide ends of the cookies in the chocolate and prop them inside narrow glasses to set, then fill with jelly beans or other sweets.

Secret Message Cookies

These fortune cookies are light and wafer-like, and what they lack in substance, they make up for in their fun capacity. These are great for older kids who can prepare birthday messages, jokes or predictions to tuck into the cookies as soon as they're baked.

Makes 18

3 egg whites
50g/2oz/½ cup icing (confectioners') sugar
40g/1½oz/3 tbsp unsalted (sweet) butter, melted
50g/2oz/½ cup plain (all-purpose) flour

1 Preheat the oven to 200°C/400°F/Gas 6. Line and lightly grease two baking sheets with baking parchment. Cut a piece of paper into 18 small strips, measuring 6 × 2cm/2½ × ¾in. Write a message on each one.

2 Lightly whisk the egg whites and icing sugar until the whites are broken up. Add the melted butter and flour and beat until smooth.

3 Using a 10ml/2 tsp measure, spoon a little of the paste on to one baking sheet and spread to a 7.5cm/3in round with the back of a spoon. Add two more spoonfuls of mixture to the baking sheet and shape in the same way.

4 Bake for 6 minutes, until the cookies are golden. Meanwhile, prepare three more cookies on the second baking sheet. Remove the first batch of cookies from the oven and replace with the second batch.

5 Working quickly, peel a hot cookie from the paper and fold it in half, tucking a message inside the fold. Rest the cookie over the rim of a glass or bowl and, very gently, fold again. (It probably won't fold over completely.) Fold the remaining two cookies in the same way.

6 Continue to bake and shape the remaining cookies in the same way, one baking sheet at a time, until all the batter and messages have been used.

Jelly Bean Cones Energy 160kcal/670kJ; Protein 1.9g; Carbohydrate 18.3g, of which sugars 15.2g; Fat 9.3g, of which saturates 5.8g; Cholesterol 18mg; Calcium 18mg; Fibre 0.4g; Sodium 66mg.
Secret Message Cookies Energy 38kcal/160kJ; Protein 0.6g; Carbohydrate 5.1g, of which sugars 3g; Fat 1.9g, of which saturates 1.2g; Cholesterol 5mg; Calcium 6mg; Fibre 0.1g; Sodium 19mg.

Cornflake Caramel Slice

A wickedly decadent caramel layer nestles between the base and the crispy cornflake topping. These cookies are simply irresistible – and fun to make too.

Makes 12
175g/6oz/³⁄4 cup butter
150g/5oz/³⁄4 cup caster (superfine) sugar
300g/10oz/2¹⁄2 cups plain (all-purpose) flour
1 egg, beaten

For the topping
30ml/2 tbsp golden (light corn) syrup
400g/14oz can sweetened condensed milk
50g/2oz/¹⁄4 cup butter
90ml/6 tbsp sour cream
about 40g/1¹⁄2oz/1¹⁄2 cups cornflakes
icing (confectioners') sugar (optional), for sprinkling

1 Preheat the oven to 190°C/375°F/Gas 5. Lightly grease and line a 28 × 18cm/11 × 7in shallow cake tin (pan) with baking parchment.

2 Put the butter in a pan and melt over a low heat, and set aside.

3 Put the sugar and flour in a bowl. Add the beaten egg and melted butter and mix well. Press the mixture evenly into the base of the prepared tin.

4 Bake for about 20 minutes, until golden brown. Leave the base to cool completely in the tin.

5 For the topping, put the syrup, condensed milk and butter in a pan over a low heat for 10–15 minutes, stirring occasionally, until the mixture is thick and turns a golden caramel colour.

6 Remove the pan from the heat and stir in the sour cream. Spread the caramel topping evenly over the base. Sprinkle over the cornflakes and leave to set. Sprinkle lightly with icing sugar, if using, and cut into bars.

Train Cookies

These cookies are so effective, especially if you let them trail across the party table. The quantity makes enough for two trains.

Makes 2 trains
150g/5oz/1¹⁄4 cups plain (all-purpose) flour
90g/3¹⁄2oz/7 tbsp unsalted (sweet) butter, chilled, diced
50g/2oz/¹⁄2 cup golden icing (confectioners') sugar
1 egg yolk
5ml/1 tsp vanilla extract

For the decoration
40g/1¹⁄2oz/3 tbsp butter, softened
75g/3oz/³⁄4 cup golden icing (confectioners') sugar
blue food colouring
large bag of liquorice allsorts

1 Put the flour and butter in a food processor. Process until the mixture resembles fine breadcrumbs. Add the sugar, egg yolk and vanilla extract and blend to a smooth dough. Wrap in clear film (plastic wrap) and chill for 30 minutes.

2 Preheat the oven to 200°C/400°F/Gas 6. Lightly grease a large baking sheet.

3 Roll out the dough and cut 7.5 × 4cm/3 × 1½ in rectangles. Cut two 3 × 2cm/1¼ × ¾ in rectangles and secure to the top of the larger rectangles for the engines (locomotives).

4 Place on the baking sheet and bake for about 10 minutes, until pale golden around the edges. Leave for 2 minutes on the baking sheet, then transfer to a wire rack to cool completely.

5 To make butter icing, put the butter and icing sugar in a bowl with a dash of blue food colouring and beat until smooth and creamy.

6 Chop plenty of the liquorice allsorts into small dice.

7 Spread a little buttercream along one long side of all the cookies except the engines and press the chopped sweets (candies) into it. Halve some square sweets and secure to the engines for windows and another piece on the front of the engine for the funnel. Secure two wheels on all the cookies.

Train Cookies Energy 174kcal/728kJ; Protein 1.8g; Carbohydrate 24.8g, of which sugars 13.3g; Fat 8.1g, of which saturates 4.9g; Cholesterol 39mg; Calcium 32mg; Fibre 0.5g; Sodium 57mg.
Cornflake Caramel Slice Energy 397kcal/1667kJ; Protein 6.5g; Carbohydrate 56.3g, of which sugars 34.6g; Fat 17.8g, of which saturates 10.8g; Cholesterol 67mg; Calcium 151mg; Fibre 0.8g; Sodium 187mg.

Gold Medals

These cookies are great for kids' parties. You can present each child with a huge cookie medal when they sit down at the table or hand them out to winners of party games. Alternatively, they make great going-home gifts when children leave.

Makes 10
50g/2oz/¼ cup unsalted (sweet) butter, at room temperature, diced

115g/4oz/generous ½ cup caster (superfine) sugar
1 egg
150g/5oz/1¼ cups self-raising (self-rising) flour
1.5ml/¼ tsp bicarbonate of soda (baking soda)

For the decoration
1 egg white
200g/7oz/1¾ cups icing (confectioners') sugar
small brightly coloured sweets (candies)

1 Preheat the oven to 180°C/350°F/Gas 4. Lightly grease two baking sheets with a little butter.

2 In a bowl, beat together the butter and sugar until smooth and creamy, then beat in the egg. Add the flour and bicarbonate of soda and mix well to combine.

3 Place large spoonfuls of the mixture on the baking sheets, spacing them well apart to allow room for spreading. Bake for about 15 minutes, or until pale golden and slightly risen.

4 Using a skewer, make quite a large hole in each cookie, 1cm/½ in from the edge. Transfer to a wire rack and leave to cool.

5 To make the icing, beat the egg white in a bowl using a wooden spoon. Gradually beat in the icing sugar to make a thick paste that just holds its shape. Spoon the icing into a piping (icing) bag and snip off the tip.

6 Write an icing message in the centre of each cookie. Secure a circle of sweets around the edge of each cookie with a little of the icing, then leave to set.

7 Thread each cookie with a piece of ribbon.

Party Bracelets

These tiny cookies are threaded on to fine ribbon along with an assortment of brightly coloured sweets that have a ready-made hole in the middle. Make the cookies a day or two in advance and thread together with the sweets on the day of the party.

Makes 22
50g/2oz/¼ cup unsalted (sweet) butter, at room temperature, diced

115g/4oz/generous ½ cup caster (superfine) sugar
5ml/1 tsp vanilla extract
pink or green food colouring
1 egg
200g/7oz/1¾ cups self-raising (self-rising) flour, plus extra for dusting

For the decoration
2 large bags of boiled sweets (hard candies) with holes in the centre
narrow pastel-coloured ribbon, for threading

1 Preheat the oven to 180°C/350°F/Gas 4. Lightly grease two baking sheets.

2 In a bowl, beat together the butter, sugar and vanilla extract until pale and creamy. Add a dash of pink or green food colouring, then beat in the egg. Add the flour and mix well to form a dough.

3 Turn the dough on to a lightly floured surface and roll out under the palms of your hands into two long, thin sausages, each about 40cm/16in long.

4 Slice each roll into 5mm/¼in rounds and space them slightly apart on the baking sheets. Chill for about 30 minutes.

5 Bake the cookies for about 8 minutes, until slightly risen and beginning to colour. Remove from the oven and, using a skewer, immediately make holes for the ribbon to be threaded through. Transfer the cookies to a wire rack to cool.

6 Thread the cookies on to 20cm/8in lengths of ribbon, alternating them with the sweets (about seven cookies on each ribbon). Tie the ends of the ribbons together in bows to finish.

Gold Medals Energy 221kcal/936kJ; Protein 2.5g; Carbohydrate 44.6g, of which sugars 33.2g; Fat 4.9g, of which saturates 2.8g; Cholesterol 30mg; Calcium 42mg; Fibre 0.5g; Sodium 46mg.
Party Bracelets Energy 72kcal/303kJ; Protein 1.2g; Carbohydrate 12.5g, of which sugars 5.6g; Fat 2.2g, of which saturates 1.3g; Cholesterol 13mg; Calcium 17mg; Fibre 0.3g; Sodium 18mg.

Peanut Butter and Jelly Cookies

These cookies are a twist on the original American peanut butter cookie and are a real hit with kids and adults alike. Give them a try – you'll love the crunchy nuts and sweet raspberry centres.

Makes 20–22

227g/8oz jar crunchy peanut butter (with no added sugar)
75g/3oz/6 tbsp unsalted (sweet) butter, at room temperature, diced
90g/3¹/₂oz/¹/₂ cup golden caster (superfine) sugar
50g/2oz/¹/₄ cup light muscovado (brown) sugar
1 large (US extra large) egg, beaten
150g/5oz/1¹/₄ cups self-raising (self-rising) flour
250g/9oz/scant 1 cup seedless raspberry jam

1 Preheat the oven to 180°C/350°F/Gas 4. Line three or four baking sheets with baking parchment.

2 Put the peanut butter and unsalted butter in a large bowl and beat together until well combined and creamy.

3 Add the caster and muscovado sugars and beat well. Add the beaten egg and blend well. Sift in the flour and mix to a stiff dough.

4 Roll the dough into 40–44 walnut-size balls between the palms of your hands (make an even number of balls). Place the balls on the prepared baking sheets, spaced well apart, and gently flatten each one with a fork to make a rough-textured cookie with a lightly ridged surface. (Don't worry if the dough cracks slightly.)

5 Bake for 10–12 minutes, or until cooked but not browned. Using a metal spatula, carefully transfer the cookies to a wire rack to cool completely.

6 Spoon a little raspberry jam on to the flat side of one cookie and top with a second. Continue to sandwich the cookies in this way.

Chocolate Birds' Nests

These delightful crispy chocolate nests make a perfect Easter teatime treat and are a real favourite with kids. They're so quick and easy to make and young children can have great fun shaping the chocolate mixture inside the paper cases and tucking the pastel-coloured eggs inside.

Makes 12

200g/7oz milk chocolate
25g/1oz/2 tbsp unsalted (sweet) butter, diced
90g/3¹/₂oz Shredded Wheat cereal
36 small pastel-coloured, sugar-coated chocolate eggs

1 Line the cups of a tartlet tray (muffin pan) with 12 decorative paper cake cases.

2 Break the milk chocolate into pieces and put in a bowl with the butter. Set the bowl over a pan of gently simmering water and stir frequently until the chocolate and butter have melted and the mixture is smooth. Remove from the heat and leave to cool for a few minutes.

3 Using your fingers, crumble the Shredded Wheat into the melted chocolate. Stir well until the cereal is completely coated in chocolate.

4 Divide the mixture among the paper cases, pressing it down gently with the back of a spoon, and make a slight indentation in the centre. Tuck three eggs into each nest and leave to set for about 2 hours.

Cook's Tip
Bags of sugar-coated chocolate eggs are widely available in supermarkets at Easter time. However, if you have trouble finding them out of season, try an old-fashioned sweet store. Often they have large jars of this type of sweet (candy), which they sell all year round. You can also buy small fluffy chicks to decorate the set nests.

Peanut Butter and Jelly Cookies Energy 169kcal/709kJ; Protein 3.4g; Carbohydrate 21g, of which sugars 15.3g; Fat 8.5g, of which saturates 3.2g; Cholesterol 18mg; Calcium 35mg; Fibre 0.8g; Sodium 89mg.
Chocolate Birds' Nests Energy 214kcal/896kJ; Protein 3.4g; Carbohydrate 24.4g, of which sugars 19g; Fat 12.1g, of which saturates 7.2g; Cholesterol 12mg; Calcium 77mg; Fibre 1g; Sodium 42mg.

Sweet Peanut Wafers

Delicate wafers filled with a sweet, peanut-flavoured buttercream make a fun, no-bake recipe that kids of any age can help with. Just remember to chill the wafer sandwiches after they have been assembled, otherwise they will be almost impossible to cut.

Makes 12
65g/2½oz/5 tbsp unsalted
   (sweet) butter, at room
   temperature, diced
65g/2½oz/generous ½ cup icing
   (confectioners') sugar
115g/4oz/½ cup crunchy
   peanut butter
12 fan-shaped wafers
50g/2oz plain
   (semisweet) chocolate

1 In a bowl beat together the butter and icing sugar until light and creamy. Beat in the peanut butter until thoroughly combined.

2 Using a metal spatula, spread a thick layer of the mixture on to a wafer and spread to the edges.

3 Place another wafer on top and press it down very gently. Spread the top wafer with more buttercream, then place another wafer on top and press down gently. Be careful not to break the wafers.

4 Use the remaining peanut buttercream and wafers to assemble three more fans in the same way. Spread any remaining buttercream around the sides of the fans. Chill in the refrigerator for at least 30 minutes until firm.

5 Using a serrated knife, carefully slice each fan into three equal wedges and arrange in a single layer on a small tray.

6 Break the chocolate into pieces and put in a heatproof bowl placed over a pan of gently simmering water. Stir frequently until melted. Remove the bowl from the heat and leave to stand for a few minutes to cool slightly.

7 Drizzle lines of chocolate over the wafers, then leave to set in a cool place for at least 1 hour.

Jammie Bodgers

These buttery cookies are an absolute classic. Sandwiched with buttercream and a generous spoonful of strawberry jam, they make a perfect snack served with a glass of milk at teatime, or are equally good in a school lunchbox as a post-sandwich treat.

Makes 20
225g/8oz/2 cups plain
   (all-purpose) flour, plus extra
   for dusting
175g/6oz/¾ cup unsalted
   (sweet) butter, chilled and diced
130g/4¼oz/⅔ cup caster
   (superfine) sugar
1 egg yolk

For the filling
50g/2oz/¼ cup unsalted
   (sweet) butter, at room
   temperature, diced
90g/3½oz/scant 1 cup icing
   (confectioners') sugar
60–75ml/4–5 tbsp strawberry
   jam

1 Put the flour and butter in a food processor and process until the mixture resembles breadcrumbs. Add the sugar and egg yolk and process until the mixture starts to form a dough.

2 Knead on a floured surface until smooth. Shape into a ball, wrap in clear film (plastic wrap) and chill for 30 minutes.

3 Preheat the oven to 180°C/350°F/Gas 4. Lightly grease two baking sheets.

4 Roll out the dough thinly on a lightly floured surface and cut out 40 rounds using a 6cm/2½in cookie cutter.

5 Place half the cookie rounds on a prepared baking sheet. Using a small heart cutter stamp out the centres of the remaining rounds. Place on the second baking sheet. Bake the cookies for about 12 minutes, until pale golden, then transfer to a wire rack and leave to cool completely.

6 To make the buttercream, beat together the butter and sugar until smooth and creamy. Spread a little buttercream on to each whole cookie. Spoon a little jam on to the buttercream, then gently press the cut-out cookies on top.

Jammie Bodgers Energy 166kcal/695kJ; Protein 1.2g; Carbohydrate 22.4g, of which sugars 13.8g; Fat 8.6g, of which saturates 5.4g; Cholesterol 22mg; Calcium 24mg; Fibre 0.4g; Sodium 65mg.
Sweet Peanut Wafers Energy 184kcal/769kJ; Protein 3.7g; Carbohydrate 19.4g, of which sugars 9.1g; Fat 10.7g, of which saturates 4.8g; Cholesterol 12mg; Calcium 30mg; Fibre 0.6g; Sodium 79mg.

Meringue Squiggles

Free from gluten, wheat and cow's milk, these wiggly wands are great for children's parties. They are fun to shape and eat and kids of all ages love making and decorating them.

Makes 14–16
2 egg whites
90g/3½oz/½ cup caster
(superfine) sugar
45ml/3 tbsp icing
(confectioners') sugar
multi-coloured sugar sprinkles,
to decorate

1 Preheat the oven to 150°C/300°F/Gas 2. Line a large baking sheet with baking parchment.

2 Put the egg whites in a large, clean bowl and whisk with a hand-held electric whisk until they form firm peaks.

3 Add a spoonful of caster sugar to the whisked egg whites and whisk for about 15 seconds to combine. Add another spoonful and whisk again. Continue in this way until all the sugar has been added.

4 Spoon the meringue mixture into a large piping (pastry) bag fitted with a large plain nozzle. Alternatively, spoon the mixture into a plastic bag, gently push it into one corner and snip off the tip so that the meringue can be pushed out in a 2cm/¾ in-thick line.

5 Pipe wavy lines of meringue, about 13cm/5in long, on to the baking sheet and bake for about 1 hour, until dry and crisp.

6 Carefully peel the meringues off the baking parchment and transfer to a wire rack to cool.

7 Put the icing sugar in a small bowl and mix in a few drops of water to make a smooth paste.

8 Using a fine pastry brush, lightly brush the tops of the meringues with a little of the sugar paste, then evenly scatter over the multi-coloured sugar sprinkles to decorate. Leave to set before serving.

Shortbread Ring Cookies

Decorated with colourful chopped sweets, these little cookies make delicious lunchbox fillers or snacks during the day.

Makes 8–10
150g/5oz/1¼ cups plain
(all-purpose) flour, plus extra
for dusting
90g/3½oz/½ cup rice flour
finely grated rind of 1 lemon
75g/3oz/6 tbsp butter

50g/2oz/¼ cup caster
(superfine) sugar
1 egg yolk
10ml/2 tsp water

For the decoration
90g/3½oz/scant 1 cup icing
(confectioners') sugar
50g/2oz/¼ cup butter
small jellied fruit sweets (candies)

1 Put the flour, rice flour, lemon rind and butter in a food processor and process briefly to combine. Add the sugar, egg yolk and water and mix to a dough.

2 Turn the dough on to a lightly floured surface and knead. Wrap in clear film (plastic wrap) and chill for about 30 minutes.

3 Preheat the oven to 180°C/350°F/Gas 4. Lightly grease a baking sheet.

4 Roll out the dough on a lightly floured surface to a thickness of about 5mm/¼in. Using a 6.5cm/2½in cookie cutter, cut out rounds and place on the baking sheet. Using a 4cm/1½in round cutter, cut out and remove the centre of each round.

5 Bake for about 20 minutes, until beginning to turn pale golden. Leave on the baking sheet for 2 minutes, then transfer to a wire rack to cool.

6 To make the topping, put the icing sugar and butter in a bowl and beat together until creamy.

7 Pipe or spoon the topping on to the ring cookies. Cut the jellied sweets into small pieces with a pair of scissors and gently press them into the cream to decorate.

Meringue Squiggles Energy 35kcal/148kJ; Protein 0.4g; Carbohydrate 8.8g, of which sugars 8.8g; Fat 0g, of which saturates 0g; Cholesterol 0mg; Calcium 5mg; Fibre 0g; Sodium 8mg.
Shortbread Ring Cookies Energy 242kcal/1008kJ; Protein 1.9g; Carbohydrate 34g, of which sugars 14.8g; Fat 10.9g, of which saturates 4.6g; Cholesterol 22mg; Calcium 16mg; Fibre 0.5g; Sodium 103mg.

Marshmallow Toasties

These soft cookie squares topped with a layer of strawberry jam and melted marshmallow make a sweet, sticky treat. When you're toasting the marshmallows, watch them very closely because once they start to colour, they brown extremely quickly.

Makes 12

130g/4¹/₂oz/generous ¹/₂ cup unsalted (sweet) butter, at room temperature, diced

75g/3oz/scant ¹/₂ cup caster (superfine) sugar
finely grated rind of 1 lemon
10ml/2 tsp vanilla extract
75g/3oz/ ³/₄ cup ground almonds
1 egg
115g/4oz/1 cup self-raising (self-rising) flour
150g/5oz/¹/₂ cup strawberry jam
200g/7oz pink and white marshmallows
icing (confectioners') sugar, for dusting

1 Preheat the oven to 180°C/350°F/Gas 4. Lightly grease the base and sides of a 23cm/9in square baking tin (pan) and line with baking parchment.

2 Put the butter, sugar and lemon rind in a bowl and beat until creamy. Beat in the vanilla extract, ground almonds and egg, then add the flour and stir well.

3 Turn the mixture into the tin and spread in an even layer. Bake for 20 minutes, until pale golden and just firm. Leave to cool in the tin for 10 minutes.

4 Spread the cookie base with jam. Using scissors, cut the marshmallows in half, then arrange them, cut sides down, in an even layer over the jam. Preheat the grill (broiler) to medium.

5 Put the tin under the grill for 2 minutes, until the marshmallows are melted. Remove from the heat and press down each marshmallow to create an even layer. Return to the grill for a minute until the surface is toasted. Leave to cool.

6 Dust lightly with icing sugar, cut into 12 bars or squares and remove from the tin.

Pink Pigs

These are what you could call rainy day cookies. They are fun to make and thoroughly absorbing when the family is stuck indoors.

Makes 10

90g/3¹/₂oz/scant 1 cup icing (confectioners') sugar, plus extra for dusting

50g/2oz/¹/₄ cup unsalted (sweet) butter, at room temperature, diced
10 rich tea (plain cookies) or digestive biscuits (graham crackers)
200g/7oz white ready-to-roll icing
pink food colouring
small, pink soft sweets (candies)
tube of black writing icing

1 To make the buttercream, put the icing sugar and butter in a bowl and beat until smooth, pale and creamy.

2 Spread the rich tea or digestive biscuits almost to the edges with the buttercream.

3 Reserve 25g/1oz of the white ready-to-roll icing. Add a few drops of pink food colouring to the remainder. Knead on a surface that has been lightly dusted with icing sugar until the pink colouring is evenly distributed. Reserve about 25g/1oz of the pink icing. Roll out the remaining pink icing thinly.

4 Using a cookie cutter that is just slightly smaller than the rich tea or digestive biscuits, cut out rounds of pink icing. Place a round over each and press it down on to the buttercream.

5 Halve five of the pink sweets. Make two small holes in each one with a wooden skewer to make a nose. Using buttercream, attach a halved sweet to the centre of each cookie.

6 Using the black writing icing, pipe two dots of icing above the nose to resemble eyes, then pipe a small, curved mouth.

7 Thinly roll out the reserved pink icing and the reserved white icing. Dampen the white icing with a little water and press the pink icing gently on top. Cut out triangles for ears. Dampen one edge of the ears with water and secure, pink side up, to the cookies. Gently curl the ears out at the ends.

Marshmallow Toasties Energy 269kcal/1131kJ; Protein 3.6g; Carbohydrate 37g, of which sugars 26.4g; Fat 13g, of which saturates 6.1g; Cholesterol 39mg; Calcium 38mg; Fibre 0.8g; Sodium 82mg.
Pink Pigs Energy 188kcal/794kJ; Protein 1g; Carbohydrate 33g, of which sugars 25.8g; Fat 6.8g, of which saturates 3.8g; Cholesterol 16mg; Calcium 25mg; Fibre 0.3g; Sodium 110mg.

Chocolate Cookies on Sticks

Let your imagination run riot when decorating these fun chocolate cookies. Use plenty of brightly coloured sweets or create a real chocolate feast by only using chocolate decorations. Whichever you choose, these cookies are very sweet so should be kept as a real treat for extra special occasions.

Makes 12
125g/4¼oz milk chocolate
75g/3oz white chocolate
50g/2oz chocolate-coated
   digestive biscuits (graham
   crackers, crumbled
   into chunks
a selection of small
   coloured sweets (candies),
   chocolate chips or chocolate-
   coated raisins
12 wooden ice lolly (popsicle)
   sticks

1 Break the milk and white chocolate into pieces and put in separate heatproof bowls. Place each bowl in turn over a pan of simmering water and heat, stirring frequently, until melted.

2 Meanwhile, draw six 7cm/2¾in rounds on baking parchment and six 9 × 7cm/3½ × 2¾in rectangles. Invert the parchment on to a large tray.

3 Spoon the milk chocolate into the outlines on the paper, reserving one or two spoonfuls of chocolate. Using the back of a spoon, carefully spread the chocolate to the edges to make neat shapes.

4 Press the end of a wooden ice lolly stick into each of the shapes, and spoon over a little more melted milk chocolate to cover the stick. Sprinkle the chocolate shapes with the crumbled cookies.

5 Pipe or drizzle the cookies with the melted white chocolate, then sprinkle the cookies with the coloured sweets, chocolate chips or chocolate-coated raisins, pressing them gently to make sure they stick.

6 Chill for about 1 hour until set, then carefully peel away the baking parchment.

Chocolate Wands

Shaping these long, wafery chocolate cookies is fun, but you need to work quickly. Only bake two cookies at a time; any more and they will become brittle before you have time to shape them into wands.

Makes 10–12
3 egg whites
90g/3½oz/½ cup caster
   (superfine) sugar
25g/1oz/2 tbsp unsalted (sweet)
   butter, melted
30ml/2 tbsp plain
   (all-purpose) flour
15ml/1 tbsp unsweetened
   cocoa powder
30ml/2 tbsp single (light) cream
90g/3½oz milk chocolate and
   multi-coloured sprinkles,
   to decorate

1 Preheat the oven to 180°C/350°F/Gas 4. Line two large baking sheets with baking parchment and grease the paper well.

2 In a bowl, briefly beat together the egg whites and sugar until the whites are broken up. Add the melted butter, flour, cocoa powder and cream to the egg whites and beat with a wooden spoon until smooth.

3 Place 2 teaspoons of the mixture to one side of a baking sheet and spread the mixture into an oval, about 15cm/6in long. Spoon more mixture on to the other side of the baking sheet and shape in the same way. Bake for 7–8 minutes, until the edges begin to darken.

4 After 30 seconds lift one off the paper and wrap it around a wooden spoon handle. As soon as it holds its shape ease it off the spoon and shape the second cookie in the same way.

5 Prepare more cookies on the second baking sheet. Repeat until all the mixture has been used up.

6 Melt the chocolate in a heatproof bowl set over a pan of gently simmering water. Dip the ends of the cookies in the chocolate, then in coloured sprinkles and place on a sheet of baking parchment. Leave for about 1 hour, until set.

Chocolate Cookies on Sticks Energy 107kcal/448kJ; Protein 1.5g; Carbohydrate 12.3g, of which sugars 10.9g; Fat 6.1g, of which saturates 3.5g; Cholesterol 2mg; Calcium 43mg; Fibre 0.2g; Sodium 30mg.
Chocolate Wands Energy 103kcal/432kJ; Protein 1.6g; Carbohydrate 14.3g, of which sugars 12.2g; Fat 4.8g, of which saturates 2.9g; Cholesterol 8mg; Calcium 28mg; Fibre 0.3g; Sodium 41mg.

Flake "99s"

You don't need a special cutter to make these party cookies. They're shaped using an ordinary round cutter to which you add a V-shaped cone when cutting them out.

Makes 15

150g/5oz/1¼ cups self-raising (self-rising) flour, plus extra for dusting
90g/3½oz/7 tbsp unsalted (sweet) butter, diced
50g/2oz/¼ cup light muscovado (brown) sugar
1 egg yolk
5ml/1 tsp vanilla extract

For the decoration

75g/3oz/6 tbsp unsalted (sweet) butter, softened
5ml/1 tsp vanilla extract
115g/4oz/1 cup icing (confectioners') sugar
2 chocolate flakes

1 Put the flour and butter in a food processor and process until the mixture resembles fine breadcrumbs. Add the sugar, egg yolk and vanilla and blend to a smooth dough. Wrap in clear film (plastic wrap) and chill for 30 minutes.

2 Preheat the oven to 200°C/400°F/Gas 6. Grease a large baking sheet.

3 Roll the dough out thinly on a floured surface. Stamp out 5cm/2in rounds using a cookie cutter. Trim two sides off to make cornets. Repeat to use up the dough. Using a sharp knife, make a pattern on each cookie.

4 Bake for 8–10 minutes until pale golden. Leave for 2 minutes, then transfer to a wire rack to cool.

5 For the buttercream, beat together the butter, vanilla and icing sugar until smooth. Add 5ml/1 tsp hot water and beat again until the mixture is light and airy. Place in a piping (pastry) bag fitted with a large plain nozzle. Pipe swirls on to the tops of the cookies so that they look like swirls of ice cream. Cut the chocolate flakes across into 5cm/2in lengths. Carefully cut each piece lengthways into four small lengths. Push a flake piece into each cookie.

Name Cookies

You could decorate these cookies for children coming to a birthday party. It can be a fun idea to prop a name cookie up against the glass at each place setting around the tea table and let the children find their own seats.

Makes 20

200g/7oz/scant 1 cup unsalted (sweet) butter, chilled and diced
finely grated rind of 1 orange
300g/10oz/2½ cups plain (all-purpose) flour, plus extra for dusting
90g/3½oz/scant 1 cup icing (confectioners') sugar
2 egg yolks

For the decoration

1 egg white
200g/7oz/1¾ cups icing (confectioners') sugar
2 different food colourings
silver balls

1 Put the butter, orange rind and flour in a food processor and process until the mixture resembles fine breadcrumbs. Add the icing sugar and egg yolks and blend until smooth. Wrap in clear film (plastic wrap) and chill for 30 minutes.

2 Preheat the oven to 200°C/400°F/Gas 6. Lightly grease two baking sheets.

3 Roll out the dough on a floured surface and stamp out cookies in a variety of shapes at least 7.5cm/3in across. Transfer to the baking sheets, spacing them slightly apart, and bake for 10–12 minutes, until pale golden around the edges.

4 Leave the cookies on the baking sheet for about 2 minutes to firm up, then transfer to a wire rack to cool completely.

5 To make the icing, put the egg white and icing sugar in a bowl and beat together until smooth and the icing just holds its shape. Divide the icing into two, then mix a few drops of food colouring into each to make two different colours.

6 Spoon the two different icings into piping (icing) bags fitted with a writing nozzle. Write the names of party guests on the cookies. Decorate as desired with icing and silver balls.

Flake "99s" Energy 198kcal/828kJ; Protein 1.8g; Carbohydrate 23.1g, of which sugars 15.5g; Fat 11.6g, of which saturates 7.1g; Cholesterol 38mg; Calcium 38mg; Fibre 0.4g; Sodium 74mg.
Name Cookies Energy 189kcal/795kJ; Protein 2g; Carbohydrate 26.9g, of which sugars 15.4g; Fat 9g, of which saturates 5.4g; Cholesterol 41mg; Calcium 33mg; Fibre 0.5g; Sodium 66mg.

Butter Gems

These tiny shortbread-based cookies are topped with rosettes of soft buttercream and a pretty sprinkling of brightly coloured sugar. They make a great treat for even the smallest of mouths.

Makes about 40
115g/4oz/1/2 cup unsalted (sweet) butter, at room temperature, diced
50g/2oz/1/4 cup caster (superfine) sugar
175g/6oz/1 1/2 cups plain (all-purpose) flour, plus extra for dusting

For the decoration
50g/2oz/4 tbsp unsalted (sweet) butter, at room temperature, diced
5ml/1 tsp vanilla extract
90g/3 1/2 oz/scant 1 cup icing (confectioners') sugar
25g/1oz/2 tbsp sugar
green, lilac or pink food colourings

1 Put the diced butter and the sugar in a large bowl and beat together until smooth and creamy. Add the flour to the creamed butter and mix well to form a thick paste.

2 Turn the dough on to a lightly floured surface and knead until smooth. Wrap the dough in clear film (plastic wrap) and chill for at least 30 minutes.

3 Preheat the oven to 180°C/350°F/Gas 4. Lightly grease two baking sheets.

4 Roll out the dough on a lightly floured surface and cut out rounds using a 3.5cm/1 1/4 in cookie cutter. Space slightly apart on the baking sheets and bake for 10 minutes, or until pale golden. Transfer to a wire rack to cool completely.

5 To decorate the cookies, beat the butter with the vanilla extract and icing sugar until smooth and creamy. Spoon the buttercream into a piping (pastry) bag fitted with a star-shaped nozzle, then pipe a rosette on to each cookie.

6 Put the sugar into a small bowl and add several drops of the food colouring. Mix the colouring into the sugar. Sprinkle a little of the sugar over the cookies.

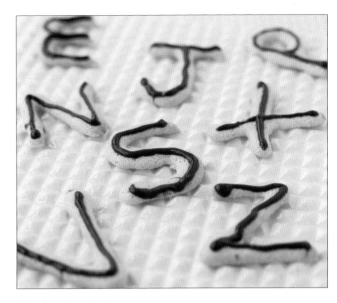

Alphabetinis

These funny little letters are great for kids – and might even be a good way to encourage them to practise their spelling. They are great fun to make and even better to eat.

Makes about 30
2 egg whites
15ml/1 tbsp cornflour (cornstarch)
50g/2oz/1/2 cup plain (all-purpose) flour
150g/5oz/3/4 cup caster (superfine) sugar
10ml/2 tsp vanilla extract
90g/3 1/2 oz milk chocolate

1 Preheat the oven to 180°C/350°F/Gas 4. Line two large baking sheets with baking parchment.

2 In a clean glass bowl, whisk the egg whites until they form soft peaks when the whisk is lifted. Sift the cornflour and plain flour over the egg whites. Add the sugar and vanilla extract. Fold in using a large metal spoon.

3 Spoon half the mixture into a plastic bag and gently squeeze it into a corner of the bag. Snip off the corner so that the cookie mixture can be squeezed out in a 1cm/1/2 in-wide line.

4 Pipe letters on to one of the lined baking sheets, making each letter about 6cm/2 1/2 in tall. Repeat with the remaining cookie mixture.

5 Bake the cookies for 12 minutes, or until crisp and golden. Transfer to a wire rack to cool.

6 Melt the chocolate in a heatproof bowl set over a pan of simmering water.

7 Spoon the melted chocolate into a small paper piping (icing) bag fitted with a plain nozzle (or use a smaller plastic bag and snip off the merest tip).

8 Pipe the chocolate in lines over the cookies to highlight the shape of each letter. Leave to set for at least 1 hour.

Butter Gems Energy 57kcal/238kJ; Protein 0.5g; Carbohydrate 6.4g, of which sugars 3.1g; Fat 3.4g, of which saturates 2.2g; Cholesterol 9mg; Calcium 8mg; Fibre 0.1g; Sodium 25mg.
Alphabetinis Energy 42kcal/178kJ; Protein 0.5g; Carbohydrate 8.5g, of which sugars 6.9g; Fat 0.9g, of which saturates 0.6g; Cholesterol 1mg; Calcium 10mg; Fibre 0g; Sodium 8mg.

Flower Power Cookies

Look for little piped sugar flower decorations in the supermarket. Some are pretty pale colours, while others are much brighter and more vibrant.

Makes 28

225g/8oz/2 cups plain (all-purpose) flour, plus extra for dusting
175g/6oz/³⁄₄ cup unsalted (sweet) butter, chilled and diced
finely grated rind of 1 orange
130g/4¼ oz/generous ½ cup light muscovado (brown) sugar
1 egg yolk

For the decoration

30ml/2 tbsp orange juice
200g/7oz/1³⁄₄ cups icing (confectioners') sugar
green, yellow and orange food colourings
multi-coloured sugared flowers

1 Put the flour, butter and orange rind into a food processor. Process until the mixture resembles fine breadcrumbs. Add the sugar and egg yolk and process until the mixture binds together.

2 Turn the mixture out on to a lightly floured surface and knead until it forms a dough. Shape the dough into a ball, wrap tightly in clear film (plastic wrap) and chill for 30 minutes.

3 Preheat the oven to 180°C/350°F/Gas 4. Lightly grease two or three baking sheets.

4 Roll out the dough thinly on a floured surface and cut out rounds using a cookie cutter about 6cm/2½in in diameter.

5 Transfer the cookies to the baking sheets, spacing them slightly apart. Bake for 12–15 minutes, until pale golden, then transfer to a wire rack to cool completely.

6 For the icing, put the orange juice in a bowl and gradually stir in the icing sugar until the mixture has the consistency of thick pouring cream. Make the icing different colours.

7 Spoon a little icing on to the cookies, spreading it to within 1cm/½in of the cookie edges. Top each one with a sugared flower. Leave to set for about 1 hour.

Dolly Cookies

These pretty cookies look like they belong at a doll's tea party. The cookies are made by simply chilling a roll of dough, then slicing off pieces on to a baking sheet. Baking doesn't get much easier than this.

Makes 14

115g/4oz/½ cup unsalted (sweet) butter, at room temperature, diced
50g/2oz/¼ cup caster (superfine) sugar
pink food colouring
5ml/1 tsp vanilla extract
175g/6oz/1½ cups plain (all-purpose) flour, plus extra for dusting
90g/3½oz white chocolate
75g/3oz multi-coloured sweets (candies)

1 Put the butter and sugar in a bowl with a dash of pink food colouring and the vanilla extract. Beat together until smooth and creamy.

2 Add the flour to the butter and sugar mixture and stir well until thoroughly combined. Turn the dough out on to a lightly floured surface and knead until smooth.

3 Using your hands, roll the dough into a thick sausage, about 12cm/4½ in long and 5cm/2in in diameter. Wrap the dough in clear film (plastic wrap) and chill for at least 30 minutes.

4 Preheat the oven to 180°C/350°F/Gas 4. Lightly grease two baking sheets.

5 Cut the dough into 5mm/¼in slices and space them slightly apart on the baking sheets. Bake for 15–18 minutes, or until the cookies begin to colour. Transfer to a wire rack to cool completely.

6 Break up the chocolate and melt it in a heatproof bowl set over a pan of gently simmering water. Using a sharp knife, cut the sweets in half.

7 Using a knife swirl a little chocolate on to each cookie and decorate with a ring of sweets. Leave to set.

Flower Power Cookies Energy 123kcal/516kJ; Protein 1g; Carbohydrate 18.7g, of which sugars 12.5g; Fat 5.4g, of which saturates 3.3g; Cholesterol 21mg; Calcium 20mg; Fibre 0.3g; Sodium 39mg.
Dolly Cookies Energy 169kcal/709kJ; Protein 1.8g; Carbohydrate 21.9g, of which sugars 12.4g; Fat 8.9g, of which saturates 5.5g; Cholesterol 18mg; Calcium 39mg; Fibre 0.4g; Sodium 59mg.

Puppy Faces

These little pups are so appealing it seems a shame to eat them. Fortunately, they taste great.

Makes 10
100g/3½oz/scant 1 cup plain
  (all-purpose) flour, plus extra
  for dusting
50g/2oz/½ cup rolled oats
2.5ml/½ tsp mixed spice (apple
  pie spice)
50g/2oz/¼ cup unsalted (sweet)
  butter, chilled and diced

100g/3½oz/½ cup caster
  (superfine) sugar
1 egg yolk

For the decoration
60ml/4 tbsp apricot jam
250g/9oz white ready-to-roll icing
10 round coloured
  sweets (candies)
black and red writing icing tubes
icing (confectioners') sugar,
  for dusting

1 Put the flour, oats and spice in a bowl. Rub in the butter until the mixture resemble breadcrumbs. Stir in the sugar, egg yolk and 5ml/1 tsp water until the mixture forms a ball.

2 Turn the dough out on to a lightly floured surface and knead until smooth. Wrap and chill for 30 minutes.

3 Preheat the oven to 200°C/400°F/Gas 6. Lightly grease a large baking sheet.

4 Roll out the dough on a floured surface and cut out rounds using a 6cm/2½in cutter. Bake for 12 minutes. Leave to cool.

5 Brush the cookies with jam. Roll out half of the icing. Stamp out 10 rounds with a 6cm/2½in cutter and place on the cookies. Halve the sweets, brush the icing with water and press on the sweets for eyes.

6 Use the writing tubes to pipe the noses and mouths, finishing with little red tongues.

7 To make the ears, divide the remaining icing into 20 pieces. Roll each piece into a ball and flatten at one end to make a flat pear shape. Brush the icing with water and secure the ears.

Gingerbread Family

You can have great fun with these cookies by creating characters with different features. By using an assortment of different gingerbread cutters you can make a gingerbread family.

Makes about 12
350g/12oz/3 cups plain
  (all-purpose) flour, plus extra
  for dusting
5ml/1 tsp bicarbonate of soda
  (baking soda)

5ml/1 tsp ground ginger
115g/4oz/½ cup unsalted
  (sweet) butter, chilled and diced
175g/6oz/¾ cup light muscovado
  (brown) sugar
1 egg
30ml/2 tbsp black treacle
  (molasses) or golden (light
  corn) syrup
50g/2oz each plain (semisweet),
  milk and white chocolate,
  to decorate

1 Preheat the oven to 180°C/350°F/Gas 4. Lightly grease two large baking sheets.

2 Put the flour, bicarbonate of soda, ginger and diced butter into the food processor. Process until the mixture begins to resemble fine breadcrumbs.

3 Add the sugar, egg and black treacle or golden syrup to the food processor and process the mixture until it begins to form into a ball.

4 Turn the dough out on to a lightly floured surface and knead until smooth and pliable. Roll out the dough on a lightly floured surface. Cut out figures using people-shaped cutters, then transfer to the baking sheets.

5 Bake for 15 minutes until slightly risen and starting to colour around the edges. Leave for 5 minutes, then transfer to a wire rack to cool.

6 To decorate the cookies, melt each type of chocolate in a separate bowl set over a pan of simmering water. Spoon the melted chocolate into piping (pastry) bags fitted with a plain tip, then pipe faces and clothes on to the cookies. Leave to set.

Tree Cookies

These cookies look really effective with their chocolate cookie "trunks" and brightly coloured "fruits". Arrange the cookies in a line on the tea table.

Makes 10
50g/2oz/¼ cup unsalted (sweet) butter, at room temperature, diced
115g/4oz/½ cup light muscovado (brown) sugar
1 egg
150g/5oz/1¼ cups self-raising (self-rising) flour
2.5ml/½ tsp bicarbonate of soda (baking soda)
finely grated rind of 1 lemon

For the decoration
50g/2oz/½ cup icing (confectioners') sugar
10ml/2 tsp lemon juice
10 milk chocolate fingers
brightly coloured sweets (candies), such as M&Ms

1 Preheat the oven to 180°C/350°F/Gas 4. Lightly grease two baking sheets.

2 In a large bowl, beat together the butter and sugar until smooth and creamy. Beat in the egg. Add the flour, bicarbonate of soda and lemon rind and mix until smooth.

3 Place 5 large spoonfuls of the mixture on to each baking sheet, spacing them well apart. Bake for 15 minutes, until the cookies have risen. Leave on the baking sheet for 5 minutes to firm up, then transfer to a wire rack to cool.

4 To decorate the cookies, mix together the icing sugar and lemon juice to make a thick paste. Use a little paste to secure one end of a chocolate finger to each cookie.

5 Attach the coloured sweets in the same way, securing each one with a little paste. Leave the cookies to set for 1 hour.

Variation
To create pretty blossoming trees, attach pastel-coloured sugar flowers to the cookies instead of coloured sweets (candies).

Marshmallow Crispie Cakes

Easy to make and guaranteed to be demolished in no time at all, these little cakes can easily be made by very young children, who like to help in the kitchen.

Makes 45
250g/9oz bag of toffees
50g/2oz/4 tbsp butter
45ml/3 tbsp milk
115g/4oz/1 cup marshmallows
175g/6oz/6 cups crisped rice cereal

1 Lightly grease a 20 x 33cm/8 x 13in roasting tin.

2 Put the toffees, butter and milk in a pan and heat gently, stirring until the toffees have melted.

3 Add the marshmallows and cereal and stir until well mixed and the marshmallows have melted.

4 Spoon the mixture into the prepared tin, level the surface and leave to set. When cool and hard, cut into squares, remove from the tin and put into paper cases to serve.

Fruit and Nut Clusters

This fun, no-cook recipe will be loved by children and adults alike.

Makes 24
225g/8oz white chocolate
50g/2oz/⅓ cup sunflower seeds
50g/2oz/⅓ cup almond slivers
50g/2oz/⅓ cup sesame seeds
50g/2oz/⅓ cup seedless raisins
5ml/1 tsp ground cinnamon

1 Break the white chocolate into small pieces. Put the chocolate into a heatproof bowl set over a pan of gently simmering water and melt. Remove from the heat.

2 Mix the sunflower seeds, almond slivers, sesame seeds, raisins and ground cinnamon into the chocolate and stir well. Using a teaspoon, spoon the mixture into paper cases and leave to set.

Tree Cookies Energy 162kcal/681kJ; Protein 1.3g; Carbohydrate 24g, of which sugars 21.6g; Fat 7.2g, of which saturates 2.8g; Cholesterol 30mg; Calcium 24mg; Fibre 0.2g; Sodium 54mg.
Marshmallow Crispie Cakes Energy 56kcal/235kJ; Protein 0.7g; Carbohydrate 9g, of which sugars 4.4g; Fat 2.2g, of which saturates 1.1g; Cholesterol 3mg; Calcium 39mg; Fibre 0g; Sodium 28mg.
Fruit and Nut Clusters Energy 93kcal/386kJ; Protein 2g; Carbohydrate 7.5g, of which sugars 7g; Fat 6.3g, of which saturates 2.1g; Cholesterol 0mg; Calcium 48mg; Fibre 0.5g; Sodium 12mg.

Traditional Sugar Cookies

Sweet and sugary, these delightful cookies can be decorated with different colours of sugar to make a pretty party spread.

Makes 36
12oz/350g/ cups plain
  (all-purpose) flour, plus extra
  for dusting
5ml/1 tsp bicarbonate of soda
  (baking soda)
10ml/2 tsp baking powder
pinch of grated nutmeg

115g/4oz/cups butter, softened
225g/8oz/ cups caster (superfine)
  sugar
2.5ml/½ tsp vanilla extract
1 egg
125ml/4fl oz milk
coloured or demerara sugar,
  for sprinkling

1 Sift the flour, bicarbonate of soda, baking powder and nutmeg into a bowl. Set aside.

2 In a bowl beat together the butter, caster sugar and vanilla extract until the mixture is light and fluffy. Add the egg and beat well to mix.

3 Add the flour to the butter and sugar mixture in batches, beating well after each addition, and alternating the flour with the milk. Stir to make a soft dough. Wrap the dough in cling film (plastic wrap) and chill in the refrigerator for at least 30 minutes, or overnight.

4 Preheat the oven to 350°F/180°C/Gas 4.

5 Roll out the dough on a lightly floured surface to a thickness of 3mm/⅛in. Stamp out rounds using a cookie cutter. Gather together the trimmings and roll and stamp out cookies until the dough has been used up.

6 Transfer the cookies to ungreased baking sheets. Sprinkle each with sugar. Bake for 10–12 minutes, until golden brown. With a metal spatula transfer the cookies to a wire rack and leave to cool completely.

Pink Sugared Hearts

Pretty and pink, these delightful cookies are always a hit. Rolling the edges in coloured sugar to accentuate their shape really adds to the decoration.

Makes 32
225g/8oz/2 cups plain
  (all-purpose) flour, plus extra
  for dusting
175g/6oz/¾ cup unsalted
  (sweet) butter, chilled and diced

130g/4¼oz/⅔ cup caster
  (superfine) sugar
1 egg yolk

For the decoration
50g/2oz/¼ cup sugar
pink food colouring
225g/8oz/2 cups icing
  (confectioners') sugar
30–45ml/2–3 tbsp lemon juice

1 Preheat the oven to 180°C/350°F/Gas 4. Lightly grease two baking sheets.

2 Put the flour and butter into a food processor, then process until the mixture resembles breadcrumbs. Add the sugar and egg yolk and process until the mixture begins to form a ball.

3 Turn the dough out on to a lightly floured surface and knead until smooth. Shape the dough into a ball, wrap in clear film (plastic wrap) and chill for at least 30 minutes.

4 Working in batches, roll out the dough thinly on a lightly floured surface and cut out heart shapes using a cookie cutter. Transfer to the baking sheets, spacing them slightly apart. Bake for 10 minutes, or until pale golden. Transfer to a wire rack to cool.

5 To decorate, put the sugar in a bowl and add a dot of pink food colouring. Mix until the sugar is pink.

6 Put the icing sugar in a separate bowl and add 30ml/2 tbsp of the lemon juice, stirring until smooth. Spread a little icing on to each cookie to within 5mm/¼in of the edge.

7 Turn each iced cookie on its side and gently roll in the coloured sugar. Leave to set for 1 hour.

Traditional Sugar Cookies Energy 85kcal/359kJ; Protein 1.2g; Carbohydrate 14.3g, of which sugars 6.9g; Fat 3g, of which saturates 1.8g; Cholesterol 12mg; Calcium 22mg; Fibre 0.3g; Sodium 23mg.
Pink Sugared Hearts Energy 265kcal/1126kJ; Protein 1g; Carbohydrate 58.2g, of which sugars 52.9g; Fat 4.8g, of which saturates 2.9g; Cholesterol 18mg; Calcium 38mg; Fibre 0.2g; Sodium 37mg.

Fruity Muesli Bars

These fruity muesli bars make an appetizing treat for a takeaway snack

Makes 10–12
115g/4oz/½ cup butter
75g/3oz/⅓ cup soft light brown sugar
45ml/3 tbsp golden (light corn) syrup

150g/5oz1¼ cups Swiss-style muesli (granola)
150g/2oz/½ cup rolled oats
5ml/1 tsp ground mixed spice (apple pie spice)
50g/2oz/⅓ cup sultanas (golden raisins)
50g/2oz/½ cup chopped ready-to-eat dried pears

1 Preheat the oven to 180°C/350°F/Gas 4. Lightly grease an 18cm/7in square cake tin (pan).

2 Put the butter, sugar and syrup in a pan and heat gently until melted, stirring.

3 Remove the pan from the heat and add the muesli, rolled oats, spice, sultanas and dried pears. Mix well with a wooden spoon until thoroughly combined.

4 Transfer the mixture to the prepared tin and level the surface, pressing down.

5 Bake for 20–30 minutes, until golden brown. Cool slightly into the tin, then mark into bars using a sharp knife.

6 When firm, remove the muesli bars from the tin and cool on a wire rack.

> **Variations**
> • A combination of rolled oats and oatmeal can be used instead of muesli (granola) for a delicious change.
> • Try using different dried fruits instead of sultanas (golden raisins) and pears —papaya and mango for a tropical taste, cranberries and apple for a hint of autumn (fall) or apricots and dates for a Middle Eastern flavour.

Jewelled Shortbread Fingers

These shortbread fingers are made using a classic, buttery shortbread base, drizzled with icing and decorated with sparkling, crushed sweets and glistening gold or silver balls.

Makes 14
90g/3½oz/7 tbsp unsalted (sweet) butter, diced
175g/6oz/1½ cups plain (all-purpose) flour

50g/2oz/¼ cup caster (superfine) sugar

To decorate
150g/5oz/1¼ cups icing (confectioners') sugar
10–15ml/2–3 tsp lemon juice
coloured boiled sweets (hard candies)
gold or silver balls

1 Preheat the oven to 160°C/325°F/Gas 3. Lightly grease an 18cm/7in square shallow baking tin (pan).

2 Put the butter and flour in a food processor and process until the mixture resembles breadcrumbs. Add the sugar and process until the ingredients form a dough.

3 Put the dough in the baking tin and press down in an even layer. Bake for 35 minutes, or until just beginning to colour. Leave to cool in the tin.

4 To make the topping, put the icing sugar in a bowl, add lemon juice to make a thick paste that just holds its shape.

5 Tap the boiled sweets (in their wrappers) with a rolling pin to break them up. Unwrap the sweets and put in a bowl.

6 Turn out the shortbread base on to a board. Cut in half, then across into fingers. Drizzle with the icing, then sprinkle with the sweets and gold or silver balls. Leave to set.

> **Cook's Tip**
> Use a serrated knife and a sawing action to cut the shortbread.

Jewelled Shortbread Fingers Energy 147kcal/618kJ; Protein 1.3g; Carbohydrate 24.7g, of which sugars 15.2g; Fat 5.5g, of which saturates 3.4g; Cholesterol 14mg; Calcium 26mg; Fibre 0.4g; Sodium 40mg.
Fruity Muesli Bars Energy 221kcal/927kJ; Protein 3.2g; Carbohydrate 32.1g, of which sugars 17.2g; Fat 9.8g, of which saturates 5.1g; Cholesterol 20mg; Calcium 32mg; Fibre 2g; Sodium 122mg.

Oaty Muesli Slices

Oaty muesli is an excellent anti-ageing food, so it makes a great ingredient in these chewy slices. As well as adding flavour, the dried apricots and apples provide an extra boost of the valuable antioxidant vitamin E.

Makes 8
75g/3oz/¹/₃ cup ready-to-eat
   dried apricots, chopped
1 eating apple, cored and grated
150g/5oz/1¹/₄ cups Swiss-style
   muesli (granola)
150ml/¹/₄ pint/²/₃ cup apple juice
15g/¹/₂ oz/1 tbsp soft butter

1 Preheat the oven to 190°C/375°F/Gas 5.

2 Place all the ingredients together in a large bowl and mix well with a wooden spoon until combined.

3 Press the mixture into a 20cm/8in non-stick sandwich tin (layer cake pan) with the back of a wooden spoon and bake for 35–40 minutes, until lightly browned and firm.

4 Using a sharp knife, mark the fruit muesli slice into eight equal-size wedges while it is still hot. Leave to cool in the tin.

Wholewheat Seed Slices

This wholewheat slice contains ingredients that are rich in nutrients, making it a healthy snack to eat.

Makes 7 slices
115g/4oz/1 cup soya flour
115g/4oz/1 cup wholemeal
   (whole-wheat) flour
115g/4oz/generous 1 cup
   rolled oats
5cm/2in preserved stem
   ginger, chopped
25g/1oz/2 tbsp sesame seeds
25g/1oz/¹/₄ cup pumpkin seeds

75g/3oz/scant 1 cup rolled oats
2.5ml/¹/₂ tsp ground ginger
2.5ml/¹/₂ tsp nutmeg
2.5ml/¹/₂ tsp cinnamon
200g/7oz/1¹/₂ cups raisins
115g/4oz linseeds
50g/2oz sunflower seeds
50g/2oz sliced almonds
300ml/¹/₂ pint soya milk
15ml/1 tbsp malt extract

1 Sift the flours into a large bowl. Tip in any bran left in the sieve (strainer).

2 Add all the dry ingredients, seeds and spices to the flour, and mix well to combine thoroughly. Slowly add the milk and malt extract, stirring well after each addition.

3 Cover the bowl for one hour, leaving the dry ingredients to soak.

4 Preheat the oven to 190°C/370°F/Gas 5. Lightly grease and line a 1lb/500g loaf tin.

5 Spoon the soaked ingredients into the cake tin and bake for up to 1 hour 15 minutes, or until golden. Leave to cool, then remove from the tin and serve cut into bars. Store in an airtight container for up to 7 days.

Sultana and Cinnamon Chewy Bars

These spicy, chewy bars are hard to resist and make a great treat, especially for children and teenagers.

Makes 16
115g/4oz/¹/₂ cup butter
25g/1oz/2 tbsp light soft
   brown sugar

25g/1oz plain toffees
50g/2oz/¹/₄ cup clear honey
175g/6oz/generous 1 cup
   sultanas (golden raisins)
10ml/2 tsp ground cinnamon
175g/6oz/6 cups crisped
   rice cereal

1 Lightly grease a shallow rectangular 23 × 28cm/9 × 11in cake tin (pan).

2 Place the butter, sugar, toffees and honey in a pan and heat gently until melted, stirring. Bring to the boil, then remove the pan from the heat.

3 Stir in the sultanas, cinnamon and crisped rice cereal and mix well. Transfer the mixture to the prepared tin and spread the mixture evenly, pressing it down firmly.

4 Leave to cool, then chill until firm. Once firm, cut into bars, remove from the tin and serve. Store the bars in an airtight container in the refrigerator.

Cook's Tip
Take care when melting the butter, sugar, toffees and honey and stir constantly to prevent the mixture from catching.

Variation
For an extra-special treat, melt 75g/3oz plain (semisweet) or milk chocolate in a heatproof bowl over a pan of gently simmering water, then spread it over the cold crisped rice cereal mixture. Alternatively, using a teaspoon or a paper piping (pastry) bag, drizzle it decoratively over the mixture. Leave to set for about 1 hour before cutting into bars.

Oaty Muesli Slices Energy 107kcals/452kJ; Protein 2.3g; Fat, total 2.7g; saturated fat 1.2g; Carbohydrate 19.6g; of which sugars 10.9g; Fibre 1.9g. **Wholewheat Seed Slices** Energy 107kcals/452kJ; Protein 2.3g; Fat, total 2.7g; saturated fat 1.2g; Carbohydrate 19.6g; of which sugars 10.9g; Fibre 1.9g. **Sultana and Cinnamon Chewy Bars** Energy 145kcal/608kJ; Protein 1.1g; Carbohydrate 22.2g; of which sugars 12.8g; Fat 6.4g, of which saturates 3.9g; Cholesterol 16mg; Calcium 60mg; Fibre 0.3g; Sodium 122mg.

Spicy Fruit Slices

A double-layered sweet cookie in which the topping combines dried fruit, with grated carrot to keep it moist. A truly indulgent teatime treat.

Makes 12–16
90g/3¹/₂oz/7 tbsp butter
75g/3oz/scant ¹/₂ cup caster (superfine) sugar
1 egg yolk
115g/4oz/1 cup plain (all-purpose) flour
30ml/2 tbsp self-raising (self-rising) flour
30ml/2 tbsp desiccated (dry unsweetened shredded) coconut
icing (confectioners') sugar, for dusting

For the topping
30ml/2 tbsp ready-to-eat prunes, chopped
30ml/2 tbsp sultanas (golden raisins)
50g/2oz/¹/₂ cup ready-to-eat dried pears, chopped
25g/1oz/¹/₄ cup walnuts, chopped
75g/3oz/³/₄ cup self-raising (self-rising) flour
5ml/1 tsp ground cinnamon
2.5ml/¹/₂ tsp ground ginger
175g/6oz/generous 1 cup grated carrots
1 egg, beaten
75ml/5 tbsp vegetable oil
2.5ml/¹/₂ tsp bicarbonate of soda (baking soda)
90g/3¹/₂oz/scant ¹/₂ cup dark muscovado (molasses) sugar

1 Preheat the oven to 180°C/350°F/Gas 4. Line a 28 × 18cm/ 11 × 7in shallow baking tin (pan) with baking parchment.

2 In a large mixing bowl, beat together the butter, sugar and egg yolk until smooth and creamy.

3 Stir in the plain flour, self-raising flour and coconut and mix together well. Press into the base of the prepared tin, using your fingers to spread the dough evenly.

4 Bake for about 15 minutes, or until firm to the touch and light golden brown.

5 To make the topping, mix together all the ingredients and spread over the cooked base. Bake for about 35 minutes, or until firm. Cool completely in the tin before cutting into bars or squares. Dust with icing sugar.

Lemon-iced Date Slices

Lemon-flavoured icing tops these scrumptious, low-fat bars, which are full of succulent fruit and crunchy seeds – the perfect mid-morning pick-me-up with a cup of decaf.

Makes 12–16
175g/6oz/³/₄ cup light muscovado (brown) sugar
175g/6oz/1 cup ready-to-eat dried dates, chopped
115g/4oz/1 cup self-raising (self-rising) flour
50g/2oz/¹/₂ cup muesli (granola)
30ml/2 tbsp sunflower seeds
15ml/1 tbsp poppy seeds
30ml/2 tbsp sultanas (golden raisins)
150ml/¹/₄ pint/²/₃ cup natural (plain) low-fat yogurt
1 egg, beaten
200g/7oz/1³/₄ cups icing (confectioners') sugar, sifted
lemon juice
15–30ml/1–2 tbsp pumpkin seeds

1 Preheat the oven to 180°C/350°F/Gas 4. Line a 28 × 18cm/ 11 × 7in shallow baking tin (pan) with baking parchment.

2 In a bowl mix together the muscovado sugar, dates, flour, muesli, sunflower seeds, poppy seeds, sultanas, yogurt and beaten egg until thoroughly combined.

3 Spread in the tin and bake for about 25 minutes, until golden brown. Leave to cool.

4 To make the topping, put the icing sugar in a bowl and stir in just enough lemon juice to make a spreading consistency.

5 Spread the icing evenly over the baked date mixture and sprinkle generously with pumpkin seeds. Leave to set before cutting into squares or bars.

> **Variation**
> *Pumpkin seeds can sometimes be rather fibrous, so if you prefer, you could substitute other seeds, such as sesame, or flaked (sliced) almonds.*

Spicy Fruit Slices Energy 228kcal/955kJ; Protein 2.7g; Carbohydrate 29.7g, of which sugars 13.9g; Fat 11.8g, of which saturates 3.8g; Cholesterol 25mg; Calcium 34mg; Fibre 1.1g; Sodium 55mg.
Lemon-iced Date Slices Energy 211kcal/893kJ; Protein 3.6g; Carbohydrate 43.6g, of which sugars 35.5g; Fat 3.6g, of which saturates 0.5g; Cholesterol 12mg; Calcium 56mg; Fibre 1.3g; Sodium 18mg.

Date and Orange Slices

These tempting wholesome slices make a tasty treat.

Makes 16
350g/12oz/2⅓ cups pitted dried dates, finely chopped
200ml/7fl oz/scant 1 cup freshly squeezed orange juice
finely grated rind of 1 orange
115g/4oz/1 cup plain (all-purpose) wholemeal (whole-wheat) flour

175g/6oz/1¾ cups rolled oats
50g/2oz/½ cup fine oatmeal
pinch of salt
175g/6oz/¾ cup butter
75g/3oz/⅓ cup soft light brown sugar
10ml/2 tsp ground cinnamon

1 Preheat the oven to 190°C/375°F/Gas 5. Lightly grease an 18 × 28cm/7 × 11in non-stick cake tin (pan).

2 Put the dates in a pan with the orange juice. Cover, bring to the boil and simmer for 5 minutes, stirring occasionally. Stir in the orange rind and set aside to cool completely.

3 Put the flour, oats, oatmeal and salt in a bowl and mix together. Lightly rub in the butter.

4 Stir in the sugar and cinnamon. Press half the oat mixture over the base of the prepared tin. Spread the date mixture on top and sprinkle the remaining oat mixture evenly over the dates to cover them completely. Press down lightly.

5 Bake for about 30 minutes, until golden brown.

6 Leave to cool slightly in the tin and mark into 16 bars, using a sharp knife. When firm, remove from the tin and cool completely on a wire rack.

> **Variation**
> *Ready-to-eat dried apricots or prunes used in place of the dates in this recipe make equally tasty slices.*

Tropical Fruit Slices

Densely packed dried exotic fruits make the filling for these deliciously moist bars. Vary the tropical fruits in different areas of the baking tray for differently-tasting snacks from the same batch.

Makes 12–16
175g/6oz/1½ cups plain (all-purpose) flour, plus extra for dusting
90g/3½oz/generous ½ cup white vegetable fat (shortening)
60ml/4 tbsp apricot jam, sieved, or ready-made apricot glaze

For the filling
115g/4oz/½ cup unsalted (sweet) butter, softened
115g/4oz/generous ½ cup caster (superfine) sugar
1 egg, beaten
25g/1oz/¼ cup ground almonds
25g/1oz/2½ tbsp ground rice
300g/11oz/scant 2 cups ready-to-eat mixed dried tropical fruits, chopped

1 Preheat the oven to 180°C/350°F/Gas 4. Lightly grease a 28 × 18cm/11 × 7in tin (pan).

2 Sift the flour into a bowl and add the vegetable fat. Cut it into the flour, then rub in with your fingertips until the mixture resembles fine breadcrumbs. Gradually add just enough water to mix to a firm dough.

3 Roll out to a rectangle on a lightly floured surface and use to line the base of the prepared tin, trimming off any excess. Spread 30ml/2 tbsp of the apricot jam or glaze evenly over the dough base.

4 To make the filling, beat together the butter and sugar in a bowl until light and creamy. Beat in the egg, then stir in the ground almonds, ground rice and mixed fruits. Spread the mixture evenly in the tin.

5 Bake for about 35 minutes, until firm and golden. Remove from the oven and brush with the remaining apricot jam or glaze. Leave to cool completely in the tin before cutting into bars.

Tropical Fruit Slices Energy 220kcal/921kJ; Protein 2.7g; Carbohydrate 26.9g, of which sugars 17.3g; Fat 12g, of which saturates 6g; Cholesterol 28mg; Calcium 41mg; Fibre 1.7g; Sodium 98mg.
Date and Orange Slices Energy 197kcals/829KJ; Protein 4.02g; Fat 5.76g; Saturated Fat 1.48g; Carbohydrate 34.06g; Fibre 1.76g; Sodium 0.08g.

Spiced Raisin Squares

Moist and aromatic, these tasty fruit bars make great any-time-of day snacks and are the perfect choice for a summer picnic basket.

Makes 30

115g/4oz/1 cup plain (all-purpose) flour
7.5ml/1½ tsp baking powder
5ml/1 tsp ground cinnamon
2.5ml/½ tsp freshly grated nutmeg
1.5ml/¼ tsp ground cloves
1.5ml/¼ tsp ground allspsice
200g/7oz/1½ cups raisins
115g/4oz/½ cup butter, at room temperature
90g/3½oz/½ cup caster (superfine) sugar
2 eggs
165g/5½oz/scant ½ cup black treacle (molasses)
50g/2oz/½ cup walnuts, chopped

1 Preheat the oven to 180°C/350°F/Gas 4. Line a 33 × 23cm/13 × 9in tin (pan) with baking parchment and lightly grease the surface.

2 Sift together the flour, baking powder, cinnamon, nutmeg, cloves and allspice into a bowl.

3 Place the raisins in another bowl and toss with a few tablespoons of the flour mixture.

4 In another bowl, beat the butter and sugar together until light and fluffy. Beat in the eggs, one at a time, then the treacle. Stir in the flour mixture, raisins and walnuts.

5 Spoon the mixture into the prepared tin and spread evenly with the back of the spoon. Bake for 15–18 minutes, until just firm to the touch. Leave to cool completely in the tin before cutting into bars or squares.

> **Variation**
> *You could also make these spicy bars with chopped dried figs instead of raisins and substitute pistachio nuts or hazelnuts for the walnuts.*

Sticky Date and Apple Squares

Combining fresh and dried fruits gives these bars a wonderful texture and fabulous flavour – truly a winning partnership.

Makes 16

115g/4oz/½ cup butter
50g/2oz/4 tbsp soft dark brown sugar
50g/2oz/4 tbsp golden (light corn) syrup
115g/4oz/⅔ cup dried dates, chopped
115g/4oz/1⅓ cup rolled oats
115g/4oz/1 cup wholemeal (whole-wheat) self-raising (self-rising) flour
2 eating apples, peeled, cored and grated
5–10ml/1–2 tsp lemon juice
walnut halves, to decorate

1 Preheat the oven to 190°C/375°F/Gas 5. Line an 18–20cm/7–8in square or rectangle loose-based cake tin (pan).

2 Put the butter, sugar and golden syrup into a large pan and melt over a low heat, stirring occasionally, until smooth and thoroughly combined.

3 Add the dates and cook until they have softened. Gradually work in the oats, flour, apples and lemon juice until well mixed.

4 Spoon into the prepared tin and spread out evenly. Top with the walnut halves.

5 Bake for 30 minutes, then reduce the temperature to 160°C/325°F/Gas 3 and bake for 10–12 minutes more, until firm to the touch and golden.

6 Cut into squares or bars while still warm if you are going to eat them straightaway, or wrap in foil when nearly cold and keep for 1–2 days before eating.

> **Variation**
> *Although not quite so sticky, these bars would also be delicious made with dried blueberries instead of dates.*

Spiced Raisin Squares Energy 84kcal/353kJ; Protein 1.2g; Carbohydrate 11.4g, of which sugars 8.4g; Fat 4.1g, of which saturates 1.8g; Cholesterol 19mg; Calcium 43mg; Fibre 0.3g; Sodium 37mg.
Sticky Date and Apple Squares Energy 150kcal/631kJ; Protein 1.9g; Carbohydrate 22g, of which sugars 11.3g; Fat 6.7g, of which saturates 3.8g; Cholesterol 15mg; Calcium 21mg; Fibre 1.1g; Sodium 56mg.

Chewy Orange Flapjacks

Flapjacks are about the easiest cookies to make and, with a little guidance, can be knocked up in minutes by even the youngest cooks. This chunky, chewy version is flavoured with orange rind, but you can substitute other fruits such as a handful of raisins, chopped prunes or apricots.

Makes 18

250g/9oz/generous 1 cup unsalted (sweet) butter
finely grated rind of 1 large orange
225g/8oz/²/₃ cup golden (light corn) syrup
75g/3oz/¹/₃ cup light muscovado (brown) sugar
375g/13oz/3³/₄ cups rolled oats

1 Preheat the oven to 180°C/350°F/Gas 4. Line the base and sides of a 28 × 20cm/11 × 8in shallow baking tin (pan) with baking parchment.

2 Put the butter, orange rind, syrup and sugar in a large pan and heat gently until the butter has melted.

3 Add the oats to the pan and stir to mix thoroughly. Tip the mixture into the tin and spread into the corners in an even layer.

4 Bake for 15–20 minutes, until just beginning to colour around the edges. (The mixture will still be very soft but will harden as it cools.) Leave to cool in the tin.

5 Lift the flapjack out of the tin in one piece and cut into fingers.

Cook's Tips
• *Flapjack is the British name for this traditional British cookie – in the United States, the term refers to pancakes. But whether you call them flapjacks or energy bars, these oaty treats are always delicious.*
• *Don't be tempted to overcook flapjacks; they'll turn crisp and dry and lose their lovely chewy texture.*

Wholemeal Flapjacks

Perfect for picnics and packed lunches, these flapjacks are really crisp and crunchy.

Makes 16

115g/4oz/¹/₂ cup butter
60ml/4 tbsp rice syrup
50g/2oz/¹/₂ cup wholemeal (whole-wheat) flour
225g/8oz/2¹/₄ cups rolled oats
50g/2oz/¹/₂ cup pine nuts

1 Preheat the oven to 180°C/350°F/Gas 4. Line a 20cm/8in shallow baking tin (pan) with oiled foil.

2 Melt the butter and rice syrup in a small pan over a low heat.

3 Add the flour, rolled oats and pine nuts and stir well until thoroughly combined.

4 Turn the mixture into the tin and pat it out evenly with the back of a spoon.

5 Bake for 25–30 minutes, until the flapjacks are lightly browned and crisp. Mark into squares while still warm.

6 Cool slightly, then lift them out of the tin and cool on a wire rack.

Cook's Tip
Rice syrup is starch- rather than sugar-based and may be available from some large supermarkets. It is also found in Japanese food stores, sometimes labelled mizuame or mizu-ame. However, this is not always made from rice and may be based on other starches from vegetable sources, such as sweet potatoes. Rice syrup is not as liquid as sugar syrups but a slightly smaller quantity of golden (light corn) syrup may be used as an alternative if you cannot find it. Whatever syrup you use, do not let the mixture boil or the flapjacks will be tacky rather than crisp.

Chewy Orange Flapjacks Energy 241kcal/1007kJ; Protein 2.7g; Carbohydrate 29.5g, of which sugars 14.3g; Fat 13.2g, of which saturates 7.2g; Cholesterol 30mg; Calcium 18mg; Fibre 1.4g; Sodium 125mg.
Wholemeal Flapjacks Energy 122kcals/513kJ; Fat, total 6.4g; saturated fat 1.2g; polyunsaturated fat 2.55g; monounsaturated fat 2.35g; Carbohydrate 14.3g; sugar, total 1.45g; starch 11.05g; Fibre 1.35g Sodium 54.1mg.

BARS, SQUARES, SLICES AND BROWNIES

Chewy Flapjacks

Flapjacks are popular with adults and children alike and they are so quick and easy to make. They are always based on rolled oats, but this standard recipe is very adaptable and all manner of variations are possible.

Makes 12

175g/6oz/³/4 cup unsalted (sweet) butter
50g/2oz/¹/4 cup caster (superfine) sugar
150g/5oz/generous ¹/3 cup golden (light corn) syrup
250g/9oz/2³/4 cups rolled oats

1 Preheat the oven to 180°C/350°F/Gas 4. Line the base and sides of a 20cm/8in square cake tin (pan) with baking parchment.

2 Put the butter, sugar and golden syrup in a pan and melt over a low heat, stirring occasionally, until smooth and thoroughly combined.

3 Add the oats and stir until all the ingredients are combined. Turn the mixture into the tin and level the surface.

4 Bake the flapjacks for 15–20 minutes, until just beginning to turn golden. Leave to cool slightly in the tin, then cut into bars or squares, carefully remove from the tin and leave on a wire rack to cool completely. Store in an airtight container for 3–4 days.

Cook's Tips
• For fruity flapjacks, stir in 50g/2oz/¹/4 cup finely chopped ready-to-eat dried apricots, peaches, apples or mangoes or 50g/2oz/scant ¹/2 cup sultanas (golden raisins) with the rolled oats in step 3.
• Try stirring in 50g/2oz/²/3 cup desiccated (dry unsweetened shredded) coconut with the oats.
• For a decadent treat, melt 75g/3oz plain (semisweet) or milk chocolate in a heatproof bowl set over a pan of gently simmering water. Remove from the heat and dip the cooled flapjacks in the chocolate to half cover.

Microwave Sticky Lemon Flapjacks

Flavoured with tangy lemon juice and grated rind, these thick and chewy flapjacks are simply scrumptious. Cooked in the microwave, they're made in minutes.

Makes 8

75g/3oz/6 tbsp butter, diced
60ml/4 tbsp golden (light corn) syrup
115g/4oz/¹/2 cup demerara (raw) sugar
175g/6oz/1³/4 cups rolled oats
juice and finely grated rind of ¹/2 lemon

1 Put the butter, syrup and sugar in a microwave bowl. Microwave on medium (50 per cent) power for 3–4 minutes, stirring halfway through.

2 Stir in the oats, lemon rind and juice. Spoon the mixture into a 20cm/8in microwave flan dish and spread out.

3 Cook on full (100 per cent) power for 3–3¹/2 minutes, or until bubbling all over. Remove from the oven and mark into wedges when warm. Leave to cool in the dish.

Cranberry Oat Flapjacks

Here's a real teatime treat for everybody to enjoy! With minimal ingredients it's quick to make and doesn't take long to bake in the oven, too.

Makes 14

150g/5oz/1¹/2 cups rolled oats
115g/4oz/¹/2 cup demerara sugar
75g/3oz/¹/2 cup dried cranberries
115g/4oz/¹/2 cup butter

1 Preheat the oven to 190°C/375°F/Gas 5. Grease a shallow 28 x 18cm/11 x 7in tin (pan).

2 Stir the rolled oats, demerara sugar and dried cranberries together in a bowl.

3 In a small pan, melt the butter over a low heat. Pour the melted butter on to the oat mixture and stir thoroughly until completely combined.

4 Press the oat and cranberry mixture into the prepared tin using the back of a wooden spoon. Bake in the oven for 15–20 minutes, until pale golden brown.

5 Remove the flapjack from the oven and mark into 14 bars, then leave to cool for 5 minutes, in the tin. Remove the bars and place on a wire rack to cool completely. Store for up to 5 days in an airtight container.

Cook's Tip
Dried cranberries, also known as craisins, are a relatively new product, available from larger supermarkets. They have a sweet yet slightly tart flavour and their bright red colour will add visual appeal. They can be used to replace more usual dried fruits, such as sultanas (golden raisins).

Chewy Flapjacks Energy 241kcal/1008kJ; Protein 2.7g; Carbohydrate 29.5g, of which sugars 14.3g; Fat 13.2g, of which saturates 7.2g; Cholesterol 30mg; Calcium 18mg; Fibre 1.4g; Sodium 125mg.
Microwave Sticky Lemon Flapjacks Energy 237kcal/995kJ; Protein 2.9g; Carbohydrate 36.9g, of which sugars 21g; Fat 9.6g, of which saturates 4.9g; Cholesterol 20mg; Calcium 23mg; Fibre 1.5g; Sodium 85mg. Cranberry Oat Flapjacks Energy 145kcal/607kJ; Protein 1.6g; Carbohydrate 18.4g, of which sugars 10.6g; Fat 7.7g, of which saturates 4.3g; Cholesterol 18mg; Calcium 16mg; Fibre 1.1g; Sodium 55mg.

Granola Bars

A gloriously dense fruity, nutty and oaty mixture, packed with goodness and delicious too, these bars are an ideal snack and perfect to pack for a school lunch.

Makes 12

175g/6oz/³⁄₄ cup unsalted (sweet) butter, diced
150g/5oz/²⁄₃ cup clear honey
250g/9oz/generous 1 cup demerara (raw) sugar
350g/12oz/3 cups jumbo oats
5ml/1 tsp ground cinnamon
75g/3oz/³⁄₄ cup pecan nut halves
75g/3oz/generous ¹⁄₂ cup raisins
75g/3oz/¹⁄₃ cup ready-to-eat dried papaya, chopped
75g/3oz/¹⁄₃ cup ready-to-eat dried apricots, chopped
50g/2oz/¹⁄₂ cup pumpkin seeds
50g/2oz/scant ¹⁄₂ cup sunflower seeds
50g/2oz/¹⁄₄ cup sesame seeds
50g/2oz/¹⁄₂ cup ground almonds

1 Preheat the oven to 190°C/375°F/Gas 5. Line a 23cm/9in square cake tin (pan) with baking parchment.

2 Put the butter and honey in a large heavy pan and heat gently until the butter has melted and the mixture is completely smooth.

3 Add the demerara sugar to the pan and heat very gently, stirring constantly, until the sugar has completely dissolved. Bring the butter mixture to the boil and continue to boil for 1–2 minutes, stirring the mixture constantly until it has formed a smooth caramel sauce.

4 Add the remaining ingredients and mix together. Transfer the mixture to the tin and press down with a spoon. Bake for 15 minutes, until the edges turn brown.

5 Leave to cool, then chill for 1–2 hours. Turn out of the tin, peel off the parchment and cut into bars.

> **Variation**
> *You can use other dried fruits, such as mango and pear.*

Apricot and Pecan Flapjacks

A tried-and-tested favourite made even more delicious by the addition of maple syrup, fruit and nuts. This is a real energy booster at any time of day – great for kids and adults alike.

Makes 10

150g/5oz/²⁄₃ cup unsalted (sweet) butter, diced
150g/5oz/²⁄₃ cup light muscovado (brown) sugar
30ml/2 tbsp maple syrup
200g/7oz/2 cups rolled oats
50g/2oz/¹⁄₂ cup pecan nuts, chopped
50g/2oz/¹⁄₄ cup ready-to-eat dried apricots, chopped

1 Preheat the oven to 160°C/325°F/Gas 3. Lightly grease an 18cm/7in square shallow baking tin (pan).

2 Put the butter, sugar and maple syrup in a large heavy pan and heat gently, stirring occasionally, until the butter has melted. Remove from the heat and stir in the oats, nuts and apricots until thoroughly combined.

3 Spread evenly in the prepared tin and, using a knife, score the mixture into ten bars. Bake for about 25–30 minutes, or until golden.

4 Remove from the oven and cut through the scored lines. Leave until completely cold before removing from the tin.

> **Cook's Tip**
> *Make sure that you stir the syrup mixture quite frequently to prevent it from sticking on the base of the pan.*

> **Variations**
> *• You can substitute walnuts for the pecan nuts, if you like, although the nutty flavour won't be so intense.*
> *• Use different dried fruits instead of the apricots, if you like. Let children choose their own.*

Granola Bars Energy 522kcal/2189kJ; Protein 8.4g; Carbohydrate 63.8g, of which sugars 40.9g; Fat 27.7g, of which saturates 8.9g; Cholesterol 31mg; Calcium 93mg; Fibre 4.3g; Sodium 108mg.
Apricot and Pecan Flapjacks Energy 240kcal/1000kJ; Protein 3.2g; Carbohydrate 18.3g, of which sugars 3.7g; Fat 17.6g, of which saturates 8.1g; Cholesterol 32mg; Calcium 21mg; Fibre 1.9g; Sodium 98mg.

Fruity Breakfast Bars

Instead of buying fruit and cereal bars from the supermarket, try making this quick and easy version – these are much tastier and more nutritious than most of the commercially-made ones. They can be stored in an airtight container for up to four days.

Makes 12

270g/10oz/1¼ cups ready-made
  apple sauce
115g/4oz/½ cup ready-to-eat
  dried apricots, chopped
115g/4oz/¾ cup raisins
50g/2oz/¼ cup demerara
  (raw) sugar
50g/2oz/scant ½ cup sunflower
  seeds
25g/1oz/2 tbsp sesame seeds
25g/1oz/¼ cup pumpkin seeds
75g/3oz/scant 1 cup rolled oats
75g/3oz/¾ cup self-raising
  (self-rising) wholemeal
  (whole-wheat) flour
50g/2oz/⅔ cup desiccated
  (dry unsweetened
  shredded) coconut
2 eggs

1 Preheat the oven to 200°C/400°F/Gas 6. Lightly grease a 20cm/8in square shallow baking tin (pan) and line with baking parchment.

2 Put the apple sauce in a large bowl with the apricots, raisins, sugar and the sunflower, sesame and pumpkin seeds and stir together with a wooden spoon until thoroughly mixed.

3 Add the oats, flour, coconut and eggs to the fruit mixture and gently stir together until evenly combined.

4 Turn the mixture into the tin and spread to the edges in an even layer. Bake for about 25 minutes, or until golden and just firm to the touch.

5 Leave to cool in the tin, then lift out on to a board and cut into bars.

Cook's Tip
It's best to sift the flour before adding it to the mixture.

Apple Crumble and Custard Slices

These luscious apple slices are easy to make using ready-made sweet pastry and custard. Just think, all the ingredients of one of the world's most popular desserts – in a cookie.

Makes 16

350g/12oz ready-made
  sweet pastry dough
1 large cooking apple, about
  250g/9oz
30ml/2 tbsp caster
  (superfine) sugar
60ml/4 tbsp ready-made
  thick custard

For the crumble topping
115g/4oz/1 cup plain
  (all-purpose) flour
2.5ml/½ tsp ground cinnamon
60ml/4 tbsp sugar
90g/3½oz/7 tbsp unsalted
  (sweet) butter, melted

1 Preheat the oven to 190°C/375°F/Gas 5. Lightly grease a 28 × 18cm/11 × 7in shallow cake tin (pan).

2 Roll out the dough and use to line the base of the tin. Prick the dough with a fork, line with foil and baking beans and bake blind for about 10–15 minutes. Remove the foil and baking beans and return the pastry to the oven for another 5 minutes, until cooked and golden brown.

3 Meanwhile, peel, core and chop the apple. Place in a pan with the sugar. Heat gently until the sugar dissolves, then cover with a lid and cook gently for 5–7 minutes, until a thick purée is formed. Beat with a wooden spoon and set aside to cool.

4 Mix the cold apple with the custard. Spread over the pastry base in an even layer.

5 To make the crumble topping, put the flour, cinnamon and sugar into a bowl and pour over the melted butter. Stir thoroughly until the mixture forms small clumps. Sprinkle the crumble over the filling.

6 Return to the oven and bake for about 10–15 minutes, until the crumble topping is cooked and golden brown. Leave to cool in the tin, then slice into bars to serve.

Fruity Breakfast Bars Energy 207kcal/871kJ; Protein 4.9g; Carbohydrate 29.3g, of which sugars 19.2g; Fat 8.7g, of which saturates 3g; Cholesterol 32mg; Calcium 65mg; Fibre 2.8g; Sodium 24mg.
Apple Crumble and Custard Slices Energy 196kcal/822kJ; Protein 2.1g; Carbohydrate 23.7g, of which sugars 8.1g; Fat 11g, of which saturates 4.9g; Cholesterol 15mg; Calcium 37mg; Fibre 0.9g; Sodium 124mg.

Creamy Fig and Peach Squares

A sweet cream cheese and dried fruit filling with a hint of mint makes these cookies really special. They are ideal for quietening hunger pangs after school or work.

Makes 24
350g/12oz/3 cups plain
   (all-purpose) flour, plus extra
   for dusting
200g/7oz/scant 1 cup unsalted
   (sweet) butter, diced
1 egg, beaten
caster (superfine) sugar,
   for sprinkling

For the filling
500g/1¼lb/2½ cups ricotta
   cheese
115g/4oz/generous ½ cup
   caster (superfine) sugar
5ml/1 tsp finely chopped
   fresh mint
50g/2oz/⅓ cup ready-to-eat dried
   figs, chopped
50g/2oz/¼ cup ready-to-eat dried
   peaches, chopped

1 Preheat the oven to 190°C/375°F/Gas 5. Lightly grease a 33 × 23cm/13 × 9in Swiss roll tin (jelly roll pan) or shallow cake tin (pan).

2 Put the flour and butter into a bowl. Rub in the butter with your fingertips until the mixture resembles fine breadcrumbs. Add the egg and enough water to mix to a firm but not sticky dough.

3 Divide the dough into two and roll out one piece on a lightly floured surface to fit the base of the prepared tin. Place in the tin and trim.

4 To make the filling, put all the ingredients in a bowl and mix together. Spread over the pastry base.

5 Roll out the remaining dough and place on top of the filling. Prick lightly all over with a fork then sprinkle with caster sugar.

6 Bake for about 30 minutes, until light golden brown. Remove from the oven and sprinkle more caster sugar thickly over the top. Cool and cut into slices to serve.

Apricot Specials

These attractive bars taste great with tea, coffee or a cold drink and fit the bill perfectly whenever you need a nutritious snack. They're surprisingly easy to make, too.

Makes 12
90g/3½oz/generous ⅓ cup soft
   light brown sugar
75g/3oz/¾ cup plain
   (all-purpose) flour
75g/3oz/6 tbsp unsalted (sweet)
   butter, chilled and diced

For the topping
150g/5oz/generous ½ cup
   ready-to-eat dried apricots
250ml/8fl oz/1 cup water
grated rind of 1 lemon
55g/2½oz/5 tbsp caster
   (superfine) sugar
10ml/2 tsp cornflour (cornstarch)
50g/2oz/½ cup chopped walnuts

1 Preheat the oven to 180°C/350°F/Gas 4.

2 In a bowl, combine the brown sugar and flour. Rub in the butter with your fingertips until the mixture resembles coarse breadcrumbs.

3 Spoon the flour and butter mixture into a 20cm/8in square baking tin (pan) and level the surface by pressing down with the back of a spoon. Bake for 15 minutes, until just set. Remove from the oven but leave the oven switched on.

4 To make the topping, put the apricots into a pan and pour in the measured water. Bring to the boil, then lower the heat and simmer for about 10 minutes, until soft. Strain, reserving the cooking liquid. Chop the apricots.

5 Return the apricots to the pan and add the lemon rind, caster sugar, cornflour, and 60ml/4 tbsp of the soaking liquid. Cook for 1 minute.

6 Cool slightly before spreading the topping over the base. Sprinkle over the walnuts and continue baking for 20 minutes more. Leave to cool in the tin before cutting into bars.

Creamy Fig and Peach Squares Energy 179kcal/747kJ; Protein 3.8g; Carbohydrate 18.8g, of which sugars 7.7g; Fat 10.3g, of which saturates 6.3g; Cholesterol 34mg; Calcium 32mg; Fibre 0.7g; Sodium 56mg. Apricot Specials Energy 169kcal/711kJ; Protein 1.8g; Carbohydrate 23.9g, of which sugars 18.3g; Fat 8.1g, of which saturates 3.5g; Cholesterol 13mg; Calcium 30mg; Fibre 1.1g; Sodium 41mg.

Blueberry Streusel Slices

The delicious melt-in-the-mouth crumbly topping on this fruity slice is packed with flavour – irresistible.

Makes about 30 slices
225g/8oz shortcrust pastry
  dough
50g/2oz/½ cup plain
  (all-purpose) flour, plus extra
  for dusting
1.25ml/¼ tsp baking powder
40g/1½oz/3 tbsp butter
25g/1oz/½ cup fresh
  white breadcrumbs
50g/2oz/⅓ cup soft light
  brown sugar
pinch of salt
50g/2oz/½ cup flaked (sliced) or
  chopped almonds
30ml/4 tbsp blackberry jelly
115g/4oz blueberries, fresh
  or frozen

1 Preheat the oven to 180°C/350°F/Gas 4. Lightly grease an 18 × 28cm/7 × 11in Swiss roll tin (jelly pan).

2 Roll out the dough on a lightly floured surface to fit the base and side of the tin. Prick the base all over with a fork.

3 Rub together the flour, baking powder, butter, breadcrumbs, sugar and salt until really crumbly, then mix in the almonds.

4 Spread the dough with the jelly, sprinkle with the blueberries, then cover evenly with the streusel topping, pressing down lightly.

5 Bake for 30–40 minutes, reducing the temperature after 20 minutes to 170°C/325°F/Gas 3.

6 Remove from the oven when golden on the top and the pastry is cooked through. Cut into slices while still hot, then leave to cool.

> **Cook's Tip**
> For best results when using frozen blueberries, leave them to thaw completely before cooking.

Banana Gingerbread Slices

Bananas make this spicy bake delightfully moist. The flavour develops on keeping, so store the gingerbread for a few days before cutting into slices, if possible.

Makes 20 slices
275g/10oz/2½ cups plain
  (all-purpose) flour
5ml/1 tsp bicarbonate of soda
  (baking soda)
20ml/4 tsp ground ginger
10ml/2 tsp mixed spice (apple
  pie spice)
115g/4oz/⅔ cup soft light
  brown sugar
60ml/4 tbsp sunflower oil
30ml/2 tbsp black treacle
  (molasses)
30ml/2 tbsp malt extract
2 eggs
60ml/4 tbsp orange juice
3 ripe bananas
115g/4oz/⅔ cup raisins or
  sultanas (golden raisins)

1 Preheat the oven to 180°C/350°F/Gas 4. Lightly grease and line a 28 × 18cm/11 × 7in shallow baking tin (pan).

2 Sift the flour, bicarbonate of soda and spices into a mixing bowl. Place the sugar in the sieve (strainer) over the bowl, add some of the flour mixture and rub through with a spoon.

3 Make a well in the centre of the dry ingredients. Add the oil, treacle, malt extract, eggs and juice. Mix thoroughly.

4 Mash the bananas on a plate. Add the raisins or sultanas to the gingerbread mixture, then mix in the mashed bananas.

5 Scrape the mixture into the prepared baking tin. Bake for about 35–40 minutes, or until the centre of the gingerbread springs back when lightly pressed.

6 Leave to cool for 5 minutes, then turn out on to a wire rack to cool completely. Cut into 20 slices to serve.

> **Cook's Tip**
> If your brown sugar is lumpy, mix it with a little flour and it will be easier to sift.

Banana Gingerbread Slices Energy 133kcal/563kJ; Protein 2.3g; Carbohydrate 25.9g, of which sugars 15.2g; Fat 3g, of which saturates 0.5g; Cholesterol 19mg; Calcium 37mg; Fibre 0.7g; Sodium 18mg.
Blueberry Streusel Slice: Energy 74kcal/309kJ; Protein 1.1g; Carbohydrate 8.5g, of which sugars 3g; Fat 4.2g, of which saturates 1.4g; Cholesterol 4mg; Calcium 15mg; Fibre 0.4g; Sodium 45mg.

Old-fashioned Gingerbread

Adding vinegar to the milk when making gingerbread is an old-fashioned trick. The extra acidity activates the two raising agents and this guarantees a lovely light result, without affecting the flavour.

Serves 8–10
15ml/1 tbsp vinegar
175ml/6fl oz/³/4 cup milk
175g/6oz/1¹/2 cups plain
  (all-purpose) flour
10ml/2 tsp baking powder
1.5ml/¹/4 tsp bicarbonate of soda
  (baking soda)
pinch of salt
10ml/2 tsp ground ginger
5ml/1 tsp ground cinnamon
1.5ml/¹/4 tsp ground cloves
115g/4oz/¹/2 cup butter, at
  room temperature
115g/4oz/generous ¹/2 cup caster
  (superfine) sugar
1 egg, at room temperature
175ml/6fl oz/³/4 cup black
  treacle (molasses)
whipped cream, for serving
chopped preserved stem ginger,
  for decorating

1 Preheat the oven to 180°C/350°F/Gas 4. Line an 20cm/8in square cake tin (pan) with baking parchment and grease the parchment and the sides of the pan.

2 Add the vinegar to the milk in a small bowl and set aside. It will curdle.

3 In another mixing bowl, sift all the dry ingredients, except the caster sugar, together three times and set aside.

4 In a bowl, beat together the butter and sugar until light and fluffy. Beat in the egg until well combined. Stir in the black treacle, mixing well.

5 Fold in the dry ingredients in four batches, alternating with the milk. Mix only enough to blend.

6 Pour the mixture into the prepared tin and bake for 45–50 minutes, until firm to the touch. Cut the gingerbread into squares and serve warm with whipped cream. Decorate with preserved stem ginger.

Sticky Marmalade Squares

These baked treats have a plain lower layer supporting a scrumptious nutty upper layer flavoured with orange and chunky marmalade. Cut into squares or bars – whichever you prefer.

Makes 24
350g/12oz/3 cups plain
  (all-purpose) flour
200g/7oz/scant 1 cup unsalted
  (sweet) butter, diced
150g/5oz/²/3 cup light muscovado
  (brown) sugar
2.5ml/¹/2 tsp bicarbonate of soda
  (baking soda)
1 egg, beaten
120ml/4fl oz/¹/2 cup single
  (light) cream
50g/2oz/¹/2 cup pecan
  nuts, chopped
50g/2oz/¹/3 cup mixed
  (candied) peel
90ml/6 tbsp chunky marmalade
15–30ml/1–2 tbsp orange juice

1 Preheat the oven to 190°C/375°F/Gas 5. Line the base of an 28 × 18cm/11 × 7in tin (pan) with baking parchment.

2 Put the flour in a bowl and rub in the butter with your fingertips. Stir in the sugar and then spread half over the base of the prepared tin. Press down firmly. Bake for 10–15 minutes, until lightly browned. Leave to cool.

3 To make the filling, put the remaining flour mixture into a bowl. Stir in the bicarbonate of soda. Mix in the egg and cream, pecan nuts, peel and half the marmalade.

4 Pour the mixture over the cooled base Bake for 20–25 minutes, or until the filling is just firm and golden.

5 Put the remaining marmalade into a small pan and heat gently. Add just enough orange juice to make a spreadable glaze. Brush the glaze over the baked cookie mixture while it is still warm. Leave to cool. Cut into bars.

> **Variation**
> *These bars would be just as delicious made with lemon, lime, grapefruit or mixed fruit marmalade instead of orange.*

Old-fashioned Gingerbread Energy 191kcal/802kJ; Protein 1.6g; Carbohydrate 24.7g, of which sugars 24.6g; Fat 10.3g, of which saturates 6.3g; Cholesterol 45mg; Calcium 128mg; Fibre 0g; Sodium 116mg.
Sticky Marmalade Squares Energy 194kcal/809kJ; Protein 2.1g; Carbohydrate 22g, of which sugars 10.9g; Fat 11.4g, of which saturates 6.2g; Cholesterol 33mg; Calcium 36mg; Fibre 0.7g; Sodium 77mg.

Walnut and Honey Bars

A sweet, custard-like filling brimming with nuts sits on a crisp pastry base. These scrumptious bars are pure heaven to bite into.

Makes 12–14

175g/6oz/1½ cups plain
  (all-purpose) flour
30ml/2 tbsp icing (confectioners')
  sugar, sifted
115g/4oz/½ cup unsalted
  (sweet) butter, diced

For the filling

300g/11oz/scant 3 cups walnut
  halves
2 eggs, beaten
50g/2oz/¼ cup unsalted (sweet)
  butter, melted
50g/2oz/¼ cup light muscovado
  (brown) sugar
90ml/6 tbsp dark clear honey
30ml/2 tbsp single (light) cream

1 Preheat the oven to 190°C/375°F/Gas 5. Lightly grease a 28 × 18cm/11 × 7in shallow tin (pan).

2 Put the flour, icing sugar and butter in a food processor and process until the mixture forms crumbs. Using the pulse button, add 15–30ml/1–2 tbsp water – enough to make a firm dough.

3 Roll the dough out on baking parchment and line the base and sides of the tin. Trim and fold the top edge inwards.

4 Prick the base, line with foil and baking beans and bake blind for 10 minutes. Remove the foil and beans. Return the base to the oven for about 5 minutes, until cooked but not browned. Reduce the temperature to 180°C/350°F/Gas 4.

5 For the filling, sprinkle the walnuts over the base. Whisk the remaining ingredients together. Pour over the walnuts and bake for 25 minutes.

Cook's Tip

Dark honey does not necessarily have a stronger flavour than paler varieties, but some types have a distinctive taste. These include chestnut, buckwheat and manuka.

Figgy Bars

Dried figs are a traditional addition to cookies but have been a little out of fashion in recent years. These tasty bars will remind you why they were once so popular.

Makes 48

3 eggs
175g/6oz/scant 1 cup caster
  (superfine) sugar
75g/3oz/¾ cup plain
  (all-purpose) flour

5ml/1 tsp baking powder
2.5ml/½ tsp ground cinnamon
1.5ml/¼ tsp ground cloves
1.5ml/¼ tsp grated nutmeg
pinch of salt
350g/12oz/2 cups coarsely
  chopped dried figs
75g/3oz/¾ cup chopped walnuts
30ml/2 tbsp brandy
icing (confectioners') sugar,
  for dusting

1 Preheat the oven to 160°C/325°F/Gas 3. Line a 30 × 20 × 3cm/12 × 8 × 1½in tin (pan) with baking parchment and lightly grease the paper.

2 In a bowl, whisk together the eggs and sugar until pale and thoroughly blended.

3 In another bowl, sift together the flour, baking powder, cinnamon, cloves, nutmeg and salt. Using a flexible spatula, gently fold the dry ingredients into the egg mixture in several batches. Stir in the figs, walnuts and brandy.

4 Scrape the mixture into the prepared tin and bake for 35–40 minutes, until the top is firm and brown. It should still be soft underneath.

5 Leave to cool in the tin for 5 minutes, then unmould and transfer to a sheet of baking parchment lightly sprinkled with icing sugar. Cut into bars.

Variation

If you prefer not to use brandy in these bars, you could substitute red grape juice or orange juice.

Walnut and Honey Bars Energy 333kcal/1386kJ; Protein 5.4g; Carbohydrate 21.4g, of which sugars 11.7g; Fat 25.7g, of which saturates 7.8g; Cholesterol 53mg; Calcium 49mg; Fibre 1.1g; Sodium 85mg.
Figgy Bars Energy 53kcal/224kJ; Protein 1g; Carbohydrate 8.9g, of which sugars 7.7g; Fat 1.6g, of which saturates 0.2g; Cholesterol 12mg; Calcium 26mg; Fibre 0.7g; Sodium 9mg.

Almond-topped Squares

Slightly chewy with a crunchy top, these squares are perfect any-time-of-day cookies whenever you feel that you deserve a treat.

Makes 18
75g/3oz/6 tbsp butter
50g/2oz/¼ cup sugar
1 egg yolk
grated rind and juice of ½ lemon
2.5ml/½ tsp vanilla extract
30ml/2 tbsp whipping cream

115g/4oz/1 cup plain
 (all-purpose) flour, plus extra
 for dusting

For the topping
225g/8oz/1 cup sugar
75g/3oz/¾ cup flaked
 (sliced) almonds
4 egg whites
2.5ml/½ tsp ground ginger
2.5ml/½ tsp ground cinnamon

1 Preheat the oven to 190°C/375°F/Gas 5. Line a 33 × 23cm/13 × 9in Swiss roll tin (jelly pan) with baking parchment and grease the paper.

2 In a bowl, beat together the butter and sugar until light and fluffy. Beat in the egg yolk, lemon rind and juice, vanilla extract and cream.

3 Gradually stir in the flour. Gather into a ball of dough with your fingertips.

4 Lightly dust your fingers with flour, then gently press the dough evenly into the base of the prepared tin. Bake for about 15 minutes, until just set. Remove the tin from the oven but leave the oven switched on.

5 To make the topping, put all the ingredients into a large heavy pan. Cook over a low heat, stirring constantly, until the mixture comes to the boil. Continue to boil, without stirring, for about 1 minute, until just golden. Pour the topping over the dough base, spreading it to cover evenly with a spatula.

6 Return to the oven and bake for about 45 minutes. Remove and score into bars or squares. Cool completely.

Pecan Squares

A melt-in-the-mouth base and a crunchy toffee-like topping make these richly coloured cookies totally impossible to resist.

Makes 36
225g/8oz/2 cups plain
 (all-purpose) flour
pinch of salt
115g/4oz/½ cup sugar
225g/8oz/1 cup cold butter, diced

1 egg
finely grated rind of 1 lemon

For the topping
175g/6oz/¾ cup butter
75g/3oz/⅓ cup clear honey
50g/2oz/¼ cup sugar
115g/4oz/½ cup dark brown
 sugar
75ml/5 tbsp whipping cream
450g/1lb/4 cups pecan halves

1 Preheat the oven to 190°C/375°F/Gas 5. Lightly grease a 37 × 27 × 2.5cm/15½ × 10½ × 1in Swiss roll tin (jelly roll pan).

2 Sift the flour and salt into a mixing bowl. Stir in the sugar. With your fingertips, rub in the butter until the mixture resembles coarse breadcrumbs.

3 Add the egg and lemon rind and blend with a fork until the mixture just holds together.

4 Spoon the mixture into the prepared tin. With floured fingertips, press into an even layer. Prick the pastry all over with a fork and chill for 10 minutes.

5 Bake the pastry crust for 15 minutes. Remove the tin from the oven, but keep the oven on while making the topping.

6 To make the topping, melt the butter, honey and both sugars. Bring to the boil. Boil, without stirring, for 2 minutes. Remove from the heat and stir in the cream and pecans. Pour over the crust and bake for 25 minutes. Leave to cool.

7 When cool, run a knife around the edge. Invert on to a baking sheet, place another sheet on top and invert again. Dip a sharp knife into very hot water and cut into squares for serving.

Almond-topped Squares Energy 127kcal/531kJ; Protein 2.4g; Carbohydrate 14.9g, of which sugars 9.9g; Fat 6.8g, of which saturates 2.9g; Cholesterol 22mg; Calcium 27mg; Fibre 0.5g; Sodium 41mg.
Pecan Squares Energy 245kcal/1016kJ; Protein 2.1g; Carbohydrate 15.5g, of which sugars 10.5g; Fat 19.8g, of which saturates 7.6g; Cholesterol 33mg; Calcium 26mg; Fibre 0.8g; Sodium 71mg.

Hazelnut and Raspberry Bars

The hazelnuts make a superb sweet pastry which is baked with a layer of raspberry jam in the middle.

Makes 30

250g/9oz/2¼ cups hazelnuts
300g/10oz/2½ cups plain (all-purpose) flour
5ml/1 tsp mixed spice (apple pie spice)
2.5ml/½ tsp ground cinnamon
150g/5oz/1¼ cups golden icing (confectioners') sugar
15ml/1 tbsp grated lemon rind
300g/10oz/1¼ cups unsalted (sweet) butter, softened
3 egg yolks
350g/12oz/1¼ cups seedless raspberry jam

For the topping

1 egg, beaten
15ml/1 tbsp clear honey
50g/2oz/½ cup flaked (sliced) almonds

1 Grind the hazelnuts in a food processor and then put in a bowl. Sift in the flour, spices and icing sugar. Add the lemon rind and mix well, then add the butter and the egg yolks and, using your hands, knead until a smooth dough is formed. Wrap in clear film (plastic wrap) and chill for 30 minutes.

2 Preheat the oven to 200°C/400°F/Gas 6. Lightly grease a 33 × 23cm/13 × 9in Swiss roll tin (jelly roll pan).

3 Roll out half the dough and fit in the base of the tin. Spread the jam over the dough base. Roll out the remaining dough and place on top of the jam.

4 To make the topping, beat the egg and honey together and brush over the dough. Sprinkle the almonds evenly over the top.

5 Bake for 10 minutes, lower the oven temperature to 180°C/350°F/Gas 4. Bake for another 20–30 minutes until golden brown. Cool, then cut into bars.

> **Cook's Tip**
> *Don't use ready-ground hazelnuts for these bars.*

Lemon Bars

These tangy lemon bars really zing with flavour and go beautifully with iced tea in summer.

Makes 36

50g/2oz/½ cup icing (confectioners') sugar
175g/6oz/1½ cups plain (all-purpose) flour
pinch of salt
175g/6oz/¾ cup butter, diced

For the topping

4 eggs
350g/12oz/1¾ cups caster (superfine) sugar
grated rind of 1 lemon
120ml/4fl oz/½ cup fresh lemon juice
175ml/6fl oz/¾ cup whipping cream
icing (confectioners') sugar, for dusting

1 Preheat the oven to 160°C/325°F/Gas 3. Lightly grease a 33 × 23cm/13 × 9in baking tin (pan).

2 Sift the sugar, flour and salt together into a large bowl. Rub the butter in with your fingertips until the mixture resembles coarse breadcrumbs.

3 Press the mixture into the base of the prepared tin using the back of a metal spoon. Bake for about 20 minutes, until golden brown.

4 For the topping, whisk the eggs and sugar together until blended. Add the lemon rind and juice and mix well.

5 Lightly whip the cream until it holds its shape and fold it into the egg mixture. Pour the liquid over the still-warm base, return it to the oven and bake for about 40 minutes, until set.

6 Leave to cool completely before cutting into bars. Dust with icing sugar.

> **Variation**
> *For an equally delicious citrus boost, substitute grated orange rind and juice for the lemon.*

Hazelnut and Raspberry Bars Energy 231kcal/962kJ; Protein 2.9g; Carbohydrate 22.1g, of which sugars 14.3g; Fat 15.1g, of which saturates 5.9g; Cholesterol 41mg; Calcium 38mg; Fibre 1g; Sodium 66mg. **Lemon Bars** Energy 124kcal/519kJ; Protein 1.3g; Carbohydrate 15.7g, of which sugars 12g; Fat 6.6g, of which saturates 3.9g; Cholesterol 37mg; Calcium 20mg; Fibre 0.2g; Sodium 39mg.

Fruity Lemon Drizzle Bars

These tangy iced, spongy bars are great for popping in lunchboxes. Experiment with other filling combinations, such as orange, dried apricots and dried pineapple.

Makes 16
250g/9oz ready-made sweet
  shortcrust pastry dough
90g/3¼ oz/¾ cup self-raising
  (self-rising) flour
75g/3oz/¾ cup fine or
  medium oatmeal
5ml/1 tsp baking powder
130g/4½oz/generous ½ cup light
  muscovado (brown) sugar
2 eggs
150g/5oz/⅔ cup unsalted
  (sweet) butter, at room
  temperature, diced
finely grated rind of 1 lemon
90g/3½oz/¾ cup sultanas
  (golden raisins)
150g/5oz/1¼ cups icing
  (confectioners') sugar
15–20ml/3–4 tsp lemon juice

1 Preheat the oven to 190°C/375°F/Gas 5 and place a baking sheet in the oven to heat through. Generously grease a 28 × 18cm/11 × 7in shallow baking tin (pan).

2 Roll out the dough thinly on a lightly floured, clean surface. Line the base of the baking tin, pressing the pastry up the sides.

3 Put the flour, oatmeal, baking powder, sugar, eggs, butter and lemon rind in a mixing bowl. Beat for 2 minutes with a hand-held electric whisk until pale and creamy. Stir in the sultanas.

4 Tip the filling into the pastry case (pie shell) and spread evenly. Place the tin on the heated baking sheet in the oven and bake for about 30 minutes, until pale golden and firm.

5 Put the icing sugar in a small bowl with enough lemon juice to mix to a thin paste, about the consistency of thin cream.

6 Using a teaspoon, drizzle the icing diagonally across the warm cake in thin lines. Leave to cool in the tin.

7 When the icing has set, use a sharp knife to cut the cake in half lengthways. Cut each half across into 8 even-size bars.

Luscious Lemon Bars

A crisp cookie base is covered with a tangy lemon topping. The bars make a delightful addition to the tea table on a warm summer's day in the garden.

Makes 12
150g/5oz/1¼ cups plain
  (all-purpose) flour
90g/3½oz/7 tbsp unsalted
  (sweet) butter, chilled and diced
50g/2oz/½ cup icing
  (confectioners') sugar, sifted

For the topping
2 eggs
175g/6oz/scant 1 cup caster
  (superfine) sugar
finely grated rind and juice of
  1 large lemon
15ml/1 tbsp plain
  (all-purpose) flour
2.5ml/½ tsp bicarbonate of soda
  (baking soda)
icing (confectioners') sugar,
  for dusting

1 Preheat the oven to 180°C/350°F/Gas 4. Line the base of a 20cm/8in square shallow cake tin (pan) with baking parchment and lightly grease the sides of the tin.

2 Put the flour, diced butter and icing sugar into a food processor and process until the mixture comes together as a smooth, firm dough.

3 Press evenly into the base of the tin and spread smoothly using the back of a tablespoon. Bake for 12–15 minutes, until lightly golden. Cool in the tin.

4 To make the topping, whisk the eggs in a bowl until frothy. Gradually add the caster sugar, a little at a time, whisking well after each addition. Whisk in the lemon rind and juice, flour and bicarbonate of soda until thoroughly combined but do not overmix. Pour the topping evenly over the cookie base.

5 Bake for 20–25 minutes, until set and golden, then remove from the oven.

6 Leave to cool slightly in the tin, then cut into 12 bars and transfer to a wire rack. Dust lightly with icing sugar and leave to cool completely.

Fruity Lemon Drizzle Bars Energy 272kcal/1141kJ; Protein 3.1g; Carbohydrate 37.3g, of which sugars 22.5g; Fat 13.3g, of which saturates 6.5g; Cholesterol 46mg; Calcium 42mg; Fibre 0.9g; Sodium 132mg. Luscious Lemon Bars Energy 189kcal/795kJ; Protein 2.5g; Carbohydrate 30.3g, of which sugars 19.8g; Fat 7.3g, of which saturates 4.2g; Cholesterol 48mg; Calcium 35mg; Fibre 0.4g; Sodium 59mg.

Fudge Nut Bars

Although your kids will be desperate to tuck into these fudgy treats, it's well worth chilling them for a few hours before slicing so that they can be cut into neat pieces. You can use any kind of nut, from mild-flavoured almonds, peanuts or macadamia nuts to slightly stronger tasting pecans or hazelnuts.

Makes 16
150g/5oz/⅔ cup unsalted
   (sweet) butter, chilled and diced
250g/9oz/2¼ cups plain
   (all-purpose) flour
75g/3oz/scant ½ cup caster
   (superfine) sugar

For the topping
150g/5oz milk chocolate, broken
   into pieces
40g/1½oz/3 tbsp unsalted
   (sweet) butter
405g/14¼oz can sweetened
   condensed milk
50g/2oz/½ cup chopped nuts

1 Preheat the oven to 160°C/325°F/Gas 3. Lightly grease a 28 × 18cm/11 × 7in shallow baking tin (pan).

2 Put the butter and flour in a food processor and process until the mixture resembles fine breadcrumbs. Add the sugar and process briefly again until the mixture starts to cling together and form a dough.

3 Tip the mixture into the prepared baking tin and spread out with the back of a wooden spoon to fill the base in an even layer. Bake for 35–40 minutes, until the surface is very lightly coloured. Remove from the oven.

4 To make the topping, put the chocolate in a heavy pan with the butter and condensed milk. Heat gently, stirring occasionally until the chocolate and butter have melted, then increase the heat and cook, stirring constantly, for 3–5 minutes, until the mixture starts to thicken.

5 Add the chopped nuts to the pan and pour the mixture over the cookie base, spreading it in an even layer. Leave to cool, then chill for at least 2 hours until firm. Serve cut into bars.

Toffee Meringue Bars

The lovely light and airy topping with its delicious caramel flavour makes these unusual bars irresistible.

Makes 12
50g/2oz/¼ cup butter
215g/7½oz/scant 1 cup soft
   dark brown sugar
1 egg
2.5ml/½ tsp vanilla extract
65g/2½oz/9 tbsp plain
   (all-purpose) flour
pinch of salt
1.5ml/¼ tsp freshly
   grated nutmeg

For the topping
1 egg white
pinch of salt
15ml/1 tbsp golden (light
   corn) syrup
90g/3½oz/½ cup caster
   (superfine) sugar
50g/2oz/⅓ cup walnuts,
   finely chopped

1 Combine the butter and brown sugar in a pan and heat until bubbling. Set aside to cool.

2 Preheat the oven to 180°C/350°F/Gas 4. Line the base and sides of a 20cm/8in square cake tin (pan) with baking parchment and oil.

3 Beat the egg and vanilla into the cooled sugar mixture. Sift over the flour, salt and nutmeg, and fold in. Spread out evenly over the base of the tin.

4 For the topping, beat the egg white with the salt until it holds soft peaks. Beat in the golden syrup, then the sugar and continue beating until the mixture holds stiff peaks. Fold in the nuts and spread on top of the dough base.

5 Bake for 30 minutes. Cut into bars when cool.

Variation
The topping also tastes terrific made with maple syrup.

Fudge Nut Bars Energy 315kcal/1317kJ; Protein 4.9g; Carbohydrate 36.6g, of which sugars 24.7g; Fat 17.5g, of which saturates 9.7g; Cholesterol 37mg; Calcium 123mg; Fibre 0.7g; Sodium 116mg.
Toffee Meringue Bars Energy 189kcal/797kJ; Protein 2g; Carbohydrate 31.9g, of which sugars 27.8g; Fat 6.8g, of which saturates 2.5g; Cholesterol 25mg; Calcium 28mg; Fibre 0.3g; Sodium 42mg.

Sticky Treacle Squares

This three-layered treat of buttery cookie base, covered with a sticky dried fruit filling, followed by an oaty flapjack-style topping, is utterly delicious.

Makes 14

175g/6oz/1½ cups plain (all-purpose) flour
90g/3½oz/7 tbsp unsalted (sweet) butter, diced
50g/2oz/¼ cup caster (superfine) sugar

For the filling
250g/9oz/generous 1 cup mixed dried fruit, such as prunes, apricots, peaches, pears and apples
300ml/½ pint/1¼ cups apple or orange juice

For the topping
225g/8oz/⅔ cup golden (light corn) syrup
finely grated rind of 1 small orange, plus 45ml/3 tbsp juice
90g/3½oz/1 cup rolled oats

1 Preheat the oven to 180°C/350°F/Gas 4. Lightly grease a 28 × 18cm/11 × 7in shallow baking tin (pan).

2 Put the flour and butter in a food processor and process until the mixture begins to resemble fine breadcrumbs. Add the sugar and mix until the dough starts to cling together in a ball.

3 Tip the mixture into the baking tin and press down in an even layer with the back of a fork. Bake for about 15 minutes, until the surface just begins to colour.

4 Meanwhile, prepare the filling. Remove the stones (pits) from any of the dried fruits. Chop the fruit fairly finely and put in a pan with the fruit juice. Bring to the boil, reduce the heat and cover with a lid. Simmer gently for about 15 minutes, or until all the juice has been absorbed.

5 Leaving the base in the tin, tip the dried fruit filling on top and spread out in an even layer with the back of a spoon.

6 For the topping, put the golden syrup in a bowl with the orange rind and juice and oats and mix together. Spoon over the fruits, spreading it out evenly. Return to the oven for 25 minutes. Leave to cool before cutting into squares.

Marbled Caramel Chocolate Slices

The classic chocolate-topped millionaire's slice is guaranteed to make you feel like a lottery winner.

Makes about 24
For the base
250g/9oz/2¼ cups plain (all-purpose) flour
75g/3oz/scant ½ cup caster (superfine) sugar
175g/6oz/¾ cup unsalted (sweet) butter, softened

For the filling
90g/3½oz/7 tbsp unsalted (sweet) butter, diced
90g/3½oz/scant ½ cup light muscovado (brown) sugar
2 × 400g/14oz cans sweetened condensed milk

For the topping
90g/3½oz plain (semisweet) chocolate
90g/3½oz milk chocolate
50g/2oz white chocolate

1 Preheat the oven to 180°C/350°F/Gas 4. Line and lightly grease a 33 × 23cm/13 × 9in Swiss roll tin (jelly roll pan).

2 Put the flour and caster sugar in a bowl and rub in the butter until it resembles fine breadcrumbs. Work with your hands until the mixture forms a dough.

3 Turn the dough into the tin and press it out with back of a tablespoon to cover the base. Prick all over with a fork and bake for about 20 minutes, or until firm to the touch. Set aside and leave in the tin to cool.

4 To make the filling, put all the ingredients into a pan and heat gently, stirring, until the sugar has dissolved. Stirring constantly, bring to the boil. Reduce the heat and simmer the mixture very gently, stirring constantly, for about 5–10 minutes, or until it has thickened and has turned a caramel colour.

5 Pour the filling over the cookie base, spread evenly, then leave until cold.

6 To make the topping, melt each chocolate separately in a heatproof bowl set over a pan of gently simmering water. Spoon plain, milk and white chocolate over the filling. Use a skewer to form a marbled effect on top.

Sticky Treacle Squares Energy 213kcal/898kJ; Protein 2.6g; Carbohydrate 39.3g, of which sugars 25.1g; Fat 6.1g, of which saturates 3.4g; Cholesterol 14mg; Calcium 35mg; Fibre 1.8g; Sodium 88mg.
Marbled Caramel Chocolate Slices Energy 305kcal/1281kJ; Protein 4.6g; Carbohydrate 39.6g, of which sugars 31.6g; Fat 15.4g, of which saturates 9.6g; Cholesterol 37mg; Calcium 132mg; Fibre 0.4g; Sodium 120mg.

Pecan Toffee Shortbread

Coffee shortbread is topped with pecan-studded toffee. Cornflour gives it a crumbly light texture, but all plain flour can be used if you like.

Makes 20
15ml/1 tbsp ground cofee
15ml/1 tbsp near-boiling water
115g/4oz/½ cup butter, softened
30ml/2 tbsp smooth
   peanut butter
75g/3oz/scant ½ cup caster
   (superfine) sugar

75g/3oz/⅔ cup cornflour
   (cornstarch)
185g/6½oz/1⅔ cups plain
   (all-purpose) flour

For the topping
175g/6oz/1¾ cup butter
175g/6oz/¾ cup soft light
   brown sugar
30ml/2 tbsp golden (light
   corn) syrup
175g/6oz/1½ cups shelled pecan
   nuts, coarsely chopped

1 Preheat the oven to 180°C/350°F/Gas 4. Lightly grease and line the base of an 18 x 28cm/7 x 11in tin (pan) with baking parchment.

2 Put the ground coffee in a small bowl and pour the hot water over. Leave to infuse (steep) for 4 minutes, then strain through a fine sieve (strainer).

3 Put the unsalted butter, peanut butter, sugar and coffee in a large bowl and beat together until light and creamy. Sift together the cornflour and flour into the bowl and mix gently to make a smooth dough.

4 Press the dough evenly into the base of the prepared tin and prick all over with a fork. Bake for about 20 minutes, until set and very lightly coloured.

5 To make the topping, put the butter, sugar and syrup into a heavy pan and cook over a medium heat, stirring occasionally, until melted. Bring to the boil, lower the heat and simmer for 5 minutes. Stir in the chopped nuts.

6 Spread the topping over the base. Leave in the tin until cold, then cut into bars.

Chocolate Butterscotch Bars

Wonderfully sticky with their sweet toffee and chocolate double topping, these rich, nutty cookie bars will be popular.

Makes 24
225g/8oz/2 cups plain
   (all-purpose) flour
2.5ml/½ tsp baking powder
115g/4oz/½ cup unsalted
   (sweet) butter, diced
50g/2oz/¼ cup light muscovado
   (brown) sugar
150g/5oz plain (semisweet)
   chocolate, melted
30ml/2 tbsp ground almonds

For the topping
175g/6oz/¾ cup unsalted
   (sweet) butter
115g/4oz/generous ½ cup caster
   (superfine) sugar
30ml/2 tbsp golden (light
   corn) syrup
175ml/6fl oz/¾ cup unsweetened
   condensed milk
150g/5oz/1¼ cups toasted
   hazelnuts
225g/8oz plain (semisweet)
   chocolate, chopped

1 Preheat the oven to 160°C/325°F/Gas 3. Lightly grease a shallow 30 x 20cm/12 x 8in cake tin (pan).

2 Sift together the flour and baking powder into a large bowl. Add the butter and rub it in until it resembles breadcrumbs.

3 Stir in the sugar. Gradually, work in the melted chocolate and ground almonds until thoroughly combined. Press the mixture into the prepared cake tin, prick the surface all over with a fork.

4 Bake for 25–30 minutes, until firm. Place the tin on a wire rack and leave to cool.

5 To make the topping, gently heat the butter, sugar, syrup and condensed milk in a pan until melted. Simmer, stirring occasionally, until golden, then stir in the hazelnuts. Pour over the base. Leave to set.

6 Melt the chocolate in a heatproof bowl set over a pan of gently simmering water. Spread over the butterscotch layer. Leave to set, then cut into bars.

Pecan Toffee Shortbread Energy 267kcal/1112kJ; Protein 1.9g; Carbohydrate 25.5g, of which sugars 14.9g; Fat 18.2g, of which saturates 8.1g; Cholesterol 31mg; Calcium 28mg; Fibre 0.7g; Sodium 95mg.
Chocolate Butterscotch Bars Energy 305kcal/1273kJ; Protein 3.5g; Carbohydrate 30g, of which sugars 22.5g; Fat 19.8g, of which saturates 9.7g; Cholesterol 29mg; Calcium 57mg; Fibre 1.2g; Sodium 89mg.

Chocolate and Coconut Slices

Very simple to make, these slices are deliciously moist and sweet. They look very tempting, too, with their sweet coconut filling and attractive, nutty topping.

Makes 24

115g/4oz/1/2 cup butter diced
175g/6oz/scant 2 1/2 cups
   crushed digestive biscuits
   (graham crackers)
50g/2oz/1/4 cup caster
   (superfine) sugar

pinch of salt
75g/3oz/1 cup desiccated
   (dry unsweetened
   shredded) coconut
250g/9oz/1 1/2 cups plain
   (semisweet) chocolate chips
250ml/8fl oz/1 cup sweetened
   condensed milk
115g/4oz/1 cup mixed nuts,
   to decorate

1 Preheat the oven to 180°C/350°F/Gas 4.

2 Melt the butter in a pan over a low heat, then remove from the heat. Mix together the biscuit crumbs, sugar and salt in a bowl and stir in the melted butter until thoroughly combined. Press the mixture evenly over the base of an ungreased 33 x23cm/13 x 9in ovenproof dish.

3 Sprinkle the coconut, then the chocolate chips, over the base. Pour the condensed milk evenly over the chocolate. Sprinkle the walnuts on top.

4 Bake for 30 minutes. Transfer to a wire rack and leave to cool, preferably overnight. When cooled, cut into slices.

Chunky Chocolate Bars

Chocolate, nuts and dried fruit are a truly enticing combination – fabulous.

Makes 12

350g/12oz plain (semisweet)
   chocolate, broken into
   small pieces
115g/4oz/1/2 cup unsalted
   (sweet) butter

400g/14oz can condensed
   (sweetened) milk
225g/8oz digestive biscuits
   (graham crackers), broken
50g/2oz/1/3 cup raisins
115g/4oz/1 1/2 cups ready-to-eat
   dried peaches, coarsely
   chopped
50g/2oz/1/2 cup hazelnuts or
   pecan nuts, coarsely chopped

1 Line a 28 × 18 cm/11 × 7 in cake tin (pan) with clear film (plastic wrap).

2 Melt the chocolate and butter in a large heatproof bowl set over a pan of simmering water. Stir until well mixed. Pour the condensed milk into the chocolate and butter mixture. Beat with a wooden spoon until creamy.

3 Add the remaining ingredients and mix until well coated in the chocolate sauce. Tip the mixture into the prepared tin. Cool, then chill until set.

4 Lift the cake out of the tin using the clear film and then peel off the film. Cut into 12 bars and serve at once.

Chocolate Walnut Bars

Once you have tasted this delicious homemade version, you will never want to eat store-bought again.

Makes 24

50g/2oz/1/2 cup walnuts
75g/3oz/1/3 cup sugar
75g/3oz/2/3 cup plain
   (all-purpose) flour, sifted
75g/3oz/6 tbsp cold unsalted
   (sweet) butter, diced
icing (confectioners') sugar,
   for dusting

For the topping
25g/1oz/2 tbsp unsalted
   (sweet) butter
75ml/5 tbsp water
40g/1 1/2oz/1/3 cup unsweetened
   cocoa powder
115g/4oz/1/2 cup sugar
5ml/1 tsp vanilla extract
pinch of salt
2 eggs

1 Preheat the oven to 180°C/350°F/Gas 4. Lightly grease a 20cm/8in square cake tin (pan).

2 Grind the walnuts with a few tablespoons of the sugar in a food processor, blender or nut grinder.

3 Mix the ground walnuts, the remaining sugar and the flour in a bowl. Rub in the butter until the mixture resembles breadcrumbs.

4 Pat the walnut mixture into the base of the prepared tin in an even layer. Bake for 25 minutes.

5 To make the topping, melt the butter with the water in a small pan over a low heat. Whisk in the cocoa and sugar. Remove from the heat, stir in the vanilla extract and salt and leave to cool for 5 minutes. Whisk in the eggs, one at a time.

6 Remove the cake tin from the oven and pour the topping evenly over the cooked walnut mixture.

7 Return the tin to the oven and bake for about 20 minutes, until set. Set the tin on a wire rack to cool. Once cooled, cut into bars and dust with sifted icing sugar. Store the bars in the refrigerator.

Chocolate and Coconut Slices Energy 217kcal/907kJ; Protein 2.8g; Carbohydrate 20g, of which sugars 15.8g; Fat 14.6g, of which saturates 7.5g; Cholesterol 18mg; Calcium 48mg; Fibre 1g; Sodium 89mg.
Chunky Chocolate Bars Energy 462kcal/1935kJ; Protein 6.3g; Carbohydrate 53.7g, of which sugars 43g; Fat 26.2g, of which saturates 13.9g; Cholesterol 42mg; Calcium 135mg; Fibre 1.9g; Sodium 220mg.
Chocolate Walnut Bars Energy 97kcal/407kJ; Protein 1.5g; Carbohydrate 9.8g, of which sugars 6.5g; Fat 6.1g, of which saturates 2.9g; Cholesterol 26mg; Calcium 16mg; Fibre 0.3g; Sodium 45mg.

White Chocolate Macadamia Slices

Keep these luxury slices for a celebratory afternoon tea. Not only do they have a superbly rich flavour, but a crunchy texture, too. For a special occasion serve with whipped cream.

Makes 16
150g/5oz/1¼ cups macadamia nuts
400g/14oz white chocolate
50g/2oz/¼ cup ready-to-eat dried apricots
75g/3oz/⅓ cup unsalted (sweet) butter
5ml/1 tsp vanilla extract
3 eggs
150g/5oz/⅔ cup light muscovado (brown) sugar
115g/4oz/1 cup self-raising (self-rising) flour

1 Preheat the oven to 190°C/375°F/Gas 5. Lightly grease two 20cm/8in sandwich tins (layer cake pans) and line the base of each with baking parchment.

2 Coarsely chop the nuts and half the white chocolate, making sure that the pieces are more or less the same size, then cut the apricots into similar-size pieces.

3 Place the remaining white chocolate and the butter in a heatproof bowl set over a pan of hot water. Melt over a gentle heat, stirring occasionally until smooth. Remove the bowl from the heat and leave to cool slightly.

4 Stir in the vanilla extract. Whisk the eggs and sugar in a mixing bowl until thick and pale, then whisk in the melted chocolate mixture.

5 Sift the flour over the mixture and fold in gently and evenly. Stir in the nuts, chopped white chocolate and apricots.

6 Spoon into the prepared tins, smooth the top level and bake for 30–35 minutes, until golden brown. Leave to cool slightly, then turn out and leave to cool on a wire rack.

7 Serve cut into slices or wedges, with a spoonful of fresh whipped cream.

Nutty Chocolate Squares

They taste wonderful and look appetizing so these cookies are sure to become a family favourite.

Makes 16
2 eggs
10ml/2 tsp vanilla extract
pinch of salt
175g/6oz/1½ cups pecan nuts, coarsely chopped
50g/2oz/½ cup plain (all-purpose) flour
50g/2oz/¼ cup caster (superfine) sugar
120ml/4fl oz/½ cup golden (light corn) syrup
75g/3oz plain (semisweet) chocolate, finely chopped
45ml/3 tbsp butter
16 pecan halves, for decorating

1 Preheat the oven to 160°C/325°F/Gas 3. Line the base and sides of a 20cm/8in square baking tin (pan) with baking parchment and grease lightly.

2 Whisk together the eggs, vanilla extract and salt. In another bowl, mix together the chopped pecan nuts and flour. Set both bowls aside.

3 In a pan, bring the sugar and golden syrup to the boil. Remove from the heat and stir in the chocolate and butter and blend thoroughly with a wooden spoon.

4 Mix in the beaten egg mixture, then fold in the pecan mixture with a flexible spatula.

5 Pour the mixture into the prepared tin and bake for about 35 minutes, until set. Leave to cool in the tin for 10 minutes before turning out. Cut into 5cm/2in squares and press pecan halves into the tops while warm. Cool completely on a rack.

Cook's Tip
The shells of pecan nuts are naturally brown but they are often sold dyed a pinkish colour, perhaps to make them more eye catching. The dye does not affect the kernels which are naturally a reddish brown colour.

White Chocolate Macadamia Slices Energy 317kcal/1326kJ; Protein 4.8g; Carbohydrate 31.6g, of which sugars 26g; Fat 20g, of which saturates 8.4g; Cholesterol 46mg; Calcium 95mg; Fibre 0.9g; Sodium 97mg. Nutty Chocolate Squares Energy 180kcal/749kJ; Protein 2.6g; Carbohydrate 16.1g, of which sugars 13.3g; Fat 12.1g, of which saturates 3.2g; Cholesterol 31mg; Calcium 30mg; Fibre 0.7g; Sodium 52mg.

Double Chocolate Slices

These delicious cookies have a smooth chocolate base, topped with a mint-flavoured cream and drizzles of melted chocolate. Perfect for a teatime treat – or at any time of day.

Makes 12
200g/7oz/1¾ cups plain
(all-purpose) flour
25g/1oz/2 tbsp unsweetened
cocoa powder

150g/5oz/⅔ cup unsalted
(sweet) butter, diced
75g/3oz/¾ cup icing
(confectioners') sugar

For the topping
75g/3oz white chocolate
mint crisps
50g/2oz/¼ cup unsalted (sweet)
butter, softened
90g/3½oz/scant 1 cup icing
(confectioners') sugar
50g/2oz milk chocolate

1 Preheat the oven to 180°C/350°F/Gas 4. Lightly grease an 18cm/7in square shallow baking tin (pan) and line with a strip of baking parchment that comes up over two opposite sides.

2 Put the flour and cocoa powder into a food processor and add the pieces of butter. Process briefly until the mixture resembles fine breadcrumbs. Add the icing sugar and mix briefly again to form a smooth soft dough.

3 Turn the flour mixture into the prepared tin and gently press out to the edges with your fingers to make an even layer. Bake for 25 minutes, then remove from the oven and leave the base to cool completely in the tin.

4 To make the topping, put the chocolate mint crisps in a plastic bag and tap firmly with a rolling pin until they are crushed. Beat the butter and sugar together until creamy, then beat in the crushed chocolate mint crisps. Spread the mixture evenly over the cookie base.

5 Melt the milk chocolate in a small heatproof bowl set over a pan of gently simmering hot water. Carefully lift the cookie base out of the tin; and remove the paper. Using a teaspoon, drizzle the melted chocolate over the topping. Leave to set, then cut into squares.

Chocolate Raspberry Macaroon Bars

Other seedless jams, such as strawberry or plum, can be used instead of the raspberry in the topping for these flavour-packed bars.

Makes 16–18 bars
115g/4oz/½ cup unsalted
(sweet) butter
50g/2oz/½ cup icing
(confectioners') sugar
25g/1oz/¼ cup unsweetened
cocoa powder
pinch of salt
5ml/1 tsp almond extract
150g/5oz/1¼ cups plain
(all-purpose) flour

For the topping
150g/5oz/scant ½ cup seedless
raspberry jam
15ml/1 tbsp raspberry-
flavour liqueur
175g/6oz/1 cup mini
chocolate chips
175g/6oz/1½ cups finely
ground almonds
4 egg whites
pinch of salt
200g/7oz/1 cup caster
(superfine) sugar
2.5ml/½ tsp almond extract
50g/2oz/½ cup flaked
(sliced) almonds

1 Preheat the oven to 160°C/325°F/Gas 3. Line a 23 × 33cm/ 9 × 13in cake tin (pan) with lightly greased foil.

2 In a bowl, beat together the butter, sugar, cocoa and salt. Add the almond extract and flour and stir until the mixture forms a crumbly dough. Turn the dough into the lined tin and smooth out. Prick with a fork. Bake for 20 minutes, until just set. Remove from the oven and increase the temperature to 190°C/375°F/Gas 5.

3 To make the topping, mix together the raspberry jam and liqueur in a bowl. Spread evenly over the chocolate crust, then sprinkle with chocolate chips.

4 In a food processor fitted with a metal blade, blend the almonds, egg whites, salt, sugar and almond extract until foamy. Pour over the raspberry layer. Sprinkle with flaked almonds.

5 Bake for 20–25 minutes, until the top is golden. Transfer to a wire rack to cool in the tin for 20 minutes. Remove to a wire rack to cool completely. Cut into bars.

Double Chocolate Slices Energy 299kcal/1248kJ; Protein 2.3g; Carbohydrate 34.4g, of which sugars 20.8g; Fat 17.3g, of which saturates 10.8g; Cholesterol 37mg; Calcium 28mg; Fibre 0.8g; Sodium 126mg. **Chocolate Raspberry Macaroon Bars** Energy 266kcal/1115kJ; Protein 4.5g; Carbohydrate 32.1g, of which sugars 26.6g; Fat 14.1g, of which saturates 5.7g; Cholesterol 16mg; Calcium 66mg; Fibre 1.2g; Sodium 79mg.

Vanilla Streusel Bars

The crumbly topping on this cake makes a crunchy contrast to the moist vanilla-flavoured sponge base underneath.

Makes about 25

175g/6oz/1½ cups self-raising (self-rising) flour
5ml/1 tsp baking powder
175g/6oz/¾ cup butter, softened
175g/6oz/¾ cup vanilla sugar
3 eggs, beaten
1½ tsp vanilla extract
1–2 tbsp milk

For the topping

115g/4oz/1 cup self-raising (self-rising) flour
75g/3oz/6 tbsp butter
75g/3oz/6 tbsp vanilla sugar
icing (confectioners') sugar, to finish

1 Preheat the oven to 180°C/350°F/Gas 4. Lightly grease and line a shallow rectangular 23 × 18cm/9 × 7in baking tin (pan) with baking parchment.

2 To make the topping, sift the flour into a bowl and rub in the butter until the mixture resembles coarse breadcrumbs. Stir in the vanilla sugar and set aside.

3 Sift the flour and baking powder into a bowl. Add the butter, vanilla sugar and eggs. Beat well until the mixture is smooth, adding the vanilla extract and just enough milk to give a soft dropping consistency.

4 Spoon the mixture into the prepared tin and level the surface. Sprinkle the streusel topping over the surface and press down to cover.

5 Bake for 45–60 minutes, until browned and firm. Cool in the tin for 5 minutes, then turn out on to a wire rack to cool completely. Cut into bars and dust with icing sugar.

Cook's Tip
Cover the cake loosely with foil if the topping browns too quickly.

Date and Honey Bars

Fresh dates are a good source of natural fibre, yet are kind and gentle on the digestive system. For a slightly different, more toffee flavour, replace the honey with real maple syrup.

Makes 16

175g/6oz/1 cup fresh dates, stoned and coarsely chopped
45ml/3 tbsp clear honey
30ml/2 tbsp lemon juice
150g/5oz/1¼ cups plain (all-purpose) flour
150ml/¼ pint/⅔ cup water
1.5ml/¼ tsp freshly grated nutmeg
115g/4oz/1 cup self-raising (self-rising) flour
25g/1oz/2 tbsp brown sugar
150g/5oz/1¼ cups rolled oats
175g/6oz/¾ cup unsalted (sweet) butter, melted

1 Preheat the oven to 190°C/375°F/Gas 5. Lightly grease the base of an 18cm/7in square cake tin (pan) and line with baking parchment.

2 Put the dates, honey, lemon juice, plain flour and measured water into a heavy pan. Gradually bring to the boil over a low heat, stirring constantly. Remove the pan from the heat and leave to cool.

3 Sift together the nutmeg and self-raising flour into another bowl and stir in the sugar, oats and melted butter until well combined. Spoon half the mixture into the prepared tin and spread it out evenly over the base with the back of the spoon, pressing down well.

4 Spread the date mixture over the top and finish with the remaining oat mixture, pressing evenly all over the surface with the back of a spoon. Bake for about 25 minutes until golden. Cool in the cake tin for 1 hour, then cut into bars.

Cook's Tip
To remove the stone (pit), split the date lengthways with a small sharp knife without cutting right through. Ease out the stone with the point of the knife.

Vanilla Streusel Bars Energy 162kcal/680kJ; Protein 2g; Carbohydrate 19.5g, of which sugars 10.7g; Fat 9g, of which saturates 5.4g; Cholesterol 44mg; Calcium 27mg; Fibre 0.4g; Sodium 70mg.
Date and Honey Bars Energy 203kcal/853kJ; Protein 3g; Carbohydrate 27g, of which sugars 7.5g; Fat 10g, of which saturates 5.7g; Cholesterol 23mg; Calcium 34mg; Fibre 1.4g; Sodium 71mg.

Chocolate Dominoes

These sweet and sugary confections are ideal for children to help to decorate.

Makes 16
175g/6oz/³/₄ cup butter
175g/6oz/³/₄ cup caster
   (superfine) sugar
3 eggs
150g/5oz/1¼ cups self-raising
   (self-rising) flour

25g/1oz/¼ cup unsweetened
   cocoa powder, sifted

For the topping
175g/6oz/³/₄ cup butter
25g/1oz/¼ cup unsweetened
   cocoa powder
300g/11oz/2½ cups icing
   (confectioners') sugar
a few liquorice strips
115g/4oz M&Ms, for decoration

1 Preheat the oven to 180°C/350°F/Gas 4. Lightly grease an 18 x 28cm/7 x 11in baking tin, and line the base and sides with baking parchment.

2 Put all the cake ingredients in a bowl and beat until smooth. Spoon into the prepared tin and level with a metal spatula.

3 Bake for 30 minutes, until the cake springs back when pressed with the fingertips. Cool in the tin for 5 mintues, then loosen the edges with a knife and transfer to a wire rack. Peel off the paper and leave to cool. Turn out and cut into 16 bars.

4 To make the topping, place the butter in a bowl, sift in the cocoa and icing sugar and beat until smooth. Spread the topping evenly over the cakes.

5 Decorate each with a strip of liquorice and M&Ms.

Variation
To make Traffic Light Cakes, omit the cocoa and add an extra 25g/1oz/3 tbsp plain (all-purpose) flour. Omit cocoa from the icing and add an extra 25g/1oz/4 tbsp icing (confectioners') sugar and 2.5ml/½ tsp vanilla extract. Spread over the cakes and decorate with red, yellow and green glacé cherries to look like traffic lights.

Chocolate Nut Slices

Although the unsliced bar looks small, it's very rich so is best sliced thinly. If you have any other plain cookies in the cupboard, you can use them instead of the rich tea, with equally good results.

Makes 10 slices
225g/8oz milk chocolate
40g/1½oz/3 tbsp unsalted
   (sweet) butter, diced
75g/3oz rich tea biscuits
   (plain cookies)
50g/2oz/½ cup flaked
   (sliced) almonds
75g/3oz plain (semisweet)
   or white chocolate,
   coarsely chopped
icing (confectioners') sugar,
   for dusting

1 Break the milk chocolate into small pieces and place in a heatproof bowl with the butter. Set the bowl over a pan of gently simmering water and heat gently, stirring frequently until melted.

2 Dampen a 450g/1lb loaf tin (pan) and line the base and sides with clear film (plastic wrap). Don't worry about smoothing out the creases in the film.

3 When the chocolate has melted and the mixture is smooth, remove the bowl from the heat and leave for 5 minutes, until slightly cooled.

4 Break the cookies into small pieces, then stir into the melted chocolate with the almonds. Add the chopped plain or white chocolate to the bowl and fold in quickly and lightly with a flexible spatula.

5 Turn the mixture into the tin and pack down with a fork. Tap the base of the tin gently on the work surface. Chill in the refrigerator for 2 hours until set.

6 To serve, turn the chocolate loaf on to a board and peel away the clear film. Dust lightly with icing sugar and slice thinly with a serrated knife.

Chocolate Dominoes Energy 326kcal/1361kJ; Protein 2.7g; Carbohydrate 29g, of which sugars 23.8g; Fat 23g, of which saturates 13.9g; Cholesterol 33mg; Calcium 44mg; Fibre 0.9g; Sodium 144mg.
Chocolate Nut Slices Energy 248kcal/1034kJ; Protein 3.7g; Carbohydrate 23.5g, of which sugars 19.4g; Fat 16.1g, of which saturates 8.2g; Cholesterol 16mg; Calcium 74mg; Fibre 0.9g; Sodium 75mg.

Rocky Road Chocolate Bars

This recipe is a dream to make with kids. They love smashing up the biscuits, and can do most of the rest, apart from melting the chocolate and lining the tin. The divine flavour of melting chocolate chips, crunchy cookies and soft marsh-mallows blended together is not just kid's stuff.

Makes 16 bars
225g/8oz/1 cup butter
115g/4oz dark (bittersweet)
chocolate with more than
60 per cent cocoa solids,
roughly broken up
30ml/2 tbsp caster
(superfine) sugar
30ml/2 tbsp golden (light
corn) syrup
30ml/2 tbsp good quality
unsweetened cocoa powder
350g/12oz mixed digestive
biscuits (graham crackers) and
ginger nuts (ginger snaps)
50g/2oz/1/2 cup mini
marshmallows
75g/3oz/1/2 cup mixed white and
milk chocolate chips
icing (confectioners') sugar, for
dusting (optional)

1 Line a 20cm/8in square cake tin (pan), measuring 2.5cm/1in deep, with baking parchment.

2 Put the butter in a pan with the chocolate, sugar, syrup and cocoa powder. Place over a gentle heat until completely melted.

3 Put the biscuits into a large plastic bag and crush with a rolling pin until broken up into coarse chunks. Stir these into the chocolate mixture. Add the marshmallows, then the chocolate chips, mixing well after each addition.

4 Spoon the mixture into the tin, but don't press down too much – it should look like a rocky road. Chill for at least 1 hour, or until firm. Remove from the tin and cut into 16 bars. Dust the bars with icing sugar before serving.

Variation
Substitute butter cookies if you don't like ginger.

Chocolate and Prune Bars

Wickedly self-indulgent and very easy to make, these fruity chocolate bars will keep for 2–3 days in the refrigerator – if they don't all get eaten as soon as they are ready. You could try adding different combinations of dried fruit.

Makes 12 bars
250g/9oz good quality
milk chocolate
50g/2oz/1/4 cup butter
115g/4oz digestive biscuits
(graham crackers)
115g/4oz/1/2 cup ready-to-
eat prunes

1 Break the chocolate into small pieces and place in a heatproof bowl. Add the butter and place the bowl over a pan of gently simmering water until the butter and chocolate have melted. Stir to mix and set aside.

2 Put the digestive biscuits in a plastic bag and seal it, then crush them into small pieces with a rolling pin.

3 Coarsely chop the prunes and stir into the melted chocolate with the biscuits.

4 Spoon the chocolate and prune mixture into a 20cm/8in square cake tin (pan) and chill for 1–2 hours until set. Remove the cake from the refrigerator and cut into 12 bars.

Cook's Tip
Do not cover the bars with cling film (plastic wrap) when chilling as condensation may spoil their texture.

Variations
• Other dried fruits are also delicious in these bars. Try dried plums, which are not quite the same as prunes and are usually made from golden rather than red varieties. Apricots would also be a good alternative.
• For extra flavour, stir 1.5ml/1/4 tsp freshly grated nutmeg or 2.5ml/1/2 tsp ground cinnamon into the chocolate mixture.

Rocky Road Chocolate Bars Energy 296kcal/1237kJ; Protein 2.7g; Carbohydrate 28.6g, of which sugars 15.7g; Fat 19.9g, of which saturates 11.6g; Cholesterol 40mg; Calcium 39mg; Fibre 0.9g; Sodium 245mg. Chocolate and Prune Bars Energy 197kcal/826kJ; Protein 2.5g; Carbohydrate 21.7g, of which sugars 16.4g; Fat 11.8g, of which saturates 6.8g; Cholesterol 18mg; Calcium 59mg; Fibre 0.9g; Sodium 102mg.

Marbled Brownies

These are the perfect brownies – made from a mixture of flavours swirled together before baking.

Makes 24
225g/8oz plain (semisweet) chocolate, chopped
75g/3oz/¹⁄₃ cup butter, diced
4 eggs
350g/12oz/1¾ cups caster (superfine) sugar
115g/4oz/1 cup plain (all-purpose) flour
pinch of salt
5ml/1 tsp baking powder
10ml/2 tsp vanilla extract
115g/4oz/1 cup walnuts, chopped

For the plain batter
50g/2oz/¹⁄₄ cup butter
175g/6oz/³⁄₄ cup cream cheese
115g/4oz/generous ¹⁄₂ cup caster (superfine) sugar
2 eggs
30ml/2 tbsp plain (all-purpose) flour
5ml/1 tsp vanilla extract

1 Preheat the oven to 180°C/350°F/Gas 4. Line a 33 × 23cm/13 × 9in tin (pan) with baking parchment.

2 Melt the plain chocolate and butter in a small pan over a low heat, stirring occasionally until smooth. Leave to cool slightly.

3 Beat the eggs until light and fluffy. Gradually add the caster sugar and beat well. Sift over the flour, salt and baking powder and fold in with a metal spoon. Fold in the chocolate mixture.

4 Set aside 475ml/16fl oz/2 cups of the chocolate batter. Stir the vanilla extract and walnuts into the rest of the mixture.

5 To make the plain batter, beat the butter and cream cheese with an electric mixer. Add the sugar and continue beating until blended. Beat in the eggs, flour and vanilla extract.

6 Spread the chocolate batter into the tin. Pour over the plain batter. Drop spoonfuls of the reserved chocolate batter on top. Swirl the mixtures to marble. Do not blend completely.

7 Bake for 35–40 minutes, until just set. Unmould when cool and cut into squares for serving.

Gingerbread Brownies

Warm and spicy, ginger liqueur is an inspired addition to this gingerbread cake with its fudge topping.

Serves 10–12
175g/6oz/³⁄₄ cup soft dark muscovado (molasses) sugar
175g/6oz/¹⁄₂ cup black treacle (molasses)
50g/2oz/¹⁄₄ cup clear honey
175g/6oz/³⁄₄ cup butter
5ml/1 tsp bicarbonate of soda (baking soda)
275g/10oz/2¹⁄₂ cups plain (all-purpose) flour
pinch of salt
15ml/1 tbsp ground ginger
10ml/2 tsp ground cinnamon
2 eggs, beaten
115g/4oz/1 cup chopped walnuts
50g/2oz/¹⁄₃ cup crystallized (candied) ginger, chopped
30ml/2 tbsp ginger liqueur
60ml/4 tbsp milk
extra chopped walnuts and crystallized (candied) ginger, to decorate

For the fudge topping
50g/2oz/4 tbsp butter
45ml/3 tbsp ginger liqueur
225g/8oz/2 cups icing (confectioners') sugar, sifted

1 Preheat the oven to 160°C/325°F/Gas 3. Grease and line a 20cm/8in square cake tin (pan).

2 Put the sugar, treacle, honey and butter into a heavy pan. Stir over a low heat until all the ingredients have melted, then cool. Stir in the bicarbonate of soda.

3 Sift the flour, salt, ginger and ground cinnamon into a bowl. Using a wooden spoon, stir in the melted ingredients.

4 Stir in the eggs, walnuts, crystallized ginger and liqueur, with enough of the milk to make a stiff cake mixture. Turn into the tin and bake for 1¼–1½ hours, until firm. Cool on a wire rack.

5 To make the fudge topping, put the butter, ginger liqueur and icing sugar into a heatproof bowl and set over a pan of barely simmering water. Stir until smooth, remove from the heat and leave to cool. Beat with a wooden spoon until it is thick enough to spread. Swirl over the cake. Cut into slices and decorate with extra walnuts and pieces of crystallized ginger.

Marbled Brownies Energy 259kcal/1083kJ; Protein 3.8g; Carbohydrate 28.8g, of which sugars 23.1g; Fat 15.1g, of which saturates 7.1g; Cholesterol 66mg; Calcium 42mg; Fibre 0.6g; Sodium 73mg.
Gingerbread Brownies Energy 387kcal/1632kJ; Protein 5.2g; Carbohydrate 68.3g, of which sugars 50.7g; Fat 11.3g, of which saturates 3.1g; Cholesterol 41mg; Calcium 151mg; Fibre 1.1g; Sodium 70mg.

Raisin Brownies

Adding dried fruit makes brownies a little more substantial, although no less moist and delicious. Try to find Californian or Spanish raisins for the best flavour and texture.

Makes 16

115g/4oz/1/2 cup butter, diced
50g/2oz/1/2 cup unsweetened
    cocoa powder
2 eggs
225g/8oz/generous 1 cup caster
    (superfine) sugar
5ml/1 tsp vanilla extract
40g/11/2 oz/1/3 cup plain
    (all-purpose) flour
75g/3oz/3/4 cup walnuts, chopped
65g/21/2oz/1/2 cup raisins
icing (confectioners') sugar,
    for dusting

1 Preheat the oven to 180°C/350°F/Gas 4. Line a 20cm/8in square baking tin (pan) with baking parchment and grease the paper lightly.

2 Melt the butter in a small pan over a low heat. Remove from the heat and stir in the cocoa.

3 In a bowl, beat together the eggs, sugar and vanilla extract with an electric mixer until light and fluffy. Add the cocoa mixture and stir to blend.

4 Sift the flour over the cocoa mixture and fold in gently with a metal spoon. Add the walnuts and raisins, mixing them in gently, then scrape the mixture into the prepared tin.

5 Bake for about 30 minutes, until firm to the touch, being careful not to overbake.

6 Leave in the tin on a rack to cool completely. Cut into 5cm/2in squares and remove from the tin. Dust with sifted icing sugar before serving.

Variation
For an adult taste, try substituting rum for the vanilla.

Nut and Chocolate Chip Brownies

These chunky chocolate brownies are moist, dark and deeply satisfying. They are delicious with a morning cup of coffee and will definitely boost morale on a dreary day.

Makes 16

150g/5oz plain (semisweet)
    chocolate, chopped
120ml/4fl oz/1/2 cup sunflower oil
215g/71/2oz/scant 1 cup light
    muscovado (brown) sugar
2 eggs
5ml/1 tsp vanilla extract
65g/21/2oz/9 tbsp self-raising
    (self-rising) flour
60ml/4 tbsp unsweetened
    cocoa powder
75g/3oz/3/4 cup chopped walnuts
60ml/4 tbsp milk chocolate chips

1 Preheat the oven to 180°C/350°F/Gas 4. Lightly grease a shallow 19cm/71/2in square cake tin (pan).

2 Melt the plain chocolate in a heatproof bowl over a pan of gently simmering water.

3 Beat together the oil, sugar, eggs and vanilla extract. Stir in the melted chocolate and beat well.

4 Sift the flour and cocoa powder into the bowl and fold in until well combined. Stir in the chopped nuts and milk chocolate chips, then tip the mixture into the prepared tin and spread evenly to the edges.

5 Bake for about 30–35 minutes, until the top is firm and crusty. Cool in the tin before cutting into squares.

Cook's Tip
These brownies freeze well and can be stored in the freezer for 3 months in an airtight container.

Variation
Substitute chopped pecan nuts for the walnuts, if you like.

Nut and Chocolate Chip Brownies Energy 235kcal/983kJ; Protein 3.4g; Carbohydrate 25.9g, of which sugars 22.2g; Fat 13.9g, of which saturates 3.8g; Cholesterol 25mg; Calcium 37mg; Fibre 1g; Sodium 49mg. **Raisin Brownies** Energy 181kcal/759kJ; Protein 2.5g; Carbohydrate 20.4g, of which sugars 18.1g; Fat 10.5g, of which saturates 4.6g; Cholesterol 39mg; Calcium 26mg; Fibre 0.7g; Sodium 86mg.

Banana Brownies

Bananas, powerhouses of energy and packed with nutrients, yet very low in fat, not only make these brownies deliciously moist but also a healthy option.

Makes 9

75ml/5 tbsp unsweetened cocoa powder
15ml/1 tbsp caster (superfine) sugar
75ml/5 tbsp milk
3 large bananas, mashed
175g/6oz/¾ cup soft light brown sugar
5ml/1 tsp vanilla extract
5 egg whites
75g/3oz/¾ cup self-raising (self-rising) flour
75g/3oz/¾ cup oat bran
15ml/1 tbsp icing (confectioners') sugar, for dusting

1 Preheat the oven to 180°C/350°F/Gas 4. Line a 20cm/8in square cake tin (pan) with baking parchment.

2 Blend the cocoa powder and caster sugar with the milk in a bowl. Add the bananas, soft brown sugar and vanilla extract.

3 In a large bowl, lightly beat the egg whites with a fork. Add the chocolate mixture and continue to beat well.

4 Sift the flour over the mixture and fold in with the oat bran. Pour the mixture into the prepared cake tin.

5 Bake for 40 minutes, or until the top is firm and crusty. Leave to cool completely in the tin before cutting into squares. Lightly dust the brownies with icing sugar before serving.

> **Variation**
> *Adding dried fruit or fresh berries would make these brownies even more of a special treat without dramatically increasing the fat content. Good extras include 50g/2oz/ scant ½ cup raisins, 50g/2oz/⅓ cup dried sour cherries or cranberries or 50g/2oz/½ cup fresh blueberries or 50g/2oz/ ⅓ cup fresh raspberries.*

Low-fat Brownies

If you ever need proof that you can still enjoy sweet treats even when you are following a low-fat diet, here it is. These brownies are not just tasty, but also very quick and easy to make.

Makes 16

100g/3½oz/scant 1 cup plain (all-purpose) flour
2.5ml/½ tsp baking powder
45ml/3 tbsp unsweetened cocoa powder
200g/7oz/1 cup caster (superfine) sugar
100ml/3½fl oz/scant ½ cup natural (plain) low-fat yogurt
2 eggs, beaten
5ml/1 tsp vanilla extract
25ml/1½ tbsp vegetable oil

1 Preheat the oven to 180°C/350°F/Gas 4. Line a 20cm/8in square cake tin (pan) with baking parchment.

2 Sift the flour, baking powder and cocoa powder into a bowl. Stir in the caster sugar, then beat in the yogurt, eggs, vanilla and vegetable oil until thoroughly combined. Put the mixture into the prepared tin.

3 Bake for about 25 minutes, until just firm to the touch. Leave in the tin until cooled completely.

4 Using a sharp knife, cut into 16 squares, then remove from the tin using a spatula.

> **Cook's Tip**
> *Low-fat yogurt is made from concentrated skimmed (low fat) milk, has a fat content of between 0.5 and 2 per cent and contains about 56 calories per 100ml/3½fl oz/scant ½ cup. Very low-fat yogurt, sometimes called low-calorie yogurt, is also available and this has a fat content of less than 0.5 per cent and contains about 41 calories per 100ml/3½fl oz/scant ½ cup. Note that soya yogurt is not a substitute in this recipe. Even though it does not contain milk, it is higher in both fat and calories.*

Banana Brownies Energy 101kcal/426kJ; Protein 4.6g; Carbohydrate 16.6g, of which sugars 10.8g; Fat 2.2g, of which saturates 1.2g; Cholesterol 0mg; Calcium 31mg; Fibre 2.8g; Sodium 167mg.
Low-fat Brownies Energy 53kcal/222kJ; Protein 2.2g; Carbohydrate 5.7g, of which sugars 0.6g; Fat 2.6g, of which saturates 0.7g; Cholesterol 24mg; Calcium 28mg; Fibre 0.5g; Sodium 41mg.

BARS, SQUARES, SLICES AND BROWNIES

Fudgy-glazed Chocolate Brownies

For a simpler brownie, omit the fudge glaze and dust with icing sugar or cocoa instead.

Makes 8–10
250g/9oz plain (semi-sweet) chocolate, chopped
25g/1oz milk chocolate, chopped
115g/4oz/½ cup unsalted (sweet) butter, diced
100g/3½oz/½ cup light brown sugar
50g/2oz/¼ cup sugar
2 eggs
15ml/1 tbsp vanilla extract
65g/2½oz/9 tbsp plain (all-purpose) flour
115g/4oz/1 cup pecans or walnuts, toasted and chopped
150g/5oz fine quality white chocolate, chopped into 5mm/¼in pieces
pecan halves, to decorate

For the fudgy glaze
170g/6oz plain (semisweet) chocolate, chopped
50g/2oz/4 tbsp unsalted (sweet) butter, diced
30ml/2 tbsp golden (light corn) syrup
10ml/2 tsp vanilla extract

1 Preheat the oven to 180°C/350°F/Gas 4. Line a 20cm/8in cake tin (pan) with foil. Lightly grease the foil.

2 In a large pan, melt the plain and milk chocolate with the butter, until smooth, stirring frequently. Remove from the heat.

3 Stir in the sugars until dissolved. Beat in the eggs and vanilla. Stir in the flour until just blended. Stir in the chopped pecans and white chocolate. Pour the batter into the prepared tin.

4 Bake for 20–25 minutes, until a skewer inserted into the centre comes out clean. Remove to a wire rack for 30 minutes, then use the foil to lift the brownies and leave to cool for 2 hours.

5 To make the glaze, in a medium pan over a medium heat, melt the glaze ingredients, stirring frequently. Remove from the heat, chill for 1 hour. Spread a layer of the glaze over the brownies. Cut into bars with a sharp knife and decorate each bar with a pecan half. Chill until set.

Chocolate and Date Brownies

Dark and full of flavour, these brownies are irresistible. They make a good teatime treat, or are perfect for accompanying a cup of coffee with friends.

Makes 20
150g/5oz/⅔ cup butter
150g/5oz/scant 1 cup stoned (pitted) dates, softened in boiling water, then drained and finely chopped
150g/5oz/1¼ cups self-raising (self-rising) wholemeal (whole-wheat) flour
10ml/2 tsp baking powder
60ml/4 tbsp unsweetened cocoa powder dissolved in 30ml/2 tbsp hot water
60ml/4 tbsp apple and pear spread
90ml/6 tbsp unsweetened coconut milk
50g/2oz/½ cup walnuts or pecan nuts, coarsely broken

1 Preheat the oven to 160°C/325°F/Gas 3. Lightly grease a 28 × 18cm/11 × 7in shallow baking tin.

2 Beat the butter and dates together in a bowl. Sift together the flour and baking powder into another bowl, then, using a flexible spatula, gradually fold the dry ingredients into the butter mixture in batches, alternating with the cocoa, apple and pear spread and coconut milk. Stir in the nuts.

3 Spoon the mixture into the prepared tin and smooth the surface with the back of the spoon.

4 Bake for about 45 minutes, or until a fine skewer inserted in the centre comes out clean. Cool for a few minutes in the tin, then cut into bars or squares. Using a metal spatula, transfer to a wire rack to cool completely.

Cook's Tip
You can use dried dates straight from the packet but they are better softened first. Put them in a small pan and add water to cover. Bring to the boil, then lower the heat and simmer gently for about 5 minutes. Drain well and pat dry with kitchen paper before chopping.

Fudge-glazed Chocolate Brownies Energy 574kcal/2393kJ; Protein 6.5g; Carbohydrate 50.3g, of which sugars 44.8g; Fat 40g, of which saturates 19.9g; Cholesterol 76mg; Calcium 88mg; Fibre 1.8g; Sodium 144mg. **Chocolate and Date Brownies** Energy 285kcal/1189kJ; Protein 4.3g; Carbohydrate 26.3g, of which sugars 13.3g; Fat 9.8g, of which saturates 5.3g; Cholesterol 56mg; Calcium 38mg; Fibre 1.3g; Sodium 62mg.

Chocolate Cheesecake Brownies

A very dense chocolate
brownie mixture is swirled
with creamy cheese to give
a marbled effect. Cut into
squares for little mouthfuls
of absolute heaven.

Makes 16
1 egg
225g/8oz/1 cup full-fat
  cream cheese
50g/2oz/¼ cup caster
  (superfine) sugar
5ml/1 tsp vanilla extract

For the brownie mixture
115g/4oz dark (bittersweet)
  chocolate (minimum
  70 per cent cocoa solids)
115g/4oz/½ cup unsalted
  (sweet) butter
150g/5oz/¾ cup light muscovado
  (brown) sugar
2 eggs, beaten
50g/2oz/½ cup plain
  (all-purpose) flour

1 Preheat the oven to 160°C/325°F/Gas 3. Line the base and
sides of a 20cm/8in cake tin (pan) with baking parchment.

2 To make the cheesecake mixture, beat the egg in a mixing
bowl, then add the cream cheese, caster sugar and vanilla
extract. Beat together until smooth and creamy.

3 To make the brownie mixture, put the chocolate and
butter in a heatproof bowl set over a pan of gently
simmering water and heat, stirring occasionally, until melted.
Remove from the heat and leave to cool slightly.

4 Stir the sugar into the chocolate mixture until dissolved, then
gradually add the beaten eggs, beating well after each addition.
Gently fold in the flour with a flexible spatula.

5 Spread two-thirds of the brownie mixture over the base
of the tin. Spread the cheesecake mixture on top, then spoon
on the remaining brownie mixture in heaps. Using a skewer,
swirl the mixtures together.

6 Bake for 30–35 minutes, or until just set in the centre. Leave
to cool in the tin, then cut into squares. Store for up to one
week in an airtight container.

White Chocolate Brownies

These irresistible brownies
are packed full of creamy
white chocolate and juicy
dried fruit. They are best
served cut into very small
portions as they are
incredibly rich.

Makes 18
75g/3oz/6 tbsp unsalted (sweet)
  butter, diced
400g/14oz white chocolate,
  coarsely chopped

3 eggs
90g/3½oz/½ cup golden caster
  (superfine) sugar
10ml/2 tsp vanilla extract
90g/3½oz/¾ cup sultanas
  (golden raisins)
coarsely grated rind of 1 lemon,
  plus 15ml/1 tbsp juice
200g/7oz/1¾ cups plain
  (all-purpose) flour

1 Preheat the oven to 190°C/375°F/Gas 5. Grease and line a
28 × 20cm/11 × 8in shallow, rectangular baking tin (pan) with
baking parchment.

2 Put the butter and 300g/11oz of the chocolate in a
heatproof bowl and set over a pan of gently simmering water,
stirring frequently until melted.

3 Remove the bowl from the heat and beat in the eggs and
sugar, then add the vanilla extract, sultanas, lemon rind and juice,
flour and the remaining chocolate. Tip the mixture into the tin
and spread into the corners.

4 Bake for about 20 minutes, until slightly risen and the surface
is only just turning golden. The centre should still be slightly soft.
Leave to cool in the tin.

5 Cut the brownies into small squares and remove from the tin.

> **Variation**
> *White chocolate is very sweet so, to compromise, make the
> brownie mixture with white chocolate as described, then stir in
> 100g/3½oz chopped milk chocolate with the flour.*

Chocolate Cheesecake Brownies Energy 226kcal/940kJ; Protein 2.4g; Carbohydrate 20.1g, of which sugars 17.7g; Fat 15.7g, of which saturates 9.4g; Cholesterol 65mg; Calcium 34mg; Fibre 0.3g;
Sodium 100mg. White Chocolate Brownies Energy 232kcal/973kJ; Protein 4g; Carbohydrate 30.3g, of which sugars 21.8g; Fat 11.4g, of which saturates 6.5g; Cholesterol 41mg; Calcium 86mg;
Fibre 0.4g; Sodium 65mg.

Butterscotch Brownies

These gorgeous treats are made with brown sugar, white chocolate chips and walnuts. Who could possibly have the will power to resist? You might want to make two batches at a time.

Makes 12
450g/1lb white chocolate chips
75g/3oz/6 tbsp unsalted (sweet) butter
3 eggs
175g/6oz/¾ cup light muscovado (brown) sugar
175g/6oz/1½ cups self-raising (self-rising) flour
175g/6oz/1½ cups walnuts, chopped
5ml/1 tsp vanilla extract

1 Preheat the oven to 190°C/375°F/Gas 5. Line the base of a 28 × 18cm/11 × 7in shallow tin (pan) with baking parchment. Lightly grease the sides.

2 Put 90g/3½oz/generous ½ cup of the chocolate chips and the butter into a heatproof bowl set over a pan of barely simmering water and heat gently, stirring occasionally, until melted and smooth. Remove the bowl from the heat and leave to cool slightly.

3 Put the eggs and light muscovado sugar into a large bowl and whisk well, then whisk in the melted chocolate mixture.

4 Sift the flour into the bowl and, using a flexible spatula, gently fold it into the mixture together with the chopped walnuts, vanilla extract and the remaining chocolate chips until thoroughly combined.

5 Spoon the mixture into the prepared tin and spread it out evenly with the back of the spoon. Bake for about 30 minutes, or until risen and light golden brown. The centre should be firm but will still be slightly soft until it cools. Leave to cool completely in the tin.

6 Cut into 12 bars when the brownie is completely cold. Store in an airtight container.

Chunky White Chocolate and Coffee Brownies

Brownies should have a gooey texture, so take care not to overcook them – when ready, the mixture will still be slightly soft under the crust, but will firm as it cools.

Makes 12
25ml/1½ tbsp ground coffee
45ml/3 tbsp near-boiling water
300g/11oz plain (semisweet) chocolate, broken into pieces
225g/8oz/1 cup butter
225g/8oz/generous 1 cup caster (superfine) sugar
3 eggs
75g/3oz/¾ cup self-raising (self-rising) flour, sifted
225g/8oz white chocolate, coarsely chopped

1 Preheat the oven to 190°C/375°F/Gas 5. Grease and line the base of an 18 × 28cm/7 × 11in shallow tin with baking parchment.

2 Put the coffee in a bowl and pour the water over. Leave to infuse for 4 minutes, then strain through a sieve (strainer).

3 Put the plain chocolate and butter in a bowl over a pan of hot water and stir occasionally until melted. Remove from the heat and leave to cool for 5 minutes.

4 In a large bowl, beat the sugar and eggs together. Stir in the chocolate and butter mixture and the coffee. Stir in the sifted flour.

5 Fold in the white chocolate pieces. Pour into the prepared tin.

6 Bake for 45–50 minutes, or until firm and the top is crusty. Leave to cool in the tin. When completely cold, cut into squares and remove from the tin.

> **Cook's Tip**
> If it's easier, make 45ml/3 tbsp strong instant coffee.

Butterscotch Brownies Energy 469kcal/1961kJ; Protein 8.1g; Carbohydrate 48.7g, of which sugars 37.7g; Fat 28.3g, of which saturates 11.4g; Cholesterol 61mg; Calcium 182mg; Fibre 1g; Sodium 151mg.
Chunky White Chocolate and Coffee Brownies Energy 480kcal/2005kJ; Protein 5.1g; Carbohydrate 51.4g, of which sugars 46.4g; Fat 29.7g, of which saturates 17.8g; Cholesterol 89mg; Calcium 88mg; Fibre 0.8g; Sodium 155mg.

Date and Walnut Brownies

These rich brownies are great for afternoon tea, but they also make a fantastic dessert. Reheat slices briefly in the microwave oven and serve with crème fraîche.

Makes 12
350g/12oz plain (semisweet) chocolate, broken into squares
225g/8oz/1 cup butter, diced
3 large (US extra large) eggs
115g/4oz/generous ½ cup caster (superfine) sugar
5ml/1 tsp vanilla extract
75g/3oz/¾ cup plain (all-purpose) flour, sifted
225g/8oz/1½ cups fresh dates, peeled, stoned (pitted) and chopped
200g/7oz/1¾ cups walnut pieces
icing (confectioners') sugar, for dusting

1 Preheat the oven to 190°C/375°F/Gas 5. Generously grease a 30 × 20cm/12 × 8in rectangular baking tin (pan) and line with baking parchment.

2 Put the chocolate squares and diced butter into a large heatproof bowl. Set the bowl over a pan of gently simmering water and heat gently until melted. Stir until smooth, then remove the bowl from the heat and leave to cool slightly.

3 In a separate bowl, beat together the eggs, sugar and vanilla. Beat into the chocolate mixture, then fold in the flour, dates and nuts. Pour into the tin.

4 Bake for 30–40 minutes, until firm and the mixture comes away from the sides of the tin. Cool in the tin, then turn out, remove the parchment and dust with icing sugar. Cut the brownies into bars or squares.

Cook's Tip
When melting the chocolate and butter, keep the water in the pan beneath simmering gently, but do not let it approach boiling point. Chocolate is notoriously sensitive to heat; it is vital not to let it get too hot or it may stiffen into an unmanageable mass.

Chocolate Chip Brownies

These easy-to-make classic brownies never fail to please and make great snacks and lunchtime treats for children and adults alike.

Makes 24
115g/4oz plain (semisweet) chocolate
115g/4oz/½ cup butter
3 eggs
200g/7oz/1 cup caster (superfine) sugar
2.5ml/½ tsp vanilla extract
pinch of salt
150g/5oz/1¼ cups plain (all-purpose) flour
175g/6oz/1 cup chocolate chips

1 Preheat the oven to 180°C/350°F/Gas 4. Lightly grease and line a 33 × 23cm/13 × 9in rectangular cake tin (pan) with baking parchment.

2 Break the chocolate into pieces and put into a heatproof bowl with the butter, then set the bowl over a pan of barely simmering water and heat gently, stirring occasionally, until melted and smooth. Remove the bowl from the heat and leave to cool slightly.

3 Beat together the eggs, caster sugar, vanilla extract and salt in a bowl until creamy. Stir in the cooled chocolate mixture. Sift the flour over the mixture and gently fold in with a flexible spatula, then add the chocolate chips and gently stir in.

4 Pour the mixture into the prepared tin and spread evenly with a metal spatula. Bake in the oven for about 30 minutes, until just set. Be careful not to overbake; the brownies should still be slightly moist inside. Remove the tin from the oven and leave to cool completely.

5 To turn out, run a round-bladed knife all around the edge of the tin and invert on to a baking sheet. Remove and discard the baking parchment. Place another baking sheet on top of the brownies and invert again so that they are the right side up. Cut into bars or squares for serving. Store in an airtight container for up to 1 week.

Date and Walnut Brownies Energy 504kcal/2097kJ; Protein 6.5g; Carbohydrate 39.9g, of which sugars 34.8g; Fat 36.5g, of which saturates 16g; Cholesterol 89mg; Calcium 54mg; Fibre 1.8g; Sodium 136mg. Chocolate Chip Brownies Energy 161kcal/674kJ; Protein 2g; Carbohydrate 21.3g, of which sugars 16.4g; Fat 8.1g, of which saturates 4.7g; Cholesterol 35mg; Calcium 22mg; Fibre 0.5g; Sodium 39mg.

Cranberry and Chocolate Cakes

There is no doubt that the contrasting flavours of tangy, sharp cranberries and sweet chocolate were made for each other – and make simply fabulous cream-topped squares.

Makes 12
115g/4oz/½ cup unsalted
   (sweet) butter
60ml/4 tbsp unsweetened
   cocoa powder
215g/7½oz/scant 1 cup light
   muscovado (brown) sugar
150g/5oz/1¼ cups self-raising
   (self-rising) flour, plus extra
   for dusting

2 eggs, beaten
115g/4oz/1 cup fresh or thawed
   frozen cranberries

For the topping
150ml/¼ pint/⅔ cup sour cream
75g/3oz/scant ½ cup caster
   (superfine) sugar
30ml/2 tbsp self-raising
   (self-rising) flour
50g/2oz/4 tbsp soft butter
1 egg, beaten
2.5ml/½ tsp vanilla extract
75ml/5 tbsp coarsely grated plain
   (semisweet) chocolate,
   for sprinkling

1 Preheat the oven to 180°C/350°F/Gas 4. Lightly grease an 18 × 25cm/7 × 10in cake tin (pan) and dust lightly with flour, shaking out any excess.

2 Combine the butter, cocoa powder and sugar in a pan and stir over a low heat until melted and smooth.

3 Remove the pan from the heat and stir in the flour and beaten eggs. Stir in the cranberries, then spread the mixture evenly in the prepared cake tin.

4 To make the topping, put the sour cream, sugar, flour, butter, beaten egg and vanilla extract into a bowl and beat well until smooth and thoroughly combined. Spoon the mixture into the tin and gently spread it evenly over the chocolate and cranberry base.

5 Sprinkle evenly with the coarsely grated chocolate and bake for about 40 minutes, or until risen and firm. Leave to cool completely in the tin, then cut into 12 squares.

Rainbow Gingerbread Cakes

These gingerbread squares have a more spongy texture than traditional gingerbread cookies and look stunning decorated with vibrantly coloured sprinkles. Ground and preserved stem ginger gives a really spicy flavour, but can easily be left out for younger children.

Makes 16
225g/8oz/2 cups plain
   (all-purpose) flour
5ml/1 tsp baking powder
10ml/2 tsp ground ginger
2 pieces preserved stem ginger,
   finely chopped
90g/3½oz/¾ cup raisins

50g/2oz/¼ cup glacé (candied)
   cherries, chopped
115g/4oz/½ cup unsalted
   (sweet) butter, diced
115g/4oz/⅓ cup golden (light
   corn) syrup
30ml/2 tbsp black treacle
   (molasses)
75g/3oz/⅓ cup dark muscovado
   (molasses) sugar
2 eggs, beaten

For the topping
200g/7oz/1¾ cups icing
   (confectioners') sugar
50g/2oz/¼ cup unsalted
   (sweet) butter, at room
   temperature, diced
multi-coloured sprinkles

1 Preheat the oven to 160°C/325°F/Gas 3. Lightly grease and line a 20cm/8in square baking tin (pan) with baking parchment.

2 Sift the flour, baking powder and ground ginger into a bowl. Add the stem ginger, raisins and cherries and stir together.

3 Put the butter, syrup, treacle and muscovado sugar in a small pan and heat gently until the butter melts. Pour the mixture into the dry ingredients. Add the eggs and stir until combined.

4 Turn into the baking tin and spread in an even layer. Bake for 55 minutes, or until risen and firm in the centre. Leave to cool.

5 To make the topping, put the icing sugar and butter in a bowl with 20ml/4 tsp hot water and beat until smooth.

6 Turn the gingerbread on to a board. Cut into 16 squares. Drizzle a thick line of icing around the top edge of each square. Scatter the coloured sprinkles over the icing.

Cranberry and Chocolate Cakes Energy 343kcal/1439kJ; Protein 4.8g; Carbohydrate 42.9g, of which sugars 30.8g; Fat 18.2g, of which saturates 8.7g; Cholesterol 76mg; Calcium 63mg; Fibre 1.4g; Sodium 164mg. **Rainbow Gingerbread Cakes** Energy 251kcal/1057kJ; Protein 2.4g; Carbohydrate 41.9g, of which sugars 31.1g; Fat 9.4g, of which saturates 5.6g; Cholesterol 46mg; Calcium 50mg; Fibre 0.6g; Sodium 100mg.

Apricot and Almond Cakes

What an utterly perfect combination. If they aren't eaten immediately, these fruity cakes will stay moist for several days if stored in an airtight container.

Makes 18
225g/8oz/2 cups self-raising (self-rising) flour
115g/4oz/¹⁄₂ cup light muscovado (brown) sugar
50g/2oz/¹⁄₃ cup semolina
175g/6oz/³⁄₄ cup ready-to-eat dried apricots, chopped
2 eggs
30ml/2 tbsp malt extract
30ml/2 tbsp clear honey
60ml/4 tbsp skimmed milk
60ml/4 tbsp sunflower oil
a few drops of almond extract
30ml/2 tbsp flaked (sliced) almonds

1 Preheat the oven to 160°C/325°F/Gas 3. Lightly grease a 28 × 18cm/11 × 7in shallow cake tin (pan) and line with baking parchment.

2 Sift the flour into a bowl and add the muscovado sugar, semolina, dried apricots and eggs. Add the malt extract, clear honey, milk, sunflower oil and almond extract. Mix well until smooth.

3 Turn the mixture into the prepared cake tin and spread to the edges. Smooth the top. Sprinkle the flaked almonds all over the surface in as even a layer as possible.

4 Bake for 30–35 minutes, until the centre of the cake springs back when lightly pressed.

5 Transfer the tin to a wire rack and leave to cool, then turn out the cake. Remove and discard the lining paper, place the cake on a board and cut it into 18 slices with a sharp knife, to serve.

Variation
You can substitute dried peaches or nectarines for the apricots; they both have an affinity with almonds.

Almond Cakes

This firm cookie-like cake has the flavour of macaroons and marzipan. It is easy to make and tastes delicious served with a cup of tea or coffee. If you can wait, the texture and flavour of the cake are improved by a few days of storage.

Serves 16
350g/12oz/3 cups ground almonds
50g/2oz/¹⁄₂ cup matzo meal
pinch of salt
30ml/2 tbsp vegetable oil
250g/9oz/generous 1 cup sugar
300g/11oz/1¹⁄₃ cups brown sugar
3 eggs, separated
7.5ml/1¹⁄₂ tsp almond extract
5ml/1 tsp vanilla extract
150ml/¹⁄₄ pint/²⁄₃ cup orange juice
75ml/5 tbsp brandy

For the topping
75ml/5 tbsp brandy
200g/7oz/1³⁄₄ cups icing (confectioners') sugar
90g/3¹⁄₂oz/scant 1 cup flaked (sliced) almonds

1 Preheat the oven to 180°C/350°F/Gas 4. Lightly grease a 30–38cm/12–15in square cake tin (pan).

2 Put the ground almonds, matzo meal and salt in a bowl and mix together.

3 Put the oil, sugars, egg yolks, almond extract, vanilla extract, orange juice and half the brandy in a separate bowl. Stir, then add the almond mixture to form a thick lumpy batter.

4 Whisk the egg whites until stiff. Fold one-third of the egg whites into the mixture to lighten it, then fold in the rest. Pour the mixture into the prepared tin and bake for 25–30 minutes.

5 To make the icing, mix the brandy with the icing sugar. If necessary, add a little water to make an icing (frosting) with the consistency of single (light) cream.

6 Remove from the oven and prick the top all over with a skewer. Pour the icing evenly over the top of the cake, then return the cake to the oven for 10 minutes, or until the top is crusty. Leave the cake to cool in the tin, then cut into squares.

Almond Cakes Energy 415kcal/1742kJ; Protein 7.6g; Carbohydrate 54g, of which sugars 51g; Fat 17.9g, of which saturates 1.7g; Cholesterol 36mg; Calcium 97mg; Fibre 2.1g; Sodium 21mg.
Apricot and Almond Cakes Energy 140kcal/589kJ; Protein 3.1g; Carbohydrate 23.6g, of which sugars 11.9g; Fat 4.3g, of which saturates 0.6g; Cholesterol 21mg; Calcium 40mg; Fibre 1.2g; Sodium 13mg.

Chocolate Orange Sponge Drops

Light as air with a melt-in-the-mouth mixture of flavours, these drops are sure to be popular.

Makes about 14
2 eggs
50g/2oz/¼ cup caster
    (superfine) sugar
2.5ml/½ tsp grated orange rind
50g/2oz/½ cup plain
    (all-purpose) flour
60ml/4 tbsp finely shredded
    orange marmalade
40g/1½oz plain (semisweet)
    chocolate, chopped into
    small pieces

1 Preheat the oven to 200°C/400°F/Gas 6. Line three baking sheets with baking parchment.

2 Put the eggs and sugar in a large heatproof bowl and whisk over a pan of simmering water until the mixture is thick and pale, and leaves a ribbon trail when the whisk is lifted. Remove the bowl from the pan of water and continue whisking until the mixture is cool.

3 Whisk in the grated orange rind. Sift the flour over the whisked mixture and fold it in gently.

4 Put spoonfuls of the mixture on the baking sheets, spacing them well apart to allow for spreading. The mixture will make 28–30 drops.

5 Bake for about 8 minutes, or until the cookies are golden. Leave them to cool on the baking sheets for a few minutes, then use a metal spatula to transfer them to a wire rack to cool completely.

6 Spread the flat sides of half the cookies with the orange marmalade, then gently press the remaining cookies on top to sandwich the drops together.

7 Melt the chocolate in a heatproof bowl set over a pan of barely simmering water. Drizzle or pipe zig-zag lines of the chocolate over the tops of the sponge drops. Leave to set completely before serving.

Coffee Sponge Drops

These are delicious on their own, but taste even better with a filling of low-fat soft cheese and chopped preserved stem ginger.

Makes 12
50g/2oz/½ cup plain
    (all-purpose) flour
15ml/1 tbsp instant coffee
    powder
2 eggs
75g/3oz/scant ½ cup caster
    (superfine) sugar

For the filling
115g/4oz/½ cup low-fat
    soft cheese
40g/1½oz/¼ cup chopped
    preserved stem ginger

1 Preheat the oven to 190°C/375°F/Gas 5. Line two or three baking sheets with baking parchment.

2 To make the filling, beat together the soft cheese and preserved stem ginger. Chill until required.

3 Sift the flour and instant coffee powder together into a bowl and set aside.

4 In a large bowl, combine the eggs and caster sugar. Beat with an electric whisk until thick and mousse-like.

5 Add the sifted flour and coffee to the egg mixture and gently fold in with a metal spoon, being careful not to knock out any air.

6 Spoon the mixture into a piping (pastry) bag fitted with a 1cm/½in plain nozzle. Pipe 4cm/1½in rounds on the prepared baking sheets, spaced well apart.

7 Bake for 12 minutes. Cool on a wire rack. Sandwich together with the filling.

Variation
For a richer, creamier filling, use mascarpone.

Chocolate Orange Sponge Drops Energy 58kcal/247kJ; Protein 1.3g; Carbohydrate 10.6g, of which sugars 8g; Fat 1.5g, of which saturates 0.7g; Cholesterol 26mg; Calcium 12mg; Fibre 0.2g; Sodium 12mg. Coffee Sponge Drops Energy 33kcal/138kJ; Protein 1.5g; Carbohydrate 5.2g, of which sugars 3.6g; Fat 0.9g, of which saturates 0.4g; Cholesterol 17mg; Calcium 13mg; Fibre 0.1g; Sodium 27mg.

Lady Fingers

These long, delicate cookies are named after the pale, slim fingers of highborn gentlewomen. They are also known, much more mundanely, as sponge fingers.

Makes 18
90g/3½oz/generous ¾ cup plain (all-purpose) flour, plus extra for dusting
pinch of salt
4 eggs, separated
115g/4oz/generous ½ cup caster (superfine) sugar
2.5ml/½ tsp vanilla extract
icing (confectioners') sugar, for sprinkling

1 Preheat the oven to 150°C/300°F/Gas 2. Lightly grease two large baking sheets, then dust lightly with flour and shake off the excess.

2 Sift the flour and salt together twice on to baking parchment and set aside.

3 With an electric mixer, beat the egg yolks with half of the sugar until thick enough to leave a ribbon trail when the beaters are lifted.

4 In another grease-free bowl, whisk the egg whites until they form stiff peaks. Gradually whisk in the remaining sugar until the mixture is very glossy.

5 Sift the flour mixture over the yolks and spoon about a quarter of the egg whites over the flour. Carefully fold in with a large metal spoon to slacken, adding the vanilla extract. Then gently fold in the remaining egg whites.

6 Spoon the mixture into a piping (pastry) bag fitted with a large plain nozzle. Pipe 10cm/4in long lines on the prepared baking sheets. Sift over a layer of icing sugar. Tip off any excess sugar.

7 Bake for 20 minutes, until crusty on the outside with soft centres. Cool slightly on the baking sheets before transferring to a wire rack.

Lemon Sponge Fingers

These sponge fingers are perfect for serving with fruit salads or light, creamy desserts and mousses.

Makes about 20
2 eggs
75g/3oz/scant ½ cup caster (superfine) sugar
grated rind of 1 lemon
50g/2oz/½ cup plain (all-purpose) flour, sifted
caster (superfine) sugar, for sprinkling

1 Preheat the oven to 190°C/375°F/Gas 5. Line two baking sheets with baking parchment.

2 Whisk the eggs, sugar and lemon rind together with a hand-held electric whisk until thick and mousse-like (when the whisk is lifted, a trail should remain on the surface of the mixture for at least 15 seconds).

3 Gently fold in the flour with a large metal spoon using a figure-of-eight action.

4 Place the mixture in a large piping (pastry) bag fitted with a 1cm/½in plain nozzle. Pipe the mixture into finger lengths on the prepared baking sheets. Sprinkle the fingers with caster sugar.

5 Bake for about 6–8 minutes, until golden brown, then transfer the sponge fingers to a wire rack to cool.

Cook's Tip
Use an unwaxed lemon, if possible. Otherwise, wash the lemon well under hot water and pat dry before grating.

Variation
To make Spicy Orange Fingers, substitute grated orange rind for the lemon rind and add 5ml/1 tsp ground cinnamon with the flour.

Lady Fingers Energy 59kcal/248kJ; Protein 1.9g; Carbohydrate 10.6g, of which sugars 6.8g; Fat 1.3g, of which saturates 0.4g; Cholesterol 42mg; Calcium 17mg; Fibre 0.2g; Sodium 16mg.
Lemon Sponge Fingers Energy 33Kcals/137KJ; Fat 0.57g Saturated Fat 0.16g; Cholesterol 19.30mg; Fibre 0.08g.

Madeleines

These little tea cakes, baked in a special tin with shell-shaped cups, were made famous by Marcel Proust, who referred to them in his memoirs. They are best eaten on the day that they are made.

Makes 12
100g/4oz/1¼ cups self-raising (self-rising) flour
5ml/1 tsp baking powder

2 eggs
75g/3oz/¾ cup icing (confectioners') sugar, plus extra for dusting
grated rind of 1 lemon or orange
15ml/1 tbsp lemon or orange juice
75g/3oz/6 tbsp unsalted (sweet) butter, melted and slightly cooled

1 Preheat the oven to 190°C/375°F/Gas 5. Generously grease a 12-cup madeleine tin (pan).

2 Sift together the flour and baking powder into a bowl and set aside.

3 Put the eggs and icing sugar into another bowl. Using a hand-held electric mixer, beat together for 5–7 minutes, until thick and creamy and the mixture leaves a ribbon trail when the beaters are lifted.

4 Gently fold in the lemon or orange rind and the lemon or orange juice. Fold in the flour and the melted butter in four batches, beginning with the flour.

5 Let the mixture stand for 10 minutes, then carefully spoon into the tin, dividing it equally among the cups. Tap gently to release any air bubbles.

6 Bake for 12–15 minutes, rotating the pan halfway through cooking, until a skewer inserted into the centre of a cake comes out clean.

7 Turn out on to a wire rack to cool completely and dust with icing sugar.

Fat Rascals

These delicious teacakes are a cross between a scone and a rock cake and are really simple to make. They would originally have been baked in a small pot oven standing over an open fire. Serve them warm or cold, just as they are or with butter.

Makes 10
350g/12oz/3 cups self-raising (self rising) flour, plus extra for dusting
175g/6oz/¾ cup butter, diced

115g/4oz/generous ½ cup caster (superfine) sugar
75g/3oz/⅓ cup mixed currants, raisins and sultanas (golden raisins)
25g/1oz/1½ tbsp chopped mixed peel
50g/2oz/⅓ cup glacé (candied) cherries
50g/2oz/½ cup blanched almonds, coarsely chopped
1 egg
about 75ml/5 tbsp milk

1 Preheat the oven to 200°C/400°F/Gas 6. Line one or two baking sheets with baking parchment.

2 Sift the flour into a large bowl. Add the butter and, with your fingertips, rub it into the flour until the mixture resembles fine breadcrumbs (alternatively process the ingredients briefly in a food processor).

3 Stir in the sugar, dried fruit, mixed peel, glacé cherries and almonds until well mixed.

4 Lightly beat the egg and stir into the flour mixture with sufficient milk to gather the mixture into a ball of soft but not sticky dough.

5 With lightly floured hands, divide the dough into 10 balls, press them into rounds about 2cm/¾in thick and arrange them on the prepared baking sheets, spaced well apart to allow room for spreading.

6 Cook for 15–20 minutes, until risen and golden brown. Transfer to a wire rack to cool.

Madeleines Energy 132kcal/557kJ; Protein 2.3g; Carbohydrate 21.1g, of which sugars 5.8g; Fat 4.9g, of which saturates 2.4g; Cholesterol 8mg; Calcium 42mg; Fibre 0.7g; Sodium 118mg.
Fat Rascals Energy 191kcal/803kJ; Protein 2.9g; Carbohydrate 28.4g, of which sugars 11.3g; Fat 8.1g, of which saturates 4.8g; Cholesterol 38mg; Calcium 45mg; Fibre 0.7g; Sodium 62mg.

Singing Hinnies

These sweet and moreish scone-like little cakes "sing" as they cook on the hot buttered griddle. Serve them warm, split and spread with butter.

Makes about 20

400g/14 oz/3½ cups self-raising (self-rising) flour, plus extra for dusting

7.5ml/1½ tsp baking powder
pinch of salt
50g/2oz/¼ cup butter, diced
50g/2oz/⅓ cup lard, diced
50g/2oz/¼ cup caster (superfine) sugar
75g/3oz/⅓ cup currants, raisins or sultanas (golden raisins)
about 150ml/¼ pint/⅔ cup milk

1 Sift the flour, baking powder and salt into a large bowl. Add the butter and lard and, with your fingertips, rub them into the flour until the mixture resembles fine breadcrumbs.

2 Stir the sugar and dried fruit into the fat and flour mixture.

3 Add the milk in batches and, with a flat-ended knife, stir the mixture until it can be gathered into a ball of soft dough. The mixture should form a dry dough. It should not be at all wet to the touch.

4 Transfer to a lightly floured surface and roll out to about 5mm/¼in thick. With a 7.5cm/3in cookie cutter, stamp out rounds, gathering up the offcuts (scraps) and re-rolling to make more rounds.

5 Heat a heavy frying pan or griddle. Rub with butter and cook the scones in batches for 3–4 minutes on each side, until well browned. Lift off and keep warm until all are cooked. Serve while warm.

Variation
Instead of making small cakes, try cooking the dough in a large, pan-sized round, cutting it into wedges first to facilitate easy turning.

Soul Cakes

These soul cakes are a cross between a biscuit texture and a cake-like crumb. They are full of fruit and spices and are deliciously sweet.

Makes about 20

450g/1lb/4 cups self-raising (self-rising) flour, plus extra for dusting
5ml/1 tsp mixed spice (apple pie spice)
2.5ml/½ tsp ground ginger
175g/6oz/¾ cup butter, softened

175g/6oz/scant 1 cup caster (superfine) sugar, plus extra for sprinkling
2 eggs, lightly beaten
50g/2oz/¼ cup currants, raisins or sultanas (golden raisins)
about 30ml/2 tbsp warm milk

1 Preheat the oven to 180°C/350°F/Gas 4. Lightly grease two baking sheets or line with baking parchment.

2 Sift the flour and spices into a bowl and set aside. Beat the butter with the sugar until the mixture is pale and fluffy.

3 Gradually beat the eggs into the mixture. Fold in the flour mixture and the dried fruit, then add sufficient warm milk to bind the mixture and gather it up into a ball of soft dough.

4 Transfer to a lightly floured surface and roll out to about 5mm/¼in thick. With a floured 7.5cm/3in cutter, cut into rounds, gathering up the offcuts (scraps) and re-rolling to make more rounds.

5 Arrange the cakes on the prepared baking sheets. Prick the surface of the cakes lightly with a fork then, with the back of a knife, mark a deep cross on top of each.

6 Put the cakes into the hot oven and cook for about 15 minutes, until risen and golden brown.

7 Sprinkle the cooked cakes with a little caster sugar and then transfer to a wire rack to cool.

Singing Hinnies Energy 132kcal/557kJ; Protein 2.3g; Carbohydrate 21.1g, of which sugars 5.8g; Fat 4.9g, of which saturates 2.4g; Cholesterol 8mg; Calcium 42mg; Fibre 0.7g; Sodium 118mg.
Soul Cakes Energy 191kcal/803kJ; Protein 2.9g; Carbohydrate 28.4g, of which sugars 11.3g; Fat 8.1g, of which saturates 4.8g; Cholesterol 38mg; Calcium 45mg; Fibre 0.7g; Sodium 62mg.

Oat and Raisin Drop Scones

Serve these scones at tea time or as a dessert with real maple syrup or honey. If you are feeling indulgent, add a spoonful of sour cream or crème fraîche.

Makes about 16

75g/3oz/¾ cup self-raising (self-rising) flour
pinch of salt
2.5ml/½ tsp baking powder
50g/2oz/scant ½ cup raisins
25g/1oz/¼ cup fine oatmeal
25g/1oz/2 tbsp caster (superfine) sugar
grated rind of 1 orange
2 egg yolks
7.5ml/1½ tsp unsalted (sweet) butter, melted
100ml/3½fl oz single (light) cream
100ml/3½fl oz/scant ½ cup water

1 Sift together the flour, salt and baking powder into a large mixing bowl.

2 Add the raisins, oatmeal, caster sugar and grated orange rind and stir well to mix. Gradually beat in the egg yolks, melted butter, cream and measured water until thoroughly combined into a creamy batter.

3 Lightly grease and heat a large frying pan or griddle and drop about 30ml/2 tbsp of batter at a time on to the pan or griddle to make six or seven small pancakes.

4 Cook over a medium heat until bubbles show on the scones' surface, then turn them over and cook for another 2 minutes until golden.

5 Transfer the scones to a plate and keep warm while cooking the remaining mixture. Serve warm.

> **Cook's Tip**
> *There are two secrets to making light-as-air drop scones. Firstly, do not leave the batter to stand once it has been mixed. The second is to heat the frying pan or griddle slowly until it is very hot before adding the batter.*

Caraway Buns

Caraway seeds were once a popular ingredient of breads and cakes.

Makes about 12

350g/12oz/3 cups plain (all-purpose) flour, plus extra for dusting
115g/4oz/⅔ cup ground rice or semolina
10ml/2 tsp baking powder
115g/4oz/½ cup butter
75g/3oz/scant ½ cup caster (superfine) sugar, plus extra for sprinkling
30ml/2 tbsp caraway seeds
2 eggs
about 75ml/5 tbsp milk

1 Preheat the oven to 200°C/400°F/Gas 6. Line a baking sheet with baking parchment.

2 Sift the flour, ground rice and baking powder together into a large mixing bowl. Add the butter and, with your fingertips, rub it into the flour until the mixture resembles fine breadcrumbs. Stir the sugar and caraway seeds into the flour mixture.

3 Lightly beat the eggs and stir them into the flour mixture, together with sufficient milk to enable you to gather the mixture into a ball of dough. Transfer to a lightly floured surface.

4 Roll out to about 2.5cm/1in thick. Using a 5cm/2in cookie cutter, cut into rounds, gathering up the scraps and re-rolling to make more.

5 Arrange the rounds on the lined baking sheet, setting them quite close together so they support each other as they rise.

6 Put into the hot oven and cook for 15–20 minutes, until risen and golden brown. Transfer to a wire rack and sprinkle with caster sugar. Leave to cool.

> **Cook's Tip**
> *Replace the caraway seeds with 50g/2oz dried fruit, such as raisins or finely chopped apricots.*

Caraway Buns Energy 244kcal/1026kJ; Protein 5.1g; Carbohydrate 36.9g, of which sugars 7.3g; Fat 9.5g, of which saturates 5.4g; Cholesterol 53mg; Calcium 60mg; Fibre 1.1g; Sodium 75mg.
Oat and Raisin Drop Scones Energy 375kcal/1574kJ; Protein 5.6g; Carbohydrate 50g, of which sugars 23.2g; Fat 18.4g, of which saturates 9.6g; Cholesterol 57mg; Calcium 93mg; Fibre 1.8g; Sodium 129mg.

Individual Apple Cakes

These delicate little cakes can be rustled up in next to no time for eating hot when visitors call. The quantities have been kept small because they really must be eaten while still fresh. To make more, simply double up on the measures.

Makes 8–10
125g/4½oz/generous 1 cup
    self-raising (self-rising) flour,
    plus extra for dusting
pinch of salt
65g/2½oz/5 tbsp butter, diced
50g/2oz/4 tbsp demerara
    (raw) or light muscovado
    (brown) sugar
1 small cooking apple, weighing
    about 150g/5oz
about 30ml/2 tbsp milk
caster (superfine) sugar,
    for dusting

1 Sift the flour and salt into a mixing bowl. Add the butter and, with your fingertips, rub it into the flour until the mixture resembles fine breadcrumbs. Stir in the sugar.

2 Peel and grate the apple, discarding the core, and stir the apple into the flour mixture with enough milk to make a mixture that can be gathered into a ball of soft, moist dough. Work it slightly to make sure the flour is mixed in well.

3 Transfer to a lightly floured surface and roll out the dough to about 5mm/¼in thick. With a 6–7.5cm/2½–3in cookie cutter, stamp out rounds, gathering up the scraps and re-rolling them to make more rounds.

4 Heat a heavy frying pan over low to medium heat. Smear a little butter on the pan and cook in batches, for about 4–5 minutes on each side, or until golden and cooked through.

5 Lift on to a wire rack and dust with caster sugar. Serve warm.

> **Cook's Tip**
> Add a pinch of ground cinnamon or nutmeg to the flour.

Hot Currant Cakes

Traditionally many cooks use half lard and half butter in this recipe. Serve the hot currant cakes warm or cold, as they are, or buttered.

Makes about 16
250g/9oz/2¼ cups plain
    (all-purpose) flour, plus extra
    for dusting
pinch of salt
7.5ml/1¼ tsp baking powder
125g/4½oz/½ cup butter, diced
100g/3½oz/½ cup caster
    (superfine) sugar, plus extra
    for dusting
75g/3oz/⅓ cup currants
1 egg
45ml/3 tbsp milk

1 Sift the flour, salt and baking powder into a large mixing bowl. Add the butter and, with your fingertips, rub it into the flour until it resembles fine breadcrumbs. Stir in the sugar and currants.

2 Lightly beat the egg and with a round-end knife and with a cutting action, stir it into the flour mixture with enough milk to gather the mixture into a ball of soft dough.

3 Transfer to a lightly floured surface and roll out to about 5mm/¼in thick. With a 6–7.5cm/2½–3in cookie cutter, stamp out rounds, gathering up the scraps and re-rolling to make more rounds.

4 Heat a heavy frying pan over medium to low heat. Smear a little butter or oil over the pan and cook the cakes, in small batches, for about 4–5 minutes on each side, or until they are slightly risen, golden brown and cooked through.

5 Transfer to a wire rack, dust with caster sugar on both sides and leave to cool.

> **Variation**
> For a change, add a large pinch of mixed spice (apple pie spice) in step 1, or a little vanilla extract in step 2.

Hot Currant Cakes Energy 128kcal/540kJ; Protein 4.1g; Carbohydrate 22.8g, of which sugars 1.3g; Fat 2.9g, of which saturates 1.4g; Cholesterol 29mg; Calcium 66mg; Fibre 0.9g; Sodium 29mg.
Individual Apple Cakes Energy 121kcal/508kJ; Protein 1.4g; Carbohydrate 16.5g, of which sugars 6.9g; Fat 6g, of which saturates 3.7g; Cholesterol 15mg; Calcium 26mg; Fibre 0.6g; Sodium 45mg.

Pineapple and Cinnamon Drop Scones

Making the batter with pineapple juice instead of milk cuts down on the amount of fat and adds a fruity piquancy to the flavour of these delicious drop scones.

Makes 24
115g/4oz/1 cup self-raising (self-rising) wholemeal (whole-wheat) flour

115g/4oz/1 cup self-raising (self-rising) white flour
5ml/1 tsp ground cinnamon
15ml/1 tbsp caster (superfine) sugar
1 egg
300ml/½ pint/1¼ cups pineapple juice
75g/3oz/½ cup semi-dried pineapple, chopped

1 Put the wholemeal flour in a mixing bowl. Sift in the white flour, add the cinnamon and caster sugar and mix together. Make a well in the centre. Add the egg with half of the pineapple juice to the well.

2 Gradually incorporate the flour to make a smooth batter, then beat in the remaining pineapple juice and stir in the chopped pineapple.

3 Heat a griddle, then lightly grease it. Drop tablespoons of the batter on to the surface, spacing them apart, and leave them until they bubble and the bubbles begin to burst.

4 Turn over the drop scones with a metal spatula and cook until the underside is golden brown. Continue to cook in successive batches.

Cook's Tips
• *Drop scones do not keep well and are best eaten freshly cooked. In any case, they are especially delicious served hot.*
• *If self-raising (self-rising) wholemeal (whole-wheat) flour is not readily available, use white self-raising flour instead.*

Drop Scones

These little scones are delicious spread with jam.

Makes 18
225g/8oz/2 cups self-raising (self-rising) flour
pinch of salt

15ml/1 tbsp caster (superfine) sugar
1 egg, beaten
300ml/½ pint/1¼ cups skimmed (low fat) milk

1 Preheat a griddle or heavy frying pan.

2 Sift the flour and salt into a mixing bowl. Stir in the sugar and make a well in the centre.

3 Add the egg and half the milk, then gradually incorporate the surrounding flour to make a smooth batter. Beat in the remaining milk.

4 Lightly grease the griddle or pan. Drop tablespoons of the batter on to the surface, leaving them until they bubble and the bubbles begin to burst.

5 Turn the drop scones over with a metal spatula and cook until the underside is golden brown. Keep the cooked drop scones warm and moist by wrapping them in a clean napkin while cooking successive batches.

Variation
For savoury scones, omit the sugar and add 2 chopped spring onions (scallions) and 15ml/1 tbsp freshly grated Parmesan cheese to the batter. Serve with cottage cheese.

Scotch Pancakes

Serve these pancakes while they're still warm, with butter and jam.

Makes 24
225g/8oz/2 cups self-raising (self-rising) flour
50g/2oz/4 tbsp caster (superfne) sugar

50g/2oz/4 tbsp butter, melted
1 egg
300ml/½ pint/1¼ cups milk
15g/½oz/1 tbsp lard

1 Mix the flour and sugar together in a bowl.

2 Add the melted butter and egg and two-thirds of the milk. Mix to a smooth batter, adding more milk, if necessary – it should be thin enough to find its own level.

3 Heat a griddle or heavy frying pan and wipe it with a little lard. When hot, drop spoonfuls of the mixture on to the hot griddle or pan. When bubbles come to the surface of the pancakes, flip them over to cook until golden on the other side. Keep the pancakes warm wrapped in a dish towel while cooking the rest of the mixture.

Pineapple and Cinnamon Drop Scones Energy 64 Kcals/270 KJ; Fat 1.09 g; Saturated Fat 0.20 g; Cholesterol 11.03 mg; Fibre 0.43 g. **Drop Scones** Energy 64 Kcals/270 KJ; Fat 1.09 g; Saturated Fat 0.20 g; Cholesterol 11.03 mg; Fibre 0.43 g. **Scotch Pancakes** Energy 67kcal/282kJ; Protein 1.6g; Carbohydrate 10.1g, of which sugars 2.9g; Fat 2.6g, of which saturates 1.3g; Cholesterol 13mg; Calcium 31mg; Fibre 0.3g; Sodium 19mg.

Lavender Scones

Lend an unusual but delicious lavender perfume to your scones – its fragrance marries well with the sweetness of summer soft fruit and makes for an elegant, romantic teatime treat. Nowadays, the flavour can seem quite surprising, because the scented quality of the lavender permeates through the well-known tea scone.

Makes 12
225g/8oz/2 cups plain
   (all-purpose) flour
15ml/1 tbsp baking powder
50g/2oz/butter
50g/2oz/sugar
10ml/2 tsp fresh lavender florets
   or 5ml/1 tsp dried culinary
   lavender, coarsely chopped
about 150ml/¼ pint/⅔ cup milk

1 Preheat the oven to 220°C/425°F/Gas 7. Lightly grease a baking sheet.

2 Sift the flour and baking powder together. Rub the butter into the flour mixture until it resembles breadcrumbs.

3 Stir in the sugar and lavender, reserving a pinch to sprinkle on the top of the scones before baking them. Add enough milk to make a soft, sticky dough. Bind the dough together and then turn it out on to a well-floured surface.

4 Shape the dough into a round, gently patting down the top to give a 2.5cm/1in depth. Using a floured cookie cutter, stamp out 12 scones. Place on the baking sheet. Brush the tops with a little milk and sprinkle over the reserved lavender.

5 Bake for 10–12 minutes, until golden. Transfer to a wire rack to cool. Serve warm, split in half and spread with plum jam and clotted or whipped cream.

> **Variation**
> *Other fragrant flowers can also be used to make these scones. Try rosemary flowers, mimosa or rose petals.*

Scones with Jam and Cream

Scones, often known as biscuits in the US, are thought to originate from Scotland, where they are still a popular part of afternoon tea with jams, jellies and thick whipped cream.

Makes about 12
450g/1lb/4 cups self-raising
   (self-rising) flour, plus extra
   for dusting
pinch of salt
50g/2oz/¼ cup butter, chilled
   and diced
15ml/1 tbsp lemon juice
about 400ml/14fl oz/1⅔ cups
   milk, plus extra to glaze
fruit jam and clotted cream or
   whipped double (heavy)
   cream, to serve

1 Preheat the oven to 230°C/450°F/Gas 8. Sift flour over a baking sheet.

2 Sift the flour and salt into a mixing bowl. Add the butter and rub it into the flour with your fingertips until the mixture resembles fine breadcrumbs.

3 Whisk the lemon juice into the milk and leave for about 1 minute to thicken slightly, then pour into the flour mixture and mix quickly to form a soft but pliable dough. The wetter the mixture, the lighter the resulting scone will be, but if they are too wet they will spread during baking and lose their shape.

4 Knead the dough lightly to form a ball, then roll it out on a floured surface to a thickness of at least 2.5cm/1in. Using a 5cm/2in cookie cutter, and dipping it into flour each time, stamp out 12 scones. Place on the baking sheet. Re-roll any trimmings and cut out more scones if you can.

5 Brush the tops of the scones lightly with a little milk, then bake for about 20 minutes, or until risen and golden brown.

6 Wrap the scones in a clean dish towel to keep them warm and soft until ready to serve. Split the scones in half and spread with fruit jam and a generous spoonful of cream.

Lavender Scones Energy 115kcal/484kJ; Protein 2.3g; Carbohydrate 18.8g, of which sugars 4.5g; Fat 3.9g, of which saturates 2.4g; Cholesterol 10mg; Calcium 46mg; Fibre 0.6g; Sodium 32mg.
Scones with Jam and Cream Energy 177kcal/749kJ; Protein 4.7g; Carbohydrate 30.7g, of which sugars 2.2g; Fat 4.8g, of which saturates 2.8g; Cholesterol 12mg; Calcium 93mg; Fibre 1.2g; Sodium 43mg.

Sunflower Sultana Scones

Traditional fruit scones are given a delightful new twist with a crunchy topping of sunflower seeds.

Makes 10–12
225g/8oz/2 cups self-raising (self-rising) flour, plus extra for dusting
5ml/1 tsp baking powder
25g/1oz/2 tbsp butter
30ml/2 tbsp golden caster (superfine) sugar
50g/2oz/⅓ cup sultanas (golden raisins)
30ml/2 tbsp sunflower seeds
150g/5oz/⅔ cup natural (plain) yogurt
about 30–45ml/2–3 tbsp milk

1 Preheat the oven to 230°C/450°F/Gas 8. Lightly grease a baking sheet.

2 Sift together the flour and baking powder into a bowl. Add the butter and rub it in with your fingertips until the mixture resembles fine breadcrumbs. Add the sugar, sultanas and half the sunflower seeds and stir well to mix.

3 Stir in the yogurt, then add just enough milk to mix to a soft but not wet dough.

4 Roll out on a lightly floured surface to about 2cm/¾in thick. Stamp out 6cm/2½in rounds with a floured cookie cutter and lift on to the baking sheet.

5 Brush the tops of the scones with milk and sprinkle with the reserved sunflower seeds.

6 Bake for 10–12 minutes, until well risen and golden brown. Transfer to a wire rack. Serve while still warm, split in half and spread with butter and jam.

Variation
You could substitute pumpkin seeds for the sunflower. Both are high in nutrients and have the essential crunch factor.

Traditional Sweet Scones

These traditional breakfast or teatime treats have a golden crust and a lovely light soft inside.

Makes 8
170g/6oz/1½ cups self-raising (self-rising) flour, plus extra for dusting
30ml/2 tbsp sugar
15ml/1 tbsp baking powder
pinch of salt
50g/2oz/4 tbsp butter, chilled and diced
120ml/4fl oz/½ cup milk

1 Preheat the oven to 425°F/220°C/Gas 7. Lightly grease a baking sheet.

2 Sift the flour, sugar, baking powder and salt into a bowl.

3 Add the butter and rub in with your fingertips until the mixture resembles fine breadcrumbs.

4 Pour in the milk and stir with a fork to form a soft dough.

5 Roll out the dough on a lightly floured surface to 3cm/1¼in thick. Stamp out rounds using a floured 5cm/2in cookie cutter.

6 Place on the baking sheet and bake for about 12 minutes, until golden. Serve hot or warm, split in half and spread with butter and jam.

Buttermilk Scones

Buttermilk was thought to be a good food for children – it certainly makes scones they'll find irresistible.

Makes 15
200g/7oz/1¾ cups plain (all-purpose) flour, plus extra for dusting
pinch of salt
5ml/1 tsp baking powder
2.5ml/½ tsp bicarbonate of soda (baking soda)
50g/2oz/¼ cup cold butter
175ml/6fl oz/¾ cup buttermilk

1 Preheat the oven to 220°C/425°F/Gas 7. Lightly grease and dust a baking sheet with flour.

2 Sift the flour, salt, baking powder and bicarbonate of soda into a bowl. Rub in the butter with your fingertips until the mixture resembles breadcrumbs.

3 Gradually pour in the buttermilk, stirring with a fork to form a soft dough.

4 Roll out the dough on a lightly floured surface to about 3cm/1¼in thick. Stamp out rounds with a 5cm/2in cookie cutter.

5 Place on the prepared baking sheet and bake for 12–15 minutes, until golden. Serve the scones warm, split in half and spread with butter.

Sunflower Sultana Scones Energy 121kcal/513kJ; Protein 3g; Carbohydrate 21.2g, of which sugars 6.9g; Fat 3.3g, of which saturates 0.6g; Cholesterol 0mg; Calcium 99mg; Fibre 0.8g; Sodium 97mg.
Traditional Sweet Scones Energy 89kcal/379kJ; Protein 2.6g; Carbohydrate 19.7g, of which sugars 3g; Fat 0.6g, of which saturates 0.2g; Cholesterol 1mg; Calcium 50mg; Fibre 0.7g; Sodium 8mg.
Buttermilk Scones Energy 74kcal/311kJ; Protein 1.7g; Carbohydrate 10.9g, of which sugars 0.7g; Fat 2.9g, of which saturates 1.8g; Cholesterol 8mg; Calcium 34mg; Fibre 0.4g; Sodium 26mg.

Wholemeal Scones

These scones make a delicious and healthy option. As you would expect, they taste great spread with jam, but they are also surprisingly good with cheese – either soft or hard.

Makes 16
225g/8oz/2 cups wholemeal (whole-wheat) flour
115g/4oz/1 cup plain (all-purpose) flour, plus extra for dusting

30ml/2 tbsp caster (superfine) sugar
pinch of salt
12.5ml/2½ tsp bicarbonate of soda (baking soda)
175g/6oz/¾ cup butter, chilled and diced
2 eggs
175ml/6fl oz/¾ cup buttermilk
40g/1½oz/⅓ cup raisins

1 Preheat the oven to 200°C/400°F/Gas 6. Lightly grease and flour a large baking sheet.

2 Sift together the flours, caster sugar, salt and bicarbonate of soda into a large bowl. Add the diced butter and rub it in with your fingertips until the mixture resembles fine breadcrumbs. Set aside.

3 In another bowl, whisk together the eggs and buttermilk. Set aside 30ml/2 tbsp for glazing.

4 Add the remaining egg mixture to the dry ingredients and stir to mix to a soft but not wet dough. Add the raisins and knead lightly until they are incorporated.

5 Roll out the dough on a lightly floured surface to about 2cm/¾in thick. Stamp out rounds with a floured cookie cutter. Place on the prepared baking sheet and brush the tops with the reserved egg mixture.

6 Bake for 12–15 minutes until golden brown. Leave to cool slightly before serving. Split the scones in half while they are still warm and spread with butter. Eat within a day of baking, or freeze for later use.

Orange and Raisin Scones

These sweet, tangy scones are really at their best served warm, in the traditional Cornish way, with thick cream and homemade jam.

Makes 16
225g/8oz/2 cups plain (all-purpose) flour, plus extra for dusting
25ml/1½ tbsp baking powder

75g/3oz/scant ½ cup caster (superfine) sugar
pinch of salt
65g/2½oz/5 tbsp butter, chopped
grated rind of 1 large orange
50g/2oz/⅓ cup raisins
115g/4oz/½ cup buttermilk
milk, for glazing

1 Preheat the oven to 220°C/425°F/Gas 7. Lightly grease and flour a large baking sheet.

2 Sift the flour, baking powder, caster sugar and salt into a large bowl. Rub in the butter with your fingertips until the mixture resembles fine breadcrumbs.

3 Add the orange rind and raisins and mix well. Gradually stir in the buttermilk to form a soft dough.

4 Roll out the dough on a lightly floured surface to about 2cm/¾in thick. Stamp out rounds with a floured 5cm/2in cookie cutter.

5 Place on the baking sheet and brush the tops with milk to glaze. Bake for 12–15 minutes, until golden brown. Serve hot or warm, split in half and spread with butter or whipped cream and jam.

Cook's Tips
• To be sure that the scones are light and delicate, handle the dough as little as possible and bake them as soon as they are ready to go in the oven.
• If you wish, split the scones when cool and toast them under a preheated grill (broiler). Butter them while they are still hot.

Wholemeal Scones Energy 207kcal/869kJ; Protein 4.9g; Carbohydrate 25.3g, of which sugars 4.6g; Fat 10.3g, of which saturates 6g; Cholesterol 48mg; Calcium 42mg; Fibre 2.3g; Sodium 82mg.
Orange and Raisin Scones Energy 145kcal/606kJ; Protein 2g; Carbohydrate 19.8g, of which sugars 6.7g; Fat 6.9g, of which saturates 2.2g; Cholesterol 9mg; Calcium 38mg; Fibre 0.6g; Sodium 63mg.

Microwave Iced Cup Cakes

Make these ever-popular
little cakes in just minutes
and with no fuss at all.

Makes about 24
115g/4oz/1 cup self-raising
 (self-rising) flour
pinch of salt
50g/2oz/4 tbsp butter
50g/2oz/4 tbsp soft brown sugar
1 egg, beaten
milk, to mix
whipped cream or glacé icing,
 to top
glacé (candied) cherries,
 to decorate

1 Sift the flour with the salt into a bowl, rub in the butter until
the mixture resembles fine breadcrumbs, then stir in the sugar.

2 Mix in the egg and enough milk to form a mixture with a
soft dropping (pourable) consistency.

3 Place six paper cases in a six-hole microwave-proof muffin
pan and place spoonfuls of the prepared cake mixture into
each, filling them each about two-thirds full.

4 Microwave on 100 per cent power for 2 minutes, giving the
dish a half-turn after 1 minute. Transfer to a wire rack to cool.
Repeat with the remaining mixture, cooking in batches of six.
Leave to cool completely before decorating.

5 To finish, pipe the tops of the cakes with swirls of whipped
cream or coat with soft glacé icing. Decorate with a cherry.

Cook's Tip
*Make and eat microwave-cooked cup cakes on the same day.
Alternatively, freeze them before adding any toppings.*

Variation
*For Chocolate Cup Cakes prepare as above but add 15ml/
1 tbsp sifted unsweetened cocoa powder to the flour mixture.
For Fairy Currant Cakes prepare the mixture as above but add
25g/1oz/2 tbsp currants to the mixture with the eggs and milk.*

Fairy Cakes with Blueberries

This luxurious way to make
fairy cakes means you can
serve them to adults and
guests as well as kids.

Makes 12–14 cakes
115g/4oz/1/2 cup butter
115g/4oz/generous 1/2 cup caster
 (superfine) sugar
5ml/1 tsp grated lemon rind
pinch of salt
2 eggs, beaten
115g/4oz/1 cup self-raising
 (self-rising) flour
120ml/4fl oz/1/2 cup whipping
 cream
75–115g/3–4oz/3/4–1 cup
 blueberries
icing sugar (confectioners') sugar,
 for dusting

1 Preheat the oven to 190°C/375°F/Gas 5. Arrange
12–14 paper cases in a small muffin tin (pan).

2 In a large bowl, beat the butter, sugar, lemon rind and salt
until pale and fluffy.

3 Gradually beat in the eggs, then gradually sift over the flour
and fold in until well mixed.

4 Spoon the mixture into the paper cake cases, and bake for
15–20 minutes, until just golden. Leave the cakes to cool.

5 Scoop out a circle of sponge from the top of each cake
using the point of a small sharp knife, and set them aside.

6 Whip the cream until stiff peaks form. Place a spoonful of
cream in each sponge, plus 2–3 blueberries. Replace the lids at
an angle and dust with sifted icing sugar.

Variation
*You can substitute other fruit, such as small strawberries, for
the blueberries, but do not prepare the cakes too far in
advance of serving them or the cream will discolour with the
juices from the fruits.*

Microwave Iced Cup Cakes Energy 43kcal/181kJ; Protein 0.7g; Carbohydrate 5.9g, of which sugars 2.3g; Fat 2g, of which saturates 1.2g; Cholesterol 12mg; Calcium 9mg; Fibre 0.2g; Sodium 16mg.
Fairy Cakes with Blueberries Energy 231kcal/962kJ; Protein 2.7g; Carbohydrate 21.5g, of which sugars 13g; Fat 15.5g, of which saturates 3.4g; Cholesterol 51mg; Calcium 63mg; Fibre 0.6g;
Sodium 151mg.

Iced Fancies

Everyone loves these pretty cakes. Utilize your artistic skills to make them look as tempting as possible.

Makes 16
115g/4oz/1/2 cup butter, at
    room temperature
225g/8oz/generous 1 cup caster
    (superfine) sugar
2 eggs, at room temperature
175g/6oz/1 1/2 cups plain
    (all-purpose) flour
pinch of salt
7.5ml/1 1/2 tsp baking powder

120ml/4fl oz/1/2 cup plus
    15ml/1 tbsp milk
5ml/1 tsp vanilla extract

For icing and decorating
2 large (US extra large)
    egg whites
400g/14oz/3 1/2 cups sifted icing
    (confectioners') sugar
1–2 drops glycerine
juice of 1 lemon
food colourings, hundreds and
    thousands, crystallized
    (candied) lemon and orange
    slices to decorate

1 Preheat the oven to 190°C/375°F/Gas 5. Arrange 16 paper cases in a muffin tin (pan).

2 In a large bowl, beat the butter and sugar until light and fluffy. Add the eggs, one at a time, beating well after each addition.

3 Sift together the flour, salt and baking powder into the butter mixture in batches, alternating with the milk. Stir in the vanilla. Beat well to combine.

4 Fill the paper cups half-full and bake for about 20 minutes until the tops spring back when touched lightly. Let the cakes stand in the tray for 5 minutes, then turn out and transfer to a rack to cool completely.

5 For the icing, beat the egg whites until stiff but not dry. Gradually add the sugar, glycerine and lemon juice, and continue beating for 1 minute. The consistency should be spreadable. If necessary, thin with a little water or add more sifted icing sugar to thicken. Divide among several bowls and tint with food colourings. Spread different coloured icings over the cakes and decorate as desired.

Daisy Cakes

What could be prettier for afternoon tea or a children's birthday party than these scrumptious little cakes decorated with daisy petals? The daisy centre is made from coloured icing.

Makes 15–20
115g/4oz/1/2 cup butter, softened
115g/4oz/generous 1/2 cup caster
    (superfine) sugar
2 eggs

115g/4oz/1 cup self-raising
    (self-rising) flour
2.5ml/1/2 tsp baking powder
10ml/2 tsp lemon juice

To decorate
115g/4oz/1 cup icing
    (confectioners') sugar
15ml/1 tbsp water
dash of yellow food colouring
2–3 daisies

1 Preheat the oven to 180°C/350°F/Gas 4. Arrange 15–20 paper cases in a small muffin tin (pan).

2 Put the butter in a bowl with the sugar and eggs. Sift the flour and baking powder into the bowl. Add the lemon juice and beat until pale and creamy.

3 Spoon the mixture into the cases and bake for about 15 minutes, until risen and golden. Transfer to a wire rack and leave to cool.

4 To decorate, beat the icing sugar with the water until the glaze thinly coats the back of the spoon. Add a dash of yellow food colouring to match the centre of the real daisy flowers.

5 Spoon a little icing on to each cake. Gently pull the petals from a daisy and use to decorate. Repeat with the remainder of the cakes.

> **Cook's Tip**
> *When using fresh flowers, make sure that they are clean and not polluted with pesticides or traffic fumes.*

Iced Fancies Energy 259kcal/1094kJ; Protein 2.7g; Carbohydrate 49.7g, of which sugars 41.4g; Fat 6.9g, of which saturates 4g; Cholesterol 40mg; Calcium 50mg; Fibre 0.3g; Sodium 66mg.
Daisy Cakes Energy 115kcal/483kJ; Protein 1.3g; Carbohydrate 16.5g, of which sugars 12.1g; Fat 5.4g, of which saturates 3.2g; Cholesterol 31mg; Calcium 18mg; Fibre 0.2g; Sodium 43mg.

Blueberry Muffins

Light and fruity, these well-known American muffins are delicious at any time of day. Serve them warm for breakfast or brunch, or as a tea-time treat.

Makes 12

2 eggs
50g/2oz/4 tbsp butter, melted
175ml/6fl oz/³⁄₄ cup milk
5ml/1 tsp vanilla extract

5ml/1 tsp grated lemon rind
180g/6¹⁄₄oz/generous 1¹⁄₂ cups plain (all-purpose) flour
60g/2¹⁄₄oz/generous ¹⁄₄ cup sugar
10ml/2 tsp baking powder
pinch of salt
175g/6oz/1¹⁄₂ cups fresh blueberries

1 Preheat the oven to 200°C/400°F/Gas 6. Arrange 12 paper cases in a muffin tin (pan) or grease the tin.

2 In a bowl, whisk the eggs until blended. Add the melted butter, milk, vanilla and lemon rind, and stir to combine.

3 Sift the flour, sugar, baking powder and salt into a large bowl. Make a well in the centre and pour in the egg mixture. With a metal spoon, stir until the flour is just moistened.

4 Add the blueberries to the muffin mixture and gently fold in.

5 Spoon the batter into the muffin tin or paper cases, leaving enough room for the muffins to rise.

6 Bake for 20–25 minutes, until the tops spring back when touched lightly. Leave the muffins in the tin, if using, for 5 minutes before turning out on to a wire rack to cool.

Variation
Muffins are delicious with all kinds of different fruits. Try out some variations using this basic muffin recipe. Replace the blueberries with the same weight of bilberries, blackcurrants, pitted cherries or raspberries.

Wholemeal Banana Muffins

Wholemeal muffins, with banana for added fibre, make a great treat at any time of the day. If you like, slice off the tops and fill with a teaspoon of jam or marmalade, then replace the tops before serving.

Makes 12

75g/3oz/³⁄₄ cup plain (all-purpose) wholemeal (whole-wheat) flour
50g/2oz/¹⁄₂ cup plain (all-purpose) white flour

10ml/2 tsp baking powder
pinch of salt
5ml/1 tsp mixed spice (apple pie spice)
40g/1¹⁄₂oz/scant ¹⁄₄ cup soft light brown sugar
50g/2oz/¹⁄₄ cup butter
1 egg, beaten
150ml/¹⁄₄ pint/²⁄₃ cup semi-skimmed (low-fat) milk
grated rind of 1 orange
1 ripe banana
20g/³⁄₄oz/¹⁄₄ cup rolled oats
20g/³⁄₄oz/scant ¹⁄₄ cup chopped hazelnuts

1 Preheat the oven to 200°C/400°F/Gas 6. Arrange 12 paper cases in a muffin tin (pan).

2 Sift together both flours, the baking powder, salt and mixed spice into a bowl, then tip the bran remaining in the sieve (strainer) into the bowl. Stir in the sugar.

3 Melt the butter in a pan over a very low heat. Remove from the heat and leave to cool slightly, then beat in the egg, milk and grated orange rind. Make a well in the centre of the flour mixture, pour in the butter mixture and beat well to incorporate the dry ingredients.

4 Mash the banana with a fork, then stir it gently into the mixture, being careful not to overmix. Spoon the mixture into the paper cases.

5 Combine the oats and hazelnuts and sprinkle a little of the mixture over each muffin.

6 Bake for 20 minutes until the muffins are well risen and golden, and a skewer inserted in the centre comes out clean. Transfer to a wire rack and serve warm or cold.

Blueberry Muffins Energy 236kcal/992kJ; Protein 4.9g; Carbohydrate 34.7g, of which sugars 12.4g; Fat 9.6g, of which saturates 5.6g; Cholesterol 54mg; Calcium 88mg; Fibre 1.4g; Sodium 82mg.
Wholemeal Banana Muffins Energy 110Kcals/465KJ; Fat 5g; Saturated Fat 1g; Cholesterol 17.5mg.

Banana Muffins

Make sure that you use really ripe bananas for these muffins, not just because those are the sweetest, but also because they are easy to mash to the proper smooth consistency.

Makes 12

225g/8oz/2 cups plain
(all-purpose) flour
5ml/1 tsp baking powder
5ml/1 tsp bicarbonate of soda
(baking soda)
pinch of salt
2.5ml/½ tsp ground cinnamon
1.5ml/¼ tsp grated nutmeg
3 large ripe bananas
1 egg
50g/2oz/¼ cup soft dark
brown sugar
50ml/2fl oz/¼ cup vegetable oil
40g/1½oz/⅓ cup raisins

1 Preheat the oven to 190°C/375°F/Gas 5. Arrange 12 paper cases in a muffin tin (pan).

2 Sift together the flour, baking powder, bicarbonate of soda, salt, cinnamon and nutmeg. Set aside.

3 Using a fork, mash the peeled bananas to a smooth consistency in a large bowl.

4 Beat the egg, sugar and oil into the mashed bananas until fully combined.

5 Add the dry ingredients and beat in gradually, using an electric whisk set at low speed. Mix until just blended. With a wooden spoon, stir in the raisins until just combined. Spoon the mixture into the muffin tins, filling them two-thirds full.

6 Bake for 20–25 minutes, until the tops spring back when touched lightly with your finger. Transfer the muffins to a wire rack to cool completely before serving.

> **Variation**
> For Banana and Chocolate Muffins, substitute 50g/2oz/⅓ cup plain (semisweet) chocolate chips for the raisins.

Honey and Spice Cakes

These golden little cakes are fragrant with honey and cinnamon. Although their appearance is traditional when cooked directly in a bun tin, they tend to rise higher and are therefore lighter when baked in paper cases.

Makes 18

250g/9oz/2¼ cups plain
(all-purpose) flour
5ml/1 tsp ground cinnamon
5ml/1 tsp bicarbonate of soda
(baking soda)
125g/4½oz/generous
½ cup butter
125g/4½oz/generous 2 cups
brown sugar
1 large (US extra large)
egg, separated
125g/4½oz/generous ½ cup
clear honey
caster (superfine) sugar,
for sprinkling

1 Preheat the oven to 200°C/400°F/Gas 6. Line a bun tin (muffin pan) with paper cases.

2 Sift together the flour, cinnamon and the bicarbonate of soda into a large bowl.

3 In another bowl, beat the butter with the sugar until light and fluffy. Beat in the egg yolk, then gradually add the honey and beat well until fully incorporated.

4 With a large metal spoon and a cutting action, fold in the flour mixture plus sufficient milk to make a soft mixture that will just drop off the spoon.

5 In a separate grease-free bowl, whisk the egg white until stiff peaks form. Using a large metal spoon, fold the egg white into the cake mixture.

6 Divide the mixture among the paper cases in the prepared tin. Bake for 15–20 minutes, or until risen, firm to the touch and golden brown.

7 Sprinkle the tops lightly with caster sugar and leave to cool completely on a wire rack.

Banana Muffins Energy 152kcal/642kJ; Protein 2.8g; Carbohydrate 29g, of which sugars 13.9g; Fat 3.6g, of which saturates 0.5g; Cholesterol 16mg; Calcium 34mg; Fibre 1g; Sodium 9mg.
Honey and Spice Cakes Energy 152kcal/639kJ; Protein 1.9g; Carbohydrate 23.6g, of which sugars 13g; Fat 6.3g, of which saturates 3.8g; Cholesterol 26mg; Calcium 30mg; Fibre 0.4g; Sodium 49mg.

Apricot and Orange Muffins

Serve these fruity muffins freshly baked and warm.

Makes 8 large or 12 medium muffins
115g/4oz/1 cup cornmeal
75g/3oz/¾ cup rice flour
15ml/1 tbsp baking powder
pinch of salt

50g/2oz/4 tbsp butter, melted
50g/2oz/¼ cup light soft
  brown sugar
1 egg, beaten
200ml/7fl oz/scant 1 cup semi-
  skimmed (low-fat) milk
finely grated rind of 1 orange
115g/4oz/½ cup ready-to-eat
  dried apricots, chopped

1 Preheat the oven to 200°C/400°F/Gas 6. Arrange 12 paper cases in a muffin tin (pan).

2 Place the cornmeal, rice flour, baking powder and salt in a bowl and mix together.

3 Stir together the melted butter, sugar, egg, milk and orange rind, then pour the mixture over the dry ingredients. Fold the ingredients gently together. The mixture will look quite lumpy, which is correct, as over-mixing will result in heavy muffins.

4 Fold in the chopped dried apricots, then spoon the mixture into the prepared paper cases, dividing it equally among them.

5 Bake for 15–20 minutes, until the muffins have risen and are golden brown and springy to the touch. Turn them out on to a wire rack to cool.

6 Serve the muffins warm or cold, on their own or cut in half and spread with a little butter or low-fat spread. Store in an airtight container for up to 1 week or seal in plastic bags and freeze for up to 3 months.

> **Variation**
> *Try substituting grapefruit rind for the orange and the same quantity of chopped dried mango for the apricots.*

Lemon Meringue Muffins

This recipe is a delightful variation on the classic fairy cake – soft lemon sponge cake is topped with crisp meringue.

Makes 18
115g/4oz/½ cup butter
200g/7oz/scant 1 cup caster
  (superfine) sugar

2 eggs
115g/4oz/1 cup self-raising
  (self-rising) flour
5ml/1 tsp baking powder
grated rind of 2 lemons
30ml/2 tbsp lemon juice
2 egg whites

1 Preheat the oven to 190°C/375°F/Gas 5. Arrange 18 paper cases in a muffin tin (pan).

2 Put the butter in a bowl and beat until soft. Add 115g/4oz/ generous ½ cup of the caster sugar and continue to beat until the mixture is smooth and creamy.

3 Beat in the eggs. Sift together the flour and baking powder over the mixture, add half the lemon rind and all the lemon juice and beat well until thoroughly combined.

4 Divide the the mixture among the paper cases.

5 To make the meringue, whisk the egg whites in a clean grease-free bowl until they stand in soft peaks. Stir in the remaining caster sugar and lemon rind. Put a spoonful of the meringue mixture on each cake.

6 Cook for 20–25 minutes, until the meringue is crisp and brown. Serve hot or cold.

> **Cook's Tip**
> *Make sure that you whisk the egg whites enough before adding the sugar – when you lift out the whisk they should stand in peaks that just flop over slightly at the top.*

Apricot and Orange Muffins Energy136kcals/572kJ; Fat, total 4.6g; saturated fat 1g; Protein2.9g; Carbohydrate 21g; sugar, total 8.5g; Fibre 0.9g; Sodium 195mg.
Lemon Meringue Muffins Energy 123kcal/514kJ; Protein 1.7g; Carbohydrate 16.6g, of which sugars 11.7g; Fat 6g, of which saturates 3.5g; Cholesterol 35mg; Calcium 19mg; Fibre 0.2g; Sodium 54mg.

Raspberry Crumble Buns

Make these stylish muffins for a special occasion in the summer when raspberries are bursting with flavour. For total luxury, serve like scones, with raspberry jam and cream.

Makes 12

175g/6oz/1½ cups plain (all-purpose) flour
10ml/2 tsp baking powder
pinch of salt
5ml/1 tsp ground cinnamon
50g/2oz/¼ cup sugar
50g/2oz/¼ cup soft light brown sugar

115g/4oz/½ cup butter, melted
1 egg
120ml/4fl oz/½ cup milk
225g/8oz/1⅓ cups fresh raspberries
grated rind of 1 lemon

For the crumble topping

50g/2oz/½ cup pecan nuts, finely chopped
50g/2oz/¼ cup soft dark brown sugar
45ml/3 tbsp plain (all-purpose) flour
5ml/1 tsp ground cinnamon
40g/1½oz/3 tbsp butter, melted

1 Preheat the oven to 180°C/350°F/Gas 4. Arrange 12 paper cases in a muffin tin (pan).

2 Sift the flour, baking powder, salt and cinnamon into a bowl. Stir in the sugars. Make a well in the centre.

3 Beat together the butter, egg and milk in a large bowl until light. Add the flour mixture to it and stir until just combined. Stir in the raspberries and lemon rind.

4 Spoon the batter into the muffin tins, filling them almost to the top.

5 To make the topping, mix the pecans, sugar, flour and cinnamon in a bowl. Stir in the melted butter.

6 Spoon a little of the crumble topping over the top of each muffin. Bake for about 25 minutes.

7 Transfer to a wire rack to cool slightly. Serve the muffins warm.

Raspberry Buttermilk Muffins

Low-fat buttermilk gives these muffins a light and spongy texture. Make them in the summer when fresh raspberries are at their seasonal best.

Makes 10–12

300g/11oz/2¾ cups plain (all-purpose) flour
15ml/1 tbsp baking powder
115g/4oz/generous ½ cup caster (superfine) sugar
1 egg
250ml/8fl oz/1 cup buttermilk
60ml/4 tbsp sunflower oil
150g/5oz/1 cup raspberries

1 Preheat the oven to 200°C/400°F/Gas 6. Arrange 10–12 paper cases in a muffin tin (pan).

2 Sift the flour and baking powder into a mixing bowl. Stir in the sugar, then make a well in the centre.

3 Mix the egg, buttermilk and sunflower oil together in a bowl, pour into the flour mixture and mix quickly until just combined.

4 Add the raspberries and lightly fold them into the mixture with a metal spoon until just combined. Spoon the mixture into the prepared paper cases, filling them about two-thirds full.

5 Bake for 20–25 minutes, until golden brown and firm in the centre. Transfer to a wire rack and serve warm or cold.

Cook's Tips
• As with other soft fruits – which can also be used in these delicious muffins – don't buy more raspberries than you require as they deteriorate quickly, although they do freeze well. If they're sold in packs, make sure that there are no squashed ones underneath. Avoid soaking them in water when washing them; just wipe with damp kitchen paper.
• Raspberry muffins make a fabulous breakfast treat with butter and honey and are great at teatime when served warm with raspberry jam and thickly whipped cream.

Raspberry Buttermilk Muffins Energy 132kcal/555kJ; Protein 4g; Carbohydrate 19g, of which sugars 5.7g; Fat 5g, of which saturates 2.7g; Cholesterol 42mg; Calcium 48mg; Fibre 1.5g; Sodium 45mg.
Raspberry Crumble Buns Energy 225kcal/940kJ; Protein 2.7g; Carbohydrate 25.2g, of which sugars 14.1g; Fat 13.3g, of which saturates 7.3g; Cholesterol 45mg; Calcium 48mg; Fibre 0.9g; Sodium 93mg.

Date and Apple Muffins

These spiced muffins are delicious and very filling. If possible, use fresh Medjool dates from Egypt, as they have sweet, dense flesh and a truly opulent flavour.

Makes 12
150g/5oz/1¼ cups self-raising (self-rising) wholemeal (whole-wheat) flour
150g/5oz/1¼ cups self-raising (self-rising) flour

5ml/1 tsp ground cinnamon
5ml/1 tsp baking powder
25g/1oz/2 tbsp butter
75g/3oz/⅓ cup light muscovado (brown) sugar
250ml/8fl oz/1 cup apple juice
30ml/2 tbsp pear and apple jam
1 egg, lightly beaten
1 eating apple
75g/3oz/½ cup chopped dates
15ml/1 tbsp chopped pecan nuts

1 Preheat the oven to 200°C/400°F/Gas 6. Arrange 12 paper cases in a muffin tin (pan).

2 Sift together both flours, the cinnamon and baking powder into a large bowl. Add the butter and rub it in with your fingertips until the mixture resembles fine breadcrumbs. Add the sugar and stir well to mix.

3 In a mixing bowl, stir a little of the apple juice with the pear and apple jam until smooth. Mix in the remaining apple juice, then add to the rubbed-in mixture with the beaten egg.

4 Quarter and core the apple, and peel it if you like, then chop the flesh finely. Add to the batter and stir in the dates. Divide the mixture among the muffin cases.

5 Sprinkle the chopped pecans on top. Bake for 20–25 minutes, until golden brown and firm in the middle. Transfer to a wire rack and serve while still warm.

> **Cook's Tip**
> *If self-raising (self-rising) wholemeal (whole-wheat) flour is not available, use more self-raising (self-rising) white flour instead.*

Apple and Cinnamon Muffins

These fruity, spicy muffins are quick and easy to make and are perfect for serving for breakfast or tea. The appetizing aroma as they bake is out of this world.

150g/5oz/1¼ cups plain (all-purpose) flour
7.5ml/1½ tsp baking powder
pinch of salt
2.5ml/½ tsp ground cinnamon
2 small eating apples, peeled, cored and finely chopped

Makes 6
1 egg, beaten
40g/1½oz/3 tbsp caster (superfine) sugar
120ml/4fl oz/½ cup milk
50g/2oz/¼ cup butter, melted

For the topping
12 brown sugar cubes, coarsely crushed
5ml/1 tsp ground cinnamon

1 Preheat the oven to 200°C/400°F/Gas 6. Arrange 6 paper cases in a muffin tin (pan).

2 Mix the egg, sugar, milk and melted butter in a large bowl. Sift in the flour, baking powder, salt and cinnamon. Add the chopped apple and mix roughly.

3 Spoon the mixture into the prepared muffin cases. To make the topping, mix the crushed sugar cubes with the cinnamon. Sprinkle over the uncooked muffins.

4 Bake for 30–35 minutes, until well risen and golden brown on top. Transfer the muffins to a wire rack to cool. Serve them warm or at room temperature.

> **Variation**
> *You can also make these muffins with pears or even quinces, both of which go well with cinnamon.*

> **Cook's Tip**
> *Do not overmix the muffin mixture – it should still be slightly lumpy when spooned into the cases.*

Date and Apple Muffins Energy 158kcal/670kJ; Protein 3.2g; Carbohydrate 30.7g, of which sugars 11.7g; Fat 3.4g, of which saturates 0.3g; Cholesterol 16mg; Calcium 45mg; Fibre 1g; Sodium 25mg.
Apple and Cinnamon Muffins Energy 236kcal/995kJ; Protein 4.3g; Carbohydrate 38.2g, of which sugars 19.1g; Fat 8.5g, of which saturates 4.9g; Cholesterol 51mg; Calcium 74mg; Fibre 1.2g; Sodium 73mg.

Apple and Cranberry Muffins

If you choose a really sweet variety of apple, it will provide a lovely contrast with the sharp flavour of the cranberries.

Makes 12
50g/2oz/¼ cup butter
I egg
90g/3½oz/½ cup caster
  (superfine) sugar
grated rind of I large orange
120ml/4fl oz/½ cup freshly
  squeezed orange juice
150g/5oz/1¼ cups plain
  (all-purpose) flour

5ml/I tsp baking powder
2.5ml/½ tsp bicarbonate of soda
  (baking soda)
5ml/I tsp ground cinnamon
2.5ml/½ tsp freshly
  grated nutmeg
2.5ml/½ tsp ground allspice
1.5ml/¼ tsp ground ginger
pinch of salt
1–2 eating apples
150g/6oz/1½ cups cranberries
50g/2oz/¼ cup walnuts, chopped
icing (confectioners') sugar, for
  dusting (optional)

1 Preheat the oven to 180°C/350°F/Gas 4. Arrange 12 paper cases in a muffin tin (pan).

2 Melt the butter over a gentle heat. Set aside to cool.

3 In a large bowl, whisk the egg lightly. Add the melted butter and whisk to combine. Add the sugar, orange rind and juice. Whisk to blend, then set aside.

4 In a mixing bowl, sift together the flour, baking powder, bicarbonate of soda, cinnamon, nutmeg, allspice, ginger and salt. Set aside.

5 Make a well in the dry ingredients and pour in the egg mixture. With a spoon, stir until just blended.

6 Quarter, core and peel the apples. Chop coarsely. Add the apples, cranberries and walnuts, and stir to blend.

7 Fill the cases three-quarters full and bake for 25–30 minutes, until the tops spring back when touched lightly. Transfer to a rack to cool. Dust with icing sugar.

Cranberry and Orange Muffins

These delicious muffins are perfect to eat at any time of day and are a real energy boost for breakfast or as a lunchbox treat. Use fresh or frozen cranberries.

Makes 10–12
350g/12oz/3 cups plain
  (all-purpose) flour, sifted
15ml/I tsp baking powder

pinch of salt
115g/4oz/generous ½ cup caster
  (superfine) sugar
2 eggs
150ml/¼ pint/⅔ cup milk
50ml/2fl oz/¼ cup corn oil
finely grated rind of I orange
150g/5oz/1¼ cups cranberries,
  thawed if frozen

1 Preheat the oven to 190°C/375°F/Gas 5. Arrange 10–12 paper cases in a muffin tin (pan).

2 Sift together the flour, baking powder and salt into a large bowl. Add the sugar and stir well to mix.

3 Lightly beat the eggs with the milk and corn oil in another bowl until thoroughly combined.

4 Make a well in the centre of the dry ingredients and pour in the egg mixture. Stir with a wooden spoon until blended to a smooth batter. Gently fold in the grated orange rind and cranberries with a metal spoon.

5 Divide the mixture among the paper cases and bake for about 25 minutes, until risen and golden. Transfer to a wire rack to cool and serve warm or cold.

Cook's Tip
The flared sides of a proper muffin tin (pan) increase the surface area, encouraging the dough to rise.

Variation
Replace half the cranberries with blueberries or raspberries.

Apple and Cranberry Muffins Energy 149kcal/624kJ; Protein 2.5g; Carbohydrate 20.4g, of which sugars 10.8g; Fat 6.9g, of which saturates 2.6g; Cholesterol 25mg; Calcium 30mg; Fibre 0.9g; Sodium 34mg. **Cranberry and Orange Muffins** Energy 184kcal/780kJ; Protein 4.3g; Carbohydrate 34.4g, of which sugars 12.2g; Fat 4.3g, of which saturates 0.9g; Cholesterol 32mg; Calcium 66mg; Fibre 1.1g; Sodium 19mg.

Dried Cherry Muffins

Cherries are always a great favourite, especially with children, so why not spoil the family and serve these scrumptious muffins freshly baked and still warm from the oven, smothered with butter and cherry jam. Dried cherries are full of antioxidants and a healthy food to eat.

Makes 16

250ml/8fl oz/1 cup natural
   (plain) yogurt
225g/8oz/1 cup dried cherries
115g/4oz/½ cup butter, softened
175g/6oz/scant 1 cup caster
   (superfine) sugar
2 eggs
5ml/1 tsp vanilla extract
200g/7oz/1¾ cups plain
   (all-purpose) flour
10ml/2 tsp baking powder
5ml/1 tsp bicarbonate of soda
   (baking soda)
pinch of salt

1 In a mixing bowl, combine the yogurt and dried cherries. Cover with clear film (plastic wrap) and leave to stand for about 30 minutes.

2 Preheat the oven to 180°C/350°F/Gas 4. Arrange 12 paper cases in a muffin tin (pan).

3 Beat together the butter and caster sugar in a bowl until light and fluffy. Add the eggs, one at a time, beating well after each addition until fully incorporated.

4 Add the vanilla extract and yogurt and cherry mixture and stir well until thoroughly mixed.

5 Sift the flour, baking powder, bicarbonate of soda and salt over the batter in batches. Gently fold in using a metal spoon after each addition.

6 Spoon the mixture into the prepared muffin tins, filling them about two-thirds full. Bake for 20 minutes, or until risen and golden and the tops spring back when touched lightly. Transfer to a wire rack to cool completely before serving or storing in an airtight container.

Oat and Raisin Muffins

Often the simplest things are the nicest and that is the case with these flavour-packed muffins.

Makes 12

75g/3oz/scant 1 cup rolled oats
250ml/8fl oz/1 cup buttermilk
115g/4oz/½ cup butter, at
   room temperature
90g/3½oz/generous ⅓ cup soft
   dark brown sugar

1 egg, at room temperature
115g/4oz/1 cup plain
   (all-purpose) flour
5ml/1 tsp baking powder
2.5ml/½ tsp bicarbonate of soda
   (baking soda)
pinch of salt
25g/1oz/2 tbsp raisins

1 In a bowl, combine the oats and buttermilk, and leave to soak for 1 hour.

2 Preheat the oven to 200°C/400°F/Gas 6. Arrange 12 paper cases in a muffin tin (pan).

3 In a bowl, cream the butter and sugar until light and fluffy. Beat in the egg.

4 Sift the flour, baking powder, bicarbonate of soda and salt into the butter mixture in batches. Alternate with batches of the oat mixture. Stir to combine after each addition. Fold in the raisins. Do not overmix.

5 Fill the prepared cups two-thirds full. Bake for about 20–25 minutes, until a skewer inserted in the centre comes out clean. Transfer to a rack to cool.

Cook's Tip
Buttermilk is made from skimmed milk fermented with a special culture under controlled conditions, resulting in an acidic product that helps dough to rise. If it is not available, add 5ml/1 tsp lemon juice or vinegar to milk and leave to stand for a few minutes until curdled.

Dried Cherry Muffins Energy 196kcal/825kJ; Protein 3.2g; Carbohydrate 32.1g, of which sugars 22.6g; Fat 7g, of which saturates 4g; Cholesterol 39mg; Calcium 67mg; Fibre 0.7g; Sodium 69mg.
Oat and Raisin Muffins Energy 177kcal/742kJ; Protein 3g; Carbohydrate 22.3g, of which sugars 10.4g; Fat 9.1g, of which saturates 5.2g; Cholesterol 37mg; Calcium 51mg; Fibre 0.8g; Sodium 77mg.

Pear and Sultana Bran Muffins

These tasty muffins are best eaten freshly baked and served warm or cold, on their own or spread with a butter, jam or honey.

Makes 12
75g/3oz/¾ cup plain (all-purpose) wholemeal (whole-wheat) flour, sifted
50g/2oz/½ cup plain (all-purpose) white flour, sifted
50g/2oz/3 cups bran
15ml/1 tbsp baking powder
pinch of salt
50g/2oz/4 tbsp butter
50g/2oz/¼ cup soft light brown sugar
1 egg
200ml/7fl oz/scant 1 cup skimmed (low fat) milk
50g/2oz/½ cup ready-to-eat dried pears, chopped
50g/2oz/⅓ cup sultanas (golden raisins)

1 Preheat the oven to 200°C/400°F/Gas 6. Arrange 12 paper cases in a muffin tin (pan).

2 Mix together the flours, bran, baking powder and salt in a bowl. Set aside

3 Gently heat the butter in a small pan until melted.

4 Mix together the melted butter, sugar, egg and milk.

5 Pour the butter mixture over the dry ingredients. Gently fold the ingredients together, only enough to combine. The mixture should look quite lumpy.

6 Fold in the pears and sultanas.

7 Spoon the mixture into the prepared muffin tins. Bake for 15–20 minutes, until well risen and golden brown. Turn out on to a wire rack to cool.

Cook's Tip
For a quick and easy way to chop dried fruit, chop with kitchen scissors.

Carrot Buns

Carrots are naturally sweet and have a moistness that makes them an ideal ingredient for cakes and muffins. If you haven't used them when baking before, you are likely to be pleasantly surprised.

Makes 12
175g/6oz/¾ cup butter, at room temperature, diced
75g/3oz/⅓ cup soft dark brown sugar
1 egg
15ml/1 tbsp water
275g/10oz/2 cups grated carrots
150g/5oz/1¼ cups plain (all-purpose) flour
5ml/1 tsp baking powder
2.5ml/½ tsp bicarbonate of soda (baking soda)
5ml/1 tsp ground cinnamon
1.5ml/¼ tsp grated nutmeg
pinch of salt

1 Preheat the oven to 180°C/350°F/Gas 4. Arrange 12 paper cases in a muffin tin (pan).

2 In a large bowl, beat the butter and sugar until light and fluffy. Beat in the egg and water.

3 Stir the grated carrots into the butter mixture until evenly combined. Sift over the flour, baking powder, bicarbonate of soda, cinnamon, nutmeg and salt. Stir to blend evenly.

4 Spoon the batter into the prepared muffin tins, filling them almost to the top.

5 Bake for about 35 minutes, until the tops spring back when touched lightly with your fingers. Leave to stand for 10 minutes before transferring to a wire rack to cool completely.

Cook's Tip
Unless the carrots are very old and coarse – in which case, they are probably not suitable for this recipe – you do not need to peel them before grating. Simply trim and wash first. Use the fine side of the grater.

Pear and Sultana Bran Muffins Energy 121kcal/510kJ; Protein 3g; Carbohydrate 18.7g, of which sugars 9.8g; Fat 4.3g, of which saturates 2.4g; Cholesterol 25mg; Calcium 51mg; Fibre 2.2g; Sodium 42mg.
Carrot Buns Energy 190kcal/791kJ; Protein 2g; Carbohydrate 18.1g, of which sugars 8.5g; Fat 12.7g, of which saturates 7.8g; Cholesterol 47mg; Calcium 32mg; Fibre 0.9g; Sodium 101mg.

Prune Muffins

Muffins with prunes are nutritious as well as delicious and perfect as a weekend breakfast treat. These are made with oil rather than butter, so are very quick to mix.

Makes 12
1 egg
250ml/8fl oz/1 cup milk
50ml/2fl oz/¼ cup vegetable oil
50g/2oz/¼ cup sugar
30ml/2 tbsp soft dark
*   brown sugar*
225g/8oz/2 cups plain
*   (all-purpose) flour*
10ml/2 tsp baking powder
pinch of salt
1.5ml/¼ tsp grated nutmeg
150g/5oz/¾ cup cooked prunes,
*   or ready-to-eat prunes, chopped*

1 Preheat the oven to 200°C/400°F/Gas 6. Arrange 12 paper cases in a muffin tin (pan).

2 Break the egg into a mixing bowl and beat with a fork. Beat in the milk and oil.

3 Stir the sugars into the egg mixture. Set aside. Sift the flour, baking powder, salt and nutmeg into a mixing bowl. Make a well in the centre, pour in the egg mixture and stir. The batter should be slightly lumpy.

4 Gently fold the prunes into the batter until just evenly distributed. Spoon into the prepared muffin tins, filling them two-thirds full.

5 Bake for about 20 minutes, until golden brown. Leave to stand for 10 minutes before transferring to a wire rack. Serve warm or cold.

Cook's Tip
When cooking prunes, if there is time, soak them overnight in 400ml/14fl oz/1⅔ cups water, then bring to the boil with 5ml/ 1 tsp lemon juice and 30ml/2 tbsp caster (superfine) sugar, if you like. Simmer for about 10 minutes, until soft.

Yogurt and Honey Muffins

Yogurt and honey are known to boost energy levels, so these muffins go well in lunchboxes.

Makes 12
50g/2oz/4 tbsp butter
75ml/5 tbsp clear honey
250ml/8fl oz/1 cup natural
*   (plain) yogurt*
1 egg
grated rind of 1 lemon
50ml/2fl oz/¼ cup lemon juice
115g/4oz/1 cup plain
*   (all-purpose) flour*
115g/4oz/1 cup wholemeal
*   (whole-wheat) flour*
7.5ml/1½ tsp bicarbonate of
*   soda (baking soda)*
pinch of grated nutmeg

1 Preheat the oven to 190°C/375°F/Gas 5. Arrange 12 paper cases in a muffin tin (pan).

2 Put the butter and honey into a small pan and heat gently, stirring frequently, until melted and smooth. Remove the pan from the heat and leave to cool slightly.

3 In a large bowl, whisk together the yogurt, egg, lemon rind and juice. Add the butter and honey mixture and whisk well until thoroughly combined.

4 In another bowl, sift together the flours, bicarbonate of soda and nutmeg. Fold the dry ingredients into the yogurt mixture just enough to blend them.

5 Fill the prepared muffin tins two-thirds full. Bake for 20–25 minutes, then leave to cool in the tins for about 5 minutes before transferring to a wire rack.

Variations
• *For Yogurt, Honey and Walnut Muffins, add 50g/2oz/½ cup chopped walnuts, folded in with the flour and substitute ground cinnamon for the nutmeg.*
• *For Honey and Hazelnut Muffins, substitute hazelnut yogurt for the natural (plain) yogurt and fold in 50g/2oz/½ cup chopped toasted hazelnuts with the flour.*

Prune Muffins Energy 190kcal/801kJ; Protein 3.7g; Carbohydrate 28.1g, of which sugars 10.7g; Fat 7.8g, of which saturates 1.2g; Cholesterol 17mg; Calcium 66mg; Fibre 1.3g; Sodium 17mg.
Yogurt and Honey Muffins Energy 155kcal/652kJ; Protein 4.7g; Carbohydrate 25.4g, of which sugars 6.9g; Fat 4.6g, of which saturates 2.5g; Cholesterol 25mg; Calcium 66mg; Fibre 1.7g; Sodium 50mg.

Raisin Bran Buns

These traditional muffins remain hugely popular. This is hardly surprising as they are delicious served warm and spread with butter and honey.

Makes 15

50g/2oz/¼ cup butter
75g/3oz/¾ cup plain (all-purpose) flour
50g/2oz/½ cup wholemeal (whole-wheat) flour
7.5ml/1½ tsp bicarbonate of soda (baking soda)
pinch of salt
5ml/1 tsp ground cinnamon
25g/1oz/½ cup bran
75g/3oz/generous ½ cup raisins
50g/2oz/¼ cup soft dark brown sugar
50g/2oz/¼ cup sugar
1 egg
250ml/8fl oz/1 cup buttermilk
juice of ½ lemon

1 Preheat the oven to 200°C/400°F/Gas 6. Arrange 15 paper cases in a muffin tin (pan).

2 Place the butter in a pan and melt over a low heat. Set aside to cool slightly.

3 In a mixing bowl, sift together both flours, bicarbonate of soda, salt and ground cinnamon. Add the bran, raisins and sugars and stir until blended.

4 In another bowl, mix together the egg, buttermilk, lemon juice and melted butter. Add the buttermilk mixture to the dry ingredients and stir lightly and quickly until just moistened; do not mix until smooth.

5 Spoon the batter into the prepared muffin tins, filling them almost to the top. Bake for about 15 minutes, or until golden. Serve warm or at room temperature.

> **Cook's Tip**
> Bran is the outer husk of cereal grains removed during milling. Wheat bran is the most widely available and popular variety, but other cereal brans are available from health food stores.

Spiced Sultana Muffins

Sunday breakfasts will never be the same again, once you have tried these delicious muffins! They are easy to prepare and take only a short time to bake.

Makes 6

75g/3oz/6 tbsp butter
1 small (US medium) egg
120ml/4fl oz/½ cup unsweetened coconut milk
150g/5oz/1¼ cups wholemeal (whole-wheat) flour
7.5ml/1½ tsp baking powder
5ml/1 tsp ground cinnamon
generous pinch of salt
115g/4oz/⅔ cup sultanas (golden raisins)

1 Preheat the oven to 190°C/375°F/Gas 5. Arrange 6 paper cases in a muffin tin (pan).

2 Beat the butter, egg and coconut milk in a bowl until well combined.

3 Sift the wholemeal flour, baking powder, ground cinnamon and salt over the beaten mixture. Fold in carefully, then beat well. Fold in the sultanas. Divide the mixture among the paper cases.

4 Bake for 20 minutes, or until the muffins have risen well and are firm to the touch. Cool slightly on a wire rack before serving warm.

> **Variation**
> The heath-conscious or those following a slimming plan can substitute the same quantity of low-fat spread for the butter. The muffins will still be utterly delicious although not quite so rich in flavour.

> **Cook's Tip**
> These muffins taste equally good cold. They also freeze well, packed in freezer bags. To serve, leave them to thaw overnight, or defrost in a microwave, then warm them briefly in the oven.

Raisin Bran Buns Energy 89kcal/373kJ; Protein 2g; Carbohydrate 13.4g, of which sugars 8.9g; Fat 3.4g, of which saturates 1.9g; Cholesterol 20mg; Calcium 34mg; Fibre 1.1g; Sodium 36mg.
Spiced Sultana Muffins Energy 240kcal/1006kJ; Protein 4.9g; Carbohydrate 30.3g, of which sugars 14.9g; Fat 11.9g, of which saturates 6.9g; Cholesterol 58mg; Calcium 35mg; Fibre 2.6g; Sodium 114mg.

Sweet Potato Muffins with Raisins

Muffins have been a part of the American breakfast for many years. This variety mixes the great colour and flavour of sweet potatoes with the more usual ingredients.

Makes 12

1 large sweet potato
350g/12oz/3 cups plain
 (all-purpose) flour
15ml/1 tbsp baking powder
1 egg, beaten
225g/8oz/1 cup butter, melted
250ml/8fl oz/1 cup milk
50g/2oz/scant 1/2 cup raisins
50g/2oz/1/4 cup caster
 (superfine) sugar
pinch of salt
icing (confectioners') sugar,
 for dusting

1 Cook the sweet potato in plenty of boiling water for 45 minutes, or until very tender. Drain the potato and when cool enough to handle peel off the skin. Place in a large bowl and mash well.

2 Preheat the oven to 220°C/425°F/Gas 7. Sift the flour and baking powder over the potatoes with a pinch of salt and beat in the egg.

3 Stir the butter and milk together and pour into the bowl. Add the raisins and sugar and mix the ingredients until everything has just come together.

4 Spoon the mixture into 12 paper muffin cases set in a muffin tin (pan).

5 Bake for 25 minutes until golden. Dust with icing sugar and serve warm.

> **Variation**
> *These muffins are delicious made with all sorts of dried fruits and would work particularly well with tropical varieties, such as pineapple, mango or papaya, as well as the more usual blueberries or cranberries.*

Maple Pecan Muffins

The smooth, rich and distinctive flavour of maple syrup complements the nuts superbly. Make sure you buy the pure syrup, as blended varieties are disappointing.

Makes 20

150g/5oz/1 1/4 cups pecan nuts
300g/11oz/2 3/4 cups plain
 (all-purpose) flour
5ml/1 tsp baking powder
5ml/1 tsp bicarbonate of soda
 (baking soda)
pinch of salt
1.5ml/1/4 tsp ground cinnamon
115g/4oz/1/2 cup sugar
50g/2oz/1/2 cup soft light
 brown sugar
45ml/3 tbsp maple syrup
150g/5oz/2/3 cup butter, softened
3 eggs
300ml/1/2 pint/1 1/4 cups
 buttermilk
60 pecan nut halves, to decorate

1 Preheat the oven to 180°C/350°F/Gas 4. Arrange 20 paper cases in a muffin tin (pan).

2 Spread the pecan nuts on a baking sheet and toast in the oven for 5 minutes. Leave to cool, then chop coarsely and set aside.

3 In a bowl, sift together the flour, baking powder, bicarbonate of soda, salt and cinnamon. Set aside.

4 Combine the sugar, light brown sugar, maple syrup and butter in a bowl. Beat until light and fluffy. Add the eggs, one at a time, beating well after each addition.

5 Pour half of the buttermilk and half of the dry ingredients into the butter mixture, then stir until blended. Repeat with the remaining buttermilk and dry ingredients. Fold the chopped pecan nuts into the batter. Spoon the mixture into the paper cases, filling them two-thirds full. Top with the pecan nut halves.

6 Bake for 20–25 minutes, until puffed up and golden brown. Leave to stand in the tins for about 5 minutes before transferring the muffins to a wire rack to cool completely before serving.

Gooey Butterscotch Muffins

Make up the two mixtures for these muffins the night before you need them and stir them together first thing next day for an irresistible mid-morning treat. Instead of butterscotch, you could try adding chocolate chips, marshmallows or blueberries.

Makes 9–12

150g/5oz butterscotch sweets (candies)
225g/8oz/2 cups plain (all purpose) flour
90g/3¹/₂oz/¹/₂ cup golden caster (superfine) sugar
10ml/2 tsp baking powder
pinch of salt
1 large (US extra large) egg, beaten
150ml/¹/₄ pint/²/₃ cup milk
50ml/2fl oz/¹/₄ cup sunflower oil or melted butter
75g/3oz/³/₄ cup chopped hazelnuts

1 Preheat the oven to 200°C/400°F/Gas 6. Arrange 9–12 paper cases in a muffin tin (pan).

2 With floured fingers, break the butterscotch sweets into small chunks. Toss them in a little flour, if necessary, to prevent them from sticking together.

3 Into a mixing bowl sift together the flour, sugar, baking powder and salt.

4 Whisk together the egg, milk and oil or melted butter, then stir the mixture into the dry ingredients with the sweets and nuts. Only lightly stir together as the mixture should be lumpy.

5 Spoon the batter evenly into the paper cases, filling about half full. Bake for 20 minutes, until well risen and golden brown. Cool in the tin for 5 minutes, then remove and transfer the muffins to a cooling rack.

6 Try spreading these with a Spanish treat called *dulce de leche* (available in larger supermarkets); it is rather like sweetened condensed milk that has been boiled in the can until caramelized. Drizzle over and eat on the day of baking.

Coffee and Macadamia Muffins

These muffins are delicious eaten cold, but are best served still warm from the oven.

Makes 12

25ml/1¹/₂ tbsp ground coffee
250ml/8fl oz/1 cup milk
50g/2oz/4 tbsp butter
275g/10oz/2¹/₂ cups plain (all-purpose) flour
10ml/2 tsp baking powder
150g/5oz/²/₃ cup light muscovado (brown) sugar
75g/3oz/¹/₂ cup macadamia nuts
1 egg, lightly beaten

1 Preheat the oven to 200°C/400°F/Gas 6. Arrange 12 paper cases in a muffin tin (pan).

2 Put the coffee in a heatproof jug (pitcher) or bowl. Heat the milk to near boiling and pour it over. Leave to infuse (steep) for 4 minutes, then strain through a sieve (strainer).

3 Add the butter to the coffee-flavoured milk mixture and stir until melted. Leave until cold.

4 Sift the flour and baking powder into a large mixing bowl. Stir in the sugar and macadamia nuts. Add the egg to the coffee-flavoured milk mixture, pour into the dry ingredients and stir until just combined – do not overmix.

5 Divide the coffee mixture among the paper cases and bake for about 15 minutes, until well risen and firm. Transfer to a wire rack and serve warm or cold.

> **Variation**
> *Macadamia nuts have a unique buttery flavour but if they are not available, cashews make a good substitute.*

> **Cook's Tip**
> *To cool the coffee-flavoured milk quickly, place the jug (pitcher) in a large bowl of iced or cold water.*

Gooey Butterscotch Muffins Energy 224kcal/941kJ; Protein 3.9g; Carbohydrate 31.7g, of which sugars 14.6g; Fat 10g, of which saturates 2.1g; Cholesterol 19mg; Calcium 66mg; Fibre 1g; Sodium 55mg.
Coffee and Macadamia Muffins Energy 221kcal/929kJ; Protein 4g; Carbohydrate 32.2g, of which sugars 14.7g; Fat 9.4g, of which saturates 3.3g; Cholesterol 26mg; Calcium 70mg; Fibre 1g; Sodium 59mg.

Chunky Chocolate and Banana Muffins

Luxurious but not overly sweet, these muffins are simple and quick to make. Serve warm while the chocolate is still gooey.

Makes 12
90ml/6 tbsp semi-skimmed (low-fat) milk
2 eggs
150g/5oz/²⁄₃ cup unsalted (sweet) butter, melted

225g/8oz/2 cups plain (all-purpose) flour
pinch of salt
5ml/1 tsp baking powder
150g/5oz/³⁄₄ cup golden caster (superfine) sugar
150g/5oz plain (semisweet) chocolate, cut into large chunks
2 small bananas, mashed

1 Preheat the oven to 200°C/400°F/Gas 6. Arrange 12 paper cases in a muffin tin (pan).

2 Place the milk, eggs and melted butter in a bowl and whisk until combined.

3 Sift together the flour, salt and baking powder into a separate bowl. Add the sugar and chocolate to the flour mixture and stir to combine. Gradually stir in the milk mixture, but do not beat it. Fold in the mashed bananas.

4 Spoon the mixture into the paper cases. Bake for about 20 minutes until golden. Cool on a wire rack.

Cook's Tips
• Use ripe bananas for this recipe and do not peel them before you are ready to use them or they will discolour. Slice thickly into a bowl before mashing with a fork; do not try to mash them while they are still whole as they are likely to slide about and fly across the kitchen.
• You can use plain (semisweet) chocolate chips instead of chunks if you prefer.

Chocolate Chip Muffins

Nothing could be easier – or nicer – than these classic muffins. The muffin mixture is plain, with a surprise layer of chocolate chips in the middle.

Makes 10
115g/4oz/¹⁄₂ cup butter
75g/3oz/¹⁄₃ cup sugar

30ml/2 tbsp soft dark brown sugar
2 eggs
175g/6oz/1¹⁄₂ cups plain (all-purpose) flour
5ml/1 tsp baking powder
120ml/4fl oz/¹⁄₂ cup milk
175g/6oz/1 cup plain (semisweet) chocolate chips

1 Preheat the oven to 190°C/375°F/Gas 5. Arrange 10 paper cases in a muffin tin (pan).

2 In a large bowl, beat the butter until pale. Add both sugars and beat until light and fluffy. Beat in the eggs, one at a time, beating well after each addition.

3 Sift the flour and baking powder together, twice. Fold into the butter mixture, alternating with the milk.

4 Divide half of the mixture among the paper cases. Sprinkle the chocolate chips on top, dividing them equally among the muffins, then cover with the remaining mixture.

5 Bake for about 25 minutes, until lightly coloured. Leave to stand for 5 minutes before transferring to a wire rack to cool.

Variation
To make Chocolate Chip and Apple Muffins, sift 2.5ml/¹⁄₂ tsp ground cinnamon, a pinch of grated nutmeg and 1.5ml/¹⁄₄ tsp mixed spice (apple pie spice) with the dry ingredients in step 2. Halve the quantity of chocolate. Peel, core and grate two eating apples and stir into the batter with the chopped chocolate in step 3. Bake as given in the recipe, but check that the muffins are cooked by inserting a skewer into the centre of one of them. If it comes out clean, then they are ready.

Chunky Chocolate and Banana Muffins Energy 240kcal/1003kJ; Protein 3.7g; Carbohydrate 26.3g, of which sugars 11.6g; Fat 14.1g, of which saturates 8.4g; Cholesterol 59mg; Calcium 47mg; Fibre 1g; Sodium 92mg. Chocolate Chip Muffins Energy 296kcal/1238kJ; Protein 4.3g; Carbohydrate 36.4g, of which sugars 22.9g; Fat 15.8g, of which saturates 3.4g; Cholesterol 40mg; Calcium 56mg; Fibre 1g; Sodium 113mg.

Chocolate Blueberry Muffins

Blueberries are one of the many fruits that combine deliciously with the richness of chocolate, while still retaining their own distinctive flavour. These muffins are best served warm.

Makes 12
115g/4oz/½ cup butter
75g/3oz plain (semisweet) chocolate, chopped
200g/7oz/scant 1 cup sugar
1 egg, lightly beaten
250ml/8fl oz/1 cup buttermilk
10ml/2 tsp vanilla extract
275g/10oz/2½ cups plain (all-purpose) flour
5ml/1 tsp bicarbonate of soda (baking soda)
175g/6oz/generous 1 cup fresh or thawed frozen blueberries
25g/1oz plain (semisweet) chocolate, melted, to decorate

1 Preheat the oven to 190°C/375°F/Gas 5. Arrange 12 paper cases in a muffin tin (pan).

2 Melt the butter and chocolate in a pan over a medium heat, stirring frequently until smooth. Remove from the heat and leave to cool slightly.

3 Stir the sugar, egg, buttermilk and vanilla extract into the melted chocolate mixture. Gently fold in the flour and bicarbonate of soda until just blended. (The mixture should be slightly lumpy.) Gently fold in the blueberries.

4 Spoon the batter into the paper cases. Bake for 25–30 minutes, until a skewer inserted in the centre comes out with just a few crumbs attached. Transfer the muffins to a wire rack.

5 To decorate, drizzle with the melted chocolate and serve warm or at room temperature.

Cook's Tip
Do not keep the batter waiting once you have folded in the blueberries. Bake the muffins immediately or they won't rise very well during cooking.

Chocolate Walnut Muffins

Walnuts and chocolate are a delicious combination and provide both smoothness and crunch while vanilla and almond extract provide extra flavour.

Makes 12
175g/6oz/¾ cup unsalted (sweet) butter, diced
150g/5oz plain (semisweet) chocolate, chopped
225g/8oz/1 cup sugar
50g/2oz/¼ cup soft dark brown sugar
4 eggs
5ml/1 tsp vanilla extract
1.5ml/¼ tsp almond extract
75g/3oz/¾ cup plain (all-purpose) flour
115g/4oz/1 cup walnuts, coarsely chopped

1 Preheat the oven to 180°C/350°F/Gas 4. Arrange 12 paper cases in a muffin tin (pan).

2 Melt the butter with the chocolate in a heatproof bowl set over a pan of gently simmering water. Transfer to a large mixing bowl.

3 Stir both the sugars into the chocolate mixture. Mix in the eggs, one at a time, beating well after each addition, then add the vanilla and almond extracts.

4 Sift the flour over the chocolate mixture and fold in with a flexible spatula until evenly combined. Stir the walnuts into the mixture.

5 Fill the paper cases almost to the top and bake for 30–35 minutes. Leave to stand for 5 minutes before transferring to a wire rack to cool.

Variation
For Chocolate Mint and Nut Muffins, omit the vanilla and almond extracts and add 2.5ml/½ tsp peppermint extract instead and substitute the same quantity of blanched almonds or hazelnuts for the walnuts.

Chocolate Mint-filled Muffins

For extra mint flavour, chop 8 mint cream-filled after-dinner mints and fold into the cake batter.

Makes 12

150g/5oz/²/₃ cup unsalted
   (sweet) butter, softened
300g/11oz/1½ cups caster
   (superfine) sugar
3 eggs
5ml/1 tsp peppermint extract
225g/8oz/2 cups plain
   (all-purpose) flour
pinch of salt
5ml/1 tsp bicarbonate of soda
   (baking soda)

50g/2oz/½ cup unsweetened
   cocoa powder
250ml/8fl oz/1 cup milk

For the mint cream filling
300ml/10fl oz/1¼ cups double
   (heavy) or whipping cream
5ml/1 tsp peppermint extract

**For the chocolate
mint glaze**
175g/6oz plain (semisweet)
   chocolate
115g/4oz/½ cup unsalted
   (sweet) butter
5ml/1 tsp peppermint extract

1 Preheat the oven to 180°C/350°F/Gas 4. Arrange 12 paper cases in a muffin tin (pan).

2 In a bowl, beat together the butter and sugar until light and creamy. Add the eggs one at a time, beating well after each addition. Stir in the peppermint extract. Sift together the flour, salt, bicarbonate of soda and unsweetened cocoa powder over the batter and mix well.

3 Fill the paper cases with the batter. Bake for 12–15 minutes, until a skewer inserted into the centre comes out clean. Remove to a wire rack and leave to cool.

4 To make the filling, in a small bowl whip the cream with the peppermint extract until stiff peaks form. Spoon into a piping (pastry) bag fitted with a plain nozzle. Pipe 15ml/1 tbsp into the centre of each muffin.

5 To make the glaze, in a pan over a low heat melt the chocolate and butter. Remove from the heat, stir in the peppermint. Leave to cool. Spread on top of each muffin.

Chocolate Muffins

These magical little treats are sure to enchant adults and children alike.

Makes 24

175g/6oz/¾ cup butter, softened
150ml/¼ pint/²/₃ cup milk
5ml/1 tsp vanilla extract
115g/4oz plain (semisweet)
   chocolate, broken into pieces
15ml/1 tbsp water
275g/10oz/2½ cups plain
   (all-purpose) flour
5ml/1 tsp baking powder

2.5ml/½ tsp bicarbonate of soda
   (baking soda)
pinch of salt
300g/11oz/1½ cups caster
   (superfine) sugar
3 eggs

For the icing
40g/1½ oz/3 tbsp butter
115g/4oz/1 cup icing
   (confectioners') sugar
2.5ml/½ tsp vanilla extract
15–30ml/1–2 tbsp milk

1 Preheat the oven to 180°C/350°F/Gas 4. Arrange 24 paper cases in a small muffin tin (pan).

2 In a bowl, beat the butter until light and fluffy. Add the milk and vanilla extract.

3 Melt the chocolate with the water in a heatproof bowl set over a pan of simmering water. Remove from the heat. Add the chocolate mixture to the butter mixture.

4 Sift the flour, baking powder, bicarbonate of soda, salt and sugar over the batter in batches and stir well to combine. Add the eggs, one at a time, and beat well after each addition. Divide the mixture evenly among the paper cases.

5 Bake for 20–25 minutes or until a skewer inserted into the centre of a cake comes out clean. Cool in the tins for 10 minutes, then turn out to cool completely on a wire rack.

6 To make the icing, in a bowl beat the butter and icing sugar together with the vanilla extract. Beat in just enough milk to make a creamy mixture.

7 Spread the top of each cake with the icing.

Chocolate Mint-filled Muffins Energy 511kcal/2129kJ; Protein 5.4g; Carbohydrate 45.2g, of which sugars 30.4g; Fat 35.6g, of which saturates 21.7g; Cholesterol 130mg; Calcium 85mg; Fibre 1.2g; Sodium 204mg. Chocolate Muffins Energy 210kcal/884kJ; Protein 2.5g; Carbohydrate 30.4g, of which sugars 21.6g; Fat 9.7g, of which saturates 5.8g; Cholesterol 44mg; Calcium 39mg; Fibre 0.5g; Sodium 67mg.

Double Chocolate Chip Muffins

These marvellous muffins are flavoured with cocoa and packed with chunky chips of plain and white chocolate so they are sure to be a success. Serve them on their own or with cherry or raspberry jam.

Makes 16
400g/14oz/3½ cups plain (all-purpose) flour
15ml/1 tbsp baking powder
30ml/2 tbsp unsweetened cocoa powder, plus extra for dusting
115g/4oz/½ cup muscovado (molasses) sugar
2 eggs
150ml/¼ pint/⅔ cup sour cream
150ml/¼ pint/⅔ cup milk
60ml/4 tbsp sunflower oil
175g/6oz white chocolate
175g/6oz plain (semisweet) chocolate

1 Preheat the oven to 190°C/375°F/Gas 5. Arrange 16 paper cases in a muffin tin (pan).

2 Sift the flour, baking powder and cocoa into a bowl and stir in the sugar. Make a well in the centre.

3 In a separate bowl, beat the eggs with the sour cream, milk and sunflower oil. Add the egg mixture to the well in the dry ingredients. Gradually incorporate the flour mixture to make a thick batter. The batter should be slightly lumpy.

4 Finely chop the white and plain chocolate and stir into the batter. Spoon the mixture into the muffin cases, filling them almost to the top.

5 Bake for 25–30 minutes, until well risen and firm to the touch. Transfer to a wire rack to cool, then dust lightly with cocoa powder before serving.

Cook's Tip
If sour cream is not available, sour 150ml/¼ pint/⅔ cup single (light) cream by stirring in 5ml/1 tsp lemon juice and letting the mixture stand until thickened.

Nutty Muffins with Walnut Liqueur

These muffins are slightly spicy and topped with a delicious crunchy sugar and nut mixture. If you're making them for children simply omit the walnut liqueur and add more milk.

Makes 12
225g/8oz/2 cups plain (all-purpose) flour
20ml/4 tsp baking powder
2.5ml/½ tsp mixed spice (apple pie spice)
pinch of salt
115g/4oz/½ cup soft light brown sugar
75g/3oz/¾ cup chopped walnuts
50g/2oz/¼ cup butter
2 eggs
175ml/6fl oz/¾ cup milk
30ml/2 tbsp walnut liqueur

For the topping
30ml/2 tbsp soft dark brown sugar
25g/1oz/¼ cup chopped walnuts

1 Preheat the oven to 200°C/400°F/Gas 6. Arrange 12 paper cases in a muffin tin (pan).

2 Sift the flour, baking powder, mixed spice and salt into a bowl. Stir in the sugar and walnuts.

3 In a small pan melt the butter over a low heat. Beat in the eggs, milk and liqueur.

4 Pour the butter mixture into the dry mixture and stir for just long enough to combine the ingredients. The batter should be lumpy. Fill the paper cases two-thirds full, then top with a sprinkling of sugar and walnuts.

5 Bake for 15 minutes, until the muffins are golden brown. Leave in the tins for a few minutes, then transfer to a wire rack to cool.

Cook's Tip
Probably the best-known walnut liqueur is brou de noix from France, which is made from green walnut husks and flavoured with cinnamon and nutmeg. Other versions are also produced.

Double Chocolate Chip Muffins Energy 281kcal/1183kJ; Protein 4.7g; Carbohydrate 41.3g, of which sugars 21.9g; Fat 11.9g, of which saturates 5.7g; Cholesterol 7mg; Calcium 94mg; Fibre 1.3g; Sodium 40mg. Nutty Muffins with Walnut Liqueur Energy 225kcal/946kJ; Protein 4.6g; Carbohydrate 29g, of which sugars 14.7g; Fat 10.6g, of which saturates 3.1g; Cholesterol 41mg; Calcium 64mg; Fibre 0.9g; Sodium 45mg.

Jam Tarts

"The Queen of Hearts, she made some tarts, all on a summer's day; the Knave of Hearts, he stole those tarts, and took them quite away!" So goes the nursery rhyme. Jam tarts have long been a treat at birthday parties and are often a child's first attempt at baking.

Makes 12

175g/6oz/1½ cups plain (all purpose) flour, plus extra for dusting
pinch of salt
30ml/2 tbsp caster (superfine) sugar
85g/3oz/6 tbsp butter, diced
1 egg, lightly beaten
jam

1 Sift together the flour and salt into a large bowl and stir in the caster sugar. Add the butter and rub it in with your fingertips until the mixture resembles fine breadcrumbs. Stir in the beaten egg and gather the mixture together into a smooth ball of dough.

2 Wrap the dough in clear film (plastic wrap) and chill in the refrigerator for about 30 minutes.

3 Meanwhile, preheat the oven to 220°C/425°F/Gas 7 and lightly grease a 12-cup bun tin (muffin pan).

4 Roll out the dough on a lightly floured surface to about 3mm/⅛in thick. Using a 7.5cm/3in fluted cookie cutter, stamp out rounds. Re-roll the scraps and stamp out more rounds to make a total of 12. Gently press the dough rounds into the prepared tray. Put a teaspoon of jam into each.

5 Bake for 15–20 minutes, until the pastry is firm and light golden brown and the jam has spread to fill the tarts. Using a metal spatula with a flexible blade, carefully transfer the tarts to a wire rack and leave to cool completely.

Cook's Tip
Take care not to overfill the tarts with jam or it will boil over, spoiling the pastry and making a sticky mess.

Maids of Honour

These little delicacies were allegedly being enjoyed by Anne Boleyn's maids of honour when the English king, Henry VIII, first met her in Richmond Palace in Surrey, and he is said to have named them. Originally they would have been made with strained curds, made by adding rennet to milk.

Makes 12

250g/9oz ready-made puff pastry, thawed if frozen
250g/9oz/generous 1 cup curd (farmer's) cheese
60ml/4 tbsp ground almonds
45ml/3 tbsp caster (superfine) sugar
finely grated rind of 1 small lemon
2 eggs
15g/½ oz/1 tbsp butter, melted
icing (confectioners') sugar, to dust

1 Preheat the oven to 200°C/400°F/Gas 6. Lightly grease a 12-cup bun tray (muffin pan).

2 Roll out the dough very thinly on a lightly floured surface and, using a 7.5cm/3in cookie cutter, stamp out 12 rounds. Press the dough rounds into the prepared tray and prick well with a fork. Chill while you make the filling.

3 Put the curd cheese into a bowl and add the almonds, sugar and lemon rind. Lightly beat the eggs with the butter and add to the cheese mixture. Mix well.

4 Spoon the mixture into the pastry cases (tart shells). Bake for about 20 minutes, until the pastry is well risen and the filling is puffed up, golden brown and just firm to the touch.

5 Transfer to a wire rack (the filling will sink down as it cools). Serve warm or at room temperature, dusted with a little sifted icing sugar.

Variation
Sprinkle the filling with a little freshly grated nutmeg at the end of step 4.

Jam Tarts Energy 114kcal/479kJ; Protein 1.1g; Carbohydrate 18.8g, of which sugars 12.5g; Fat 4.3g, of which saturates 2.6g; Cholesterol 18mg; Calcium 16mg; Fibre 0.3g; Sodium 39mg.
Maids of Honour Energy 236kcal/993kJ; Protein 2.5g; Carbohydrate 36.7g, of which sugars 22.4g; Fat 9.8g, of which saturates 5.2g; Cholesterol 37mg; Calcium 43mg; Fibre 1g; Sodium 70mg.

Chocolate Whirls

These cookies are so easy to make. They're made with ready-made puff pastry rolled up with a chocolate filling. They're not too sweet and are similar to Danish pastries, so you could even make them as a special treat for breakfast.

Makes about 20
75g/3oz/scant ½ cup golden caster (superfine) sugar
40g/1½oz/⅓ cup unsweetened cocoa powder
2 eggs
500g/1lb 2oz ready-made puff pastry, thawed if frozen
25g/1oz/2 tbsp butter, softened
75g/3oz/generous ½ cup sultanas (golden raisins)
90g/3½oz milk chocolate, broken into small pieces

1 Preheat the oven to 220°C/425°F/Gas 7. Lightly grease two baking sheets.

2 Put the sugar, cocoa powder and eggs in a bowl and mix to a paste. Set aside.

3 Roll out the pastry on a lightly floured surface to make a 30cm/12in square. Trim off any rough edges using a sharp knife.

4 Dot the pastry all over with the butter, then spread the chocolate paste evenly over the pastry surface. Sprinkle the sultanas over the top.

5 Roll the pastry into a sausage, then cut the roll into 1cm/½in slices.

6 Place the slices on the baking sheets, spacing them apart. Bake the cookies for 10 minutes, until risen and pale golden. Transfer to a wire rack and leave to cool.

7 Melt the chocolate in a heatproof bowl set over a pan of gently simmering water.

8 Spoon or pipe lines of melted chocolate over the cookies, taking care not to completely hide the swirls of chocolate filling.

Ricotta and Marsala Tarts

These sweet, melt-in-the-mouth tarts have a crisp puff pastry base. The light cheese filling is flavoured in the Italian way with Marsala.

Makes 12
375g/13oz ready-made puff pastry, thawed if frozen
250g/9oz/generous 1 cup ricotta cheese
1 egg, plus 2 egg yolks
45–60ml/3–4 tbsp caster (superfine) sugar
30ml/2 tbsp Marsala
grated rind of 1 lemon
50g/2oz/scant ½ cup sultanas (golden raisins)

1 Preheat the oven to 190°C/375°F/Gas 5. Lightly grease a muffin tin (pan).

2 Roll out the pastry. Stamp out 12 9cm/3½in rounds of pastry and line the prepared tin. Leave to rest in the refrigerator for 20 minutes.

3 Put the ricotta cheese in a bowl and add the egg, extra yolks, sugar, Marsala and lemon rind. Whisk until smooth, then stir in the sultanas.

4 Spoon the mixture into the lined tins. Bake for about 20 minutes, or until the filling has risen and the pastry is golden and crisp.

5 Cool the tarts slightly before easing each one out with a metal spatula. Serve warm.

Variations
• *You could use ready-made shortcrust pastry instead of puff, but the tarts will not be quite so light or crisp.*
• *Instead of Marsala, you could use Madeira or sweet sherry, but if you prefer a non-alcoholic version, substitute 5ml/1 tsp vanilla extract.*
• *You can substitute curd (farmer's) cheese, strained cottage cheese or mascarpone for the ricotta but neither the texture nor the flavour will be quite the same.*

Chocolate Whirls Energy 165kcal/689kJ; Protein 2.9g; Carbohydrate 18.6g, of which sugars 9.4g; Fat 9.5g, of which saturates 1.9g; Cholesterol 23mg; Calcium 34mg; Fibre 0.4g; Sodium 117mg.
Ricotta and Marsala Tarts Energy 222kcal/928kJ; Protein 29g; Carbohydrate 27.3g, of which sugars 10.1g; Fat 11.4g, of which saturates 3.4g; Cholesterol 16mg; Calcium 64mg; Fibre 1.7g; Sodium 119mg.

Filo Crackers

These can be prepared a day in advance, brushed with melted butter and kept covered with clear film in the refrigerator or freezer before baking.

Makes 24
2 x 275g/10oz packets frozen filo pastry, thawed
115g/4oz/½ cup butter, melted
thin foil ribbon, to decorate
sifted icing (confectioners') sugar, to decorate

For the filling
450g/1lb eating apples, peeled, cored and finely chopped
5ml/1tsp ground cinnamon
25g/1oz/2 tbsp soft light brown sugar
50g/2oz/½ cup pecan nuts, chopped
50g/2oz/1 cup fresh white breadcrumbs
25g/1oz/3 tbsp sultanas (golden raisins)
25g/1oz/2 tbsp currants

For the lemon sauce
115g/4oz/ generous ½ cup caster (superfine) sugar
finely grated rind of 1 lemon
juice of 2 lemons

1 Unwrap the filo pastry and cover it with clear film (plastic wrap) and a damp cloth to prevent it from drying out. Mix all the filling ingredients together in a bowl.

2 Take one sheet of pastry at a time and cut it into 115 x 30cm/6 x 12in strips. Brush with butter. Place a spoonful of the filling at one end and fold in the sides, so the pastry measures 13cm/5in across. Brush the edges with butter and roll up. Pinch the "frill" at each end and tie with ribbon. Brush with butter.

3 Place the crackers on baking trays, cover and chill for 10 minutes. Preheat the oven to 190°C/375°F/Gas 5. Brush each cracker with melted butter. Bake the crackers for 30–35 minutes, or until they are golden brown. Let them cool slightly on the baking trays and then transfer them to a wire rack to cool completely.

4 To make the lemon sauce, put all the ingredients in a small pan and heat gently to dissolve the sugar. Serve the sauce warm. Finally, dust the crackers with sifted icing sugar.

Mince Tarts

Taste the difference in these luxurious pies filled with homemade mincemeat.

Makes 36
425g/15oz/3¾ cups plain (all-purpose) flour
150g/5oz/1¼ cups icing (confectioners') sugar
350g/12oz/1½ cups butter, chilled and diced
grated rind and juice of 1 orange
milk, for glazing

For the filling
175g/6oz/1½ cups finely chopped blanched almonds
150g/5oz/⅔ cup ready-to-eat dried apricots, chopped
175g/6oz/generous 1 cup raisins
150g/5oz/⅔ cup currants
150g/5oz/scant 1 cup glacé (candied) cherries, chopped
150g/5oz/scant 1 cup cut mixed (candied) peel, chopped
115g/4oz/⅔ cup chopped suet
grated rind and juice of 2 lemons
grated rind and juice of 1 orange
200g/7oz/scant 1 cup soft dark brown sugar
4 cooking apples, peeled, cored and chopped
10ml/2 tsp ground allspice
250ml/8fl oz/1 cup brandy
225g/8oz/1 cup cream cheese
30ml/2 tbsp caster (superfine) sugar
icing (confectioners') sugar, for dusting

1 Mix the first 13 filling ingredients together. Cover and leave in a cool place for 2 days.

2 For the pastry, sift the flour and icing sugar into a bowl. Rub in the butter. Stir in the orange rind and enough juice to bind. Chill for 20 minutes.

3 Preheat the oven to 220°C/425°F/Gas 7. Lightly grease two or three bun trays (muffin pans).

4 Roll out the dough, stamp out 36 8cm/3in rounds and put into the trays. Half fill with mincemeat. Beat the cream cheese and sugar and add a teaspoonful to each pie. Roll out the trimmings and stamp out 36 5cm/2in rounds. Brush the edges with milk and cover the pies. Cut a slit in each.

5 Brush lightly with milk. Bake for 15–20 minutes, then leave to cool. Dust with icing sugar.

Filo Crackers Energy 149kcal/629kJ; Protein 2.2g; Carbohydrate 23.9g, of which sugars 9.6g; Fat 5.7g, of which saturates 2.7g; Cholesterol 10mg; Calcium 34mg; Fibre 1g; Sodium 46mg.
Mince Tarts Energy Energy 301kcal/1258kJ; Protein 2.9g; Carbohydrate 33g, of which sugars 23.5g; Fat 16.8g, of which saturates 8.8g; Cholesterol 29mg; Calcium 58mg; Fibre 1.6g; Sodium 96mg.

Simple Mince Pies

These small pies have become synonymous with Christmas. To eat one per day for the 12 days of Christmas was thought to bring happiness for the coming year.

Makes 12
225g/8oz/2 cups plain
   (all-purpose) flour, plus extra
   for dusting
pinch of salt
45ml/3 tbsp caster (superfine)
   sugar, plus extra for dusting
115g/4oz/½ cup butter, diced
1 egg, lightly beaten
about 350g/12oz mincemeat

1 Sift the flour and salt and stir in the sugar. Rub in the butter until the mixture resembles breadcrumbs. Stir in the egg and gather into a smooth dough.

2 Chill the dough for 30 minutes. Meanwhile, preheat the oven to 220°C/425°F/Gas 7 and lightly grease a 12-cup bun tray (muffin pan).

3 Roll out the dough on a lightly floured surface to about 3mm/⅛in thick and, using a 7.5cm/4in cutter, cut out 12 rounds. Press into the prepared tray. Gather up the scraps and roll out again, cutting slightly smaller rounds to make 12 lids. Spoon mincemeat into each case (shell), dampen the edges and top with a pastry lid. Make a small slit in each pie.

4 Bake for 15–20 minutes until light golden brown. Transfer to a wire rack to cool and serve dusted with sugar.

Galettes

These simple round flat pastries, whose name comes from the French word for a flat weather-worn pebble, are made from a sweet pastry such as pâte sucrée.

Makes 10
150g/5oz/1¼ cups plain
   (all-purpose flour)
pinch of salt
75g/3oz/6 tbsp chilled
   butter, diced
25g/1oz/¼ cup icing
   (confectioners') sugar, sifted
2 egg yolks

1 Sift the flour and salt together. Make a well in the centre and put in the butter and sugar, then the egg yolks on top.

2 Rub in the mixture until it resembles scrambled eggs, and then a smooth paste. Work quickly. Lightly knead the dough for about 1 minute.

3 Shape the dough into a ball, then flatten slightly to make it easier to start rolling out. Wrap in clear film (plastic wrap) and chill for 1 hour. Preheat the oven to 200°C/400°F/Gas 6.

4 Roll out the dough to 5mm/¼in thick. Stamp out 6cm/2½in rounds. Place on a baking sheet and prick with a fork. Gather up the scraps and roll out more cookies. Bake for 10 minutes, until golden brown.

Almond Mincemeat Tarts

These little tartlets are a welcome change from traditional mince pies. Serve them warm with brandy butter. They freeze well and can be reheated for serving.

Makes 36
275g/10oz/2½ cups plain
   (all-purpose) flour, plus extra
   for dusting
75g/3oz/generous ¾ cup icing
   (confectioners') sugar
5ml/1 tsp ground cinnamon
175g/6oz/¾ cup butter
50g/2oz/½ cup ground almonds
1 egg yolk

45ml/3 tbsp milk
450g/1lb mincemeat
15ml/1 tbsp brandy or rum

For the filling
115g/4oz/½ cup butter
115g/4oz/generous ½ cup caster
   (superfine) sugar
175g/6oz/1½ cups self-raising
   (self-rising) flour
2 large (US extra large) eggs
finely grated rind of 1 large lemon

For the icing
115g/4oz/1 cup icing
   (confectioners') sugar
15ml/1 tbsp lemon juice

1 Sift the flour, icing sugar and cinnamon into a bowl or a food processor and rub in the butter until it resembles fine breadcrumbs. Add the ground almonds and bind with the egg yolk and milk to a soft dough. Knead the dough until smooth, wrap in clear film (plastic wrap) and chill for 30 minutes.

2 Preheat the oven to 190°C/375°F/Gas 5.

3 On a lightly floured surface, roll out the pastry and stamp out 36 rounds with a cookie cutter. Mix the mincemeat with the brandy or rum and put a teaspoonful in the bottom of each pastry case (tart shell). Chill.

4 For the filling, whisk all the ingredients together until smooth. Spoon on top of the mincemeat, dividing it evenly, and level the tops. Bake for 20–30 minutes, or until golden brown and springy to the touch. Remove and leave to cool on a wire rack.

5 For the icing, sift the icing sugar and mix with the lemon juice to a smooth, thick, coating consistency. Spoon into a piping (pastry) bag and drizzle a zig-zag pattern over each tart.

Simple Mince Pies Energy 182kcal/758kJ; Protein 5.2g; Carbohydrate 12.6g, of which sugars 5.1g; Fat 12.9g, of which saturates 3g; Cholesterol 43mg; Calcium 31mg; Fibre 0.4g; Sodium 85mg.
Galettes Energy 83kcal/352kJ; Protein 3.4g; Carbohydrate 14.3g, of which sugars 2.9g; Fat 1.75g, of which saturates 0.4g; Cholesterol 43mg; Calcium 27.9mg; Fibre 4..9g; Sodium 6mg.
Almond Mincemeat Tarts Energy 177kcal/746kJ; Protein 1.8g; Carbohydrate 26.4g, of which sugars 16.9g; Fat 7.8g, of which saturates 4.4g; Cholesterol 34mg; Calcium 32mg; Fibre 0.6g; Sodium 57mg.

Mini Mille Feuilles

This pâtisserie classic is a delectable combination of crisp puff pastry with luscious pastry cream. As a large one is difficult to cut, making individual servings is a great solution.

Serves 4

450g/1lb ready-made puff pastry, thawed if frozen

6 egg yolks

65g/2½oz/⅓ cup caster (superfine) sugar
45ml/3 tbsp plain (all-purpose) flour
350ml/12fl oz/1½ cups milk
30ml/2 tbsp Kirsch or cherry liqueur
450g/1lb/2⅔ cups raspberries
icing (confectioners') sugar, for dusting

1 Lightly grease two large baking sheets and sprinkle them with a little very cold water.

2 On a lightly floured surface, roll out the pastry to a thickness of 3mm/⅛in. Using a 10cm/4in cookie cutter, stamp out 12 rounds. Place on the baking sheets and prick each with a fork. Chill for 30 minutes. Preheat the oven to 200°C/400°F/Gas 6.

3 Bake the pastry rounds for 15–20 minutes, until golden, then transfer to wire racks to cool.

4 Whisk the egg yolks and sugar for 2 minutes until light and creamy, then whisk in the flour until just blended. Bring the milk to the boil over a medium heat and pour it over the egg mixture, whisking to blend. Return to the pan, bring to the boil and boil for 2 minutes, whisking constantly.

5 Remove from the heat and whisk in the Kirsch or liqueur. Pour into a bowl and press a piece of clear film (plastic wrap) on to the surface to prevent a skin from forming. Set aside.

6 To assemble, carefully split the pastry rounds in half. Spread each round with a little pastry cream. Arrange a layer of raspberries over the cream and top with a second pastry round. Spread with a little more cream and a few more raspberries. Top with a third pastry round and dust with icing sugar.

Almond Cream Puffs

These sweet little pies consist of crisp, flaky layers of pastry surrounding a delicious, creamy filling. They are best served warm, so reheat any that become cold before eating.

Makes 10

275g/10oz ready-made puff pastry, thawed if frozen

2 egg yolks

15ml/1 tbsp plain (all-purpose) flour
30ml/2 tbsp ground almonds
30ml/2 tbsp caster (superfine) sugar
a few drops of vanilla or almond extract
150ml/¼ pint/⅔ cup double (heavy) cream, whipped
milk, to glaze
icing (confectioners') sugar, for dusting

1 Preheat the oven to 200°C/400°F/Gas 6. Lightly grease a patty or cupcake tin (pan).

2 Roll out the pastry thinly on a lightly floured surface, and stamp out ten 7.5cm/3in plain rounds and ten 6.5cm/2½in fluted rounds. Keep the smaller fluted rounds for the lids and use the larger ones to line the tin. Chill in the refrigerator for about 10 minutes.

3 Whisk the egg yolks with the flour, almonds, sugar and vanilla extract. Fold in the cream and spoon into the pastry cases (pie shells).

4 Brush the rims with milk, add the lids and seal the edges. Glaze with milk.

5 Bake for 20–25 minutes, until puffed up and golden. Using a metal spatula carefully transfer the puffs to a wire rack to cool slightly. Dust with icing sugar.

Variations
Other tasty options are to use desiccated (dry unsweetened shredded) coconut or ground hazelnuts instead of ground almonds in the filling.

Mini Mille Feuilles Energy 702kcal/2943kJ; Protein 16.5g; Carbohydrate 79.1g, of which sugars 30.4g; Fat 37.8g, of which saturates 3.4g; Cholesterol 308mg; Calcium 258mg; Fibre 3.2g; Sodium 406mg.
Almond Cream Puffs Energy 225kcal/933kJ; Protein 3.2g; Carbohydrate 14.9g, of which sugars 3.9g; Fat 17.6g, of which saturates 5.5g; Cholesterol 61mg; Calcium 39mg; Fibre 0.3g; Sodium 91mg.

Surprise Fruit Baskets

Almost too pretty to eat, these crisp filo baskets are filled with fresh fruit set on a rich creamy base with a surprise flavour.

Serves 6
4 large or 8 small sheets of
  frozen filo pastry, thawed
65g/2½oz/5 tbsp butter, melted
250ml/8fl oz/1 cup double
  (heavy) or whipping cream
45ml/3 tbsp strawberry jam
15ml/1 tbsp Cointreau or other
  orange-flavoured liqueur

For the topping
15g/4oz seedless black
  grapes, halved
115g/4oz seedless white
  grapes, halved
150g/5oz fresh pineapple,
  cubed, or drained canned
  pineapple chunks
115g/4 oz/⅔ cup raspberries
30ml/2 tbsp icing
  (confectioners') sugar
6 sprigs of fresh mint,
  to decorate

1 Preheat the oven to 350°F/180°C/Gas 4. Lightly grease six cups of a bun tray (muffin pan).

2 Stack the filo sheets and cut with a sharp knife or scissors into 24 squares each 11cm/4¼in.

3 Place 4 squares of pastry in each of the six greased cups. Press the pastry firmly into the cups, rotating slightly to make star-shaped baskets.

4 Lightly brush the pastry baskets with melted butter. Bake for about 5–7 minutes, until the pastry is crisp and golden brown. Using a metal spatula, carefully transfer the baskets to a wire rack to cool.

5 In a bowl, lightly whip the cream until soft peaks form. Gently fold the strawberry jam and Cointreau into the cream with a flexible spatula.

6 Just before serving, spoon a little of the cream mixture into each pastry basket. Top with the grapes, pineapple and raspberries. Sprinkle with icing sugar and decorate each basket with a small sprig of mint.

Plum and Marzipan Pastries

These Danish pastries can be made with any stoned fruit. Try apricots, cherries, damsons or greengages, adding a glaze made from clear honey or a complementary jam.

Makes 6
375g/13oz ready-made puff
  pastry, thawed if frozen
90ml/6 tbsp plum jam

115g/4oz/¾ cup white
  marzipan, coarsely grated
3 red plums, halved and stoned
1 egg, beaten
50g/2oz/½ cup flaked
  (sliced) almonds

For the glaze
30ml/2 tbsp plum jam
15ml/1 tbsp water

1 Preheat the oven to 220°C/425°F/Gas 7.

2 Roll out the pastry, cut it into six equal squares and place on one or two dampened baking sheets.

3 Spoon 15ml/1 tbsp jam into the centre of each pastry square. Divide the marzipan among them. Place half a plum, hollow side down, on top of each marzipan mound.

4 Brush the edges of the pastry with beaten egg. Bring up the corners and press them together lightly, then open out the pastry corners at the top.

5 Brush the pastries all over with a little beaten egg to glaze. Divide the flaked almonds between the six pastries and press all over the tops and sides.

6 Bake the pastries for 20–25 minutes, until crisp and golden brown. Keep a close eye on them towards the end of the cooking time as the almonds can scorch quite quickly, spoiling the appearance and flavour of the pastries.

7 To make the glaze, heat the jam and water in a small pan, stirring until smooth. Press the mixture through a sieve (strainer) into a small bowl, then brush it over the tops of the pastries while they are still warm. Leave to cool on a wire rack.

Surprise Fruit Baskets Energy 619kcal/2569kJ; Protein 3.9g; Carbohydrate 37.9g, of which sugars 15.6g; Fat 50.9g, of which saturates 20.9g; Cholesterol 80mg; Calcium 76mg; Fibre 1.6g; Sodium 80mg.
Plum and Marzipan Pastries Energy 416kcal/1746kJ; Protein 6.6g; Carbohydrate 51.8g, of which sugars 29.2g; Fat 22.4g, of which saturates 0.6g; Cholesterol 0mg; Calcium 73mg; Fibre 1.2g; Sodium 205mg.

Marzipan Buns

These delicious buns are perfumed with aromatic light spices, and filled with thick cream and marzipan.

Makes 12
275ml/9fl oz/generous 1 cup double (heavy) cream
40g/1½oz fresh yeast
100g/4oz/½ cup unsalted (sweet) butter, melted
5ml/1 tsp ground cardamom
30ml/2 tbsp sugar
450g/1lb/4 cups plain (all-purpose) flour, plus extra for dusting
pinch of salt
1 egg, beaten
icing (confectioners') sugar, to decorate

For the filling
100g/4oz good quality marzipan
275ml/16fl oz/2 cups double (heavy) cream

1 Pour the cream into a pan and heat until warm to the touch.

2 In a large bowl, blend the yeast with a little of the warmed cream and then add the butter, cardamom and sugar. Add the flour and salt and mix together to form a dough.

3 Turn the dough on to a lightly floured surface and knead for 10 minutes, until firm and elastic. Shape into a ball, put in a clean bowl and cover with a clean dish towel. Leave to rise in a warm place for about 1½ hours, until the dough has doubled in size.

4 Turn the dough on to a lightly floured surface and knead for 2–3 minutes. Divide into 12 equal pieces. Shape each into a round bun and place on a greased baking sheet. Cover and leave to rise in a warm place until doubled in size.

5 Preheat the oven to 180°C/350°F/Gas 4. Brush the tops of the buns with beaten egg, then bake for about 10 minutes until golden brown. Transfer to a wire rack and leave to cool.

6 To serve, cut the tops off the buns and reserve. Remove half of the crumbs from the buns and put in a bowl. Grate the marzipan on top and mix. Replace the mixture in the buns. Whisk the cream until stiff, top the buns with the cream and then replace the tops. Sprinkle the icing sugar on top.

Apricot Triangles

These quite substantial pastries have a luscious filling of dried apricots poached with cinnamon, but a variety of other fillings are also popular. If serving them as snacks, you can make the pastry cases smaller and more delicate.

Makes about 24
115g/4oz/½ cup unsalted (sweet) butter, softened
250g/9oz/generous 1cup sugar
30ml/2 tbsp milk
1 egg, beaten
5ml/1 tsp vanilla extract
pinch of salt
200–250g/7–9oz/1¼–2¼ cups plain (all-purpose) flour, plus extra for dusting
icing (confectioners') sugar, for dusting (optional)

For the filling
250g/9oz/generous 1 cup dried apricots
1 cinnamon stick
45ml/3 tbsp sugar

1 Beat the butter and sugar until pale and fluffy. In another bowl mix together the milk, egg, vanilla extract and salt.

2 Add one-third of the flour, stir, then add the rest in batches, alternating with the milk mixture. Cover and chill for 1 hour.

3 To make the filling, put the ingredients in a pan and add enough water to cover. Heat gently, then simmer for 15 minutes, until the apricots are tender and most of the liquid has evaporated. Remove the cinnamon stick, then purée the apricots in a food processor or blender with a little of the cooking liquid until they form a consistency like thick jam.

4 Preheat the oven to 180°C/350°F/Gas 4. On a lightly floured surface, roll out the dough to 5mm/¼in thick, then cut into 7.5cm/3in rounds using a cookie cutter.

5 Place 15–30ml/1–2 tbsp of filling in the centre of each round, then pinch the pastry together to form three corners.

6 Place on a baking sheet and bake for 15 minutes, or until pale golden. Serve warm or cold, dusted with icing sugar.

Marzipan Buns Energy 465kcal/1938kJ; Protein 5.3g; Carbohydrate 38.2g, of which sugars 9.6g; Fat 33.4g, of which saturates 19.9g; Cholesterol 96mg; Calcium 85mg; Fibre 1.3g; Sodium 69mg.
Apricot Triangles Energy 125kcal/528kJ; Protein 1.6g; Carbohydrate 21.3g, of which sugars 14.9g; Fat 4.4g, of which saturates 2.6g; Cholesterol 18mg; Calcium 28mg; Fibre 0.9g; Sodium 35mg.

Mallorcan Ensaimadas

These spiral-shaped sweet breads are a popular Spanish breakfast treat. The butter adds a delicious richness.

Makes 16

225g/8oz/2 cups strong white
   bread flour, plus extra
   for dusting
pinch of salt
50g/2oz/¼ cup caster
   (superfine) sugar
15g/½ oz fresh yeast
75ml/5 tbsp lukewarm milk
1 egg
30ml/2 tbsp sunflower oil
50g/2oz/¼ cup butter, melted
icing (confectioners') sugar,
   for dusting

1 Lightly grease two baking sheets. Sift the flour and salt into a large bowl. Stir in the sugar. Make a well in the centre.

2 Cream the yeast with the milk, pour into the centre of the flour, then sprinkle a little of the flour mixture over the top of the liquid. Leave in a warm place for 15 minutes, or until frothy.

3 In a small bowl, beat the egg and sunflower oil together. Add to the flour mixture and mix to a smooth dough. Turn out on to a lightly floured surface and knead for 8–10 minutes, until smooth and elastic. Place in a lightly oiled bowl, cover with lightly oiled clear film (plastic wrap) and leave to rise in a warm place for 1 hour, or until doubled in bulk.

4 Turn out the dough on to a lightly floured surface. Knock back (punch down) and divide into 16 equal pieces. Shape each piece into a rope about 38cm/15in long. Pour the melted butter on to a plate and dip the ropes into the butter to coat.

5 On the baking sheets, curl each rope into a loose spiral, spacing well apart. Tuck the ends under to seal. Cover with lightly oiled clear film and leave to rise in a warm place for about 45 minutes, or until doubled in size.

6 Preheat the oven to 190°C/375°F/Gas 5. Brush the rolls with water and dust with icing sugar. Bake for 10 minutes, or until light golden brown. Cool on a wire rack. Dust again with icing sugar and serve warm.

Saffron Buns

Sweet, filling and infused with saffron, these delicious buns are great for eating at any time of day.

Makes 20

300ml/½ pint/1¼ cups milk
130g/4½oz/9 tbsp unsalted
   (sweet) butter
a pinch of saffron threads
50g/2oz fresh yeast
700g/1½lb/6 cups plain
(all-purpose) flour, plus extra
   for dusting
5ml/1 tsp salt
150g/5oz/¾ cup caster
   (superfine) sugar
40 raisins
beaten egg, to glaze

1 Put the milk and butter in a pan and heat until the butter has melted. Remove from the heat, add the saffron threads and leave to cool until warm to the touch.

2 In a large bowl, blend the fresh yeast with a little of the warm saffron milk. Add the remaining saffron milk, then add the flour, salt and sugar. Mix together to form a dough that comes away from the sides of the bowl.

3 Turn the dough on to a lightly floured surface and knead for about 10 minutes, until the dough feels firm and elastic. Shape into a ball, put in a clean bowl and cover with a clean dish towel. Leave to rise in a warm place for about 1 hour, until the dough has doubled in size.

4 Turn the dough on to a lightly floured surface and knead again for 2–3 minutes. Divide the dough into 20 equal pieces. Roll each into an S shape and place on greased baking sheets.

5 Place a raisin at the end of each bun. Cover with a clean dish towel and leave to rise in a warm place for about 40 minutes, until doubled in size.

6 Preheat the oven to 200°C/400°F/Gas 6. Brush the tops of the buns with beaten egg to glaze and bake for 15 minutes, until golden brown.

Mallorcan Ensaimadas Energy 327kcal/1371kJ; Protein 8.7g; Carbohydrate 38.6g, of which sugars 4.3g; Fat 16.1g, of which saturates 9.3g; Cholesterol 117mg; Calcium 172mg; Fibre 1.4g; Sodium 162mg.
Saffron Buns Energy 423kcal/1788kJ; Protein 9.2g; Carbohydrate 81.7g, of which sugars 15.1g; Fat 8.8g, of which saturates 5g; Cholesterol 20mg; Calcium 161mg; Fibre 2.8g; Sodium 69mg.

Chocolate Eclairs

These crisp pastry fingers are filled with fresh cream, sweetened with vanilla.

Makes 12
65g/2½oz/9 tbsp plain
    (all-purpose) flour
pinch of salt
50g/2oz/¼ cup butter, diced
150ml/¼ pint/⅔ cup water
2 eggs, lightly beaten

For the filling
300ml/½ pint/1¼ cups double
    (heavy) cream
10ml/2 tsp icing (confectioners')
    sugar, sifted
1.5ml/¼ tsp vanilla extract

For the glaze
115g/4oz plain (semisweet)
chocolate
25g/1oz/2 tbsp butter

1 Preheat the oven to 200°C/400°F/Gas 6. Grease and line a baking sheet. For the pastry, sift the flour and salt on to a sheet of baking parchment.

2 Melt the butter with the water in a pan, then bring to a rolling boil. Remove from the heat, add all the flour and beat until combined. Return to a low heat, beating until the mixture leaves the side of the pan and forms a ball. Leave to cool for 2–3 minutes. Gradually beat in the eggs to make a smooth, shiny paste.

3 Spoon the pastry into a piping (pastry) bag fitted with a 2.5cm/1in plain nozzle. Pipe 10cm/4in lengths on to the baking sheet. Use a wet knife to cut off the pastry at the nozzle. Bake for 25–30 minutes, until risen and golden.

4 Make a slit along the side of each éclair to release the steam, lower the oven temperature to 180°C/350°F/Gas 4 and bake for 5 minutes more. Cool on a wire rack.

5 For the filling, whip the cream with the sugar and vanilla. Spoon into a piping bag and use to fill the éclairs.

6 Melt the chocolate with 30ml/2 tbsp water in a heatproof bowl over a pan of simmering water. Remove from the heat and gradually stir in the butter. Dip the top of each éclair in the chocolate. Leave to cool until set.

Chocolate Profiteroles

These mouth-watering desserts are served with ice cream and drizzled with chocolate sauce.

Serves 4–6
75g/3oz/¾ cup plain
    (all-purpose) flour
pinch of salt
pinch of ground nutmeg
175ml/6fl oz/¾ cup water

75g/6 tbsp unsalted (sweet)
    butter, diced
3 eggs

For the filling and glaze
275g/10oz plain (semisweet)
    chocolate
120ml/4fl oz/½ cup water
750ml/1¼ pints/3 cups vanilla
    ice cream

1 Preheat the oven to 200°C/400°F/Gas 6. Lightly grease a large baking sheet.

2 To make the profiteroles, sift the flour, salt and nutmeg into a bowl.

3 In a medium pan, bring the water and butter to a boil. Remove from the heat and add the dry ingredients all at once. Beat with a wooden spoon for about 1 minute, until well blended, then set the pan over a low heat and cook for about 2 minutes, beating constantly. Remove from the heat.

4 Beat one egg in a small bowl and set aside. Add the remaining eggs, one at a time, to the flour mixture, beating well after each addition. Add the beaten egg by teaspoonfuls until the dough is smooth and shiny; it should pull away and fall slowly when dropped from a spoon.

5 Using a tablespoon, drop the dough on to the baking sheet in 12 mounds. Bake for 25–30 minutes until the pastry is well risen and browned. Turn off the oven and leave the puffs to cool with the door open.

6 To make the sauce, melt the chocolate and water in a heatproof bowl over a pan of gently simmering water, stirring occasionally. Split the pastry in half, add a scoop of ice cream and pour over the chocolate sauce.

Chocolate Eclairs Energy 253kcal/1050kJ; Protein 2.5g; Carbohydrate 11.6g, of which sugars 7.4g; Fat 22.2g, of which saturates 13.5g; Cholesterol 80mg; Calcium 29mg; Fibre 0.4g; Sodium 56mg.
Chocolate Profiteroles Energy 647kcal/2707kJ; Protein 11.7g; Carbohydrate 68.2g, of which sugars 52.4g; Fat 36.9g, of which saturates 22.7g; Cholesterol 155mg; Calcium 182mg; Fibre 1.7g; Sodium 189mg.

Double Chocolate Cream Puffs

These cream puffs are made with double helpings of chocolate and cream.

Makes 12
150g/5oz/1¼ cups plain
   (all-purpose) flour
25g/1oz/2 tbsp unsweetened
   cocoa powder
250ml/8fl oz/1 cup water
2.5ml/½ tsp salt
15ml/1 tbsp sugar
115g/4oz/½ cup unsalted
   (sweet) butter, diced
4–5 eggs

For the cream
150g/5oz plain (semisweet)
   chocolate, melted

475ml/16fl oz/2 cups milk
6 egg yolks
100g/3½oz/scant ½ cup sugar
50g/2oz/½ cup plain
   (all-purpose) flour
120ml/4fl oz/½ cup whipping
   cream

For the glaze
300ml/10fl oz/1¼ cups
   whipping cream
55g/2oz/4 tbsp unsalted (sweet)
   butter, diced
225g/8oz plain (semisweet)
   chocolate, chopped
15ml/1 tbsp golden (light corn)
   syrup

1 Preheat the oven to 200°C/400°F/Gas 6. Lightly grease a large baking sheet. To make the cream puffs, sift the flour and cocoa powder into a bowl.

2 In a medium pan, bring the water, salt, sugar and butter to a boil. Continue to make and bake the cream puffs following the recipe for Chocolate Profiteroles.

3 To make the cream, melt the chocolate and set it aside. Bring the milk to a boil. In a bowl, beat the egg yolks with the sugar until pale and thick. Stir in the flour. Slowly pour over half of the hot milk, stirring constantly. Return the yolk mixture to the milk pan and cook until boiling. Stir in the melted chocolate. Cool to room temperature. Whip the cream. Fold into the cooled custard mixture. Fill each puff with pastry cream using a piping (pastry) bag.

4 Melt the glaze ingredients in a medium pan over a low heat, stir until smooth. Cool slightly and pour over the cream puffs.

Coffee Cream Profiteroles

Crisp-textured coffee choux pastry puffs are filled with cream and drizzled with a white chocolate sauce.

Serves 6
65g/2½oz/9 tbsp plain
   (all-purpose) flour
pinch of salt
50g/2oz/¼ cup butter, diced
150ml/¼ pint/⅔ cup freshly
   brewed coffee
2 eggs, lightly beaten

For the filling and sauce
50g/2oz/¼ cup sugar
100ml/3½fl oz/scant ½ cup
   water
150g/5oz good-quality white
   chocolate, broken up
25g/1oz/2 tbsp butter
300ml/½ pint/1¼ cups double
   (heavy) cream
30ml/2 tbsp coffee liqueur, such
   as Tia Maria or Kahlúa

1 Preheat the oven to 220°C/425°F/Gas 7. To make the pastry, sift the flour and salt on to a sheet of baking parchment and set aside. Put the butter into a pan with the coffee. Bring to a rolling boil, then remove from the heat and add all the flour. Beat vigorously with a wooden spoon until the mixture forms a ball and comes away from the side. Let stand for 2 minutes.

2 Gradually add the beaten eggs to the flour mixture, beating thoroughly after each addition. Spoon into a piping (pastry) bag fitted with a 1cm/½in plain nozzle.

3 Pipe 24 buns on to a damp baking sheet and bake for about 20 minutes. Transfer to a wire rack. Pierce each one to let out the steam. Leave to cool.

4 To make the sauce, put the sugar and water in a pan and heat until the sugar has dissolved. Bring to the boil, then simmer for 3 minutes. Remove from the heat and add the chocolate and butter, stirring until smooth. Stir in 45ml/3 tbsp of the cream and the coffee liqueur.

5 To assemble, whip the remaining cream in a small bowl until soft peaks form. Spoon into a piping bag and use to fill the buns through the slits in the sides. Pour a little sauce over.

Double Chocolate Cream Puffs Energy 576kcal/2401kJ; Protein 9.2g; Carbohydrate 46.9g, of which sugars 33.7g; Fat 40.4g, of which saturates 23.5g; Cholesterol 235mg; Calcium 133mg; Fibre 1.6g; Sodium 166mg. **Coffee Cream Profiteroles** Energy 579kcal/2401kJ; Protein 6g; Carbohydrate 32.6g, of which sugars 24.4g; Fat 46.8g, of which saturates 28.4g; Cholesterol 159mg; Calcium 123mg; Fibre 0.3g; Sodium 138mg.

Nutty Cream Cheese Spirals

These light and sweet, cream cheese and nut-filled spirals taste heavenly.

Makes 32
225g/8oz/1 cup butter
225g/8oz/1 cup cream cheese
10ml/2 tsp sugar
225g/8oz/ 2 cups plain
    (all-purpose) flour, plus extra
    for dusting

1 egg white beaten with
    15ml/1 tbsp water, for glazing
sugar, for sprinkling

For the filling
115g/4oz/1 cup walnuts or
    pecans, finely chopped
75g/3oz/1/2 cup light brown sugar
5ml/1 tsp ground cinnamon

1 In a bowl, beat the butter, cream cheese and sugar until pale and creamy.

2 Sift over the flour and mix to a form a dough. Gather into a ball and divide into two. Flatten each peice, wrap in clear film (plastic wrap) and chill in the refrigerator for at least 30 minutes.

3 To make the filling, mix together the chopped walnuts, or pecans, brown sugar and cinnamon.

4 Preheat the oven to 190°C/375°F/Gas 5. Lightly grease two baking sheets.

5 On a lightly floured surface, roll out each half of dough thinly into a circle about 28cm/11in in diameter. Trim the edges with a knife using a dinner plate as a guide.

6 Brush the surface with egg white glaze and sprinkle the dough evenly with half the filling.

7 Cut the dough into quarters and each quarter into four sections to form 16 triangles. Starting from the base of the triangles (the rounded end) roll up to form spirals.

8 Place on the prepared baking sheets and brush with the remaining glaze. Sprinkle with sugar. Bake for 15–20 minutes until golden. Transfer to a wire rack to cool completely.

Spiced Nut Palmiers

Created at the beginning of the last century, these dainty French cookies are designed to be served with afternoon tea. They are said to look like the foliage of palm trees.

Makes 40
75g/3oz/3/4 cup chopped
    almonds, walnuts or hazelnuts
30ml/2 tbsp caster (superfine)
    sugar, plus extra for sprinkling
2.5ml/1/2 tsp ground cinnamon
225g/8oz ready-made rough-puff
    or puff pastry dough, thawed
    if frozen
1 egg, lightly beaten

1 Lightly butter two large baking sheets, preferably non-stick. In a food processor fitted with a metal blade, process the nuts, sugar and cinnamon until finely ground.

2 Sprinkle the work surface with caster sugar and roll out the dough to a rectangle 50 × 20cm/20 × 8in and about 3mm/1/8in thick. Lightly brush the dough all over with beaten egg and sprinkle evenly with about half of the nut mixture.

3 Fold in the long edges of the dough to meet in the centre and flatten with the rolling pin. Brush with egg and sprinkle with most of the remaining nut mixture. Fold in the folded edges to meet in the centre, brush with egg and sprinkle with the remaining nut mixture. Fold one side of the dough over the other.

4 Cut the dough crossways into 8mm/3/8in slices and place 2.5cm/1in apart on the baking sheets.

5 Spread the dough edges apart to form dough wedges. Chill the palmiers for at least 15 minutes. Preheat the oven to 220°C/425°F/Gas 7.

6 Bake the palmiers for about 8–10 minutes, until the pastry is crisp and golden. Carefully turn them over halfway through the cooking time using a metal spatula. Keep a watchful eye on them as the sugar can easily scorch. Carefully transfer to a wire rack to cool completely.

Nutty Cream Cheese Spirals Energy 150kcal/621kJ; Protein 1.7g; Carbohydrate 9.7g, of which sugars 4.3g; Fat 11.8g, of which saturates 6g; Cholesterol 28mg; Calcium 24mg; Fibre 0.3g; Sodium 67mg.
Spiced Nut Palmiers Energy 37kcal/155kJ; Protein 0.9g; Carbohydrate 3g, of which sugars 0.9g; Fat 2.6g, of which saturates 0.1g; Cholesterol 5mg; Calcium 9mg; Fibre 0.1g; Sodium 20mg.

Tunisian Almond Cigars

These light-as-air pastries are filled with a subtly flavoured almond mixture that is sure to delight your guests but will also keep them guessing.

Makes 8–12
250g/9oz almond paste
1 egg, lightly beaten
15ml/1 tbsp rose water or orange flower water
5ml/1 tsp ground cinnamon
1.5ml/¼ tsp almond extract
8–12 sheets filo pastry, thawed if frozen
melted butter, for brushing
icing (confectioners') sugar and ground cinnamon, for dusting

1 Knead the almond paste until soft, then put in a bowl and mix in the egg, flower water, cinnamon and almond extract. Chill for 1–2 hours.

2 Preheat the oven to 190°C/375°F/Gas 5. Lightly grease a baking sheet.

3 Place a sheet of filo pastry on a piece of baking parchment, keeping the remaining pastry covered with a damp cloth, and brush with the melted butter.

4 Shape 30–45ml/2–3 tbsp of the filling into a cylinder and place at one end of the pastry. Fold the pastry over to enclose the ends of the filling, then roll up to form a cigar. Place on the baking sheet and make 7–11 more cigars in the same way.

5 Bake for about 15 minutes, or until golden brown. Leave to cool completely, then serve, dusted with icing sugar and ground cinnamon.

Variation
Instead of dusting with sugar, drench the pastries in syrup. In a pan, dissolve 250g/9oz/generous 1 cup sugar in 250ml/8fl oz/1 cup water and boil until thickened. Stir in a squeeze of lemon juice and a few drops of rose water and pour over the pastries. Leave the syrup to soak in before serving.

Butterfly Cookies

Melt-in-the-mouth puff pastry interleaved with sugar, nuts and cinnamon produces a slightly outrageous-looking cookie that teams well with ice creams and fruit salads.

Makes about 12
500g/1¼lb ready-made puff pastry, thawed if frozen
1 egg, beaten
115g/4oz/½ cup sugar
25g/1oz/¼ cup chopped mixed nuts
5ml/1 tsp ground cinnamon

1 Preheat the oven to 200°C/400°F/Gas 6.

2 Roll out the dough on a lightly floured surface to a rectangle 50 × 17cm/20 × 6½in. Using a sharp knife, cut the rectangle widthways into four pieces. Lightly brush each piece with the beaten egg.

3 Mix together 75g/3oz/6 tbsp of the sugar, the nuts and cinnamon in a bowl. Sprinkle this mixture evenly over three of the pieces of dough. Place the pieces one on top of the other, ending with the uncoated piece, placing this one egg side down on the top of the stack. Press lightly together with the rolling pin.

4 Cut the stack of dough sheets widthways into 5mm/¼in slices. Carefully place one strip on a non-stick baking sheet and place the next strip over it at an angle. Place a third strip on top at another angle so that it looks like a butterfly. Don't worry if the strips separate slightly when you are transferring them to the baking sheet. However, try to handle the dough as little as possible.

5 Using your fingers, press the centre very flat. Sprinkle with a little of the reserved sugar. Continue in this way to make more cookies until all the dough is used up.

6 Bake the cookies for about 10–15 minutes, or until golden brown all over. Leave to cool completely on the baking sheet before serving with a dessert such as ice cream or fruit salad.

Tunisian Almond Cigars Energy 109kcal/458kJ; Protein 2.2g; Carbohydrate 18.9g, of which sugars 14.2g; Fat 3.2g, of which saturates 0.4g; Cholesterol 16mg; Calcium 25mg; Fibre 0.6g; Sodium 10mg.
Butterfly Cookies Energy 212kcal/889kJ; Protein 3.4g; Carbohydrate 25.6g, of which sugars 10.6g; Fat 11.8g, of which saturates 0.2g; Cholesterol 16mg; Calcium 37mg; Fibre 0.2g; Sodium 136mg.

Rugelach

These crisp, flaky cookies, rolled around a sweet filling, resemble a croissant. They are thought to have come from Poland, where they are a traditional sweet treat. Chocolate chip rugelach are very popular in the United States.

Makes 48–60

115g/4oz/½ cup unsalted (sweet) butter
115g/4oz/½ cup full-fat soft white (farmer's) cheese
15ml/1 tbsp sugar

1 egg
pinch of salt
about 250g/9oz/2¼ cups plain (all-purpose) flour, plus extra for dusting
about 250g/9oz/generous 1 cup butter, melted
250g/9oz/scant 2 cups sultanas (golden raisins)
130g/4½oz/generous 1 cup chopped walnuts
about 225g/8oz/generous 1 cup caster (superfine) sugar
10–15ml/1–2 tsp ground cinnamon

1 To make the pastry, put the butter and cheese in a bowl and beat until creamy. Beat in the sugar, egg and salt.

2 Fold the flour into the mixture, a little at a time, until the dough can be worked with the hands. Continue adding the flour, kneading with the hands, until it is a consistency that can be rolled out. (Add only as much flour as needed.)

3 Shape the dough into a ball, then cover with clear film (plastic wrap) and chill in the refrigerator for at least 2 hours or overnight. Preheat the oven to 180°C/350°F/Gas 4.

4 Divide the dough into six equal pieces. On a lightly floured surface, roll out each piece into a round about 3mm/⅛in thick, then brush with a little of the melted butter and sprinkle over the sultanas, chopped walnuts, a little sugar and the cinnamon.

5 Cut the rounds into eight to ten wedges and carefully roll the large side of each wedge towards the tip. (Some of the filling will fall out.) Arrange on baking sheets, brush with a little butter and sprinkle with the sugar. Bake for 15–30 minutes, until lightly browned. Leave to cool before serving.

Fig and Date Ravioli

These irresistible cushions of sweet pastry are filled with a delicious mixture of figs, dates and walnuts and dusted with icing sugar. They are ideal for serving with coffee.

Makes about 20

375g/13oz ready-made sweet shortcrust pastry dough, thawed if frozen

milk, for brushing
icing (confectioners') sugar, sifted, for dusting

For the filling

115g/4oz/⅔ cup ready-to-eat dried figs
50g/2oz/scant ½ cup stoned (pitted) dates
15g/½oz/1 tbsp chopped walnuts
10ml/2 tsp lemon juice
15ml/1 tbsp clear honey

1 Preheat the oven to 180°C/350°F/Gas 4. To make the filling, put all the ingredients into a food processor and blend to a paste.

2 Roll out just under half of the shortcrust pastry dough on a lightly floured surface to a square. Place spoonfuls of the fig paste on the dough in neat rows at equally spaced intervals.

3 Roll out the remaining dough to a slightly larger square. Dampen all around each spoonful of filling, using a pastry brush dipped in cold water. Place the second sheet of dough on top and press together around each mound of filling.

4 Using a zig-zag pastry wheel, cut squares between the mounds of filling. Place the cookies on non-stick baking sheets and lightly brush the top of each with a little milk. Bake for 15–20 minutes, until golden.

5 Using a metal spatula, transfer the cookies to a wire rack to cool. When cool, dust with icing sugar.

Cook's Tip
If you don't have a pastry wheel, use a sharp knife to cut out the ravioli, although it will not produce a fluted edge.

Rugelach Energy 143kcal/596kJ; Protein 1.9g; Carbohydrate 13.2g, of which sugars 5.3g; Fat 9.5g, of which saturates 4.7g; Cholesterol 18mg; Calcium 32mg; Fibre 0.6g; Sodium 48mg.
Fig and Date Ravioli Energy 111kcal/464kJ; Protein 1.5g; Carbohydrate 13.9g, of which sugars 5.3g; Fat 5.9g, of which saturates 1.7g; Cholesterol 3mg; Calcium 31mg; Fibre 0.9g; Sodium 79mg.

Gazelles' Horns

Originating from Morocco, these horn-shaped pastries are filled with fragrant sweet almond paste – an unusual and lovely treat.

Makes about 16
200g/7oz/1¾ cups plain
    (all-purpose) flour, plus extra
    for dusting
pinch of salt
25g/1oz/2 tbsp butter, melted
about 30ml/2 tbsp orange
    flower water
1 egg yolk, beaten
60–90ml/4–6 tbsp chilled water

For the filling
200g/7oz/scant 2 cups
    ground almonds
115g/4oz/1 cup icing
    (confectioners') sugar, plus
    extra for dusting
30ml/2 tbsp orange flower water
25g/1oz/2 tbsp butter, melted
2 egg yolks, beaten
2.5ml/½ tsp ground cinnamon

1 Mix the almonds, icing sugar, orange flower water, butter, egg yolks and cinnamon in a bowl to make a smooth paste.

2 To make the dough, sift the flour and salt into a large bowl, then stir in the melted butter, orange flower water and about three-quarters of the egg yolk. Stir in enough chilled water to make a fairly soft dough.

3 Quickly and lightly, knead the dough until it is smooth and elastic, then place it on a lightly floured surface and roll it out thinly. Cut the dough into long strips 7.5cm/3in wide. Preheat the oven to 180°C/350°F/Gas 4. Grease a baking sheet.

4 Roll small pieces of the almond paste into thin sausages about 7.5cm/3in long with tapering ends. Place these in a line along one side of the strips of dough, about 3cm/1¼in apart. Dampen the dough edges with water, then fold the other half of the strip over the filling and press the edges together firmly.

5 Cut around each dough sausage to make a crescent shape. Make sure that the edges are firmly pinched together. Prick the crescents with a fork and place on the baking sheet. Brush with the remaining egg yolk and bake for 12–16 minutes until lightly coloured. Leave to cool, then dust with icing sugar.

Baked Sweet Ravioli

These rich pastries are flavoured with lemon and filled with ricotta cheese, fruit and chocolate, for a sweet and rich treat.

Serves 4
225g/8oz/2 cups plain
    (all-purpose) flour
65g/2½oz/⅓ cup caster
    (superfine) sugar
90/3½oz/scant ½ cup
    butter, diced
2 eggs
5ml/1 tsp finely grated lemon
    rind, plus extra for sprinkling

For the filling
175g/6oz/¾ cup ricotta cheese
50g/2oz/¼ cup caster
    (superfine) sugar
4ml/¾ tsp vanilla extract
1 egg yolk, beaten
15ml/1 tbsp mixed candied fruits
25g/1oz dark (bittersweet)
    chocolate, finely chopped
icing (confectioners') sugar,
    for sprinkling
grated dark (bittersweet)
    chocolate, for sprinkling

1 For the dough, process the flour, sugar and butter in a food processor. Add one egg and the lemon rind and process to form a dough. Wrap in clear film (plastic wrap) and chill.

2 Press the cheese through a sieve (strainer) into a bowl. Stir in the sugar, vanilla, egg yolk, fruits and chocolate.

3 Halve the dough and roll out each half between sheets of clear film to a 15 x 56cm/6 x 22in rectangle.

4 Preheat the oven to 180°C/350°F/Gas 4. Lightly grease a baking sheet.

5 Place mounds of filling, 2.5cm/1in apart, in two rows on one dough strip. Beat the remaining egg and brush between the mounds. Top with the second dough strip and press to seal. Stamp out ravioli around each mound with a 6cm/2½in cookie cutter. Gently pinch to seal the edges.

6 Place on the baking sheet and bake for 15 minutes, until golden. Sprinkle with lemon rind, icing sugar and chocolate.

Baked Sweet Ravioli Energy 628kcal/2636kJ; Protein 13.1g; Carbohydrate 81.4g, of which sugars 38.5g; Fat 30.1g, of which saturates 17.7g; Cholesterol 162mg; Calcium 119mg; Fibre 2.1g; Sodium 186mg.
Gazelles' Horns Energy 182kcal/762kJ; Protein 4.4g; Carbohydrate 18.1g, of which sugars 8.2g; Fat 10.7g, of which saturates 2.5g; Cholesterol 44mg; Calcium 56mg; Fibre 1.3g; Sodium 23mg.

Fruit-filled Empanadas

Imagine biting through crisp buttery pastry to discover a rich fruity filling flavoured with oranges and cinnamon.

Makes 12

275g/10oz/2½ cups plain
  (all-purpose) flour, plus extra
  for dusting
25g/1oz/2 tbsp sugar
90g/3½ oz/scant ½ cup butter,
  chilled and diced
1 egg yolk
iced water

milk, to glaze
caster (superfine) sugar,
  for sprinkling
whole almonds and orange
  wedges, to serve

For the filling

25g/1oz/2 tbsp butter
3 ripe plantains, peeled
  and mashed
2.5ml/½ tsp ground cloves
5ml/1 tsp ground cinnamon
225g/8oz/1⅓ cups raisins
grated rind and juice of 2 oranges

1 Combine the flour and sugar in a mixing bowl. Add the butter and rub in with your fingertips until the mixture resembles fine breadcrumbs.

2 Beat the egg yolk and add to the flour mixture. Add iced water to make a smooth dough. Shape it into a ball.

3 For the filling, melt the butter in a pan. Add the plantains, cloves and cinnamon and cook over a medium heat for 2–3 minutes. Stir in the raisins, with the orange rind and juice. Lower the heat so that the mixture barely simmers. Cook for about 15 minutes, until the raisins are plump and the juice has evaporated. Set aside to cool.

4 Preheat the oven to 200°C/400°F/Gas 6. Roll out the dough on a lightly floured surface. Stamp out 10cm/4in rounds using a cookie cutter. Place on a baking sheet and spoon on a little of the filling. Dampen the rim of the dough rounds with water, fold the dough over the filling and crimp the edges to seal.

5 Brush with milk. Bake in batches if necessary, for about 15 minutes, or until they are golden. Leave to cool a little, sprinkle with caster sugar and serve warm, with whole almonds and orange wedges.

Microwave Date-filled Pastries

Made traditionally these pastries are labour-intensive, but making a small quantity in the microwave is not such a lengthy procedure.

Makes about 25

75g/3oz/6 tbsp butter, softened
175g/6oz/1½ cups plain
  (all-purpose) flour
5ml/1 tsp rose water
5ml/1 tsp orange flower water

45ml/3 tbsp water
20ml/4 tsp sifted icing
  (confectioners') sugar, for
  sprinkling

For the filling

115g/4oz/⅔ cup stoned (pitted)
  dried dates
50ml/2fl oz/¼ cup boiling water
2.5ml/½ tsp orange flower water

1 To make the filling, chop the dates finely and place in a bowl. Add the boiling water and orange flower water, then beat the mixture vigorously with a wooden spoon. Set aside and leave to cool.

2 For the pastries, rub the butter into the flour with your fingertips. Mix in the rose and orange flower waters and the water to make a firm dough.

3 Shape the dough into about 25 small balls.

4 Press your finger into a ball of dough to make a small container, pressing the sides round and round to make the sides thinner. Put 1.5ml/¼ tsp of the date mixture into the dough. Seal by pressing the pastry together.

5 Repeat with the remaining dough and filling.

6 Arrange the date pastries, seam side down, on lightly greased baking parchment and prick each one with a fork. Microwave on HIGH (100 per cent) power for 3–5 minutes, rearranging twice during cooking. Leave to stand for 5 minutes before transferring to a rack to cool.

7 Put the cooled pastries on a plate and sprinkle over the icing sugar. Shake lightly to make sure they are covered.

Fruit-filled Empanadas Energy 276kcal/1161kJ; Protein 4g; Carbohydrate 45.4g, of which sugars 15.7g; Fat 9.9g, of which saturates 5.9g; Cholesterol 40mg; Calcium 59mg; Fibre 1.7g; Sodium 80mg.
Microwave Date-filled Pastries Energy 59kcal/246kJ; Protein 0.8g; Carbohydrate 8.6g, of which sugars 3.3g; Fat 2.6g, of which saturates 1.6g; Cholesterol 6mg; Calcium 12mg; Fibre 0.4g; Sodium 19mg.

Greek Fruit and Nut Pastries

Aromatic Greek pastries are packed with candied citrus peel and walnuts, soaked in a coffee syrup.

Makes 16
450g/1lb/4 cups plain
  (all-purpose) flour, plus extra
  for dusting
2.5ml/¹/₂ tsp ground cinnamon
2.5ml/¹/₂ tsp baking powder
pinch of salt
150g/5oz/10 tbsp unsalted
  (sweet) butter
30ml/2 tbsp caster (superfine)
  sugar

1 egg
120ml/4fl oz/¹/₂ cup milk, chilled

For the filling
60ml/4 tbsp clear honey
60ml/4 tbsp strong freshly
  brewed coffee
75g/3oz/¹/₂ cup mixed candied
  citrus peel, finely chopped
175g/6oz/1¹/₂ cups
  walnuts, chopped
1.5ml/¹/₄ tsp freshly-grated
  nutmeg
milk, to glaze
caster (superfine) sugar,
  for sprinkling

1 Preheat the oven to 180°C/350°F/Gas 4. To make the dough, sift the flour, ground cinnamon, baking powder and salt into a bowl. Rub in the butter until the mixture resembles fine breadcrumbs. Stir in the sugar. Make a well in the middle.

2 Beat the egg and milk together and add to the well in the dry ingredients. Mix to a soft dough. Divide the dough into two and wrap in clear film (plastic wrap). Chill for 30 minutes.

3 To make the filling, mix the honey and coffee. Add the peel, walnuts and nutmeg. Stir well and leave to soak for 20 minutes.

4 Roll out a portion of dough on a lightly floured surface to about 3mm/¹/₈in thick. Stamp out 10cm/4in rounds.

5 Place a heaped teaspoonful of filling on one side of each round. Brush the edges with milk, then fold over and press the edges together to seal. Repeat until all the filling is used.

6 Put the pastries on non-stick baking sheets, brush with milk and sprinkle with caster sugar. Prick each with a fork and bake for 35 minutes. Cool on a wire rack.

Fruit and Nut Turnovers

A tasty mixture of dried fruit and nuts is enclosed in crisp little pastry crescents.

Makes 16
225g/8oz/2 cups plain
  (all-purpose) flour
1.5ml/¹/₄ tsp baking powder
pinch of salt
10ml/2 tsp caster (superfine)
  sugar
50g/2oz/4 tbsp unsalted (sweet)
  butter, chilled
25g/1oz/2 tbsp white cooking fat
120–175ml/4–6fl oz/¹/₂–³/₄ cup
  iced water

For the filling
350g/12oz/2 cups mixed
  dried fruit, such as apricots
  and prunes
75g/3oz/generous ¹/₂ cup raisins
115g/4oz/1¹/₂ cup soft light
  brown sugar
65g/2¹/₂oz/generous ¹/₂ cup pine
  nuts or chopped almonds
2.5ml/¹/₂ tsp ground cinnamon
oil, for frying
45ml/3 tbsp caster (superfine)
  sugar mixed with 5ml/1 tsp
  ground cinnamon, for sprinkling

1 For the dough, sift the flour, baking powder, salt and sugar into a bowl and rub in the fats until the mixture resembles fine breadcrumbs. Mix in enough iced water to form a dough. Shape into a ball, cover and chill for 30 minutes.

2 Place the dried fruit in a pan and add cold water to cover. Bring to the boil, then simmer for 30 minutes, until the fruit is soft enough to purée. Drain and place in a food processor or blender. Process until smooth, then return the purée to the pan.

3 Add the brown sugar and cook for 5 minutes, stirring constantly, until thick. Remove from the heat and stir in the nuts and cinnamon. Leave to cool.

4 Roll out the dough to 3mm/¹/₈in thick. Stamp out rounds with a 10cm/4in cookie cutter. Put a spoonful of fruit in the centre of each round. Brush the edges of the rounds with water, fold in half and crimp the edges with a fork.

5 Heat a 1cm/¹/₂in depth of oil in a frying pan. Fry the pastries, in batches, for 1¹/₂ minutes on each side, until golden. Drain, sprinkle with cinnamon sugar and serve.

Greek Fruit and Nut Pastries Energy 278kcal/1162kJ; Protein 5g; Carbohydrate 30.2g, of which sugars 8.7g; Fat 16.1g, of which saturates 5.7g; Cholesterol 32mg; Calcium 69mg; Fibre 1.5g; Sodium 80mg. **Fruit and Nut Turnovers** Energy 199kcal/840kJ; Protein 3.2g; Carbohydrate 33.6g, of which sugars 22.7g; Fat 6.7g, of which saturates 2.5g; Cholesterol 8mg; Calcium 54mg; Fibre 2.2g; Sodium 27mg.

Baklava

Turkish coffee is black, thick, very sweet and often spiced. Here it is used in this famous pastry confection served throughout the Middle East.

Makes 16
50g/2oz/¹⁄₂ cup blanched
  almonds, chopped
50g/2oz/¹⁄₂ cup pistachio
  nuts, chopped
75g/3oz/scant ¹⁄₂ cup caster
  (superfine) sugar

115g/4oz filo pastry, thawed
  if frozen
75g/3oz/6 tbsp unsalted (sweet)
  butter, melted and cooled

For the syrup
115g/4oz/generous ¹⁄₂ cup
  caster (superfine) sugar
7.5cm/3in piece cinnamon stick
1 whole clove
2 cardamom pods, crushed
75ml/5 tbsp strong freshly
  brewed coffee

1 Preheat the oven to 180°C/350°F/Gas 4. Lightly grease an 18 × 28cm/7 × 11in tin (pan) with melted butter.

2 Mix the nuts and sugar together. Cut the pastry to fit the tin. Place a sheet of pastry in the tin and brush with butter. Repeat with three more sheets and spread with half the nut mixture.

3 Layer up three more sheets of pastry as before, then spread the remaining nut mixture over them. Top with the remaining pastry and butter. Press down the edges to seal. Mark the top into diamonds. Bake for 20–25 minutes, until golden.

4 Put the syrup ingredients in a pan and heat gently until the sugar dissolves. Cover and leave to stand for 20 minutes.

5 Remove from the oven. Re-heat the syrup and strain over the pastry. Leave to cool in the tin. Cut into diamonds, remove from the tin and serve.

Cook's Tip
Keep the filo pastry covered with a damp cloth to stop it drying out and becoming brittle, which makes it difficult to use.

Pan Dulce

These "sweet breads" of various shapes are made throughout Mexico and are eaten as a snack or with jam or marmalade for breakfast.

Makes 12
120ml/4fl oz/¹⁄₂ cup lukewarm
  milk
10ml/2 tsp active dried yeast
450g/1lb/4 cups strong white
  bread flour, plus extra
  for dusting
75g/3oz/scant ¹⁄₂ cup caster
  (superfine) sugar

25g/1oz/2 tbsp butter, softened
4 large (US extra large) eggs,
  beaten

For the topping
75g/3oz/6 tbsp butter, softened
115g/4oz/¹⁄₂ cup sugar
1 egg yolk
5ml/1 tsp ground cinnamon
115g/4oz/1 cup plain
  (all-purpose) flour

1 Pour the milk into a small bowl, stir in the dried yeast and leave in a warm place until frothy.

2 Put the flour and sugar in a mixing bowl, add the yeast mixture, butter and eggs and mix to a soft, sticky dough.

3 Place the dough on a lightly floured surface and dredge it with flour until it is completely covered. Cover it with lightly oiled clear film (plastic wrap) and leave to rest for 20 minutes.

4 Meanwhile, make the topping. Beat the butter and sugar in a bowl, then mix in the egg yolk, cinnamon and flour.

5 Grease two baking sheets. Divide the dough into 12 equal pieces and shape each of them into a round. Space well apart on the baking sheets. Sprinkle the topping over the breads, dividing it more or less equally among them, then press it lightly into the surface.

6 Leave the rolls in a warm place to stand for about 30 minutes, until they are about one and a half times their previous size. Preheat the oven to 200°C/400°F/Gas 6 and bake the breads for about 15 minutes. Leave to cool slightly.

Baklava Energy 161kcal/675kJ; Protein 2.3g; Carbohydrate 21.3g, of which sugars 16.3g; Fat 8g, of which saturates 2.6g; Cholesterol 8mg; Calcium 27mg; Fibre 0.7g; Sodium 70mg.
Pan Dulce Energy 358kcal/1510kJ; Protein 6.5g; Carbohydrate 65.2g, of which sugars 17.6g; Fat 9.6g, of which saturates 5.6g; Cholesterol 39mg; Calcium 110mg; Fibre 1.9g; Sodium 68mg.

Brioches au Chocolat

These lovely buttery and chocolate-filled breads are the ultimate luxury breakfast treat.

Makes 12
250g/9oz/2¼ cups strong white
   bread flour, plus extra
   for dusting
pinch of salt
30ml/2 tbsp caster
   (superfine) sugar
1 sachet easy-blend dried yeast
3 eggs, beaten, plus extra beaten
   egg, for glazing
45ml/3 tbsp hand-hot milk
115g/4oz/½ cup unsalted
   (sweet) butter, diced
175g/6oz plain (semisweet)
   chocolate, broken into squares

1 Sift the flour and salt into a large bowl and stir in the sugar and yeast. Make a well in the centre and add the eggs and milk. Beat the egg and milk mixture well, gradually incorporating the surrounding dry ingredients to make a fairly soft dough.

2 Turn the dough on to a lightly floured surface and knead well for about 5 minutes, until smooth and elastic.

3 Add the butter to the dough, a few pieces at a time, kneading until each addition is absorbed before adding the next. When all the butter has been incorporated and small bubbles appear in the dough, wrap it in clear film (plastic wrap) and chill for at least 1 hour.

4 Lightly grease 12 individual brioche tins (pans) set on a baking sheet. Divide the dough into 12 and shape each into a smooth round. Place a chocolate square in the centre of each round. Bring up the sides of the dough and press the edges firmly together to seal, use a little beaten egg if necessary.

5 Place the brioches, join side down, in the prepared tins. Cover and leave them in a warm place for about 30 minutes, or until doubled in size. Preheat the oven to 200°C/400°F/Gas 6.

6 Brush the brioches with beaten egg. Bake for 12–15 minutes, until well risen and golden brown. Leave to cool slightly on wire racks.

Churros

Churros are long, golden doughnuts which are deep-fried and rolled in sugar while still hot.

Serves 2
200g/7oz/1¾ cups plain
   (all-purpose) flour
150ml/¼ pint/⅔ cup milk
150ml/¼ pint/⅔ cup water
2 eggs, beaten
vegetable oil, for deep-frying
caster (superfine) sugar,
   for dusting

1 Sift the flour on to a sheet of baking parchment.

2 Bring the milk and water to a boil in a pan. Tip in the flour and beat vigorously with a wooden spoon, stirring until the dough forms a ball.

3 Remove the pan from the heat and let the dough cool a little. Gradually beat in the eggs, adding just enough to give a piping consistency. Spoon the mixture into a piping (pastry) bag fitted with a large fluted nozzle.

4 Preheat the oven to 150°C/300°F/Gas 2.

5 To cook the churros, heat the oil in a deep-fat-fryer or heavy frying pan to 190°C/375°F or until a piece of dough sizzles as soon as it hits the oil. Squeeze the piping bag over the deep-fryer or pan, snipping off 10cm/4in lengths with kitchen scissors. Fry the churros, in batches of four to six, for 3–4 minutes, until golden brown.

6 Remove with a slotted spoon and drain on kitchen paper. Dust with caster sugar and keep warm in the oven while you cook the remaining batches.

Cook's Tip
Kids will love these served Spanish-style scooped into a cone of rolled paper – perhaps with a mug of hot chocolate.

Churros Energy 378kcal/1561kJ; Protein 9.1g; Carbohydrate 40.7g, of which sugars 2.6g; Fat 20.6g, of which saturates 3.2g; Cholesterol 10mg; Calcium 130mg; Fibre 1.6g; Sodium 53mg.
Brioches Au Chocolat Energy 236kcal/988kJ; Protein 4.3g; Carbohydrate 27g, of which sugars 11g; Fat 13.1g, of which saturates 7.6g; Cholesterol 69mg; Calcium 48mg; Fibre 1g; Sodium 79mg.

Buñuelos

These lovely little puffs look like miniature doughnuts and taste so good it is hard not to over-indulge. Make them for brunch, or simply serve them with coffee.

Makes 12
225g/8oz/2 cups plain (all-purpose) flour, plus extra for dusting
pinch of salt
5ml/1 tsp baking powder
2.5ml/½ tsp ground aniseed
115g/4oz/½ cup caster (superfine) sugar
1 large (US extra large) egg
120ml/4fl oz/½ cup milk
50g/2oz/¼ cup butter, melted
oil, for deep frying
10ml/2 tsp ground cinnamon
cinnamon sticks, to decorate

1 Sift the flour, salt, baking powder and ground aniseed into a mixing bowl. Add 30ml/2 tbsp of the caster sugar.

2 Place the egg and milk in a small jug (pitcher) and whisk together well. Pour the egg mixture gradually into the flour, stirring constantly, then add the butter. Mix with a wooden spoon and then with your hands to make a soft dough. Turn out the dough on to a lightly floured surface and knead for about 10 minutes, until smooth.

3 Divide the dough into 12 pieces and roll into balls. Slightly flatten each ball with your hand and then make a hole in the centre with the floured handle of a wooden spoon.

4 Heat the oil to 190°C/375°F, or until a cube of dried bread, added to the oil, floats and then turns golden in 30–60 seconds. Fry the buñuelos in small batches until they are puffy and golden brown, turning them once or twice during cooking. As soon as they are golden, lift them out of the oil using a slotted spoon and place on a double layer of kitchen paper to drain.

5 Mix the remaining caster sugar with the ground cinnamon in a small bowl. Add the buñuelos, one at a time, while they are still warm, toss them in the mixture until they are lightly coated and either serve at once or leave to cool. Decorate with cinnamon sticks.

Chocolate Cinnamon Doughnuts

Packed with flavour, these doughnuts really are an extra special treat.

Makes 16
500g/1¼lb/5 cups strong white bread flour, plus extra for dusting
30ml/2 tbsp unsweetened cocoa powder
pinch of salt
1 sachet easy-blend dried yeast
300ml/½ pint/1¼ cups lukewarm milk
40g/1½oz/3 tbsp butter, melted
1 egg, beaten
115g/4oz plain (semisweet) chocolate, broken into 16 pieces
sunflower oil, for deep-frying

For the coating
45ml/3 tbsp caster (superfine) sugar
15ml/1 tbsp unsweetened cocoa powder
5ml/1 tsp ground cinnamon

1 Sift the flour, cocoa and salt into a large bowl. Stir in the yeast. Make a well in the centre and add the milk, melted butter and egg. Stir, gradually incorporating the surrounding dry ingredients, to make a soft and pliable dough.

2 Knead the dough on a lightly floured surface for about 5 minutes, until smooth and elastic. Return to the clean bowl, cover and leave to rise in a warm place for 1 hour.

3 Knead the dough lightly again, then divide into 16 pieces. Shape each into a round, press a piece of plain chocolate into the centre, then fold the dough over to enclose the filling, pressing firmly to make sure the edges are sealed. Re-shape the doughnuts when sealed, if necessary.

4 Heat the oil for frying to 180°C/350°F or until a cube of day-old bread browns in 30–45 seconds. Deep fry the doughnuts in batches. As each doughnut rises and turns golden brown, turn it over carefully to cook the other side. Drain the cooked doughnuts well on kitchen paper.

5 Mix the sugar, cocoa and cinnamon in a shallow bowl. Toss the doughnuts in the mixture to coat them evenly. Pile on a plate and serve warm.

Buñuelos Energy 296kcal/1235kJ; Protein 9.9g; Carbohydrate 22.5g, of which sugars 0.6g; Fat 18.9g, of which saturates 10.5g; Cholesterol 184mg; Calcium 156mg; Fibre 0.9g; Sodium 223mg.
Chocolate Cinnamon Doughnuts Energy 235kcal/989kJ; Protein 5.1g; Carbohydrate 33.2g, of which sugars 9g; Fat 10.1g, of which saturates 2.7g; Cholesterol 14mg; Calcium 76mg; Fibre 1.5g; Sodium 48mg.

Lover's Knots

These attractive cookies are eaten at carnival time in Italy but as they are so charming they're sure to be welcome at any time of year.

Makes 24

150g/5oz/1¼ cups plain (all-purpose) flour, plus extra for dusting
2.5ml/½ tsp baking powder
pinch of salt
30ml/2 tbsp caster (superfine) sugar, plus extra for dusting
1 egg, beaten
about 25ml/1½ tbsp rum
vegetable oil, for deep-frying

1 Sift the flour, baking powder and salt into a bowl, then stir in the sugar. Add the egg. Stir with a fork until it is evenly mixed with the flour, then add the rum gradually and continue mixing until the dough draws together.

2 Knead the dough on a lightly floured surface until it is smooth. Divide the dough into quarters.

3 Roll each piece out to a 15 x 7.5cm/6 x 3in rectangle and trim to make them straight. Cut each rectangle lengthways into six strips, 1cm/½in wide, and tie into a simple knot without stretching the dough.

4 Heat the oil in a frying pan to a temperature of 190°C/375°F or until a cube of day-old bread browns in about 30 seconds. Deep-fry the knots, in batches, for 1–2 minutes, until crisp and golden. Transfer to kitchen paper with a slotted spoon. Serve warm, dusted with sugar.

Variations
• If you don't like the flavour of rum, substitute another sweet spirit or liqueur, such as Amaretto or Kirsch.
• For a chocolate treat, replace 30ml/2 tbsp of the flour with the same quantity of unsweetened cocoa powder and use crème de cacao instead of rum.

Ladies' Navels

This is a classic fried pastry, an invention from the Topkapı Palace kitchens. Garnish it with whole or chopped pistachios and serve with cream.

Serves 4–6
50g/2oz/¼ cup butter
pinch of salt

175g/6oz/1½ cups plain (all-purpose) flour
60g/2oz/⅓ cup semolina
2 eggs
sunflower oil, for deep-frying

For the syrup
450g/1lb/scant 2¼ cups sugar
juice of 1 lemon

1 To make the syrup, put the sugar and 300ml/½ pint/1¼ cups water into a heavy pan and bring to the boil, stirring constantly. When the sugar has dissolved, stir in the lemon juice and lower the heat, then simmer for about 10 minutes, until the syrup has thickened a little. Leave to cool.

2 Put the butter, salt and 250ml/8fl oz/1 cup water in another heavy pan and bring to the boil. Remove from the heat and add the flour and semolina, beating all the time, until the mixture becomes smooth. Leave to cool.

3 Beat the eggs into the cooled mixture so that it gleams. Add 15ml/1 tbsp of the cooled syrup and beat well.

4 Pour enough oil for deep-frying into a deep-sided pan. Heat until just warm, then remove from the heat. Wet your hands and take an apricot-size piece of dough. Roll it into a ball, flatten it, then make an indentation in the middle.

5 Drop the dough into the pan of warmed oil. Repeat with the rest of the mixture to make about 12 navels.

6 Place the pan back over the heat. As the oil heats up, the pastries will swell, retaining the dip in the middle. Swirl the oil until the navels turn golden all over.

7 Remove with a slotted spoon. Toss them in the cooled syrup. Leave to soak for a few minutes, and spoon some syrup over.

Lover's Knots Energy 56kcal/236kJ; Protein 0.9g; Carbohydrate 6.2g, of which sugars 1.4g; Fat 3.1g, of which saturates 0.4g; Cholesterol 8mg; Calcium 11mg; Fibre 0.2g; Sodium 3mg. **Ladies'** Navels Energy 517kcal/2190kJ; Protein 6.3g; Carbohydrate 108.8g, of which sugars 78.9g; Fat 9.3g, of which saturates 4.9g; Cholesterol 81mg; Calcium 93mg; Fibre 1.1g; Sodium 80mg.

French Quarter Beignets

These airy puffs are even lighter than fritters, so they're sure to disappear in no time at all.

Makes about 20

225g/8oz/2 cups plain
   (all-purpose) flour, plus extra
   for dusting
pinch of salt
15ml/1 tbsp baking powder
5ml/1 tsp ground cinnamon
2 eggs
50g/2oz/¼ cup sugar
175ml/6fl oz/¾ cup milk
2.5ml/½ tsp vanilla extract
oil for deep-frying
icing (confectioners') sugar,
   for sprinkling

1 To make the dough, sift the flour, salt, baking powder and ground cinnamon into a medium mixing bowl.

2 In a separate bowl, beat together the eggs, sugar, milk and vanilla. Pour the egg mixture into the dry ingredients and mix together quickly to form a ball.

3 Turn the dough out on to a lightly floured surface and knead until it is smooth and elastic.

4 Heat the oil in a deep-fryer or large, heavy pan to 190°C/375°F.

5 Roll out the dough to 5mm/¼in thick. Slice diagonally into diamonds about 7.5cm/3in long.

6 Fry in the hot oil, turning once, until golden brown on both sides. Remove with tongs or a slotted spoon and drain well on kitchen paper. Sprinkle the beignets with icing sugar before serving warm.

Cook's Tip
For a special treat, heat a few tablespoons of strawberry or raspberry jam or golden (light corn) or maple syrup until runny. Pour into a sauceboat and serve with the warm beignets for a delicious dessert.

Chelsea Buns

Soft, sweet and scrumptious, no wonder these lightly spiced buns are so popular.

Makes 12

225g/8oz/2 cups strong
   white bread flour, plus extra
   for dusting
pinch of salt
40g/1½oz/3 tbsp unsalted
   (sweet) butter
7.5ml/1½ tsp easy-blend
   (rapid-rise) dried yeast
120ml/4fl oz/½ cup milk
1 egg, beaten
75g/3oz/½ cup mixed dried fruit
25g/1oz/2½ tbsp chopped mixed
   (candied) peel
50g/2oz/¼ cup soft light
   brown sugar
clear honey, to glaze

1 Sift the flour and salt into a bowl, then rub in 25g/1oz/2 tbsp of the butter until the mixture resembles breadcrumbs.

2 Stir in the yeast and make a well in the centre. Slowly pour the milk and egg into the well, stirring the ingredients together, then beat until the dough leaves the sides of the bowl clean.

3 Turn out the dough on to a lightly floured surface and knead until smooth and elastic. Place in an oiled bowl, cover with oiled clear film (plastic wrap) and leave at room temperature for about 2 hours, until doubled in volume. Place on a lightly floured surface, then roll out to a rectangle about 30 x 23cm/ 12 x 9in.

4 Mix the dried fruit, peel and sugar. Melt the remaining butter and brush over the dough. Sprinkle over the fruit mixture, leaving a 2.5cm/1in border. Starting at a long side, roll up the dough. Seal the edges, then cut into 12 slices.

5 Lightly grease a 18cm/7in round tin (pan). Put the slices, cut side up, in the prepared tin. Cover with a clean dish towel and leave to rise in a warm place for about 30 minutes, until doubled in size.

6 Preheat the oven to 190°C/375°F/Gas 5. Bake for 30 minutes, until a rich golden brown. Brush the tops with honey and leave to cool slightly in the tin before turning out.

French Quarter Beignets Energy 99kcal/415kJ; Protein 2g; Carbohydrate 11.8g, of which sugars 3.2g; Fat 5.2g, of which saturates 0.8g; Cholesterol 20mg; Calcium 30mg; Fibre 0.4g; Sodium 11mg.
Chelsea Buns Energy 287kcal/1208kJ; Protein 6.1g; Carbohydrate 43.5g, of which sugars 16.6g; Fat 11.1g, of which saturates 2.3g; Cholesterol 26mg; Calcium 85mg; Fibre 1.3g; Sodium 243mg.

Sticky Buns

Sweet, gooey and sheer delight, these lightly spiced buns are irresistible.

Makes 18

170ml/5½fl oz/scant ¾ cup milk
15ml/1 tbsp active dried yeast
30ml/2 tbsp caster (superfine) sugar
425–450g/15oz–1lb/3½–4 cups strong white bread flour, plus extra for dusting
pinch of salt
115g/4oz/½ cup butter, diced
2 eggs, lightly beaten
grated rind of 1 lemon

For the topping and filling

275g/10oz/1¼ cups soft dark brown sugar
65g/2½oz/5 tbsp butter
120ml/4fl oz/½ cup water
75g/3oz/½ cup walnuts, chopped
45ml/3 tbsp caster (superfine) sugar
10ml/2 tsp ground cinnamon
165g/5½oz/generous 1 cup raisins

1 Heat the milk to lukewarm. Add the yeast and sugar, and leave until frothy, about 15 minutes.

2 Put the flour and salt in a bowl. Rub in the butter until the mixture forms breadcrumbs. Make a well in the centre and add the yeast mixture, eggs and lemon rind. Mix to a rough dough.

3 Transfer to a floured surface and knead until smooth and elastic. Cover with a plastic bag and leave to rise in a warm place until doubled in volume, about 2 hours.

4 To make the topping, boil the sugar, butter and water in a pan for 10 minutes, until thick. Put 15ml/1 tbsp of the syrup in each muffin cup. Sprinkle lightly with nuts. Mix the remaining nuts with the sugar, cinnamon and raisins in a bowl.

5 Knock back (punch down) the dough. Roll out to a 45 × 30cm/18 × 12in rectangle. Sprinkle the filling over it and roll up from a long side. Cut into 2.5cm/1in rounds and put into the muffin cups, cut side up. Leave to rise in a warm place for 30 minutes. Preheat the oven to 180°C/350°F/Gas 4.

6 Bake for 25 minutes. Invert on a baking sheet, leave for 3–5 minutes, then remove the tins. Transfer the buns to a wire rack.

Banana and Apricot Chelsea Buns

Old favourites are given a low-fat twist with a delectable fruit filling.

Serves 9

225g/8oz/2 cups strong white bread flour, plus extra for dusting
10ml/2 tsp ground allspice
pinch of salt
2.5ml/½ tsp easy-blend (rapid-rise) dried yeast
25g/1oz/2 tbsp butter
75g/3oz /scant ½ cup caster (superfine) sugar
90ml/6 tbsp skimmed (low-fat) milk
1 egg

For the filling

1 large ripe banana
175g/6oz/¾ cup chopped ready-to-eat dried apricots
30ml/2 tbsp light brown sugar

1 Sift the four, allspice and salt into a bowl and stir in the yeast. Rub in the butter, then stir in 50g/2oz/¼ cup of the sugar. Make a well in the centre. Lightly beat the milk and egg, pour into the well and gradually mix in the flour.

2 Turn the dough on to a floured surface. Knead for 5 minutes, until smooth and elastic. Return to the clean bowl, cover and leave in a warm place to rise for 2 hours.

3 Turn out and knead the dough on a floured surface for 2 minutes. Roll out to a 30 × 23cm/12 × 9in rectangle.

4 Mash the banana in a bowl, stir in the apricots and sugar and spread the filling over the dough. Roll up lengthways like a Swiss (jelly) roll, with the join underneath. Cut the roll into nine slices. Grease an 18cm/7in square cake tin (pan). Put the slices in the tin, cut side down, cover and leave to rise in a warm place for 30 minutes.

5 Preheat the oven to 200°C/400°F/Gas 6. Bake the buns for 20–25 minutes, until golden.

6 Meanwhile, mix the remaining caster sugar with 30ml/2 tbsp water in a pan. Bring to the boil, stirring constantly, then boil for 2 minutes. Brush the glaze over the buns, then transfer to a wire rack to cool.

Sticky Buns Energy 438kcal/1844kJ; Protein 6.1g; Carbohydrate 66.3g, of which sugars 37.6g; Fat 18.4g, of which saturates 8.6g; Cholesterol 64mg; Calcium 100mg; Fibre 1.7g; Sodium 119mg.
Banana and Apricot Chelsea Buns Energy 193kcal/816kJ; Protein 4.3g; Carbohydrate 38.3g, of which sugars 19.1g; Fat 3.5g, of which saturates 0.3g; Cholesterol 22mg; Calcium 70mg; Fibre 2.1g; Sodium 147mg.

Cheese and Pineapple Wholemeal Scones

These cheese and pineapple scones are delicious eaten freshly baked, warm or cold, with a little butter and jam.

Makes 14–16
225g/8oz/2 cups self-raising (self-rising) wholemeal (whole-wheat) flour, sifted, plus extra for dusting
5ml/1 tsp baking powder, sifted
pinch of salt
40g/1½oz/3 tbsp butter
5ml/1 tsp mustard powder
75g/3oz/¾ cup mature (sharp) Cheddar cheese, finely grated
50g/2oz/¼ cup ready-to-eat dried pineapple, finely chopped
150ml/¼ pint/⅔ cup skimmed (low fat) milk

1 Preheat the oven to 220°C/425°F/Gas 7. Line a baking sheet with baking parchment.

2 Sift the flour, baking powder and salt into a bowl.

3 Rub in the fat until the mixture resembles breadcrumbs.

4 Fold in the mustard powder, cheese, pineapple and enough milk to make a fairly soft dough.

5 Turn the dough on to a lightly floured surface and knead lightly. Lightly roll out to 2cm/¾in thickness.

6 Using a 5cm/2in cookie cutter, stamp out rounds and place them on the prepared baking sheet.

7 Brush the tops with milk and bake for about 10 minutes, until well risen and golden brown. Transfer to a wire rack to cool and serve warm or cold.

Variation
Other mature (sharp) cheese, such as Emmenthal, Mahon, Appenzeller or Gouda, would also taste good in these scones.

Wholemeal Parmesan Scones

These are very good warm with a little butter and are ideal for children's lunches and picnics. Fill them with ham, cheese, chicken or salad.

Makes 15
450g/1lb/4 cups wholemeal (whole-wheat) flour, plus extra for dusting
pinch of salt
10ml/2 tsp baking powder
115g/4oz Parmesan cheese, finely grated
50g/2oz/¼ cup butter
150–300ml/¼–½ pint/⅔–1¼ cups buttermilk

1 Preheat the oven to 200°C/400°F/Gas 6.

2 Mix the flour, salt, baking powder and Parmesan cheese in a bowl and rub in the butter with your fingertips until the mixture resembles breadcrumbs. Working quickly and lightly, stir in enough of the buttermilk to make a moist dough using a knife at first and then gathering up the dough with your fingertips.

3 Pat out the dough on a lightly floured board to a thickness of about 4cm/1½in.

4 Using a 7cm/2¾in cutter, stamp out 15 rounds. Place the rounds on a floured baking sheet and bake for about 10 minutes. The exact cooking time will depend on the depth of the scones. They should be well risen and lightly browned. Serve warm, cut in half, spread with butter.

Cook's Tips
• These scones will keep well in an airtight container for up to 3 days. Before serving, reheat them for 4–5 minutes in a preheated oven at 200°C/400°F/Gas 6.
• Baked scones can also be frozen for up to 3 months. Thaw thoroughly at room temperature and reheat before serving, as described above.

Cheese and Pineapple Wholemeal Scones Energy 99Kcals/418KJ; Protein 4.22g; Fat 3.62g; Saturated Fat 1.05g; Carbohydrate 13.28g; Fibre 1.74g; Added Sugar 1.33g; Sodium 0.06g.
Wholemeal Parmesan Scones Energy 160kcals/674kJ; Fat, total 5.95g; saturated fat 2.25g; polyunsaturated fat 1.55g; monounsaturated fat 1.7g; Carbohydrate 20.4g; sugar, total 1.65g; starch 18.8g; Fibre 2.7g; Sodium 196.6mg.

Cornmeal Scones

These are delicious served hot, straight from the oven, and spread with butter. They are great for breakfast and also go well with soup for a light lunch.

Makes 12
50g/2oz/¹/₂ cup cornmeal, plus extra for sprinkling
175g/6oz/1¹/₄ cups plain (all-purpose) flour, plus extra for dusting
12.5ml/2¹/₂ tsp baking powder
pinch of salt
175g/6oz/³/₄ cup butter, diced
175ml/6fl oz/³/₄ cup milk

1 Preheat the oven to 230°C/450°F/Gas 8. Sprinkle a large baking sheet lightly with a little cornmeal.

2 Sift together the flour, baking powder and salt into a bowl. Stir in the cornmeal. Add the butter and rub into the dry ingredients with your fingertips until the mixture resembles coarse breadcrumbs.

3 Make a well in the centre and pour in the milk. Stir in quickly with a wooden spoon until the dough begins to pull away from the sides of the bowl.

4 Turn the dough out on to a lightly floured surface and knead lightly 8–10 times only. Roll it out to a thickness of 1cm/¹/₂in. Stamp out into rounds with a floured 5cm/2in cookie cutter.

5 Arrange the dough rounds on the prepared baking sheet, spacing them about 2.5cm/1in apart. Sprinkle with a little cornmeal, then bake for about 10–12 minutes, until golden brown.

Cook's Tip
Cornmeal usually has a beautiful golden colour that makes the scones look particularly appetizing. Blue cornmeal, once used exclusively by Native Americans, is blue-black in colour and could also be used with striking results.

Cheese Scones

These delicious scones make a good teatime treat. They are best served fresh and still slightly warm.

Makes 12
225g/8oz/2 cups plain (all-purpose) flour, plus extra for dusting
12.5ml/2¹/₂ tsp baking powder
2.5ml/¹/₂ tsp dry mustard powder
pinch of salt
50g/2oz/4 tbsp butter, chilled and diced
75g/3oz/³/₄ cup Cheddar cheese, grated
150ml/¹/₄ pint/²/₃ cup milk
1 egg, beaten

1 Preheat the oven to 230°C/450°F/Gas 8.

2 Sift the flour, baking powder, mustard powder and salt into a mixing bowl. Add the butter and rub into the flour mixture until the mixture resembles breadcrumbs.

3 Stir 50g/2oz/¹/₂ cup of the cheese into the butter and flour mixture.

4 Make a well in the centre and gently stir in the milk and egg with a wooden spoon until a soft dough forms. Turn the dough on to a lightly floured surface.

5 Roll out the dough and cut it into triangles or squares with a sharp knife. Put the scones on to one or two baking sheets, brush lightly with milk and sprinkle evenly with the remaining grated cheese. Leave to rest for 15 minutes, then bake for 15 minutes, until well risen and golden.

Cook's Tip
While ready-grated cheese is convenient, it does dry out quickly once the packet has been opened and it is rarely a top-quality variety. For maximum flavour, it is always better to grate cheese freshly just before you are going to use it and there's likely to be less waste, too.

Cornmeal Scones Energy 180kcal/750kJ; Protein 2.3g; Carbohydrate 15.2g, of which sugars 1g; Fat 12.6g, of which saturates 7.8g; Cholesterol 32mg; Calcium 41mg; Fibre 0.5g; Sodium 95mg.
Cheese Scones Energy 133kcal/557kJ; Protein 4.3g; Carbohydrate 15.2g, of which sugars 0.9g; Fat 6.4g, of which saturates 3.8g; Cholesterol 32mg; Calcium 91mg; Fibre 0.6g; Sodium 82mg.

Feta Cheese and Chive Scones

Salty feta cheese makes an excellent substitute for butter in these tangy savoury scones. They not only go well with hot soup, but also make a delicious snack at any time of day.

Makes 9
115g/4oz/1 cup self-raising (self-rising) flour, plus extra for dusting

150g/5oz/1¼ cup self-raising wholemeal (self-rising whole-wheat) flour
pinch of salt
75g/3oz feta cheese
15ml/1 tbsp chopped fresh chives
150ml/¼ pint/⅔ cup skimmed (low fat) milk, plus extra for glazing
1.5ml/¼ tsp cayenne pepper

1 Preheat the oven to 200°C/400°F/Gas 6.

2 Sift together both the flours and the salt into a large bowl, adding any bran left over from the flour in the sieve (strainer).

3 Coarsely crumble the feta cheese into the bowl and rub it into the dry ingredients with your fingertips until the mixture resembles breadcrumbs. Stir in the chives, then add the milk and mix lightly with a wooden spoon or your hands to form a soft, but not sticky dough.

4 Turn out the dough on to a floured surface and knead lightly until smooth. Roll out to 2cm/¾in thick and stamp out nine scones with a floured 6cm/2½in cookie cutter.

5 Transfer to a non-stick baking sheet. Lightly brush the tops with skimmed milk, then sprinkle over the cayenne pepper. Bake for 15 minutes, until golden brown. Serve warm or cold.

> **Cook's Tip**
> Try to obtain genuine sheep's milk feta, as it has the best flavour. Much modern feta is made from cow's milk, but some Greek and, surprisingly, Bulgarian feta is still made in the traditional manner.

Cheddar and Chive Scones

These soft scones are delicious warm, split and spread with butter; serve with soup or to accompany a savoury meal.

Makes 20
200g/7oz/1¾ cups plain (all-purpose) flour
10ml/2 tsp baking powder
2.5ml/½ tsp bicarbonate of soda (baking soda)
pinch of salt

1.5ml/¼ tsp black pepper
65g/2½oz/5 tbsp unsalted (sweet) butter, chopped
50g/2oz/½ cup grated mature (sharp) Cheddar cheese
30ml/2 tbsp chopped fresh chives
175ml/6fl oz/¾ cup buttermilk

1 Preheat the oven to 200°C/400°F/Gas 6. Lightly grease two baking sheets.

2 Sift the flour, baking powder, bicarbonate of soda, salt and pepper into a large bowl. Add the butter and rub it into the dry ingredients with your fingertips until the mixture resembles coarse breadcrumbs. Add the grated cheese and chives and stir well to mix.

3 Make a well in the centre of the mixture. Add the buttermilk and stir vigorously until the batter comes away from the sides of the bowl.

4 Drop 30ml/2 tbsp mounds spaced 5–7.5cm/2–3in apart on the prepared baking sheets. Bake for 12–15 minutes, until golden brown.

> **Variations**
> • For Cheddar and Bacon Scones, substitute 45ml/3 tbsp crumbled cooked bacon for the chives.
> • For Cheese and Ham Scones, substitute grated Parmesan or Pecorino for the Cheddar cheese and 50g/2oz/⅓ cup chopped prosciutto for the chives.

Feta Cheese and Chive Scones Energy 121kcal/514kJ; Protein 5.2g; Carbohydrate 21.4g, of which sugars 1.4g; Fat 2.3g, of which saturates 1.2g; Cholesterol 6mg; Calcium 75mg; Fibre 1.9g; Sodium 128mg.
Cheddar and Chive Scones Energy 124kcal/524kJ; Protein 5.2g; Carbohydrate 21.5g, of which sugars 1.5g; Fat 2.5g, of which saturates 1.4g; Cholesterol 7mg; Calcium 74mg; Fibre 1.9g; Sodium 128mg.

Cheese and Mustard Scones

Depending on their size, these cheese scones can be served as little canapé bases, teatime treats or even as a quick pie topping or cobbler.

Makes 12

250g/9oz/2¼ cups self-raising (self-rising) flour, plus extra for dusting
5ml/1 tsp baking powder
pinch of salt
40g/1½oz/3 tbsp butter

175g/6oz/1½ cups grated mature (sharp) Cheddar cheese, plus extra for sprinkling
10ml/2 tsp wholegrain mustard
about 150ml/¼ pint/⅔ cup milk, buttermilk or natural (plain) yogurt
1 egg yolk beaten with 5ml/1 tsp water, to glaze (optional)
ground black pepper
garlic-flavoured cream cheese, chopped fresh chives and sliced radishes, to serve (optional)

1 Preheat the oven to 220°C/425°F/Gas 7.

2 Sift the flour, baking powder and salt into a bowl, then rub in the butter until the mixture resembles fine breadcrumbs. Season with pepper and stir in the cheese.

3 Mix the mustard with the milk, buttermilk or yogurt. Add to the dry ingredients and mix quickly until the mixture just comes together. Do not over-mix or the scones will be tough.

4 Knead the dough lightly on a lightly floured surface, then pat it out with your hands to a depth of 2cm/¾in. Cut into squares, or use a 5cm/2in cutter to stamp out rounds, re-rolling the dough as necessary.

5 Place the squares or rounds on a non-stick baking sheet. Brush with the egg glaze, if using, and sprinkle with extra grated cheese.

6 Bake for about 10 minutes, until risen and golden. You can test scones by pressing the sides, which should spring back. Transfer to a wire rack to cool.

7 Serve spread with garlic-flavoured cream cheese. Top with chopped chives and sliced radishes, if using.

Cheese and Marjoram Scones

Amaze unexpected guests with your culinary skills and these mouthwatering made-in-minutes savoury treats.

Makes 18

115g/4oz/1 cup wholemeal (whole-wheat) flour
115g/4oz/1 cup self-raising (self-rising) flour, plus extra for dusting

pinch of salt
40g/1½oz/3 tbsp butter, diced
1.5ml/¼ tsp dry mustard
10ml/2 tsp dried marjoram
50–75g/2–3oz/½–⅔ cup Cheddar cheese, finely grated
about 125ml/4fl oz/½ cup milk
50g/2oz/¼ cup pecans or walnuts, chopped

1 Sift the two types of flour into a bowl and add the salt. Rub the butter into the flour with your fingertips until the mixture resembles fine breadcrumbs.

2 Add the mustard, marjoram and grated cheese, then mix in sufficient milk to make a soft, but dry dough. Knead the dough lightly.

3 Roll out the dough on a floured surface to 2cm/¾in thick and cut out about 18 scones using a 5cm/2in square cutter. Push the offcuts together and roll out and cut out more scones.

4 Brush the scones with a little milk and sprinkle the chopped pecans or walnuts over the top. Place the scones on a piece of baking parchment in the microwave, spacing them well apart. Microwave on HIGH (100 per cent) power for 3–3½ minutes, repositioning the scones twice during cooking.

5 Brown under a preheated hot grill (broiler) until golden, if you like. Serve warm, split and buttered.

> **Variation**
> For Herb and Mustard Scones, use 30ml/2 tbsp chopped fresh parsley or chives instead of the dried marjoram and 5ml/1 tsp Dijon mustard instead of the dry mustard.

Cheese and Marjoram Scones Energy 121kcal/504kJ; Protein 3g; Carbohydrate 9.8g, of which sugars 0.9g; Fat 8g, of which saturates 2.4g; Cholesterol 8mg; Calcium 44mg; Fibre 1.1g; Sodium 39mg.
Cheese and Mustard Scones Energy 169kcal/706kJ; Protein 6.4g; Carbohydrate 16.8g, of which sugars 1g; Fat 8.5g, of which saturates 5.2g; Cholesterol 39mg; Calcium 156mg; Fibre 0.7g; Sodium 146mg.

Cheese and Potato Scones

The unusual addition of creamy mashed potato gives these wholemeal scones a light moist texture and a crisp crust. A sprinkling of cheese and sesame seeds adds the finishing touch.

Makes 9
115g/4oz/1 cup wholemeal (whole-wheat) flour, plus extra for dusting
pinch of salt
20ml/4 tsp baking powder
40g/1½oz/3 tbsp unsalted (sweet) butter
2 eggs, beaten
50ml/2fl oz/¼ cup semi-skimmed (low-fat) milk or buttermilk
115g/4oz/1⅓ cups cooked, mashed potato
45ml/3 tbsp chopped fresh sage
50g/2oz/½ cup grated mature (sharp) Cheddar cheese
sesame seeds, for sprinkling

1 Preheat the oven to 220°C/425°F/Gas 7. Lightly grease a baking sheet.

2 Sift the flour, salt and baking powder into a bowl. Rub in the butter using your fingers until the mixture resembles fine breadcrumbs, then mix in half the beaten eggs and all the milk or buttermilk. Add the mashed potato, sage and half the Cheddar and mix to a soft dough with your hands.

3 Turn out the dough on to a floured surface and knead lightly until smooth. Roll out the dough to 2cm/¾in thick, then stamp out nine scones using a 6cm/2½in fluted cutter.

4 Place the scones on the prepared baking sheet and brush the tops with the remaining beaten egg. Sprinkle the rest of the cheese and the sesame seeds on top and bake for 15 minutes, until golden. Transfer to a wire rack and leave to cool.

> **Variations**
> • Use unbleached self-raising (self-rising) flour instead of wholemeal (whole-wheat) flour and baking powder, if you wish.
> • Fresh rosemary, basil or thyme can be used in place of the sage.

Caramelized Onion and Walnut Scones

These scones are very good buttered and served with cheese. Make small ones as a base for cocktail canapés, topped with a little soft goat's cheese.

Makes 10–12
90g/3½oz/7 tbsp butter
15ml/1 tbsp olive oil
1 Spanish (Bermuda) onion, chopped
5ml/1 tsp cumin seeds, lightly crushed
200g/7oz/1¾ cups self-raising (self-rising) flour
5ml/1 tsp baking powder
25g/1oz/¼ cup fine oatmeal
5ml/1 tsp light muscovado (molasses) sugar
90g/3½oz/scant 1 cup chopped walnuts
5ml/1 tsp chopped fresh thyme
120–150ml/4–5fl oz/½–⅔ cup buttermilk
a little milk
salt and ground black pepper

1 Melt 15g/½oz/1 tbsp of the butter with the oil in a small pan and cook the onion gently, covered, for 10–12 minutes. Uncover, then continue to cook gently until it begins to brown.

2 Add half the cumin seeds and increase the heat slightly. Continue to cook, stirring occasionally, until the onion begins to caramelize. Cool. Preheat the oven to 200°C/400°F/Gas 6.

3 Sift the flour and baking powder into a bowl and add the oatmeal, sugar, salt and black pepper. Add the remaining butter and rub in until the mixture resembles fine breadcrumbs.

4 Add the cooled onion and cumin mixture, chopped walnuts and chopped fresh thyme, then bind to make a soft, but not sticky, dough with the buttermilk.

5 Roll out the dough to a thickness of 1cm/½in. Stamp out 10–12 scones using a 5–6cm/2–2½n cookie cutter. Place the scones on a floured baking tray, glaze with the milk and sprinkle with a little salt and the remaining cumin seeds. Bake the scones for 12–15 minutes, until well-risen and golden brown. Allow to cool for a few minutes on a wire rack.

Cheese and Potato Scones Energy 124kcal/517kJ; Protein 4.9g; Carbohydrate 10.5g, of which sugars 0.7g; Fat 7.1g, of which saturates 4g; Cholesterol 57mg; Calcium 60mg; Fibre 1.3g; Sodium 87mg.
Caramelized Onion and Walnut Scones Energy 131kcal/543kJ; Protein 1.8g; Carbohydrate 3g, of which sugars 1.3g; Fat 12.6g, of which saturates 4.6g; Cholesterol 17mg; Calcium 23mg; Fibre 0.5g; Sodium 51mg.

Herb and Sesame Seed Triangles

Stuffed with cooked chicken and salad, these make a good lunchtime snack, and are also an ideal accompaniment to a bowl of steaming soup.

Makes 8

225g/8oz/2 cups wholemeal (whole-wheat) flour
115g/4oz/1 cup plain (all-purpose) flour, plus extra for dusting
pinch of salt
2.5ml/½ tsp bicarbonate of soda (baking soda)
5ml/1 tsp cream of tartar
2.5ml/½ tsp chilli powder
50g/2oz/½ cup butter, chilled and diced
60ml/4 tbsp chopped mixed fresh herbs
250ml/8fl oz/1 cup skimmed (low fat) milk
15ml/1 tbsp sesame seeds

1 Preheat the oven to 220°C/425°F/Gas 7. Lightly dust a baking sheet with flour.

2 Put the wholemeal and plain flours in a mixing bowl. Sift in the salt, bicarbonate of soda, cream of tartar and chilli powder, then rub in the butter.

3 Add the herbs and milk and mix to a soft dough. Turn on to a lightly floured surface. Knead only very briefly or the dough will become tough.

4 Roll the dough out to a 23cm/9in round and place on the prepared baking sheet. Brush lightly with water and sprinkle the top evenly with the sesame seeds.

5 Carefully cut the dough round into eight wedges, separate them slightly and bake for 15–20 minutes. Transfer to a wire rack to cool. Serve warm or cold.

> **Variation**
> To make Sun-dried Tomato Triangles, replace the fresh mixed herbs with 30ml/2 tbsp drained chopped sun-dried tomatoes in oil and add 15ml/1 tbsp each mild paprika, chopped fresh parsley and chopped fresh marjoram.

Chive and Potato Drop Scones

These little scones should be fairly thin, soft, and crisp on the outside. Serve them for breakfast.

Makes 20

450g/1lb potatoes
115g/4oz/1 cup plain (all-purpose) flour
30ml/2 tbsp olive oil, plus extra for brushing
30ml/2 tbsp chives, chopped
pinch of salt
ground black pepper

1 Cook the potatoes in a pan of salted boiling water for 20 minutes, until tender, then drain thoroughly. Return the potatoes to the clean pan and mash them well with a potato masher. Alternatively, pass them through a potato ricer.

2 Preheat a griddle or heavy frying pan.

3 Add the flour, olive oil, chives and a little salt and pepper to the mashed potato. Mix to a soft dough.

4 Roll out the dough on a well-floured surface to a thickness of 5mm/¼in and stamp out rounds with a floured 5cm/2in plain cookie cutter. Lightly grease the griddle or frying pan with a little olive oil.

5 Reduce the heat to low, add the scones to the pan, in batches, and cook for about 5 minutes on each side, until golden brown and crisp on the outside. Keep the cooked scones warm while you cook the remaining batches. Serve immediately.

> **Cook's Tips**
> • Cook the scones over a constant low heat and do not try to hurry them or the outsides will burn before the insides are properly cooked through.
> • The easiest way to keep the cooked scones warm is to tuck them into a folded dish towel.

Herb and Sesame Seed Triangles Energy 204kcal/860kJ; Protein 6.4g; Carbohydrate 30.6g, of which sugars 2.2g; Fat 7.1g, of which saturates 3.6g; Cholesterol 14mg; Calcium 84mg; Fibre 3.2g; Sodium 54mg. **Chive and Potato Drop Scones** Energy 45kcal/191kJ; Protein 0.9g; Carbohydrate 8.1g, of which sugars 0.4g; Fat 1.2g, of which saturates 0.2g; Cholesterol 0mg; Calcium 9mg; Fibre 0.4g; Sodium 3mg.

Ham and Potato Scones

These make an ideal accompaniment to soup. Choose a strongly flavoured ham and chop it fairly finely, so that a little goes quite a long way.

Makes 12
225g/8oz/2 cups self-raising
  (self-rising) flour, plus extra
  for dusting
5ml/1 tsp dry mustard
5ml/1 tsp paprika, plus extra
  for sprinkling
pinch of salt
25g/1oz/2 tbsp butter
15ml/1 tbsp chopped fresh basil
50g/2oz/1/2 cup drained sun-dried
  tomatoes in oil, chopped
50g/2oz/1/3 cup ham, chopped
90–120ml/3–4fl oz/1/2–2/3 cup
  skimmed (low-fat) milk, plus
  extra for brushing

1 Preheat the oven to 200°C/400°F/Gas 6. Lightly dust a large baking sheet with flour.

2 Sift the flour, mustard, paprika and salt into a bowl. Add the butter and rub it in with your fingertips until the mixture resembles breadcrumbs.

3 Stir in the basil, sun-dried tomatoes and ham and mix lightly. Pour in enough milk to mix to a soft dough.

4 Turn the dough out on to a lightly floured surface, knead lightly and roll out to a 20 × 15cm/8 × 6in rectangle. Cut into 5cm/2in squares and arrange on the baking sheet.

5 Brush the tops lightly with milk, sprinkle with a little paprika and bake for 12–15 minutes, until golden. Transfer to a wire rack to cool slightly. Serve warm.

> **Cook's Tip**
> If you want to use sun-dried tomatoes from a packet, rehydrate them first by soaking in hot water until softened. Drain and pat dry before chopping.

Rosemary Scones

Serve these aromatic scones with a starter or main meal instead of rolls or bread. They're great with lamb dishes.

Makes 12
225g/8oz/2 cups self-raising
  (self-rising) flour
pinch of salt
5ml/1 tsp baking powder
10ml/2 tsp chopped fresh
  rosemary
50g/2oz/1/4 cup butter
150ml/1/4 pint/2/3 cup milk
1 egg, beaten

1 Preheat the oven to 230°C/450°F/Gas 8. Lightly grease a baking sheet.

2 Sift together the flour, salt and baking powder into a bowl and stir in the rosemary. Add the butter and rub it in with your fingertips until the mixture resembles breadcrumbs.

3 Add the milk and mix lightly with a wooden spoon or your hands to form a soft, but not sticky dough.

4 Turn out the dough on to a lightly floured surface and knead very gently. Roll out to about 2cm/3/4in thick. Stamp out 12 scones with a 5cm/2in plain round cookie cutter. Lightly brush the tops with beaten egg and place them on the prepared baking sheet.

5 Bake for 8–10 minutes, until risen and golden brown. Transfer the scones to a wire rack to cool slightly, then serve warm.

> **Variations**
> • When serving these scones with soup, sprinkle the tops with a little grated cheese before baking.
> • For scones to serve with fish dishes, substitute 15ml/1 tbsp chopped fresh dill for the rosemary.
> • For serving with chicken or vegetarian dishes, substitute 15ml/1 tbsp chopped fresh basil.

Sweet Potato Scones

These are scones with a difference. A sweet potato gives them a pale orange colour and they are meltingly soft in the centre, just waiting for a knob of butter.

Makes about 24

150g/5oz/1¼ cups plain
  (all-purpose) flour, plus extra
  for dusting
20ml/4 tsp baking powder
pinch of salt
15g/½oz/1 tbsp soft light
  brown sugar
150g/5oz mashed sweet potatoes
150ml/¼ pint/⅔ cup milk
50g/2oz/4 tbsp butter, melted

1 Preheat the oven to 230°C/450°F/Gas 8. Lightly grease a baking sheet.

2 Sift together the flour, baking powder and salt into a bowl. Mix in the sugar.

3 In a separate bowl, mix the mashed sweet potatoes with the milk and melted butter. Beat well to blend.

4 Add the flour to the sweet potato mixture and stir to make a dough. Turn out on to a lightly floured surface and knead until soft and pliable.

5 Roll or pat out the dough to a 1cm/½in thickness. Cut into rounds using a 4cm/1½in cutter. Push the offcuts together and roll and cut out more scones.

6 Arrange the rounds on the baking sheet. Bake for about 15 minutes until risen and lightly golden. Serve warm.

> **Cook's Tip**
> *To cook the sweet potatoes, wash them but do not peel. Cook in unsalted boiling water for about 30 minutes, until tender. Drain and leave to cool slightly, then peel off the skins and mash the flesh with a potato masher.*

Three Herb Potato Scones

These flavoursome scones are perfect served warm and split in two with hand-carved ham and Parmesan shavings as a filling.

Makes 12

225g/8oz/2 cups self-raising
  (self-rising) flour, plus extra
  for dusting
5ml/1 tsp baking powder

pinch of salt
50g/2oz/4 tbsp butter, diced
25g/1oz potato flakes
15ml/1 tbsp fresh parsley,
  chopped
15ml/1 tbsp fresh basil, chopped
15ml/1 tbsp fresh oregano,
  chopped
150ml/¼ pint/⅔ cup milk

1 Preheat the oven to 180°C/350°F/Gas 4. Lightly grease a baking sheet.

2 Sift the flour into a bowl with the baking powder. Add a pinch of salt. Rub in the butter with your fingertips until the mixture resembles fine breadcrumbs.

3 Place the potato flakes in a separate bowl and pour over 200ml/7fl oz/scant 1 cup boiling water. Beat well and cool slightly.

4 Stir the potatoes into the dry ingredients with the parsley, basil, oregano and milk.

5 Bring the mixture together to form a soft dough. Turn out on to a floured surface and knead the dough very gently for a few minutes, until soft and pliable.

6 Roll the dough out on a floured surface to about 4cm/1½in thick and stamp out rounds using a 7.5cm/3in cookie cutter. Reshape any remaining dough and re-roll for more scones. Place the scones on to the prepared baking sheet and brush the surfaces with a little more milk.

7 Bake for 15–20 minutes, until golden brown. Transfer to a wire rack to cool slightly and serve warm. They can be eaten plain, or with a filling.

Sweet Potato Scones Energy 48kcal/200kJ; Protein 0.9g; Carbohydrate 7.1g, of which sugars 1.4g; Fat 1.9g, of which saturates 1.2g; Cholesterol 5mg; Calcium 18mg; Fibre 0.3g; Sodium 18mg.
Three Herb Potato Scones Energy 46kcal/193kJ; Protein 1g; Carbohydrate 8.1g, of which sugars 0.4g; Fat 1.3g, of which saturates 0.2g; Cholesterol 0mg; Calcium 12mg; Fibre 0.5g; Sodium 3mg.

Bacon and Cornmeal Muffins

Serve these tasty muffins fresh from the oven for an extra special breakfast. They would also be ideal as part of a weekend brunch menu, served with scrambled eggs or an omelette.

Makes 14

8 bacon rashers (strips)
50g/2oz/¼ cup butter
50g/2oz/¼ cup margarine
115g/4oz/1 cup plain
   (all-purpose) flour
15ml/1 tbsp baking powder
5ml/1 tsp caster (superfine) sugar
pinch of salt
175g/6oz/1½ cups cornmeal
250ml/8fl oz/1 cup milk
2 eggs

1 Preheat the oven to 200°C/400°F/Gas 6. Lightly grease 14 cups of two muffin tins (pans), or line with paper cases.

2 Remove and discard the bacon rinds, if necessary. Heat a heavy frying pan, add the bacon and cook over a medium heat, turning occasionally, until crisp. Remove with tongs and drain well on kitchen paper. When cool enough to handle, chop into small pieces and set aside.

3 Melt the butter and margarine in a pan over a low heat, then remove from the heat and set aside.

4 Sift together the flour, baking powder, caster sugar and salt into a large mixing bowl. Stir in the cornmeal, then make a well in the centre.

5 Pour the milk into a small pan and heat gently until just lukewarm, then remove from the heat. Lightly whisk the eggs in a small bowl, then add the lukewarm milk. Stir in the melted butter and margarine.

6 Pour the milk and egg mixture into the centre of the well and stir in the dry ingredients until smooth and well blended.

7 Fold in the bacon. Spoon the batter into the prepared tin, filling the cups halfway. Bake for about 20 minutes, until risen and golden.

Chilli Cheese Muffins

Prepare for a whole new taste sensation with these fabulous spicy muffins – they're hot stuff.

Makes 12

115g/4oz/1 cup self-raising
   (self-rising) flour
1 tbsp baking powder
pinch of salt
225g/8oz/2 cups fine cornmeal
150g/5oz/1¼ cups grated
   mature (sharp) Cheddar cheese
50g/2oz/4 tbsp butter, melted
2 large (US extra large)
   eggs, beaten
1 tsp chilli purée (paste)
1 garlic clove, crushed
300ml/½ pint/1¼ cups milk

1 Preheat the oven to 200°C/400°F/Gas 6. Thoroughly grease 12 deep muffin tins (pans) or line the tins with paper cases.

2 Sift the flour, baking powder and salt together into a bowl, then stir in the cornmeal and 115g/4oz/1 cup of the grated cheese until well mixed.

3 Pour the melted butter into a bowl and stir in the eggs, chilli purée, crushed garlic and milk.

4 Pour on to the dry ingredients and mix quickly and lightly until just combined.

5 Spoon the batter into the prepared muffin tins, sprinkle the remaining grated cheese evenly on top and bake for about 20 minutes, until risen and golden brown. Leave to cool for a few minutes in the tin before transferring the muffins to a wire rack to cool completely.

> **Cook's Tip**
> Chilli purée (paste) is available in both jars and tubes from most supermarkets. If you are unable to find it, you can substitute a generous pinch of hot chilli powder, 2.5ml/½ tsp chilli flakes or even a seeded and chopped fresh red or green chilli. Stir any of them into the mixture with the grated cheese in step 2.

Bacon and Cornmeal Muffins Energy 176kcal/735kJ; Protein 5.2g; Carbohydrate 16.7g, of which sugars 1.3g; Fat 10g, of which saturates 3.2g; Cholesterol 43mg; Calcium 39mg; Fibre 0.5g; Sodium 203mg.
Chilli Cheese Muffins Energy 208kcal/871kJ; Protein 7.8g; Carbohydrate 22.3g, of which sugars 1.5g; Fat 9.6g, of which saturates 5.4g; Cholesterol 54mg; Calcium 162mg; Fibre 0.7g; Sodium 176mg.

Corn Muffins with Ham

These delicious little muffins are simple to make. If you like, serve them unfilled with a pot of herb butter.

Makes 24

50g/2oz/scant ¹/₂ cup
   yellow cornmeal
65g/2¹/₂ oz/9 tbsp plain
   (all-purpose) flour
30ml/2 tbsp sugar
7.5ml/1¹/₂ tsp baking powder
pinch of salt
50g/2oz/4 tbsp butter, melted
120ml/4fl oz/¹/₂ cup
   whipping cream
1 egg, beaten
1–2 jalapeño or other medium-hot
   chillies, seeded and finely
   chopped (optional)
pinch of cayenne pepper
butter, for spreading
grainy mustard or mustard with
   honey, for spreading
50g/2oz oak-smoked ham

1 Preheat the oven to 200°C/400°F/Gas 6. Lightly grease a muffin tin (pan) with 24 4cm/1¹/₂in cups.

2 In a large bowl, combine the cornmeal, flour, sugar, baking powder and salt. In another bowl, whisk together the melted butter, cream, beaten egg, chopped chillies, if using, and the cayenne pepper.

3 Make a well in the cornmeal mixture, pour in the egg mixture and gently stir in just enough to blend (do not over-beat – the batter does not have to be smooth).

4 Drop 15ml/1 tbsp batter into each muffin cup. Bake for 12–15 minutes, until golden. Leave to cool completely.

5 Split the muffins, spread each bottom half with a little butter and mustard and top with ham.

> ### Cook's Tip
> *Muffins can be made in advance and stored in airtight containers. Bring to room temperature or warm slightly before filling and serving.*

Cheese Muffins

Puffed up and golden with their yummy cheese filling and the merest hint of hot spice, these must top the list of everyone's favourite savoury muffins.

Makes 9

50g/2oz/4 tbsp butter
175g/6oz/1¹/₂ cups plain
   (all-purpose) flour
10ml/2 tsp baking powder
30ml/2 tbsp caster
   (superfine) sugar
pinch of salt
5ml/1 tsp paprika
2 eggs
120ml/4fl oz/¹/₂ cup milk
5ml/1 tsp dried thyme
50g/2oz mature (sharp) Cheddar
   cheese, diced

1 Preheat the oven to 190°C/375°F/Gas 5. Lightly grease a nine-cup muffin tin (pan) or line with paper cases.

2 Melt the butter in a small pan over a low heat. Remove the pan from the heat and set aside to cool slightly.

3 Sift together the flour, baking powder, caster sugar, salt and paprika into a large mixing bowl.

4 Combine the eggs, milk, melted butter and dried thyme in another bowl and beat lightly with a balloon whisk or a fork until thoroughly blended.

5 Add the milk mixture to the bowl of dry ingredients and stir lightly with a wooden spoon until just moistened and combined. Do not mix until smooth.

6 Place a heaped tablespoonful of the mixture in each of the prepared muffin cups. Divide the pieces of cheese equally among them, then top with another spoonful of the mixture, making sure that the cheese is covered.

7 Bake for about 25 minutes, until puffed and golden. Leave to stand for 5 minutes before transferring to a wire rack to cool slightly. These muffins are best served while they are still warm or at room temperature.

Corn Muffins with Ham Energy 54kcal/227kJ; Protein 1.5g; Carbohydrate 6.8g, of which sugars 1.6g; Fat 2.5g, of which saturates 1.4g; Cholesterol 14mg; Calcium 13mg; Fibre 0.2g; Sodium 43mg.
Cheese Muffins Energy 166kcal/698kJ; Protein 5.1g; Carbohydrate 19.3g, of which sugars 4.4g; Fat 8.1g, of which saturates 4.6g; Cholesterol 60mg; Calcium 93mg; Fibre 0.6g; Sodium 96mg.

Poppy Seed and Sea Salt Crackers

These attractive little crackers are ideal to use as the base of drinks party canapés, or they can be served plain as tasty snacks in their own right.

Makes 20
115g/4oz/1 cup plain
   (all-purpose) flour, plus extra
   for dusting
pinch of salt
5ml/1 tsp caster (superfine) sugar
15g/¹/₂oz/1 tbsp butter
15ml/1 tbsp poppy seeds
about 90ml/6 tbsp single
   (light) cream

1 Preheat the oven to 150°C/300°F/Gas Mark 2.

2 Sift together the flour, salt and sugar into a bowl. Add the butter and rub in with your fingertips until the mixture resembles fine breadcrumbs. Stir in the poppy seeds. Add just enough cream to mix to a stiff dough.

3 Turn the dough on to a lightly floured surface and roll out to a 20 x 25cm/8 x 10in rectangle. Cut into 20 squares with a sharp knife.

4 Put the crackers on to one or two ungreased baking sheets and brush lightly with milk. Sprinkle a few flakes of sea salt over each cracker.

5 Bake for about 30 minutes, until crisp but still quite pale. Using a metal spatula, carefully transfer the crackers to a wire rack to cool completely.

Variations
• You can substitute white poppy seeds for the black ones used here or use a mixture of the two.
• Vary the flavour of these crackers by using other small seeds: for example, celery seeds for sharpness, caraway for piquancy or sesame for a slight sweetness.

Festive Cheese Nibbles

Shape these spicy cheese snacks in any way you wish – stars, crescent moons, triangles, squares, hearts, fingers or rounds. Serve them with drinks from ice-cold cocktails to hot and spicy mulled wines.

Makes 60
115g/4oz/1 cup plain
   (all-purpose) flour, plus extra
   for dusting

5ml/1 tsp mustard powder
pinch of salt
115g/4oz/¹/₂ cup butter
75g/3oz/³/₄ cup Cheddar
   cheese, grated
pinch of cayenne papper
30ml/2 tbsp water
1 egg, beaten
poppy seeds, sunflower seeds or
   sesame seeds, to decorate

1 Preheat the oven to 200°C/400°F/Gas 6. Lightly grease two baking sheets.

2 Sift the flour, mustard powder and salt into a bowl and rub in the butter until the mixture resembles fine breadcrumbs.

3 Stir in the cheese and cayenne pepper and sprinkle on the water. Add half the beaten egg, mix to a firm dough and knead lightly until smooth.

4 Roll out the dough on a lightly floured surface and cut out a variety of shapes. Re-roll the trimmings and cut more shapes until all the dough has been used up.

5 Place the shapes on the prepared baking sheets and brush with the remaining egg. Sprinkle on the seeds. Bake for 8–10 minutes until puffed and golden. Leave to cool on the baking tray for a few minutes before carefully removing to a wire rack with a metal spatula.

Cook's Tip
Serve these nibbles as they are with pre-dinner drinks, or add them to the cheeseboard at the end of a meal.

Poppy Seed and Sea Salt Crackers Energy 39kcal/164kJ; Protein 0.8g; Carbohydrate 4.8g, of which sugars 0.4g; Fat 2g, of which saturates 1g; Cholesterol 4mg; Calcium 17mg; Fibre 0.2g; Sodium 6mg.
Festive Cheese Nibbles Energy 27kcal/113kJ; Protein 0.6g; Carbohydrate 1.5g, of which sugars 0g; Fat 2.1g, of which saturates 1.3g; Cholesterol 8mg; Calcium 13mg; Fibre 0.1g; Sodium 22mg.

Classic Oatcakes

These are very simple to make and are an excellent addition to a cheeseboard.

Makes 24
225g/8oz/1²/₃ cups medium oatmeal, plus extra for sprinkling
75g/3oz/³/₄ cup plain (all-purpose) flour
pinch of bicarbonate of soda (baking soda)
pinch of salt
25g/1oz/2 tbsp hard white vegetable fat (shortening)
25g/1oz/2 tbsp butter
60–90ml/4–6 tbsp boiling water

1 Preheat the oven to 220°C/425°F/Gas Mark 7.

2 Put the oatmeal in a large bowl. Sift together the flour, bicarbonate of soda and salt into the bowl and mix well.

3 Put the vegetable fat and butter into a small pan and melt over a low heat, stirring occasionally.

4 Add the mixture of melted fats to the dry ingredients, stirring well to combine. Stir in enough boiling water to mix to a soft, but not sticky dough.

5 Sprinkle a work surface with a little oatmeal and turn out the dough. Knead lightly, then roll out thinly. Stamp out 24 rounds with a 5cm/2in plain cookie cutter and place them on ungreased baking sheets.

6 Bake for about 15 minutes, until light golden brown and crisp. Leave to cool on the baking sheets, then using a metal spatula, remove them carefully.

> **Cook's Tips**
> • You can store these oatcakes in an airtight container in a cool place for up to 1 week.
> • Oatcakes are traditionally made with lard so if you want an authentic flavour, use this instead of vegetable fat (shortening).

Oatcake Triangles

These oatcakes are delicious served as a snack with grapes and wedges of cheese. They are also good topped with thick honey for breakfast.

Makes 8
175g/6oz/1 cup medium oatmeal, plus extra for sprinkling
pinch of salt
pinch of bicarbonate of soda (baking soda)
15ml/1 tbsp pure vegetable margarine
75ml/5 tbsp water

1 Preheat the oven to 150°C/300°F/Gas 2. Put the oatmeal into a large mixing bowl, add the salt and bicarbonate of soda and mix well.

2 Melt the margarine with the water in a small pan over a low heat. Bring to the boil, then add to the oatmeal mixture and mix to a moist dough.

3 Turn the dough on to a surface sprinkled with extra oatmeal and knead to a smooth ball. Turn a large baking sheet upside-down, grease it, sprinkle it lightly with oatmeal and place the ball of dough on top. Sprinkle the dough with oatmeal, then roll out to a 25cm/10in round.

4 Using a sharp knife, cut the round into eight equal triangular sections, ease them apart slightly and bake for about 50–60 minutes until crisp.

5 Leave to cool on the baking sheet, then carefully remove the oatcakes with a metal spatula.

> **Cook's Tip**
> To achieve a neat round, place a 25cm/10in plate upside down on top of the oatcake dough. Cut away any excess dough with a knife, then gently remove the plate.

Classic Oatcakes Energy 102kcal/429kJ; Protein 2.7g; Carbohydrate 16g, of which sugars 0g; Fat 3.4g, of which saturates 1g; Cholesterol 4mg; Calcium 12mg; Fibre 1.5g; Sodium 142mg.
Oatcake Triangles Energy 101kcals/428kJ; Protein 2.7g; Fat 3.4g; Saturated fat 0.7g; Carbohydrate 15.9g; Sugar 0g; Fibre (NSP) 1.5g; Calcium 12mg.

Herby Seeded Oatcakes

The addition of thyme and sunflower seeds to this traditional recipe makes these oatcakes an especially good accompaniment to cheese – try them spread with goat's cheese or ripe Brie or Camembert.

Makes 32

rolled oats, for sprinkling
175g/6oz/1½ cups plain wholemeal (all-purpose whole-wheat) flour, plus extra for dusting
175g/6oz/1½ cups fine oatmeal
pinch of salt
1.5ml/¼ tsp bicarbonate of soda (baking soda)
75g/3oz/6 tbsp white vegetable fat (shortening)
15ml/1 tbsp fresh thyme leaves, chopped
30ml/2 tbsp sunflower seeds

1 Preheat the oven to 150°C/300°F/Gas 2. Sprinkle two ungreased, non-stick baking sheets with rolled oats. Set aside.

2 Put the flour, oatmeal, salt and bicarbonate of soda in a bowl and rub in the fat until the mixture resembles fine breadcrumbs. Stir in the thyme.

3 Add just enough cold water (about 90–105ml/6–7 tbsp) to the dry ingredients to mix to a stiff, but not sticky dough.

4 Gently knead the dough on a lightly floured surface until smooth, then cut roughly in half and roll out one piece on a lightly floured surface to make a 23–25cm/9–10in round.

5 Sprinkle sunflower seeds over the dough and press them in with the rolling pin. Cut into triangles and arrange on one of the baking sheets. Repeat with the remaining dough. Bake for 45–60 minutes until crisp but not brown. Cool on wire racks.

> **Variation**
> *These oatcakes are also great sprinkled with sesame seeds.*

Oatmeal Crackers

Although not as neat as bought ones, these home-made oatmeal crackers make up in flavour and interest anything they might lose in presentation – and they make the ideal partner for many cheeses, especially with some fresh fruit to accompany them.

Makes about 18

75g/3oz/¾ cup plain (all-purpose) flour
pinch of salt
1.5ml/¼ tsp baking powder
115g/4oz/1 cup fine pinhead oatmeal, plus extra for sprinkling
65g/2½oz/generous ¼ cup white vegetable fat (shortening)

1 Preheat the oven to 200°C/400°F/Gas 6. Lightly grease one or two baking sheets.

2 Sift together the flour, salt and baking powder into a mixing bowl. Add the oatmeal and mix well. Add the white vegetable fat and rub it in with your fingertips until the mixture is crumbly.

3 Blend in just enough water to work the mxture into a stiff dough.

4 Turn out the dough on a work surface sprinkled with a little fine oatmeal and knead lightly until smooth and manageable. Roll out to about 3mm/⅛in thick and cut into rounds, squares or triangles with a plain cookie cutter or a sharp knife. Transfer to the prepared baking sheets.

5 Bake in the preheated oven for about 15 minutes, until crisp. Using a metal spatula, carefully transfer the crackers to a wire rack and leave to cool completely.

> **Cook's Tip**
> *Store the crackers when absolutely cold in an airtight container lined with baking parchment. Check for crispness before serving; reheat for 4–5 minutes in a preheated oven at 200°C/400°F/ Gas 6 to crisp up if necessary.*

Herby Seeded Oatcakes Energy 62kcal/259kJ; Protein 1.6g; Carbohydrate 7.7g, of which sugars 0.2g; Fat 3g, of which saturates 0.9g; Cholesterol 0mg; Calcium 6mg; Fibre 0.9g; Sodium 21mg.
Oatmeal Crackers Energy 72kcal/301kJ; Protein 1.2g; Carbohydrate 7.9g, of which sugars 0.1g; Fat 4.2g, of which saturates 1.8g; Cholesterol 3mg; Calcium 9mg; Fibre 0.6g; Sodium 57mg.

Rosemary Crackers

Here rosemary flowers are used to flavour and garnish the top of savoury rosemary crackers, which are really delicious either on their own or with a mild-flavoured cheese. Use freshly-picked rosemary leaves for the best flavour in these crackers.

Makes about 25

225g/8oz/2 cups plain (all-purpose) flour, plus extra for dusting
2.5ml/½tsp baking powder
good pinch of salt
2.5ml/½tsp curry powder
75g/3oz/6 tbsp butter
30ml/2tbsp finely chopped young rosemary leaves
1 egg yolk
milk, to glaze

To decorate

30ml/2tbsp cream cheese
rosemary flowers

1 Put the flour, baking powder, salt and curry powder in a food processor. Add the butter, cut into small pieces, and blend until the mixture resembles fine breadcrumbs.

2 Add the rosemary, egg yolk and 30–45ml/2–3 tbsp cold water and mix to a firm dough. (Alternatively, sift the flour, baking powder, salt and curry powder together into a bowl, add the butter and rub in with your fingertips until the mixture resembles fine breadcrumbs. Stir in the rosemary, egg yolk and water and mix to a firm dough.) Chill for 30 minutes.

3 Thinly roll out the dough on a lightly floured surface and stamp out about 25 crackers using a 5cm/2in plain or fluted round cookie cutter.

4 Transfer to a large baking sheet and prick with a fork. Brush with milk to glaze and bake for about 10 minutes, until pale golden. Transfer to a wire rack and leave to cool.

5 Spread a little cream cheese on to each cracker and secure a few rosemary flowers on top, using tweezers to position the flowers, if that makes it easier.

Wheat Thins

These classic wheat crackers are especially delicious with rich-tasting creamy cheeses, and also make a quick snack simply spread with butter when you are in a hurry.

Makes 18

175g/6oz/1½ cups fine stoneground wholemeal (whole-wheat) flour, plus extra for dusting
pinch of salt
5ml/1 tsp baking powder
50g/2oz/½ cup coarse oatmeal
40g/1½oz/3 tbsp sugar
115g/4oz/½ cup unsalted (sweet) butter, chilled and diced

1 Preheat the oven to 190°C/375°F/Gas 5.

2 Put all the ingredients into a food processor and process until the mixture starts to clump.

3 (Alternatively, sift the flour, salt and baking powder into a bowl. Tip in the bran remaining in the sieve (strainer) and stir in the oatmeal and sugar. Add the butter and rub in with your fingertips until the mixture resembles breadcrumbs.)

4 Tip out on to a lightly floured surface, gather the dough together with your hands and roll out.

5 Stamp out 18 rounds with a 7.5cm/3in cookie cutter. Place on an ungreased baking sheet.

6 Bake for 12 minutes until just beginning to colour at the edges. Leave to cool slightly, then transfer to a wire rack to cool completely.

> **Cook's Tip**
> *These crackers are perfect for serving with a cheeseboard and look very pretty cut into different shapes. You could make star-shaped crackers for Christmas, or heart-shaped ones for Valentine's Day.*

Rosemary Crackers Energy 61kcal/254kJ; Protein 1g; Carbohydrate 7g, of which sugars 0.2g; Fat 3.4g, of which saturates 2g; Cholesterol 16mg; Calcium 15mg; Fibre 0.3g; Sodium 22mg.
Wheat Thins Energy 98kcal/408kJ; Protein 1.6g; Carbohydrate 10.6g, of which sugars 2.6g; Fat 5.7g, of which saturates 3.4g; Cholesterol 14mg; Calcium 8mg; Fibre 1.1g; Sodium 73mg.

Thyme and Mustard Crackers

These aromatic crackers are delicious served with herbed cheese as a light, savoury last course. Alternatively, wrap them in cellophane and tie with string for a pretty gift.

Makes 40
175g/6oz/1½ cups wholemeal
   (whole-wheat) flour, plus extra
   for dusting
50g/2oz/²⁄₃ cup rolled oats
25g/1oz/2 tbsp caster
   (superfine) sugar
10ml/2 tsp baking powder
30ml/2 tbsp fresh thyme leaves
pinch of salt
50g/2oz/¼ cup butter, diced
25g/1oz/2 tbsp white vegetable
   fat (shortening), diced
45ml/3 tbsp milk
10ml/2 tsp Dijon mustard
30ml/2 tbsp sesame seeds
ground black pepper

1 Preheat the oven to 200°C/400°F/Gas 6. Lightly grease two or three baking sheets.

2 Put the flour, oats, sugar, baking powder and thyme leaves into a bowl, season with salt and pepper and mix together. Add the butter and white vegetable fat and rub in with your fingertips until the mixture resembles breadcrumbs.

3 Pour the milk into a small bowl, add the mustard and whisk lightly with a fork until combined. Add to the dry ingredients and stir well to make a soft dough.

4 Turn out the dough on to a lightly floured surface and knead briefly. Roll out to a thickness of 5mm/¼in. Stamp out rounds with a 5cm/2in fluted round cookie cutter. Place them, spaced slightly apart to allow room for spreading, on the prepared baking sheets. Gather up the scraps, knead together lightly and re-roll. Stamp out more rounds until all the dough is used up.

5 Prick the biscuits with a fork and sprinkle them evenly with the sesame seeds. Bake for 10–12 minutes, until golden.

6 Leave to cool completely on the baking sheets. Store in a cool place in an airtight container for up to 5 days.

Blue Cheese and Chive Crisps

Advance preparation is the key with these crisps. You need to begin the day before you want to serve them. They are perfect for serving after a special festive meal.

Makes 48
225g/8oz/2 cups blue
   cheese, crumbled
115g/4oz/½ cup unsalted
   (sweet) butter
1 egg
1 egg yolk
30ml/2 tsp chopped fresh chives
black pepper
225g/8oz/2 cups plain
   (all-purpose) flour, sifted

1 In a large bowl, beat together the blue cheese and butter until well blended using an electric mixer. Add the egg, egg yolk, chopped chives and a little pepper, and beat until just blended.

2 Add the flour in three batches, folding in well with a metal spoon between each addition.

3 Divide the dough into two and roll each half into a log about 5cm/2in in diameter. Tightly wrap each log in baking parchment and chill overnight in the refrigerator.

4 Preheat the oven to 190°C/375°F/Gas 5. Light grease two or three baking sheets.

5 Cut the dough logs into slices about 3mm/⅛in thick. Place the slices on the prepared baking sheets. Bake in the oven for about 10 minutes, until just golden around the edges.

6 Leave to firm up slightly on the baking sheets for a few minutes. Using a metal spatula, transfer the crisps to a wire rack and leave to cool completely.

> **Cook's Tip**
> *The cheese crisps will keep for up to 10 days in an airtight container.*

Thyme and Mustard Crackers Energy 40kcal/168kJ; Protein 0.9g; Carbohydrate 4.5g, of which sugars 0.8g; Fat 2.2g, of which saturates 1g; Cholesterol 3mg; Calcium 9mg; Fibre 0.5g; Sodium 21mg.
Blue Cheese and Chive Crisps Energy 55kcal/229kJ; Protein 1.7g; Carbohydrate 3.8g, of which sugars 0.1g; Fat 3.8g, of which saturates 2.3g; Cholesterol 18mg; Calcium 32mg; Fibre 0.2g; Sodium 77mg.

Savoury Cocktail Crackers

Serve these savoury snacks at a party or with pre-dinner drinks. Each of the spice seeds contributes to the flavour.

Makes 20–30

150g/5oz/1¼ cups plain (all-purpose) flour, plus extra for dusting
10ml/2 tsp curry powder
115g/4oz/½ cup butter, chopped
75g/3oz/¾ cup grated Cheddar cheese
10ml/2 tsp poppy seeds
5ml/1 tsp black onion seeds
1 egg yolk
cumin seeds, to garnish

1 Lightly grease two baking sheets. Sift the flour and curry powder into a large mixing bowl.

2 Add the butter and rub in with your fingertips until the mixture resembles breadcrumbs.

3 Stir in the cheese, poppy seeds, black onion seeds and egg yolk and mix to a firm dough. Wrap in clear film (plastic wrap) and chill for 30 minutes.

4 Dust a rolling pin and roll out the dough on a floured surface to a thickness of about 3mm/⅛in.

5 Stamp out 20–30 rounds with a floured plain cookie cutter. Arrange the rounds on the prepared baking sheets, spaced slightly apart, and sprinkle with the cumin seeds. Chill in the refrigerator for 15 minutes.

6 Preheat the oven to 190°C/375°F/Gas 5. Bake for 20 minutes, until the cookies are crisp and golden. Cool slightly and serve warm or cold.

> **Variation**
> Try using caraway or sesame seeds in place of the poppy seeds, if you wish.

Sunflower and Almond Sesame Crackers

You might be surprised to learn that crackers aren't always based on flour. Here, ground nuts and seeds are the basis for crisp crackers that are just as tasty with cheese or pâté as their more usual counterparts.

Makes about 24

130g/4½ oz/1 cup ground sunflower seeds
90g/3½ oz/generous ¾ cup ground almonds
5ml/1 tsp baking powder
30ml/2 tbsp milk
1 egg yolk
25g/1oz/2 tbsp butter, melted
25g/1oz/¼ cup sesame seeds

1 Preheat the oven to 190°C/375°F/Gas 5.

2 Reserve 25g/1oz/¼ cup of the ground sunflower seeds for rolling out, and mix the remaining ground seeds with the ground almonds and baking powder in a bowl.

3 Blend together the milk and egg yolk and stir into the ground seed and almond mixture with the melted butter, mixing well. Gently work the mixture with your hands to form a moist dough.

4 Roll out the dough to 5mm/¼in thickness on a cool surface, lightly dusted with a little of the reserved ground sunflower seeds, with a little more sprinkled on top to prevent sticking.

5 Sprinkle the dough with sesame seeds and cut into rounds using a 5cm/2in cookie cutter. Place on a non-stick baking sheet.

6 Bake for about 10 minutes, until lightly browned. Remove from the oven and leave for a minute or two. Transfer to a wire rack and leave to cool.

> **Variation**
> Sprinkle some poppy seeds on top of a few of the crackers.

Savoury Cocktail Crackers Energy 62kcal/257kJ; Protein 1.3g; Carbohydrate 4g, of which sugars 0.1g; Fat 4.5g, of which saturates 2.6g; Cholesterol 17mg; Calcium 32mg; Fibre 0.3g; Sodium 43mg.
Sunflower and Almond Sesame Crackers Energy 72kcal/296kJ; Protein 2.2g; Carbohydrate 1.3g, of which sugars 0.3g; Fat 6.4g, of which saturates 1.1g; Cholesterol 11mg; Calcium 25mg; Fibre 0.7g; Sodium 8mg.

Swedish Crispbread

This is a very traditional Swedish crispbread with a lovely rye flavour. The texture is crunchy. Pile with paté, spread or cream cheese-type toppings, then add fruit or chopped raw vegetables.

Makes 8
450g/1lb/4 cups rye flour, plus extra for dusting
pinch of salt
50g/2oz/¼ cup butter
20g/¾ oz fresh yeast
275ml/9fl oz/generous 1 cup lukewarm water
75g/3oz/2 cups wheat bran

1 Preheat the oven to 230°C/450°F/Gas 8. Lightly grease two baking sheets. Mix the rye flour and salt in a large bowl. Add the butter and rub in with your fingertips until the mixture resembles breadcrumbs. Make a well in the centre.

2 Cream the yeast with a little water until smooth, then stir in the remaining lukewarm water. Pour into the well in the centre of the flour, mix to a dough, then mix in the bran. Knead on a lightly floured surface for 5 minutes until smooth and elastic.

3 Divide the dough into 8 equal pieces and roll each one out on a lightly floured surface, to a 20cm/8in round.

4 Place 2 rounds on the prepared baking sheets and prick all over with a fork. Cut a hole in the centre of each round, using a 4cm/1½in cutter.

5 Bake for 15–20 minutes, or until the crispbreads are golden and crisp. Transfer to a wire rack to cool. Repeat with the remaining crispbreads.

Cook's Tip
The hole in the centre of these crispbreads is a reminder of the days when breads were strung on a pole, which was hung across the rafters to dry. Make smaller crispbreads, if you like, and tie them together with bright red ribbon for an unusual Christmas gift.

Malted Wheat and Mixed Seed Crackers

These large crackers have plenty of crunch and flavour provided by the selection of different seeds that are used. They taste simply fabulous with robust farmhouse cheeses.

Makes 12–14
250g/9oz/2¼ cups Granary (whole-wheat) or malted wheat flour, plus extra for dusting
pinch of salt
2.5ml/½ tsp baking powder
115g/4oz/½ cup butter, chilled and diced
1 egg, beaten
30ml/2 tbsp milk, plus extra for brushing
15ml/1 tbsp pumpkin seeds
15ml/1 tbsp sunflower seeds
15ml/1 tbsp sesame seeds
2.5ml/½ tsp celery salt

1 Preheat the oven to 180°C/350°F/Gas 4. Put the flour, salt, baking powder and butter in a bowl. Rub together.

2 Add the egg and milk and mix to a stiff dough. Roll out on a floured surface to about 5mm/¼in thick.

3 Using a pastry brush, brush a little milk over the dough. Sprinkle all the pumpkin, sunflower and sesame seeds over the top in an even layer, then sprinkle the celery salt over the top.

4 Very gently, roll the rolling pin back and forth over the seeds to press them into the dough.

5 Stamp out rounds using a 10cm/4in cookie cutter and place on a non-stick baking sheet, spacing them slightly apart.

6 Bake the crackers for about 15 minutes, or until just beginning to brown. Transfer to a wire rack to cool completely.

Cook's Tip
To make celery salt, grind five parts lightly toasted celery seeds with one part sea salt.

Swedish Crispbread Energy 253kcal/1070kJ; Protein 6.1g; Carbohydrate 44.9g, of which sugars 0.3g; Fat 6.7g, of which saturates 3.5g; Cholesterol 13mg; Calcium 29mg; Fibre 9.5g; Sodium 41mg.
Malted Wheat and Mixed Seed Crackers Energy 140kcal/586kJ; Protein 3.4g; Carbohydrate 12.1g, of which sugars 0.5g; Fat 9.1g, of which saturates 4.6g; Cholesterol 31mg; Calcium 14mg; Fibre 1.8g; Sodium 126mg.

Parmesan Tuiles

These lacy tuiles look very impressive, but they couldn't be easier to make. Believe it or not, they use only a single ingredient – grated Parmesan cheese.

Makes 8–10

115g/4oz Parmesan cheese

1 Preheat the oven to 200°C/400°F/Gas 6. Line two baking sheets with baking parchment.

2 Grate the cheese using a fine grater, pulling it down slowly to make long strands.

3 Spread the grated cheese out in 7.5–9cm/3–3½in rounds. Do not spread the cheese too thickly; it should only just cover the parchment. Bake for 5–7 minutes, until bubbling and golden brown.

4 Leave the tuiles on the baking sheet for about 30 seconds, and then carefully transfer them, using a metal spatula, to a wire rack to cool and set. Alternatively, drape them over a rolling pin while they are still warm so that they set in a curved shape.

Cook's Tip
Parmesan cheese will keep for months if stored properly. Wrap it in foil and store in a plastic box in the least cold part of the refrigerator, such as the salad drawer or one of the compartments in the door.

Variation
Tuiles can be made into little cup shapes by draping over an upturned egg cup. These little cups can be filled to make tasty treats to serve with drinks. Try a little cream cheese flavoured with herbs.

Rye and Caraway Seed Sticks

Wonderful with cocktails or pre-dinner drinks and a great addition to the cheeseboard, these long sticks are made with rye flour and have crunchy caraway seeds inside and out.

Makes 18–20

*90g/3½oz/generous ¾ cup plain
    (all-purpose) flour*
75g/3oz/¾ cup rye flour
pinch of salt
2.5ml/½ tsp baking powder
*90g/3½oz/7 tbsp unsalted
    (sweet) butter, diced*
10ml/2 tsp caraway seeds
60ml/4 tbsp boiling water

1 Preheat the oven to 180°C/350°F/Gas 4. Put the flours, salt and baking powder in a bowl and mix together. Add the butter and rub in gently with your fingertips until the mixture resembles fine breadcrumbs.

2 Stir in 5ml/1 tsp of the caraway seeds. Add the water and mix well to form a soft dough.

3 Divide the dough into about 18 even-size pieces and, using your fingers, gently roll each one out to a long thin stick about 25cm/10in long. Do not use any flour when rolling out the sticks unless the mixture is a little too moist. Try to make the sticks as uniform as possible.

4 Place the sticks on a non-stick baking sheet. Sprinkle over the remaining caraway seeds, rolling the sticks in any spilled seeds.

5 Bake the sticks in the oven for about 20 minutes, until crisp. Remove from the oven and transfer carefully to a wire rack. Leave to cool completely.

Cook's Tip
Rye flour has a rich and distinctive flavour that complements smoked fish. Try serving these sticks with a dip, such as taramasalata or smoked fish pâté, as part of a party buffet table. They are also delicious served with a seafood soup.

Rye and Caraway Seed Sticks Energy 64kcal/269kJ; Protein 0.9g; Carbohydrate 6.4g, of which sugars 0.1g; Fat 4.1g, of which saturates 2.4g; Cholesterol 10mg; Calcium 12mg; Fibre 0.6g; Sodium 77mg.
Parmesan Tuiles Energy 52kcal/216kJ; Protein 4.5g; Carbohydrate 0g, of which sugars 0g; Fat 3.8g, of which saturates 2.4g; Cholesterol 12mg; Calcium 138mg; Fibre 0g; Sodium 125mg.

Sun-dried Tomato Butter Crackers

These buttery crackers have all the flavours of classic pizza – cheese, tomato, oregano and olives.

Makes about 25
175g/6oz/1½ cups plain (all-purpose) flour
150g/5oz/⅔ cup unsalted (sweet) butter, chilled and diced
150g/5oz/1¼ cups grated mature (sharp) Cheddar cheese
15ml/1 tbsp sun-dried tomato paste
25g/1oz semi-dried sun-dried tomatoes, coarsely chopped
15ml/1 tbsp oregano
15g/½oz/2 tbsp pitted black olives, drained
15–30ml/1–2 tbsp cold water
50g/2oz sesame seeds

1 Put all the ingredients, except the water and sesame seeds, into a food processor. Process until the mixture forms fine crumbs.

2 Add enough water to mix to a soft dough, then shape it into a neat log about 25cm/10in long.

3 Spread out the sesame seeds over a sheet of baking parchment or on a large plate. Roll the dough log in the seeds until the sides are thoroughly coated. Wrap in clear film (plastic wrap) and chill for about 2 hours.

4 Preheat the oven to 180°C/350°F/Gas 4. Using a long, sharp knife, slice the unwrapped log into 1cm/½in slices and place on non-stick baking sheets, spaced slightly apart. Bake for 15–20 minutes, or until golden brown. Transfer the cookies to a wire rack to cool.

> **Variations**
> • If you don't like olives, you can still retain the pizza theme by substituting the same quantity of drained, chopped capers or caper berries.
> • If you prefer, roll the dough log in chopped pine nuts instead of sesame seeds.

Three-cheese Crumble Crackers

A delicious combination of mozzarella, Red Leicester and Parmesan cheese and the fresh taste of pesto make these crackers totally irresistible. Make mini ones to serve with drinks.

Makes 10
225g/8oz/2 cups self-raising (self-rising) flour
50g/2oz/¼ cup butter, diced
50g/2oz mozzarella cheese, diced
50g/2oz Red Leicester cheese, diced
15ml/1 tbsp fresh pesto
1 egg
60ml/4 tbsp milk
15g/½oz/2 tbsp Parmesan cheese, grated
15ml/1 tbsp mixed chopped nuts

1 Preheat the oven to 200°C/400°F/Gas 6.

2 Put the flour in a large mixing bowl, add the butter and rub in with your fingertips until the mixture resembles fine breadcrumbs.

3 Add the diced mozzarella and Red Leicester cheeses to the bowl and stir to mix well. In a separate bowl, beat together the pesto, egg and milk, then pour into the flour and cheese mixture. Stir together quickly until well combined.

4 Using a tablespoon, place in rocky piles on non-stick baking sheets, spaced slightly apart. Sprinkle over the Parmesan cheese and chopped nuts. Bake for 12–15 minutes, until well risen and golden brown. Using a metal spatula carefully transfer to a wire rack to cool.

> **Variations**
> You can vary any or all of the cheeses in this recipe according to taste, but it is best to keep to the same types. Try feta or curd (farmer's) cheese instead of mozzarella, or substitute a creamy blue cheese, such as Bleu d'Auvergne or Gorgonzola. Other semi-hard cheeses, such as Provolone, sage Derby or Cantal could replace the Red Leicester, and pecorino is a good substitute for Parmesan.

Polenta Dippers

These tasty Parmesan-flavoured batons are best served warm from the oven with a spicy, tangy dip such as Thai chilli dipping sauce or creamy guacamole.

Makes about 80
1.5 litres/2½ pints/6¼ cups
   water
10ml/2 tsp salt
375g/13oz/3¼ cups
   instant polenta
150g/5oz/1½ cups freshly grated
   Parmesan cheese
90g/3½oz/scant ½ cup butter
10ml/2 tsp cracked black pepper
olive oil, for brushing

1 Put the water in a large heavy pan and bring to the boil over a high heat. Reduce the heat, add the salt and pour in the polenta in a steady stream, stirring constantly with a wooden spoon. Cook over a low heat, stirring constantly, until the mixture thickens and comes away from the sides of the pan – about 5 minutes.

2 Remove from the heat and add the cheese, butter and pepper and salt to taste. Stir until the butter melts and the mixture is smooth.

3 Pour on to a smooth surface, such as a baking sheet. Spread the polenta to a thickness of 2cm/¾in and shape into a rectangle. Leave for at least 30 minutes to become quite cold.

4 Preheat the oven to 200°C/400°F/Gas 6. Lightly oil two or three baking sheets with some olive oil.

5 Cut the polenta slab in half, then cut into even-size strips. Bake for about 40–50 minutes, until dark golden brown and crunchy. Turn the strips over from time to time during cooking. Serve warm.

> **Cook's Tip**
> The dough can be made a day ahead, then wrapped in clear film (plastic wrap) and kept chilled until ready to bake.

Fennel and Chilli Ring Crackers

Based on an Italian recipe, these cookies are made with yeast and are dry and crumbly. Try them with drinks, dips or with a selection of antipasti.

Makes about 30
500g/1lb 2oz/4½ cups type 00
   flour, plus extra for dusting
115g/4oz/½ cup white vegetable
   fat (shortening)
5ml/1 tsp easy-blend (rapid-rise)
   dried yeast
15ml/1 tbsp fennel seeds
10ml/2 tsp crushed chilli flakes
15ml/1 tbsp olive oil
400–550ml/14–18fl oz/
   1⅔–2½ cups lukewarm water
olive oil, for brushing

1 Put the flour in a bowl and rub in the fat until the mixture resembles fine breadcrumbs. Add the yeast, fennel and chilli and mix well. Add the oil and enough water to make a soft but not sticky dough. Turn out on to a floured surface and knead lightly.

2 Take small pieces of dough and shape into sausages about 15cm/6in long. Shape into rings and pinch the ends together.

3 Place the rings on a non-stick baking sheet and brush lightly with olive oil. Cover with a dish towel and set aside at room temperature for 1 hour to rise slightly.

4 Meanwhile, preheat the oven to 150°C/300°F/Gas 2.

5 Bake the cookies for 1 hour, until they are dry and only slightly browned. Leave on the baking sheet to cool completely.

> **Cook's Tip**
> Type 00 is an Italian grade of flour used for pasta. It is milled from the centre part of the endosperm so that the resulting flour is much whiter than plain (all-purpose) flour. It contains 70 per cent of the wheat grain. It is available from Italian delicatessens and some large supermarkets. If you cannot find it, try using strong white bread flour instead.

Polenta Dippers Energy 34kcal/142kJ; Protein 1.2g; Carbohydrate 3.4g, of which sugars 0g; Fat 1.7g, of which saturates 1g; Cholesterol 4mg; Calcium 23mg; Fibre 0.1g; Sodium 27mg.
Fennel and Chilli Ring Crackers Energy 92kcal/385kJ; Protein 1.6g; Carbohydrate 13g, of which sugars 0.3g; Fat 4.1g, of which saturates 1.5g; Cholesterol 1mg; Calcium 24mg; Fibre 0.5g; Sodium 31mg.

Herb and Garlic Twists

These twists are very short and crumbly, made with garlic-flavoured dough sandwiches with fresh herbs and some chilli flakes for an extra kick. A very popular party nibble.

Makes about 20
90g/3½oz/scant ½ cup butter, at room temperature, diced
2 large garlic cloves, crushed
1 egg
1 egg yolk
175g/6oz/1½ cups self-raising (self-rising) flour
large pinch of salt
30ml/2 tbsp chopped fresh mixed herbs, such as basil, thyme, marjoram and flat leaf parsley
2.5–5ml/½–1 tsp dried chilli flakes
paprika or cayenne pepper, for sprinkling

1 Preheat the oven to 200°C/400°F/Gas 6. Put the butter and garlic into a bowl and beat well. Add the egg and yolk and beat in thoroughly. Stir in the flour and salt and mix to a soft but not sticky dough.

2 Roll the dough out on a sheet of baking parchment to a 28cm/11in square. Using a sharp knife, cut it in half to make two rectangles.

3 Sprinkle the herbs and chilli flakes over one of the rectangles, then place the other rectangle on top. Gently roll the rolling pin over the herbs and chilli flakes to press them into the dough.

4 Cut the dough into 1cm/½in sticks. Make two twists in the centre of each one and place on a non-stick baking sheet.

5 Bake the twists for 15 minutes, or until crisp and golden brown. Leave on the baking sheet to cool slightly, then carefully transfer to a wire rack to cool completely. To serve, sprinkle with a little paprika or cayenne pepper, according to taste.

Cook's Tip
If the dough is too soft to handle, wrap it in clear film (plastic wrap) and chill to firm up. It will be much easier to roll it out.

Microwave Sesame Cheese Twists

These savoury snacks are perfect to serve with soups or salads.

Makes 36
115g/4oz/1 cup plain (all-purpose) flour, plus extra for dusting
pinch of salt
pinch of mustard powder
50g/2oz/¼ cup butter, diced and chilled
50g/2oz/½ cup finely grated strong-flavoured cheese, such as Cheddar
1 egg yolk
10ml/2 tsp cold water
30ml/2 tbsp sesame seeds

1 Sift the flour, salt and mustard powder into a bowl. Rub in the butter until the mixture resembles fine breadcrumbs, then stir in the cheese.

2 Mix the egg yolk and water together, sprinkle over the dry ingredients and mix to a firm dough. Turn out and lightly knead on a floured surface.

3 Roll out the dough to 5mm/¼in thickness and cut into sticks about 7.5cm/3in long and 5mm/¼in wide.

4 Hold the ends of the sticks and twist them in opposite directions. Sprinkle the sesame seeds on a plate and roll the twists in them until coated. Line a microwave tray with baking parchment and arrange 12 twists in a circle on it.

5 Cook on full (100 per cent) power for 2–2½ minutes, until firm to the touch. Leave to stand for 2 minutes, then transfer to a wire rack to cool. Cook the remaining cheese twists in the same way.

Cheese and Herb Twizzles

These tasty cheese-and-herb flavoured sticks are great for serving with dips and are a popular choice for children's packed lunches.

Serves 6–8
225g/8oz/2 cups plain (all-purpose) flour, plus extra for dusting
115g/4oz/½ cup butter, diced
15ml/1 tbsp dried mixed herbs
50g/2oz/½ cup mature (sharp) Cheddar cheese, grated
cold water, to mix
salt and ground black pepper

1 Preheat the oven to 190°C/375°F/Gas 5. Lightly grease a baking sheet.

2 Put the flour and the butter in a bowl. Rub in the butter, then stir in the herbs, grated cheese and seasoning and add enough water to be able to pull the mixture together and knead it into a firm dough.

3 Roll out the dough on a lightly floured surface to 5mm/¼in thick and cut it into 15cm/6in strips, about 1cm/½in wide. Twist each strip once or twice and arrange them in rows on the baking sheet. Cook for 15–20 minutes, until golden brown. Cool on a wire rack.

Herb and Garlic Twists Energy 71kcal/295kJ; Protein 1.4g; Carbohydrate 6.9g, of which sugars 0.2g; Fat 4.4g, of which saturates 2.5g; Cholesterol 29mg; Calcium 19mg; Fibre 0.3g; Sodium 32mg.
Microwave Sesame Cheese Twists Energy 34kcal/140kJ; Protein 0.9g; Carbohydrate 2.5g, of which sugars 0.1g; Fat 2.3g, of which saturates 1.1g; Cholesterol 10mg; Calcium 21mg; Fibre 0.2g; Sodium 19mg. Cheese and Herb Twizzles Energy 229kcal/955kJ; Protein 4.3g; Carbohydrate 22g, of which sugars 0.5g; Fat 14.2g, of which saturates 8.9g; Cholesterol 37mg; Calcium 88mg; Fibre 0.9g; Sodium 133mg.

Caraway Bread Sticks

Ideal to nibble with drinks, these can be made with all sorts of other seeds – try cumin seeds, poppy seeds or celery seeds.

Makes about 20
150ml/¼ pint/⅔ cup lukewarm
    water
2.5ml/½ tsp active dried yeast
pinch of sugar
225g/8oz/2 cups plain
    (all-purpose) flour, plus extra
    for dusting
pinch of salt
10ml/2 tsp caraway seeds

1 Grease two baking sheets. Put the warm water in a jug (pitcher). Sprinkle the yeast on top. Add the sugar, mix well and leave for 10 minutes.

2 Sift the flour and salt into a mixing bowl, stir in the caraway seeds and make a well in the centre. Stir the yeast mixture to a smooth paste. Add the yeast mixture and gradually incorporate the flour to make a soft dough, adding a little extra water if necessary.

3 Turn on to a lightly floured surface and knead for 5 minutes, until smooth. Divide the mixture into 20 pieces and roll each one into a 30cm/12in stick. Arrange on the baking sheets, leaving room to allow for rising, then leave for 30 minutes until well risen.

4 Preheat the oven to 220°C/425°F/Gas 7.

5 Bake the bread sticks for about 10–12 minutes until golden brown. Cool on the baking sheets.

> **Variation**
> *To make Coriander and Sesame Sticks, replace the caraway seeds with 15ml/1 tbsp crushed coriander seeds. Dampen the bread sticks lightly and sprinkle them with sesame seeds before baking.*

Cheese Straws

Cheese-flavoured pastries became popular when it was customary (for gentlemen, particularly) to eat a small savoury at the end of a long, sophisticated meal. Now we are more likely to eat cheese straws as an appetizer with pre-dinner drinks or as a party snack.

Makes about 10
75g/3oz/¾ cup plain (all-purpose)
    flour, plus extra for dusting
40g/1½oz/3 tbsp butter, diced
40g/1½oz mature (sharp)
    hard cheese, such as Cheddar,
    finely grated
1 egg
5ml/1 tsp ready-made mustard
salt and ground black pepper

1 Preheat the oven to 180°C/350°F/Gas 4. Line a baking sheet with baking parchment.

2 Sift together the flour and seasoning into a bowl and add the butter. Rub in with your fingertips until the mixture resembles fine breadcrumbs. Stir in the grated cheese until thoroughly incorporated.

3 Crack the egg into another bowl, add the mustard and lightly whisk together with a fork. Add half the egg mixture to the flour and stir gently until the mixture can be gathered together into a smooth ball of dough.

4 Roll out the dough on a lightly floured surface to a square measuring about 15cm/6in. Cut into ten lengths with a sharp knife. Place on the prepared baking sheet and brush with the remaining egg mixture.

5 Bake for about 12 minutes, until golden brown. Using a metal spatula, carefully transfer the cheese straws to a wire rack to cool slightly. Serve warm.

> **Variation**
> *You can sprinkle some or all of the cheese straws with sesame, poppy or sunflower seeds before baking or dust with paprika or cayenne pepper afterwards.*

Caraway Bread Sticks Energy 41kcal/176kJ; Protein 1.2g; Carbohydrate 8.7g, of which sugars 0.2g; Fat 0.4g, of which saturates 0.1g; Cholesterol 0mg; Calcium 19mg; Fibre 0.4g; Sodium 0mg.
Cheese Straws Energy 78kcal/325kJ; Protein 2g; Carbohydrate 5.9g, of which sugars 0.1g; Fat 5.2g, of which saturates 3.1g; Cholesterol 33mg; Calcium 43mg; Fibre 0.2g; Sodium 54mg.

Curry Crackers

Crisp curry-flavoured crackers are very good with creamy cheese or yogurt dips and make an unusual nibble with pre-dinner drinks. Add a pinch of cayenne pepper for an extra kick.

Makes about 30
175g/6oz/1½ cups self-raising (self-rising) flour, plus extra for dusting
pinch of salt
10ml/2 tsp garam masala
75g/3oz/6 tbsp butter, diced
5ml/1 tsp finely chopped fresh coriander (cilantro)
1 egg, beaten

For the topping
beaten egg
black onion seeds
garam masala

1 Preheat the oven to 200°C/400°F/Gas 6. Put the flour, salt and garam masala into a bowl. Rub in the butter until the mixture resembles fine breadcrumbs. Stir in the coriander, add the egg and mix to a soft dough.

2 Turn out on to a lightly floured surface and knead gently until smooth. Roll out to a thickness of about 3mm/⅛in.

3 Cut the dough into neat rectangles measuring about 7.5 × 2.5cm/3 × 1in. Brush with a little beaten egg and sprinkle each cracker with a few black onion seeds. Place on non-stick baking sheets and bake in the oven for about 12 minutes, until the crackers are light golden brown all over.

4 Remove from the oven and transfer to a wire rack using a metal spatula. Put a little garam masala in a saucer and, using a dry pastry brush, dust each cracker with a little of the spice mixture. Leave to cool before serving.

Cook's Tip
Garam masala is a mixture of Indian spices that usually contains a blend of cinnamon, cloves, peppercorns, cardamom seeds and cumin seeds. You can buy it ready-made or make your own.

Low-fat Curry Thins

These spicy, crisp little crackers are very low fat and are ideal for serving with drinks.

Makes 12
50g/2oz/1½ cups plain (all-purpose) flour, plus extra for dusting
pinch of salt
5ml/1 tsp curry powder
1.5ml/¼ tsp chilli powder
15ml/1 tbsp chopped fresh coriander (cilantro)
30ml/2 tbsp water

1 Preheat the oven to 180°C/350°F/Gas 4.

2 Sift the flour and salt into a mixing bowl. Add the curry powder and the chilli powder. Make a well in the centre and add the coriander and water. Gradually incorporate the flour and mix to a firm dough.

3 Turn out on to a lightly floured surface, knead until smooth and leave to rest for 5 minutes.

4 Cut the dough into 12 equal pieces and knead each into a small ball. Roll out each ball very thinly to a 10cm/4in round, sprinkling more flour over the dough if necessary to prevent it from sticking to the rolling pin.

5 Arrange the rounds on two ungreased baking sheets, spaced apart, then bake for 15 minutes, turning them over once during cooking. Using a metal spatula, carefully transfer the crackers to a wire rack to cool.

Cook's Tip
Commercial curry powders vary enormously in flavour and their degree of heat, depending on the specific spices used and their proportions. The best-quality ones tend to be more expensive, but this is not invariably the case. Try different brands until you find one that you like.

Curry Crackers Energy 39kcal/164kJ; Protein 0.6g; Carbohydrate 4.6g, of which sugars 0.1g; Fat 2.2g, of which saturates 1.3g; Cholesterol 5mg; Calcium 11mg; Fibre 0.3g; Sodium 17mg.
Low-fat Curry Thins Energy 17kcal/73kJ; Protein 0.5g; Carbohydrate 3.6g, of which sugars 0.1g; Fat 0.2g, of which saturates 0g; Cholesterol 0mg; Calcium 14mg; Fibre 0.4g; Sodium 6mg.

Hot Cheese Crescents

Cheesy, spicy and peppery, these tiny crescents are small pastries packed with flavour. Serve them as a snack or with pre-dinner drinks.

Makes about 40

225g/8oz/2 cups plain (all-purpose) flour, plus extra for dusting
1.5ml/¼ tsp grated nutmeg
pinch of salt
150g/5oz/²₃ cup cold butter, lard or white cooking fat (shortening), diced
60ml/4 tbsp iced water

For the filling
2 eggs
115g/4oz mature (sharp) Cheddar cheese, grated
hot pepper sauce, to taste
15ml/1 tbsp finely chopped mixed fresh herbs, such as thyme, chives and sage

1 For the dough, sift the flour, nutmeg and salt into a bowl. Using your fingertips, rub the fat into the dry ingredients until the mixture resembles breadcrumbs.

2 Sprinkle the iced water over the flour mixture. Combine with a fork until the dough holds together. Divide the dough in half. Wrap each portion in clear film (plastic wrap) and chill for 20 minutes.

3 Preheat the oven to 220°C/425°F/Gas 7.

4 To make the filling, in a large bowl, beat the eggs with a fork. Add the cheese, hot pepper sauce to taste and the herbs.

5 On a lightly floured surface, roll out the dough to a thickness of 3mm/⅛in. Cut out rounds using a 7.5cm/3in cookie cutter.

6 Place 5ml/1 tsp of the filling in the centre of each dough round. Fold over to make half-moon shapes, and press the edges together with the tines of a fork. Cut a few small slashes in the top of each pastry with the point of a sharp knife.

7 Place on ungreased baking sheets. Bake for 18–20 minutes, until the pastries start to darken slightly. Serve warm with drinks.

Mini Cocktail Savouries

Tiny savoury crackers always make lovely party snacks. Try making a range of shapes and flavouring them with different cheeses and spices.

Makes 80

350g/12oz/3 cups plain (all-purpose) flour, plus extra for dusting
pinch of salt
2.5ml/½ tsp ground black pepper
5ml/1 tsp wholegrain mustard
175g/6oz/¾ cup unsalted (sweet) butter, diced
115g/4oz/1 cup grated Cheddar cheese
1 egg, beaten
5ml/1 tsp chopped nuts
10ml/2 tsp dill seeds
10ml/2 tsp curry paste
10ml/2 tsp chilli sauce

1 Line several large baking sheets with baking parchment and set aside.

2 Sift the flour into a large mixing bowl and add the salt, pepper and wholegrain mustard. Mix well.

3 Add the butter and rub it in with your fingertips until the mixture resembles fine breadcrumbs. Stir in the cheese with a fork until it is incorporated. Add the egg and mix together to form a soft dough.

4 Turn out the dough on to a floured surface, knead lightly until smooth, then divide it into four equal pieces.

5 Knead chopped nuts into one piece, dill seeds into another, and curry paste and chilli sauce into the remaining pieces. Wrap each piece in clear film (plastic wrap) and chill for 1 hour.

6 Preheat the oven to 200°C/400°F/Gas 6. Roll out each piece of dough in turn. Use a floured cookie cutter to stamp out about 20 shapes from the curry-flavoured dough. Use a different cutter to cut out the chilli-flavoured dough. Repeat with the remaining dough.

7 Arrange the shapes on the baking sheets and bake for 6–8 minutes, until pale gold. Cool on wire racks.

Hot Cheese Crescents Energy 63kcal/263kJ; Protein 1.6g; Carbohydrate 4.4g, of which sugars 0.1g; Fat 4.4g, of which saturates 2.7g; Cholesterol 20mg; Calcium 34mg; Fibre 0.2g; Sodium 48mg.
Mini Cocktail Savouries Energy 39kcal/162kJ; Protein 0.9g; Carbohydrate 3.5g, of which sugars 0.1g; Fat 2.4g, of which saturates 1.5g; Cholesterol 8mg; Calcium 18mg; Fibre 0.1g; Sodium 25mg.

Nutty Cheese Balls

These tasty morsels are perfect for nibbling at any time of day.

Makes 32

115g/4oz/½ cup cream cheese

115g/4oz Roquefort cheese
115g/4oz/1 cup walnuts, chopped
fresh parsley, chopped
paprika
salt and ground black pepper

1 Beat the two cheeses together until smooth using a whisk. Stir in the chopped walnuts and season with salt and pepper.

2 Shape into small balls. Chill on a baking sheet until firm. Roll half the balls in the chopped parsley and half in the paprika. Serve on cocktail sticks (toothpicks).

Cheddar Pennies

Serve these tasty snacks with pre-dinner drinks. Choose a strong-flavoured Cheddar, or Caerphilly or substitute Parmesan, pecorino or a farmhouse Lancashire cheese.

Makes 20

50g/2oz/4 tbsp butter at room
    temperature, diced
115g/4oz/1 cup grated
    Cheddar cheese
40g/1½oz/⅓ cup plain
    (all-purpose) flour
pinch of salt
pinch of chilli powder

1 With an electric mixer, beat the butter until soft. Stir in the cheese, flour, salt and chilli powder. Gather to form a dough.

2 Using your hands and a spatula, shape the dough into a long cylinder about 3cm/1¼in in diameter. Wrap in baking parchment and chill for 1–2 hours.

3 Preheat the oven to 180°C/350°F/Gas 4. Grease one large or two medium-size baking sheets.

4 Cut the dough into 5mm/¼in thick slices and place on the prepared baking sheets. Bake for about 15 minutes.

Tiny Cheese Puffs

These choux pastry bites go perfectly with chilled white wine. They are delicious on their own, but are also good filled with garlic-flavoured cheese.

Makes 45

115g/4oz/1 cup plain
    (all-purpose) flour

pinch of salt
5ml/1 tsp mustard powder
pinch of cayenne pepper
250ml/8fl oz/1 cup water
115g/4oz/½ cup butter, diced
4 eggs
75g/3oz Gruyère cheese, diced
15ml/1 tbsp fresh chives, chopped

1 Preheat the oven to 200°C/400°F/Gas 6. Lightly grease two large baking sheets.

2 Sift together the flour, salt, mustard powder and cayenne pepper into a bowl.

3 In a pan, bring the water and butter to the boil over a medium heat. Remove from the heat. Add the flour mixture all at once, beating with a wooden spoon until a dough ball forms. Return the pan to the heat and beat constantly for 2 minutes. Remove from the heat and cool for 5 minutes.

4 Beat three of the eggs into the dough, one at a time, beating well after each addition.

5 Beat the fourth egg in a small bowl, then add a little at a time, beating until the dough is smooth and falls slowly when dropped from a spoon. (You may not need all of it.)

6 Stir the diced cheese and chives into the dough.

7 Drop small mounds of dough, spaced about 5cm/2in apart, on to the prepared baking sheets. Beat any remaining egg with 15ml/1 tbsp water and brush the tops with the glaze.

8 Bake for 8 minutes, then reduce the temperature to 180°C/350°F/Gas 4 and bake for another 7–8 minutes, until puffed and golden. Transfer to a wire rack to cool. Serve warm.

Nutty Cheese Balls Energy 53kcal/218kJ; Protein 1.4g; Carbohydrate 0.1g, of which sugars 0.1g; Fat 5.2g, of which saturates 2g; Cholesterol 6mg; Calcium 24mg; Fibre 0.1g; Sodium 55mg.
Cheddar Pennies Energy 49kcal/205kJ; Protein 1.7g; Carbohydrate 1.6g, of which sugars 0.1g; Fat 4g, of which saturates 2.6g; Cholesterol 11mg; Calcium 46mg; Fibre 0.1g; Sodium 57mg.
Tiny Cheese Puffs Energy 41kcal/172kJ; Protein 1.2g; Carbohydrate 2g, of which sugars 0.1g; Fat 3.2g, of which saturates 1.8g; Cholesterol 24mg; Calcium 20mg; Fibre 0.1g; Sodium 34mg.

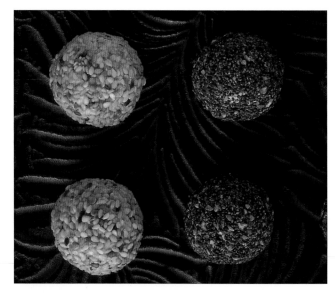

Savoury Cheese Balls

These colourful little cheese balls are made in four different flavours, each variety coated with a different herb or seed.

Makes about 48
450g/1lb/2 cups cream cheese, at room temperature
25g/1oz/¼ cup mature (sharp) Cheddar cheese, grated
2.5ml/½ tsp dry mustard powder, prepared
5ml/1 tsp mango chutney, chopped (optional)
cayenne pepper
pinch of salt
50g/2oz Roquefort or Stilton cheese

15ml/1 tbsp spring onions (scallions) or fresh chives, finely chopped
5–10ml/1–2 tsp pesto sauce
15ml/1 tbsp chopped pine nuts
1–2 garlic cloves, finely chopped
30ml/2 tbsp chopped mixed fresh herbs, such as parsley, tarragon, chives, dill or coriander (cilantro)

To coat
30ml/2 tbsp paprika
30ml/2 tbsp fresh parsley, chopped
30ml/2 tbsp toasted sesame seeds
ground black pepper mixed with poppy seeds

1 Divide the cream cheese equally among four small bowls. Into one mix the Cheddar cheese, mustard and mango chutney, if using. Season with cayenne pepper and a little salt. Into the second bowl, mix the Roquefort or Stilton cheese and spring onions or chives and season with a little cayenne.

2 Mix the pesto sauce and pine nuts into the third bowl and season with a little cayenne. Mix the chopped garlic and mixed fresh herbs into the last bowl of cream cheese.

3 Cover and chill all four bowls for about 30 minutes, until the cheese is firm enough to handle. Roll each of the different cheese mixtures into small balls, keeping them separate.

4 Lightly dust the Cheddar-flavoured balls with paprika, rolling to cover completely. Roll the pesto balls in chopped parsley and the Roquefort balls in sesame seeds. Roll the garlic-herb cheese balls in coarsely ground black pepper and poppy seeds. Arrange the balls on a plate and serve with cocktail sticks (toothpicks).

Cheeselets

These crispy cheese crackers are irresistible, and will disappear in moments. Try using different cheeses sprinkled with a variety of seeds to give alternative flavours and colours.

Makes about 80
115g/4oz/1 cup plain (all-purpose) flour
pinch of salt

½ tsp cayenne pepper
½ tsp mustard powder
11g/4oz/½ cup butter, diced
50g/2oz/½ cup Cheddar cheese, grated
50g/2oz/½ cup grated Gruyère cheese
1 egg white, beaten
15ml/1 tbsp sesame seeds

1 Preheat the oven to 220°C/425°F/Gas 7. Line several baking sheets with baking parchment.

2 Sift the flour, salt, cayenne pepper and mustard into a mixing bowl. Add the butter and rub into the flour mixture until it begins to cling together.

3 Divide the mixture in half, add the Cheddar to half, and the Gruyère to the other half. Using a fork, work each mixture into a soft dough and knead on a floured surface until smooth.

4 Roll out both pieces of dough very thinly and cut into 2.5cm/1in squares. Repeat the process until you have used up all the cookie dough. Transfer to the lined baking sheets.

5 Brush the squares with beaten egg white, sprinkle with sesame seeds and bake in the oven for 5–6 minutes, or until slightly puffed up and pale gold in colour.

6 Cool on the baking sheets, then carefully remove with a metal spatula.

Variation
For a milder flavour, substitute paprika for the cayenne.

Savoury Cheese Balls Energy 55kcal/225kJ; Protein 0.9g; Carbohydrate 0.2g, of which sugars 0g; Fat 5.6g, of which saturates 3.2g; Cholesterol 10mg; Calcium 24mg; Fibre 0.1g; Sodium 45mg.
Cheeselets Energy 22kcal/93kJ; Protein 0.6g; Carbohydrate 1.2g, of which sugars 0g; Fat 1.7g, of which saturates 1g; Cholesterol 4mg; Calcium 13mg; Fibre 0.1g; Sodium 19mg.

Praline Pavlova Cookies

Melt-in-the-mouth meringue with a luxurious velvety chocolate filling is topped with nutty praline – just the thing for a special tea party.

Makes 14
2 large (US extra large) egg whites
large pinch of ground cinnamon
90g/3½oz/½ cup caster (superfine) sugar
50g/2oz/½ cup pecan nuts, finely chopped

For the filling
50g/2oz/¼ cup unsalted (sweet) butter, at room temperature, diced
100g/3½oz/scant 1 cup icing (confectioners') sugar, sifted
50g/2oz plain (semisweet) chocolate

For the praline
60ml/4 tbsp caster (superfine) sugar
15g/½oz/1 tbsp finely chopped toasted almonds

1 Preheat the oven to 140°C/275°F/Gas 1. Line two baking sheets with baking parchment.

2 In a bowl, whisk the egg whites until stiff. Stir the cinnamon into the sugar. Add a spoonful of sugar to the egg whites and whisk. Continue adding sugar, a spoonful at a time, whisking until the mixture is thick and glossy. Stir in the chopped pecan nuts.

3 Place 14 spoonfuls of meringue on the baking sheets, spaced well apart. Using the back of a wetted teaspoon, make a small hollow in the top of each. Bake for 45–60 minutes, until dry and just beginning to colour. Set aside to cool.

4 To make the filling, beat together the butter and icing sugar until light and creamy. Melt the chocolate in a heatproof bowl set over a pan of simmering water and stir occasionally. Remove and leave to cool slightly. Add the chocolate to the butter mixture and combine. Divide among the meringue hollows.

5 To make the praline, heat the sugar gently in a small non-stick pan until melted. When it begins to turn brown, stir in the nuts. When the mixture is a golden brown, remove from the heat. Pour on to a non-stick baking sheet. Leave to cool and then break into small pieces. Sprinkle over the meringues.

Pastel Meringues

A cut-glass cake stand piled high with meringues in pretty pastel shades makes a decorative centrepiece before being dismantled and sampled at the end of the meal.

Makes 30
3 egg whites
175g/6oz/1½ cups icing (confectioners') sugar
mauve and pink food colouring
silver or sugar balls to decorate

1 Preheat the oven to 120°C/250°F/Gas ½. Line two baking sheets with baking parchment.

2 Whisk the egg whites in a heatproof grease-free bowl until they are really stiff, then gently fold in the icing sugar, a little at a time, with a metal spoon. Set the bowl over a pan of gently simmering water and whisk the mixture for a few seconds until it is firm enough for piping. The mixture should form stiff peaks when a metal spoon is pulled away from it.

3 Remove the bowl from the heat and divide the mixture into two batches. Tint one batch with a little mauve food colouring and the other with pink.

4 Gently spoon one batch of meringue into a piping (pastry) bag fitted with a small star nozzle and pipe little mounds of the mixture on to one of the prepared baking sheets. Spoon the second batch of meringue into a clean piping bag fitted with a small plain nozzle and pipe little heart shapes on to the other baking sheet. Decorate the meringues with silver or sugar balls.

5 Bake for 1 hour, until the meringue lifts off the parchment easily. Leave to cool completely, then pile the meringues on to a cake stand.

> **Cook's Tip**
> *Use a metal, ceramic or glass bowl for whisking egg whites. Plastic bowls are easily scratched and then it becomes almost impossible to wash away all traces of grease from the bowl.*

Praline Pavlova Cookies Energy 148kcal/621kJ; Protein 1.3g; Carbohydrate 21.2g, of which sugars 21.1g; Fat 7g, of which saturates 2.7g; Cholesterol 8mg; Calcium 16mg; Fibre 0.3g; Sodium 32mg.
Pastel Meringues Energy Energy 24kcal/103kJ; Protein 0.3g; Carbohydrate 6.1g, of which sugars 6.1g; Fat 0g, of which saturates 0g; Cholesterol 0mg; Calcium 3mg; Fibre 0g; Sodium 6mg.

Coconut Meringues

Make these tiny meringues to serve with a fruit salad, or make the bigger ones and sandwich with cream or crème fraîche to serve for tea.

175g/6oz/1½ cups caster (superfine) sugar
50g/2oz/½ cup desiccated (dry unsweetened shredded) coconut
whipped cream or crème fraîche, and lemon curd (optional), to serve

Makes 16

3 egg whites, at room temperature

1 Preheat the oven to 160°C/325°F/Gas 3. Line two baking sheets with baking parchment.

2 Whisk the egg whites in a large, grease-free bowl, until stiff. Whisk in half the sugar until smooth and glossy.

3 Carefully fold in the rest of the sugar and the coconut with a metal spoon. When well blended, place tablespoonfuls, spaced well apart, on the prepared baking sheets.

4 Bake the meringues for 20 minutes, then change the positions of the baking sheets over and reduce the temperature to 140°C/275°F/Gas 1 for a further 40 minutes, or until crisp and slightly golden.

5 Using a metal spatula, carefully remove the meringues from the baking sheets while they are still warm and transfer to a wire rack to cool completely. When they are cold, sandwich the meringues together in pairs with whipped cream, crème fraîche or a mixture of whipped cream and lemon curd. Serve within 30 minutes of filling.

Cook's Tip
You could use this mixture to make one large meringue gâteau. Spread out the mixture in two 18cm/7in rounds and bake as above, then sandwich with one of the suggested fillings.

Muscovado Meringues

These light brown meringues are extremely low in fat and are delicious served on their own or sandwiched together with a fresh fruit and soft cheese filling, or melted chocolate and soft cheese.

Makes about 20

115g/4oz/½ cup light muscovado (brown) sugar
2 egg whites
5ml/1 tsp finely chopped walnuts

1 Preheat the oven to 160°C/325°F/Gas 3. Line two baking sheets with baking parchment.

2 Press the sugar through a metal sieve (strainer) into a bowl.

3 Whisk the egg whites in a grease-free bowl until very stiff and dry, then whisk in the sugar, about 15ml/1 tbsp at a time, until the meringue is very thick and glossy.

4 Spoon small mounds of the mixture on to the prepared baking sheets.

5 Sprinkle the meringues with the chopped walnuts. Bake for 30 minutes. Leave to cool for 5 minutes on the baking sheets, then using a metal spatula, carefully transfer to a wire rack to cool completely.

Cook's Tip
When separating the eggs, make sure that no traces of yolk fall into the egg whites, as this will prevent them from foaming properly when whisked.

Variation
For a sophisticated filling, mix 115g/4oz/½ cup low-fat soft cheese with 15ml/1 tbsp icing (confectioners') sugar. Chop 2 slices of fresh pineapple and add to the mixture. Use to sandwich the meringues together in pairs.

Coconut Meringues Energy 64kcal/270kJ; Protein 0.8g; Carbohydrate 11.6g, of which sugars 11.6g; Fat 1.9g, of which saturates 1.7g; Cholesterol 0mg; Calcium 7mg; Fibre 0.4g; Sodium 13mg.
Muscovado Meringues Energy 26kcal/109kJ; Protein 0.4g; Carbohydrate 6g, of which sugars 6g; Fat 0.2g, of which saturates 0g; Cholesterol 0mg; Calcium 3mg; Fibre 0g; Sodium 6mg.

Orange, Mint and Coffee Meringues

These tiny, crisp meringues are flavoured with orange, coffee and mint chocolate sticks and liqueurs. Pile into dry, airtight glass jars or decorative containers.

Makes 90
25g/1oz/8 chocolate mint sticks
25g/1oz/8 chocolate orange sticks
25g/1oz/8 chocolate coffee sticks
2.5ml/½ tsp crème de menthe
2.5ml/½ tsp orange curaçao or Cointreau
2.5ml/½ tsp Tia Maria
3 egg whites
175g/6oz/¾ cup caster (superfine) sugar
5ml/1 tsp unsweetened cocoa powder

1 Preheat the oven to 110°C/225°F/Gas ¼. Line 2–3 baking sheets with baking parchment.

2 Chop each flavour of chocolate stick separately and place each into separate bowls, reserving a teaspoonful of each flavour stick. Stir in the liquid flavourings to match the chocolate sticks.

3 Place the egg whites in a grease-free bowl and whisk until stiff. Gradually add the sugar, whisking well after each addition until thick. Add a third of the meringue to each bowl of chopped chocolate sticks and fold in gently using a flexible spatula until evenly blended.

4 Place about 30 teaspoons of each mixture on to the baking sheets, spaced well apart. Sprinkle the top of each meringue with the reserved chopped chocolate sticks, matching the flavours to the meringues.

5 Bake for 1 hour, or until crisp. Leave to cool slightly on the baking sheets, then using a metal spatula, carefully transfer the meringues to a wire rack to cool completely. Dust lightly with unsweetened cocoa powder.

> **Cook's Tip**
> *These meringues are great served with vanilla ice cream.*

Mint Chocolate Meringues

These mini meringues are perfect for a buffet dessert at a birthday party and could be tinted pink or green. Alternatively, you could tint the filling with cocoa powder. Any spares are delicious crunched into your next batch of vanilla ice cream.

Makes about 50
2 egg whites
115g/4oz/generous ½ cup caster (superfine) sugar
50g/2oz/16 chocolate mint sticks, chopped
unsweetened cocoa powder, sifted (optional)

For the filling
150ml/¼ pint/⅔ cup double (heavy) or whipping cream
5–10ml/1–2 tsp crème de menthe, or peppermint extract

1 Preheat the oven to 110°C/225°F/Gas ¼. Line two large baking sheets with baking parchment.

2 Whisk the egg whites in a grease-free bowl until stiff, then gradually whisk in the sugar, a little at a time, until the meringue is thick and glossy. Gently fold in the chopped mint sticks with a metal spoon or flexible spatula. Place teaspoonfuls of the mixture on to the prepared baking sheets, spaced a little apart.

3 Bake for 1 hour, or until crisp. Remove from the oven and allow to cool, then dust with cocoa powder, if using.

4 Lightly whip the cream, stir in the crème de menthe or peppermint extract, and sandwich the meringues together in pairs just before serving.

> **Cook's Tips**
> • *Crème de menthe may be either a brilliant green or "white", that is, colourless. The flavour is no different, so it is a matter of personal taste which you use to flavour the filling. (Peppermint extract is always colourless.)*
> • *You can store these meringues in an airtight container for several days, but do not fill them until ready to serve.*

Nutty Nougat

Nougat is an almost magical sweetmeat that emerges from honey-flavoured meringue made with boiled syrup. Since any other nuts or candied fruits can be used instead of almonds, as long as you have eggs, sugar and honey, you have the potential for making an impromptu gift or dinner-party treat.

Makes about 500g/1¼lb
225g/8oz/generous 1 cup sugar
225g/8oz/1 cup clear honey or golden (light corn) syrup
1 large (US extra large) egg white
115g/4oz/1 cup flaked (sliced) almonds or chopped pistachio nuts, roasted

1 Line a 17.5cm/7in square cake tin (pan) with rice paper.

2 Place the sugar, honey or syrup and 60ml/4 tbsp water in a large, heavy pan and heat gently, stirring frequently, until the sugar has completely dissolved.

3 Bring the syrup to the boil and boil gently until it reaches the soft crack stage or the temperature registers 129–135°C/264–275°F on a sugar thermometer. To test for soft crack stage, drop a little syrup into a bowl of iced water. If it separates into hard, but not brittle threads that remain supple when pressed between your fingers, it is ready.

4 Meanwhile, whisk the egg white until very stiff, but not crumbly, then slowly drizzle in the syrup while whisking constantly.

5 Quickly stir in the nuts and pour the mixture into the prepared tin. Leave to cool but, before the nougat becomes too hard, cut it into squares. Store in an airtight container.

Cook's Tip
Warm the sugar thermometer in hot water (and dry) before placing it in the syrup. Make sure the bulb is covered by the syrup but is not touching the base of the pan, as this would give an inaccurate reading.

Guirlache

This is an Arab sweetmeat from the Pyrenees, combining toasted nuts and caramel to produce a crisp nut brittle – a forerunner of some familiar chocolate bar fillings.

Makes about 24 pieces
115g/4oz/1 cup almonds, half blanched, half unblanched
115g/4oz/1 cup hazelnuts, half blanched, half unblanched
5ml/1 tsp almond oil or a flavourless oil
200g/7oz/1 cup sugar
15ml/1 tbsp lemon juice

1 Preheat the oven to 150°C/300°F/Gas 2. Spread out the nuts on a baking sheet and toast for about 30 minutes, shaking the sheet occasionally. The nuts should smell pleasant and have turned brown and be very dry.

2 Coarsely chop the toasted nuts or crush them coarsely with a rolling pin. Cover another baking tray with foil and grease it generously with the oil.

3 Put the sugar in a pile in a small pan and pour the lemon juice around it. Cook over a high heat, shaking the pan, until the sugar turns a coffee colour. (As it cooks, the pile of sugar will melt and collapse into caramel.) If the heat is too high the sugar will burn and will taste unpleasant.

4 Immediately tip in the nuts and stir once to mix, then pour the mixture on to the foil and spread out into a thin, even layer with a metal spatula. Leave the mixture to cool completely and harden.

5 Once set, break up the caramel into pieces and store in an airtight container.

Cook's Tip
Guirlache may be served as an after-dinner treat. It is also very good pulverized and used as a topping for mousses and whipped cream. It also makes wonderful ice cream.

Nutty Nougat Energy 1177kcal/4907kJ; Protein 29.9g; Carbohydrate 85g, of which sugars 83.4g; Fat 82.2g, of which saturates 38.9g; Cholesterol 163mg; Calcium 799mg; Fibre 4.6g; Sodium 483mg.
Guirlache Energy 94kcal/395kJ; Protein 1.7g; Carbohydrate 9.3g, of which sugars 9.1g; Fat 5.8g, of which saturates 0.5g; Cholesterol 0mg; Calcium 23mg; Fibre 0.7g; Sodium 1mg.

Sweet Nutty Confections

If you love chocolate, condensed milk, nuts and crumb crust then these are the cookies for you. It's fortunate that they are incredibly easy to make because they are even easier to eat and are sure to become firm favourites with all the family as a treat for special occasions. Children enjoy helping to make them.

Makes 16–18
250g/9oz digestive biscuits (graham crackers)
115g/4oz/½ cup butter, melted
150g/5oz/scant 1 cup milk chocolate chips
200g/7oz mixed whole nuts, such as pecan nuts, hazelnuts, Brazil nuts, walnuts and almonds
200ml/7fl oz/scant 1 cup sweetened condensed milk

1 Preheat the oven to 180°C/350°F/Gas 4.

2 Put the digestive biscuits in a plastic bag and crush them with a rolling pin.

3 Put the crumbs in a bowl and stir in the melted butter. Mix well. Press the mixture evenly into the base of a 10 x 36cm/4 x 14in cake tin (pan).

4 Sprinkle the chocolate chips evenly over the crumb base. Arrange the nuts on top and pour the sweetened condensed milk over the top evenly.

5 Bake for 25 minutes, or until bubbling and golden. Cool in the tin, loosen from the sides, then cool completely and slice into thin bars.

Variation
Use crushed ginger nuts (ginger snaps) for the base of the bars.

Cook's Tip
If you prefer, use a shallow 20cm/8in square cake tin (pan) instead, and cut the cookies into squares.

Apple and Date Balls

Although these sweetmeats take quite a long time to cook, they are very easy to make and you are certain to agree that the time spent was worthwhile when you sample this rich, fruity combination of flavours.

Makes 20
1kg/2¼lb cooking apples
115g/4oz/⅔ cup dried, stoned (pitted) dates
250ml/8fl oz/1 cup apple juice
5ml/1 tsp ground cinnamon
50g/2oz/½ cup finely chopped walnuts

1 Cut the apples in half and core them but do not peel. Put them into a large, heavy pan and add the dates, apple juice and ground cinnamon. Cook over a very low heat, stirring occasionally, for 4–6 hours, or until the mixture has reduced to a dry paste.

2 Remove the pan from the heat and using a metal spatula, scrape the mixture into a bowl. Leave to cool completely.

3 Meanwhile, spread out the nuts on a baking sheet and toast under a preheated grill (broiler) for a few minutes, until golden. Take care that they do not scorch. Remove from the heat and leave to cool.

4 Take spoonfuls of the cooled fruit mixture and roll them into bitesize balls between the palms of your hands. Roll the balls in the toasted nuts to coat.

5 Wrap each apple and date ball in a twist of cellophane and store in an airtight container.

Variations
• *Halve the quantity of cinnamon and add 2.5ml/½ tsp ground ginger to the mixture.*
• *These fruit balls are just as delicious made with pears instead of apples. Try to find a cooking variety or an all-purpose pear. As with apples, the time taken to cook to a dry paste may vary quite considerably.*

Sweet Nutty Confections Energy 42kcals/176kJ; Fat, total 2.3g; saturated fat 0.55g; polyunsaturated fat 0.8g; monounsaturated fat 0.8g; Carbohydrate 4.95g; sugar, total 4.85g; starch 0.05g; Fibre 0.5g; Sodium1.9mg. **Apple and Date Balls** Energy 47kcals/198kJ; Fat, total 1.8g; saturated fat 0.15g; polyunsaturated fat 1.25g; monounsaturated fat 0.3g; Carbohydrate 7.6g; sugar, total7.6g; starch 0g; Fibre 1g; Sodium 1.9mg.

Chocolate Nut Clusters

These delightful chocolate-coated cookies are packed with chunky nuts and are an ideal way to end a dinner party or the perfect gift for a special friend.

Makes 30
550ml/18fl oz/2¼ cups double (heavy) cream
25g/1oz/2 tbsp unsalted (sweet) butter, diced
350ml/12fl oz/1½ cups golden (light corn) syrup
200g/7oz/scant 1 cup sugar
90g/3½oz/scant ½ packed cup soft light brown sugar
pinch of salt
15ml/1 tbsp vanilla extract
425g/15oz/3¾ cups hazelnuts, pecan nuts, walnuts, Brazil nuts or unsalted peanuts
400g/14oz plain (semisweet) chocolate, chopped
25g/1oz/2 tbsp white vegetable fat (shortening)

1 Lightly grease two baking sheets. Put the cream, butter, syrup, both kinds of sugar and the salt in a heavy pan and cook over a medium heat, stirring constantly until the sugars dissolve and the butter melts. Bring to the boil and cook, stirring frequently, for about 1 hour, until the caramel reaches 119°C/238°F (soft ball stage) on a sugar thermometer.

2 Plunge the base of the pan into cold water to stop further cooking. Cool slightly, then stir in the vanilla extract.

3 Stir the nuts into the caramel until well-coated. Using an oiled tablespoon, drop spoonfuls of the mixture on to the baking sheets, about 2.5cm/1in apart. If the mixture hardens, return to the heat. Chill for 30 minutes, until firm and cold.

4 Transfer to a wire rack placed over a baking sheet. Melt the chocolate with the white vegetable fat in a pan over a low heat, stirring until smooth. Remove from the heat and leave to cool.

5 Using a fork, dip each cluster into the chocolate mixture and lift out, shaking off the excess chocolate.

6 Place the nut clusters on the wire rack over the baking sheet. Leave to set for about 2 hours, until hardened.

Microwave Cinnamon Balls

Ground almonds make these little treats very moist. When cooked, they should be soft inside, with a very strong cinnamon flavour. They harden, however, with keeping, so it is a good idea to freeze some as they can be thawed very quickly when required.

Makes about 15
175g/6oz/1½ cups ground almonds
75g/3oz/scant ½ cup caster (superfine) sugar
15ml/1 tbsp ground cinnamon
2 egg whites
icing (confectioners') sugar, for dusting

1 Mix together the ground almonds, sugar and cinnamon in a bowl. Whisk the egg whites in another grease-free bowl until they begin to stiffen, then fold enough into the almonds to make a fairly firm mixture.

2 Wet your hands with cold water and roll small spoonfuls of the mixture into smooth balls. Place these well apart on baking parchment.

3 Microwave on full (100 per cent) power for 2½–3½ minutes, rearranging their positions twice, until cooked but still slightly soft inside.

4 Slide a metal spatula under the balls to release them from the paper and leave to cool.

5 Sift a few tablespoons of icing sugar on to a plate and when the cinnamon balls are cold slide them on to the plate. Shake gently to completely cover the cinnamon balls in sugar.

Cook's Tips
• When completely cold, store the cinnamon balls in layers interleaved with baking parchment in an airtight container for 2–3 days.
• To freeze, interleave the cinnamon balls in the same way and freeze for up to 6 months.

Chocolate Nut Clusters Energy 311kcal/1298kJ; Protein 2.7g; Carbohydrate 28.3g, of which sugars 27.9g; Fat 21.6g, of which saturates 9.2g; Cholesterol 27mg; Calcium 36mg; Fibre 1.1g; Sodium 46mg.
Microwave Cinnamon Balls Energy 93kcal/386kJ; Protein 2.9g; Carbohydrate 6g, of which sugars 5.7g; Fat 6.5g, of which saturates 0.5g; Cholesterol 0mg; Calcium 31mg; Fibre 0.9g; Sodium 10mg.

Stuffed Prunes

Chocolate-covered prunes, soaked in brandy liqueur, hide a melt-in-the-mouth coffee filling.

Makes about 30

225g/8oz/1 cup unstoned (unpitted) prunes
50ml/2fl oz/¼ cup Armagnac
30ml/2 tbsp ground coffee
150ml/¼ pint/⅔ cup double (heavy) cream
350g/12oz plain (semisweet) chocolate, broken into squares
10g/¼oz/½ tbsp white vegetable fat (shortening)
30ml/2 tbsp unsweetened cocoa powder, for dusting

1 Put the unstoned prunes in a bowl and pour the Armagnac over. Stir, then cover with clear film (plastic wrap) and set aside for 2 hours, or until the prunes have absorbed the liquid.

2 Make a slit along each prune to remove the stone (pit), making a hollow for the filling, but leaving the fruit intact.

3 Put the coffee and cream in a pan and heat almost to boiling point. Cover, infuse (steep) for 4 minutes, then heat again until almost boiling. Put 115g/4oz of the chocolate into a bowl and pour over the coffee cream through a sieve (strainer).

4 Stir until the chocolate has melted and the mixture is smooth. Leave to cool.

5 Fill a piping (pastry) bag with a small plain nozzle with the chocolate mixture. Pipe into the cavities of the prunes. Chill in the refrigerator for 20 minutes.

6 Melt the remaining chocolate in a bowl over a pan of hot water. Using a fork, dip the prunes one at a time into the chocolate to give them a generous coating. Place on baking parchment to harden. Dust each with a little cocoa powder.

Cook's Tip
Fresh dates can be used instead of prunes, if preferred.

Chocolate-coated Nut Brittle

Equal amounts of pecan nuts and almonds set in crisp caramel, then coated in dark chocolate, make a truly sensational gift – if you can bear to give them away.

Makes 20–24

115g/4oz/1 cup mixed pecan nuts and whole almonds
115g/4oz/generous ½ cup caster (superfine) sugar
60ml/4 tbsp water
200g/7oz plain (semisweet) chocolate, chopped

1 Lightly grease a baking sheet. Mix the nuts, sugar and water in a heavy pan. Cook over a low heat, stirring until the sugar has dissolved.

2 Bring the ingredients to the boil, then lower the heat to medium and cook, without stirring, until the mixture turns a rich golden brown and registers 148°C/300°F on a sugar thermometer.

3 To test without a thermometer, drop a small amount of the mixture into iced water. It should become brittle enough to snap.

4 Quickly remove the pan from the heat and tip the mixture on to the prepared baking sheet, spreading it evenly. Leave until completely cold and set hard. Break the nut brittle into pieces.

5 Place the chocolate in a heatproof bowl set over a pan of gently simmering water and heat gently until melted. Remove the chocolate from the heat and carefully dip the pieces of nut brittle into it to half-coat them. Leave the nut brittle on a sheet of baking parchment to set. Store the nut brittle in an airtight container.

Cook's Tip
This brittle looks best in coarse chunks, so don't worry if the pieces break unevenly, or if there are a few small gaps in the chocolate coating.

Stuffed Prunes Energy 100kcal/419kJ; Protein 0.9g; Carbohydrate 10.1g, of which sugars 9.9g; Fat 6.3g, of which saturates 3.8g; Cholesterol 8mg; Calcium 10mg; Fibre 0.8g; Sodium 7mg.
Chocolate-coated Nut Brittle Energy 94kcal/395kJ; Protein 0.9g; Carbohydrate 10.6g, of which sugars 10.4g; Fat 5.7g, of which saturates 1.7g; Cholesterol 1mg; Calcium 8mg; Fibre 0.4g; Sodium 1mg.

Chocolate Kisses

These rich little balls look attractive mixed together on a plate and dusted with icing sugar. Serve with ice cream or simply with a cup of coffee.

Makes 24

75g/3oz plain (semisweet) chocolate, chopped
75g/3oz white chocolate, chopped
115g/4oz/½ cup butter, at room temperature, diced
115g/4oz/generous ½ cup caster (superfine) sugar
2 eggs, beaten
225g/8oz/2 cups plain (all-purpose) flour
icing (confectioners') sugar, to decorate

1 Put the plain and white chocolate into separate small, heatproof bowls and melt the chocolates, in turn, over a pan of hot, but not boiling water, stirring until smooth. Remove the bowls from the heat and set them aside to cool slightly.

2 Beat together the butter and caster sugar until pale and fluffy. Beat in the eggs a little at a time, beating well after each addition.

3 Sift the flour over the butter, sugar and egg mixture and mix in lightly and thoroughly.

4 Halve the mixture and divide it between the two bowls of chocolate. Mix each chocolate in well. Knead the doughs until smooth, wrap in clear film (plastic wrap) and chill in the refrigerator for 1 hour.

5 Preheat the oven to 190°C/375°F/Gas 5. Grease two baking sheets.

6 Take rounded teaspoonfuls of the doughs and shape them roughly into balls. Roll the balls between the palms of your hands to make neater ball shapes. Arrange the balls on the prepared baking sheets and bake for about 12 minutes. Remove from the oven.

7 Dust with sifted icing sugar, then, using a metal spatula, transfer the balls to wire racks. Allow to cool completely.

Praline Chocolate Bites

These delicate, mouth-watering little bites never fail to impress guests, but are quite simple to make. They are perfect for serving with coffee after dinner. Dust with icing sugar for a decorative finish, if you like.

Makes 16

115g/4oz/1 cup caster (superfine) sugar
115g/4oz/1 cup whole blanched almonds
200g/7oz plain (semisweet) chocolate

1 Lightly brush a baking sheet with oil. Put the sugar in a heavy pan with 90ml/6 tbsp water. Stir over a gentle heat until the sugar has dissolved. Bring the syrup to the boil and cook for about 5 minutes, without stirring, until the mixture is golden and caramelized.

2 Remove the pan from the heat and add the almonds, gently swirling the pan to immerse them in the caramel. Tip the mixture on to the prepared baking sheet and spread out evenly with a metal spatula. Set aside and leave to cool for about 15 minutes, until hardened.

3 Meanwhile, break the chocolate into pieces and melt in a heatproof bowl set over a pan of gently simmering water. Remove the bowl from the heat.

4 Cover the surface of the hardened caramel with a sheet of clear film (plastic wrap) and hit it with a rolling pin to break it up. Put the pieces in a food processor and process until finely chopped. Transfer to a bowl and stir in the melted chocolate. Chill in the refrigerator until sufficiently set to roll into balls. Roll small pieces of the mixture into 16 balls between the palms of your hands. Place in mini paper cases to serve.

> **Cook's Tip**
> The mixture for these bites can be made ahead and stored in the freezer for up to 2 weeks. To use, thaw the mixture at room temperature until soft enough to roll into balls.

Chocolate Kisses Energy 125kcal/524kJ; Protein 1.9g; Carbohydrate 16.1g, of which sugars 9g; Fat 6.4g, of which saturates 3.7g; Cholesterol 26mg; Calcium 28mg; Fibre 0.4g; Sodium 39mg.
Praline Chocolate Bites Energy 544kcal/2280kJ; Protein 8.7g; Carbohydrate 63.8g, of which sugars 62.6g; Fat 30.1g, of which saturates 9.7g; Cholesterol 3mg; Calcium 101mg; Fibre 3.4g; Sodium 9mg.

Rich Chocolate Truffles

These irresistible after-dinner truffles melt in the mouth. Use a good-quality chocolate with a high percentage of cocoa solids to give a real depth of fabulous flavour.

Makes 20–30
175ml/6fl oz/¾ cup double (heavy) cream
1 egg yolk, beaten
275g/10oz plain (semisweet) chocolate, chopped

25g/1oz/2 tbsp unsalted (sweet) butter, diced

For the coatings
unsweetened cocoa powder
finely chopped pistachio nuts or hazelnuts
400g/14oz plain (semisweet), milk or white chocolate, or a mixture

1 Bring the cream to the boil, then remove the pan from the heat and beat in the egg yolk. Add the chocolate, then stir until melted and smooth. Stir in the butter, then strain into a bowl and leave to cool. Cover and chill for 6–8 hours.

2 Line a large baking sheet with baking parchment. Using two teaspoons, form the mixture into 20–30 balls and place on the paper. Chill if the mixture becomes too soft.

3 To coat the truffles with cocoa, sift some powder into a small bowl, drop in the truffles, one at a time, and roll to coat well. To coat them with nuts, roll the truffles in finely chopped pistachio nuts or hazelnuts.

4 To coat with chocolate, freeze the truffles for at least 1 hour. In a small bowl, melt the plain, milk or white chocolate in a heatproof bowl set over a pan of gently simmering water, stirring until melted and smooth, then leave to cool slightly.

5 Using a fork, dip the frozen truffles into the cooled chocolate, one at a time, tapping the fork on the edge of the bowl to shake off the excess. Place on a baking sheet lined with baking parchment and chill in the refrigerator for several hours before serving.

Liqueur Chocolate Truffles

Truffles can be simply dusted with cocoa, icing sugar, finely chopped nuts or coated in melted chocolate.

Makes 20 large or 30 medium truffles
250ml/8fl oz/1 cup double (heavy) cream
285g/10oz fine quality dark (bittersweet) or plain (semisweet) chocolate, chopped

45g/1½oz 3 tbsp unsalted (sweet) butter, diced
45ml/3 tbsp brandy, whisky or other liqueur

To decorate
unsweetened cocoa powder, for dusting
finely chopped pistachios
400g/14oz dark (bittersweet) chocolate

1 In a pan over medium heat, bring the cream to a boil. Remove from the heat and add the chocolate. Stir gently until melted. Stir in the butter until melted, then stir in the brandy or liqueur. Strain into a bowl and leave to cool to room temperature. Cover and chill for 4 hours or overnight.

2 Line one or two baking sheets with baking parchment. Using a small ice cream scoop, scrape up the chocolate mixture into 30 small or 20 medium balls and place them on the prepared baking sheets.

3 If dusting with cocoa, sift a thick layer of unsweetened cocoa powder on to a dish or pie plate. Roll the truffles in the cocoa, rounding them between the palms of your hands. (Dust your hands with cocoa powder to prevent the truffles from sticking.) Do not worry if the truffles are not perfectly round as the irregular shape looks more authentic.

4 Alternatively, roll the truffles in very finely chopped pistachios, to coat.

5 If coating with chocolate, do not roll in cocoa or nuts, but freeze for 1 hour. In a heatproof bowl set over a pan of gently simmering water melt the chocolate. Using a fork, dip each truffle into the melted chcolate. Place on a baking parchment lined baking sheet to set.

Rich Chocolate Truffles Energy 152kcal/634kJ; Protein 1.3g; Carbohydrate 14.4g, of which sugars 14.2g; Fat 10.3g, of which saturates 6.2g; Cholesterol 18mg; Calcium 11mg; Fibre 0.6g; Sodium 8mg.
Liqueur Chocolate Truffles Energy 172kcal/718kJ; Protein 1.3g; Carbohydrate 14.7g, of which sugars 14.4g; Fat 12.1g, of which saturates 7.4g; Cholesterol 16mg; Calcium 12mg; Fibre 0.6g; Sodium 12mg.

Coffee Chocolate Truffles

Because these classic chocolates contain fresh cream, they should be stored in the refrigerator and eaten within a few days.

Makes 24
350g/12oz plain (semisweet)
   chocolate
75ml/5 tbsp double
   (heavy) cream

30ml/2 tbsp coffee liqueur,
   such as Tia Maria, Kahlua
   or Toussiant
115g/4oz good quality
   white chocolate
115g/4oz good quality
   milk chocolate

1 Melt 225g/8oz of the plain chocolate in a bowl over a pan of barely simmering water. Stir in the cream and liqueur, then chill the mixture for 4 hours, until firm.

2 Divide the mixture into 24 equal pieces and quickly roll each into a ball. Chill for 1 more hour, or until they are firm again.

3 Melt the remaining plain, white and milk chocolate in separate small bowls. Using two forks, carefully dip eight of the truffles, one at a time, into the melted milk chocolate.

4 Repeat with the white and plain chocolate. Place the truffles on a board, covered with baking parchment or foil. Leave to set before removing and chill in the refrigerator for several hours before placing in a serving bowl or individual paper cases.

Variations
Ring the changes by adding one of the following to the truffle mixture. Ginger – Stir in 40g/1½ oz/¼ cup finely chopped crystallized (candied) ginger. Candied fruit – Stir in 50g/2oz/⅓ cup finely chopped candied fruit, such as pineapple and orange. Pistachio – Stir in 25g/1oz/¼ cup chopped skinned pistachio nuts. Hazelnut – Roll each ball of chilled truffle mixture around a whole skinned hazelnut.

Fruit and Nut Chocolates

When beautifully boxed, these chocolates make perfect presents.

Makes 20
50g/2oz ready-to-eat prunes or
   dried apricots
50g/2oz/⅓ cup sultanas (golden
   raisins) or raisins

25g/1oz/2 tbsp ready-to eat dried
   apples, figs or dates
25g/1oz/¼ cup flaked (sliced)
   almonds
25g/1oz/¼ cup hazelnuts
   or walnuts
30ml/2 tbsp lemon juice
50g/2oz good-quality dark
   (bittersweet) chocolate

1 Chop the fruit and nuts in a food processor or blender until fairly small. Add the lemon juice and process to mix.

2 Melt the chocolate in a heatproof bowl set over a pan of simmering water. Roll the fruit mixture into small balls. Using tongs, roll the balls in the melted chocolate, then place them on oiled foil to cool and set.

Malt Whisky Truffles

Blending rich chocolate with cool cream and potent whisky makes a mouth-watering end to any meal.

Makes 25–30
200g/7oz dark (bittersweet)
   chocolate, broken into pieces

150ml/¼ pint/⅔ cup double
   (heavy) cream
45ml/3 tbsp malt whisky
115g/4oz/1 cup icing
   (confectioners') sugar
unsweetened cocoa powder,
   for coating

1 Melt the chocolate in a heatproof bowl set over a pan of simmering water, stirring constantly. Leave to cool slightly.

2 Using a wire whisk, whip the cream with the whisky in a bowl until thick enough to hold its shape. Stir in the melted chocolate and icing sugar and leave until firm enough to handle.

3 Dust your hands with cocoa powder and shape the mixture into bitesize balls. Coat in cocoa powder.

Coffee Chocolate Truffles Energy 143kcal/599kJ; Protein 1.5g; Carbohydrate 15.2g, of which sugars 15.1g; Fat 8.7g, of which saturates 5.3g; Cholesterol 6mg; Calcium 30mg; Fibre 0.4g; Sodium 11mg.
Fruit and Nut Chocolates Energy 33kcal/139kJ; Protein 0.6g; Carbohydrate 4.7g, of which sugars 4.7g; Fat 1.4g, of which saturates 0.5g; Cholesterol 0mg; Calcium 10mg; Fibre 0.4g; Sodium 2mg.
Malt Whisky Truffles Energy 93kcal/387kJ; Protein 0.5g; Carbohydrate 10g, of which sugars 9.9g; Fat 5.5g, of which saturates 3.3g; Cholesterol 9mg; Calcium 8mg; Fibre 0.2g; Sodium 2mg.

Truffle Christmas Puddings

These truffles disguised as
Christmas puddings are
great fun to make and
receive. Make any flavoured
truffle, and decorate them
as you like.

Makes 20
20 plain (semisweet)
  chocolate truffles
15ml/1 tbsp unsweetened
  cocoa powder

15ml/1 tbsp icing
  (confectioners') sugar
225g/8oz/1 1/3 cups white
  chocolate chips, melted
50g/2oz/1/3 cup white marzipan
green and red food colourings
yellow food colouring
  dust (optional)

1 Make the rich chocolate truffles following the recipe on the previous page. Sift the cocoa powder and sugar together and coat the truffles in the mixture.

2 Spread about two-thirds of the melted white chocolate over a piece of baking parchment with a metal spatula. Carefully pick up the corners of the parchment and shake gently to level the surface. Leave until just set.

3 Using a 2.5cm/1in daisy cookie cutter, stamp out 20 shapes. Place a truffle on the centre of each daisy shape, securing it with a little of the reserved melted white chocolate. Leave to set completely.

4 Colour two-thirds of the marzipan green and one-third red using the food colourings. Roll out the green marzipan thinly and stamp out 40 leaves using a tiny holly leaf cutter. Mark the veins with a knife. Mould lots of tiny red beads.

5 If you like, colour the remaining melted white chocolate with yellow food colouring dust and spoon into a baking parchment piping (pastry) bag. Fold down the top, cut off the point and pipe the chocolate over the top of each truffle to resemble custard. Alternatively, leave the melted chocolate uncoloured and pipe it to resemble cream. Arrange two marzipan holly leaves and some red berries on the top.

Gingered Truffles

Wonderfully creamy, these
rich chocolate truffles are
flecked with ginger, coated
in dark chocolate and piped
with swirls of melted
white chocolate.

Makes about 30
150ml/1/4 pint/2/3 cup double
  (heavy) cream
150g/5oz dark (bittersweet)
  chocolate
25g/1oz/2 tbsp butter, diced

30ml/2 tbsp brandy
15ml/1tbsp glacé (candied)
  ginger or preserved stem
  ginger, finely chopped

To decorate
15ml/1 tbsp unsweetened
  cocoa powder
225g/8oz dark (bittersweet)
  chocolate, broken into pieces
glacé (candied) ginger, chopped
50g/2oz white chocolate

1 Put the cream in a heavy pan and bring it to the boil. Remove the pan from the heat. Break the dark chocolate into pieces and add to the cream with the butter. Leave to stand for 5 minutes, stirring occasionally, until the chocolate and butter have melted.

2 Gradually stir in the brandy and then, using an electric whisk, beat for 5–10 minutes, until the mixture is thick. Stir in the ginger. Cover and chill for 2–3 hours, until firm.

3 Put the cocoa powder on a plate. Lightly dip a teaspoonful of mixture in cocoa and then roll it into a ball with your hands. Continue until all the mixture is used up. Chill the truffles for several hours until hard.

4 Melt the chocolate pieces in a heatproof bowl set over a pan of gently simmering water. Hold a truffle on a fork and coat it completely with chocolate. Transfer to a baking sheet lined with baking parchment.

5 To decorate, coarsely chop the ginger, sprinkle it over the truffles and then leave to cool and harden. Melt the white chocolate in the same way. Spoon the chocolate into a baking parchment piping (pastry) bag, snip off the tip and pipe squiggly lines over the truffles. Chill to harden.

Truffle Christmas Puddings Energy 148kcal/616kJ; Protein 1.3g; Carbohydrate 11.9g, of which sugars 10.3g; Fat 10.5g, of which saturates 6.2g; Cholesterol 22mg; Calcium 19mg; Fibre 0.5g; Sodium 31mg.
Gingered Truffles Energy 118kcal/490kJ; Protein 1g; Carbohydrate 10.3g, of which sugars 10.1g; Fat 8.1g, of which saturates 4.9g; Cholesterol 10mg; Calcium 13mg; Fibre 0.4g; Sodium 14mg.

Truffle-filled Filo Tulips

These cups can be prepared a day ahead and stored in an airtight container.

Makes about 24

3–6 sheets filo pastry, thawed
    if frozen
45g/1½oz/3 tbsp unsalted
    (sweet) butter, melted
sugar for sprinkling
lemon rind, to decorate

For the truffles
250ml/8fl oz/1 cup double
    (heavy) cream
225g/8oz dark (bittersweet)
    or plain (semisweet)
    chocolate, chopped
55g/2oz/4 tbsp unsalted (sweet)
    butter, diced
30ml/2 tbsp brandy or
    other liqueur

1 In a pan over a medium heat, bring the cream to the boil. Remove from the heat and add the chocolate, stirring until melted. Beat in the butter and add the brandy. Strain into a bowl. Chill for 1 hour until thick.

2 Preheat the oven to 200°C/400°F/Gas 6. Grease a bun tray (muffin pan) with 24 x 4cm/1½in cups.

3 Place the filo sheets on a work surface. Cut each sheet into 6cm/2½in squares. Cover the sheets with a damp dish towel to prevent them from drying out while you are working. Keeping the filo squares covered, place one square on a work surface. Brush lightly with melted butter, turn over and brush the other side in the same way. Sprinkle with sugar. Brush melted butter on another square, place it over the first at an angle and sprinkle with sugar. Butter a third square and place it over the first two squares, so that the corners form an uneven edge. Press the layered square into the tray. Continue to fill the tray with filo squares in this way.

4 Bake the filo cups for 4–6 minutes, until golden. Cool for 10 minutes on a wire rack in the tray. Remove from the tray and leave to cool completely.

5 Stir the chocolate mixture; it should be just thick enough to pipe. Spoon it into a piping (pastry) bag with a star nozzle and pipe a swirl into each cup. Decorate with lemon rind.

Chocolate Christmas Cups

These charming petits fours, served with coffee, provide the perfect finishing touch to an elegant festive meal and – most importantly – they taste just as wonderful as they look.

Makes 35

275g/10oz plain (semisweet)
    chocolate, broken into pieces
175g/6oz cooked, cold
    Christmas pudding
75ml/5 tbsp brandy or whisky
chocolate leaves and crystallized
    (candied) cranberries,
    to decorate

1 Place the chocolate in a heatproof bowl set over a pan of gently simmering water and heat gently until melted.

2 Using a pastry brush, brush the bottom and sides of about 35 paper petit fours cases with the melted chocolate. Leave to set, then repeat, reheating the melted chocolate if necessary, applying a second coat. Leave to cool and set completely, for 4–5 hours or overnight. Reserve the remaining chocolate.

3 Crumble the Christmas pudding into a small bowl, sprinkle with brandy or whisky and leave to stand for 30–40 minutes, until the brandy is absorbed.

4 Spoon a little of the pudding mixture into each chocolate cup, smoothing the top. Reheat the remaining chocolate and spoon over the top of each cup to cover the surface of each cup to the edge. Leave to set.

5 When completely set, carefully peel off the cases and place in clean foil cases. Decorate with chocolate leaves and crystallized cranberries.

Cook's Tip
To crystallize (candy) cranberries, beat an egg white until frothy. Dip each berry first in the egg white, then in caster (superfine) sugar. Leave to dry completely on a sheet of baking parchment before using.

Truffle-filled Filo Tulips Energy 147kcal/612kJ; Protein 1.1g; Carbohydrate 9.4g, of which sugars 6.1g; Fat 11.7g, of which saturates 7.2g; Cholesterol 24mg; Calcium 15mg; Fibre 0.4g; Sodium 28mg.
Chocolate Christmas Cups Energy Energy 59kcal/249kJ; Protein 0.6g; Carbohydrate 7.5g, of which sugars 6.6g; Fat 2.7g, of which saturates 1.3g; Cholesterol 0mg; Calcium 7mg; Fibre 0.3g; Sodium 10mg.

Chocolate Box Cookies

These prettily decorated, bitesize cookies look as though they've come straight out of a box of chocolates.

Makes about 50
175g/6oz/1½ cups self-raising (self-rising) flour, plus extra for dusting
25g/1oz/¼ cup unsweetened cocoa powder
5ml/1 tsp mixed spice (apple pie spice)
50g/2oz/¼ cup unsalted (sweet) butter, softened, diced
115g/4oz/generous ½ cup caster (superfine) sugar
1 egg
1 egg yolk

For the decoration
150g/5oz milk chocolate
150g/5oz white chocolate
100g/3¾oz plain (semisweet) chocolate
whole almonds or walnuts
unsweetened cocoa powder, for dusting

1 Preheat the oven to 180°C/350°F/ Gas 4. Lightly grease two baking sheets.

2 Put the flour, cocoa powder, spice and butter into a food processor. Process until the ingredients are thoroughly blended. Add the sugar, egg and egg yolk and mix to a smooth dough.

3 Turn out on to a lightly floured surface and knead. Cut the dough in half and roll out each piece into a 33cm/13in long log. Cut each log into 1cm/½in slices. Place on the baking sheets, spaced slightly apart, and chill for 30 minutes. Bake for 10 minutes, until slightly risen. Transfer to a wire rack to cool.

4 To decorate, melt the chocolate in three separate heatproof bowls set over pans of gently simmering water.

5 Divide the cookies into six batches. Completely coat three batches, then half-coat the other three batches in plain, milk and white chocolate. Place on a sheet of baking parchment. Press a nut on to the tops of the plain chocolate-coated cookies. Drizzle white chocolate lines over some cookies. Dust the white chocolate-coated cookies with cocoa powder.

White Chocolate Snowballs

These little spherical cookies are particularly popular during the Christmas season. They're simple to make, yet utterly delicious and bursting with creamy, buttery flavours. If you like, make them in advance of a special tea as they will keep well in the refrigerator for a few days.

Makes 16
200g/7oz white chocolate
25g/1oz/2 tbsp butter, diced
90g/3½oz/generous 1 cup desiccated (dry unsweetened shredded) coconut
90g/3½oz syrup sponge or Madeira cake
icing (confectioners') sugar, for dusting

1 Break the chocolate into pieces and put in a heatproof bowl with the butter. Set the bowl over a pan of gently simmering water and stir frequently until melted. Remove the bowl from the heat and set aside for a few minutes.

2 Meanwhile, put 50g/2oz/⅔ cup of the coconut on a plate and set aside. Crumble the cake and add to the melted chocolate with the remaining coconut. Mix well to form a chunky paste.

3 Take spoonfuls of the mixture and roll into balls, about 2.5cm/1in in diameter, and immediately roll them in the reserved coconut. Place the balls on baking parchment and leave to set.

4 Before serving, dust the snowballs generously with plenty of sifted icing sugar.

Cook's Tips
• You'll need to shape the mixture into balls as soon as you've mixed in the coconut and cake; the mixture sets very quickly and you won't be able to shape it once it hardens.
• If you have any brandy or rum butter left over from Christmas lunch, substitute it for the plain butter to give these cookies an extra special flavour.

Rose Petal Truffles

An indulgent treat that demands the finest quality chocolate with at least 60 per cent cocoa solids.

Makes 80
500g/1¼lb plain (semisweet) chocolate

300ml/½ pint/1¼ cups double (heavy) cream
15ml/1 tbsp triple-distilled rose water
2 drops rose essential oil
250g/9oz plain (semisweet) chocolate, for coating
crystallized (candied) rose petals

1 Melt the chocolate and cream together in a heatproof bowl set over a pan of gently simmering water. Add the rose water and essential oil.

2 Pour into a baking tin lined with baking parchment. Leave to cool and when the mixture is nearly firm, shape teaspoonfuls of it into balls. Chill the truffles.

3 To finish, melt the chocolate in a heatproof bowl set over a pan of gently simmering water. Skewer a truffle and dip it into the melted chocolate, coating it completely. Place a crystallized rose petal on each before the chocolate sets.

Swedish Rose Chocolate Balls

This is a very rich and delicious chocolate sweet.

Makes 20–30
150g/5oz good quality milk chocolate
30ml/2 tbsp ground almonds
30ml/2 tbsp caster (superfine) sugar

2 egg yolks
10ml/2 tsp strong coffee or coffee extract
15ml/1 tbsp dark rum
15ml/1 tbsp triple-distilled rose water
40g/1½ oz/¼ cup chocolate vermicelli

1 Grind the chocolate in a processor and add to the other ingredients except the rose water and vermicelli. Make into tiny balls by rolling small spoonfuls between your fingers. Chill well. Dip into the rose water and roll in the chocolate vermicelli.

Chocolate and Cherry Colettes

Luxurious and sophisticated, these unique handmade petits fours add that indefinable distinctive touch to any special occasion meal.

Makes 18–20
115g/4oz plain (semisweet) or dark (bittersweet) chocolate, chopped into small pieces

75g/3oz white or milk chocolate, chopped into small pieces
25g/1oz/2 tbsp unsalted (sweet) butter, melted
15ml/1 tbsp Kirsch
60ml/4 tbsp double (heavy) cream
18–20 maraschino cherries or liqueur-soaked cherries
milk chocolate curls, to decorate

1 Melt the plain or dark chocolate in a heatproof bowl set over a pan of gently simmering water, stirring occasionally. Remove the bowl from the heat.

2 Spoon the melted chocolate into 18–20 foil petits four cases, dividing it equally among them. Using a small brush, spread the chocolate evenly up the sides of the cases, then leave to cool until the chocolate has set completely.

3 Put the white or milk chocolate and the butter in another heatproof bowl and melt over a pan of gently simmering water, stirring occasionally. Remove from the heat and leave to cool slightly. Stir in the Kirsch, then stir in the cream. Leave to cool until the mixture is just thick enough to hold its shape.

4 When the chocolate cups are set, carefully peel off and discard the foil cases. Place one cherry in each chocolate cup. Spoon the chocolate and cream mixture into a piping (pastry) bag fitted with a small star nozzle. Pipe the mixture over the cherries to fill each of the cases, then pipe a generous swirl on top to decorate. Top each colette with two or three milk chocolate curls. Leave to set before serving.

Variation
Substitute brandy or Drambuie for the Kirsch, if you like.

Rose Petal Truffles Energy 47kcal/197kJ; Protein 0.9g; Carbohydrate 5g, of which sugars 3.9g; Fat 2.5g, of which saturates 1.1g; Cholesterol 15mg; Calcium 16mg; Fibre 0.1g; Sodium 5mg.
Swedish Rose Chocolate Balls Energy 66kcal/276kJ; Protein 0.5g; Carbohydrate 6.01g, of which sugars 5.93g; Fat 4.63g, of which saturates 0.01g; Cholesterol 5.7mg; Calcium 4.9mg; Fibre 0.23g; Sodium 1.38mg.
Chocolate and Cherry Colettes Energy 79kcal/327kJ; Protein 0.7g; Carbohydrate 6.8g, of which sugars 6.8g; Fat 5.4g, of which saturates 3.3g; Cholesterol 7mg; Calcium 14mg; Fibre 0.2g; Sodium 13mg.

Double Chocolate Dipped Fruit

Make the most of your favourite soft seasonal fruit by double dipping them in chocolate – a perfect and light dessert or treat.

Makes 24 coated pieces
*fruits – about 24 pieces
(strawberries, cherries, orange
segments, large seedless*

*grapes, physalis, kumquats,
stoned (pitted) prunes, stoned
(pitted) dates, dried apricots,
dried peaches or dried pears)
115g/4oz white chocolate,
chopped into small pieces
115g/4oz dark (bittersweet) or
plain (semisweet) chocolate,
chopped into small pieces*

1 Clean and prepare fruits; wipe strawberries with a soft cloth or brush gently with a pastry brush. Wash firm-skinned fruits such as cherries and grapes and dry well. Peel and leave whole or cut up any other fruits being used.

2 Put the white chocolate into a heatproof bowl and melt over a pan of gently simmering water. Remove from the heat and cool, stirring frequently, until tepid (about 29°C/84°F).

3 Line a baking sheet with baking parchment. Holding each fruit by the stem or end and at an angle, dip one by one into the melted chocolate so that they are about two-thirds coated. Allow the excess to drop off back into the bowl, then place on the prepared baking sheet. Chill in the refrigerator for about 20 minutes, until the chocolate has set.

4 Put the pieces of dark or plain chocolate into a heatproof bowl and melt over a pan over gently simmering water, stirring frequently until smooth. Remove the bowl from the heat and leave the chocolate to cool to just below body temperature (about 30°C/86°F).

5 Take each white chocolate-coated fruit in turn from the baking sheet and, holding by the stem or end and at the opposite angle, dip the bottom third of each piece into the melted chocolate, creating a chevron effect. Set on the baking sheet. Chill for 15 minutes or until set. Before serving, allow the fruit to stand at room temperature for 10–15 minutes.

Cognac and Ginger Creams

You will need plastic moulds to create these luxurious chocolates with just the right touch of expertise, but the technique is quite straightforward. All you need is a little patience.

Makes 18–20
*300g/11oz/ dark (bittersweet)
chocolate, chopped into
small pieces*

*45ml/3 tbsp double
(heavy) cream
30ml/2 tbsp cognac
4 pieces of preserved stem ginger,
drained and finely chopped,
plus 15ml/1 tbsp syrup from
the jar
crystallized (candied) ginger,
to decorate*

1 Polish the insides of 18–20 chocolate moulds carefully with cotton wool (absorbent cotton). Melt about two-thirds of the chocolate in a heatproof bowl over a pan of barely simmering water, then remove from the heat. Spoon a little melted chocolate into each mould. Reserve a little of the melted chocolate for sealing the creams.

2 Using a small brush, gently sweep the chocolate up the sides of the moulds to coat them evenly, then invert them on to a sheet of baking parchment and set aside until the chocolate sets.

3 Melt the remaining chopped chocolate over simmering water. Remove from the heat and stir in the cream, cognac, preserved stem ginger and ginger syrup, mixing well. Spoon into the chocolate-lined moulds. If the reserved chocolate has solidified, melt it again, then spoon a little into each mould to seal.

4 Leave the chocolates in a cool place, but not in the refrigerator, until set.

5 To remove them from the moulds, gently press them out on to a cool surface, such as a marble slab. Decorate with small pieces of crystallized ginger. Keep the chocolates cool if not serving them immediately.

Double Chocolate Dipped Fruit Energy 54kcal/227kJ; Protein 0.8g; Carbohydrate 6.8g, of which sugars 6.8g; Fat 2.8g, of which saturates 1.7g; Cholesterol 0mg; Calcium 17mg; Fibre 0.3g; Sodium 7mg.
Cognac and Ginger Creams Energy 93kcal/390kJ; Protein 0.8g; Carbohydrate 10.2g, of which sugars 10g; Fat 5.4g, of which saturates 3.3g; Cholesterol 4mg; Calcium 6mg; Fibre 0.4g; Sodium 3mg.

Fruit Fondant Chocolates

These chocolates are simple to make using pre-formed plastic moulds, yet look very professional. Fruit fondant is available from sugarcraft stores and comes in a variety of flavours including coffee and nut. Try a mixture of flavours using a small quantity of each, or use just a single flavour.

Makes 24
225g/8oz plain (semisweet), milk or white chocolate
115g/4oz/1 cup real fruit liquid fondant
15–20ml/3–4 tsp cooled boiled water

For the decoration
15ml/1 tbsp melted plain (semisweet), milk or white chocolate

1 Melt the chocolate. Use a piece of cotton wool (absorbent cotton) to polish the insides of the chocolate moulds, ensuring that they are spotlessly clean. Fill up the shapes in one plastic tray to the top, leave for a few seconds, then invert the tray over the bowl of melted chocolate allowing the excess chocolate to fall back into the bowl. Sit the tray on the work surface and draw a metal spatula across the top to remove the excess chocolate and to neaten the edges. Chill until the chocolate has set. Repeat to fill the remaining trays.

2 Sift the fruit fondant mixture into a bowl. Gradually stir in enough water to give it the consistency of thick cream. Place the fondant in a baking parchment piping (pastry) bag, fold down the top and snip off the end. Fill each chocolate case almost to the top by piping in the fondant. Leave for 30 minutes or until a skin has formed on the surface of the fondant.

3 Spoon the remaining melted chocolate over the fondant to fill each mould level with the top. Chill until the chocolate has set hard. Invert the tray and press out the chocolates one by one. Place the melted chocolate of a contrasting colour into a baking parchment piping bag, fold down the top, snip off the point and pipe lines across the top of each chocolate. Leave to set, then pack into pretty boxes and tie with ribbon.

Chocolate Almond Torrone

Serve this Italian speciality in thin slices.

Makes 20
115g/4oz plain (semisweet) chocolate, chopped
50g/2oz/4 tbsp unsalted (sweet) butter
1 egg white
115g/4oz/generous ½ cup caster (superfine) sugar
50g/2oz/½ cup ground almonds

75g/3oz/¾ cup chopped toasted almonds
75ml/5 tbsp mixed chopped (candied) peel

For the coating
175g/6oz white chocolate, chopped
25g/1oz/2 tbsp unsalted (sweet) butter
115g/4oz/1 cup flaked (sliced) almonds toasted

1 Melt the chocolate with the butter in a heatproof bowl over a pan of hot water, stirring until the mixture is smooth.

2 In a clean, grease-free bowl, whisk the egg white with the sugar until stiff. Gradually beat in the melted chocolate, then stir in the ground almonds, chopped toasted almonds and peel.

3 Tip the mixture on to a large sheet of baking parchment and shape into a thick roll. As the mixture cools, use the parchment to press the roll firmly into a triangular shape. Twist the parchment over and chill until completely set.

4 To make the coating, melt the white chocolate with the butter in a heatproof bowl set over a pan of hot water. Unwrap the chocolate roll and spread the white chocolate quickly over the surface. Press the almonds in a thin even coating over the chocolate, working quickly before the chocolate sets.

5 Chill again until firm, then cut the torronne into fairly thin slices to serve.

> **Cook's Tip**
> The mixture can be shaped into a simple round roll instead of the triangular shape, if you prefer.

Chocolate and Coffee Mint Thins

These coffee-flavoured chocolate squares contain pieces of crisp minty caramel and are perfect for serving with after-dinner coffee.

Makes 16
75g/3oz/scant ½ cup sugar
75ml/5 tbsp water

3 drops oil of peppermint
15ml/1 tbsp strong-flavoured ground coffee
75ml/5 tbsp near-boiling double (heavy) cream
225g/8oz plain (semisweet) chocolate
10g/¼oz/½ tbsp unsalted (sweet) butter

1 Line an 18cm/7in square tin (pan) with baking parchment. Gently heat the sugar and water in a heavy pan until the sugar has dissolved. Add the peppermint oil, and boil until a light caramel colour.

2 Pour the caramel on to an oiled baking sheet and leave to harden, then crush into small pieces.

3 Put the coffee in a small bowl and pour the hot cream over. Leave to infuse (steep) for about 4 minutes, then strain through a fine sieve (strainer). Melt the chocolate and butter in a bowl over barely simmering water. Remove from the heat and beat in the hot coffee cream. Stir in the mint caramel.

4 Pour the mixture into the prepared tin and smooth the surface level. Leave in a cool place to set for at least 4 hours, preferably overnight.

5 Carefully turn out the chocolate on to a board and peel off the parchment. Cut the chocolate into squares with a sharp knife and store in an airtight container until needed.

> **Cook's Tip**
> Don't put the chocolate in the refrigerator to set, or it may lose its glossy appearance and become too brittle to cut easily into neat squares.

Chocolate Boxes

These tiny chocolate boxes make the perfect containers for handmade chocolates or other sweets. Make them as you need them.

Makes 4
225g/8oz/plain (semisweet), or milk chocolate, melted
50g/2oz white chocolate

For the decoration
handmade chocolates or sweets (candies), to fill
2m/2yd ribbon, 1cm/½in wide

1 Line a large baking sheet with baking parchment.

2 Pour all but 15ml/1 tbsp of the chocolate over the parchment paper and quickly spread to the edges using a metal spatula. Pick up 2 corners of the paper and drop; do this several times on each side to level the surface of the chocolate.

3 Leave the chocolate until almost set but still pliable. Place a clean piece of baking parchment on the surface, invert the chocolate sheet and peel the parchment away from the back of the chocolate. Using a ruler and a craft knife, measure and cut the chocolate sheet into 16 squares each 5cm/2in to form the sides of the boxes. Measure and cut out 8 squares each 5.5cm/2¼in for the lids and bases of each of the boxes.

4 To assemble the boxes, paint a little of the remaining melted chocolate along the top edges of a chocolate square using a fine brush.

5 Place the side pieces in position one at a time, brushing the side edges to join the four squares together to form a box. Leave to set. Repeat to make the remaining three boxes.

6 Melt the white chocolate and spoon into a baking parchment piping (icing) bag. Fold down the top and snip off the point. Pipe 20 chocolate loops on to a sheet of baking parchment and leave them to set. Remove from the parchment with the tip of a brush. Stick them in place on each side of the box using melted chocolate.

Chocolate Boxes Energy 353kcal/1479kJ; Protein 3.8g; Carbohydrate 43g, of which sugars 42.5g; Fat 19.6g, of which saturates 11.8g; Cholesterol 3mg; Calcium 52mg; Fibre 1.4g; Sodium 17mg.
Chocolate and Coffee Mint Thins Energy 118kcal/494kJ; Protein 0.8g; Carbohydrate 13.9g, of which sugars 13.8g; Fat 7g, of which saturates 4.3g; Cholesterol 9mg; Calcium 10mg; Fibre 0.4g; Sodium 6mg.

Peppermint Chocolate Sticks

With their double flavour, these are so much nicer than any kind of chocolate sticks you can buy.

Makes about 80
115g/4oz/½ cup sugar
150ml/¼ pint/⅔ cup water

2.5ml/½ tsp peppermint extract
200g/7oz plain (semisweet)
   chocolate, chopped into
   small pieces
60ml/4 tbsp toasted desiccated
   (dry unsweetened
   shredded) coconut

1 Lightly grease a large baking sheet. Place the sugar and water in a small, heavy pan and heat gently, stirring, until the sugar has dissolved.

2 Bring to the boil and boil rapidly without stirring until the syrup registers 138°C/280°F on a sugar thermometer. Remove from the heat and stir in the peppermint extract.

3 Pour the mixture on to the prepared baking sheet and leave until set.

4 Break up the peppermint mixture into a small bowl and use the end of a rolling pin to crush it into small pieces.

5 Melt the chocolate in a heatproof bowl set over a pan of gently simmering water. Remove the bowl from the heat and stir in the mint pieces and desiccated coconut.

6 Place a 30 × 25cm/12 × 10in sheet of baking parchment on a flat surface. Spread the chocolate mixture over it, leaving a narrow border all around, to make a rectangle 25 × 20cm/10 × 8in. Leave to set.

7 When the chocolate rectangle is firm, use a sharp knife to cut into thin sticks, each about 6cm/2½in long.

> **Variation**
> *You can also use dark (bittersweet) chocolate for these sticks.*

Chocolate Peppermint Crisps

If you do not have a sugar thermometer, test cooked sugar for "hard ball stage".

Makes 30
50g/2oz/¼ cup sugar
50ml/2fl oz/¼ cup water
5ml/1 tsp peppermint extract
225g/8oz plain (semisweet)
   chocolate, chopped
unflavoured oil, for greasing

1 Lightly brush a large baking sheet with unflavoured oil. In a pan over a medium heat, heat the sugar and water, swirling the pan gently until the sugar dissolves. Boil rapidly until the temperature registers 138°C/280°F on a sugar thermometer. Remove the pan from the heat and add the peppermint extract and swirl to mix. Pour on to the prepared baking sheet and leave to set and cool completely.

2 When the mixture is cold, break it into pieces. Place in a food processor fitted with a metal blade and process to fine crumbs but do not over-process it.

3 Line two baking sheets with baking parchment. Place the chocolate in a small heatproof bowl set over a pan of gently simmering water. Place over a very low heat until the chocolate has melted, stirring frequently until smooth. Remove from the heat and stir in the peppermint mixture.

4 Using a teaspoon, drop small mounds on to the prepared baking sheets. Using the back of the spoon, spread to 4cm/1½in rounds. Cool, then chill in the refrigerator for about 1 hour, until set. Peel off the parchment and store in airtight containers with baking parchment between the layers.

> **Cook's Tip**
> *To test for "hard ball stage", drop a little of the syrup into a bowl of ice cold water. Gather it together with your fingertips and if it forms a hard ball, the syrup has reached the required temperature.*

Peppermint Chocolate Sticks Energy 23kcal/96kJ; Protein 0.2g; Carbohydrate 3.1g, of which sugars 3.1g; Fat 1.2g, of which saturates 0.8g; Cholesterol 0mg; Calcium 2mg; Fibre 0.2g; Sodium 0mg.
Chocolate Peppermint Crisps Energy 45kcal/188kJ; Protein 0.4g; Carbohydrate 6.5g, of which sugars 6.4g; Fat 2.1g, of which saturates 1.3g; Cholesterol 0mg; Calcium 3mg; Fibre 0.2g; Sodium 1mg.

Marshmallows

These light and fragrant mouthfuls of pale pink mousse are flavoured with rose water.

Makes 500g/1¼lb

45ml/3 tbsp icing
    (confectioners') sugar
45ml/3 tbsp cornflour
    (cornstarch)
50ml/2fl oz/¼ cup cold water
45ml/3 tbsp rose water
25g/1oz powdered gelatine
pink food colouring
450g/1lb/2 cups sugar
30ml/2 tbsp liquid glucose (clear
    corn syrup)
250ml/8fl oz/1 cup boiling water
2 egg whites

1 Lightly grease a 28 × 18cm/11 × 7in Swiss roll tin (jelly roll pan). Sift together the icing sugar and cornflour and use some of this mixture to coat the inside of the tin evenly. Shake out the excess.

2 Mix together the cold water, rose water, gelatine and a drop of pink food colouring in a heatproof bowl. Place over a pan of hot water and stir occasionally until the gelatine has dissolved.

3 Place the sugar, liquid glucose and boiling water in a heavy pan. Stir over a low heat to dissolve the sugar completely. Ensure that there are no sugar crystals around the water line; if so, wash these down with a brush dipped in cold water.

4 Bring the syrup to the boil and boil without stirring until the temperature reaches 127°C/260°F on a sugar thermometer. Remove from the heat. Stir in the gelatine mixture.

5 Whisk the egg whites stiffly in a large grease-free bowl using an electric hand whisk. Pour a steady stream of syrup on to the egg whites, constanly whisking for about 3 minutes, or until the mixture is thick and foamy.

6 Pour the mixture into the prepared tin and leave to set overnight. Sift the remaining icing sugar mixture over the surface and over a board. Ease the mixture away from the tin with an oiled metal spatula and invert on to the board. Cut into 2.5cm/1in squares, coating the cut sides with the sugar mixture.

Marzipan Logs

Shiny gold-coated sweets, sometimes called dragées, give these irresistible petits fours an air of luxury. They would make a welcome gift to a dinner-party hostess for serving at the end of a meal.

Makes about 12

225g/8oz marzipan, at
    room temperature
115g/4oz/⅔ cup candied orange
    peel, chopped
30ml/2 tbsp orange-flavoured
    liqueur
15ml/1 tbsp soft light
    brown sugar
edible gold powder
75g/3oz plain (semisweet)
    chocolate, melted
gold-coated sweets (candies)

1 Knead the marzipan well, then mix in the chopped peel and liqueur. Set aside for about 1 hour to dry.

2 Break off small pieces of the mixture and roll them into log shapes with your hands.

3 Dip the tops of half of the marzipan logs in the sugar and brush them lightly with edible gold powder.

4 Dip the remaining logs in the melted chocolate. Place on baking parchment and press a gold-coated sweet in the centre of each. Leave to set.

5 Arrange all the logs on a plate and decorate the arrangement with extra gold-coated sweets.

> **Cook's Tips**
> • Store the marzipan logs in an airtight container, interleaved with baking parchment, for a maximum of 2 days. After this, they will start to dry out and become hard and brittle.
> • Edible gold powder may also be labelled gold lustre or sparkle dust. A silver version is also available, as too are silver dragées.

Marshmallows Energy 2228kcal/9504kJ; Protein 8.5g; Carbohydrate 584.1g, of which sugars 529.3g; Fat 0.3g, of which saturates 0g; Cholesterol 0mg; Calcium 275mg; Fibre 0g; Sodium 220mg.
Marzipan Logs Energy 137kcal/580kJ; Protein 1.3g; Carbohydrate 23.6g, of which sugars 23.6g; Fat 4.2g, of which saturates 1.2g; Cholesterol 0mg; Calcium 28mg; Fibre 1g; Sodium 31mg.

Marzipan Fruits

These eye-catching and realistic fruits will make a perfect gift for lovers of marzipan.

Makes 450g/1 lb
450g/1lb white marzipan
yellow, green, red, orange and burgundy food colouring dusts
30g/2 tbsp whole cloves

1 Line a baking sheet with baking parchment. Quarter the marzipan and cut a quarter into ten equal pieces. Put small heaps of the food colouring dust on a plate. Halve two-thirds of the cloves, making a stem and core end.

2 Roll each of the 10 pieces into a ball. Dip a ball into the yellow colouring and roll between the palms of your hands. Dip it into the green colouring and roll to a greenish yellow. Roll one end of the ball with your finger to make a pear shape. Press a clove stem and core into each end. Make 9 more pears and place on the baking sheet.

3 Cut another marzipan quarter into 10 and roll into balls. Dip each into green colouring and roll in your hands. Add a spot of red and roll again. Indent the top and base of each ball with a ball tool or the end of a paintbrush to make apples. Add stems and cores.

4 Repeat as above using another piece of the marzipan to make 10 orange coloured balls. Roll each over the surface of a fine grater to give the texture of an orange skin. Press a clove core into the base of each.

5 Reserve a small piece of the remaining marzipan, roll the rest into tiny beads and colour them burgundy. Put a whole clove on the baking sheet and arrange a cluster of beads to make a bunch of grapes. Make three more.

6 Roll out the remaining tiny piece of marzipan thinly and brush with green food colouring dust. Using a small vine leaf cutter, cut out 8 leaves, mark the veins with a knife and place 2 on each bunch of grapes, bending to give a realistic appearance. When all the marzipan fruits are dry, pack into gift boxes.

Coconut Ice

A great favourite with both adults and children, the ice is always sweet and juicy. However, if you've only ever eaten sweets made with dried coconut, you are about to experience an unforgettable taste explosion.

Makes 16 squares each 5cm/2in
1 coconut
450g/1lb sugar
120ml/4fl oz/½ cup coconut milk
25g/1oz butter
red food colouring
flavourless oil, for greasing

1 Grease a 20cm/8in square cake tin (pan) or brush with a little flavourless oil.

2 Crack the coconut and drain off the milk into a bowl. Break open the shell, remove the flesh and grate it.

3 Put the sugar, reserved coconut milk and butter into a pan and bring to the boil over a low heat, stirring frequently, until the sugar has dissolved and the butter has melted. Gradually stir in the grated coconut and continue to boil, stirring constantly, for 10 minutes, until thickened. Remove the pan from the heat.

4 Divide the mixture between two bowls. Add a few drops of red food colouring to one batch and mix well to colour it pink. Leave the second batch uncoloured.

5 Firmly press the uncoloured coconut mixture into the prepared tin to make an even layer. Cover with the pink coconut mixture, pressing it down into an even layer. Leave to set, then cut into squares with a sharp knife. The squares can be wrapped in individual cellophane parcels, if you like.

Cook's Tip
To crack a coconut, hold it firmly in one hand and pierce the eyes with a skewer. Pour the milk into a bowl. Hit the coconut all around the centre with a hammer and lever apart. Scoop out the flesh with a small knife and peel off the skin.

Marzipan Fruits Energy 1837kcal/7752kJ; Protein 28.3g; Carbohydrate 314.7g, of which sugars 304.2g; Fat 61g, of which saturates 5.2g; Cholesterol 0mg; Calcium 351mg; Fibre 8.6g; Sodium 100mg.
Coconut Ice Energy 162kcal/683kJ; Protein 0.5g; Carbohydrate 30.2g, of which sugars 30.2g; Fat 5.2g, of which saturates 4.2g; Cholesterol 3mg; Calcium 19mg; Fibre 0.9g; Sodium 21mg.

Turkish Delight

You either love or loathe this somewhat chewy sweetmeat – there are no half measures. Fans will certainly welcome this versatile recipe that can be made in minutes.

Makes 450g/1lb
450g/1lb/2 cups sugar
300ml/¹/₂ pint/1 ¹/₄ cups water

25g/1oz powdered gelatine
2.5ml/¹/₂ tsp cream of tartar
30ml/2 tbsp rose water
pink food colouring
25g/1oz/3 tbsp icing
   (confectioners') sugar, sifted
15ml/1 tbsp cornflour
   (cornstarch)

1 Wet the insides of 2 × 18cm/7in shallow square tins (pans) with water. Place the sugar and all but 60ml/4 tbsp of water into a heavy pan. Heat gently, stirring occasionally, until the sugar has dissolved.

2 Blend the gelatine and remaining water in a small bowl and place over a pan of hot water. Stir occasionally until dissolved. Bring the sugar syrup to a boil and boil steadily for about 8 minutes or until the syrup registers 127°C/260°F on a sugar thermometer. Stir the cream of tartar into the gelatine, then pour into the boiling syrup and stir until well blended. Remove from the heat.

3 Add the rose water and a few drops of pink food colouring to tint the mixture pale pink. Pour the mixture into the prepared tins and leave to set for several hours or overnight. Dust a sheet of baking parchment with some of the sugar and cornflour. Dip the base of the tin in hot water. Invert on to the paper. Cut into 2.5cm/1in squares using an oiled knife. Toss in icing sugar to coat evenly.

> **Variation**
> *Try substituting the same quantity of orange flower water or crème de menthe or a few drops of lemon extract for the rose water, and using orange, green or yellow food colouring.*

Rose Turkish Delight

In the Middle East, these sweets are served with tiny cups of very strong coffee.

Makes 450g/1lb
60ml/4tbsp triple-distilled
   rose water
30ml/2tbsp powdered gelatine
450g/1lb/1³/₄ cups sugar
150ml/¹/₄ pint/²/₃ cup water

cochineal colouring
9 drops rose essential oil
25g/1oz/¹/₄ cup coarsely chopped
   blanched almonds
20g/³/₄oz/scant ¹/₄ cup cornflour
   (cornstarch)
65g/2¹/₂oz/¹/₃ cup icing
   (confectioners') sugar

1 Lightly brush a 15–18cm/6–7in square baking tin (pan) with flavourless oil.

2 Pour the rose water into a bowl and sprinkle the gelatine over the surface. Set aside to soften and become spongy.

3 Meanwhile put the sugar and measured water into a pan and bring to the boil over a low heat, stirring until the sugar has dissolved. When the syrup is clear, boil until the mixture registers 116°C/234°F on a sugar thermometer.

4 Remove the pan from the heat and add the gelatine and rose water. Return the pan to a low heat and cook, stirring constantly, until the gelatine has dissolved.

5 Remove the pan from the heat and stir in a few drops of cochineal to colour the mixture pale pink, then stir in the rose oil and almonds.

6 Pour the mixture into the prepared tin and leave to set. Using a sharp knife, cut the Turkish delight into pieces. Sift the cornflour and icing sugar together, then sprinkle it over the pieces.

> **Cook's Tip**
> *Although it is expensive, cochineal produces the purest red colouring.*

Turkish Delight Energy 1944kcal/8295kJ; Protein 2.5g; Carbohydrate 515.4g, of which sugars 501.6g; Fat 0.1g, of which saturates 0g; Cholesterol 0mg; Calcium 257mg; Fibre 0g; Sodium 37mg.
Rose Turkish Delight Energy 2368kcal/10080kJ; Protein 36.7g; Carbohydrate 558.3g, of which sugars 539.2g; Fat 14.1g, of which saturates 1.1g; Cholesterol 0mg; Calcium 336mg; Fibre 1.9g; Sodium 45mg.

Macaroon Candies

These tasty little macaroons, decorated with almonds and cherries, make delightful petits fours to serve with after-dinner liqueurs and coffee or with a glass of sweet dessert wine.

Makes 30
50g/2oz/1½ cup ground almonds
50g/2oz/¼ cup caster (superfine) sugar

15ml/1 tbsp cornflour (cornstarch)
1.5–2.5ml/¼–½ tsp almond extract
1 egg white, whisked
15 flaked (sliced) almonds
4 glacé (candied) cherries, quartered
icing (confectioners') sugar or unsweetened cocoa powder, for dusting

1 Preheat the oven to 160°C/325°F/Gas 3. Line two baking sheets with baking parchment.

2 Place the almonds, sugar, cornflour and almond extract into a bowl and mix together well using a wooden spoon.

3 Stir in enough egg white to form a soft piping consistency. Spoon the mixture into a nylon piping (pastry) bag fitted with a 1cm/½in plain nozzle.

4 Pipe about 15 rounds of mixture on to each baking sheet, well spaced apart. Press a flaked almond on to half the macaroons and quartered glacé cherries on to the remainder.

5 Bake for 10–15 minutes, until firm to touch. Leave to cool on the baking sheets and dust with sugar or the unsweetened cocoa powder before removing from the baking parchment.

> **Variation**
> To make chocolate macaroons, replace the cornflour (cornstarch) with the same quantity of unsweetened cocoa powder. Decorate with pieces of marrons glacés and dust with sifted unsweetened cocoa powder when cold.

Creamy Fudge

A good selection of fudge always makes a welcome change from chocolates and won't melt like chocolate. Mix and match the flavours.

Makes 900g/2lb
50g/2oz/4 tbsp unsalted (sweet) butter
450g/1lb/2 cups sugar
300ml/½ pint/1¼ cups double (heavy) cream
150ml/¼ pint/⅔ cup milk

45ml/3 tbsp water (this can be replaced with orange, apricot or cherry brandy, or strong coffee)

For the flavourings
225g/8oz/1 cup plain (semisweet) or milk chocolate chips
115g/4oz/1 cup chopped almonds, hazelnuts, walnuts or Brazil nuts
115g/4oz/½ cup chopped glacé (candied) cherries, dates or dried apricots

1 Grease a 20cm/8in shallow square tin (pan). Place the butter, sugar, cream, milk and water into a heavy pan. Heat very gently, stirring occasionally, until the sugar has dissolved.

2 Bring the mixture to the boil and boil steadily, stirring constantly to prevent the mixture from burning on the base of the pan. Boil until the fudge reaches just under soft ball stage, 113°C/230°F for a soft fudge.

3 If you are making chocolate flavoured fudge, add the chocolate at this stage. Remove the pan from the heat and beat thoroughly until the mixture starts to thicken.

4 Alternatively, add the chopped nuts for a nutty fudge, or glacé cherries or dried fruit for a fruit-flavoured fudge. Beat well until evenly blended.

5 Pour the fudge into the prepared tin. Leave the mixture until cool and almost set. Using a sharp knife, mark the fudge into small squares and leave in the tin until quite firm.

6 Turn the fudge out on to a board and invert. Using a long-bladed knife, cut into neat squares. Dust some squares with icing sugar and drizzle other squares with melted chocolate, if you like.

Macaroon Candies Energy 102kcal/426kJ; Protein 2.8g; Carbohydrate 7.8g, of which sugars 7.5g; Fat 6.9g, of which saturates 0.6g; Cholesterol 13mg; Calcium 33mg; Fibre 0.9g; Sodium 5mg.
Creamy Fudge Energy 5886kcal/24635kJ; Protein 40.4g; Carbohydrate 708.8g, of which sugars 704.5g; Fat 340.8g, of which saturates 171g; Cholesterol 540mg; Calcium 874mg; Fibre 14.1g; Sodium 512mg.

Easy Hazelnut Fudge

The sweetness of the nuts combines beautifully with plain chocolate in this truly scrumptious fail-safe recipe.

350g/12oz/2 cups plain (semisweet) chocolate chips
5ml/1 tsp hazelnut liqueur (optional)

Makes 16 squares
150ml/¼ pint/⅔ cup evaporated milk
375g/13oz/1¾ cups sugar
pinch of salt
50g/2oz/½ cup halved hazelnuts

1 Generously grease a 20cm/8in square cake tin (pan).

2 Combine the evaporated milk, sugar and salt in a heavy pan. Bring to the boil over a medium heat, stirring constantly. Simmer gently, stirring, for about 5 minutes.

3 Remove the pan from the heat and add the hazelnuts, chocolate chips and liqueur, if using. Stir until the chocolate has completely melted.

4 Quickly pour the fudge mixture into the prepared tin and spread it out evenly. leave to cool.

5 When the fudge has set completely, cut it into 2.5cm/1in squares. Store in an airtight container, separating the layers with sheets of baking parchment.

Variation
• For Easy Peanut Butter Fudge, substitute peanut butter chips for the chocolate chips and replace the hazelnuts with the same quantity of peanuts.
• If can't find hazelnut liqueur, suitable substitutes include Cointreau (orange), Drambuie (honey and heather), Galliano (honey and vanilla) or Tia Maria (coffee). For a non-alcoholic alternative, use orgeat (sugar-free) syrup.

Vanilla Fudge

Perennially popular, home-made fudge ends a meal beautifully when served as a petit four. This meltingly good vanilla version is sure to become a favourite.

Makes 60 pieces
175g/6oz/¾ cup butter
900g/2lb/4 cups soft light brown sugar
400g/14oz condensed milk
2.5ml/½tsp vanilla extract, or to taste

1 Butter a shallow tin (pan), about 18 x 28cm/7 x 11in. Put the butter and 150ml/¼ pint/⅔ cup water into a large, heavy pan and warm very gently over a low heat until the butter melts.

2 Add the sugar and stir over a low heat until it has completely dissolved. Raise the heat and bring the mixture to the boil. Boil hard until it reaches hard crack stage (168°C/336°F on a sugar thermometer). Test by pouring a small amount into a saucer of cold water to form strands that can be cracked.

3 Remove from the heat and beat in the condensed milk with a wooden spoon. Return to a medium heat, stirring, for a few minutes. Remove from the heat again, add the vanilla extract, and beat again with a spoon until glossy. Pour the mixture into the tin. Leave to cool.

4 Cut the fudge into cubes and store in an airtight tin until required. Place in petits fours cases to serve.

Cook's Tip
It is essential to keep stirring the fudge mixture while it is boiling, as it may otherwise catch on the base of the pan. Even if this does not taint the flavour, the mixture will not set properly and the fudge will be spoiled.

Variation
For Coffee Fudge, add 30ml/2 tbsp coffee extract.

Easy Hazelnut Fudge Energy 234kcal/987kJ; Protein 2.4g; Carbohydrate 39.5g, of which sugars 39.3g; Fat 8.5g, of which saturates 4.1g; Cholesterol 3mg; Calcium 48mg; Fibre 0.8g; Sodium 14mg.
Vanilla Fudge Energy per piece 103kcal/435kJ; Protein 0.7g; Carbohydrate 19.4g, of which sugars 19.4g; Fat 3.1g, of which saturates 1.9g; Cholesterol 9mg; Calcium 28mg; Fibre 0g; Sodium 28mg.

Chocolate Fudge Triangles

These attractive white and plain chocolate fudge "sandwiches" are very rich and almost impossible to resist, so cut them into quite small triangles.

Makes about 48 triangles

600g/1lb 5oz fine quality white chocolate, chopped into small pieces
375g/13oz can sweetened condensed milk
15ml/1 tbsp vanilla extract
7.5ml/1½ tsp lemon juice
pinch of salt

175g/6oz/1½ cups hazelnuts or pecan nuts, chopped (optional)
175g/6oz plain (semisweet) chocolate, diced
40g/1½oz/3 tbsp unsalted (sweet) butter, diced
50g/2oz dark (bittersweet) chocolate, for drizzling
oil, for greasing

1 Line a 20cm/8in square baking tin (pan) with foil. Brush the foil lightly with oil. In a pan over a low heat, melt the white chocolate and condensed milk until smooth, stirring frequently. Remove from the heat and stir in the vanilla extract, lemon juice and salt. Stir in the nuts, if using. Spread half the mixture in the tin. Chill for 15 minutes.

2 In a pan over a low heat, melt the plain chocolate and butter until smooth, stirring frequently. Remove from the heat, cool slightly, then pour over the chilled white layer and chill for 15 minutes, until set.

3 Gently reheat the remaining white chocolate mixture and pour over the set chocolate layer. Smooth the top, then chill for 2–4 hours, until set.

4 Using the foil to help, remove the fudge from the tin and turn it on to a chopping board. Lift off the foil and use a sharp knife to cut the fudge into 24 squares. Cut each square into two triangles. Melt the dark chocolate in a heatproof bowl set over a pan of barely simmering water. Cool slightly, then drizzle over the triangles to decorate.

Rich Chocolate Pistachio Fudge

This top-of-the-range fudge is truly a special treat. Fudge is not difficult to make and is a great activity to share with children, who may like to make the sweet confection as a wonderful gift for a special grandparent.

Makes 36

250g/9oz/generous 1 cup sugar
400g/14oz can sweetened condensed milk
50g/2oz/¼ cup unsalted (sweet) butter
5ml/1 tsp vanilla extract
115g/4oz dark (bittersweet) chocolate, grated
75g/3oz/¾ cup pistachio nuts, almonds or hazelnuts

1 Grease a 19cm/7½in square cake tin (pan) and line it with baking parchment.

2 Put the sugar, condensed milk and butter into a heavy pan and cook over a low heat, stirring occasionally, until the sugar has dissolved and the mixture is smooth.

3 Bring the mixture to the boil, stirring occasionally, and boil until it registers 116°C/240°F on a sugar thermometer or until a small amount of the mixture dropped into a cup of iced water forms a soft ball.

4 Remove the pan from the heat and beat in the vanilla extract, chocolate and nuts. Beat vigorously until the mixture is smooth and creamy.

5 Pour the mixture into the prepared tin and spread evenly. Leave until just set, then mark into squares. Leave to set completely, then cut into squares and remove from the tin.

Cook's Tip
Store in an airtight container for 2–3 days. Remember that all handmade sweets (candies), while tasting far superior to most commercial ones, will not keep for so long.

Chocolate Fudge Triangles Energy 120kcal/503kJ; Protein 1.5g; Carbohydrate 15.3g, of which sugars 15.1g; Fat 6.3g, of which saturates 3.8g; Cholesterol 6mg; Calcium 28mg; Fibre 0.4g; Sodium 17mg.
Rich Chocolate Pistachio Fudge Energy 104kcal/435kJ; Protein 1.5g; Carbohydrate 15.6g, of which sugars 15.6g; Fat 4.3g, of which saturates 2.1g; Cholesterol 7mg; Calcium 40mg; Fibre 0.2g; Sodium 36mg.

Pomerantzen

This candied citrus peel is a speciality of Jews whose origins lie in Germany. At festivals people often offer a box of pomerantzen as a gift, usually dipped in dark chocolate. They are easy to make, and appeal to the frugal as the peel would usually be thrown away, rather than being transformed into such a special treat.

Serves 4–6
3 grapefruit and 5–6 oranges or
6–8 lemons, unwaxed
300g/11oz/1¾ cups sugar
300ml/½ pint/1¼ cups water
30ml/2 tbsp golden (light
corn) syrup
caster (superfine) sugar (optional)

1 Score the fruit to remove the peel neatly, then peel. Put the peel in a pan, fill with cold water and bring to the boil. Simmer for 20 minutes, then drain.

2 When the peel is cool enough to handle, gently scrape off as much of the white pith as possible. Cut the peel lengthways into narrow strips.

3 Put the sugar, water and golden syrup in a pan and bring to the boil. When clear, add the peel and simmer for 1 hour, until translucent, taking care that it does not burn.

4 Stand a rack over a baking sheet. Remove the peel from the pan and arrange it on the rack. Leave to dry for 2–3 hours, then put in a plastic container or jar, cover and store in the refrigerator until required.

5 If serving as a sweetmeat, cover a large flat plate with caster sugar and toss the peel in it. Leave to dry for 1 hour. Sprinkle with sugar again and store in a covered container.

> **Cook's Tip**
> *If you find it too much trouble to remove the pith from the fruit, omit this step as once the pith has been simmered, its bitterness fades.*

Candied Peel Ribbons

Make this in the latter part of winter when the new season's citrus fruit is available. It will keep all year and can be used in apple pies or baked apples, to enliven a bought mincemeat for mince pies or even added to a beef stew to give a deep, rich flavour. Any syrup that is left over from the candying process can be used in fruit salads or drizzled over a freshly baked sponge cake. To preserve the individual flavour of each fruit – lemons, limes and oranges – they should all be candied separately. The same process may be used to candy orange slices and larger pieces of citrus peel.

Makes about 675g/1½lb
5 large oranges or 10 lemons or
limes, unwaxed
675g/1½lb/3 cups sugar, plus
extra for sprinkling

1 Halve the fruit, squeeze out the juice and discard the flesh, but not the peel.

2 Cut the peel into strips about 1cm/½in wide and place in a pan, cover with boiling water and simmer for 5 minutes. Drain, then repeat this four times, using fresh water each time to remove the peel's bitterness.

3 In a heavy pan, pour 250ml/8fl oz/1 cup water over the sugar. Heat to dissolve the sugar. Add the peel and cook slowly, partially covered, for 30–40 minutes until soft. Leave to cool thoroughly, then sprinkle with sugar.

> **Cook's Tip**
> *Citrus fruits may be waxed to extend their shelf life and keep the skins looking bright and fresh. It involves treating the fruit with an ethylene gas called diphenyl. It's not really possible to tell whether fruit has been waxed just from its appearance, so unless it is labelled "unwaxed", assume that it has been treated. In that case, scrub the fruit thoroughly in hot water and pat dry with kitchen paper before squeezing the juice and slicing the peel.*

Pomerantzen Energy 116kcal/492kJ; Protein 0.2g; Carbohydrate 29.6g, of which sugars 29.6g; Fat 0.5g, of which saturates 0g; Cholesterol 0mg; Calcium 65mg; Fibre 2.4g; Sodium 140mg.
Candied Peel Ribbons Energy 1559kcal/6642kJ; Protein 2g; Carbohydrate 398.9g, of which sugars 398.9g; Fat 6.1g, of which saturates 0g; Cholesterol 0mg; Calcium 878mg; Fibre 32.4g; Sodium 1890mg.

Orange Spoon Preserve

Spoon preserves are made with various types of fruit in a luscious syrup. Make orange peel preserve in late autumn with navel oranges and in winter use Seville oranges. Orange peel preserve is the easiest type to make and will happily keep for one or two years.

Makes about 30 pieces
8–9 thick-skinned oranges, total
    weight about 1kg/2¼ lb, rinsed
    and dried
1kg/2¼ lb/4½ cups caster
    (superfine) sugar
juice of 1 lemon

1 Grate the oranges lightly and discard the zest. Slice each one vertically into 4–6 pieces (depending on the size), remove the peel from each segment, keeping it in one piece, and drop it into a bowl of cold water. Use the flesh for another recipe.

2 Have ready a tapestry needle threaded with strong cotton string. Roll up a piece of peel and thread the needle through it. Continue this process until there are 10–12 pieces on the string, then tie the ends together. String the remaining peel in the same way. Put the strings in a bowl of cold water and leave for 24 hours, changing the water 3–4 times.

3 The next day, drain the strings of peel and put them in a large pan. Pour in about 2.8 litres/4½ pints/11 cups water. Bring to the boil, partially cover the pan and continue to boil for 15 minutes. Drain. Return the peel to the pan, cover with same amount of water and boil for 10 minutes until the peel feels soft. Tip into a colander and leave to drain for at least 1 hour.

4 Put the sugar in a large, heavy pan and add 150ml/¼ pint/ ⅔ cup water. Stir over a gentle heat until the sugar dissolves, then boil gently without stirring for about 4 minutes until a thick syrup forms. Remove the fruit from the threads. Simmer for 5 minutes, then take off the heat and leave to stand overnight.

5 The next day, boil the syrup very gently for 4–5 minutes, until it starts to set. Stir in the lemon juice, take the pan off the heat and cool. Pack into sterilized jars. Seal and label when cool.

Popcorn

What do you do with the kids on a wet Saturday or Sunday afternoon? Hire the latest Disney blockbuster and make a big batch – or two – of popcorn, of course. To amuse teenagers – or adults – change the movie, but not the snack.

Serves 10–15
15ml/1 tbsp vegetable oil
175g/6oz popcorn kernels

1 Put the vegetable oil in a large pan. Pour in the popcorn kernels and stir with a wooden spoon to coat them in the oil.

2 Place the lid on the pan and heat gently, for about 5 minutes, until you hear the popcorn starting to pop. Do not be tempted to remove the lid.

3 When the popping noises have slowed down, remove the lid. Popcorn can be eaten plain or coated.

Variations
Popcorn can be coated with sweet and savoury ingredients to give added flavour:
• Season the popped corn with ground sea salt, stirring well to coat lightly. Add only a small amount at a time and taste between additions.
• Sieve 30ml/2 tbsp of granulated sugar over the top of the popped corn. Replace the lid on the pan and holding the lid in place, shake the pan well to distribute the sugar evenly over the corn. Taste and add more sugar to sweeten, if required.

Cook's Tip
You can buy microwave popcorn which is especially for cooking in the microwave.

Orange Spoon Preserve: Energy 131kcal/560kJ; Protein 0.3g; Carbohydrate 34.8g, of which sugars 34.8g; Fat 0g, of which saturates 0g; Cholesterol 0mg; Calcium 31mg; Fibre 0g; Sodium 3mg.
Popcorn Energy 84kcal/352kJ; Protein 1.4g; Carbohydrate 8.3g, of which sugars 0.3g; Fat 5.3g, of which saturates 0.7g; Cholesterol 1mg; Calcium 10mg; Fibre 0.2g; Sodium 16mg.

Index